W9-AON-866
R03000 08611

EDGAR LEE MASTERS:
A BIOGRAPHY

Edgar Lee Masters

A Biography

HERBERT K. RUSSELL

UNIVERSITY OF ILLINOIS PRESS
URBANA AND CHICAGO

Manufactured in the United States of America
♾ This book is printed on acid-free paper.

Frontispiece photograph courtesy of the
Illinois State Historical Library

Library of Congress Cataloging-in-Publication Data
Russell, Herbert K., 1943–
Edgar Lee Masters : a biography / Herbert K. Russell.
p. cm.
Includes bibliographical references and index.
ISBN 0-252-02616-0 (alk. paper)
1. Masters, Edgar Lee, 1868–1950.
2. Authors, American—20th century—Biography.
I. Title.
PS3525.A83Z86 2001
811'.52—dc21 00-009471

C 5 4 3 2 1

As I shall die, let your belief
Find in these words too poor and brief
My soul's essential self.

—Edgar Lee Masters

CONTENTS

ACKNOWLEDGMENTS

I am particularly grateful to Edgar Lee Masters's son Hilary Masters for permission to quote from his father's letters, diaries, and unpublished chapters and drafts of *Across Spoon River.* Mr. Masters also granted permission to quote from letters and other documents written by his mother, Ellen Coyne Masters; to reproduce a family photograph in his possession; and to quote from his own family history, *Last Stands: Notes from Memory,* as well as from his letters to his father. Hilary Masters gave generously of his time through correspondence, telephone calls, and meetings as I worked on this book throughout the decade of the 1990s and much of 2000; I value his friendship.

I am also grateful to Marcia Cavell, the granddaughter of Edgar Lee Masters and his first wife, Helen Jenkins Masters. Ms. Cavell kindly permitted me to quote from her grandmother's letters to Edgar Lee Masters and from Helen Masters's fifty-seven-page typescript, "Mrs. Edgar Lee Masters." Ms. Cavell also granted permission to quote from her May 6, 1994, letter to me and from poems written by her mother, Marcia Lee Masters.

I also appreciate the cooperation of the following: Jenna Owen Rose for permission to quote from William Jennings Bryan's June 28, 1904, letter to Masters; the Newberry Library for permission to quote from Dorothy Dow's "An Introduction to Some Letters" and the Masters/Dow correspondence; Nicholas C. Lindsay for permission to quote from Vachel Lindsay's letters to Masters on June 16, 1926, and June 8, 1927, and also from a letter by Elizabeth Conner Lindsay to Masters dated May 27, 1933; the Trustees under the Will of Amy Lowell to quote from a December 18, 1915, letter from Lowell to Masters and from Lowell's *A Critical Fable;* Jane J. Ficke for offering no objection to quoting from Arthur Davison Ficke's "Notes on Edgar Lee Masters, 1938–39"; and the Darrow Family for offering no objection to quoting from Clarence Darrow's letters to Masters on November 29, 1907, February 3, 1912, and November 10, 1919.

I also appreciate permission to reprint portions of my own work copyrighted in several publications: various details of this book were first printed in the *Dictionary of Literary Biography,* 1987, and *Concise Dictionary of American Lit-*

erary Biography, 1988, both published by Gale Research, Inc.; portions of this book were first accepted by the *Dictionary of Midwestern Literature,* Indiana University Press (in press); portions of this book also appeared in my Introduction for *The Enduring River: Edgar Lee Masters' Uncollected Spoon River Poems* published by Southern Illinois University Press, copyright © 1991 by the Board of Trustees, Southern Illinois University; portions of my discussion of *Toward the Gulf* first appeared in *ICarbS* 3 (1977): 149–51; portions of this book first appeared under the title of "Edgar Lee Masters' Final Years in the Midwest" in *Essays in Literature* (Macomb) 4 (1977): 212–20; much of my discussion of *Domesday Book* was first printed as "Edgar Lee Masters' 'Finest Achievement': *Domesday Book,*" *Western Illinois Regional Studies* 14 (1991): 65–70; and much of my discussion of satires on *Spoon River* first appeared as "Imitations of *Spoon River:* An Overview," *Western Illinois Regional Studies* 2 (1979): 173–82.

Forty-three institutions and dozens of individuals provided information for this book. I am particularly indebted to the Harry Ransom Humanities Research Center at the University of Texas at Austin, where I spent five pleasant months of research; to the Lauinger Library at Georgetown University; and to the Newberry Library, Chicago, which in 1976 awarded me a research fellowship that served as the germ of this book.

I also appreciate the positive influence of my 1977 dissertation director, Professor Henry Dan Piper of Southern Illinois University, Carbondale. I have often relied on Southern Illinois University's Morris Library for various research needs supplied by David Koch, Barbara Preece, Chris Desai, an entire generation of inter-library loan staff, and by my librarian wife, Thyra Russell. The university's Frederick Williams kindly translated Masters's Greek and Latin expressions for me.

Some others who have helped me include Jean Rosen of Marion, Indiana, Dorothy Belle Hill of Danville, Kentucky, and Cathie Henderson and Pat Fox, both of the Harry Ransom Humanities Research Center. I have been aided too by Masters scholar Charles E. Burgess, whose years of solid research make him the world authority on Masters's paternal ancestry; Kimball Flaccus performed complementary work on Masters's maternal ancestry and on various other parts of his story. Professor John E. Hallwas of Western Illinois University, Macomb, and Professor James Hurt of the University of Illinois, Champaign, both read the manuscript and critiqued it. The University of Illinois Press's Richard Wentworth and Bruce Bethell offered cordial and sound advice at various times.

I appreciate too the support of the John A. Logan College Board of Trustees, which provided me with two mini-sabbaticals, and the John A. Logan College Foundation, which provided me with financial support. I was also aided by a 1991 Travel to Collections Grant from the National Endowment for the Humanities. I was helped too by my college secretary, Sonnie Walker, and by Olise Mandat, who keyboarded the entire manuscript, the drafts of which were confusing, and whose intelligence and patience are deservedly recognized.

EDGAR LEE MASTERS:

A BIOGRAPHY

INTRODUCTION

Edgar Lee Masters was one of America's most prolific authors, publishing fifty-three books during his long lifetime: twenty-nine volumes of verse, seven novels, seven plays, five biographies, a book of essays, and an autobiography, as well as two histories and one edited volume. He also published at least ten pamphlets and a large number of newspaper and magazine pieces in addition to book prefaces and miscellaneous prose and poetry in festschrifts. A posthumous collection of poems added a fifty-fourth volume to this prodigious output.

Masters was a public man in that several of his best-known artistic works are autobiographical, but there has not heretofore been a full-length biography of him, and much of what has been published is inaccurate. Nor was Masters himself cooperative where details of his private life were concerned. He worked on his autobiography intermittently for a decade but finally suppressed its final third and routinely turned down requests from scholars wishing to make use of his letters. Several years after his death, five small boyhood diaries were made available for scholarly use, but the diaries from his adult years have until recently remained locked in the family vault. One wonders why. Why was a man so public in some ways so guarded in others?

Edgar Lee Masters (1868–1950) was one of "the prairie poets" who, along with Carl Sandburg, Vachel Lindsay, and others, fled the midwestern villages of their youths and made their ways to Chicago to pursue various careers while nourishing hopes of becoming successful artists. Masters was particularly hardworking and idealistic, and one spring (when he was more than a little lucky as well) he realized his dreams beyond his wildest expectations.

In May 1914, using the pseudonym "Webster Ford," Masters began publishing some two hundred poems about talkative ghosts in a midwestern cemetery, the work appearing in the St. Louis magazine *Reedy's Mirror.* His identity was revealed the following November, and in 1915 the poems were collected in book form as the *Spoon River Anthology.* The volume became an international popular and critical success and heralded with a flourish the literary phenomenon known as the Chicago Renaissance.

Readers had never before seen anything quite like these poetic monologues, or "epitaphs." Literary critics accused Masters of showing too little respect for poetic rules; a wide variety of people felt he had written too realistically about subjects that had hitherto been regarded as inappropriate for verse. For these very reasons, however, Masters's book soon became "the most read and most talked-of volume of poetry that had ever been written in America."[1]

Spoon River Anthology was reported to have sold 80,000 copies in its first year of publication, and although Masters's own words indicate that this figure is too high, it was believable at the time because of the book's "notorious" reputation. In the years since its publication, *Spoon River Anthology* has maintained both popular and critical audiences, though less as an item of sensational writing than as a landmark of American literature. It has spawned dozens, perhaps hundreds, of imitative writings and is the direct literary antecedent of creations as diverse as Sherwood Anderson's short stories (*Winesburg, Ohio*), Sinclair Lewis's novels (*Main Street*), and one of Thornton Wilder's plays (*Our Town*). *Spoon River Anthology* has never been out of print and has been translated in whole or in part into at least eighteen foreign languages.[2]

Unfortunately, *Spoon River* was to be Masters's only lasting success. Before it appeared, he published a dozen undistinguished books (poems, plays, and political preachments); after its publication, he slowly abandoned his successful law practice to pursue writing full time, publishing another forty titles (poetry, plays, novels, biographies, and histories), but he never duplicated his one-time phenomenal achievement. As Louis Untermeyer said in 1923 of the writer's dramatic rise and subsequent decline, "With *Spoon River Anthology* Masters arrived—and left."[3]

Masters himself did little to contradict this impression when he paused in 1936 to publish his autobiography. Its title, *Across Spoon River,* reminded readers of his most significant title of twenty years earlier, and its chronological boundaries seemed to affirm that he had indeed "arrived and left" in the 1910s: he told of his life through 1916 and a part of 1917 and then suddenly broke off his story, saying simply, "All the years after 1917—to—to when?—remain to be told."[4]

Readers who desired more information about the latter part of his life until his death in 1950 were confined to brief sketches about him in biographical dictionaries and a handful of articles about his post–*Spoon River* career. Much of this information was managed by Masters himself in interviews or in reference-book material he approved, and much of it was repetitive. Although he occasionally complained about his low visibility, saying, "There is no decent sketch of me anywhere," he was consistently unhelpful in producing a better one. He was known to keep a tight rein on biographical profiles and called off interviews if denied the chance to "revise" the results. Those who sought genuinely new information were turned away or warned to be careful: "I am in the midst of preparations for a trip and cannot give the time for an interview," he told the newsman David Karsner. "Instead I have dictated and corrected the enclosed statement, which is all I have to say. . . . I do not want anything added to the biographical matter contained in it, which as far as it goes is authentic."[5]

As a result, more than a quarter of a century would elapse after Masters's death before scholars had even a rough outline of his life between 1917 and 1923, when he was divorced and left the Midwest for New York. There is much that remains to be dealt with in this six-year period, however, and there is no published record at all concerning what he did from the time he left Chicago, in 1923, until the time of his second marriage, in 1926.[6]

Nor is there much published information on the remainder of his life. Midwestern scholar John T. Flanagan correctly remarked in his 1974 book *Edgar Lee Masters: The Spoon River Poet and His Critics* that "most of the essays dealing with Masters after the appearance of *Spoon River Anthology* in book form in 1915 discuss the work rather than the man and yield little biographical detail." Flanagan listed only four instances of "biographical data" completed while Masters was alive, to which might be added various newspaper articles (also repetitive in that many of them carry the same obligatory information about *Spoon River* as a "literary bombshell").[7]

Similarly, there has been little biographical delving during the half-century since Masters's death. Masters's paternal ancestry has been explored by Charles E. Burgess in several useful articles, and the writer's maternal ancestry has been traced by the poet and scholar Kimball Flaccus. The writer August Derleth and the poet Gertrude Claytor have provided glimpses of Masters's old age, but there is nothing that even comes close to being a complete biography. Hardin Wallace Masters, the writer's son from his first marriage, completed *Edgar Lee Masters: A Centenary Memoir-Anthology* (a book of poems with a foreword) and *Edgar Lee Masters: A Biographical Sketchbook about a Famous American Author* (a book of short anecdotes). Hilary Masters, the only child from Masters's second marriage, has published a family biography, *Last Stands: Notes from Memory,* a well-written book concerning Masters, his second wife, and her parents, but this book is limited by the fact that Hilary spent most of his boyhood and young manhood away from his father. Twayne's United States Author Series book on Masters is principally critical in nature, with minor mistakes troubling some of the biographical data.[8]

The illegibility of Masters's handwritten source materials, such as letters, has been another major obstacle to a completed biography. Masters was frequently in turmoil (about love and money in particular), and the legibility of his handwriting decreased as his agitation increased, so that much of his post–*Spoon River* history has literally been a blur.

That blur also reflects his lifestyle for several years. When *Spoon River Anthology* made him famous in 1915, Masters suddenly found himself in charge of two successful careers, each of which (for different reasons) was under public scrutiny and required a great deal of time to manage properly. The forty-six-year-old Masters, married with three children, needed to decide whether to continue with the law, which he disliked immensely, or to try to survive as a poet. It was to be a major decision of his life, but he failed to make a clean choice. Instead he compromised, continuing half-heartedly with his legal business for several years while also publishing numerous books, thereby giving full-time attention to neither career and eventually damaging both.

For a time, however, he seemed to be able to handle this duality. He had a ready market for his writing and capitalized on it in 1916 with an augmented edition of *Spoon River* (which added thirty-one new poems and an epilogue), as well as two volumes of miscellaneous verses. The following year he made so much money from a single law case ($27,000) that he was able to follow up on a boyhood dream of buying a rural "haven" and devoting himself to poetry: "I decided to buy a country place and to have apple trees and bees, flowers and vegetables, and to work in the open air and to have tranquillity for writing." He purchased a small farm with an old house at Spring Lake, Michigan, and renovated it, but he had barely gotten settled when he fell into a feud with his neighbors and into an argument with a family member and stormed out to return to Chicago. It was September 13, 1917—the point at which he ended his autobiography, *Across Spoon River.*[9]

"I have written this autobiography with an eye to the truth," Masters wrote in the epilogue that closes the book, "but what is truth? There are levels of truth, lower and higher." Masters had the capacity to write successful literary biography, as witnessed by his 1935 life of Vachel Lindsay, but Masters also felt that writing anyone's life story was complicated by what he called the author's "web of motive," a term he touched on (but did not quite explain) to a friend of his later years, Gertrude Claytor: "Most biographies, he said, were fakes because no one can really penetrate the web of motive in himself and to unravel the life of another is almost impossible, so the biographer must resort to fiction—intentional or otherwise." So too with autobiography, it seems, for *Across Spoon River* has several fictions in it.[10]

One of these fictions opens the book, another closes it, and there are several more in between. The fiction that begins the book is on line 1 of the first page: "I was born at Garnett, Kansas, on August 23, 1869." The correct year was 1868. The fiction that ends the book concerns the year in which Masters gave up his Michigan house and farm; he lets the reader believe it was 1917: "As it turned out I had left them for good." The correct year was 1923. Masters cannot be forgiven the first error for he had known exactly in what year he was born (1868) when he provided that information to the 1910–1911 edition of *Who's Who in America.* Nor can he be forgiven the second error, for it would require him to have forgotten the post-1917 visits to his Michigan farm from such people as his best friend, William Marion Reedy, who first published the Spoon River poems in *Reedy's Mirror*; the dozens of letters he addressed and mailed from Spring Lake after 1917; the experience of standing in the Michigan snow in February 1922 to add a kitchen to his house; and his readily documentable grief at losing this beloved farm in his much-publicized 1923 divorce.[11]

This is not to say that *Across Spoon River* is flawed throughout. Not only is his autobiography interesting, but it remains the best single source of information about Masters. Because he relied on boyhood diaries to write it and had an excellent memory (and because he had been recalling parts of his story for many years in his poems and novels), the book has a sense of recency. So how does one explain inaccuracies such as those just cited? What "web of motive" led Edgar Lee Masters to "resort to fiction" about his own life and to end his story prematurely?[12]

This book was begun in an attempt to answer these questions, to examine the author's life through his letters and other documents. More than sixty repositories of Mastersiana were consulted, either directly or through copies of documents, and all promising leads were pursued. The richest collection of materials (containing perhaps 95 percent of the source documents) was at the Harry Ransom Humanities Research Center (HRC) at the University of Texas at Austin. This research facility has a voluminous collection of Masters materials, including manuscripts and galleys; the author's personal library; materials pertinent to his two marriages and several girlfriends; and information about his children, various books, and business transactions. It also houses hundreds of photographs, 12,000 items of correspondence, boyhood diaries, and other documents, including many of the research materials collected by Dr. Kimball Flaccus (1911–72), who researched the life of Masters for a biography but died before completing his work. The present biography constitutes the first sustained use of these materials.

The HRC also yielded an unexpected boon: the final part of the manuscript of Masters's autobiography. These ten and one-half unpublished draft chapters show unambiguously that Masters's 1936 autobiography of eighteen chapters (plus epilogue) is the truncated version of a manuscript that once stretched to twenty-eight chapters (plus epilogue). Other important details are these: the new chapters discuss, in varying detail, Masters's life from the fall of 1917 through a small portion of 1934; they emphasize the years 1919 through 1926; six of the chapters appear to be complete (they are typed with a minimum of handwritten insertions and run about as long as chapters published in *Across Spoon River*); and four chapters appear incomplete (by dint of their brevity, density, or lack of focus). The half-chapter is the final part of the autobiography's chapter 18, which Masters broke off with the events of September 13, 1917, the point at which he ended the published version of his story. Relevant portions of this new information are here made public for the first time.

This biography also marks the first use of all the author's known diaries. While writing his autobiography, Masters relied on diary entries from as early as 1884 to recall portions of his boyhood. He saved diaries from other years as well, and diaries for thirty-three years or parts of years were available for use in this study. Masters's first diaries were simply school tablets in which he sporadically posted news of some of his boyhood activities. During his *Spoon River* years and later, he used small vest-pocket organizers measuring about three by five inches. He carried these journals everywhere, using a pencil to scrawl in a space of about two square inches per day a summary of the people and events he wanted to remember.[13]

The content of individual diary entries depends, of course, on the content of the relevant day. Entries for some days seem relatively straightforward, as do these excerpts from 1919, when Masters was dividing his time between New York and the Midwest and doing much of his writing at Spring Lake, Michigan ("S.L."): "Arrive N.Y. 8 A.M. Ran into Lindsay at Brevoort" (February 4); "Breakfast at Players. Visit with Dreiser" (February 5); "Wrote Dedication to *Domesday Book*" (May 25); "At S.L." (June 22).

Excerpts from this same year are useful in a second, unexpected way: they show what Masters did not do, correcting certain assumptions about his professional and domestic lives. For example, Masters insisted privately and publicly for upward of thirty years that "poetry killed [his] law business" ("law business daily proved that a name in poetry frightens clients away"), but his diary for 1919, a pivotal year in his Chicago legal career, shows that he was often not available to practice law. He was instead in New York with literary personages for a week at a time (a day was required just to get there), cavorting with a girlfriend in Indiana (five hours from Chicago by train), in St. Louis roistering with his old friend Reedy (occasionally), enjoying the life of a country squire in Michigan (frequently), or—far less often—making money from lecturing. Likewise, while he sometimes suggested that his first son and two daughters drifted away from him during this year, it might be more accurate to say that he drifted away from them. His diary for 1919, for example, has only one entry reading "dinner at home with children." In other words, the occurrence was rare enough to note.[14]

Finally, there are a good many diary entries (still from 1919, a time representative of his active years) that pique the imagination but offer no understandable information: "5200 Harper. High Ho" (July 6). And some are coded but need no explanation: "Left 10:30 for Peggy's. Couch X" (April 16). A good many entries are simply lists, names of people from New York, Chicago, or elsewhere, most of them long since gone, nearly all unknown today. Some days show "Nothing." Some days are blank.

The lacunae in Masters's life have been literature's loss, for his biography has all the ingredients of a good story, that of a boy from the country who, against great odds, dreams, struggles, and succeeds in his quest to be recognized as a world-class writer, only to be brought down by weaknesses inherent in his own being. Shakespeare and the Greek tragedians recognized this type of person and left dramas concerning figures who exemplified it; Masters left us with a portrait of the artist from the Midwest.

The son of badly mismatched parents, Masters was raised in a household with too little love and sought in literature and writing an escape from his parents' turmoil and a way to gain the attention denied him at home. College seemed his best means to success. Masters's father refused to support more than one year of higher education, however, and after convincing his son that he was constitutionally unfit to go to college and work simultaneously, he maneuvered Masters into law with the hope that he would work for the family firm in the Illinois county seat of Lewistown. Frustrated in his attempts to get an education and write, Masters abandoned Lewistown for turn-of-the-century Chicago, where he channeled his urge to succeed in two other directions: he married success (that is, he married the beautiful daughter of a Chicago railroad baron), and he became such a good lawyer that he replaced former Illinois governor Peter Altgeld in Clarence Darrow's law firm.[15]

But Masters was not intellectually satisfied (for he hated the law), emotionally fulfilled (for he had married principally for money), or financially secure (for he was a spendthrift and spent all that he made). He addressed all three problems by continuing to write. He paid to have his writings published with the hopes that he might become famous as an author and make so much money that he could retire from the law and attract a woman who he felt was right for him.[16]

The by now familiar story of how *Spoon River Anthology* vaulted Masters to international fame is one of the great tales of America's literary history, but Masters's bullheaded drive to succeed literarily did not make him happy. *Spoon River* did not make him independently wealthy; it did not satisfy him intellectually, for he thought his true talents lay in other directions; and it did not address his emotional needs, for fame did not deliver to him the perfect soulmate of whom he often dreamed.

Instead it brought him Lillian Wilson, a young widow who had a great deal of money, satisfied his emotional needs for a time, and satisfied him intellectually in some ways, for she was clever, funny, and reasonably well read. Unfortunately, she was also the means to Masters's divorce, which paupered him, helped ruin his good name as a lawyer in Chicago, and left him with the need to publish as rapidly as possible to keep body and soul together.[17]

This bitter denouement to Masters's pursuit of success had a terrible effect on him. He had assumed that hard work and ambition would help him realize his dream to be known as a writer, but he attained this goal only to be let down by the bitter fruits of his success. Nothing worked out as he had hoped it would, and his life was finally an American success story in which the final chapters all went terribly wrong. By the time of his divorce at age fifty-four, he was in many ways worse off than he had been before he became famous: he was still restless and wanted to produce great literature, but he was no longer young and was broke as well.

In 1923 he quit Chicago, his home for thirty years, and moved to New York

City, where he took out his anger in his writings. He published works that focused on the nation's abuse of its artists and wrote autobiographical stories in which he compared himself to the British writer John Keats, a talented poet who was "killed by the critics" (as a popular myth had it) and died before he could marry his beloved. Other works also revealed Masters as a malcontent, a man who was out of step with both his peers and the times. He developed a reputation as a brooding and bitter man, and literary people and the public finally steered a wide berth around him.[18]

What Masters failed to see was that he himself was responsible for many of his problems, in part because his chief goal lacked focus. Did he want to be known as a writer of poetry (with the emphasis on the quality of his writings), or did he want to be known foremost as a famous poet (with the emphasis on the collateral benefits sometimes associated with writing—money, attention, and favors from the opposite sex)? Based on what he said, one would think Masters wanted to write great poetry, but based on his actions, one would assume he was far more interested in the collateral attractions. Unsure of what he wanted, Masters got what the world gave him, along with what his own frequently reckless actions generated.[19]

Anxious for signs of success, Masters pursued short-term gratification as if there were no tomorrows. He married for status and money, for example, and then pursued other women while telling himself (and occasionally the public) that he was lonely and looking for love. He often published with the same abandon. Ignoring his editors' advice, he would assemble poorly done and contradictory volumes, rushing new titles into print to gain recognition and money. By the end of his life, he thought his chief problems were stony-hearted publishers and an uncaring public; his real problem was his lifelong misunderstanding of himself.[20]

Many years after Masters's death, his son Hilary surveyed the wreckage of his father's life and encapsuled it in one word: "Sad." A granddaughter, also a writer, commented on the overriding irony of Masters's existence, his ability to understand almost anything except the flaws in his own personality: "One pities him, the man so celebrated for his knowledge of human nature in *Spoon River,* so lacking insight into himself . . . , so consistently refusing to accept responsibility for who he was and what he did, and through that very trait of character rendering himself less in control of his fate than he might have been." Masters's final opportunity to address these matters came to a definite end in December 1943, when he was overtaken by pneumonia and malnutrition in his New York hotel room. He would be an invalid or semi-invalid for the rest of his life.[21]

A man of many words, Edgar Lee Masters would have preferred to tell this story, and he did tell much of it, but circumstances and his own strong will prevented him from publishing a complete account. He wanted his life story told, however, else he would not have written it or have spent so much time explaining his point of view in his many letters. He was a prodigious letter writer. It is doubtful that any biographer could observe all the "fine understandings" Masters sometimes mentioned with regard to a biography of himself, a euphemism meaning he wished certain things left unsaid, but he understood well the role of unpublished source materials and left this note to a future biographer in an expurgated chapter of his autobiography: "It is pertinent now to say that I wrote letters along the way which may contain material that could properly be used here, and that should be incorporated in these pages in order to attain a full characterization of me, my feelings and beliefs and attitudes."[22]

Because these "feelings and beliefs and attitudes" were far more important to Masters than the tools of their conveyance, such as spelling, punctuation, and capitalization (and the related typing concerns of strikeovers and fused words), he usually depended on his editors to look after such things. For example, he depended on William Marion Reedy, who was "particular and expert," to look after his things published in *Reedy's Mirror.* A little later Masters told the publisher of *Spoon River Anthology,* "I punctuate . . . as carefully as I know how, not being any too expert at that. . . . If there are grammatical slips that I have missed, any good reader [editor] should get them." Much later, in 1936, when *Across Spoon River* was being readied for publication, Masters sent a letter to Farrar and Rinehart saying, "I appreciate the care you are taking by having the [manu]script edited." Because Masters left behind an endless stream of grammatical, stylistic, and typing errors in his letters, correcting them in the traditional way would have produced an equally endless stream of scholarly brackets and comments. Such items, which mattered little to him, have been silently emended to avoid detracting from his story, which mattered greatly and which was on his mind at the end of his active life: "Do you realize," he asked a friend in 1942, "that no biography of me has been written at all?"[23]

CHAPTER 1

Road to Spoon River

Along the road a wagon chuckles,
Loaded with corn, going to Atterbury.
And an old man sits under a tree asleep . . .
And a boy lies in the grass
Near the feet of the old man,
And looks up at the sailing clouds,
And longs, and longs, and longs
For what, he knows not.

—Edgar Lee Masters, "Jonathan Houghton,"
Spoon River Anthology

In mid-1914 Edgar Lee Masters began publishing in *Reedy's Mirror* some 200 free verse poems about the inhabitants of an Illinois cemetery and by the end of the year had reshaped his own future and that of American literature. Everything that followed in Masters's life was influenced by the book that grew out of this time—*Spoon River Anthology*—and any biography of him must recognize the two distinct parts of his story divided by it. Between his birth in 1868 and the publication of *Spoon River* in 1915, Masters grew up, became a lawyer, moved to Chicago, and married. Then, at the age of forty-six, this respected lawyer and family man suddenly achieved his boyhood dream of becoming a famous writer. His life changed almost overnight. To understand the magnitude of these changes, it is necessary to know certain facts about Masters, how he lived in the years both before and after *Spoon River.*

Masters grew up in the Illinois towns of Petersburg, on the Sangamon River, and Lewistown, near the Spoon River, two Corn Belt county seats that would provide him with models for his literary village of "Spoon River." From age one to eleven Masters lived in or near Petersburg, where his father, Hardin (1845–1925), had grown up with a love of sports, horses, and dancing but with few serious interests, despite having attended an "academy" near Petersburg, the preparatory school of Illinois College in Jacksonville, and the University of Michigan in Ann Arbor. Hardin Masters had ostensibly gone to the latter to study law but made so little impression on the school that years later, when Masters sought to verify his father's presence there, the school could find no record of his attendance. Perhaps this was owing to poor record keeping; perhaps the university lacked information because Hardin soon dropped out of Michigan and journeyed to Philadelphia to learn the dry goods business. When he lost interest in dry goods, he worked for a time as a streetcar conductor in Philadelphia before returning to Petersburg, where he failed as a pharmacist and succeeded as a grocer before again showing interest in the law. He studied under the Petersburg attorney W. McNeely and also made plans to marry a woman named Kate Gardner. Before they could be married, however, Hardin encountered a woman who interested him far more than Miss Gardner.[1]

Emma Dexter (1849–1926) was only "about sixteen" when she left the home of her New England Methodist minister-father (a man of "fiery temper") and went to Illinois, where she visited a sister in Pana (or possibly a different sister in Petersburg) and met and fell in love with Hardin. They were married on September 10, 1867, when she was barely eighteen and he twenty-one. After their marriage they stayed with Hardin's parents until May 1868, when they moved to Garnett, Kansas. Emma Dexter Masters had a sister who was married to a successful attorney in Kansas, and the couple may have thought Hardin could practice law there. Then, too, they may have followed the example of other Illinoisans who had successfully migrated to Garnett, including a judge named Abram Bergen, a supposed acquaintance of the Masters family. Or perhaps Hardin thought the move could allay a youthful indiscretion that grew out of the Civil War. Shortly after the firing on Fort Sumter, fifteen-year-old Hardin had attempted to run away and join the Union Army but was soon caught and returned home by his father. Hardin subsequently developed Southern sympathies and one night joined a posse intent on "releasing from jail some [Northern] men who had resisted the draft." He was later called on to reckon with and explain this act, and it may have been a factor in directing him to Kansas. In any event, law cases were limited in Kansas, and after Edgar Lee was born on August 23, 1868, the family returned to Illinois to live with Hardin's parents. When this arrangement failed to work, the young family moved a mile away to a log cabin on Shipley's Hill and then to a farm in nearby Atterberry before living in a series of houses in Petersburg. Each of these was small, cold, or unhealthy, and when Hardin's new work as a farmer and teacher failed to show promise, Emma Masters began to grow unhappy.[2]

Emma was a woman of considerable sensitivity and prettiness, but her New England upbringing had provided her few if any skills for cooking or keeping house in the rough environment of the Sangamon River valley. Her tart tongue and developing hatred of the Middle West worsened matters. Masters described her as follows in an early draft of his autobiography: "When she was happy, she was ecstatic; and when she was depressed, she was dark, sometimes with a tender melancholy, at other times with threats of storm; and when she was indignant, all her energies came to hand. Then she did not merely give way to little chidings or half articulate scoldings . . . but she sent bolts of lightning right and left, and settled things with emphasis."[3]

One of the things she did "with emphasis" was to undertake to change her husband. They had both been raised as Methodists, but she was of the New England variety (Vermont and New Hampshire), while Hardin was of the Middle West. They soon disagreed on one of the few things on which they might have agreed—religion—and after that they found they disagreed on many things. Masters described their rather hopeless situation thus: "Her will was unconquerable, and as my father had the same indomitable disposition, their marriage was the union of conflicting and irresistible forces. She had imbibed a sort of theological doctrine, probably from her father, which was that the will had to be broken. She set out to break my father's will, and utterly failed all her life." Hardin felt compelled to prove his independence in such a scenario; Emma countered by using her sharp tongue to make sure he regretted such attempts.[4]

It was impossible for Hardin's parents not to notice this, for the families lived in one small house for a time, and Emma and her mother-in-law were soon at odds, even though Hardin was receiving financial help from his father. If Hardin had not become state's attorney for Menard County in 1872, family tensions would probably have grown worse. As it was, "he was much away" (as Masters twice wrote in *Across Spoon River*) and "was out late at night" and was eventually "deep in all the revels of Petersburg"—a euphemism meaning he had developed an eye for the ladies (a trait he would pass to his son), had extramarital affairs, and stayed too long at saloons. (Hardin Masters may to this day be the only member of the Illinois bar whose son proudly identified him as a "playboy" in his funeral eulogy, which was printed on page 1 of the local newspaper and reprinted in pamphlet form.) Together, Mr. and Mrs. Hardin Masters made a particularly handsome couple, but one often out of sorts owing to the difficulties already suggested and to troubles over meals (never hot or on time), money (never enough), and the needs of their four children: Edgar Lee, the eldest; Madeline (called "Mat" or "Mattie"), born 1870; Alexander, born 1873; and Thomas Davis ("T.D."), born 1877.[5]

These family problems left Masters with two clear impressions that guided much of his adult thinking. Marriage is a trap, though a difficult one to avoid, given the nature of "love," and sectionalism is a divisive force: his mother represented the East, his father represented "the West" (as it was then known), and their values were never reconciled.

Matched against the confusion of Masters's parents' household was the well-regulated farm of his paternal grandparents, Squire Davis ("Squire" was his given name) and Lucinda Masters. They lived five and one-half miles north of Petersburg on a farmstead of 200 acres in Sand Ridge Township, where everything seemed in order: the rolling pastures and well-kept fields; the orchard and arbor; the brick walk to the house and its shaded lawn; the lilacs, tulips, and roses (yellow and red); the tasty meals (served hot and on time); and Uncle Wilbur (or sometimes a hired hand) serving as an older brother for "Lee." In addition, there were books, quantities of them by Masters's account—so many, in fact, that at Squire Masters's death in 1904 they constituted one-eighth the value of his chattel property. Even Squire Masters himself seemed "in order." A devout Christian, he was active in his church, where he sometimes spoke, and was an intimate of the nineteenth century's best-known backwoods minister, Peter Cartwright ("Cartwright made my grandfather's house a sort of station in his travels to the Spoon River country"). Plus, the elder Masters was financially well off and seemed always to make a profit on his various agricultural transactions (he was essentially a cattle dealer, owning as much as 500 acres at one time). And with it all, he was a gentleman (when farm animals were to be bred, he retired to his living room with the *Petersburg Observer,* sat down under the picture of the author Washington Irving, and let others attend to the details). He was a transplanted southerner, with roots in Virginia and Tennessee, where he had been born, and he usually behaved as a gentleman farmer. "He never had worked to hurt himself," noted his busy wife, Lucinda.[6]

The mother of eight children, Lucinda Masters was the unrecognized head of this peaceable kingdom, living to age ninety-five before dying in 1910, shortly before Masters immortalized her as "Lucinda Matlock" (and her late husband as "Davis Matlock") in *Spoon River Anthology.* Masters contrasted his parents' harried and unhappy domestic setting with that of his grandmother's cheerful management. "What a happy relief it was to get away from this home life and to go out to my grandmother's," he wrote in his autobiography. "Often I went on Saturday to stay over Sunday, and in the summertime I would be there for weeks, or for just as long as my mother allowed me to stay. . . . There was such order, such comfort at that old house." Its comfort knew no comparison in part because these were the only grandparents Masters knew: his New England grandparents "never visited," nor did Masters visit them, and so Lucinda Masters's home was the best that he experienced. Like her husband, Lucinda was of southern origin (North Carolina and Tennessee, which she had left at age six) and had what Masters described as "a wonderful sense of aesthetics." From her, Masters received the first active encouragement to pursue his artistic side: "My grandmother was sending me to a music teacher; for my mother and she fancied that because of my long fingers and my passion for committing rhymes to memory I was destined to be a musician."[7]

Masters himself thought he was destined to be a farmer, like his grandfather. In fact, many of the Masterses had been of this occupation. Masters believed that his paternal ancestors had come from the British Isles in the eighteenth century, when an uncaring stepmother drove one Notley (or Knottley) Masters and his sister from home; they found their way to an island off the coast of Wales, where a passing ship captain saw their smoke and carried them (or perhaps only Notley) to Virginia. (More recent scholarship has suggested that Masters erred in the name of this first ancestor in America, in his arrival time—it could have been in the seventeenth century—and in the family's American locations: Maryland and the Carolinas should be added to Virginia.) In any event, Notley and his kinsman Hillery (or Hillory) are among the first family members who show up in family lore. Hillery may have served as a soldier in the Revolutionary War before moving to Overton County, Tennessee. Hillery's son Thomas, born 1787, moved with his son Squire Davis (Masters's grandfather) to central Illinois and the Jacksonville area about 1829 to take advantage of fertile farm land. Thomas left a legacy of six hundred dollars to Squire Davis, who used it to buy the Petersburg farm where Masters played and to which he now went regularly on a new pony his father had bought him.[8]

These trips gained importance later, for they gave Masters a usable geography for the countryside of "Spoon River"—a memory bank of hills, lanes, creeks, woods, ponds, trails, wagon roads, fords, ferries, and churchyards both old and new. A glance at the landmarks young Lee Masters passed by on an average day in the late 1870s as he made his way to his grandparents illustrates the geography.

To get to the farm, he and his pony, Rock, went north out of Petersburg up Estill Hill, by the Menard County Fairgrounds, and on for a long "country mile" on Bowman's Lane. Then he had a choice of routes. He could angle north-northwest toward New Hope Church and the village of Oakford, or he could take a longer way, northeasterly down Shipley's Hill, the road following the base of the hill with the trees overhanging on one side and the Sangamon River bottoms opening out on the other. He would then angle northwest and upward on a winding road before reaching the uplands and a view of the Mason County hills to the north. He would proceed westward by Shipley's Hill Cemetery and the Shipley Schoolhouse (the Shipleys were large landowners), and then his grandparents' place would come into view. The farmhouse stood on a hill, and although situated on the prairie, it was surrounded in every direction by streams: to the south and passing through the farm (and neighbor Sevigne Houghton's woods) was Concord Creek, by which Masters played as a boy; to the west the headwaters of the Latimore grew significant enough for that stream to have a name; and the Sangamon River flowed three miles to the east, turning near the crossing of Sheep Ford to pass north of the farm on its way to Miller's Ferry.[9]

But the people Masters saw on the Petersburg square and those he heard of there were also to be important to him. In the 1870s Petersburg was sixteen blocks long and half that many wide, a town of 3,000 in a valley framed by hills. The Sangamon River, the Menard County Courthouse, and most of the people occupied the valley or the slopes. The hilltops held other homes, along with the town's two principal cemeteries, Rose Hill, where some of the models for *Spoon River* are buried, and Oakland, where other *Spoon River* names are found, along with the graves of several pioneers associated with Abraham Lincoln. The town's business assets included two railroads, coal mines, and a brewery and winery, in addition to numerous saloons, two flour mills, a woolen mill, a tile factory, tailors and bootmakers, lumber yards, wagon shops, and other businesses and offices. Hardin Masters's law office (or the one his son liked for its view of circuses and Fourth of July celebrations) was on the west side of the square on the second floor of a business building. Masters played about the town and river or went two miles south to New Salem, where he and his chums, "the Hill Gang," played among the ruins of Lincoln's vanished village. Most of New Salem's buildings had tumbled to decay by the time Masters came along, but foundation stones remained, along with the gristmill, rebuilt at the river's edge in the early 1850s.[10]

The Sangamon River was as much a liability as an asset, however. It had brought Lincoln to New Salem, but it was not suitable for shipping and occasionally flooded parts of Petersburg, as well as guaranteeing that winters there would be damp, foggy, and cold. Masters blamed the river's unhealthful climate for the death of his brother Alex ("a boy as beautiful as Shelley"), killed by diphtheria at age five in 1878. The Sangamon nearly killed Masters as well. When he was "about ten years old" (as he reckoned later), he and his father and friends went on a fishing outing to the New Salem mill, where he mistook a twenty-foot-deep mill run for a "pool" and went in over his head. He was saved by a neighbor, Jim Arnold, after he "had sunk for the third time" and was "18 inches below the surface." "You were clean dead," Arnold told him much later. "I took you and stood you on your head. The water just gushed out of your mouth; and your dad came over and helped to bring you back."[11]

It was at about this time, too, that Masters survived a brush with lightning (it knocked him down). He had already nearly died from a combination of measles and pneumonia, which he contracted simultaneously and which he was left to fight alone one night while his parents (getting along for a change) went off to a party. (This incident helped fuel the grievance against his sharp-tongued mother that Masters nursed throughout his life.) He also claimed to have been kicked by horses. Petersburg was not a gentle place, nor was Masters's rearing in it easy. A playmate named Lee died of diphtheria, and shortly after Masters survived his near drowning, his best friend, George Mitchell "Mitch" Miller, died when he fell under the wheels of a train.[12]

Some days the gas and smoke from the coal mines drifted into the village and mixed oppressively with the humidity, to be cleared at last by one of the numerous tornadoes and windstorms that visited the area during Masters's youth. Masters would sit with one of his dogs, Queen or Gyp, on a step of the house and watch the storm approach, his attention diverted by two contradictory sounds: while one neighbor played the religious tune "Depths of Mercy" on the organ, a second neighbor coughed up his diseased lungs. Meanwhile, the storm clouds swirled nearer. Masters would watch them for a time and then go nervously inside to stand in the middle of a room when the lightning flashed or else retreat to his feather bed. The home of his devout grandfather seemed a safe place to be in an environment filled with cyclones and lightning, but even here a visit might bring intimations of early death and other confoundments.[13]

When Masters stayed with his grandparents on Saturday night (as he often did in the summers), they would go to nearby Concord Church on Sunday morning, but before the service he and Lucinda Masters might wander for a time among the graves and read the inscriptions on the tombstones. The melancholy of the churchyard carried over to the church's interior, where the quavering voices of the elder members added a plaintiveness to "Rock of Ages," Cowper's hymn of "a fountain filled with blood," and other songs of the grave, damnation, and grace. Some of the tunes brought tears to Masters's eyes, and he would look sideways through the wavy windows to where the headstones of the pioneers shimmered in the summer sun or otherwise conceal his emotions ("I would bend my head and close my eyes to hide my feelings"). On the way home they might pass by yet another burial ground, the Old Concord Cemetery, where Ann Rutledge was buried: "My grandmother and I walked about the graves, always to look at the grave of Ann Rutledge with its simple gray stone bearing her simple name. 'Linkern's sweetheart,' my grandmother would say in a reverent and tender voice, as if speaking to herself."[14]

So it was little wonder, perhaps, that Masters would sometimes seek out less somber pursuits, as he occasionally did with his uncle Wilburne (called "Wilbur" or "Will"), Squire Masters's youngest son, who was nine years older than Masters. Sometimes they hunted ducks, fished, or gathered pecans, or maybe they would visit Atkinson, "a famous fiddler" who lived in a log house in the middle of a nearby woods:

> Perhaps the next night after the Concord [Church] experience we would go to see this fiddler. Down the road we went, up the hill, into the beginning of the grove, over the bridge which crossed Concord Creek, and up a steeper hill at whose top we climbed the rail fence and made our way through the brush and the darkness of the shadowing oaks to the midst of the forest where the hut of the fiddler stood. The stars shone over us or perhaps the moon; the whippoorwills were calling from mysterious vastness around us; and my heart danced with the magical wonder of the hour. When we came to the front of the hut, there sat Atkinson, the fiddler, resting under the stars and in the refreshing coolness of the night from the hot toil of the day. "Howdy, Will," was his welcome to my uncle. His children came forth, shy as young quails.

Atkinson was only a hunter-gatherer (wild turkeys, squirrels, and honey), but he could send forth tunes such as "Susannah" and "The Arkansas Traveler" into acres of trees and offered Masters one of his first views of an artist, one who had become "famous" through his art. (Masters tried to play, but lacking proper instruction, he learned only a fiddler's jig, "Paddy, Won't You Drink Some Good Old Cider?")[15]

On days when the hunting, fishing, and fiddling were done (and no horse racing, camping, or swimming was planned), Masters might simply go off by himself to lie in the large meadow west of his grandparents' farmhouse and send his kite into the sky or a toy sailboat "scudding across the pond in the meadow." The blue skies, water, and breezes, he remembered, were as perfect as "a Mother Goose illustration." And he didn't even have to walk back to the house: the mules wouldn't carry him, but if he roused the horses out of their horsey dreams under the poplar trees, Old Pepperdog or Molly would. Happy in these surroundings, he acquired his childhood nickname, "Giggle."[16]

Unfortunately this rural environment provided Masters only a minimal education that offered him little but bad memories. His first school was such a foul affair in terms of ventilation and outhouses that he later said he had "nothing but loathing for those days." He briefly attended the Shipley School, staying with his grandparents, who lived nearby, but two boys from the school died, including one named John Garver. Masters would recall to the end of his days Garver's interment in the Shipley's Hill Cemetery adjacent to the schoolhouse: "They opened up the coffin to let people look at him. I saw him, and by God I saw him in my mind's eye in the dark for days after, and it terrified me. Blood was running out of the corner of his mouth." The other public schools Masters attended in Petersburg "did not have a particle of charm" or effective teachers, and when one of the teachers at last grew weary with Masters's chronic misbehaving (he was eating an apple in class), she beat him with a pointer until he was black and blue. (The teacher, Clara McDougal, subsequently stepped into a drop-off while fishing in the Sangamon River and drowned, one more death for Masters to confront.) Masters's parents withdrew him from this school and sent him to a private school serving the area's many German farmers, but the discipline was even more lax there (the boys chewed tobacco, fought, and did whatever they wanted, with no semblance of "school order"). Masters did learn elementary German at this school, however, which would be important to him later.[17]

School thus played a relatively minor role in Masters's intellectual development at this time, much of it coming instead from the books he found at his grandparents' farm. His grandfather loved the poetry of the Scottish poet Robert Burns, and Lucinda Masters and her son Will both kept numerous books around the house. Some were in bookcases; some were in trunks on the second floor in a gloomy corner whose dormer windows let in so little light that the family called it "the Dark Ages." *The Babes in the Wood,* Grimm's *Fairy Tales,* and Thomas Bailey Aldrich's *Story of a Bad Boy* became some of Masters's first literary influences. Masters's parents had only a "few books" in the house, and although his mother occasionally read the poems of Burns to him, she seems to have been more interested in Petersburg's social and artistic activities; she enjoyed, for example, her role in a local production of Gilbert and Sullivan's drama *H.M.S. Pinafore.* During these years Masters also got to know Mark Twain's *Tom Saw-*

yer, the poems of Thomas Moore, and the graveyard verse of Edgar Allan Poe—influences that would later find their way into his own writing. So, despite being reared in a family and town with limited literary interests, Masters by age twelve had firsthand exposure to the three literary genres that would interest him most as an adult: poetry, plays, and novels.[18]

In the summer of 1880 Masters's association with the Petersburg–New Salem area changed dramatically when his father decided to move his family forty miles northwest to Lewistown, the Fulton County seat. Masters wrote in *Across Spoon River* that his father had hopes for greater opportunities in Lewistown, but it was also true that Hardin Masters had made several enemies as state's attorney in Petersburg and had to carry a pistol after dark. In any event, the family one day loaded its goods on one train and themselves on another and proceeded to the town of Havana, where they stayed the night before crossing the Illinois River and continuing by stage on the morning of July 3. Along the way Masters made his first, if unprepossessing, crossing of Spoon River: "It was July and very hot. The black flies bit the stage horses, and smells of dank weeds, dead fish, and the green scum of drying pools smote our nostrils. At Duncan's Mills, a place of one store and a post office, we crossed Spoon River on a covered wooden bridge, and ascending a long hill a mile beyond reached the uplands that surround Lewistown."[19]

Lewistown and Petersburg were both small county seats, but they were quite different, much like Masters's father and mother. Petersburg was essentially southern in its ancestry and values, whereas Lewistown was mixed but more northern than southern. Petersburg had been settled by natives of Virginia, Kentucky, and Tennessee, whereas Lewistown was dominated intellectually by people who had migrated from more eastern regions. Petersburg was tolerant of drink, casual about education, and relatively relaxed about religion and religious strictures; it was an easy-going town. Lewistown was not. It was thought to be serious about education (it had a high school with a Princeton man in charge of it), and the town was also serious about strong drink: prominent church members wanted it kept out permanently. Unfortunately, Hardin Masters enjoyed a drink, and although he might have handled this matter covertly, news of his Civil War attempts to free northern draft resisters (or "Copperheads") reached Lewistown "and prevented him from getting business." If Hardin had seemed to be in his element in Petersburg, he was decidedly out of it now—and although his wife could glory in her new surroundings (which were more like those of her native New England), she too suffered, since her immediate well-being was tied to Hardin's. He might have been helped by one of his father's old friends, Lewis Ross, a local lawyer for whom Lewistown was named, but Ross never did anything for Hardin other than to invite him to dinner and rent him a drafty house. It was not until the late 1880s, after Hardin was involved in a sensational murder trial, that the family's fortunes changed greatly. Before this happened (in 1887), Masters had gotten into the habit of returning to his grandfather's farm near Petersburg each summer, in part to recover from the bad colds to which the family's substandard housing made him prone. Masters would later recall living in five houses in Lewistown, none of which, seemingly, was proof against Lewistown's winter winds.[20]

The move to Lewistown was probably hard on Masters's mother as well. Emma had been active in Petersburg's social affairs and looked with jaundiced eyes on the shadeless lot and unimpressive house Hardin had picked for her in Lewistown. She may have anticipated being let down by Lewistown, for before she would sign the bill of sale for their Petersburg place, she made Hardin promise to give her sufficient money for a trip to New Hampshire to visit her mother in the summer of 1880. Certainly, the neat New England houses and staid New Englanders would offer a marked contrast to the ups and downs of life with Hardin Masters—or perhaps she merely wanted to revisit her roots.[21]

Emma's first ancestor in America had probably been the Englishman Gregory Dexter, a printer reputed to have printed one of John Milton's pamphlets. Gregory Dexter migrated to the New World, where he was a friend of the Rhode Island leader Roger Williams. In addition, Emma could claim other well-known Dexters as kin, although these were offset by equally visible and more humble ties to a farmer or two, one of whom, James, was her grandfather. His son, the Reverend Deming Dexter, was a dour divine who may have inadvertently prompted Emma to marry Hardin. In his later years Dexter was rather poor, but he still had daughters who needed husbands. Because the Civil War had thinned the ranks of New England bachelors, Emma followed two older sisters west, where she met Hardin. He was high-spirited, handsome, and carefree—just the opposite of Emma's stern father—and it is easy to see why she was attracted to him.[22]

Despite the move to Lewistown, Masters's home life and many of his social activities remained about the same. He soon made a new set of friends and enjoyed his rambles about the new countryside: "I spent happy days skating and fishing and hunting with boy chums. We used to go to Thompson's Lake about four miles from Lewistown . . . , there to fish and hunt; and to the Spoon River to swim." He also played baseball, wrestled, learned roller skating and ice skating, and became one of the swiftest runners in town. (He had previously taken a few lessons in boxing and the use of parallel bars at a gymnasium in Petersburg.) In addition, he met the town's colorful characters and learned the gossip about them, and he was introduced to village heroes as well, including Major Walker, "who had talked / With venerable men of the revolution." Unfortunately, Masters's family life continued with its strains, the result of parental bickering, poor housing, and insufficient money. Matters were especially strained in 1885 when Hardin Masters cut a finger while slaughtering some family hogs and came down with blood poisoning. Emma took in sewing to support the family while her husband lay near death for several weeks. It was during these years that Masters experienced what he would later describe as "real labor"—carrying coal, delivering newspapers, and picking berries for a penny a quart.[23]

Hardin Masters had a long-range goal of becoming a circuit judge, but he refused to enhance his image with the electorate by attending church or giving up whisky and gambling on such things as poker and horse racing. Nevertheless, he may have impressed the villagers by his willingness to work without compensation when he encountered a deserving client who had no money—although this could be risky: one story had it that some of Lewistown's lawyers would accept sexual favors as payment from women seeking divorces and that Hardin contracted a venereal disease in this manner. In any event, his womanizing seems to have continued more or less openly. After his important 1887 murder trial (his client, the defendant, received twenty-five years instead of death), Hardin's legal abilities were recognized, but his antiprohibition stand on the "wet" versus "dry" issue alienated many voters. His home itself was split by the wet/dry controversy when Emma joined the fashionable but very dry Presbyterian Church in 1881. So the topic of alcohol came up at home as well as in shops around the square and in adjoining townships.[24]

Hardin's lifestyle had at least two important effects on Masters: it presented him with a role model who was honest about his vices and opinions, even when he himself was wounded thereby, and it provided more evidence that tension is the natural state of marriage. Tensions were worst at the holidays, as Masters remembered for the rest of his life: "Christmas . . . brings to me nothing but unpleasant reflections. In my home there in Lewistown, it was never celebrated. I remember staying awake half the night, sleeping and coming to, and in my disordered mind making red top boots out of pieces of quilt or other objects in the room. We got no presents; we had no dinner. There was neither good will nor peace." Masters's diaries for these days affirm the austerity of certain holidays at the Masters house: "Christmas morning dawned revealing few and simple presents in stockings and on the table. Mat woke up and came down to see what Santa had left for her but went back to bed with a whimper carrying a stocking with a little candy therein." (Masters was being somewhat disingenuous here: not all New England Christians who were transplanted to Illinois celebrated Christmas, and Masters's mother may have been influenced by these; Masters's diary for 1884 shows unambiguously that the family did celebrate the Thanksgiving holiday that year.)[25]

Masters's emotional development in Lewistown was not favorable. It would be too much to say that he was emotionally starved in his parents' household, for they did show him some attention, but Masters's perceptions were colored by his belief that his parents did not really care for him, as he made clear in his autobiography: "I made my own way, finding the path after many misjudgments of the directions, and after many obstacles of circumstances, of my own making, and that of my parents. As I look back at it now it seems to me that my parents did not really care for me, or have any proper interest in me." He felt that his mother in particular was "indifferent." He thus learned how to be uncaring, too, and to be self-centered, a future overachiever looking for something but not knowing what. He would spend much of the rest of his life looking for love, although his parental examples showed him not how to give or receive it but only how to turn his back on those close to him.[26]

By the time he was sixteen, the environment of Lewistown had begun to shape him. Like Petersburg, Lewistown was steeped in history (it had once been the county seat for much of northern Illinois, including Chicago), and it offered Masters viewpoints he had not previously encountered. One morning Amos Bronson Alcott, the father of novelist Louisa May Alcott, passed through town and told the assembled high school students how his daughter had become a writer. "It was my first contact with anyone who had ever had anything to do with the making of a real book," Masters wrote in a draft of his autobiography, "and became an unforgettable circumstance." Masters secured a part-time job as an apprentice on the *Lewistown News,* and in 1884, with the help of printer Grant Hyde, he set in print thirty to forty copies of his "first verses": "I set them in type one night and ran them off clandestinely toward midnight on the job press." The resulting poem, "The Minotaur," is both interesting and not: its rhymey four-line stanzas did not seem likely to revolutionize American verse, but its story of a bad-to-the-bone village editor flowed straight from the same source as *Spoon River.* (Its subject was the prohibitionist editor of Lewistown's *Fulton Democrat,* William Davidson, who was not really bad to the bone but only inflexible in opposing Hardin Masters on the subject of saloons.) The poem consisted of ten stanzas and a nonsensical prefatory note, all phrased in youthful overkill, as these excerpts suggest:

THE MINOTAUR

Bill Davidson
National Ode
Dedicated to His Majesty
King Satan

* * *

By the Author

In that vile sheet the "Democrat,"
Bill doth weekly boast.
To read it some all night have sat.
In Hell he'll surely roast.

At slandering Bill doth oft excel.
This truth all can conceive.
Lies from his mouth escape pell mell
As water from a sieve.

* * *

Because "The Minotaur" had not been printed through normal editorial channels involving selection and rejection, Masters sometimes listed another poem as his first: "My first printed poem was in . . . a paper in Quincy. I was about 17. The poem was called 'Zueline,' and is pretty bad, even for juvenilia."[27]

What started Masters writing, he later told Amy Lowell and others, was "music running through [his] brain" and the beauty of the Spoon River countryside: "I began to write verses when about sixteen years old, attempting to put in words universal emotions excited by music, by phenomena of nature, the fall of the year and its calms . . . , winds, and skies." The poetry of Robert Burns and Percy Bysshe Shelley and stories and poems of Edgar Allan Poe formed other, academic influences, along with the Lewistown teacher Esther Sparks and assistant principal Mary Fisher, who loaned Masters books and encouraged his literary aspirations. Fisher met with Masters and four or five others after school to encourage them in their reading of American authors Emerson and Ingersoll and the British mainstays Dickens, Scott, Thackeray, Byron, and Shakespeare. (Masters aspired to be her favorite student, but his friend Will Worley affected a "Byronic despair" and convinced her that he had the most promise.) Ingersoll's *Mistakes of Moses* soon turned Masters into an atheist; other books opened his eyes to what he had been missing at home: "All this was a new life to me; for at home there were no books but Bryant's *A New Library of Poetry and Song,* a copy of Burns, *The Arabian Nights,* which I didn't enjoy, and my Grimm from the Masters farm, which I read over and over; a few paper-bound plays of Shakespeare, and a copy of Crabbe's poems, which I never looked into." (Nevertheless, Masters's commonplace book from these years shows a quotation copied from Crabbe—"Beauties are tyrants, and if they reign / They have no feelings for their subjects [*sic*] pain"—so perhaps he did look at Crabbe.) Masters's new reading led him to John Alden's inexpensive editions of major authors and to translations of Greek and Roman authors. Mary Fisher also visited the Masters home and talked with his mother about books (Emma gave her son at least one book, a copy of Tennyson). It was in his Lewistown years, too, that Masters tried out the first of his many pseudonyms, that of "Adam Casebolt," at the end of one of his diaries.[28]

The precise date of Masters's first writings is hard to pin down since he gave contradictory dates, sometimes in the same sentence: "I began to write when I was 17—indeed when I was ten." The narrative made at ten was of a railroad trip to visit Masters's Kansas aunt and resulted in his first "reading" of one of his works—to his grandfather in the living room of the farmhouse north of Petersburg. Squire Masters tried to appreciate the narrative, but it was too calm even for a doting grandparent, and the old man nodded off.[29]

Lewistown's high school soon took a disappointing turn, for the Princeton man left (as did Mary Fisher after the 1883–84 school year), and successive principals let the school devolve into "a riot of disorder," as Masters said in his autobiography: "Boys arose from their seats and fought in the aisles. Chalk whizzed about the room, sometimes striking the principal. Erasers were hurled across the room. The principal expelled scholars; they laughed at him and kept their seats." Reportedly, Masters was also expelled but returned the next day. "We stomped and just raised thunder," Masters wrote in his diary following one incident. When the teacher tried to discipline the class or speak to them, the students "laughed at him." By the spring of 1884 Masters was missing school every sixth day on the average, and within the year he decided that "the time was past to really progress in the school," choosing instead "to learn the printer's trade." He at first worked at the *Lewistown News* before and after classes but dropped out of school to work full-time as a printer in the fall of 1885, when his school was overtaken by genuine "pandemonium." He returned to school in the same season in time to plan for graduation but did so with the knowledge that his schooling had been "casual," "intermittent," and "interrupted at the very time of life when it should have been continuous and systematic": "When I was taking stock of what I had learned in order to see whether I could graduate from the high school, I was forced to do some piecing. I could then see that I had not finished the courses along the way as I should have done." He graduated in a class of four in the spring of 1886 and delivered an oration entitled "A Tribute to the Memory of Robert Burns" on the stage of Beadles Opera House in Lewistown. His father was gaining in respectability and also spoke.[30]

Masters's graduation from high school did not mark the end of his useful relations with his former teacher, Mary Fisher. Even after she left, she continued to write him, from the time he was sixteen until he was nearly twenty-four: "She kept up a steady correspondence with me about books and life. On her annual trips to Europe she wrote me frequently; and so it continued until I went to Chicago in 1892. . . . I was reading under the tutelage of Miss Fisher's letters; and with one chance and another I was being educated."[31]

Masters's continuing newspaper experience also helped educate him. If the *Lewistown News* editor "Lute" Breedon had not been the son of a wealthy physician, he might have felt compelled to spend more time working at his newspaper and thus inadvertently denied Masters the experiences he gained in writing, editing, and preparing copy for print. As it was, Breedon liked to begin the day with two strong drinks before a big breakfast, after which he tippled sleepily through the rest of the day. Masters's apprenticeship turned into an important job as he prepared the newspaper for print, thus providing himself with an education in publishing with each successive issue. He also wrote a social column and other material and served as correspondent for papers as far away as St. Louis and Chicago.[32]

During his first three years out of high school, Masters not only wrote poetry and "did stories" but also worked as a telephone operator (at two dollars per week) while clerking in his father's law office. After his father decided to send him to college, Masters studied Latin and mathematics at an academy in Lewistown. It was during these years, too, that Masters read extensively from the library of a Lewistown lawyer, John ("Judge") Winter, who provided him with copies of Addison, Steele, Dryden, Pope, and other literary mainstays. Masters also spent some of his Sunday afternoons studying informally with a physician from nearby Bernadotte, Dr. William Strode. The doctor's interest in fauna (especially clams) in the Spoon River brought him national and some international attention far beyond the sleepy hollow of Bernadotte, a fishing hamlet with a picturesque mill and dam. More important for Masters, Strode encouraged his membership (about 1887) in the Fulton County Scientific Association, where Masters had a chance to meet monthly with fifteen to twenty other intellectuals interested in literature and science and before whom he read papers on the poet Walt Whitman, clairvoyance, and science and religion. (Masters repaid Strode with a kindly epitaph in *Spoon River Anthology,* that of naturalist William Jones.)[33]

One day in 1886, returning to Lewistown from his grandparents' farm during his first summer out of high school, Masters encountered an influence that was to be greater than any of these. Masters's decision to forgo his usual train route through the village of Atterberry and take a different train yielded the following result: "My grandmother gave me $15 when I departed. . . . When I got to Mason City I had an hour to wait for the train on to Havana, and I spent it walking about and looking into the store windows. In one of them I saw a book bound in red with golden scrolls and decorations, and the words 'Shelley's Poems.' . . . I took the necessary $2 from the money my grandmother had given me, and walked out with the book, into what proved to be a new world." Masters had read some of Shelley's verses before, but this experience leading him to a "new world" gave a sense of direction to his post–high school life—"to more metaphysics, to Plato, to the Greek writers"—and eventually to his quest to become a famous author. But before his literary life could unfold much further, he had to discover that he had no future in Lewistown.[34]

First, however, he experienced an overdose of Shelleyan platonic love and became enamored with a local poet named Margaret George ("Anne" of the autobiography), with whom he rambled the hills of nearby Big Creek and read the Elizabethan dramatists Marlowe and Webster. He said he was engaged to her in an early draft of his autobiography, and some townspeople thought they would marry, but he downgraded the relation to "friendship" in the published version. The latter is probably the better term, since he was becoming infatuated with Margaret's friend and neighbor Winnogene Eichelberger, known as "Winnie" and "Winks" (the autobiography's "Alfreda"), during some of the same months that he was seeing Margaret. Margaret's father, a minister, made the best of the situation by loaning Masters books from his personal library, including Wordsworth and George Eliot, and by teaching him a smattering of Latin and Greek.[35]

Largely as a result of his readings, Masters settled on a tentative vocation at this time: "I had about made up my mind to be a short-story writer." He read one of his short stories at a local Chautauqua meeting, but the reading went poorly, and perhaps this caused him to change his mind and to publish a flurry of poems in local papers in Bushnell and Quincy, in Eugene Field's "Sharps and Flats" column in the *Chicago Daily News,* and in the *Chicago Inter-Ocean* (which published more than sixty of his poems during an eight-year period beginning in 1888). The poems were written "mostly under pseudonyms": "I was diffident about being known as their author, both because of their sentimental nature, and because I knew that the opinion of the people about me was that poetry was not a virile avocation." He thus chose pen names that had absolutely no relation to his own, such as "Joseph Bilge," "Willis Aronkeil," and at least once each, "Julia Brown" and "George Proctor." (Aronkeil was derived from the Petersburg family name of Ahrenkeil, George Proctor was a Lewistown acquaintance, and Julia Brown was a Lewistown friend; Masters appropriated all the names without asking their owners' permission.)[36]

As for Lewistown itself, Masters felt its rough edges from the very beginning: "It was a rough, ignorant town, save for a few cases, and my companions were Huckleberry Finns and boys who were working, or who were the sons of lawyers and had every possible contempt for what I was doing." As a result he spent many days trying to please others as well as himself, as his diary for April 8, 1889, shows: "Arose at 7—Was at the office by 8 prompt. Worked till half past nine at my Caesar. . . . Read Blackstone until eleven. Rushed eagerly to the post office to get a copy of the daily news expecting to find my ballad. Not there. Laughed it off with a very good face—but inwardly felt enraged and dissatisfied." The reason he felt enraged, of course, was because his writing meant far more to him than the study of his father's law tomes (Blackstone) or the slow process of self-education (Caesar). He was a young man pulled in several directions, but he wanted most of all the sense of achievement he supposed writing would bring. This, in turn, might bring him the attention his parents failed to give him and compensate in part for an unhappy home life—although nothing was guaranteed: "Fame," he confided to his diary, "is many years off from me if I ever have it."[37]

It was the search for fame, however, that encouraged the development of two personality traits that would characterize Masters's adult behavior: personal ambition and tenacity. For example, when the *Atlantic Monthly* routinely rejected one of Masters's poems in 1889, he submitted the same poem a second time, drawing this comment from a nameless editor: "I return your poem, which I do not need to see twice." He was luckier with two other East Coast publications, *Waverly Magazine* and *The Writer,* which published, respectively, two short stories and an article on how to write. Masters's comments in *The Writer* show his awareness that both style and substance are important in writing: "It is the business of a literary performance to please the ear as well as the intellect, and the reverse." He also told how he worked on his style and a larger vocabulary: "I have copied pages from my favorite books, and when I have come to write at some future time, many of the words which were strikingly used, I have found to my glowing satisfaction, were unconsciously added to my own vocabulary, and flocked willingly to assist me in the etching out of my thoughts." But he had not completely mastered either style or substance in 1889. "Try to be natural in your writing," the editor of *The Writer* counseled him. "Why waste your time on the vapor of a dream?" *Waverly* asked. "Give to literature more vital stuff; waking life furnishes a million stirring themes. Try one of them."[38]

Unfortunately, waking life also furnished a million complications as far as Masters's emotional life was concerned. He and Margaret George had a lovers' tiff, which left him feeling lonely, as he would throughout the rest of his life when he had no woman to share his experiences. A friendship with a Havana, Illinois, intellectual named May Heberling would also come to nothing (Heberling is one of two women nicknamed "Louise" in the autobiography). His writing offered an outlet for his emotions, but he was doing so much reading and writing—in his father's law office; for the *Lewistown News;* for the *Chicago Inter-Ocean;* and for a newspaper in nearby Canton, where he published letters—that he experienced a nervous disorder in the summer of 1889. A local doctor suggested he needed to be out of doors more, at which point Hardin Masters saw a means of collecting some old debts from his clientele. As a result Masters and a Lewistown friend named Edwin Parsons Reese were soon driving around the Spoon River countryside in a badly used one-horse vehicle collecting Hardin's bills. The young men returned home at the end of two weeks, and Masters was pronounced well. In future years he would repeatedly return to the rural images of the Spoon River valley (or to those of the Sangamon) to replenish himself when feeling dispirited.[39]

In the fall of 1889 Masters traveled to nearby Galesburg to attend Knox College but discovered to his "mortification" that he was not prepared academically. He had gone to "the college building" on September 4 and found that his "present attainments" were insufficient ("I could not even enter the freshman class"). He had to attend the college's middle preparatory school, Knox Academy, for a year to address deficiencies in Latin (too little) and Greek (almost none). (The academy was housed in the same five buildings as the college itself.) Masters enjoyed this year of education as much as he did any year of his life ("everything was magical about this fresh-water college and this little city of Galesburg"), but he chafed at the thought of being as old as he was and not yet ready for college. His Lewistown friend Edwin Reese had come with him to Knox College, and he and Masters roomed together on Cedar Street, "just across the street from the campus," and studied, read, or daydreamed about the girls who came to the tennis courts. Masters joined two clubs, E.O.D. and K.E.K. The latter was a dining society—the Knox Epicurean Klub—and provided both food and fellowship; the former drew its name from a Greek phrase meaning "to be, not to seem," and offered food for the mind: weekly debates, orations, and declamations. Masters also studied German, spent much time in the town and college libraries, enjoyed professionally performed plays in Galesburg, and saw some of his poetry accepted for college outlets. The poetry won him the nickname of "Old Soph" (after Sophocles), since he was behaving as a poet, although he was also known as "the atheist." His background in reading and writing finally earned him the respect of his peers, and the college yearbook for 1890 referred to him as "a mighty wonder bred among our quiet crew." His name at last established, Masters went home to Lewistown for the summer of 1890. He never returned to his studies.[40]

Hardin Masters had agreed to send his son to college if he met certain demands: he had to leave off "all scribbling, including that for the local newspapers"; he had to abandon "idle" habits (including girlfriend Margaret George, the daughter of the "dry" Presbyterian minister and thus Hardin's enemy); and he had to prepare for a career in law. Perhaps Hardin now felt that his son had not upheld his end of this bargain, perhaps Hardin was chafing over the fact that he himself was a political liberal while Knox was known for its conservatism, or maybe his law practice was doing less well than usual. (His wife hinted that Hardin was drinking too much whisky.) Or maybe Hardin discerned that the Presbyterian minister's daughter Margaret George had simply been replaced by the Presbyterian deacon's daughter Winnie Eichelberger (Masters became so enamored of Winnie during the Christmas break of his college year that he considered himself "engaged"). During Hardin's own student days, he had spent a year in the "Preparatory Department" of nearby Illinois College at Jacksonville, but he seemed to forget the tedium of preparatory units and the fact that his own father had later allowed him to attend the University of Michigan. In any event, he refused to give Masters the $200 he needed for another year at Knox. (Tuition for the college's thirty-seven-week school year was only $25; Masters's room cost $2 per week and food cost $2.50, making a total of $191.50 per year.) Nor was Masters's mother impressed with his college work. She had expected him to "dig right into preparations for entering college" but instead observed that he was pursuing his own interests. "The fact of it is," she told him later, "the glamour of writing shut your eyes to everything else." Now she sided against him, too—an act for which he never forgave her—saying that his giddy sister, Madeline, needed his college money to travel east "to relieve the embarrassment of a broken engagement." Plus, there was another son, Tom, to consider. The family would eventually find money to send Tom (then thirteen) to a half-dozen schools (Abington, Illinois College, Morgan Park Academy, Notre Dame, the University of Michigan, and possibly Northwestern), but as the fall of 1890 came on, there was no money for Masters's education. He appealed to his grandfather for the loan of one hundred dollars for one more term, but he was turned down there, too. Masters was stuck in Lewistown. Meanwhile, his friend Edwin Reese returned to Knox.[41]

Commenting on Masters's one year of college, Reese recalled that Masters did not seem to place a great value on his education and, at age twenty-one, did not seem overly mature. He remembered that Masters spent much less time on his lessons—Latin, Greek, mathematics, "and other essentials"—than he did on reading Kant, Hegel, and Spinoza and having fun. Having fun included daydreaming about a girl or girls, writing endless poems about the fairer sex, or participating in college highjinks. In those days the great amusement at Knox was to put a cow in the college library overnight, tie a pig in the president's office, or some such thing. Masters put a rooster in the bed of a boy at the house and invited "the gang" to come in at midnight to share the merriment. (More prankish young scholars inverted the college bell, tied it in place, and filled it with water that would freeze solid and immobilize the clapper in Galesburg's iron winters.) Masters awarded himself "a blue ribbon in deviltry" at the end of the year, but this may simply have been an attempt to be one of "the gang."[42]

Somehow Hardin Masters got the impression that his son was not taking his college work seriously. In addition, both Hardin and Emma doubted the efficacy of college, as well they might when Masters returned home and began telling his stories: "My father looked at me with wide noncommittal eyes. But I took him thus to say that it was hardly worth while to send me away to gather humorous material about the rooster of the college janitor, and about the boys who played pranks on one another." Masters confused them further by saying that he "felt a constriction" at Knox and asking that his father send him elsewhere. (This must have been perplexing to his parents, for he seemed at ease at the college and would later claim to have received "a hundred in all [his] studies.") Meanwhile, Madeline, who had not even attended high school, took in these conversations with her mother "and looked as if she thought she should be in Knox." And in a very short time Madeline was at Knox—and Masters was looking for work.[43]

Masters's departure from college would have a number of long-term effects on him, all of them harmful. It made him permanently resentful of his parents' judgment in allowing Madeline to go to college instead of himself; it laid the foundation for a resentment at least as great against his brother, Tom, who would also enjoy the benefits of family support for college; and—more important—it left Masters without the critical training he needed to distinguish his good writing from his bad. As it was, he had little more formal training in literature than did the tobacco-chewing opinionists who loafed under the awnings of the Lewistown square, a failing that would leave him vulnerable to the attacks of literary critics who would later judge his work and find it lacking. In addition, Masters's inability to complete his hoped-for course of study left him at cross-purposes socially with those who did have college degrees and bred in him a smoldering resentment of such people, particularly when they claimed to know more about writing than he did.

The pity is that Masters might have gone to college—might have worked his way through, as many young men did—but his father apparently convinced him that he was constitutionally unfit to work and go to school at the same time ("in your state of health . . . , you'll break down for sure"). This advice, articulated in Masters's autobiographical novel *Skeeters Kirby,* may have been the deciding factor in ending Masters's pursuit of a college degree. In any event, by the time he had weathered several Chicago winters and discovered that he was physically able to do whatever he wanted, his life was set in a different direction.[44]

His attempts at education thwarted, Masters failed as a book salesman and then took a job in the fall of 1890 as a schoolteacher at a railroad flagstop named Bybee, a few miles north of Lewistown. Each day a train on the Fulton County Narrow Gauge Railway passed by not far from the school on its way to its northern terminus of Galesburg and Knox College, but it did not stop for him. Masters did not enjoy teaching and came to dislike it so intensely that he did what the bored have always done in schools; he escaped: "During the school hours I read Homer while the students were getting their lessons, keeping my book behind a large geography." He abandoned teaching after the fall semester of 1890 and returned to Lewistown to do what his father wanted him to, study law.[45]

Masters and a Lewistown friend named Will Winter, the son of Judge Winter, studied law together and examined each other at night. Masters was very unhappy at this time and mixed his legal studies with French and Italian lessons, the study of Homer in Greek, work on the *Lewistown News,* his own creative writing, and a great deal of nostalgia about his one happy year at Knox. Overriding everything was his observation that the law career for which he was preparing was at odds with what he really wanted to do, as he noted in his diary for May 4, 1891, shortly before taking the Illinois bar exam: "I never can think of myself as a lawyer, though had I been properly started that might have been my ambition with pleasure. But at sixteen, like a fool, I began to write verses (I think my first were written at fifteen). . . . So here I am, at twenty-two, financially stranded, with an ill cultivated talent, no audience, no prospects, fighting the habit of years to give half of my mind to law when, alas, either law or poetry demands the whole attention."[46]

Such gloominess notwithstanding, Masters subsequently passed the State of Illinois's spring 1891 bar exam in first place (he said) among sixty applicants. (His diary shows that twenty-eight took the exam and that twenty-six passed.) He did not seek law work, however, but applied for a job on the *Chicago Inter-Ocean,* which turned him down. At about the same time, his father concluded that Minneapolis had a favorable business climate, and so Masters spent July there. He lived at 232 Fremont, working briefly for both a law publishing house and the Swinburne Printing establishment, but he was mostly unemployed and returned to Lewistown, where his father proposed a partnership.[47]

His father's office (shared with partner William Dyckes) was on the second floor of the Beadles Block, a large building occupying most of the north side of the Lewistown square. It incorporated Beadles Opera House (in which Masters had delivered his graduation oration on Robert Burns), and the top center of its front sported a colored plaster bust of Shakespeare—Masters's daily reminder that literature had been supplanted by law; occasional presentations of *East*

Lynne and *Uncle Tom's Cabin* had the same effect. Masters tried at least one case, which he lost, but his chief activities were conducting legal research for his father, interviewing witnesses, and collecting bills. He also watched his father try cases, although Hardin Masters was hardly a model lawyer; as Masters later observed, his father was "incapable of systematic work. He practiced law a good deal by ear, by inspiration, by great bursts of energy when he was cornered." The partnership lasted a year—from August 1891 to July 1892—and although Masters's chances boded well to advance from his starting salary of $5 a week to $2,000 a year as master in chancery, he was finally overtaken by what he described as the "vast futility" of village life:

> My father's office was on the second floor of the Beadles Block, just across from the courthouse yard and with two sides of the square visible. In fact, the square had but three sides; for at the east was an open space of at least a block which was in front of the Presbyterian Church. Thus at the window where I sat in study I could glance up and see what was going on about town as men went here and there on their business, and as the farmers came into town, tied their horses to the rack and started forth to see merchants, lawyers, or what not. This spectacle so affected me at times with its vast futility that I had to go forth and find companions to shake off the depressing feeling.[48]

But he sometimes argued with these same companions and with his parents as well. His mother, for example, had become unbearable on the subject of his need to give up writing for the law. She herself had taken up writing, getting a story or two printed in an adjoining town's paper, but she was insistent that her son cease his efforts to write. In this she showed the same inflexible nature, her need to dominate, that had caused tension with her husband for many years. One hot July day she attempted to settle one of her recurrent disputes with Masters by hitting him over the head with a rolled-up window shade. The result was that he decided at last "to go to Chicago, to get away from the village spites, the melancholy of the country, and from the bad will that followed me everywhere." He confided matters to his diary: "If I were out of Lewistown, I could be myself, and that means some happiness." He might also escape a recent humiliation: Winnogene Eichelberger, to whom he had once considered himself engaged, had thrown him over for a mere "ribbon clerk" working in one of Lewistown's dry goods stores.[49]

On July 20, 1892, when Masters's strain of "the village virus" became too much, he packed a valise and "about 400 poems" and gathered his life savings of about twelve dollars. Then he left Lewistown on the narrow-gauge railroad, "The Peavine" (so named "because it twisted and turned every which way"), and went to the town of Havana, on the Illinois River. There he waited in the super-humid air for the midnight train to Chicago.[50]

Masters would later characterize many of his Lewistown years as "largely wasted," a mishmash of juvenile longings, family bickering, poor-paying jobs, and patternless reading—and this is the impression one gets from his autobiography—but by the time he left Lewistown, he had developed both the character and the curiosity necessary to succeed in the city, both as an attorney and as an author. As had happened in his first hometown of Petersburg, he had learned more than he realized, many of his out-of-school experiences being more important than the lessons he learned within schoolhouse walls.[51]

It had taken character for Masters to read on his own the works of the essayists Addison and Steele and the poets Dryden and Pope, not to mention the philosophers John Locke and David Hume. Nor could Masters have found it easy to pursue the writings of Bishop Berkeley, and those of the astronomer-mathematician Sir William Hamilton, even if the source of such books had a daughter as welcome to Masters's eyes as Margaret George. And how many students then (or a century later) would have consulted Fulton County schoolteacher Homer Roberts to gain a better understanding of the evolutionists Thomas Henry Huxley and Herbert Spencer? A similar question could be asked regarding Masters's youthful self-study of Rousseau, Flaubert, Gautier, Virgil, Cervantes, Tolstoy, Goethe, Tennyson, Plutarch, and others.[52]

Much later, when Masters compiled a lengthy list of his readings between ages seventeen and twenty-one, only a few of the works he named were on the subject of law. Instead, most were squarely in the mainstream of American and European literature: "Poe's tales over and over, and his poems too; also Hawthorne's novels . . . , Virgil entire . . . , all of Shakespeare, except seven plays (most for the second time), Chaucer . . . , *Paradise Lost* for the third or fourth time," and so on. Because Masters had not studied these in a formal way in a classroom, however, he felt self-conscious about his education.[53]

He need not have felt this way. Masters had not only read but understood much concerning all the authors of his study. Consider, for example, the critical understanding (as well as the interesting last line) of the following, which he wrote in his diary shortly before passing the Illinois bar exam: "I look on the work of [William Dean] Howells and [Henry] James as merely preparatory to a school of fiction *purely American* and perhaps surpassing anything the world has seen. America's great poet is yet to be. He will be higher and better than any idea of him which can now be found; and he will most astonishingly vary from everything of which we know. What we want is a modern poet."[54]

Surprisingly, Masters sensed he had the raw materials for important literary writings even in Lewistown but did not know how to approach them, as his diary also makes clear: "I have been thinking today that a Shakespeare in America at this day would toss off ten thousand aphorisms, witty, exquisite, and sublime. . . . Think of truths peculiarly American contemporaneous with us and being quoted everywhere. What enrages me is that these things are under my nose and everyone else's, yet we can't see them." The "truths peculiarly American" would, of course, later be enunciated in *Spoon River Anthology.*[55]

In other words, Masters's Lewistown years left him with a far better education than he knew. Thus, when he finally boarded his midnight train to Chicago, it was perfectly in character for him to stay up all night simply because he wanted "to see the first traces of Chicago, to see how and where it began." He was curious about such things as that, too, and so Chicago would also become part of his education.[56]

CHAPTER 2

A Dark, Poetic Hamlet

You are a dark, poetic Hamlet who constantly leaves the plow to lean on the rail fence, study a dusty landscape and brood on love, slavery and death.

—Theodore Dreiser to Edgar Lee Masters, February 6, 1939

Masters entered Chicago as a "round-faced, dark-eyed rube" of twenty-three, his long hair hanging over his collar as he perspired into his clothing and toted his canvas suitcase along the rails of Chicago's grimy Polk Street train station. "There were also poems," his son Hilary later said, "many poems, packed among the underwear and shirts along with the same portfolio for success all country boys lug into the city, bound in ambition and edited by dreams." If Masters had wanted a change in his life, this was his chance: he was broke, virtually friendless, and had no way to go but up.[1]

He also had a limited market for his poems. Chicago in 1892 had a million-plus souls, all of them there to make money. Noisy, dirty, and ambitious, Chicago's polyglot multitudes toiled in the workshops of the wealthy, in grain terminals, railroad yards, meatpacking houses, machinery factories, and manufacturing concerns. Most of these people had no interest whatsoever in poetry. The few who were interested in writing were mostly reporters or the socially privileged. If they were the latter, they might be interested in literature—but only from New England (Longfellow, Whittier, and Holmes) or old England (Shelley, Keats, and Browning).[2]

There were a few places in Chicago that dealt intimately with literary subjects, but these were limited. The Little Room was representative. Begun in the 1890s, its members typically met in Chicago's salons, where the artistically established had the opportunity to meet and mingle with the financially well off. Its purpose was as much social as artistic, and its very existence turned on an afterthought: patrons at Friday matinee performances of the Chicago Symphony needed something to do after the performances; the Little Room was the result.

Its outlook was unambiguously genteel, and a literary revolutionary—or a boy fresh from the country—would have felt out of place. Typical attendees might have included editors of *The Dial* (which published university professors and presidents), the founders of the publishing house Stone and Kimball (vendors of fine books printed at Harvard), and others from Chicago's literary elite.[3]

Masters stayed initially with his uncle, Augustus Ladd, who ran a boardinghouse and helped him find his first job contacts: the newsman William Busbey of the *Chicago Inter-Ocean,* who sized up Masters and told him to go into law, and a lawyer who told him to go back to the country. Masters's tiny room overlooking an alley behind the boardinghouse seemed almost inviting after meetings with these two. Masters soon formed a romantic liaison with one of the tenants of his boardinghouse, a French nurse. Masters followed up on job possibilities by day and in the evenings sat with the nurse (Madam Y, he called her) on the boardinghouse steps and watched Chicago's millionaires sweep by: "Before us passed the endless procession of millionaires riding behind docked horses, out to refresh themselves against the heat of the day."[4]

Masters's first Chicago position was as a bill collector for Samuel Insull's Edison Company, work he called "galling." The job required Masters to tramp from one end of the city to the other in all types of weather, collecting old debts and prosecuting debtors in court, where the cases were often thrown out. His pay was fifty dollars a month (about a third what he could have made in Lewistown), and the job left him too exhausted for study of any type and too broke to buy books. His Lewistown friend Will Winter had also come to Chicago, and he and Masters had an occasional talk about Greek writers and French playwrights, but for the most part Masters's intellectual side was not being fed. One of his few writings from this time was an article entitled "Tennyson," printed in the November 1892 issue of a Knox College student publication, the *Coup D'Etat.* Tennyson's death was the occasion for the piece; its acceptance no doubt resulted from Masters's recent attendance at the school. Meanwhile, his new work became more intolerable when he discovered he was being underpaid. After ten months of working for Insull, Masters heard of a young lawyer who was looking for a partner and soon left bill collecting behind him.[5]

On May 1, 1893, Masters joined this new partner, Kickham Scanlan, in the Ashland Building and began his slow progress up the city's overpopulated legal ladder. There was one problem from the start, however: life as a lawyer was not what Masters really wanted, so that every case and every association was tinged with the expediency of making money—more specifically, with the hope of making so much money that he could quit the law and devote himself to writing. "I was . . . writing verses and occasionally publishing a few. When I did so, I had to run the fire of comment from lawyers at the courthouse and elsewhere; and I soon saw that I could not advance as a lawyer and have this indulgence known about me; so I resolved again to go on in secret and abide the day when the law would make me financially independent." At his 1893 salary of fifty dollars a month, plus what he could "pick up," retirement from the law did not seem imminent, but this did not greatly bother him at the time.[6]

Masters enjoyed immensely the endless variety of Chicago in the Gay Nineties. The two young men opened their law office on the same day that the Columbian Exposition (or Chicago World's Fair) opened. Masters would later describe it as "the most beautiful thing that has ever existed on this earth." He pursued a variety of young women to help him enjoy it and remained in their pursuit after the fair was over. He lost one (without remorse) to the boxer "Gentleman Jim" Corbett. Others had the distressing tendency of growing too serious, at least one turned out to be married, and some were prostitutes. One day he was visiting in Lewistown when he was diagnosed with syphilis by his naturalist-friend, Dr. Strode. Masters was devastated, for there was no cure at this time, and he decided to commit suicide. First, however, he journeyed to Petersburg, because, he said, "I wanted to see the old farm again before I took my life." While he was there, his complaint cleared up; a second doctor found nothing wrong with him, and he was soon back to his usual habits.[7]

According to Masters, his sexuality was always a prominent part of his being and had begun at age six or seven, when he was attracted to "an older girl" named Nettie Robbins (who subsequently died in childbirth and became the character of "Edith Conant" in *Spoon River*). When Masters was seven or eight, a worldly ten-year-old named Cora Williams "explained the technique of love-making" to him, after which his "emotions became directed toward satisfaction." He experienced a serious case of puppy love for Petersburg's Zueline Wallace at age eleven or so and thereby learned, he said, how to harden his heart in such a way as to avoid emotional involvements. He was aware of this ability to hold back a part of himself (he had learned it to perfection in the emotionally stinted environment of his parents' house) and would never thereafter give himself completely to anyone. He commented on this tendency in an unpublished chapter of his autobiography: "Few can [be] or ever have been closely intimate with me. My double personality always works. I keep back a part of myself, an inner self which is aloof and in a protecting and watchful mood." He seems to have been a bit too forward, however, with his first Lewistown girlfriend, Delia Proctor, and her father ended the relationship. It was at about this time, too, during Masters's teenage, Lewistown years, that he developed a dual attitude toward women as whores or angels, an attitude that would sometimes characterize his adult relations as well. He explained the phenomenon thus: "Wherever my idealism was involved I kept its object high and afar; where my passion was the only thing with which I was concerned I was bold enough." His Lewistown sweetheart Margaret George had been in the "angel" category; other women fell easily into the latter, including an untold number of serving maids in Lewistown with whom he had achieved what he called "natural gratification." (One location for these trysts, it is interesting to note, was the Lewistown graveyard.)[8]

An emerging problem in Chicago was that other people sometimes failed to understand Masters's values as clearly as he did—not Lena, who followed Madam Y and who liked him well enough to marry him, or Stella, who was apparently pregnant, possibly by him. It is doubtful, too, whether a gambler named Jake would have understood Masters's easy approach to sexual relations. Masters was having an affair with Jake's girl, Julia, in one of the rooming houses, but Jake was probably armed, and Masters was always a little afraid of being discovered and shot. His emotional life became more tangled one day in early 1895 when Margaret George contacted him to let him know that she was considering marriage to Lewistown's prohibitionist editor William T. Davidson, his father's long-time enemy and the subject of Masters's first printed poem, "The Minotaur." Masters felt she was "angling for a proposal of marriage" from him, but he was no longer interested and told her to marry Davidson; she subsequently did so and died only two years later. Masters would later characterize her as "one of the most inspiring friends of [his] youth," one who had greatly encouraged his intellectual development.[9]

His new work as a lawyer left him with more time and energy to follow his intellectual passions. In addition, the law settled his identity: prior to this he had usually been "Lee Masters" or "E. L. Masters," but one day he found his partner had used his full name on the office door and began using it himself. Masters had more time for himself than he preferred, for business fell off when the World's Fair ended and grew still worse as a national depression manifested itself in Chicago in the mid-1890s. Many of his cases yielded only small fees, in part because Masters often helped those who had only a limited ability to pay, a phenomenon that he attributed to his "intercessor spirit" (learned from his father) and that, he said, "the study of Shelley had magnified." So from the very start of his legal career, Masters was guided by his readings from his Lewistown days.[10]

He was guided as well by two new acquaintances in Chicago, Victor and Rachel (or Rachelle) Yarros, two recent Russian émigrés who were both exceptionally well read. The wife was a physician and expert not only in Russian literature but also in English, French, and American writings. She was especially interested in Herbert Spencer and in the matter of philosophical anarchy, a subject that would form the nucleus of Masters's U.S. Supreme Court case a few years later. Dr. Yarros's husband was even more helpful: "He read French, German, Russian and English equally well and there was no book, especially in economics or philosophy, which he did not, as it seemed, know. He was a man of infinite dialectic, fluent and profuse, and with his definite convictions clarified many of my ideas." Both Yarroses were authorities on the subject of personal freedom, something that Masters would pursue in one way or another for several decades.[11]

Meanwhile, he drifted out of one relationship into another, and from one boardinghouse to another, pausing in 1896 to share an apartment with a new law associate (and minor poet), Ernest McGaffey, who encouraged him in his writing ("He lived with me at my apartment in the Groveland [Hotel,] where we wrote ballades[,] and ate at Mrs. Allison's Strictly Home Cooking restaurant"). McGaffey—the autobiography's "Maltravers" and a model for "Petit, the Poet" in *Spoon River*—was a restless spirit and remained with the firm of Scanlan and Masters for only a year, but before he left, he introduced Masters to the Chicago Press Club. Masters met writer Opie Read and others there, but these individuals offered only momentary balm to his loneliness, and for a variety of reasons, he more and more contemplated marriage and a home.[12]

Sometimes, however, circumstances themselves seemed to suggest that he should remain single. One evening in 1896, while weighing the advice of Jake's girlfriend, Julia ("get married"), against a complaint from another sweetheart, Marcella ("you never let yourself go"), Masters decided to fall in love with "Honoria" (Helen Runyon), a young woman from a fashionable address on Chicago's North Side. He had recently discerned an "affinityship in feeling and thinking" with Honoria and started for her father's house. He had barely gotten started, however, when he was overtaken by his former girlfriend Stella. Stella no longer interested him, and when an argument ensued, he informed her that she had fallen in his estimation. Stella replied that she would remove herself from his life forever if he would make love to her one last time. Masters consulted his watch. "It was now only about six o'clock," he wrote in his autobiography, "so we went to a hotel, and she parted from me in tears as I went to the North Side. On my way I bought a large bunch of roses for Honoria." But Honoria had an illness, and her mother refused to let Masters enter, remarking that it would be some time before he could see her. In the end Honoria went the way of Stella, Marcella, and Julia, along with Anne, Cecile, Gertrude, and Grace. Indeed, she went the way of a great many women with identities ranging from *A* to *Z,* from Alfreda to Zueline (many of them are identified only by aliases in his autobiography), and Masters went on to another fashionable address and to another bank of brightly lit windows beckoning him in from the street.[13]

He was drawn to a good many shabby addresses as well, but within two years of his arrival in Chicago, two events encouraged Masters in his quest for upward mobility: in 1893 his sister, Madeline, married into Chicago's polite society (as Mrs. Carl Stone) and soon suggested to her brother that he might also marry well (Masters's eyes must have opened in wonder when the private railroad car carrying Madeline and her wealthy husband pulled out of Lewistown after the wedding); a year later, in 1894, Masters argued his first case before the Illinois Supreme Court. His ensuing victory increased his social standing only a little, but it increased his self-confidence a great deal and showed him that he could compete on even terms with men from more favored circumstances: "My winning it gave me a certain name at the bar but brought me no substantial results. I must say, however, that I rather gloried in my shingle flung to the winds without the help or the backing of anyone, and rather looked down upon the young college men who were beginning in the great [law] offices, and whom by reason of my initiative and self-discipline I was able to handle for the most part so easily."[14]

This in turn caused him to see that he might compete favorably against such men in other arenas as well. He observed that young men like himself ("young men of the soil, or those who had worked their way through college") sometimes needed only to have a plan to marry well:

> Some of these men with nothing but dinner coats and a suit case established themselves at the less expensive hotels located near the fashionable districts, and from that vantage point schemed for invitations to dinners and dances, where they used their college wit and their practiced feet to win the daughters of great magnates who were looking for husbands. My opportunity to know these heiresses was greater than nearly any of these soldiers of fortune. For my sister, suddenly introduced into the most elect of the city's social life, was ambitious for me and tried to settle me with a wife who would mean something to my financial independence.

Madeline Masters never did find the ideal spouse for her brother (or for herself), but after this, visions of a grim future loomed whenever Masters considered marriage to a woman of humble circumstances.[15]

Other factors old and new also encouraged his upward mobility. Masters felt he had to work harder than others because he was not well connected and because he had not received a college education—and he was teased, too, with what might have been if his paternal grandfather had managed his affairs a little differently more than sixty years earlier. In 1832, after serving in northern Illinois in a company of mounted volunteers during the Blackhawk War, Squire Masters had passed through Fort Dearborn near what would later be some of the most valuable real estate in downtown Chicago. He was riding a "wonderful Indian pony" sufficiently impressive that it led someone to offer as a trade "a large piece of land" near the junction of the Chicago River and Lake Michigan. The land was sandy and unproductive, however, and not at all suitable for corn, which inclined Squire Masters to keep the pony. In addition, he had recently met a girl he admired on a hayrack ride to a party for young people at Murrayville. The pony was his quickest conveyance back to her. He had subsequently married the girl, now Lucinda Masters, and was happy with her—but as anybody could see, he had passed up the deal of a lifetime.[16]

So all this was behind Masters and shaping him when he one night in 1896 encountered the pretty daughter of a Chicago railroad executive, the respected president of one of the elevateds. Masters was greatly attracted to both her beauty and her character: "I was impressed by her piety, which I took as the equivalent of goodness, by her chastity which was fuel to my passion." He also saw in her an opportunity to address the need of greater financial security, for his law practice did not prosper in its early days: "I imagined that I should have no trouble in finding a place in the railroad office by grace of its president if he became my father-in-law." And so, in November 1896, Masters became engaged to Helen Mary Jenkins, daughter of Robert E. and Marcia Jenkins.[17]

Masters's story of what ensued has always puzzled readers of his autobiography, for he willingly entered into a relation that seemed cursed from the start. "He made a marriage against his best judgment," said a reviewer of *Across Spoon River,* and his union with Helen Masters certainly came to be the most galling thing in his life, robbing him of his peace of mind and his modest fortune and disturbing his writing as well. Thus, what he says about his courtship and marriage in *Across Spoon River* says a great deal about Edgar Lee Masters the man.[18]

Above all, Masters was legitimately concerned about the divergent opinions he and his prospective bride held on almost every issue about which men and women can argue: politics, religion, money, sex, and personal habits such as drinking and smoking. They differed as well in mood and temperament, as Masters himself remarked: "The lady did nothing impulsively. She deliberated on everything. . . . When I proposed to her, she calmly took the matter under advisement, promising an answer by a given day; and when she accepted the proposal, she as deliberately said that no marriage could be for at least a year. This delay was to furnish the time within which we could know each other." Thus, while Masters greatly admired Helen's face, figure, and moral virtues, he always found her a little dull ("I never had any madness for her"), and finally he came up with an analysis of them both that was simultaneously accurate and pathetic: "She really was . . . a beautiful woman with a character in which there were many virtues, too many for me."[19]

As the months went by, Masters had serious second thoughts about his approaching nuptials. He talked with his friends, his father, his sister, and his betrothed about why he should not marry her, but none of these offered him a means to break off the relation. Conventions of the time obligated him to consider marriage after a sustained relation, and an engagement announcement virtually demanded it. Nevertheless, he went to her house one night determined to end the relation. He delivered his news: they would have to break up. The poor girl burst into tears. He told her she could say that she ended the engagement; she told him she could not lie. Forty-five years later (after Masters had thought of this evening for more years than he wished), he summed it up as follows: "If I had walked out of the house never to return the night I told her we must not go on, everything would have been different in respect to happiness of myself. Tears and forecasts of social shame overcame my will." In fact, tears, social shame, and precedent all played a part. Masters had once before given in to circumstances when asked to make a major life decision—when his father insisted that he become a lawyer and Masters reluctantly agreed. Now his father suggested that he had little choice but to marry Helen, and Masters again acquiesced.[20]

Masters should probably have remained single, because he lacked the capacity to remain faithful to one woman. He had in fact once decided "never to marry" but was overcome by "the unending loneliness of having no one intimately in [his] life" and by the storybook side of marriage as well as its practical aspects: "I fancied myself settled with a wife with my books around me during long peaceful evenings, when I could turn to write a poem." Needless to say, the prospective Mrs. Masters admired his verses and might in her way contribute to them: "I had to do everything for myself, such as to sew on buttons and to get my laundry gathered up and sent out, which always bothered me more than it should have done. It made no matter how much I was worn down and distracted, how much I felt my talent for writing wasting away under the attritions of the city, living the hurly-burly life that I lived, I still kept my passion for poetry, and there was a hurt always in my heart that I was forced to neglect the call that I felt." If he had a helpmate to look after such bachelor drudgeries, he reasoned, he would be free to write his poems.[21]

In the end, ambivalent to the last, Masters presented himself on the evening of Tuesday, June 21, 1898, at the home of his prospective father-in-law at 4200 Drexel Boulevard. He took his place in the bridal party at 8:00 P.M., feeling, he wrote later, "like a man going to the electric chair." Almost immediately, as if the marriage vows were a script, his life changed for both better and worse: his honeymoon was miserable ("everything I did displeased her"), his wife soon became pregnant, and he felt imprisoned by marriage's constraints—but his shirts were all laundered and had buttons as well, and he had ample time for his verse, for all his evenings were long.[22]

Because home life was stressful and because he saw that he and his wife might never grow closer, his early years of marriage proceeded under a cloud: "My heart was unsatisfied. I was not unhappy, but I was heavily worked and my life seemed scrappy and unmanageable. And my wife was not happy. She tried to make herself over into what she fancied I wanted her to be, but it tore her to do so." The couple often had "sharp words" followed by his "peace offerings" of jewelry, and "she was in tears both for my offenses and for my contrition for them." Uneasy at home and unhappy at law, he turned to his writings for comfort.[23]

It all made a rather sad story.

It was not, however, an entirely true one. In fact, this account of his courtship, engagement, and marriage, which appears in *Across Spoon River*, led Helen Jenkins Masters to draw up her own summary of these events. This document (a fifty-seven-page typescript at the University of Texas Harry Ransom Humanities Research Center) is entitled "Mrs. Edgar Lee Masters" and is dated April 10, 1950. It is interesting for at least three reasons: Masters had been dead for a month by then, the Masterses themselves had been divorced for more than a quarter of a century, and the story Helen Masters told differs from that in *Across Spoon River*. Although the importance of her unpublished document might be minimized on the grounds that former domestic partners often have opposing views of the same events, even to the grave, this case constitutes an exception:

in letters he wrote to Helen from 1897 through 1903, Masters affirmed what she wrote while contradicting what he published in his autobiography.[24]

Far from behaving "like a man going to the electric chair," Edgar Lee Masters wrote letters both before and after his marriage suggesting that he was very much in love. He called Helen Jenkins "My Dearest Love," "My Dearest Dolly Girl," "Darling Child," and "Lamb." He referred to himself as her "hubby to be":

> May 13, 1897
> My Dearest Helen:
> It is reported in the "Boo-le-vard" that Miss J—— is engaged to a young man who writes—both reports being false. I did write, but don't—Miss J—— is not engaged—that anybody knows of.
> I am being quite good, having smoked but once yesterday and once to-day.
> Ever Lovingly Yours,
> Edgar[25]

It was true that she was trying to change him—he had to quit smoking and start going to church—but he said he could accommodate that: "What you are and have been make up to me for all efforts to be as you want me to be. . . . I shall go to the church without you and with you." It was a promise easier made than kept—with Masters once scheduling a Sunday morning meeting with his law partner to avoid church attendance. "I could not keep my appointment with my partner and go to church too," he explained. (A few years later, however, Helen was happy to report that he was the president of the church's men's club.) Smoking was another matter. He had begun using tobacco regularly by the time he left Knox College and smoked a pipe, cigars (less often), or cigarettes (far less often) most of his days thereafter; he also chewed tobacco.[26]

In any event, he was going to change her, too, as he explained in letters dated August and September 1897: "It is evident that my study has made my mind and its expressions on many things a somewhat new experience to you. Will you not see if there is any profit in it to you, exercising at the same time your intellectual freedom?" "I am glad you enjoy the *Iliad*—the *Odyssey* will please you more. . . . Oh you shall be the most learned girl in town."[27]

When Helen Jenkins expressed concerns about the differences in their temperaments, Masters told her she was behaving immaturely: "I think, dolly dear, that your 'girlish misgivings' occasionally expressed are quite impossible and not to be thought of. . . . Think of the Norse proverb 'Be brave, be brave' and have *some* confidence in the man who loves you truly." Sometimes, however, the man who loved her truly had strange ways of expressing it: "I don't think you mean to ask me to be upright and faithful. To extract such a promise suggests a doubt as to my course in that regard. . . . We must adopt the doctrine of freedom. Each is to do as he pleases so long as neither commits a trespass against the other." But then he soon reassured her: "I have been fearfully ambitious and with it all, outside of the pleasure of mental excitement, I have known little peace of mind. The last year, which includes my association with you, has been fraught with keener pleasure than any other portion of my life." In addition, he bragged about her, doing so here four months before their marriage: "Helen is the real source of judgment and information and I am so used to deferring to her that if I did not know what she knew I would not know anything." Obviously, he needed her: "I love you so sincerely that I can in a way overlook my short-comings." Really, he could be very winning.[28]

Helen Jenkins was twenty-two, or nearly so, when she met her future husband at a fund-raising bazaar of the Chicago Friendly Aid Society held next door to her home. Blondish, with yellow-gray eyes, she had attended nearby Rockford College and had graduated from its Conservatory of Music with an ongoing interest in voice and piano. Her father, an affluent lawyer, was president of both the Metropolitan Elevated Railroad and the Chicago Congregational Club, a religious organization (he would serve also as treasurer for the Chicago Bar Association). He sent his son, George, to Harvard Law School and provided his wife and two daughters with a sheltered and genteel lifestyle. On the night that Helen Jenkins met Masters, she and her fellow fund-raisers were pursuing the arm's-length aid to the poor that her class practiced, and if she was not actually leading a fairy-tale life, she certainly looked it: "All the helpers were in costumes as Mother Goose characters," she noted in her unpublished memoir. "I was dressed as Jill."[29]

Masters was then a "budding young lawyer" living in bachelor quarters at the Groveland Hotel. He was escorting the wife of a local judge (Mrs. John Barton Payne) on the night of the bazaar, and it was she who introduced him to Helen Jenkins. The judge's wife was something of a matchmaker, and Masters soon found himself alone with Miss Jenkins, taking her around to the booths and buying her some trifles and ice cream. But something about her intrigued him. He was soon visiting her at home, sending her books, and taking her to the opera. On the way home from one of the operas (and quite unexpectedly), he proposed. She accepted, despite the reservations of her father, who was also a deacon and Sunday school superintendent. Masters's future mother-in-law put up less resistance and was soon going with her daughter to his Groveland Hotel apartment to gather his laundry and see it returned.[30]

Helen Jenkins hoped then and for several years afterward to assist Masters in his writing, which she felt had lacked proper encouragement. During the year and a half of her engagement, she had time to consider the subject:

> His frequent letters always made me want to weep. I used to go to the bathroom where I could lock the door and be undisturbed, and read them and cry over them. For one thing, he had always wanted to write and his parents had discouraged him. They wanted him to concentrate on the law and be a successful lawyer. He used to write me about this and I resolved that my first concern would be to encourage

> him in writing his poetry and I carried out that resolve and thenceforth he came to depend on me for that help.

Not surprisingly, as time went on, his writing and their romance somehow became intertwined. She was especially hopeful, for example, that his first book would turn out well and scolded him when he failed to report on its progress—and when he failed to report just how he spent his evenings away from her: "I think it is very naughty in you not to tell me how far you have progressed in our precious book, and whether you work on it every night, and if not, what you do. You haven't told me about your evenings. . . . I always think of you when I close my eyes at night, and I like to be able to place you—to know just where you are." Any reservations she held were surely removed when it was discovered that she and Masters were distant cousins—tenth-generation descendants of one Lieutenant Putnam, grandfather of the Revolutionary War patriot Israel Putnam.[31]

As she grew to be more a part of his life, Helen became more and more determined that their relationship work out. "You are now my knight and my hero," she wrote him in February 1898, "and someday you will be my husband forever." She sent him a snippet of a romantic poem:

> I have you fast in my fortress
> and will not let you depart,
> But put you into the dungeon,
> in the round tower of my heart.

"Fate cannot separate us, can it, darling?" she asked on Valentine's Day. They were married in the spring of 1898 and subsequently honeymooned in the East, including Concord, Massachusetts, where they took away pictures of the homes of Hawthorne and Emerson. Masters's wedding gifts to Helen included two lots in Chicago deeded to her the day after their marriage.[32]

The newlyweds settled into the third floor of the Jenkins home on Drexel Boulevard, where their son, Hardin Wallace Masters (named for Masters's father but called "Ittie Boy" and "Bug"), was born in April 1899. As their first anniversary approached, Masters left this note for his wife before he traveled out of town:

> Darling Child,
> I want to write you a little before leaving to tell you how much I love you and also to ask forgiveness for any little sorrow I may have caused you. . . . We have a little boy now, and surely no couple was ever blessed with a better child.

Nor could he ask for a better wife, as he said in this letter of August 14, 1899: "I am so happy in the possession of you, darling, for I have never seen anyone like you and never expect to see your like again. You are so wise, gentle, loving, forgiving, progressive, dutiful, etc., etc., and with the coming of 'Ittie Boy' have shown yourself equal to any duty in life. . . . If I ever am unjust to you, always remember that my head errs and not my heart for the latter is with you always." "Life," he assured her in March 1900, "will never be sweeter than now"; "we will go along together in life believing that you will receive everything your perfect goodness merits."[33]

As the third anniversary of their marriage approached in 1901, Masters reiterated Helen's wifely virtues: "We are exceedingly happy. And I am always regretful in thinking of times when I have been fretful. I don't believe there is another woman like you; equally patient and sweet, equally generous and loving." Not surprisingly, perhaps, he wanted to share with her a large family:

> You are Queen of my Heart and I always hate to be away from you and our darling boy. You are in every way a high-minded and noble girl and I hope we can develop together in every way all the years of our lives. You are as necessary to me as I am to you. . . . I cannot help but remember how beautiful you were [during a recent outing], how much superior to all who were there. Your spirit is written in your face—a spirit of love and loveliness. You have transmitted to Hardin a remarkable nature—sweet, generous, and wise. If we only had a little girl exactly like your dear self. . . . Kiss Bug for me.

Masters's love letters to Helen continued in much the same vein through 1903 and part of 1904.[34]

While such letters are not numerous, their content is consistent and raises the question of why Masters's letters say one thing and his autobiography another. The answer rests (as does so much with him) in his 1923 divorce. Bitterly angry over circumstances surrounding it, Masters tried in his autobiography to inflict a lasting revenge on Helen Masters by denying that he had ever cared for her, even in their best days. Unfortunately, his decision to inflict this revenge warped the accuracy of his own story. All evidence suggests that Masters had a "good" if somewhat dull early marriage to Helen (or "Jingle," as he called her); when she began to bore him, he sought excitement elsewhere. His father had done the same thing when faced with the stress of his own unhappy marriage, a fact to which Masters referred more or less openly in his poem "So We Grew Together," whose title refers to the similarities between father and son, a chief similarity being their inability to commit themselves to any one woman.[35]

Masters, however, had good reasons to look elsewhere, or so he said. Quoting Schopenhauer in the pages of *Poetry,* he wrote that "life's problem is how to escape boredom." Some nights he sought escape at a house of prostitution managed by Minna and Ada Everleigh at 2131 South Dearborn. The Everleigh Sisters (or "the Ladies Everleigh," as one reporter put it) managed the best services of their kind in Chicago. Their three-story house was "to pleasure what

Christ was to Christianity," the same reporter averred, and their prices (ten to fifty dollars per girl) reflected this. They flourished from 1900 to 1911, with a clientele that consisted of the affluent and well known, including Masters, who speaks in several places of being a patron. A quarter of a century after Chicago mayor Carter Harrison closed the house, Masters reminisced with Harrison about the days when the Everleigh "club" had been a popular tourist attraction: "Next to the stockyards, it was the great thing in Chicago to see. For that matter, I believe it was, and in fact I would put it ahead of the stockyards."[36]

Masters also spoke candidly of the Everleigh Club in an article he later published with *Town and Country* magazine, where he claimed that he had enjoyed conversations about English and American poets while visiting at the Everleigh house and that some guests ended up staying for days at a time. Food and drink were available at the establishment, so that a gentleman might address several of his appetites at once, enjoying fried chicken and wine while talking with the girls about life's perplexities. Pleasant times at the Everleigh house were still on Masters's mind as late as 1938, when he was one day "loafing with Dreiser" and telephoned the Everleigh sisters, then retired and living under assumed names in New York, "just to talk over old days and canvas the general situation on Eros."[37]

In any event, during the early years of his marriage Masters was indiscriminate and opportunistic in his relations with women, justifying his behavior on the grounds that he felt lonely or trapped: "Not finding all in my home that I wanted for the stuff of living, I . . . always kept my own way." One of his ways was to associate with a group called "The Cook County Democracy" or "Cook County Democrats" about 1904. The group consisted of men with similar tastes in politics (liberal) and women (loose); a dominant force among Chicago Democrats, the group's idea of a good time was to charter a train to New Orleans and drink its way into Dixie. Masters speaks of making such trips several times.[38]

During these same years Masters strenuously applied himself to his law practice, "consoling" himself "with Sir Walter Scott's example, who wrote under a pseudonym while he was a lawyer." He also borrowed from his studies of philosophy and literature and learned a formidable means of cross-examination based in part on his "observation of the ways in which Socrates in the *Dialogues* confuted his adversaries." (Unlike Socrates, Masters kept a revolver in his office in case his adversaries resented such confutations.) Masters appeared before the Illinois Supreme Court several times during these years, beginning in 1894, and helped prepare a personal-use 4,000-page summary of Illinois tort cases to streamline his legal research. (He would later claim to have written about 10,000 pages of briefs for court cases tried at the appellate level alone.) If he could not be the poet he wanted to be, he would achieve at the law, as he once explained to Robert Morss Lovett: "I plunged into the law with all possible energy, intending to devote my knowledge to the best uses of people who were wronged, making that my poem, so to speak."[39]

He was also attracted to politics as an agency of change, both for "the people" and for himself. A galvanizing moment had come during the 1896 Democratic National Convention, held in Chicago. Masters and his father (a loyal Democrat and then a delegate) heard candidate William Jennings Bryan deliver his famous "Cross of Gold" speech in the Chicago Coliseum:

> It was a spectacle never to be forgotten. It was the beginning of a changed America. Bryan's voice, so golden and winning, came clearly to my ears as he said, "You shall not press down upon the brow of labor this crown of thorns, you shall not crucify mankind upon a cross of gold. . . ." A new life had come to me as well as to the Democracy. And at night at the apartment my father and I talked. Bryan would sweep the country, and it would be reclaimed from the banks and the syndicates who had robbed the people since 1861 and whose course had made it so impossible for a young man to get along in the world, save by allying himself with financial oligarchs.

Bryan, it was thought, would alleviate the plight of the masses through the increased coinage of silver, "cheap" money that would flow to the farmers, the laborers, and urban poor. Masters bought the idea outright: "I sat there thinking of what I had read in Milton, in Mill, in More, in Bacon's *New Atlantis,* in Shelley, and resolving that I would throw myself into this new cause, which concerned itself with humanity."[40]

After studying the writings of John Stuart Mill, Adam Smith, and the population theorist David Ricardo, Masters drafted a pamphlet called *Bimetallism,* which the state Democratic committee permitted him to read to some skeptical listeners on the Petersburg square. He also repeated part of the pamphlet to an audience at the Shipley Schoolhouse, near his grandfather's farm. Neither event went well, largely because Masters read the material to his listeners instead of delivering it extemporaneously and because he mispronounced words, which the wife of a local farmer called to his attention. This lackluster performance and an earlier, poor reception given a short story at a Chautauqua meeting convinced Masters that he was a poor speaker and helped lay the foundation for his nervousness and defensiveness when he was called on to speak to groups later in life. Meanwhile, his political idealism received an important jolt when Bryan's Republican opponent, William McKinley, swept the election of 1896.[41]

Political matters turned against Masters again one day in 1898 when he was visiting in Lewistown and heard the church bells pealing to announce the U.S. declaration of war against Spain. Masters felt the Spanish-American War was an imperialistic venture in both Cuba and the Philippine Islands, and the peace that soon followed convinced him of this. As he said, "I began to see more clearly than before where I was," by which he meant that he was now radicalized against Republicans and all they stood for and was in a mood to ally himself with others who felt the same.[42]

One of those who often held similar political views happened to be a Bryan supporter and to work under the same roof as Masters. The attorney Clarence Darrow's office was in the Ashland Building not far from Masters's, and the two met in 1897 when Masters steered a case there. Darrow's firm was shorthanded despite having recently added former Illinois governor John Peter Altgeld, and in 1898 Darrow offered Masters a position. Masters turned him down, noting that Darrow "was not in good odor in Chicago." Masters subsequently worked with Altgeld on a new constitution and by-laws for the Cook County Bar Association, and although this project came to nothing, it did give Masters experience in working with one of Darrow's law partners. At the same time, Masters's legal practice with Kickham Scanlan was growing "very poor," with personal relations strained as well, and after the hoped-for position with his father-in-law's railroad failed to materialize, Masters reconsidered Darrow's offer.[43]

Masters would always suspect—but could never prove—that a Chicago lawyer named Frank Walker (the autobiography's "Frank Winkler") used his influence with Masters's father-in-law, Robert Jenkins, to block the desired position with the railroad. Jenkins and Walker were friends (Masters had met and spoken with Walker at Jenkins's home), and even though Masters was married to Jenkins's daughter, he seemed to have less influence than this outsider. The situation bothered Masters, because this hope for advancement had offered the financial incentive for his marriage to Helen. Matters were made a little worse when his father-in-law began to suffer long-term business reverses within a year after Masters's marriage. (Jenkins was eventually forced to rent his Drexel Boulevard mansion and move into a boarding house.) At the same time, Masters's own real estate investments seem not to have been profitable; he had interests in lots in Chicago and Alabama, but these business ventures were fruitless. Clarence Darrow's offer now seemed like Masters's best hope, and in April 1903, after Altgeld died, the firm of Darrow, Masters, and Wilson came into being.[44]

A journalist familiar with the law firm called it "an alliance calculated to greatly instruct a man or to land him in nervous prostration." Although Masters got along reasonably well with the third principal member of the firm, Francis S. Wilson (later an Illinois Supreme Court judge), he never thought much of Clarence Darrow: "He seemed an old-fashioned soul, easy and lounging and full of generosities. As a matter of fact, he was penurious, grasping, and shrewd." Still, Darrow and Masters had much in common: both favored the rights of the oppressed and downtrodden over those of big business, both were Democrats, and both regarded themselves as liberals. In other words, Darrow was somewhat like Masters's father and even practiced law as Hardin Masters did, depending as much on eloquence and inspiration as on preparation when he went to court. Chicago's bubbling labor problems might sooner or later have brought Masters and Darrow together, but regardless, they were together now.[45]

Masters was immediately plunged into a case in which he fought an injunction against striking workers. It had by now become his habit to rely heavily on his literary and philosophical readings whenever possible, and he eventually drafted "a brief of about 350 pages in which every point was argued with Mill, Spencer, Adam Smith" and other liberal interpreters of the law. Masters carried the suit to the Illinois Supreme Court, where it became the first case of "government by injunction," but he lost.[46]

The high point of Masters's work with Darrow came in 1904 when the two went to Washington to argue a case before the U.S. Supreme Court, but the Court was not friendly to them or to the viewpoints of their client (an "anarchist"), and they lost the case. Masters felt Darrow had been improperly prepared and said so in his autobiography: "His wings wobbled, and in five minutes more he came down. He made a very bad talk." But perhaps Masters should not have blamed Darrow entirely. Masters himself had spoken to the Court for over an hour (by his own reckoning), and since Masters spoke before Darrow, he or his arguments ("all my piled-up learning") may have antagonized the Court well before Darrow's speech, which lasted only twenty minutes. At some point the Free Speech League of New York sold the brief as a pamphlet on free speech, probably under the title of *United States ex rel. John Turner* or *United States versus John Turner,* thus giving Masters another pamphlet.[47]

The Turner case was representative of much of Masters's legal work in that it involved individual rights against a larger, much richer, much stronger, and better organized entity. As Masters phrased it in a newspaper interview, "I am keenly interested in championing the cause of the underdog, particularly in the field of labor." He described himself as a radical. (The bust of Jefferson in his law office reminded him that he occasionally had to be a "revolutionary.") Despite his civil law preoccupations, however, Masters developed through Darrow a reputation as a "criminal lawyer," a description he was sometimes at pains to deny. Masters later summarized the activities that were representative of his life as a lawyer in Chicago:

> I was never a criminal lawyer. When I first went to Chicago, I was associated with a lawyer [Kickham Scanlan] who was expert in the trial of criminal cases. A few times, not to exceed a half dozen, I sat at the trial table and took notes while he tried the case. Once, I believe, I made a speech and a poor one, for this was not my forte. Later, I wrote or helped to write some briefs where knotty questions of law were involved in criminal cases tried by a partner [Darrow], not by me. That's all. For the rest, my practice was always in civil cases, election cases, cases involving the constitutionality of laws, will cases, handwriting cases, and the like.[48]

Despite its partners' occasional differences, the firm of Darrow, Masters, and Wilson prospered for several years, with each man reportedly earning as much as $25,000 to $35,000 annually, the equivalent of about a quarter-million dollars each in late twentieth-century buying power. Masters once generated $10,000 from a single case and said he made $20,000 per year in his best years, but because he failed to keep proper records (a trait discussed later), and because Darrow "never kept strict account," the two may not have known what they earned. (There was no federal income tax at the time.) The third member of the firm apparently kept records no better than did his partners, although Masters liked him better: "Frank Wilson, my law partner, and I used to imagine obscene visitations on judges that beat us in court, to which could be added transactions in which Minnie Everleigh figured."[49]

Masters used his share of the profits to pamper family members and to acquire new living quarters, moving successively to two apartments on Ellis Avenue before locating in a third apartment at 4406 Greenwood Avenue. He also felt affluent enough to fund the Edgar Lee Masters Prize Essay Contest at Knox College by 1903, to assume the presidency of the college's alumni group, and, in 1906, to take Helen to Europe, where they visited eight countries. Their daughter Madeline (named for Masters's sister) was born at the Greenwood Avenue apartment in 1907, as was daughter Marcia Lee (named for Masters's mother-in-law, a deceased sister of Helen's, and Masters himself) in 1909.[50]

But both his law partnership and marriage had distinct problems. Masters and Darrow were alike in their Democratic Party politics and literary interests (in 1904 Darrow had published an autobiographical novel called *Farmington*), but while Darrow brought a great many important clients to the office, such as the Hearst newspaper chain (which Masters said he defended in a libel suit brought by sharpshooter Annie Oakley), he did little of the technical work behind his court appearances. Worse, in Masters's eyes, he often failed to remit clients' checks to the firm's general treasury. Relations were worsened in 1905 when Darrow, his son, and Masters were involved in a banking scheme in which Masters lost $5,000. They were made still worse in 1906 when Darrow undertook the successful defense of "Big Bill" Haywood, the union activist indicted in Idaho for the dynamite murder of a former governor of that state. Darrow was gone from Chicago for two years and generated a fee of $50,000 in the Haywood case but paid only $14,000 of it into the firm's treasury; he was broke when he returned in 1908.[51]

Masters was in a position to know how much Darrow contributed to the firm's treasury because he was responsible for auditing the firm's financial reports. Since Masters never enjoyed the minutiae of financial management (a trait that would bother him greatly later), he turned over this job to Helen, as she noted in her memoir: "Lee was supposed to audit the firm accounts but he did not want to. I offered to do it and he was glad to be relieved of the task." She was not paid for her work, and only Masters knew she did it. It was on the basis of his wife's accounting, however, that Masters was to write the treasurer of Bill Haywood's union headquarters in 1908 to say that the union had in the past "done business with [the] firm as a firm" and not with its members. In other words, the union's checks should be sent to Chicago rather than directly to Darrow. Darrow sidestepped such matters by writing Masters that he would quit the firm rather than surrender his fees in the case: "If the firm cannot get along on the amount received[,] then I will be obliged to pull out—for I cannot at my time of life afford to lose what I have. If you can pull it along there until I am back[,] I believe we can put it on its feet all right and can adjust any differences for overdraughts OK." Darrow refused even to consider any other approach: "I would feel very badly if it was necessary to quit the game, but I am absolutely obliged to hold what I get here until the pinch is over." Masters was never to be successful in this accounting and it helped create an enmity with Darrow that lasted until the latter's death in 1938.[52]

Masters's home life was equally stressful. A few years after his marriage, he had developed ample proof that he and his wife "were not mated," as he phrased it, and began a series of extramarital affairs. He had already developed a wandering eye and noticed the attractiveness of his wife's sister and the widowed wife of a third cousin (about whom he had fashioned a play in 1908, *The Trifler*); now he graduated to more serious strayings. Early in 1909 he encountered the artist Tennessee Mitchell, a sculptor and musician. He had met her once before (she was the music teacher to his two nieces, for his sister had remained in Chicago), but now he discovered her as the roommate of Marcella, a former girlfriend. Tennessee Mitchell (the "Deirdre" of his autobiography) was a thin, sandy-haired woman with two facial characteristics to which Masters was invariably drawn—a distinctive nose and a prominent smile. He subsequently "contracted madness in her kiss" (as he put it), and when his wife and children left Chicago during the summer of 1909, he fell in love. The relationship lasted from August 20, 1909, until May 23, 1911 (if a poem on the subject is to be believed, and it probably should be), in the course of which Masters determined to divorce his wife.[53]

To soothe his conscience and perhaps to prepare for the inevitable, he now agreed to his wife's demands for a house. Helen Masters had excellent taste in homes, and in August 1909 she chose a $12,000 house at 4853 Kenwood Avenue, in fashionable Hyde Park, near the University of Chicago. It was a three-story Georgian brick structure with a thirty-two-foot-long living room and large fireplace, an immense front porch with columns, and, in the backyard, a big oak tree surrounded by an attractive circular seat.[54]

Helen also had a social position and three young children to defend, however, and she was not in the mood to throw over her marriage for the sake of a skinny redhead whose face, figure, and morals were far inferior to her own. She refused outright Masters's request for divorce. The turning point of this eternal triangle came when Helen threatened to expose the relationship and thus end Mitchell's piano-teaching practice among the wealthy. Not long after this, Mitchell came to Masters's home one day when he was gone and, approaching Helen, "knelt in penitence at her feet." Oddly, only a few seasons before this, Masters had described a similar situation in his 1907 play *Althea*, in which a poor working girl (Rene) ends her extramarital relation with Lucien Hardcastle (based on Masters) by "dropping down upon her knees" before the wronged wife. Life imitates art. Tennessee Mitchell went on to become the wife of the novelist Sherwood Anderson (and possibly to influence the character of "Tennessee Claflin Shope" in *Spoon River Anthology*), and Masters found himself frustrated at home and at work. He thought of writing a play about "a lonely home to which a broken-hearted man has returned" but apparently never completed it.[55]

Despite a busy law schedule and marital infidelities, Masters continued during many of these years to read English, American, German, and Greek writings. He read "all the English poets," he said, along with Goethe, Whitman, Crane, Dickinson, the New and Old Testaments, "the prose poems of Turgenev and the French schools"; he studied "the ideas of Ibsen, of Shaw, of the Irish theater, of advancing science." He also tackled Swedenborg, Spinoza, and others (including, he said, "books that I did not like, but which I thought I should read"), but none of these could help him with his real-life problems in his home and office.[56]

He and Darrow still agreed on certain progressive political goals, but not much else. They had met with William Jennings Bryan, for example, to discuss Democratic Party strategies in Chicago for the 1908 presidential race, but office relations between Masters and Darrow were permanently strained. Masters said Darrow never paid him his share of the Haywood case (which was $9,000), but since Masters later offered to sue other people for far less cause, it might be inferred that he had no clear claim on this money. (Masters once said he did not sue Darrow because he was "deep in literature" and "didn't want it known" that he and Darrow had once been partners, but one of the other members of the firm later said Darrow owed Masters nothing.) When Darrow once again turned west, this time to Los Angeles as defense counsel in the 1910–12 McNamara brothers case (another union, more dynamite, and more deaths), Masters knew it was time to end the relation.[57]

He was aided in his decision to leave by a large fee that came his way via his sister, Madeline. The Chicago estate of her late father-in-law (Mr. Stone) was to be settled, in the course of which a State Street property valued at $500,000 was to be sold. Masters's responsibility was to look after the financial well-being of Madeline and her children, all of whom had an interest in the property. Masters eventually "made an $8,000 fee in this matter," after which he felt he could afford to sever his partnership with Darrow: "Ultimately, there was a fee for me in this litigation of considerable amount; and I saw that I did not have to depend upon my partnership for a living." In 1911 Masters started in practice for himself and moved from the Ashland Block (where he had been since 1893) to the Marquette Building. He could not escape his former partner as cleanly as he wished, however, not only because their names were linked in certain cases on appeal but also because Darrow was soon involved in a jury-tampering incident.[58]

As the McNamara case was getting underway in November 1911, a member of Darrow's law team was apprehended on a Los Angeles street corner while offering a bribe to a prospective juror. Darrow was standing only a few feet away, thereby generating for himself a future charge of jury tampering. When Darrow pleaded the McNamara brothers guilty three days later, many people felt that he had struck a deal, that he had pleaded his clients guilty in exchange for a future innocent verdict in his own case. Masters was absolutely sure of this, not only because the guilty pleas followed on the heels of the attempted bribe, but also because he felt that Darrow's correspondence to him indicated as much. Writing a quarter-century later to his old friend Carter Harrison, Masters phrased his opinion thus: "It is a fact, however, that [Darrow] was promised immunity for pleading his clients guilty. I have letters here that indicate that—letters from him." What Masters was probably remembering was a letter that Darrow wrote him in February 1912, after the attempted bribe but before the trial; Darrow had commented on his situation but stopped short of admitting guilt: "As you know the ax has fallen—but I feel very confident that I shall win—though of course it is a hard blow—well I chose my life and must stand the consequences."[59]

Masters stood some of the consequences as well, for after Darrow had been indicted for jury tampering, he appealed to Masters to travel about Chicago and solicit depositions attesting to his integrity as a lawyer. Masters was furious with the request but felt forced to honor it, "all the while," he later said, "cursing myself that our association of years before entailed this consequence upon me." He would later say, too, that he "had gone around Chicago and borrowed the money" Darrow needed for his California expenses and that he was never reimbursed. Masters also said, somewhat confusingly, that he drew $1,000 from a Chicago bank: "I got him $1,000 and sent it to him. Then he wrote me that he needed depositions as to his good reputation in Chicago, and I got these for him." Family members looking at Masters's reduced financial condition later wondered whether the "depositions" might have been IOUs that Masters himself had to pay back, but this is unlikely, for the third-party loans seem to have been made specifically to Darrow rather than to Masters. In any event, Masters joined together the money and the depositions in his autobiography, where he describes Darrow as "that lawyer for whom I had gathered depositions and to whom I sent money when he was broke."[60]

One has also to note the contents of two unexpected letters touching on this matter. The California newsman Fremont Older sent Masters a letter dated February 2, 1912, in which he urged Masters to help him establish a defense fund for Darrow, whom he characterized as being both physically weak and broke. Older enclosed a handwritten letter from Darrow's wife in which she claimed Darrow had lost everything, that he had a debt load as high as $60,000, and that he was suffering from poor health. Mrs. Darrow also made it clear that it was she and not Darrow who was soliciting money from her handwritten list of twenty-two men who she felt might help her husband. The list included newsmen, lawyers, politicians, a bank president, a professor, and a philanthropist, as well as writers, including Masters, Hamlin Garland, and William Marion Reedy. So Masters may have been led to help Darrow through the intercession of Mrs. Darrow rather than by Darrow himself. Regardless, he now came to the aid of his former partner while hating every minute of it.[61]

Such unpleasantness looked as if it might come to an end for good when the country elected Democrat Woodrow Wilson to the White House in 1912, and the possibility of a federal judgeship in Chicago's U.S. Court of Appeals opened for Masters. Masters had worked for Democratic Party principles from 1896 through part of 1908, and while he did not know Wilson, he did know the Democratic Party's three-time nominee for the presidency, William Jennings Bryan. Masters had been won over to Bryan's thinking at the 1896 convention in Chicago; he then met Bryan at Hardin Masters's Lewistown home in 1899 and soon established a friendship with "the Great Commoner." Bryan, in turn, eventually came to know and like the Masters family, as is suggested by this friendly letter to Masters in 1904: "I had the pleasure of meeting your father and mother at Canton[, Illinois,] the other day, and am still looking forward with pleasure to making the acquaintance of that republican wife of yours. She is the only fact that I know of that raises a question as to the persuasiveness of your democratic arguments." Masters also saw much of Bryan at the Jefferson Club, a group Masters founded in 1905 and guided as its first president; it was "devoted to the radical movement in the Democratic Party," Masters explained, and "gave many banquets to Bryan from 1905 on." Bryan and Masters also communicated in London during Masters's 1906 trip abroad and came home on the same ship. After Bryan had asked for and received help with his 1908 campaign (they met at Masters's Greenwood Avenue apartment), Masters was in a position to seek a favor from Bryan. The favor came in the form of advice: "In the spring of 1913, Bryan wrote me a letter from Florida saying that he wished me to stand for the appointment to the Federal Circuit Court of Appeals in Chicago." Being the politician that he was, Bryan would receive something in return, as Masters astutely observed: he "wanted a radical above him to sustain his decisions occasionally." In any event, after Masters discussed the matter with one of his Sunday afternoon walking partners (Judge Kenesaw Mountain Landis), he decided to pursue the judgeship: "I secured the endorsement of all the Supreme Court judges of Illinois as well as those of the lower courts; and finally I had the support of the Democratic Congressional [D]elegation of Illinois. . . . Bryan took up the matter with President Wilson in a conversation or two." Masters also wrote the president twice.[62]

As time went on, the judgeship came to be more and more attractive to Masters, in part because Judge Landis convinced him he would have time to "write opinions with one hand and poetry with the other" and also because the new position would help ensure his family's financial well-being. It might be mentioned, however, that his family was not exactly suffering. Masters claimed to make very good money after leaving Darrow ("I was making $20,000 a year by 1914"), but the judgeship would provide him with security, and that was no doubt attractive. Unfortunately, the governor of Illinois withheld his support for the judgeship, as did an Illinois senator, and when Masters withdrew his portfolio of recommendations to copy some letters, another man was quickly appointed. (The latter would hold the position until 1937.)[63]

Masters was nonplussed. "I was living in suburban respectability with the woman I had married," he later wrote. What more did the public and politicians want? Privately he had worried about the "ugly publicity" of an unnamed "society paper" linking him and Tennessee Mitchell; of his "former senior partner," Darrow, who had been indicted for jury tampering; and of his own reputation as a liberal lawyer and writer of political tracts: "I was known as a radical." (He would later say that President Wilson had discovered his political writings and had consequently refused to name him to the judgeship, but Masters would finally blame Darrow: "What beat me for a federal judgeship in 1913 was the smell of Darrow on me.") Masters was disappointed about losing the judgeship but tried to be philosophical. "Certainly," he wrote in *Across Spoon River,* "it would have been out of key for a Federal judge to have written some of the *Spoon River* pieces." It was these that would next occupy him.[64]

CHAPTER 3

White Stones in a Summer Sun

Better than granite, Spoon River,
Is the memory-picture you keep of me . . . ,
My voice mingling with the June wind
That blew over wheat fields from Atterbury;
While the white stones in the burying ground
Around the Church shimmered in the summer sun.

—Edgar Lee Masters, "Aaron Hatfield," *Spoon River Anthology*

In its background and composition, *Spoon River Anthology* makes a fascinating story in itself, not only because writing it was the most important act of Masters's life, but also because it yielded a literary and social uproar unlike that of any other book of American poetry published before or after. At least a half-dozen major factors contributed to the book's creation along with an untold number of minor influences—people, places, and reading—but in the end there is only one fact that is important: from this wide variety of influences Masters fashioned in *Spoon River Anthology* what another poet described as a remarkable "world in microcosm, new in form, timeless in essence."[1]

Spoon River Anthology's impact on American poetry was so significant that it can obscure the book's literary relationships, the stirrings in both prose and poetry that preceded Masters's realistic poems. The rise of midwestern literary realism had begun by at least 1871, when the prose writer Edward Eggleston published his account of life in rural Indiana in *The Hoosier Schoolmaster.* Joseph Kirkland had brought literary realism to Illinois by 1887 in his Danville-based novel *Zury, the Meanest Man in Spring County.* Other prominent prose exercises in midwestern literary realism had come with the work of E. W. Howe's *Story of a Country Town* (1883), Mark Twain's *Adventures of Tom Sawyer* (1876), and Hamlin Garland's *Main-Travelled Roads* (1891). Two of these books were in the Masters household. Masters's father had presented him with a copy of *Tom*

Sawyer, which Masters "read to tatters" in Petersburg, and Hardin Masters had received a gift copy of *The Story of a Country Town* when he was ill with blood poisoning in 1885; Masters reported, "We all read it with great delight."[2]

Realism's effects on poetry and the development of a "new" poetry distinct from that of the nineteenth century were slower in coming. The most popular midwestern poet of the day was James Whitcomb Riley, whose sentimental poems of rural subjects found favor with at least two generations of readers through the time of World War I. The most-read poet in Chicago through the mid-1890s was probably Eugene Field, who had a daily newspaper column called "Sharps and Flats" and who had published some of Masters's poems. Field never really matured as a poet, however, and the only Chicago poet of merit who was writing on realistic subjects was William Vaughn Moody, a neighbor of Masters in Chicago's Hyde Park area, but one he never met. Moody's 1901 *Poems* had dealt with contemporary political events of interest to Masters and may have influenced him. "I read his verse as it appeared," Masters once wrote. "We were similarly influenced by the times."[3]

The years preceding *Spoon River* were not happy ones for Masters. His affair with Tennessee Mitchell had soured and left him lonely; circumstances had gone against him in his quest for the federal judgeship; and important national events had also moved against his preferences: the American involvement in the Spanish-American War (and subsequent control of islands such as Puerto Rico and the Philippines) had convinced him that the nation had caved in to the lures of imperialism and had illegally occupied foreign lands, and Democrat William Jennings Bryan's unsuccessful strivings for the White House had left Masters in a rancorous mood toward Republicans. The Spanish-American War and Bryan's candidacies for president are important to Masters's story, however, for they activated him politically and help to explain why some of his early writings are more closely focused on politics than one might expect. His pamphlet *Bimetallism* is one such example; the sale of his Supreme Court brief as a free-speech tract is another. A review of other pre–*Spoon River* writings sheds additional light on Masters's turn-of-the-century interests.

To write about what he regarded as America's venture into colonialism, Masters set out to understand the legal basis for such behavior: "I determined to master the history that went to the making of the Constitution and our republican system, and plunged myself into Montesquieu, More, Plato, Aristotle, and into histories like those of Gibbon, Motley, Macaulay, to give my understanding a sense of history and of general background. I read almost untold books to this end, and began to write articles for the Chicago *Chronicle.*" The constitutional articles published in the *Chronicle* and in Tom Watson's *Jeffersonian Magazine* led, around 1900, to Masters's pamphlet entitled *The Constitution and Our Insular Possessions,* a discussion in which he said that the United States had adopted imperialistic attitudes toward island peoples unable to defend themselves. This same mind-set carried over to a short, separately published poem called *Samson and Delilah* (about 1903), in which Masters argued for the rights of "the People" (Samson) against the powerful and privileged (Delilah). (Masters was aided in his activism by reading "the notes to Shelley's *Queen Mab,*" the political rhetoric of which convinced him he was doing the right thing.) It is interesting to speculate on what might have become of Masters had he been a little more successful with his political writings. He would probably have been more like his father, who after finally being accepted in Lewistown was elected to municipal offices and appointed to various positions in the Democratic Party's political machine. Indeed, Masters once "thought the Democratic Party might take [him] up for something" or send him to the legislature.[4]

Unlike his father, however, Masters also wanted to write verse, although his turn-of-the-century poems—genteel, derivative, and dull—were not likely to make a name for him. Certainly little in his early poetry anticipated the Spoon River poems. An endless mix of *moon, June,* and *spoon* (and *yearn, learn,* and *spurn*), Masters's alliterative ripples from fairyland wearied even their composer at times, as occurred in the mid-1890s when he sent six stanzas to Marcia Patrick (the autobiography's "Marcella"), along with a note that these were "assuredly the last" that he would write: "It is a profitless sort of art when it is that, and otherwise the only excuse for it is that it may please someone. My efforts are sophomorical, but happily the law has nipped them in the bud, and if I have inflicted the public in the past, at least I shall spare it in the future. Then I hate to be known as a writer of verse, and especially from a business standpoint do I object to it." But he soon had a change of heart.[5]

His first volume of poetry, *A Book of Verses* (1898), was a collection of conventional juvenilia derived from the four hundred poems from his Lewistown and Knox College days that Masters had brought with him to the city, along with a few poems composed in Chicago. Its title also came from his Lewistown days—or more precisely, from *The Rubaiyat of Omar Khayyam,* which Masters had read with the Fulton County schoolteacher Homer Roberts. One of the poems ("Under the Pines") had been written around 1886; several others had been published in the *Chicago Inter-Ocean.* The volume came into being in part because Masters's law associate and sometimes roommate Ernest McGaffey "genuinely admired" the poems and urged publication. Encouragement notwithstanding, Masters had to fight to get the book in print: "That book was written in Lewistown before I went to Chicago in 1892. I carried the manuscript around with me for several years, from boarding place to boarding place, until about 1896 when I turned it over to [the Chicago publisher] Way & Williams, who had it for two years before doing anything. Then I threatened to sue them; then they set it up." (Way and Williams insisted on a contract saying that Masters would pay the company $450 if the book failed to pay its expenses.) The form of the new book was traditional, as were its themes of love, fellow poets, mythical heroes, and the seasons:

In our rough clime where skies are gray
O'er leafless trees in winter's time
We dreamed of a serener day
Through books of rhyme.

Although Masters long retained a fondness for portions of this book, his publisher had second thoughts (declaring bankruptcy on the day it was to be released), and the few reviews resulted from Masters's own efforts in circulating copies.[6]

Nor did a new effort at political writing, *The New Star Chamber and Other Essays* (1904), or his second volume of miscellaneous poetry, *The Blood of the Prophets* (1905), attract long-term attention. Some of the thirteen political essays in *The New Star Chamber* had been printed previously in the Chicago *Chronicle* and established for Masters a certain fame as a radical, or "protester" of Republican Party policies (its title essay was issued in pamphlet form). *The Blood of the Prophets* added to Masters's name as a radical, for some of the poems were simply extensions of his thoughts in the political essays. The book is of some interest, however, as the first that Masters published under a pseudonym, one derived from his mother's maiden name and his father's middle name, that of Dexter Wallace.[7]

For five years following this, Masters attempted no new volumes of poetry but concentrated on the publication and circulation of his plays. He had by this time written at least two verse plays. One, "Benedict Arnold" (about 1895), remained in manuscript form, while a second, *Maximilian* (1902, an indirect comment on America's role in the Philippines and other islands), was in print through Richard G. Badger of Boston. Both works had been largely ignored by the actors to whom they were sent, and in 1907 Masters began concentrating on prose plays, publishing six between then and 1911. Of these, he later recalled, he "printed about 30 copies of each to send around to theatrical men"; they were "bound copies in brown paper" and carried the imprint of the Rooks Press of Chicago. *Althea* (1907), *The Trifler* (1908), and *The Leaves of the Tree* (1909) all deal with unhappy relations between men and women and are autobiographical in that sense, as are *Eileen* (1910) and *The Locket* (1910), both of which reflect Masters's love affair with Tennessee Mitchell. *The Bread of Idleness* (1911) incorporates the themes of domestic relations and labor relations and reflects Masters's ongoing interest in political questions. Masters never claimed his motives were other than mercantile where these early plays were concerned, nor did he delude himself as to their quality. They were "all trash" and written "for money," he said. "I do not list these among my works because I do not regard them as literature." The actors and others who received the plays felt the same way, and only one of the plays came close to being produced. This, *The Trifler,* spent part of a year under consideration by Mr. and Mrs. Harrison Grey Fiske (he was the editor of New York's *Dramatic Mirror;* she was a very popular actress), but in the end, *The Trifler* also failed, leaving only a disagreement between the Masterses: Helen Masters claimed she sent the manuscript to Mrs. Fiske; Masters seems to have thought he sent it to Mr. Fiske. The failure of the prose plays also marked the end of play publishing by the Rooks Press (albeit for unexpected reasons): "The Rooks Press was a little corporation of my own formation. I used it to publish my prose plays of those days of 1907 et seq. . . . The Rooks Press just lapsed; it was not dissolved—I left it where Jesus flang it." In other words, he was no happier as a playwright than as a husband or the law partner of Clarence Darrow. On a trip to the East in 1908, he journeyed to the grave of one of his literary heroes, Ralph Waldo Emerson, and admitted to the shades that he was a failure: "Fate had cornered me—and perhaps it did not matter."[8]

After his plays had circulated unsuccessfully, Masters turned back to poetry in 1910 and 1912, publishing under the name of Webster Ford (two British dramatists) miscellaneous verses entitled *Songs and Sonnets* and *Songs and Sonnets: Second Series.* The first was issued in thirty-forty copies, and the second, in an indeterminate number. Both books alluded to women other than Helen Masters, so their publication probably heightened tensions at home. These pre–*Spoon River* poems are of little biographical use except for those that reflect Masters's serious extramarital affair with Tennessee Mitchell, but critics neither knew nor cared about his fallen hopes with her, and in the end neither volume of *Songs and Sonnets* attracted much attention. Both books were published under the Rooks Press imprint (as was *The Blood of the Prophets*), thus bringing to nine the number of volumes he self-published under that "little corporation of [his] own formation." Since he later admitted to Amy Bonner (associated with *Poetry* magazine) that all his "books of verse before *Spoon River* . . . were privately printed," only two of his early books might have been published through more competitive means. These—*Maximilian* and *The New Star Chamber*—may also have been underwritten by Masters (although he claimed that "*Maximilian* was not published privately"). Masters also published a pamphlet entitled *Browning as a Philosopher,* probably in 1912, and as that year came to an end, he was the author of at least sixteen separately printed books and pamphlets, most of which (and probably all) had been printed at his own expense. He had drafted one more play (about the law) by October 1913, but as none of his previous efforts with plays had succeeded, he did not print this one. He also published a conventional poem about a favorite teacher at Knox College in *The Dial* in late 1913. His personal and professional lives remained without major changes until the spring of 1914, when several factors coalesced to launch the epitaphs of *Spoon River Anthology.*[9]

It should be mentioned that in the months preceding the composition of *Spoon River,* Masters had breathed an atmosphere increasingly friendly to original expression. In 1909 Francis Hackett's *Friday Literary Review* had begun to offer a weekly literary supplement to Chicago newspaper readers. Maurice Brown offered Chicago's theatergoers a new perspective with his Little Theatre beginning in 1912. In addition, Harriet Monroe's first issue of *Poetry: A Magazine of Verse* had appeared in November 1912 and did much to ignite the literary phenomenon now known as the "Chicago Renaissance." "We shall read with special interest poems of modern significance," Monroe wrote in the circular announcing her new magazine, and she did precisely that. Within a short time she had published many of the poets who were to make a name for themselves in the early twentieth century, including Ezra Pound, William Butler Yeats, John Masefield, Richard Aldington, Edwin Arlington Robinson, Amy Lowell, Carl Sandburg, Vachel Lindsay, William Vaughn Moody, Robert Frost, William Carlos Williams, and eventually Masters himself.[10]

Masters's acceptance by *Poetry* was the conclusion to a long apprenticeship. From late adolescence on, he had dreamed of making his mark as a writer, and as early as 1906 he had contemplated a novel about the towns of his boyhood, explaining to his father his plans for someday writing such a book: "I told him that my life in Chicago had shown me that the country lawyer and the city lawyer were essentially the same; that the country banker and the city banker had the same nature; and so on down through the list of tradespeople, preachers, sensualists, and all kinds of human beings." It was such a gallery of diverse types that would ultimately serve to universalize the people of Spoon River—but in 1906 Masters did not think to express his thoughts in poetry, and so what he characterized as this early "germ" of *Spoon River* was for a time dormant.[11]

A year later, in 1907, Masters met William Marion Reedy, the editor of the St. Louis magazine *Reedy's Mirror.* Masters had sent Reedy a copy of his 1902 book *Maximilian* and had been sending poems to him since 1904. (He may have been encouraged to do so by his former roommate and law associate Ernest McGaffey, who had himself been encouraged by Reedy.) Masters had not enjoyed much luck in placing his poems, but he and Reedy had begun to correspond regularly: "From about 1904 I was in communication with Reedy but did not meet him until about 1907 when I was passing through St. Louis on my way to Hannibal to try a case." In the course of a long relationship, Reedy published many items by Masters, including most of the poems of *Spoon River Anthology* (which Masters first published under his pseudonym Webster Ford for fear they would hurt his law business). One of Reedy's most important acts was to recommend or give to Masters a copy of *Epigrams from the Greek Anthology.* These highly compressed ancient writings did much to shape Masters's book, a fact he publicly acknowledged shortly after *Spoon River*'s publication: "It was you," Masters said with reference to Reedy, "who pressed upon my attention in June, 1909, the *Greek Anthology.* It was from contemplation of its epitaphs that my hand unconsciously strayed to the sketches . . . of *The* [*sic*] *Spoon River Anthology.*"[12]

A second literary influence of major importance was the American novelist Theodore Dreiser, with whom Masters was corresponding by late 1912. Dreiser by then had solid plans to trounce the tenets of the so-called "genteel tradition" in American literature and was already doing for the American novel what Masters would shortly do for poetry—forcing its reevaluation. Masters admired Dreiser's books for their frankness about American society, his 1912 comments about Dreiser's novel *The Financier* prefiguring what others would soon say of his own *Spoon River:* "I believe no American writer understands the facts of modern American life as well as you do. And your 'sceptical daring' is immense. Your treatment of evil, and sin, and such things is such an unmasking of the passing show. . . . If you ever get a theme which focuses all your powers and which comes forth fused and molten, you will add that illumination to your work which makes art." He offered to give Dreiser (then in New York) "some facts" on the "labor question" and extended an invitation for a meeting: "If you are in Chicago, look me up." Because Dreiser was then researching his trilogy on the life of the Chicago streetcar baron C. T. Yerkes, he welcomed the invitation and relied on Masters for finding legal documents and for providing access to those who had known Yerkes, such as former Chicago mayor Carter Harrison.[13]

Dreiser and Masters continued to correspond through 1913, when Masters read and admired Dreiser's one-act play *The Girl in the Coffin* (Masters still recalled the play two years later, at the time of *Spoon River,* writing in a letter to Dreiser, "I remember the play . . . and . . . retain the impression that it made upon me"). The friendship and letters continued into 1914, when Dreiser sent Masters galleys of *The Titan* so that Masters could check details concerning legal matters. Masters praised Dreiser for the "frankness" of his work, the shocking nature of which reminded him of "an aeroplanist dropping bombs from the skies." Nevertheless, he began to feel that Dreiser had made small mistakes in *The Titan,* an important observation, for it meant that by 1914 Masters was regarding Dreiser's writing in terms of its expression as well as its social themes. "Where in hell did you get those names?" he asked, finding fault with Dreiser for not using "names closer to the spirit of the story." He even offered Dreiser advice on the development of appropriate names. "Do you keep a book to jot down names in? Signs and windows are fruitful." Finally, Masters thanked Dreiser for his help in 1914—without knowing at this point just how helpful he had been: "It has added much to the richness of my life that I have known you."[14]

Meanwhile, Masters's own writing did not go well. Family medical bills made a "heavy drain" on his finances in late 1913 and early 1914, and while the law business was flourishing ("I am heavy as hell with cases"), his responsibilities left him too tired for more than occasional writing: "I'm loaded to the gunnels; go home at night spent and after dinner fall asleep and sleep and sleep." On March 30, 1914, he was still laboring under a heavy load, remarking to Dreiser that he had time for only "one or two" conventional poems per week: "The poems are accumulating, one or two every Sunday. But you must imagine how a life harried by other intellectual interests and by the burdens of a growing family must strain and resolve to do anything with literature." Then things changed abruptly, not because the "strain" had let up, but because Masters was suddenly in the mood for writing.[15]

As early as September 1913, Masters had told Dreiser that he had "a wealth of material for Illinois stories." He wrote a short prose sketch called "The Oakford Derby" and thought of writing some short plays with his Illinois material, as he wrote to Dreiser on April 13, 1914: "I am trying to find a theme for a play that interprets a bit the spirit of the times. As yet, all is nebula, whirling about, emitting sparks and smoke. These central Illinois stories and episodes would make playlets." In the same letter Masters remarked on the rejuvenation he felt with the coming of spring 1914: "Spring strikes me this time with a dynamic urge. I feel like a snake with a new skin." Within a week that "dynamic urge" had translated itself into what was probably the first of the Spoon River poems, "Theodore the Poet," later published in *Spoon River Anthology.* It was the direct result of Masters's association with the two friends he valued most, Reedy, who had suggested the form and tone through the *Greek Anthology,* and Dreiser, who was principally responsible for the frankness of the poem while also serving as its subject:

THEODORE THE POET

As a boy, Theodore, you sat for long hours
On the shore of the turbid Spoon
With deep-set eye staring at the door of the craw-fish's burrow,
Waiting for him to appear, pushing ahead,
First his waving antennæ, like straws of hay,
And soon his body, colored like soap-stone,
Gemmed with eyes of jet.
And you wondered in a trance of thought
What he knew, what he desired, and why he lived at all.
But later your vision watched for men and women
Hiding in burrows of fate amid great cities,
Looking for the souls of them to come out,
So that you could see
How they lived, and for what,
And why they kept crawling so busily
Along the sandy way where water fails
As the summer wanes.[16]

Masters commented on both the source of the poem and its subject when he mailed a copy of it to Dreiser on April 20, 1914: "Drop in some bookstore and buy Bohn's edition of the *Greek Anthology*—good book for spring days—for the mood when one watches a craw-fish. Moreover, you will there see the original of which the enclosed is my imitation." Dreiser was by this time familiar with both the Spoon River region and some of its inhabitants, having met John Armstrong (the son of a man Lincoln defended) by late 1912 or early 1913; in addition, Dreiser had visited the Spoon River region in 1913 or 1914 when Masters showed him around Springfield, Oakford, and environs near Petersburg. Dreiser would finally say that it was he himself who was behind Masters's success with *Spoon River*, as he years later wrote H. L. Mencken: "It was I who persuaded him to crystallize his bitter broodings into the *Spoon River Anthology.*" Masters did not at first contemplate a book-length collection of his verses, and his plans were still tentative on May 31, when he mailed Dreiser clippings of the first-published Spoon River poems: "I am including Reedy's critique of *The Titan*, also some things of my own, published in this week's *Mirror*, under my pseudonym, or one of them, that is. I wish you would give me your opinion of these *imagiste* ventures into rural delineations of fate and sorrow."[17]

This reference to "*imagiste* ventures" is one of Masters's few acknowledgments of his debt to the so-called imagist school of poetry. Created by a variety of English and American poets—Ezra Pound, Amy Lowell, Richard Aldington, and others—imagism abandoned traditional rhymed stanzas in favor of ordinary speech and freedom of form and subject. Masters may have first heard the term about 1912, when Pound popularized it, or in 1914, when Pound collected imagist poems by English and American authors and published *Des Imagistes*. There is no doubt that imagism helped prepare the way for acceptance of Masters's poems, but he seldom acknowledged this fact—in part because he preferred to derive from Walt Whitman, if anyone, and in part because he developed a dislike for the chief American proponent of imagism, Amy Lowell. He referred to her in his letters as being intellectually "shallow" and politically "injurious"; she was also "the fat nervous type," he said. "I've never been more annoyed or bored with a human being than with Amy Lowell." Her fellow poets fared no better. "The imagists are merely tad-poles of this day," he wrote *Poetry* magazine's Alice Corbin Henderson. "None of them amount to anything." This opinion was not universally held, of course, especially not in Chicago, where Harriet Monroe and the emerging poet Carl Sandburg were both disciples of imagism.[18]

Monroe's involvement with Masters's poems was minimal and occurred at the end of his effort (she proofed the galleys). Monroe might have asked Masters to publish the Spoon River poems in *Poetry*, but she had no way of knowing who he was: Masters published many of his writings under pseudonyms (from a "press" of his own invention), and besides, he was better known in Chicago as a writer of political essays. Masters had become familiar with *Poetry* shortly after it was founded in 1912, but he regarded it as "one of the habitual manifestations of Chicago's amateur spirit" and did not then think to publish in it. In this, he differed from one of his new acquaintances, Carl Sandburg.[19]

The two men met in early 1914 when Sandburg was a reporter and visited Masters's office for information about a labor case Masters was trying. They soon became friends and went on walks about the city while Sandburg shared with Masters his interest in free verse. ("Sandburg generally had poems to show me.") The appearance of Sandburg's famous poem "Chicago" in *Poetry* in March 1914 underscored his talent in this regard and preceded the first Spoon River poems by a few weeks. In mid-April 1914 Masters wrote Theodore Dreiser that he had planned a Sunday "tramp to the sand dunes with a Swede bard. He is a new find and I think has the right fibre." Numerous lunches and dinners, sometimes with each other's families, were a part of the relation, along with an occasional swim. The two were still taking walks in August when Masters wrote Alice Corbin Henderson that he had been "consorting of evenings" with "old man Sandburg, the Swedish bard." Sandburg did not offer advice on Masters's new poems, but he was close enough, he later said, to observe the composition of *Spoon River:* "I saw Masters write this book. He wrote it in snatched moments between fighting injunctions against a waitresses' union striving for the right to picket and gain one day's rest a week, battling from court to court . . . amid affairs as intense as those he writes of." Masters publicly acknowledged the influence of Sandburg's verse and *Poetry* at a Chicago "editor's night" in February 1915; Harriet Monroe summarized Masters's comments in her 1938 autobiography, but Masters's exact words seem not to have survived the occasion.[20]

Perhaps that does not matter. What Sandburg did was to help free Masters from his reliance on socially correct models of verse and make him see the poetry in the commonplace of Illinois. Masters's comments about the waitresses he defended in a court case that ran concurrent to the composition of much of *Spoon River* illustrate this new understanding:

> This getting down among people who worked, who endured the deprivations of life, whose experiences had given them wisdom and pity, and sympathy, and courage and resolution did something quite marvelous and hardly describable for my emotional life. It entered into the composition of *Spoon River Anthology* by way of an emotional resurgence, a spiritual regeneration that I can scarcely analyze. I can only say that like music or like scenery, or like love, or like any emotional rebirth, it played a great part in the writing of that book.

Although Masters had occasionally written about down-to-earth subjects prior to *Spoon River,* he had not left behind a written record like this. Masters felt the waitresses had played a part in the composition of *Spoon River,* and they probably did.[21]

Another person who helped indirectly with Masters's success was the Springfield poet Vachel Lindsay. He had been born and schooled but a few miles from Petersburg, and although Masters had completed *Spoon River* well before he and Lindsay met, the two men's mothers were friends, and Masters was well aware of Lindsay's success. Lindsay had burst on the literary scene with "General William Booth Enters into Heaven" in January 1913 and followed it a short time later with "The Congo," both of which were regarded as radical in form and content. Lindsay did not influence Masters as directly as did Sandburg and Dreiser, but he did offer living proof that a writer from the cornfields of Illinois could succeed as readily as one writing from New York or Paris. As Alice

Corbin Henderson phrased it (in the June 1914 issue of *Poetry,* at a time when Masters was in the midst of composing *Spoon River*), "Mr. Lindsay did not go to France for 'The Congo' or for 'General William Booth Enters into Heaven.' He did not even stay on the eastern side of the Alleghenies." Masters was more succinct, once remarking to Sherwood Anderson that "it was Lindsay who led the way."[22]

Two of Masters's law partners may also have played roles in causing Masters to look homeward for literary material. Around 1894 Masters and Ernest McGaffey rambled about the Petersburg-Lewistown area for several days while Masters explained why the region "fascinated [his] youth and possessed [his] affectionate memory." A decade or so later, about 1905, McGaffey lived for a time in rural Lewistown while writing articles and searching for "literary material." McGaffey thus demonstrated by example that the Spoon River country could be a source of various writings. A little before McGaffey returned to Lewistown, Clarence Darrow was putting the final touches on a novel about the small town of his boyhood, *Farmington* (1904), in which the narrator-hero asks about old acquaintances, only to find that they are now under "white stones" on "the hill," the local graveyard. Masters had worked with Darrow for about a year at the time of the book's appearance and was probably aware of its contents either by reading it or through his daily association with Darrow.[23]

The real catalyst to *Spoon River,* however, the one that Masters said started him writing, was a May 1914 visit by his mother. In the course of her visit to Chicago, the two reminisced about the towns of his boyhood:

> We went over the whole past of Lewistown and Petersburg, bringing up characters and events that had passed from my mind. . . . The psychological experience of this was truly wonderful. Finally on the morning she was leaving for Springfield we had a last and rather sobering talk. It was Sunday, too, and after putting her on the train at 53rd Street I walked back home full of strange pensiveness. The little church bell was ringing, but spring was in the air. I went to my room and immediately wrote "The Hill" [the introductory poem], and two or three of the portraits of *Spoon River Anthology.*[24]

Oddly, nothing concerning his mother appears in Masters's diary for this important day. According to the diary, Emma Masters visited him in Chicago on April 2, a Thursday; the next day's entry says, "Took mother to train at 12th St." There is no diary reference to Emma at all in May, and the first diary reference to the "anthologies" (as Masters first called his poems) is for Sunday, May 24: "Walk with Hardin through Lake Side Park. Wrote nine anthologies. Sans Souci [probably the restaurant] with Albert McArthur. Saw George in P.M." Masters had an excellent memory, and it is difficult to explain the discrepancies between his diary and his autobiography. Like all writers, Masters sometimes collapsed the boundaries of time to tell a better story, and perhaps this discrepancy is an instance of that tendency. Or perhaps the fuzziness of detail is related to Masters's initial uncertainty about the value of his poems. Unsure of just what he was on to, he sent at least eight of the poems to Reedy, who published them on May 29, 1914. Between the time the poems were mailed and their publication, Masters toyed with the idea of going to Europe for the summer. As things turned out, it was fortunate he did not.[25]

Those first eight poems were to make all the difference to Masters's life and career. Nevertheless, although Reedy immediately recognized their merit, Masters did not. There are few references to the poems in Masters's diary for 1914, and it is clear that he regarded the first Spoon River poems as "rampant yokelisms," poems turned out in sheer "buffoonery," as he remarked in a letter of August 20, 1914, to Alice Corbin Henderson. Because there have been differences of opinion about Masters's first impression of his work, and because his letter is unambiguous, it will be useful here to present his comments in unedited form:

> Let me tell you about this Spoon River venture, so that you may never be able to accuse me of not taking the most loyal pride and interest in Poetry—in not desiring to contribute to its achievement. I sent this Spoon River stuff that first garland, in pure self derision, buffoonery, Reedy had written me concerning "The Altar" which you saw "damn it man you're not Doric, you're American." I then dUmped on him "The Hill" "Hod Putt" "Chase Henry" etc rampant yokelisms, and with the comment: "Here Bill, is this American?"[26]

Eunice Tietjens repeated a variation of this same scenario in her autobiography, namely, that the poems were begun after Reedy had wearied of receiving Masters's dull and watery old-fashioned poems devoted to long-dead Greeks (or Dorics) and urged him to "write about life." Masters had puzzled over the new directions—he thought his poems were full of life—and then rolled up his sleeves and sat down to draft a reply: "Something answered in Masters one day, some burst of creative energy engendered by rage, which swept away his complexes, his ideas of what poetry should be like, as a flood sweeps away dykes. 'You want life?' he answered. 'Very well, you shall have life, and by God you shall have it raw.'" Sometimes his friends had it "raw" as well. Dreiser, for example, discovered in one declarative sentence that the poem about himself had become a permanent part of the collection: "I have you pickled in my Anthology as 'Theodore the Poet.'"[27]

Whatever the impulse, Masters now used his spare moments to jot down on the margins of newspapers and on the backs of envelopes, menu cards, and other scraps of paper more short poems about his talkative ghosts. His secretary, a would-be lawyer named Jake Prassel, then typed the new pieces, and these were sent to Reedy. By July 11 Masters knew he was on to something significant and wrote Dreiser that he was at work on the "Spoon River stuff[,] into which I am pouring divers philosophies—taking the emptied tomato cans of the rural dead to fill with the waters of the macrocosm." The tomato cans became, in turn, literary shrapnel raining down on an unsuspecting public, a metaphor reinforced in part by a comment Masters made at this time to Henderson: "We aeroplanists dropping bombs on the multitude must keep our nerves hard and taut." (This was, of course, the same metaphor he had used with reference to Dreiser and underscores the affinity he felt with that author.) If Masters ran out of ammunition, he could always return home for more, as he did in September 1914, when he went to the Petersburg-Springfield area "on business and to look about a little for some good types to work up." The types did not all come from there, of course, as he later explained to Henderson: "*Spoon River* came from nowhere except it came from everywhere as my life and living took things out of the soil, and air, from other men and books." At some point it occurred to Masters that his characters should know some of the same confused personal relations he had, and so he had them interact, thus giving life (so to speak) to the dead: "When I sent [Reedy] the first poems of *Spoon River Anthology,* he exclaimed that I had opened a new vein, and to go on with it. The interrelating of the poems and the characters came as an afterthought on my part." Many of these poems seem to have been as spontaneous as those he first sent to Reedy; others, Masters said, were "rewritten several times." (It might be noted, too, that Masters wrote at least two old-fashioned or conventional poems while composing his early Spoon River pieces. These—"The Moon Rises" and "Simon Peter"—may also underscore Masters's uncertainty about the value of his new verses.)[28]

The unusual title of the emergent work came from the name of a sleepy prairie stream, the Spoon River, that passed within a few miles of Lewistown, the village of Masters's Fulton County years. By an odd coincidence, there had once been a Fulton County post office in a hamlet named Spoon River, but it was obscure and short-lived (1838–47). By 1914 Masters had often passed by the supposed location of the defunct village of Spoon River (near a point where the Spoon empties into the Illinois River), but he apparently went to his grave assuming the town name of "Spoon River" was original with him; U.S. postal records prove otherwise. In any event, because Masters's intentions with the poems were at least partly satiric—to send Reedy verses so frank as to surprise him—he chose a title that struck him as uniquely unpoetic: "When I wrote these first pieces, and scrawled at the top of the page 'Spoon River Anthology,' I sat back and laughed at what seemed to me the most preposterous title known to the realm of books. Hence when I saw that [Reedy] really liked the work[,] I wanted to change the title to 'Pleasant Plains Anthology.'" Pleasant Plains was a village near Masters's first Illinois home of Petersburg, but its name struck Reedy as far too euphonic, mellifluous, and pleasant for the unpleasant lives of Spoon River, and he convinced Masters to keep his original title.[29]

That, at least, is the usual story of the naming of *Spoon River Anthology.* Helen Masters told a somewhat different version in her recollections:

> Lee came in one afternoon from a visit to his parents in Springfield and asked me what I thought of the name Sangamon River Anthology. I said it was too long and not striking enough. Then he said, "What about Spoon River Anthology," and I replied, "You couldn't beat it. It is short and unusual." He said, "Spoon River was just a dried up stream," and I replied, "Even if it didn't exist, it is still a good name." Bill Reedy, by letter, confirmed my opinion, so the book was named.[30]

Despite his sometimes unflattering attitude toward his work, Masters's writing went well during the summer of 1914, in part because the year was a calm one for him. In his professional life, the angry breach with his former law partner Darrow was behind him. At home, his slowly failing marriage had reached a stage that he described as "one of splendid neutrality"—indifference. He had two girlfriends: the woman described as "E.A." in his diary remains hidden in shadow, but "E.T." is clearly *Poetry* magazine's Eunice Tietjens, with whom Masters had a quiet affair through the fall of 1914. He was not serious about either of them, however, and neither would have a disruptive effect on his writing. Nor was he at odds with anyone else or troubled by contemporary events. Courthouse America—"the old America," he once called it—was still flourishing in the Midwest, and World War I had not made its effects felt on the country.[31]

It was this "old America," especially the unindustrialized village, that had recently been occupying his thoughts during his spare moments. Time and travel had done much to offer perspective and to place the American village in its larger context. Because he had dreamed from boyhood of being a writer, he had regarded humanity with a writer's eye all along, and this served him well as he returned in his thoughts to incidents and people of his youth. Also, his excellent memory helped make the details of his poems exact and the individuals in them believable.

He also relied on several sources more substantive than memory. He explained the full range of his *Spoon River* resources in an early draft of his autobiography:

> Into it I poured all that I had thought, read, suffered, observed and experienced in the long years of study and living which I had passed through before that time, going back to old notebooks where in youth I had set down apothegms or comments on life; to commonplace books where I had preserved the fruits of my readings; to briefs and records of cases that I had tried or had known about; to what I had known from my father and mother or reports from them about their own lives, or lives that they had known. And as I tapped this long-stored material, every newspaper, every magazine, every personal contact day by day awoke some recollection, some image stored in my memory and covered over by the refuse of the years, until I found myself overwhelmed with voices and imaginative persons begging for expression through me.

The fact that many of the people described were based on people Masters had known or heard of in Petersburg and Lewistown added to the realism of many of the pieces.[32]

He saw his Spoon River characters as people with no illusions left and let them speak plainly and to the point. The point to which so many of them address themselves is that their lives were not lived as they had wished, and now, too late, they see this. They blame others, events, and occasionally themselves while expressing themselves unambiguously in free verse, the controversial poetry form that was at last gaining some acceptance.

This verse form proved to be just right for Masters, for its plainness complemented the matter-of-factness with which his Spoon River inhabitants told of their lives and deaths. In their epitaphs most of them confront eternity armed with only a simple truth or two, a few lines distilled as the essence of their existences. The epitaphs of two of Spoon River's better-known characters illustrate:

KNOWLT HOHEIMER

I was the first fruits of the battle of Missionary Ridge.
When I felt the bullet enter my heart
I wished I had staid at home and gone to jail
For stealing the hogs of Curl Trenary,
Instead of running away and joining the army.
Rather a thousand times the county jail
Than to lie under this marble figure with wings,
And this granite pedestal
Bearing the words, "*Pro Patria.*"
What do they mean, anyway?

LYDIA PUCKETT

Knowlt Hoheimer ran away to the war
The day before Curl Trenary
Swore out a warrant through Justice Arnett
For stealing hogs.
But that's not the reason he turned a soldier.
He caught me running with Lucius Atherton.
We quarreled and I told him never again
To cross my path.
Then he stole the hogs and went to the war—
Back of every soldier is a woman.

Had Masters used conventionally rhymed and metered verse, the *Spoon River* poems would have been vastly different, as evidenced by the following quatrain published only two years earlier in Masters's *Songs and Sonnets: Second*

Series; the subject is again tombstone epitaphy, but the overall effects are changed:

> Thus be well known, and after that be crammed
> Tight in a coffin, dead at last and damned,
> With money left to build a tomb, well chiseled
> With words that show your little life was fizzled.

A second poem in the same volume also anticipated the dead of *Spoon River* but bore no resemblance to the later epitaphs:

> The cock crows faintly, far away;
> A troop of age and grief appears.
> Ye shadows of a distant day,
> What do ye, pioneers?[33]

Literary America did not know what to make of Masters's Spoon River poems as they were published in groups, or "garlands," of a half-dozen or so in *Reedy's Mirror* during the summer and fall of 1914. There had never been anything quite like them before except, perhaps, parts of Walt Whitman's *Leaves of Grass,* and those poems had not been addressed to the audience of a popular magazine. Like Whitman's, the poems by Masters also aroused disputes among the critics concerning poetry and morality. Literary critics often accused him of showing lack of respect for poetic rules, for his poems were formally poetic only through a vague dependence on the sonnet structure. That is, they consisted of two or three parts with a concluding summary statement. ("Poetry," he would say in this regard, is "a question of form only so far as form is necessary to convey the idea in its entirety.") What he wanted to do was to make people *see.* The "rampant yokelisms" had been intended to make Reedy see the quality of life in an American small town. Masters had not realized how well he was doing this at first but eventually recognized that this realism lay at the heart of his success: "I am for the 'Key Hole' school of philosophers and poets," he wrote Henderson, "by which I mean that two lines in which something is seen is worth a whole epic of sound." It was really not surprising, then, when critics of various sorts complained that Masters made his readers see too much by writing realistically about hitherto ignored views of village life. Regardless, people wanted to talk and write about the poems, and they also wanted to communicate with their author.[34]

Reedy's Mirror served as a conduit between Masters and the public. Readers who wished to write "Webster Ford" could send their correspondence to the *Mirror,* where Reedy or one of his subordinates forwarded letters to Masters. Many of those who commented were struck with the characterizations in the verses or, just as often, with the realistic starkness of Masters's country graveyard: "I seem to see this shunned God's acre, baking under an August sun, the parched grass crackling over and amid the marked, unmarked and sunken graves, thirsty geraniums wilting on those remembered, obscene tinfoil shining through the wreaths of one of yesterday; the soldiers' monument, bumptious, arresting, in the center, its *Pro Patria* newly illumined by 'Kno[w]lt Hoheimer.' It stands along the brow of a yellow claybank shelving down to the Spoon, a creek now, never a river but in freshet season."[35]

Masters had gone on with his law business while writing the epitaphs, and when a complicated case experienced a lengthy recess, he spent part of the summer of 1914 at the Michigan resort town of Spring Lake. There he rented a summer place called "The Oaks" and continued writing epitaphs:

> In the summer of 1914, I took the lower part of a house on the lake where there was a great yard of maple trees, a back yard of flowers and apple trees and grapes, and in front a dock with boats and a springboard for diving. *Spoon River* was now going, I was writing, and every mail brought me letters, first from Reedy, then from his assistant, of the reception that the work was receiving, frequently enclosing me letters from admiring readers addressed to the *Mirror,* or clippings from the enthusiastic publications over the country.

"Every week," he wrote in *Across Spoon River,* the poems were published in the *Mirror,* and "the country began to ask, Who is Webster Ford?"[36]

Every week also brought him closer to a decision he needed to make about publicly mingling his two careers of law and literature. His wife was pleased with his success and along with Reedy pleaded with him to reveal himself as the author of the Spoon River poems. He refused, replying, "My law business would be ruined if I were known so generally as a poet"; "a man was a weakling and a fool who wrote poetry, according to the judgement of the time—and knowing that judgement and having a family to support by the practice of law, I hid."[37]

These concerns did not, however, prevent him from being perfectly candid with some of his numerous admirers. For example, a letter from a "Mr. Woodruff" sent to Masters care of the *Mirror* yielded a reply from him in which he listed both his Michigan and Chicago addresses and signed his real and pseudonymous names as well:

> "THE OAKS"
>
> Spring Lake, Michigan
> August 7 '14
>
> Dear Mr. Woodruff:
>
> Your kind letter of the 3rd was forwarded to me here from St. Louis, where I am recreating for a time in the cool breezes and refreshing shadows of this ideal place.

I thank you heartily for your encouraging words on the "Spoon River Anthology." I begin to feel that I am making myself understood, and conceiving a certain view of destinies. A good many letters reach me now. If I should tell you that I had written and published four volumes of verses, three of them under pseudonyms, and that none of them reached as far or as generally as the anthology you might be as surprised as I am that the anthology appeals. I think I shall have to bring the latter out in a book as soon as a good medium offers itself. My address is Marquette Building, Chicago, Ill. And if ever you pass through there it would give me much pleasure to see you.

Truly yours,
(Webster Ford) Edgar L. Masters[38]

A week later he responded to the poet Witter Bynner's letter of admiration, again making his identity known: "This is me—Webster Ford of Spoon River, also the Loop. Many thanks for your hearty words of encouragement. I know your work and the work of all the boys around here and across the water. You're doing things all right. So is Lindsay. Glad if I can add a bit to the circle."[39]

On August 24 he again wrote Bynner and told how the Spoon River poems differed from those of the Victorians. Masters also remarked in the margin of his letter that he would soon be back in Chicago "for another year's pull at the old cart," a comment reflecting his frequent metaphor that he was only a "pack horse" in the field of law:

"THE OAKS"

Spring Lake, Michigan
August 24th 1914

Dear Mr. Bynner:
Your kind letter of the 18th forwarded here. I appreciate greatly your offer to interest your publishers in the Anthology, and I may avail myself of it. My plans—really I have no plans about publishing. I don't want to contend with squeamishness. . . . My purpose has been to speak what I have seen. The truth, the truth, the truth all the time. The Victorian poetry had great music, but stripped of its music the residue of truth was small in too many cases. The truth has a music of her own. One can use beautiful words, but they adumbrate too frequently something beside the naked thought the poet had—because he went for phrases, etc., etc. . . .

Truly yours, E. L. Masters[40]

He returned to Chicago to resume work on his interrupted legal case (concerning the right of waitresses to strike), and he also continued writing. In September 1914 *Current Opinion* gave the poems what Masters called their "first magazine recognition" by quoting several of them, and it also printed a favorable review:

> One of the most interesting experiments in verse, or semi-verse, that we have seen in some time is published in *Reedy's Mirror,* of St. Louis. It is entitled "Spoon River Anthology," and consists of a series of thumb-nail portraits, usually autobiographical in form, of the occupants of the graves in a village cemetery! Spoon River is a veritable stream in Central Illinois and apparently the portraits are based to a considerable degree upon fact. They are written in very free verse, destitute of either rhyme or rhythm, yet they seem to compel recognition as poetry rather than prose.

Current Opinion reprinted three of the poems, including that of "Griffy the Cooper":

> The cooper should know about tubs.
> But I learned about life as well,
> And you who loiter around these graves
> Think you know life.
> You think your eye sweeps about a wide horizon, perhaps,
> In truth you are only looking around the interior of your tub.
> You cannot lift yourself to its rim
> And see the outer world of things,
> And at the same time see yourself.
> You are submerged in the tub of yourself—
> Taboos and rules and appearances,
> Are the staves of your tub.
> Break them and dispel the witchcraft
> Of thinking your tub is life!
> And that you know life![41]

In October *Poetry* gave public notice to the epitaphs. All the staff at the magazine probably knew by then that Masters had authored the poems in *Reedy's Mirror,* but its editorial writers were not yet at liberty to use his name: "Mr. Webster Ford unites something of the feeling and method of the Greek Anthology with a trace of the spirit of Villon; but the 'tradition' has only served to lead him to a little cemetery in a small town—it might be any small town—in the United States, where death reveals life in a series of brief tragic epitaphs."[42]

Poetry reprinted three of the poems in its October 1914 issue, but Harriet Monroe wanted previously unpublished pieces and solicited Masters for some new epitaphs from Spoon River. He replied with an ambiguous answer in the third week of November: "I'm going to give you some anthologies, but I'm under a sort of contract to finish up with the *Mirror.* My goal has been 200, and it may run a little over. I have finished 190; the excess will be free contributions or contributions freed from my present arrangement. I have written for you a poem called 'Silence.'" He knew, however, that "Silence" (while an excellent poem) was not a replacement for the epitaphs. He subsequently sent Monroe a conciliatory Christmas gift of a small classical dictionary, noting, "The old myths are perennially interesting to me." Then he let her have "Silence" for free: "Oh no, Harriet—couldn't think of it—making too much money anyway. Add this in to the price of something you accept by a bard who is going without a coat for the sake of Apollo." He also complimented her on being the driving force behind "the Chicago Renaissance": "You see what you've done. You've started a cultus and it's moving fast. Hold on to the magazine. It has done more for Chicago authors than anything we've had." What Monroe really wanted, of course, was to turn back the clock—to have been the discoverer and first publisher of the Spoon River poems. As *Poetry*'s foreign correspondent, Ezra Pound, phrased it, "The St. Louis *Mirror* scored in getting the *Spoon River Anthology*—that is the one big hole in our record." Masters phrased it in more personal tones. "It almost broke Harriet's heart that she did not get it."[43]

On November 20, 1914, Masters voluntarily ended his anonymity, allowing Reedy to publish a discussion of the Spoon River poems and their author:

> THE WRITER OF SPOON RIVER
>
> By William Marion Reedy
>
> For twenty-one weeks now there has been running in the *Mirror* a sequence of poems under the general title, "Spoon River Anthology." They were printed as by Webster Ford—palpably a pen-name, though the poetry under it was not like anything of Webster's or Ford's. Inquiry as to the identity of the author has been widespread and persistent. . . . Well, the interest, the curiosity of the discerning is justified. The readers who know the work are entitled to know who is the man behind the work. The author is Edgar Lee Masters, of Chicago, a lawyer and a good one.

Masters spent this important day like many others: he worked on a legal case, met girlfriend Eunice Tietjens for dinner and lovemaking at a Chicago hotel, and then swam and went home.[44]

As December came on and the new year approached, Masters continued writing, his reputation growing by the week as Reedy published the poems in new issues of the *Mirror.* At some point Reedy sent Dreiser copies of the poems in the *Mirror,* and Dreiser approached the John Lane Publishing Company to see about a book, but Lane rejected the poems, and before Dreiser tried a second publisher, the Macmillan Company reached an agreement with Masters via Reedy. (Macmillan had contacted Masters—probably through *Reedy's Mirror*—as early as August, after which Masters and Reedy spoke of copyrighting the poems.) Masters himself said, "The Macmillan Company . . . chased me for the manuscript." He was never very clear about these details, remarking to Lew Sarrett, "My life was in such a whirl in 1914 that many things got obscured in the dust." In any event, Masters signed Macmillan's contract on the final day of 1914 and at last had a commercial book of verse.[45]

He had also arrived literarily. Through the last two-thirds of 1914 Masters the lawyer had set upright 200 mythical stones in a central Illinois cemetery and had at last been identified as Masters the author. Now, as Reedy would soon note, "Spoon River [was] in flood," and neither Masters's life nor American literature would ever be quite the same.[46]

The writer's maternal grandparents, Jerusha Humphrey Dexter and the Reverend Deming S. Dexter, "a man of fiery temper." (Photography Collection, Harry Ransom Humanities Research Center, the University of Texas at Austin)

Lucinda and Squire Davis Masters, the poet's paternal grandparents. Masters said she "used to love me so" and chose to be buried beside her. (Photography Collection, Harry Ransom Humanities Research Center, the University of Texas at Austin)

Masters's parents, Emma Jerusha Masters and Hardin Wallace Masters. "Their marriage was the union of conflicting and irresistible forces." (Photography Collection, Harry Ransom Humanities Research Center, the University of Texas at Austin)

The future poet as a serious young man of four. (Photography Collection, Harry Ransom Humanities Research Center, the University of Texas at Austin)

A Masters family photo in the early 1880s. Seated: Madeline, Thomas, and Hardin. Standing: Emma and "Lee." (Dartmouth College Library)

The mill and dam on the Spoon River at Bernadotte. (Dartmouth College Library)

Masters as a young man in Lewistown. (The Flaccus-Masters Archive, Special Collections Division, Georgetown University Library)

Margaret George, Masters's first important girlfriend. (The Flaccus-Masters Archive, Special Collections Division, Georgetown University Library)

Masters shortly after he arrived in Chicago, about 1893. (Photography Collection, Harry Ransom Humanities Research Center, the University of Texas at Austin)

Out on the town: Masters and Chicago law partner Kickham Scanlan about 1898. (Photography Collection, Harry Ransom Humanities Research Center, the University of Texas at Austin)

A Masters family portrait about 1898. First row: Madeline Masters Stone and daughter Elizabeth, Lucinda Masters, Squire Davis Masters, Helen Jenkins Masters. Second row: Dr. Carl Stone, Hardin Masters, Emma Masters, Edgar Lee Masters. (Property of Hilary Masters)

CHAPTER 4

When Spoon River Was in Flood

America has discovered a poet.

—Ezra Pound, "Webster Ford"

During 1915 and for several years thereafter, *Spoon River Anthology* dominated the American literary scene. After January 15, 1915—when *Reedy's Mirror* announced that the epitaph series had concluded and that plans were underway for a book—editors everywhere found room for news of Masters and his poems. Writing *Spoon River Anthology* had left him physically drained, not only because he had put a great deal of energy into the book's composition, but also because he had written portions of it in the midst of a particularly grueling law case. During this same time he had continued his usual conversations with friends, his recreational swimming, and his ongoing self-education through reading, all the while addressing the after-hours demands of his law clientele. He had sensed a weariness overtaking him early in 1915 as he mailed the last of *Spoon River*'s original 214 poems to William Marion Reedy at the *Mirror:* "In the January 15th number I epitaphed myself under the pseudonym 'Webster Ford' which I had used for the work. That was the last. And I was about ready to be laid way and given a stone with these verses. For with the waitress' case and this writing I was exhausted."[1]

He suffered a severe bout of pneumonia beginning January 25 and nearly died, becoming so sick that his father and brother, Tom, visited his home in Chicago. Tom Masters—who had received ample money to pursue his education at a half-dozen schools—had passed the bar exam and (forever the family pet) had taken over much of his father's law practice, now relocated to Springfield. Tom offered to provide Helen with $200 per week while her husband lay ill, but Masters did not accept his offer (perhaps because he did not then know he had pneumonia), and so he faced his bills and illness as best he could. He was saved, he said, by a "charming nurse" (Bertha Bauman) who kept his sickroom "in a gale of laughter" and by "the expected arrival" of the proofs for *Spoon River,* which he felt he had to correct "before stepping off" (his euphemism for dying). Even as he lay ill, however, the growing momentum of the epitaphs continued. It was clear by now that he would probably enjoy that rarest of publications, a poetry best-seller; as if to affirm this, *Poetry*'s editor Harriet Monroe herself visited his sickroom to proof the galleys of the forthcoming book. He also sent proof sheets to Dreiser.[2]

By March 1915 people were writing Masters to inquire about the publication date of *Spoon River* and to offer him other writing opportunities. Hamlin Garland, the author of the American classic *Main-Travelled Roads* and an emissary of *Collier's* magazine, sought him out to urge him to write something significant for that publication. Masters did not turn him down immediately, although it would have been clear to any observer that he could not then accept the assignment. He was still on his sickbed, his law business stood in the neglected state it had when his illness struck, and just as important (retrospectively), 1915 was the year he became famous: he did not have time to work on a sustained writing project. What did matter was that Masters was now accepted by a prominent midwestern author whose work he respected and who was treating him as an equal; Masters's March 15 letter to Garland illustrates his response: "I appreciate more than I can say your kind letter which came this morning with its words of welcome to *Spoon River*'s arrival in the world. I am gratified. There is even a touch of surprise in my feeling at the hand of friendship which has been extended me by fellow writers over the country. But it only proves what a writer should not forget, that creators, equally with readers, respond to what they believe to be a reality." Masters also remarked that he was surprised at the success of the Spoon River poems and offered to exchange signed volumes with Garland: "I may say to you that *Spoon River* is as foreign to what I imagined myself finally doing, and therefore to my plans, as anything could be—which only shows that with many of us, if not with all, we do not what we dream, but what something beyond us or over us dictates. I venture to ask you, hereby expressing my appreciative thanks, to inscribe a copy of 'Main Travelled Roads' to me, i.e., if you have one at hand—don't bother to get one. Can I bribe you by promising a copy of *Spoon River* when it comes out?"[3]

Masters also began sustained correspondence with other writers, including Amy Lowell, the leading female poet of the day, telling her he was using his winter illness "to further acquaint [him]self with [her] work" and congratulating her on the "variety of [her] music and . . . abundant imagination." He was in the mood to be complimentary, in part because he himself was receiving a good many compliments. In addition, he had discovered to his complete surprise that he did not have to battle his way to prominence, as he explained to the writer Ridgely Torrence: "Truly, I have been gratified at the interest which authors have taken and with their generous words. I never expected it. I had always imagined that even if I ever wrote a good thing I'd have to fight my way, particularly against authors." Now, however, many of them accepted him outright. Harriet Monroe saw to it that he reviewed her book *You and I* in the January 1915 issue of her magazine. And a week before *Spoon River* was published, the leading American verse innovator, Ezra Pound, chatted familiarly with Masters in a letter from England, noting that he was just "back from visiting [the famed Irish poet William Butler] Yeats in Sussex." Masters had arrived.[4]

Meanwhile, a crisis began in his law office and with his family's financial well-being. When Masters returned to his office in the third week of March, he was so weak that he could work only a few hours a day ("my head swims like a cork above the dam at Bernadotte," he told Monroe). The number of those seeking legal assistance had declined, both because of his enforced absence while ill and also because of the notoriety caused by the controversial epitaphs as they appeared in serial form; nor did the number of clients increase after *Spoon River Anthology* was published in book form in April. With his reputation as a lawyer damaged by his book's sensational publicity and his literary career on the ascendancy, Masters needed to decide which of his careers to pursue more actively. He took off ten days with his friend Sam Morgan, a court reporter, and traveled to the Indiana resort town of French Lick, where he walked the hilly countryside, tried his hand at local amusements, and sat in his room "reading *Spoon River* in book form, and wondering about this creation."[5]

Suddenly, however, he was interrupted by an urgent message from his sister, Madeline, who implored him to return to Chicago to offer her advice about her second marriage. (Her first husband, Dr. Carl Stone, had died, and she was now married to a Danish diplomat named Neils Gron, the man Masters referred to in his autobiography as "the Great Dane.") His problems unsolved and his musings undone, Masters returned to the city. He later recalled his ambivalence about the future as he sat in his law office in the summer of 1915:

> In these days now back in the office I could see at once that clients did not come to me. I heard that the report was about that I had closed my office, that I was in New York, that I had gone to England. But, on the other hand, suppose I did get clients again, what should I do with these surging themes that rolled up in my mind, with the material that I had which I had not yet touched? Should it be killed and buried?
>
> I sat in my office waiting for law business, troubled beyond measure about money. Clients did not come in, but people from New York and over the country called to see me as the man who wrote *Spoon River*.[6]

His health still bothered him as late as July 6, when he wrote Witter Bynner that he was in need of a "beach to bake on and get [his] strength back": "My illness of February has left me disengaged and decentralized." When a significant case came in July, it turned out to be a physically demanding one involving more than three weeks of arguments before a jury while the opposing lawyer made references to him as "the author of the atrocious *Spoon River Anthology*."[7]

When the case went to the Illinois appellate court in early August, Masters traveled to New York, where novelist Theodore Dreiser was his host for several days: "He entertained me at his place on West 10th Street in New York City where a party given in my honor was attended by many celebrities and many pretty young women. We had a glorious time. And I read to them from the *Spoon River*." It was on this trip, too, that Masters brought with him the manuscript of Carl Sandburg's "Chicago Poems" and tried unsuccessfully to market it. Masters was "the new man of the hour" (as he expressed it), and enjoyed the get-togethers, readings, and acceptance. "I gave [William Stanley] Braithwaite a long interview for the *Transcript*," he wrote Helen Masters after a side trip to Boston. "I seem to be the rage up there." He subsequently spent three weeks in Michigan, returning to Chicago in mid-September. He talked poetry with Harriet Monroe and one night heard the British lecturer John Cowper Powys describe him as "the reincarnation of Chaucer." As Masters went home that night, he wondered about his ability "to sustain that role which had been thrust upon" him and about what to do with his law business and daily expenses.[8]

What he was experiencing, of course, was the establishment of a new identity. As one of his Chicago friends later remarked, "It was almost as if the triumph of *Spoon River* had caused the then middle-aged man to be reborn." In fact, the process of assuming a new identity had begun even before *Spoon River* appeared in book form, as he had explained to Dreiser two weeks before its publication: "I am E. Masters in New York; in high circles here, Ed Masters; among the ladies, Eddie Masters; in public circles, Edgar Lee Masters; in Spoon River [Petersburg and Lewistown], Lee Masters." He even thought of becoming Masters the novelist (for Macmillan would have published such a work) but turned down the idea for lack of time.[9]

Throughout the rest of 1915, Masters continued to build literary friendships, corresponding with people such as the critic and poet Joseph Warren Beach, Iowa writer Arthur Davison Ficke, and Harriet Monroe, who visited his home on November 2. He also visited Vachel Lindsay in Springfield. Much of Masters's time, however, was consumed by the appeals process of the case he was now trying (known as the Helen Lee case or Bermingham case), and he spent many of his days reading legal material while turning down various (and to him infinitely more interesting) literary offers. Amy Lowell was particularly insistent about meeting him and let him know that in Boston, at least, he was now on the same plane as the respected British writer John Masefield: "The Executive Committee of our little Poetry Club has asked me to ask you if you would not come to one of its other meetings, as you could not come to the last one. They are on the first Wednesday of the month, and we should be delighted to have you come any month when you could, with the exception of January, when we are giving a reception for Mr. Masefield." But Masters could accept none of her offers, replying to one of them with a lengthy explanation of his law-related duties and noting, "These days I need the eyes of Argus."[10]

Hamlin Garland and the *Collier's* offer for a sustained piece of writing also continued to occupy Masters's attention, with Garland visiting Masters at his home in mid-December, but Garland's offer collided with Masters's legal responsibilities and lack of time: "One of the questions that is troubling me," he wrote Garland on December 21, "is just how to get the leisure to do this and to do it right." Joseph Warren Beach had to settle for a similar response: "I only wish that I had more time." Beach was searching out Masters's early writings and requesting copies of his early books, and this type of attention greatly buoyed Masters's confidence, as is visible in a note he addressed to Beach: "I saw your poem in *The Atlantic*. . . . You are in the right track without any question. As it is in swimming, after you have learned the secret of the stroke, all you need to do is to go on." As if to prove this, Masters went on writing poems for *Spoon River Anthology* through the summer and fall of 1915 until he had enlarged the original 214 pieces by an additional thirty-one epitaphs and "The Epilogue" (published in the augmented edition in 1916, with illustrations by Oliver Herford).[11]

Unfortunately, Beach's interest in Masters's early works encouraged his belief that these verses were as good as those in *Spoon River*. It should be remembered that the Spoon River poems were begun after Reedy had irritated Masters with comments critical of Masters's work; Masters had responded by forwarding the first of the Spoon River poems—a literary chip on his shoulder that he expected Reedy to knock off. Instead Reedy surprised him and asked for more ("I was astonished," wrote Masters). He had been equally amazed when the American Poetry Society's Edward Wheeler wrote him in early April 1915 to remark that the prospective volume had occasioned debate as to whether it was "poetry." "Who the 'ell said it was?" Masters asked Dreiser. "I don't know whether it's poetry or not." It was for this reason that he did not in the future plan similar writings, as he explained to Dreiser in July: "But *S.R.* is not what I expected to do. It seems to me by the way, not in the line. My attitude toward it is therefore detached and impersonal. And I feel if I can get my steady hand back I can beat it in another direction." Now, in mid-1915, with the poems in book form, Masters was still teased with the thought that the epitaphs were "foreign" to his true talents, as he had just explained to Hamlin Garland. Eunice Tietjens also observed his ambivalence toward the Spoon River poems when he read them at the office of *Poetry*: "He used to look at me with a puzzled expression showing through his very justifiable pride, and ask: 'But why are these so much better than my other things?'" As Reedy summed up matters, "I don't think he quite appreciates how big a thing he's done."[12]

Instead, Masters had to ask others. Two days after *Spoon River*'s appearance in book form, Masters mailed to Harriet Monroe his first two volumes of poems, *A Book of Verses* and *The Blood of the Prophets*, along with a request that Monroe "look into them a little": "I am wondering if there is anything in either of these books worthy of preservation. I know their faults well enough, but I am not clear about their merits, if they have any." The former was essentially rhymed juvenilia composed during his first twenty-three years, and the latter, his political opinions expressed in verse. Tietjens was right: he really did not know why his Spoon River poems were better. Nor did he learn more through the summer.[13]

For example, when he submitted an inferior poem called "The City" to Wilbur Cross of the *Yale Review* in September 1915, it was summarily rejected in seven days. (Even the man of the hour was not guaranteed publication of everything.) Around the same time Masters received a compliment from Arthur Davison Ficke on his use of Dreiser in one of the Spoon River portraits ("Theodore the Poet"). Masters's reply was only half-serious, but it is important for it shows that it was the concept of self-criticism that was really foreign to him: "You and the rest of you must quit picking out such things for admiration. My judgement in my work is already sufficiently undermined, and if this keeps up, I will have to have some of you around to tell me when I hit it and when I don't."[14]

As 1915 went on, however, there was no shortage of individuals ready to offer an opinion on that or to try to arrange a meeting with the author of *Spoon River.* Masters enjoyed some of these, but from the start of his fame he showed an impatient and antisocial side and often tried to avoid people. He was now faced with the demands of the literati, who wanted dinners and public exposure, but such demands conflicted with his habit of trying to protect his law practice from the low esteem often accorded poets. Moreover, his education had left him vulnerable where a more conventional one might have helped: he had painstakingly learned much more through self-education than many of his admirers had learned through formal means, and since he did not suffer fools gladly, he had a contempt for many of those with whom fraternization was now expected. Worse, both the public and the literati seemed always to want a speech, and he knew from experience that he was no speechmaker. Even if he had been, how could he make endless patter about a book that was basically an accident and of which he himself did not think much? Fame itself thus became an irritant to the extent that it did not pay very well, introduced him to people he did not like, and ate up time at an alarming rate.[15]

He was exceptionally sensitive to the fact that fame had not led to emotional fulfillment, had not brought him the perfect and understanding woman who could admire him during the apex of his acclaim. The closest he had come to such a being during *Spoon River*'s composition was Eunice Tietjens, the horsey, bespectacled girl Friday of *Poetry* magazine. As tall as Masters, she had far too much sense to render unto him the adulation he required and was obviously not the girl of his dreams. So from the very start of his success, Masters experienced tensions between himself and his public, and between his expectations and reality, while gaining little of the elation he had supposed fame would bring him. In short, he had achieved success without achieving satisfaction.

It was this combination of events that gave Masters's life its unusual dynamics and made him appear as a man who was never satisfied. Indeed, there was always something wrong with Masters's life, from the days in his parents' loveless house and his fractured college plans through the time of his own loveless marriage—after which he had hammered the American political system in his pamphlets, tried unsuccessfully to flee his dull wife, and finally (in *Spoon River*) planted an ugly mud daub squarely on the Christmas card image Americans preferred when they thought of their little towns. And every meeting he went to brought him more flatterers and bores, and every evening when he came home, he encountered his patient, smiling wife, so that after he had gone upstairs and shut the door to his second floor study, he sat at his desk and pondered again the phenomenon of renown without reward. There were characters in *Spoon River* who were less trapped than he was.

Meanwhile his book seemed to have a life of its own. When *Spoon River* appeared in book form (at $1.25 a copy) on April 15, 1915, it succeeded wildly, going through seven printings in seven months and finally exhausting nineteen printings before the augmented edition of 1916 added new parts and more sales. It would take the better part of a decade to put the book in perspective, but when the literary critic Percy Boynton commented in the mid-1920s on *Spoon River*'s several years' domination of the literary scene, he explained the phenomenon thus: "Mr. Masters' *Spoon River Anthology* (1915) in the first years after publication was altogether the most read and most talked-of volume of poetry that had ever been written in America. . . . People who really knew poetry were interested and amused at [the] combination of a very old Greek form with the doings of an Illinois town. People who were allured but disappointed by the glitter and the hollowness of much of the new poetry were refreshed by the grim substance of this book." Although no one review, article, or comment was significant enough to alter the course of Masters's life, the collective impact of the commentary did; because this is so, it will be useful to examine several of the critical assessments that contributed to his transition from lawyer to man of letters.[16]

Commentary on Masters and his book appeared in every type of publication and from a wide variety of critics. In general, older and established writers disliked *Spoon River*'s literary form and subjects, while younger or emerging writers admired its energy and frankness. To nineteenth-century traditionalists such as William Dean Howells (the editor of *Harper's* magazine), Masters was not writing poetry at all but producing only "shredded prose." Despite certain "truths," Masters's verse was doomed: "It is when the strong thinking of Mr. Masters makes us forget the formlessness of his shredded prose that we realize the extraordinary worth of his work. It is really something extraordinary, that truth about themselves which his dead folk speak from their village graveyard. . . . Yet as to the form of their record, it is shredded prose without even a slow, inscriptional pulse in it, and we doubt if it will last." Genteel innovators such as poet Amy Lowell were sometimes critical of the content: "*Spoon River* is one long chronicle of rapes, seductions, liaisons, and perversions," she wrote.

"One wonders, if life in our little Western cities is as bad as this, why everyone does not commit suicide."[17]

Literary radical Ezra Pound disagreed. "AT LAST!" Pound shouted in the pages of the *Egoist,* "At last America has discovered a poet." "The silly will tell you . . . : 'It isn't poetry.' The decrepit will tell you it isn't poetry. There are even loathsome atavisms, creatures of my own generation who are so steeped in the abysmal ignorance of generations, now, thank heaven, fading from the world, who will tell you: 'It isn't poetry.'" Nevertheless, it was poetry, and Pound ranked the epitaphs alongside the poems of another midwesterner, T. S. Eliot: "He and Masters are the best of the bilin' [boiling—i.e., the best of the bunch]." Pound ignored for the moment the emerging talent of Chicagoan Carl Sandburg, himself swept along by the current of *Spoon River.* Sandburg wrote that he had discovered in the work "the people of life itself" and hoped Masters had "other books in him as vivid and poignant."[18]

The diversity of commentary continued in one form or another throughout 1915–16 and on through 1917 and America's involvement in World War I. A frequent question was whether *Spoon River* was really poetry: "A really remarkable series of character-studies, though the half would be much better than the whole; but for poetry—cui bono?" Another frequent remark was that the book was in bad taste: "Spoon River is in Illinois, and in the two hundred and more sketches—perhaps they can be called poems only by courtesy—that make up this volume the author reproduces the life of the community, its ugliness, its vulgarity, its hypocrisy, its depravity and, more rarely, its nobility and beauty." Some said *Spoon River* told too much about the American village: "The village knows everything, comments upon everything, judges everything." Some said *Spoon River* told too little: "A grave limitation is the book's inattention—to the warmer and brighter side of village life—its humor, courage, and frank honesty." Some said Masters was a very sick man: "The Anglo-Saxon is a lover of superficial speciousness, of quasi-materialism, of cheap novelty. He also takes a secret delight in boldness of expression and morbid sexual details—the hypocritical Freudian reaction to a zymotic puritanism. These things are all summed up and emphasized in the *Spoon River Anthology.*" Some said the book was a literary triumph: "It is indeed a triumph—and one not likely to be duplicated—for *Spoon River Anthology* is a unique as well as a great contribution." To others, it brought up the question of genre—maybe it was really a novel: "It is the first successful novel in verse we have had in American literature." To others, it was really a movie: "What Mr. Masters has accomplished is the cinematographing of narrative-verse." To others, it was really an epic: "What then is *Spoon River Anthology?* Let me humbly suggest that it is an epic." To still others, it was really a "fotograf album." The opinions proliferated, the whole making a kaleidoscope of commentary, with some comparing Masters to Shakespeare and some calling for his resignation from the human race. Perhaps William Marion Reedy summed up things best: "*Spoon River* is like that mythical river in some old mythology that flows all around the whole world."[19]

At the height of the discussions, it was not unusual for a publication to take two entirely different editorial stances on *Spoon River,* and in one notable instance (the January 1916 issue of *The Forum*), a journal provided four analyses by four different writers. The *New York Times Book Review* noted this unusual phenomenon and provided an article about the articles.[20]

Bowled over by such attention, Masters paused occasionally to thank some of his admirers, among them William Stanley Braithwaite, whose recent article had been particularly laudatory: "I want to thank you for your fine article in *The Forum.* I do not know how I can repay you and so many others for the expression of your interest except by doing better work, and that I shall endeavor to do." Around this same time (1916), however, he was still responsible for overseeing his clients' interests in legal cases and told Dreiser he was "up to [his] ears in litigation." There was also his family to consider. His children would probably see even less of him if he pursued his opportunities in literature while honoring his commitments to the law.[21]

Edgar Lee Masters could be a loving father, though one who appeared somewhat gruff, as Tietjens recalled in describing her first meeting with him on a *Poetry* magazine outing to the Indiana Dunes: "Masters proved to be a heavy-set man with a roughly molded face which in repose was more like that of Beethoven than any I have seen. . . . He had his two little daughters with him and he sat patiently, trying to talk, while the pretty little girls clambered over him, pulled his ears, and mussed his hair." If the daughters tired, he might amuse them with a fairy tale of his own invention, as his son Hardin recalled: "The animals of his fancy were the Geraufaklus, twice the size of a lion; the Spitzdoodle, a snake with a head like a bear; and that horrific of birds, the Jubjub Bird, as big as a cow but with the talons of an eagle. He told endless stories about these fantastic creatures. His ability to invent new tales, concerning the ferocity of this triumvirate, seemed to be endless." Not surprisingly, perhaps, the children grew up with some of the same interests as their parents. Madeline and Marcia, called "Lamb" and "Little" (or "Leetle"), respectively, enjoyed presenting Saturday afternoon plays during their little-girl years. Hardin played the drums, while his mother accompanied him on the piano.[22]

But Masters could also be a distant father. He was often physically removed to another city by his law and literary obligations and removed in other ways as well. With the door to his second-floor study shut and his children out of his mind, he could be as cold as "wind around the moon"—a phrase later used by Marcia—or as indifferent as the stars in her poem "Running Away When I Was Very Young":

> The winter's night I ran away
> Father was writing,
> Stern as Zeus
> Behind his thunderbolts of verse.
> Light scowled beneath his door.

* * *

I walked and walked,
And once a street-car passed me,
Oblivious with snow.
The streets grew longer,
Whiter—as if about to end
Someplace that had no people,
No lights, no homes.

And suddenly I thought of home,
Its rich, though lost, connections,
And I turned back.

* * *

Nothing had changed:
The house sat high, detached,
Upon its icy bluff,
And at my father's window
His white lamp burned
Indifferent as a star.[23]

Masters's other daughter, Madeline, chose to live a private life and left few public impressions of her father, while Hardin, a businessman and military man, remembered his father's scholarly side as well as his warmer one. Even as an old man Hardin Masters recalled his mother's admonishments to adopt a church-mouse quietness when his father was writing ("silence was the order of the day"), but he also remembered the pleasant walks with his father about Chicago and the boat trips across Lake Michigan to one or another of the Michigan summer houses Masters rented before buying one: "I always enjoyed these junkets, usually taken on Friday night and returning on Sunday night. We sometimes talked late into the night on the leeside of the boat, stretched out in deck chairs. Here was talk at its best for my father—night, starlight, mystical splash of prow water, and the darkness stretching away into eternity."[24]

As to his relations with his wife, Masters in the years immediately before and after *Spoon River*'s publication was both a good provider and a terrible husband. When he left home in the morning with his three-piecer, derby, and confident scowl, he looked and seemed like any other member of Chicago's professional community. He walked no further than the curb, however, for Edward the chauffeur would be there with the Studebaker EMF 30 (EMF meant "Every Man's Favorite," Masters said), and he rode in it to the Illinois Central station. There, at Forty-seventh Street, he caught a train to the city. ("Going to the office to make money," he would have said on his way out the door.) In fact, he made so much money (in 1913 and thereabouts) that the family could afford four other servants as well (a cook, maid, janitor, and yardman).[25]

And he spent a lot of money too. He and Helen had taken a trip west to the Rockies in 1904 and gone to Europe in 1906 before making a trip to Vancouver and Seattle in 1910. He traveled frequently to New York while working as a lawyer with Darrow, went once to Cuba (business unspecified), and liked to unwind in New Orleans. In addition, the Masterses went frequently to one resort town or another in Michigan. They also liked to entertain friends from the nearby University of Chicago, lawyers from the neighborhood (there were a good many), and, between 1905 and 1908, Democrat Party faithful from the Jefferson Club. At other times they followed up on one of Masters's more esoteric interests. He had a long-term curiosity about occult matters, as witnessed by his early paper on clairvoyance read to the Fulton County Scientific Association, and at least once invited a spiritualist to the house along with five or six couples. Perhaps that was the evening he had his palm read and found that he would someday come to a difficult crossroads, here described by Helen Masters: "Lee always wanted to talk to the fortune tellers or to have them tell his fortune where ever [*sic*] we encountered them. One evening he had his hand read by a woman who had made a study of psychology and spiritualism, and had made quite a reputation for herself in that regard. She said to Lee, 'You will come to a cross-roads and you will take the wrong path.' He was always disturbed by this."[26]

In actuality, he was at a crossroads each day but failed to recognize it. The affluence he had so successfully sought was in part drained by the need to support a house that relied on servants—domestics who were supposed to provide him with time to write but instead kept him on a treadmill supporting them. Thus, he each day went to his car and was driven by Edward, apparently failing to note that he could live on less money and have more time for verse if he drove his own car. None of the American writers he admired had relied on servants (Poe, Whitman, and Emerson, for example), nor did any of the contemporary writers whose work influenced his (e.g., Sandburg and Dreiser). It was true that Masters's mother often had a maid in her employment, as did his grandparents (who had a maid and hired men), but the only writers who had servants were generally those Masters would claim to dislike—effete easterners, Ivy League graduates, and the spoiled sons of the very rich. So why did Masters maintain a lifestyle that was defeating the attainment of his one avowed passion, time to write? The answer is that Helen Masters had lived this kind of life and expected it, and after a time the Masters children expected it, too; more important, for all his avowals regarding poetry as his passion, Masters liked several other things equally well. Having servants was one of them.[27]

He relaxed from his labors through music, reading, and exercise. Masters enjoyed Strauss waltzes and Sousa marches and such pieces as Dvorak's *New World Symphony* and the score from *The Merry Widow.* He and Helen even collaborated on a musical piece called "The Lark" (he wrote the lyrics, and she composed the music, adapted from Mendelssohn). Because he knew he worked too hard and read too late, he tried to reserve Sunday afternoons for a walk at the Indiana

Dunes, a natural area with an abundance of plant and animal life. Sometimes he took his children on these rambles but more often went with fellow professionals such as Judge Kenesaw Mountain Landis, Charles Gates Dawes (vice-president under Coolidge), or his friend Sam Morgan. When Morgan experienced the travails of a divorce, he rented a room and bath on the third floor of Masters's house about 1914 and ended up staying for seven years, until Masters's own marital problems caused Morgan to side with Helen Masters.[28]

During the early and middle years of her marriage, Helen Masters steadfastly maintained her prenuptial commitment to encourage her husband in his writing. For example, when they moved from her father's house to an apartment on Ellis Avenue two blocks away, she and Hardin (still a small boy) moved Masters's unsold copies of *A Book of Verses* to their new address: "Lee used to say he had the largest collection of his own books of any author living. I felt sure they would sell some day and packed them carefully in a wheelbarrow and hired a boy to take them over to the Tudor apartments. Hardin and I walked beside the wheelbarrow as a guard of honor." Helen Masters also said that she researched the historical background for Masters's 1902 play, *Maximilian,* and encouraged him during his spate of play writing between 1907 and 1911: "Lee always brought his evening's work to me and we talked it over before we went to bed. We were both especially desirous that he write a play and we studied plays by Ibsen, Pinero, Rostand, etc." She offered indirect support at other times as well: "In the evenings when we had no engagements and Lee was home, he wrote on the second floor. I used this period to practice on the piano. He always said the rhythm of the music helped him to write. So these hours were an inspiration to us both." He subsequently dedicated *Spoon River Anthology* to his wife (because Reedy urged him to do so), and although he did not mention this dedication in his autobiography, she did so in her manuscript: "Lee told me he was dedicating *Spoon River Anthology* to me because I had always believed in him and had helped him so much and he felt he could not have completed it without me." She also kept a scrapbook of its reviews and served as hostess for her husband's dinner guests, including the poets Carl Sandburg and Robert Nichols, the novelists Theodore Dreiser and Henry Blake Fuller, and the future British poet laureate John Masefield and his countryman John Cowper Powys (the latter sometimes stayed at the house). The socialist writer and poet John Reed (later buried near the Kremlin) visited one evening, a reminder that Masters's political essays were once considered as "radical" as his free verse poems. These and others visited the Masters household, a pleasant place (most would have said) with three truly beautiful children and a series of pet dogs to round out the domestic scene.[29]

Between these events Helen Masters pursued her cultural interests with The Cordon (a club composed of women with husbands and households rather similar to her own) and started a local musical group, the Kenwood Fortnightly Club. Masters usually pooh-poohed such diversions, telling Alice Corbin Henderson in 1916 that "madam has no life except through me—never thinks or plans independently, and has no friends or interests of her own that cut any figure in particular." When Helen looked for new ways to branch out, Masters discouraged her. For example, she wanted to learn how to drive the automobile, but even though Masters was inexpert with it (he had an accident and gave up driving), he did not wish his wife to drive.[30]

There were also other tensions. Despite all the appearances of a happy home, Masters spent many evenings out of the house, general whereabouts known (Chicago), exact location and company not. One night his ramblings and his home life collided when the Masterses had a party and he demonstrated an unknown capacity for dancing; Helen Masters recalled this very clearly more than thirty years later: "He had never danced, but he must have taken lessons somewhere unbeknownst to me, for he astonished me and everyone else by dancing very well." He had, in fact, been dancing since about 1910, practicing with other women as he could and would, sometimes at the bachelor apartment of his friend Bill Slack, another attorney. He had more time for such things, having essentially given up on politics in 1908 when Bryan lost his third bid for the presidency. Masters's Jefferson Club for radical Democrats expired at the same time (the members could not afford their dues), and Masters stilled the loneliness he sometimes felt by going "back to Aeschylus, Sophocles and Euripedes."[31]

Meanwhile, magazines and newspapers continued to devote extraordinary amounts of space to Masters during the first six months of 1916. There was "More about 'Spoon River,'" and "More Hot News from Spoon River"; Masters was regarded as "Another Walt Whitman." His correspondents old and new (Braithwaite, Hamlin Garland, Amy Lowell, and Louis Untermeyer) asked for articles, pictures, or meetings with him; the former president Theodore Roosevelt also wrote him (Masters felt he was "most cordial and hospitable": "[he] invites me to come to Sagamore"). People who had never bought a book of poems (or even read one) now heard of Masters, for he and *Spoon River* were a subject of general as well as literary interest. (Some may have bought his book because they thought the *spoon* of the title was synonymous with the word *smooch*.) Masters augmented his publicity with lectures in the East and Chicago.[32]

By early March 1916 he had so many activities underway that he had given up his weekly walk on the dunes and leisurely restaurant meals and had only limited time for writing: "I have been following a rule this winter of not dining out at all," he told one admirer. "I have no time, literally none, except Sunday for writing." There is a likelihood, however, that even this time was compromised, as he suggested to Henderson on March 27: "I've been so busy for ten days that my eyes are blinding, reading 1,000 pages of print, correcting proof of a brief, dictating, etc. . . . I'm pulling a heavy load trying to get through law business, prepare a lecture, get hold of some money, and then—then—create again—oh la, what a climb!"[33]

He had been the subject of so much attention by mid-1916 that he reacted in a perfectly normal way: he decided that the furor over his poetry would soon burn itself out and that he should continue as a lawyer. (His practice at the time of *Spoon River* came largely "from lawyers who wanted something done in the [Illinois] Supreme Court, or some matter attended to requiring . . . particular skill in cases of disputed handwriting, in will contests and the like.") In mid-May he moved his Chicago law office from the Marquette Building to the Portland Block and had it redone, explaining in a letter to Amy Lowell that he did not think the present interest in poetry would last: "I begin to feel that poetry will pass into a more settled interest soon. There has been too much of a fury for the game to last as it has been going the past year or so." Nevertheless, he added, "I've been writing some things."[34]

In late July he rented a lakeside vacation place at Belle Pointe in Spring Lake, Michigan, first sending his family to stay with his parents, then at nearby Saugatuck. He wrote Monroe that he was doing some writing, but seems to have spent most of this time simply enjoying the scenery and luxuriating in his success as a writer. For the first time in his life, perhaps, he was satisfied with himself and his surroundings: "Altogether I was never so happily situated, and begin to see why millionaires are unhappy, if they are—since when every want is filled, what is there to want or to do? . . . I roll in, and arise with the lark, thoroughly regenerated by a long night breathing fresh air laden with the smell of green leaves and pine needles. Hurrah for life anyway!"[35]

But even Eden was lonely without a mate, and this long-looked-for happiness would soon require a "long-looked-for woman" (as he would later style her). On August 3 he told a friend that someone such as novelist Theophile Gautier's libertine character Mademoiselle de Maupin might do: "I want for nothing—still, if you meet Mademoiselle de Maupin, you might mention this bower and its sedate inhabitant ready to give lessons in philosophy." A more accurate gauge of his feelings would be revealed a few years later through an autobiographical character in *The New Spoon River* (1924) and its story of a writer who is finally "a name in the world, / After thirty years of obscurity":

> Here I was on the heights at last—
> But my chum of thirty years was there:
> Old Loneliness still held my arm,
> As I stood on the peaks, and was known at last.[36]

Masters turned down an offer in late August to write a play ("I'm pressed with so many things I can't concentrate my mind on this") and refused numerous lecture offers in the East, explaining in October that he was lecturing as often as he could in Chicago and practicing law simultaneously: "I am booked by J. B. Pond Lyceum Bureau in a number of places near at hand, so as to permit me to practice law and wedge in lectures when I can. . . . I am lecturing rather than reading." Nor could he free himself to see Amy Lowell in Boston: "It is hard for me to leave—has been very hard the past year. I am practicing law, even though people forget it."[37]

The reason people forgot it, of course, was that he was so much in the news as a writer. In November *Poetry* announced it had awarded him the 1916 Helen Haire Levinson Prize of $200, in December Amy Lowell requested biographical data for "a series of lectures on a few of the more important American poets," and the *Yale Review* now reconsidered its earlier rejection and made him an offer: "Would you care to publish . . . a poem of one or two pages?" He accepted, asking $100 for a piece called "Boyhood Friends." (He received $50 instead.)[38]

As Christmas 1916 approached, the strain of being several different things to many different people was beginning to take its toll, as Masters remarked to Lowell, at the same time commenting about his privately circulated plays: "I have been asked at times to give a sketch of myself. I can't do it. I can't get the focus so as to produce a telling picture. Maybe I shall sometime. . . . But I am known as a lawyer, as a democrat in politics, as a writer of prose plays, etc.—by which I mean people know these phases of my life, and each one is likely to take that phase as I."[39]

Being different things to different people has often been standard behavior for poets, but Masters sometimes found it difficult. An example concerning two of his acquaintances illustrates. In 1916 Witter Bynner and Arthur Davison Ficke undertook a successful spoof of modern poetry while writing under the assumed names of "Emanuel Morgan" and "Anne Knish." They satirized the new schools of poetry (including free verse) through a combination of poems and critical gobbledygook and sent a copy of their book (*Spectra*) to Masters. He fell for the ruse. "Have you seen 'Spectra' by Emanuel Morgan and Anne Knish?" Masters asked Harriet Monroe on December 1. "I got it a week ago and it's good, and in the right way." Masters also wrote to Emanuel Morgan (Bynner) to say that "Spectrism" was "at the core of things" (Bynner and Ficke subsequently threw dice to see who would keep this letter from the most-important American poet of the day). After the joke was over, Ficke and Bynner had a good laugh and took off for the Orient; Masters remained in Chicago, his money from *Poetry*'s Levinson Prize going up the chimney (he "paid the coal bill" with it). In other words, while certain of Masters's friends felt free to pursue whatever new interests they chose, he was different. No matter what phase of his life he focused on—lawyer, poet, dramatist, or Democrat—he still had his family responsibilities (a Chicago newspaper had described him as "very domestic"). He was more and more pulled in different directions.[40]

On the one hand, there was his need to continue as a lawyer for the sake of his family's financial well-being, as well as his belief that the literary controversy over *Spoon River* must soon end; on the other, there was the undeniable fact that the furor over *Spoon River* did not end, and this daily or weekly suggested to him that he should write for a living. His friend Tietjens described *Spoon River*'s ongoing appeal thus: "The critics throughout the country were carried away by it in a wave that almost amounted to hysteria. They kowtowed in rows, bumping their heads on the ground and grovelling. No words in the language were spared in praise. Masters was a second Shakespeare, a giant of almost legendary proportions." As the editors of the *Literary History of the United States* wrote several years later, "Several planets conjoined to make the book in its completed form one of the most momentous in American literature."[41]

Masters finally learned to enjoy the several years' literary storm his book occasioned, writing in his autobiography, "I could fill a page with the names that I was called, and put beside them the high praises that were given me." He once remarked that he had "received a room full of letters from over the world" and summarized these in "The Genesis of *Spoon River*" in H. L. Mencken's *American Mercury:*

> It was called the greatest American book since Whitman, and on the other hand one of the evilest books of all time. It was compared by the American *Review of Reviews* to Homer, and by some critics to Zola and the worst French writers. It was called as lofty as Dante by some critics, and as vile as Rabelais by others. It was said to be as sublime as Aeschylus on the one hand, and as misanthropical and hateful as Byron on the other. Some reviewers attacked it for lack of originality, saying that it was nothing but an imitation of the *Greek Anthology;* others likened it, for fertility, invention and variety, to Shakespeare.
>
> Some said its style was as simple and dignified as that of the *Iliad;* others denounced the baldness, bleakness, harshness of the words. . . . Van Wyck Brooks and the *Literary Digest* committee, which he headed to pick the ten greatest books of the Twentieth Century, put the book on the list. The Boston *Transcript* gave it a place among the masterpieces; the Peoria papers and the village papers for fifty miles south along the Spoon River valley took it as a gross attack by a disloyal son.[42]

This battle of words about *Spoon River*—the big-time battle by critics writing for newspapers, magazines, and learned journals—was waged entirely in prose and was a mostly serious affair by well-credentialed specialists. But there was another, now largely forgotten series of discussions phrased in verse. These, the poems and parodies written in reaction to Masters's epitaphs, are important to this discussion, too, for they underscore how Masters's controversial book captured the nation's popular imagination.

Masters himself was well aware of the imitative verses he had inspired, remarking in "The Genesis of *Spoon River*" that the epitaphs were "parodied all over America" shortly after they were serialized in *Reedy's Mirror.* Just how many of these satiric verses were published is not known, but they began appearing in great abundance after *Spoon River* was published as a book in April 1915. At one point Reedy had seen so many that he declared, "Everybody seems to be doing something in imitation of *Spoon River Anthology.*"[43]

Some of these continued the battle as to whether the anthology was really poetry, as did writer Bliss Carman's "Spoon River Anthology" in *The Forum:* "His Anthology is a morgue of souls, / A Charnel house of decayed characters . . . , / Every one of them a plot for a short story."[44]

Most of the satiric discussions, however, took place in newspapers. Between June 17 and November 11, 1915, the *New York Tribune* alone provided space for nineteen different parodies in its famous "Conning Tower" column, edited by Franklin P. Adams. These often began by "bowing to Edgar Lee Masters," were said to be written "by our own Edgar Lee Masters," or otherwise strove to make the appropriate literary connection: "If I were Mr. Masters / And Mr. Masters I," and so on. Several of these titles continued for two days to a week, with the result that for the first half-year after *Spoon River* appeared as a book, Adams's nationally read column was awash with "river anthologies." They came from the banks of the Hudson, the Thames, the Connecticut, and (it had to be) "Loon River." There was a "Schroon Lake Anthology," a "Fox Meadow Tennis Club Anthology," an "Anthracite Anthology," an "Illustrator's Anthology," a "Week-Ender's Anthology," a "Subfluminal Anthology," and others.[45]

Because all the parodies that appeared in Adams's column read about the same, their collective worth—that they exist and that they were spawned by *Spoon River*—is probably more significant than any individual poem, with one possible exception, a satire called "Maurice Vernon" composed by the well-known eastern poet and critic Louis Untermeyer. What chiefly distinguishes it is that in a letter dated November 8, 1915, Masters wrote Untermeyer to thank him for sending a copy of "Maurice Vernon" and to say that he liked this poem better than any of the other satires on *Spoon River.* Since "Maurice Vernon" is only an average effort, however—it is not a great parody or good poetry—one suspects Masters's admiration for the poem stemmed from the attention he was getting from the eastern literary establishment that Untermeyer represented:

> I was just sixteen,
> In the queer twistings of a delayed adolescence,
> When I came to New York;
> To study the classics, as my mother said.
> And, according to my father, to become a man.
> I liked the prep school I attended—
> It was such a pleasant place to get away from.
> Often I neglected Terence for the tango;
> Or Livy for Lillian Lorraine.
> I was just learning to wear my dinner-jacket
> In that "carefully careless" manner endorsed by "Vogue,"
> When my father died bankrupt,
> Throwing me upon my own resources.
> Then I found I hadn't any.

So, knowing how to use neither my hands nor my brain,
I remembered my feet,
And became a chorus man. . . .
Then one night I turned my ankle.
When I was able to get up again
The public had flocked to another favorite.
So I entered an Endurance Dancing Carnival
And waltzed myself to death.[46]

The attention visited on Masters was not confined to the nation's literary capital of New York City, however, or exclusively to the year 1915. Indeed, the satires, parodies, and lookalike verses traceable to *Spoon River Anthology* continued for years, both at home and overseas. Quoting one of these foreign satires will be useful here, not only to demonstrate *Spoon River*'s international appeal, but also to show something of the skill, humor, and care that went into the best of these.[47]

The finest overseas parody by far (and the one against which all other satires of *Spoon River* should be measured) was published in 1917 by the British humorist J. C. Squire. His transatlantic double parody spoofed not only *Spoon River* but also the English language's best-known sentimental poem, Thomas Gray's "Elegy Written in a Country Churchyard." Squire relied on the form of Gray's eighteenth-century poem, as well as "echoes" of it, but the content came from Spoon River:

IF GRAY HAD HAD TO WRITE HIS ELEGY IN THE CEMETERY OF SPOON RIVER INSTEAD OF IN THAT OF STOKE POGES

The curfew tolls the knell of parting day,
    The whippoorwill salutes the rising moon,
And wanly glimmer in her gentle ray,
    The sinuous windings of the turbid Spoon.

Here where the flattering and mendacious swarm
    Of lying epitaphs their secrets keep,
At last incapable of further harm
    The lewd forefathers of the village sleep.

* * *

For them no more the whetstone's cheerful noise,
    No more the sun upon his daily course
Shall watch them savouring the genial joys
    Of murder, bigamy, arson and divorce.

Here follows a not-quite-exhaustive list of crimes, misdeeds, and disasters that can overtake humanity (especially when humanity cooperates), after which the author observes that in this world—and particularly in Spoon River—evil often triumphs over good:

> Full many a vice is born to thrive unseen,
>   Full many a crime the world does not discuss,
> Full many a pervert lives to reach a green
>   Replete old age, and so it was with us.

There are a good many other parodies that might be mentioned—by well-known personalities and obscure ones—but they all affirm the ancient adage that imitation is the sincerest form of flattery. In 1915 and 1916 in particular, *Spoon River Anthology* was the most imitated book in America.[48]

There has of course been a great deal of more serious commentary on *Spoon River,* and because it is this one book that lends significance to Masters's life, it will be useful to pause here and examine some of these reflections on *Spoon River* and to see how this critical commentary provides both an estimate of his poetic vision and a gloss on his life.

CHAPTER 5

Reflections on Spoon River

It was the vision, vision, vision of the poets Democratized!

—Edgar Lee Masters, "Lydia Humphrey," *Spoon River Anthology*

The remarkable reception given *Spoon River Anthology* logically elicits the question of why nothing else by Masters ever came close to equaling it. Also important is the interplay between Masters's personal life and literary influences and his literary success. One wonders, too, whether *Spoon River* offers biographical insights about issues that are fundamental both to Masters's being and to the book's success, and if so, why these important factors failed to work harmoniously in other books. Interpretive insights can shed light on all these matters and are useful in highlighting important parts of Masters's life story.

It is clear that what Masters regarded as a chief misfortune of his youth—the conflicts and stresses in his parents' household—actually worked to his advantage when he sat down to describe the complexities of the 200-plus individuals in *Spoon River Anthology.* In his autobiography, for example, he tells of the tension of living with two feuding parents who were as different as day and night, or North and South (or East and West), which they in their ways resembled. Moreover, the divisive nature of the little towns in which they lived added to their own divisiveness, so that Masters's earliest environment was fractured from boyhood. One might also mention the adversarial relations Masters experienced with his sister and brother (both of whom received college money Masters felt should have come to him), as well as the adversarial nature of Masters's profession (and that of his father)—of lawyer versus lawyer and client versus client. And of course there is the greatest tension of all: Masters's desire to live as a poet while forced by his father into the law. Many of these tensions found expression in *Spoon River,* which is replete with family stress and people pulled in two directions. So Masters's early family life provided an unexpected foundation for the villagers he would later depict.[1]

Masters's turbulent relations with women also deserve a closer examination. He was torn, for example, between Lewistown's Margaret George, whom he idealistically admired, and her better-looking and more sensual friend Winnie Eichelberger; between his wife, Helen, who offered him status and respectability, and the whores of the Everleigh house, who amused him; between his ongoing desire for a woman who had the intellectual wherewithal to understand him and the equally insistent urge to be with a woman who excited him physically. When one simply lists the ways in which Masters represented a divided personality (both in his parents' house and in his own), it is no wonder that many of his Spoon River inhabitants emerge similarly divided. Yet it was the addition of this extra dimension and the understanding of the dichotomous nature of humankind that did much to make Masters's *Spoon River* folk real.

So close are some parallels between Masters and his book that it is occasionally difficult to determine where the reality of *Spoon River* ends and the biography of Masters begins. For example, a character named "Robert Fulton Tanner" says that life is like a giant rat trap, and Masters, too, felt "trapped" at virtually every stage of his existence: in his parents' loveless home, in his engagement to Helen Jenkins, at their wedding, and in his marriage, which he likened to a "prison." He felt trapped, too, in his daily work as a lawyer, as one who might simply "drop dead" from overwork. When he placed these experiences in perspective and weighed them in the light of his readings of naturalistic authors such as Dreiser and Stephen Crane (in whose works many characters are trapped), it opened Masters's eyes to his own situation and helped guide his treatment of his *Spoon River* characters, many of whom are similarly locked in bad marriages, loveless homes, and meaningless work they despise.[2]

Masters also felt trapped by the times in which he lived (preferring an earlier America instead) and in this respect was influenced sharply by an American statesman who was one of his heroes, Thomas Jefferson. Masters was frank about Jefferson's influence, saying in the conclusion of his autobiography that Jefferson was one of those who helped lay "the foundation for many things in *Spoon River Anthology.*" Thus, Masters tried whenever possible (e.g., in his autobiography and in interviews) to trace his intellectual roots to Jefferson and his genealogical roots to Virginia, Jefferson's home state and the home of Squire Davis Masters's forebears. Masters was guided by Jefferson's comments in *Notes on the State of Virginia,* particularly the famous observation that "those who labour in the earth are the chosen people of God." Masters needed look no further than his Petersburg grandparents to see this wonderfully illustrated—in their harmonious relations with others, in their fruitful farming endeavors, and in their uncomplicated belief in God. (The two grandparents also served him in *Spoon River* when he wanted to show people who were not torn by circumstances, as the epitaphs of "Aaron Hatfield" and "Lucinda Matlock" illustrate.) What caused Masters so much trouble—in both his writing and his personal relation to the age—was that America had changed from the days of Jeffersonian ideals:

> The democratic ideal that originated with Jefferson was realized on the Jacksonian frontier in the lives of the uncorrupted (Adamic) pioneers, who held fast to the American vision, but the Civil War destroyed that idyllic agrarian democracy and allowed materialistic and repressive forces to dominate the country. In short, America degenerated from primal innocence. *Spoon River Anthology* is a kind of objective correlative of this idea, a microcosmic reflection of America's spiritual condition after the Edenic culture had been displaced by those subversive forces.[3]

Many of Masters's other books would also reflect this displacement, and this tendency would play a major role in determining his literary reputation both during his life and afterward: seeing that honesty, hard work, and principle (represented by his grandparents' generation) had been replaced with the greed and expediency that often characterized later years of American history, Masters frequently overreacted in his many books. Instead of writing poems and stories (and histories and biographies) that dealt with the dualities of human life, he too often presented one-dimensional characters whose sole reason for being was to reflect his own biases against modern times.

This helps to explain why many of Masters's pioneer characters can do no wrong and why their children and grandchildren can do so little good. Equally important, it helps to explain a more subtle design in *Spoon River,* Masters's attempt to turn back the clock and, in characters such as those based on his grandparents, to recover a better time: "In one sense *Spoon River Anthology* was a spiritual quest for [America's earlier environment], an attempt to recover what had vanished—from his life and from American culture—by memorializing it in his poetry." This was a challenging undertaking, and Masters might not have succeeded had he not had the example of the poet with whom he has been most frequently compared, Walt Whitman.[4]

Whitman figured early in Masters's intellectual development. Masters had studied Whitman with Margaret George in his Lewistown days and presented a paper on him before the Fulton County Scientific Association. Much later, in his autobiography, Masters correctly linked Whitman's vision of America with Jefferson's: "What had enthralled me with Whitman . . . was his conception of America as the field of a new art and music in which the people would be celebrated instead of kings; and the liberty of Jefferson should be sung until it permeated the entire popular heart. . . . In that America Whitman would be the Hesiod and someone yet to rise the Homer." This is not unlike Whitman's own mythic view of America in "Song of Myself," of a country of comrades working with an affection for the nation and one another to make the nation reach its idealistic potential. Like Whitman's, however, Masters's vision had been splintered by the post–Civil War era, corruption in high public offices, the visible effects of Gilded Age materialism, and (in Masters's case) turn-of-the-century imperialism. Thus, Masters's view of America was also like Whitman's in *Democratic Vistas,* in which the poet had to deal with his own cynicism with the American experience.[5]

This potentially devastating vision worked ultimately to Masters's advantage in *Spoon River.* Like Whitman in "Song of Myself," Masters consciously or unconsciously created in *Spoon River* what has been described as "a single poem," one "in which the characterizations are a multifaceted mask for the poet's discordant and struggling literary mind, which eventually does assert its dominion, creating his new identity." As has already been suggested, Masters's characters often reflect his own divided nature, and their cumulative effect was to create a new identity for their author, "the Spoon River Poet."[6]

From Whitman, too, Masters found precedent to discuss the theme of human sexuality that threads its way through many of his writings. In a world of disunity and divided natures, romantic love and sex offered Masters not only a sense of unity but a glimpse of heaven as well, as he once explained in verse;

> Man's genius in the love embrace
> Finds secrets of infinitude,
> And fathoms heaven's mystic space,
> And for a moment is one with God.

He would repeat the same idea in one of his autobiographical novels: "The union of one personality with another overcomes the spiritual lacuna": "Psychologically considered, the thing that comes nearest to annihilating . . . loneliness is love—romantic love. While it lasts it really does blot out the loneliness." He would explain in his biography of Whitman that humankind's urgings toward love and sex come from deep within: "The *irrepressible yearning* with which Whitman credited the human soul is nothing less than that lacuna at its center which sex, by some trick of nature, fills. It lifts human beings out of their soul loneliness while it stays, if only for a moment, the desolate gap of eternity which tortures the soul all through its earth pilgrimage." Masters phrased matters even more concisely to one of his male friends: "Then [comes] this awful loneliness that nothing ever eased and blotted except the wonder of sex!" Thus, what Masters refers to as "cosmic longing" or "the secret of the mystery of life" is simply what Whitman refers to by other names, such as "the procreant urge" of the world. Whatever its name, the yearning for romantic love shows up frequently both in Masters's personal behavior and in the characters of *Spoon River,* whose lives such yearning often shapes. (Masters in his later years would say he was glad he had explored the theme of sexuality in his writings since none of his peers were doing so.) So in these ways, too, Masters's reading and personal beliefs meshed to provide portraits for *Spoon River.*[7]

But perhaps it was Whitman's emphasis on the common that provided Masters with his most important insights. Whitman's "Song of Myself" focuses on the common person throughout, and Masters may have seen that he needed look no further than the village townships of his youth to discover all the poetry he needed. One scholar phrased the matter thus, while quoting from Masters's biography of Whitman: "In the kind of lyrics Whitman sang, Masters looked for [a] technique that 'extracts the essential from landscapes and the souls of men and women in their daily life and in heroic moments.' Through Whitman, Masters didn't feel the need to look anywhere else but more deeply into where he already was." In other words, he had learned that examples lying close at hand might lead to universal truths. Like Whitman, Masters would express these truths in language some people felt was coarse.[8]

Spoon River also shows the influence of one of Whitman's principal teachers, Ralph Waldo Emerson. Masters was studying Emerson by the time he was in high school and found him to be a congenial tutor, perhaps because Masters did not find in Emerson the regional condescension that other easterners often displayed. Emerson's dictum to trust oneself might have directed Masters to use his own indigenous materials; certainly Emerson's views on the appropriate role of influences were thought provoking (he counseled readers to use authors from the past to achieve their own ends). Some years after *Spoon River,* while editing a selection of Emerson's works, Masters chose a quotation from Emerson's "Circles" as the epigraph for the book: "Life travels upwards in spirals. He who takes pains to search the shadows of the past below us, then, can better judge the tiny arc up which he climbs." This is essentially what Masters did in *Spoon River:* he searched the shadows of his own past and combined what he found with his reading. Emerson might also be credited with informing Masters that he need not feel ashamed of his small-town roots, for Emerson himself lived in a village, and that he should not worry about affronting orthodoxy. In other words, Emerson helped Masters find not only himself but his way to *Spoon River* as well. Writing in the early 1940s (in the introduction to his collection of Emerson's selected works), Masters reminisced about what he needed as a young intellectual in central Illinois: "Out in middle Illinois when I was in high school we eager young found ourselves stifled by the parochial orthodoxy that surrounded us. The unsmoked sky was above us, the fields and woods were around us, yet we needed air. We could not be free without knowing what we were, and what we possibly could do. . . . We needed someone to say that we had possibilities, and moreover in the encouraging doctrine of Emerson that we were potential geniuses, ready to expand wings and fly. . . . Emerson did this."[9]

In addition to family and readings in American literature, various European authors also greatly influenced Masters. The British romantic poet Percy Bysshe Shelley had a particularly important role in shaping Masters's life and attitudes and several of the *Spoon River* poems. In his autobiography Masters told of being introduced to Shelley's poems in high school and of buying a volume of Shelley's poems that opened "a new world" to his eyes. That book had helped to direct Masters to wider reading and to his vocation as a writer; later, Shelley's influence would help Masters put into perspective his boyhood yearnings for beauty, an urge that continued through his young manhood and through the time of his ill-fated marriage and numerous girlfriends:

> As a boy on the Masters farm the silence of the prairie had seemed to me to be the silence of my own heart. And in the stillness of evenings when the sun set beyond the farthest farmhouses I walked about the pasture where I flew kites with something choking in my breast, with a longing that I could not understand. When I found Shelley and read such lines as "I thirst for the music that is divine" I saw that eternity and the mystery about life beckon sensitive souls to realms that lie below life's horizon. At last I understood that my passion for beauty in women, and my attempts to realize myself through erotic love, were just futile searches to fill the void in my heart.[10]

It is sometimes said (no doubt correctly) that Masters's mother created this void in his heart by failing to provide him with sufficient mother love and that his subsequent devotion to his grandmother Lucinda Masters began when he sensed that she offered a substitute love. Thus, he was cursed with the need to search all his life for the love his mother failed to give him and doomed not to recognize genuine love, since he had been deprived of it in the most fundamental stages of his existence. Masters himself was well aware of his chronic fascination with women, remarking in his autobiography that "the pursuit of the eternal feminine was deeply fated in my nature." Such a "fate" would ultimately play itself out in a life involving many women and many wanderings until, his physical energies exhausted, he would end old and alone. Before this time, however, he would turn to the literary personages he admired to see how they coped with this problem.[11]

Masters was especially drawn to Shelley's depictions of idealized eroticism and for years actively pursued such a will-o'-the-wisp in his private life. In *Across Spoon River* he explained Shelley's influence by contrasting him with another romantic writer, Edgar Allan Poe: "There is an apostrophe to woman in Poe's 'The Poetic Principle,' where he rhapsodizes on the grace of her step, the luster of her eye, the melody of her voice, her soft laughter and the angelic rustling of her robes. That sort of lush romanticism was not mine. I saw my divinities through the poetry of Shelley, clothed in woven wind, and innocently walking before me in their immaculate nudeness, willing to yield their loveliness in obedience to unashamed passion."[12]

Much of Masters's autobiography is little more than a description of his search for an ideal woman of the type Shelley might have described—or pursued. (Like Shelley, Masters would eventually abandon his first wife in preference for another woman.) Indeed, many of the sections of *Across Spoon River* that offended its first readers directly resulted from Shelley's influence on Masters. It was one thing, for example, when Masters remarked, "There grew up in me a passion for intellectual beauty fed by the poems of Shelley." It was quite another thing for Masters to illustrate over and over the belief that sex is the uniting force in life, what he called "the union of two souls" and "the Secret Power." Nevertheless, it was perfectly natural for Masters to come to this conclusion, not only because some of his reading informed him that this was so, but also because his fragmented world filled him with a chronically perceived need to seek unity, to address the loneliness he felt by being at one with another. Thus, the world that Shelley showed Masters was too appealing in that respect: it could not be realized and permanently sustained in the real world.[13]

By the time Masters came to be an old man, he realized that Shelleyan visions of an idealized eroticism had done much to shape his life, that he had not consummated the erotic ideal he sought, and that he would never address the longings he had felt since young manhood. The dream could not be reached ("it is distant now, and will ever be so"). Nonetheless, he felt closest to Shelley of all authors regarding attitudes on love and sex: "I do not find in Shakespeare, in Goethe, in Byron, in Browning, in Keats the same attitude toward passional love that I have felt almost from boyhood. Perhaps Shelley is nearest to me." "I dwell upon this subject," he added, "because I feel that a good deal of my secret is contained in it."[14]

Masters would eventually rework many Shelleyan themes in poems composed early and late and would conduct portions of his professional life as Shelley had conducted his own. Indeed, a part of Masters's impulse to help humanity's downtrodden through his law practice had its origin in Shelley's writings. Masters's reformist tendencies, political liberalism, support for William Jennings Bryan, and concern for people in islands dominated by the United States through the Spanish-American War might also be traced to liberal influences from Shelley. Shelley thus had a tremendous effect on Masters's conduct of his life as well as his creative works, including *Spoon River,* in which scholars have found several poems showing a Shelleyan vision or influence. There is even a character named "Percy Bysshe Shelley" in *Spoon River;* like his namesake, he dies in an accident involving water.[15]

Masters was also influenced by the nineteenth-century German romantic Johann Wolfgang von Goethe, particularly by Goethe's *Faust.* Masters studied German in both grade school and college and first encountered *Faust* in translation at age twenty when he purchased a copy in a Lewistown bookstore. Masters spoke of an "enthrallment with Goethe's *Faust*" and of its being "a lifelong delight" to him, perhaps because he discerned that the character of Faust was much like himself, part artist seeking higher meaning and part sensualist seeking an ideal woman. Alternatively, he may have identified with Goethe himself, a lawyer who had money problems and domestic difficulties as well as a strong interest in erotic attractions. Or maybe Masters simply liked Goethe's appearance: Masters's parents owned a book entitled *Album of Authors,* and Masters once remarked that he had "studied constantly the faces of these notables, picking Goethe and Shelley as the best of all." Goethe's potential influence on *Spoon River* is well documented since Masters speaks of reading *Faust* in January 1915, when he had drafted some but not all of the poems.[16]

Most telling is Masters's comment that he often had the sensation of being "two persons" and having "two personalities," of being both the idealist who composed the romantic verses of his first book and the realist who lived in "that Hittite city called Chicago." Of course, Masters's sense of being two persons while writing *Spoon River* parallels Goethe's most famous work, in which Faust represents the questing and idealistic side of humankind and his opponent, Mephistopheles, represents the cynical and realistic side. Masters may have found that, in his divided nature, Faust was much like the characters in *Spoon River,* several of whom have sensitive and questing natures but are brought up hard against the limits imposed by reality—like Faust or, for that matter, Edgar Lee Masters himself in his search for the right woman, a place for poetry, and the fame he hoped poetry would bring. In any event, it seems likely that Faust's divided nature is reflected both in Masters and in the divided natures of some of his *Spoon River* characters.[17]

Because Masters found in Goethe's famous work a literary influence that was congruent with his own personality, one is again faced with a question of determining where literary influence ends and autobiography begins. We shall never define these limits exactly, for Masters himself did not know. Writing about different treatments of love, for example, Masters commented both on the final chorus of *Faust* and on its relation to his own values: "Goethe declares here that in the transitory life of earth[,] love is only a symbol of its diviner being, and that the possibilities of love, which earth can never fulfill, become realities in a higher life which follows, and that the spirit which woman interprets to us here still draws us upward. So here is expressed all that I have felt of love, both as a giver of life and as a forecast of a higher sphere, as a delusion, a satiety and a deathless force." Masters's yearnings ultimately found expression in the strivings of his characters in *Spoon River,* many of whom (like their creator) attempt to articulate what is most heartfelt and shape their lives and epitaphs accordingly.[18]

It is clear, too, that the writings of the seventeenth-century Dutch philosopher Baruch Spinoza influenced Masters's personal philosophy and the epitaphs of *Spoon River.* Masters read Spinoza at Knox College and was attracted to the concept that mind and matter are merely two aspects of the larger reality of God. God is everywhere in the Spinozistic world, a belief to which Masters was receptive (for his heroes Shelley and Goethe were receptive to it). Masters would consider Spinoza's teachings for much of his life, declaring near the end of his days that God and the mind are one and the same: "As to God, after thinking it over all my life, I have come to the conclusion that there is a mind as large as the universe that is in everything"; "all we see in the heavens and in the earth is Mind." According to Spinoza, immortality can be achieved simply by understanding this, but humankind has to make the appropriate intellectual effort. "Immortality is something to be earned," Masters once wrote a friend. "Years ago I expressed this idea in the epitaph of 'The Village Atheist'" in *Spoon River.* Masters then quoted the final four lines of that epitaph:

Immortality is not a gift,
Immortality is an achievement;
And only those who strive mightily
Shall possess it.[19]

There is also evidence of Spinoza's influence in numerous other epitaphs from *Spoon River,* including those for some of the unhappiest personalities (who represent only their fragmented selves, as do Ollie and Fletcher McGee) and some of the happiest (who see the unity that guides their lives, as do the two identified jointly as "William and Emily"). The concluding piece of *Spoon River,* the "Epilogue," is also a manifestation of Spinozistic thought, as the penultimate speaker asserts:

Ever aspire.
Worship thy power,
Conquer thy hour,
Sleep not but strive,
So shalt thou live.

Thus, the individual finds God and "Infinite Life" by vigorous intellectual striving and through that exercise earns a measure of happiness denied others. To one pulled in as many ways as Masters was, this offered a type of peace, both in the present world and in preparation for the one to come. "I have been called an atheist," Masters once said in an interview, "but my atheism is that of Spinoza, in whom I find my profoundest satisfaction—and he was an all-God man, not an atheist." Spinoza's views on religion seem to have been sufficient for Masters from his college days on, for he himself was never baptized (at least not as an adult), nor did he ever join a church. When he felt particularly stressed, as he did at the time of World War I, he achieved peace of mind by reflecting on Spinoza's works: "In these days, Spinoza helped me."[20]

Masters and his epitaphs were also shaped by one of England's most popular nineteenth-century poets, Robert Browning, who in some ways was more important than all the other influences. Masters had read a paper on Browning and Tennyson before a Chicago literary group in 1911 or 1912 and had it printed as a small pamphlet entitled *Browning as a Philosopher* about 1912. Masters admired the spirit of Browning's artists and intellectuals, who attempt to turn life into a successful quest, often in the face of discouraging odds. This, of course, is what Masters faced in his parents' loveless household, from which he had eventually fled with the aspiration that writing might bring him the attention and companions he wanted to end the loneliness he felt. Masters could easily have identified with Browning's fledgling knight in "Childe Roland to the Dark Tower Came": the young man traveled alone through an environment choked with discouragement and malevolent misdirection (as Masters sometimes did in Lewistown and Chicago) and succeeded simply because he refused to give up. Masters had primed himself for similar strivings since childhood, as he suggested in connection with an art object belonging to his grandmother: "As a boy on the Masters farm my grandmother kept a paper knight, an embossed figure it was, in her bureau drawer. I am unable to describe the emotion that this simple object gave me, of the thrilling association of fancy which it stirred in me."[21]

Like Masters, Browning had derived much of his liberal thinking from Shelley. In addition, both Masters and Browning devoted portions of their early days to the seemingly futile writing of plays, an exercise that paid off when it provided them both with genius insight into the speech patterns they would use in their dramatic monologues. It is sometimes said that Browning's use of the dramatic monologue influenced all the practitioners who followed him, and in Masters's case this turned out to be a very beneficial influence. *Spoon River Anthology* would have turned out far differently had it not been phrased as a series of dramatic monologues (a claim amply demonstrated by the unsuccessful and now forgotten tombstone epitaphy Masters expressed in conventional, rhymed lines, reproduced in chapter 3).[22]

Moreover, the dramatic monologue provided Masters a fortunate opportunity to apply his law background to his creative works. As one Masters scholar summarized it, "Masters' experience with courtroom testimony sharpened his sensitivity to the poetic possibilities in a montage of different perspectives on the same event." Thus, Masters's characters not only comment on one another but provide telling glimpses of their own personalities and inner beings. (The observer of all this—the reader—sits to one side, like a member of a jury.)[23]

Masters's challenge in *Spoon River* was to mesh the form of the dramatic monologue with the stories from his own experience and reading. Here the finely wrought depictions of Browning's characters served as excellent models for Masters and his often intense characters: "In the eternal quests of Browning's heroes and villains, Masters found intriguing models for the character sketches of his own monologues. His deepest debt to Browning was the use of dramatic technique to achieve objectified intensity of feeling. Masters knew the standard dramatic monologues, parleyings, and character pieces which Browning conceived. These tight, polished forms helped him to present his own controversial themes with impact and precision."[24]

Masters left behind a permanent reminder of his reliance on Browning in the penultimate epitaph in *Spoon River,* which he named "Elijah Browning." Unfortunately, after *Spoon River,* Masters too often threw aside the Browningesque personae or masks that had served him better than they had any other writer of his generation, so that readers saw Masters's own personal frustrations instead of his characters'. The new results were seldom felicitous, since Masters needed such a form to objectify the many inner conflicts he felt.

Of all the influences on Masters, however, that of Greek writers may have been the most deeply seated, not only because Masters borrowed his title for *Spoon*

River and the concept of the anthology from *Epigrams from the Greek Anthology* (and its "microbiographies" of individuals), but also because Masters valued Greek culture above all others. As he explained in his autobiography, Shelley had first led him to the Greeks, and by the summer of 1886, Masters was reading Greek writers in translation. He told Kimball Flaccus that he also learned a smattering of Greek from Margaret George's father—but this was so insignificant that he said in his autobiography that he had "no start at all in Greek" until he went to Knox College, where he studied under Professor Newcomer. "Greek fascinated me beyond anything I had ever studied," he wrote, adding, "My Greek studies proved the happiest of all." By the end of his one year of college preparatory work, Masters was reading Homer and the *Anabasis* in the original. He later borrowed the classics from the library of Judge Winter, the father of Will Winter, the Lewistown youth with whom he studied law in 1890–91. Masters would later say he reread Homer each spring until 1914, when he was busy with *Spoon River.*[25]

Masters admired the "wholeness" of Greek culture, finding it to have been a higher and richer culture than that of other societies. Poetry in "its purest form" came from the Greeks, he said, and neither American culture in the aggregate nor any of its writers could measure up to them. From that belief, it was only a short step for Masters to remember his boyhood days in Lewistown (and his youthful readings in Shelley) and to discover that a chief stumbling block to American cultural advancement lay in religion.[26]

Masters had grown skeptical of religion while still a teenager, not long after Lewistown's assistant principal Mary Fisher had directed her best students to the lectures of Robert Ingersoll: "For myself I read the Bible through and through; and by the time I was fourteen or so I was skeptical of it as a revelation. The attitude of some leading citizens toward my father helped to solidify my opposition to the churches and to the religion they preached." Nor did his views mellow with time. His opinions in 1915 were congruent with his thinking at the end of his life: "In a word I think that Christianity has falsified and enervated the world, America included. It has bred the hypocrite, who was a far less prevalent character in pagan days. I think I can say this with as much justification in reason as I could say that a great pestilence and a vast slaughter in war were disasters to the world. To my mind there is hardly an utterance of Jesus that is sound and true, while his mind and his character are inferior to those of Socrates, Confucius, Aristotle, and Plato."[27]

This was hardly the kind of utterance that would play in Peoria, as a phrasemaker of a later day would put it, and as Peoria and all its middle-class connotations were geographically and spiritually close to the heartland Masters was describing in *Spoon River,* it is evident that he was on a collision course with his readership. He looked about. It was clear to him that Greek ideals could not simply be grafted onto the American middle class, and it was clear, too, that America would be slow in creating its own ideals based on Greek models (as

Emerson might have suggested). Yet America and countries far away had recognized and rewarded Masters when he found fault with its small towns. Might he not receive equal or greater rewards if he were to criticize the nation's other constituent parts? He believed he might. Thus, by a circuitous route (through Greece and his own wide reading), Masters would be led to what amounted to a permanent war against some of the nation's institutions.

In many future works he would come across as one of American literature's truly angry men as he searched in vain for a country that met the ideals of Jefferson, Emerson, Whitman, and the Greeks and found instead a country as fractionated and far from its ideals as he himself was. Married to the wrong woman and living in the transitional era of World War I, Masters by the time of *Spoon River* had developed a poetic vision that was essentially tragic, like that of the Greek dramatists he admired. "I am a Hellenist," he once said—and that said much. Like the Greek writers, he too spoke much of warring states and of individuals at war with themselves, particularly with their own sexual yearnings. A book such as *Spoon River* could give voice to his wide intellectual range and the many conflicts within him, but it remained to be seen whether he could bring his energies and feelings under control in future books or whether new writings would simply show an inchoate, sprawling mass of ideas.[28]

The first book to follow *Spoon River* suggested it would be the latter, for Masters did what many authors of best-sellers have done following a literary success: he sifted through his files to find poems he might quickly assemble in a new book and thus capitalize on his fame. The result was his first volume of 1916, *Songs and Satires,* an uneven book of miscellaneous poems, about which there would be far less said, written, or remembered than there was about *Spoon River.* One reason for this difference is that *Spoon River* enjoyed the effective, if unplanned, strategy of being brought out in four different marketing efforts (once in serial form in 1914, once as a first edition in 1915, once through magazine reprints, and again as an augmented edition in 1916); a better reason is that Masters's first book after *Spoon River* really was not very satisfying.[29]

Published by Macmillan in the spring of 1916, *Songs and Satires* is a mixture of new poems and old, many of them written years before those in *Spoon River.* Four of the poems were carried over from Masters's 1898 volume *A Book of Verses,* and most of that volume had been drafted in his Lewistown days, as he once explained to Amy Lowell: "I published *A Book of Verses* in 1898 through Way and Williams of Chicago, the same being what I brought up with me from Spoon River in 1892 when I came here weeded out of several hundred." Moreover, he added, "several others in *Songs and Satires* were written years ago, indeed were printed years ago." Thus, while Masters once said of *Songs and Satires* that "most of it was new," he must have meant simply that many of the poems had not been previously printed in book form. Certainly reviewers found little of the "new poetry" in its selections, at least one of which, "Helen of Troy," had been printed more than twenty years earlier:

Helen of Troy, Greek art
Hath made our heart thy heart,
    Thy love our love.
For poesy, like thee,
Must fly and wander free
    As the wild dove.[30]

About a third of the poems in *Songs and Satires* stress achievement or dedication to a goal and concern romantic idealists, many of whom, like Masters himself, undergo major tests on their long march to success. In this respect one might discern the influence of Robert Browning, who created similar heroes, but with one major difference: Masters relied on Browning's favorite storytelling device, the dramatic monologue, in only some of his poems—with the result that he drifted away from the objectivity of *Spoon River* and into what sometimes seemed like personal discussions. (The abandonment of the brief epitaph form also encouraged Masters's tendency toward long-windedness.) One respected poet and critic, T. S. Eliot, examined *Songs and Satires* and arrived at a criticism that could stand both for it and for many of Masters's other books: "He must have a personage, and this personage must be detached from himself in order to give his peculiar meditative irony its opportunity; it must not appear as an element in a supposed autobiographical situation, or the incisive comment tends to dissolve in sentiment."[31]

As a result, what should have been a marketing director's dream—selling *Spoon River*'s successor—became instead a critical hodgepodge, with reviewers looking in vain for vestiges of *Spoon River*'s insights and psychoanalyses. Many critics were generous enough to find something good to say, but few found what they expected: "Mr. Masters has not, apparently, any definite theory of poetry, classical or romantic; he is a medley of conflicting influences. . . . Yet behind all this absurdity there is some of the original force which made 'Spoon River Anthology' a notable book."[32]

Unfortunately, Masters learned little or nothing from reviews of *Songs and Satires,* except to develop a dormant hostility toward reviewers and critics: "I was pretty indifferent to what they said; for in many critical quarters it was well received. It had a decent sale and I was too occupied with writing, with using my long-gathered material, to stop to listen to men who had nothing to tell me." He chose to ignore the fact that readers might reasonably assume that a new volume of poems by a writer of his stature would mean new poems rather than old. When serious critics wrote serious commentary about his old poems but misread them as new ones, he found it amusing. In the same letter in which he told Lowell that many of the poems in *Songs and Satires* had been written years before, he also commented on critics who thought the poems were of recent vintage: "I mention as it occurs to me now to express to you the amusement I had at the critics who spoke of some of these as evidencing a genuine lyricism—

an ability to write poetry, perhaps, which *Spoon River* did not foreshadow. The critics make me laugh."[33]

Nor was William Marion Reedy always helpful in this regard. Masters valued his opinions above those of all others, but after Reedy had read the manuscript of *Songs and Satires*, he described it as "one hell of a good book" and told Masters he "need not fear the verdict of any critic whose opinion is worth a tinker's dam." Reedy correctly suggested that Masters's best work was in free verse, but he also told him that form did not matter: "It isn't the form that matters so much after all. The main thing is to get your thought over, and your feeling too." This advice, issued in late 1915 or early 1916, turned out to be absolutely wrong for Masters, for he now felt free to move away from the highly successful succinctness of the *Spoon River* poems to the meandering subjectivity that characterized many of his other works. In fact, a good deal of Reedy's post–*Spoon River* advice was bad. He encouraged Masters to pursue drama (an area in which Masters had limited talent), occasionally praised poor books and poems, and told Masters some of his conventional verses were better than *Spoon River.* Many other critics found terrible flaws in Masters's poems published after *Spoon River,* but Reedy was uneven in this respect, although he did warn Masters of the perils of using poetry to attack enemies: "Be a little foxy, Lee." Perhaps Reedy himself had been bowled over with the success of *Spoon River* and could not always criticize his old friend's work; perhaps Reedy's judgment was compromised because of his poor health. In any event, he failed now to provide Masters with what he needed most: a touchstone to identify his good writing from his bad.[34]

The effect on Masters was predictable: he interpreted certain polite comments from the critics as a license to publish more of his older verses, particularly those written soon after his 1892 arrival in Chicago. His April 1916 comments to Alice Henderson illustrate this attitude: "What gratifies me is that these things that were produced in that period [the 1890s] have enough vitality to interest people of this period. And it encourages me to slip in other things in future books."[35]

With this encouragement, in the fall of 1916 Masters published a volume of miscellaneous poems similar to *Songs and Satires.* This, *The Great Valley,* had the Jeffersonian ideal of memorializing Illinois pioneers such as his grandparents (to whom the book was dedicated), but some of its traditionally arranged rhymes and nineteenth-century themes also suggested "long-gathered material." The book had begun well enough, with Masters telling a friend in the summer of 1916 that he had "rented the loveliest cottage of all [his] days" ("The Little House in the Woods") on Spring Lake's Belle Point and that he was enjoying himself with his children: "My boy . . . rented a sailboat, and we sail, and eat and sleep, and I have written some. The little girls are divinely happy, brown, fat, etc., and I am as happy as I have ever been."[36]

Unfortunately, Masters's sister, Madeline, had again separated from her husband, Neils Gron, and appealed to her brother for help. When Masters ignored her, she "appeared at Spring Lake with Buddie" (her son), after which the atmosphere for writing new poems or reviewing old ones deteriorated. Masters's wife was furious with the interruption of their vacation, and their friends took a dislike to Madeline, while the boys "snapped each other like two dogs." Masters was "disturbed" and "without tranquility." The summer ended without other problems, but he knew his writing had not received the time and attention it should have: "In the fall of 1916 *The Great Valley* was published. On my soul I wish that the poems about the Illinois country were better."[37]

Worse, he had again disappointed the critics, including one from *The Dial*, who wrote this assessment of Masters's chief challenges and flaws in 1916:

> This leading exponent of a new medium, midway between prose and poetry, shows himself quite impartial in his employment of traditional metres and of those free rhythms more peculiar to himself—blank verse, the rhymed pentameter couplet, and *vers libre.* It would be hard to say in which he displays the greater artistic ineptitude. . . . Not that there do not occur flashes of the power and penetration, coupled with the harsh felicities of word and phrase, that made of the "Spoon River Anthology," with all its obvious crudities, a really notable performance. But they are relatively few, and largely lost in the welter of words.
>
> The truth is, of course, that Mr. Masters, who seemed at one time to give a certain artistic promise, is not primarily an artist at all, but a moralist and social philosopher of vague ideological tendencies. For the moment, in the "Spoon River Anthology," his discursive instincts were held in check by the sheer mechanical requirements of the restricted form he imposed upon himself, in the brief space and inscriptional succinctness of the epigram. This artificial restraint once removed, however, the poet appears in his proper guise as a popular preacher of semi-literary, pseudo-scientific pretensions.

The Macmillan Company may have realized that it had a stiffer marketing challenge with *The Great Valley* and sent only 325 copies to foreign publishers, 75 to Canada and 250 to England.[38]

The summer over, Masters returned to Chicago, and as *The Great Valley* gathered poor reviews, he sat in his law office and again pondered his two careers. Just then neither was doing well financially. His law business had fallen off, although he did have a major case on appeal (the Helen Lee case, or Bermingham case, as he sometimes called it in reference to his client's uncle). If he won it, he would make a great deal of money. For the most part, however, he felt that law and literature mixed no better than oil and water: "My books were making money, but the days of settlement were long delayed by the terms of the contracts. Law business daily proved that a name in poetry frightens clients away." Nor did his attitude help. The idealism that had once prompted him to devote his legal talents to "people who were wronged" was slowly being replaced by a cynicism about people in general, as he had recently suggested to Nathan Haskell Dole: "I am occupied in the pleasant duty of trying a difficult and hotly contested lawsuit where people are quarreling with all the venom that can be evoked about matters of property. I have noticed that hogs in a meadow are friendly towards each other and at peace until a basket of yellow corn is emptied before them, when they begin to bite off each other's ears and disembowel each other in order to get all the corn. People are much the same." Meanwhile, at about this time (and a little before and after), *Spoon River* exploded at home.[39]

In Masters's two hometowns of Petersburg and Lewistown, near the Sangamon and Spoon Rivers, the people had looked up one day (or had just driven Dobbin and Beauty to town, or stepped onto the village square) and suddenly found their parents, grandparents, or themselves made grist for the grisly mill of the sordid *Spoon River Anthology.* Worse, someone they knew had done it. In 1915 and 1916 most of the citizens of rural Petersburg and Lewistown could not have cared less about a poetry best-seller, their attentions focusing instead on grain and livestock prices, church affairs, an annual trip or two to Springfield or Peoria, and increasingly, the war in Europe. But nearly all of them knew the lawyer Hardin Masters (a former state's attorney and Democratic Party worker), and a good many remembered "Hardy's" boy Lee. They knew Lee had attended college for a year or two and had gone to Chicago after a false start up north somewhere (Minneapolis). They also knew he had married a city woman and worked as a lawyer with the famous (or infamous) Clarence Darrow. Neither of the towns had heard much at all about Lee Masters for several years, or at least since 1909, when he had returned to the area to see his grandmother one last time. And now he had done this to them. People began to talk.[40]

Edward Laning, an Illinois artist acquainted with Masters, was a generation younger than the writer but just the right age to note how his own grandfather reacted to Masters's book. "The keeper of Petersburg's conscience" and "the fundamentalist teacher of the men's Sunday school class," this gentleman ("Papa" Smoot) never learned to enjoy modern views and amusements, so it was not surprising that he hated *Spoon River Anthology:*

> That Damned Book. When *Spoon River Anthology* appeared and won national fame, all hell broke loose. Half the town found itself mirrored there; and all the righteous were condemned, and all the sinners were pardoned. Perhaps the worst of it to Papa Smoot was the poem about Ann Rutledge, especially those lines, "Beloved in life of Abraham Lincoln, Wedded to him, not through union. But through separation." This smacked to Papa of some peculiarly horrible moral turpitude which by association he attributed to Edgar Lee. "If that man came to this door and rang the bell, I wouldn't let him in the house!" he would thunder in his courtroom manner.

So the towns of Masters's youth also became part of the critical process in weighing the merits of *Spoon River,* and when literary fame at last came to him, it came with a begrudging bitterness in the boyhood haunts where he had once supposed he would value it the most. Not even the epitaphs of *Spoon River* could rival the cruel irony of that success.[41]

Village self-esteem may have suffered in Petersburg and Lewistown, but the fate of tiny Hanover, Illinois, was in a way worse. Located in northwestern Illinois, Hanover had done nothing except be Hanover before Amy Lowell got it into her head that it had furnished the real-life model for *Spoon River.* Worse, she said as much in an important book-length study of the new verse, *Tendencies in Modern American Poetry:* "Spoon River purports to be a small town in the Middle West. It is said that Hanover, Illinois, served as its prototype. The poems are supposed to be the epitaphs in the cemetery of this town." Lowell's book turned out to be widely read, and since she was highly regarded as a poet and critic and was something of a newsmaker as well, people for several years searched their maps for Hanover when they went looking for the "real model" for Spoon River. (Lowell's claim is technically true to the extent that every American village is the village of Spoon River, but since this is not literally so and is based on a mistake, and because Lowell's book is still read, it is probably advisable to straighten out the record one more time.) In the end Hanover returned to its peaceful obscurity, while Petersburg and Lewistown were identified as the towns of Masters's boyhood and youth. William Marion Reedy had been right once again; *Spoon River* was like a flood: rapid in its ascent but indiscriminate in its sweep, it roiled into the new year of 1917, one of Masters's best and one of his worst.[42]

Masters would find himself adrift on this flood. Unable to rely wholly on Reedy's judgment, and with little critical discernment of his own, he had no idea whether his next book would draw bouquets or brickbats. He glowed when critics and reviewers praised him but developed lingering hatreds when they questioned the value of his work. Unable to learn from society's critical reflections on *Spoon River* and its immediate successors, he lowered his head into this storm of his own creation and daydreamed of a means to escape. He had in mind a rural retreat where he might simply write or seek the solace of a kind and understanding woman.

CHAPTER 6

A Country Place

You must have the satisfaction of realizing that you have achieved immortality if anyone alive today has.

—Amy Lowell to Edgar Lee Masters, July 20, 1917

Edgar Lee Masters spent much of his early manhood and middle years wishing he owned a country place, a rural retreat where he could live permanently if he made money enough to abandon law and pursue literature full-time. He admired men who were situated thus. From boyhood on he had been drawn to the story of the British author Sir Walter Scott and his writing haven of Abbotsford. Masters also had the example of his grandfather, who had lived on a farm of large acreage. Later, after Masters was married, he rented various country places for summer vacations and wrote a substantial portion of *Spoon River Anthology* at one, "The Oaks," in Spring Lake, Michigan. He also enjoyed being around people who lived on rural property, especially when it was substantial, and in 1921 began a lengthy friendship with a wealthy Illinois farmer named George Stokes. Masters's daydreams about a country place also showed up in his published and unpublished writings. Masters included a more ideal mate in his vision of a country place (especially when things were not going well with his wife), someone with whom he would write and relax, put in a garden and some trees, and putter with his acres until they were perfect.[1]

In the spring of 1917 he at last realized a portion of this dream, purchasing a house on a rural parcel of land near the Michigan resort town of Spring Lake. Unfortunately, his happiness and satisfaction with his new retreat lasted scarcely a hundred days. The former owner of the place became his enemy, and an old girlfriend showed up as a new neighbor. When the United States entered World War I, Masters's son ignored his father and tried to enlist. In addition, Masters was still mired in the same unhappy marriage, and when he sat down to write—at last on a full-time basis—he had less to say than he thought.

Masters had begun 1917 with the hope of pursuing both literature and law by compartmentalizing them. "Industry and concentration are my means to achievement," he told one correspondent seeking information about him: "When I work at writing, I work. When I practice law, I forget writing. I accumulate my subjects, jot down realities, thoughts, etc. When I have time for writing, I have my material at hand and produce much and rapidly, revising little, though sometimes correcting and re-writing until the picture gets clear." Despite this plan, however, time for writing often competed unfavorably with the law and with the many invitations and diversions that came to Masters as a celebrity.[2]

An example from 1916 illustrates these demands. After the Republican National Convention was held in Chicago in that year, Theodore Roosevelt's sister Corinne (Mrs. Douglas Robinson), herself a poet, visited Masters at his home and invited him to New York to meet her famous brother; Roosevelt himself also invited Masters to his house. Although Masters's 1904 volume *The New Star Chamber* had excoriated President Roosevelt and his expansionist policies, Masters now leaped at the opportunity to meet the former chief executive. (The temperamental Masters would often develop a strong hate only to set it aside if the other party offered friendship.) Roosevelt had prepared the way for the meeting through correspondence in which he had complimented Masters on his writing ("he had fine words to say of *Spoon River*"). Masters was too "tangled in lawsuits" to go at Corinne Robinson's preferred time, however, and so delayed his trip east until late January 1917, when he and Reedy could travel together.[3]

In addition to meeting Teddy Roosevelt on this trip, Masters was a guest of honor at a dinner sponsored by the Poetry Society of America at the National Arts Club in New York. He was not much of a club man, however, and looked forward more to seeing Roosevelt and his sister. Masters's diary summarizes the day of the dinner and meetings: "Poetry dinner, NY. Lunched with Mrs. R. Breakfast with TR." Masters sat in Roosevelt's New York hotel room and found himself liking the former president and his conversational fluency on a wide range of subjects. Roosevelt was like Masters in that respect. This meeting also heightened Masters's restlessness, however, for it focused the question of whether he should continue with the law or try to be a full-time writer, as he shortly explained to his friend Alice Corbin Henderson: "Oh I have so many things to write, and so many requests to write things. And here I am divided, distracted, worried—I don't know what to do sometimes. I'd like to run away."[4]

His marriage, also a chronic distraction, added to his problems. The success of *Spoon River Anthology* and the social doors it opened reminded Masters constantly of how happy he might have been—or might be still—if he were married to the right woman. Something was wrong in his life, as he remarked to his friend Dorothy Harvey: "But after all, the thing one desires is not the very thing when it comes. It has then been realized, departs from you, and is yours no more. . . . So it is a question whether one wants that as life, or merely life itself, which may be more. Life is greater of itself than life captured for an artistic purpose or through the [medium] of an artistic vision." In other words, his newfound prominence had quieted neither the restlessness nor the loneliness he often felt. He had gained the fame he sought as a boy but now discovered that there was no emotional payoff for the unhappiness he had endured in both his parents' house and his own. After work and on weekends, as he swam and walked, he pondered a way out of his problems.[5]

In February 1917 a way suddenly opened up: the Illinois appellate court decided in his favor in the Helen Lee/Bermingham case, and his client received $200,000; Masters received a fee of $27,000. He used $5,000 to pay off a bank loan and spent $2,000 on other debts and then planned a brief vacation to Indiana, as he explained to Dorothy Harvey in late February 1917: "I'm off to the dunes Sunday and Monday and expect to go away south or west for a recreation of a few weeks. I have not been well . . . , so much on my mind." He ended by going to New Orleans with his friend Sam Morgan, his wife and daughters following in about a week as he lectured at Tulane University.[6]

This period of social acceptance and financial affluence in early 1917 marked the high-water mark of Masters's dual careers as successful lawyer and man of letters. He had widespread name recognition, and as he explained in his autobiography, he had at last achieved his goal of making money enough to retire from the law and devote himself to his writing: "I had over $20,000 when my debts were all paid. To the reader it must be clear that I was now free to leave the law, to go to the country and to settle down to the literary life in earnest." Perhaps country living would yield a book that was real poetry and not the "yokelisms" of *Spoon River*. Perhaps such a book would even lead to happiness.[7]

Unfortunately, few writers other than journalists were able to make a comfortable living from their pens in the 1910s, and Masters was not to be an exception to this rule. Despite his international literary success, Masters several times complained that he received limited royalties from overseas sales of *Spoon River*. The best market was England, but the English public simply did not show much interest in literature from "the colonies." World War I shipping perils were also a consideration. Nor were domestic sales what Masters might have hoped. It should be remembered that *Spoon River Anthology* was a *poetry* best-seller, but it was not the overall national best-seller for books published in 1915, nor was it the runner-up or even in third place. In fact, *Spoon River* is not even mentioned in many end-of-the-year best-seller lists, a fact that shows its notoriety as a controversial book of poetry far exceeded the size of its royalty checks. These same circumstances prevailed in 1916 and 1917. In fact, the story that *Spoon River* sold 80,000 copies in its first year alone is just that, a story. Masters himself said in 1927 that the book required four years to reach the 80,000 mark: "sale of the book . . . reached 80,000 copies in four years, and broke the record in America for the sale of a book of verse."[8]

Masters's actual proceeds from the book can be reckoned roughly as follows. Assuming that *Spoon River* sold 20,000 copies each year during its first four years (the 80,000 copies mentioned previously), and using Masters's royalty rate of 10 percent on the first 3,000 copies and 15 percent afterward, his first year of sales would have generated $5,700 at the 1916 price of $2.00 per copy and $6,000 in the three subsequent years. Because Masters usually revised galleys, however, and because such author-generated expenses are sometimes deducted from royalties, this might have affected his earnings (we know that Masters's friend Harriet Monroe made certain editorial markings on *Spoon River*). By October 1915, six months after *Spoon River* was issued as a book and after Masters had some idea of the income it might produce, he offered Dreiser a satiric summary of the profits from poetry: "If I could sing like the angel Israfel, I couldn't make $1,000 a year—must practice law." In any event, royalty income of $6,000 per year was about one-fourth what Masters had been accustomed to making in a good year as a lawyer. In other words, if he were now "to leave the law" and "settle down to the literary life in earnest," he would have to produce four *Spoon Rivers* per year if he were to maintain his pre–*Spoon River* lifestyle. Except for his wife's equity in the family house and some life insurance, Masters had saved little of his previous earnings as a lawyer and none of his 1915–16 royalties from *Spoon River.* If he had, he would not have needed to spend $7,000 from the Bermingham case fee to get out of debt. It was the $20,000 remaining from the fee in that case that now allowed Masters to purchase his long-dreamed-of writing retreat.[9]

Masters acquired his country place at about the same time as America entered World War I (on April 6, 1917), a watershed time in his history just as in the nation's. The war and the writing retreat were related temporally and to a degree causally, and he bracketed them together in one paragraph in his autobiography:

> I decided to buy a country place and to have apple trees and bees, flowers and vegetables, and to work in the open air and to have tranquillity for writing. If there was forever to be war, first the Spanish-American War, which changed the form of our government, and now war upon Germany, which would solidify that change, I wanted to get to the hills. It didn't look much now as though I should ever have an estate such as Walter Scott's Abbotsford, which had teased my fancy always to live as he did. But I could get a country place, and I set about to do so.

To get a jump on things, he bought an incubator in late April and "hatched out 40 chickens for [his] own and the children's amusement."[10]

By the spring of 1917, the children constituted Masters's principal reason to stay married. For one thing, he knew that divorce involving a wife and three children would be very costly; for another, Masters had a genuine affection for his son and two little girls. Sometimes their attraction was so great that he could almost set aside the problems of his marriage to maintain their happiness. He explained the matter thus to Alice Corbin Henderson in May 1917: "Everything seems all right with us—the little girls too beautiful, like little wooley chickens, and my boy, blue eyed and strong. The hell of life is that one can't see his own blessings. What right has a hand to write about love when he has wedded a woman who has produced his heart's ideals?" To aid in the merriment of his "heart's ideals," particularly the daughters, he moved the container of chickens into the dining room of 4853 Kenwood pending their transfer to a more rural environment. (He also had his daughters learn the quilting stitches of their great-grandmother Lucinda Masters so that the rural crafts and "old America" would not be forgotten.)[11]

Masters had begun the serious search for a country place soon after returning from New Orleans. He looked in parts of northern Illinois (near the town of Oregon) and then saw an advertisement for a little farm in Spring Lake, Michigan, in an area he had known since 1903. The prospective property was "beautifully situated" and adjacent to the rental site where he had written much of *Spoon River* in the summer of 1914. He (or Helen—this is unclear) contacted the owner and found that title to the little farm and its house was not free and clear but the subject of a contract for deed by a third party. That individual was far behind in his payments but had spent the last several summers at the place along with his wife and children and had plans to return in the summer of 1917. This would-be buyer of the place turned out to be one of Masters's former acquaintances, Frank Walker, the man he suspected of having influenced his father-in-law to keep him out of the elevated railroad office. That suspicion notwithstanding, Masters and his wife had earlier become friendly with the Walker family and had seen a good deal of them in the summer of 1914 as Masters worked on *Spoon River* at Spring Lake. Since Walker could not meet his contractual obligations, he gave up his interest in the farm (though not without bitterness), and by May 25, 1917 (or a little before), Masters had taken possession of the property.[12]

The farm consisted of an old house and some outbuildings on a twelve-acre rectangle, two sides of which fronted on Spring Lake near the Grand Haven River. The property had been advertised for $8,500, but the seller was an old friend of Helen Masters who had served as a pallbearer at her father's funeral, and after she paid him a visit (Masters was ill with a cold), the owner lowered his price to $6,500. Masters told the rest of the story in his autobiography:

> And so I bought the place, after going to Spring Lake and walking over the twelve acres which it contained, and looking through the old house and sheds on it. In a few days I was sojourning at Arbutus Banks, a summer hotel about a half a mile from my place, and walking from there to rake leaves and clean up the grounds. I raked five years' accumulation of leaves, I cut and burned brush, I made a flower garden and a vegetable garden, I trimmed apple trees, and cut away alder bushes and piled dead branches for burning, and cleared my 1,000 feet of water front. . . . Truly these were happy days.
>
> There was glorious sunshine, and the birds sang to the echo in my orchard. Could I not have bees as Virgil and Horace had them? John [Wierenga, a hired hand,]

would attend to that for me. Already I had an incubator and was raising some chickens. At night tired to the bone with labor, I fell asleep at nine o'clock. I was up at five and off to the place at six to meet John and go to work again. I was hastening, for I wanted to get the place habitable for the writing of a book.

Nor did he confine himself to natural improvements:

I had a contractor making the house over. I built a beautiful outside chimney with two large fireplaces, one in the living room downstairs, the other in my study upstairs. I laid hardwood floors, and put in a hot and cold water system, and built an icehouse, and a fine concrete pier into the lake. I dug a cellar in which the 500-gallon tank for the water system was installed. . . . I had to have some kind of car to get in and out from the village which was two miles away, Grand Haven being five miles away. So I bought a car which had been run 200 miles for $600.

A tennis court rounded out the list of amenities. The total improvements added several thousand more to the purchase price of his lakefront property: "I had a good bank account and went into improvements to the tune of about $3,000 without embarrassment, having cash for everything." His total outlay on his new property and car now totaled $10,100, or about half the cash reserves he had set aside to begin life anew as a full-time writer.[13]

He did not, however, do any writing. "What is poetry anyhow?" he asked Harriet Monroe. "I haven't an idea more'n a potato," a reference to some gardening he had been doing. He did, however, provide Amy Lowell with a bibliography for use in her forthcoming book *Tendencies in Modern American Poetry.* "I found more to say about you than any one else," she wrote him. Unfortunately, she could not read his handwriting (it never got any better) and had to ask for his bibliographic information a second time. Meanwhile, Masters was spending the days at his farm, but as late as July 11 he was still sleeping at Spring Lake's Arbutus Banks Hotel, where he had neither ink nor table. Sometime in late July or early August, the carpentry and cleanup were finished, Masters and his family moved in, and he sat down to his long-deferred dream of a writing retreat in the country:

I set to work to write *Toward the Gulf,* taking my exercise by working in the flower and vegetable garden. . . . I became so infatuated with my flower garden that I could not stay away from it. I was still retiring early and rising early, sometimes by four o'clock. I would get up to look at the poppies, the calendulas, the zinnias, which danced in the white dawn, and seemed to thrill as the golden sun came up behind the sand hill at the rear of my acres. My daughter Madeline, as mystical and beautiful as a dryad, would sometimes hear me as I arose, and would follow me to the flower garden.[14]

A letter from Amy Lowell on July 20 made the summer a little more "golden." She affirmed that Masters was right in laughing at the critics ("we have reviewers, but of critics we are sadly bereft"), and she added her opinion that he had achieved literary immortality: "As to 'Spoon River' I do not think anything can kill it. You must have the satisfaction of realizing that you have achieved immortality if anyone alive today has." Elsewhere, William Marion Reedy looked at Masters's 1917 work and decided he did not like it ("Old Bill . . . doesn't like my recent poems," Masters confided to Monroe. "He is a hard taskmaster"). Reedy nevertheless had confidence in his friend, and as was typical of his uneven approach to Masters's post–*Spoon River* career, he contemplated an article on Masters and the need for a national poet laureate. Things seemed to be going well.[15]

Harriet Monroe paid Masters "a long visit" in his new place, as did other guests, but Masters was free to spend virtually as much time as he wished in preparing the manuscript of *Toward the Gulf.* Just how little attention he did devote to this new book can be determined by combining information in his autobiography with information in letters he exchanged with Paul Carus, the editor of the philosophical journal *The Monist* (and representative of many intellectuals who wanted to meet the author of *Spoon River*). Carus began the significant part of the correspondence on August 2, 1917, inviting Masters and his family to meet him at his Michigan summer place in Benton Harbor. Masters declined the invitation on August 7, saying that he had recently purchased his country estate and that since his arrival on May 25 he had found himself occupied with maintenance and repair. Because of these labors he had only recently begun to write and therefore felt that he should postpone his visit to Benton Harbor for a month. Carus took Masters's request for a thirty-day delay literally and proposed on August 23 that they meet at Benton Harbor on September 7. Masters had to defer this invitation also, writing Carus a candid letter on August 26: "Do you know we have just sat through a list of guests, after being most of the summer repairing the house; and now I have just settled down to writing, and getting an article. I'm afraid—indeed I know—I can't come around September 7th." In other words, if his letter is to be taken at face value, he was only then, in the fourth week of August, getting around to his writing. For these reasons Masters again suggested a later meeting.[16]

His writing did not go well, however, in part because Spring Lake turned out to be too charming. "It would be lovely to live here so far as vacations are concerned," he later wrote Monroe, "but I believe I couldn't write a thing, would go to pieces, need my old toil after all." Moreover, he began to doubt (as Reedy had) the value of his present work. He explained his concerns to Monroe in a letter of September 8, touching on a problem central to his creative life: "I wish a big critic would come along, and if I can't write I wish he'd say so. I'd quit so quick everybody could hear the silence. For this game is just crucifixion—a man has no time for living or loving or anything; and if the contribution is worthless, I'd be glad to take up living and loving." In no other utterance does Masters define so clearly the two poles of his artistic existence, showing he was less interested in making the sacrifices (or "crucifixion") required to write great poetry than he was in enjoying the life of a prominent poet and spending his days "living and loving."[17]

It was five days later, on September 13, that Masters stormed out of his writing "haven" following feuds with both his family and his neighbors. He wrote in his autobiography that he took with him "the script of *Toward the Gulf*" and that "there were 46 poems in the book, nearly all written that summer." He also left the impression that he was finished with the volume: "My book was written." Although he indicated in his autobiography that he had begun *Toward the Gulf* by July of 1917, his letters suggest that he wrote, revised, or reviewed for publication the volume's forty-six poems in only five weeks (from August 7 to September 13). Indeed, if his August 26 letter to Carus is taken at face value, he may have worked only about two and one-half weeks on this book, the third to follow *Spoon River.*[18]

Several of the poems were well done, but most of the pieces were far too long, disorganized, and diffuse to satisfy the critics. Some of the poems in this new volume seemed more recent than those in *The Great Valley*—the title poem, for example, was "dedicated to Theodore Roosevelt" and explored Masters's new relation with that former president; others examined family realities without the cynicism of *Spoon River.* But reviewers made the inevitable comparisons to *Spoon River,* as did Masters and his publisher. The first words in the new book were Masters's prefatory note "To William Marion Reedy" thanking him for his earlier help ("it would have been fitting had I dedicated *Spoon River Anthology* to you"); the last words, from the Macmillan Company, advertised a deluxe leather edition of *Spoon River Anthology* at $2.50. (The trade edition remained at its 1916 price of $2.00.) By itself, *Toward the Gulf* is merely one book in Masters's list of fifty-plus volumes, but seen in the light of his total development, reputation, and personal happiness, it is very important: when he did briefly achieve the economic independence he needed to devote himself full-time to his writing, he found he lacked the artistic discipline to do so; equally important, the $2,500 advance he received for *Toward the Gulf* may have convinced him that publishers would print anything with his name on it, regardless of quality. The result was a mediocre volume instead of the literary equal to *Spoon River* he was seeking.[19]

Nor did the writing retreat itself turn out as he had planned. His problems began not long after he had arrived. Some residents did not trust this well-known outsider whose *Spoon River Anthology* had made startling declarations about a community not unlike Spring Lake. America's entry into World War I intensified their suspicions, as he said in his autobiography: "For myself, *Spoon River* was anything but an assurance of my blind patriotism; my radical life and ideas were easy to intrepret [*sic*] my guarded speech into a secret sympathy with Germany." To allay such suspicions, he purchased $3,000 worth of war bonds, thus lowering his cash reserves to less than $7,000. In addition, in a matter of weeks after getting settled, Masters had disagreements with the farm's previous tenant, Frank Walker, who "rented a house on the lake and proceeded to circulate the story that I had cheated him out of his beloved place." (Mrs. Walker called it "Walker's Point.") At the same time, Masters's wife was "rather friendly" with Walker's wife, Walker having been an old friend of her late father.[20]

Then a second ghost from the past appeared. "Cecile" had been a girlfriend of Masters in 1896; now she showed up as a permanent resident across the lake. Masters's growing son disobeyed him and insisted on visiting a sister of this old friend, all of which left Masters very uneasy. When he discovered that his son had developed a sexual relation with the sister, or was likely to do so, he was even more disturbed. Not surprisingly, Masters's relationship with his family also developed new tensions. On September 13 things came to a head. As a novel by Masters relates, the precipitating factor occurred when he wanted his son to help him repair the water system and found that Hardin was once more across the lake with the former girlfriend's sister.[21]

Other details of this important day at Spring Lake are sketchy; the autobiography describes them as follows:

> One day, it was September 13th, something unusually exasperating happened, and I packed to leave, and to abandon my orchard and my house, and to turn over to the family the car, the garden, letting the enchantress across the lake do as she would. A sturdier spirit, perhaps, would have sent the family back to Chicago. Somehow I could have gone on with the negro cook. But my book was written, I was tired and I wanted a change. I started across the porch followed by the cook who begged me not to leave. But I went, acting as I have always acted, suddenly and without turning back after my patience has been exhausted.
>
> I returned to Chicago to find everything changed, my friends occupied with the war or gone to France. The *Poetry* office was not what it had been. Studios of happy assemblage were silent. . . . This is what I found in a few hours after leaving the wind-swept hill of my lawn, and the stars between the oak trees that overlooked my roof at Spring Lake. As it turned out I had left them for good.

Masters never elaborated on the events of this day, nor was he more helpful shortly thereafter when he published a poem called "Spring Lake." The poem's Greek epigraph seemed to affirm that Masters and his character were one and the same: "And down he came from the peak of Olympus, angry at heart." Details of the poem affirmed the appropriateness of the epigraph; the artist-hero leaves Spring Lake following a feud with his neighbors. Circumstances were different from those Masters reported in *Across Spoon River,* but the results were exactly the same: the hero departs permanently.[22]

These comments notwithstanding, Masters returned to Spring Lake within three weeks of his departure. He was there on October 2 and October 6, and he returned to it in the spring of 1918, the fall of 1918, and many times thereafter.

In fact, the estate at Spring Lake was to serve as Masters's warm-weather headquarters for several years (as well as a part of the winter of 1922), and he did not quit it entirely until it was taken from him during his 1923 divorce. Nor did his decision to walk out on September 13, 1917, mark the end of his living with his family, although comments from his autobiography suggest as much: "Leaving Spring Lake that fall of 1917 I was again in Chicago, where the war was roaring. And immediately the Fates begin to spin and to weave. I went wandering and roaming troubled by the distressing days of war. I was in New York, Boston, New England, and Grand Rapids. Much later in 1921 I was in Egypt, riding a camel over the sand about the pyramids of Gizeh. From Egypt I went to Athens and saw its wonders; and then to Rome."[23]

What he actually did on September 13 was to return to Chicago, calm down, read his mail, examine the sorry state of his law business, grow lonely, and search for female companionship. Finding none, he unburdened himself on September 21 to Dorothy Harvey (Theodore Dreiser's eventual biographer), who was then in New York City: "I have been in this hellish city since last Thursday, having returned in rage and vexation. And as there is no one here I want to see, I am alone. . . . If this war doesn't abolish matrimony and leave people free (and make them feel free too) to live their lives it will have failed in one important result. . . . I must return to Spring Lake October 1st to close up. . . . My plans are cloudy but I'll be here a good deal."[24]

Actually, most of Masters's plans worked out as he had made them two weeks earlier. Writing Harriet Monroe from Spring Lake on September 8, Masters had noted that his family was well, adding: "I am going east next week to take Hardin to a school. Then back here to build a hot bed and a pier and close up, returning to Chicago (alas) about the 1st." That done, and with Hardin at Exeter Academy for a time (but not for a long time—lonely and unhappy with the school, he came home in a matter of weeks), Masters settled in for several more seasons of unhappy matrimony at 4853 Kenwood. He did not spend "that fall of 1917 . . . wandering and roaming," as he claimed in his autobiography, but pursued far tamer diversions instead, writing Theodore Roosevelt on October 31 that he had "last night . . . read to the family [an] article in this month's *Atlantic.*" Nor did Masters spend time trying to "abolish matrimony." Six months later, for example, when he was in Virginia researching a book on Robert E. Lee, he mailed Helen a very domestic-sounding reminder that it was time to think of returning to Michigan: "I'm wondering if you hadn't better be getting ready for Spring Lake. It's so devilish hot here that it makes me think I must get my corn in." It was about a year later, in late March or early April 1919, that Masters finally decided on divorce, and it was then—and not September 1917—that the important rupture with Helen came.[25]

Essentially, Masters's misinformation telescoped what happened over several years into an easier-to-narrate day. Thus, although Masters's 1919–22 separation and 1923 divorce were prolonged and messy (sensational enough to earn him page

1 treatment in the Chicago press), what happened on September 13, 1917, did not amount to much. As to his comments that "something unusually exasperating happened" that day, it is clear that the blowup with Hardin was probably not very significant in itself but simply the final item in a long line of frustrations from that summer. What mattered far more was that Masters had at last enjoyed the leisure to prepare a new manuscript of poems and had discovered (to his great consternation) that he did not have in him another book as good as *Spoon River.* That was the important fact to emerge from the summer of 1917, not the tiff with "the enchantress across the lake." In any event, he would soon have had to leave Spring Lake anyway, for his place was a summer place and hard to heat, and more important, he would shortly be low on money.[26]

It should be remembered that Masters could easily spend money at the rate of about $2,500 per month ($30,000 a year). This is approximately what he was making in a good year with Clarence Darrow, and he seems to have made this much and more in at least one of the years after leaving Darrow: "The last year that I really practiced, I made $35,000." If he followed this customary rate of expenditure in 1917, his cash reserves of $20,000 received in February would be depleted by September, which, interestingly, is when he returned to Chicago. His finances were then under control, but barely so. On December 24 he returned an advance royalty check of $2,500 to the Macmillan Company, commenting as he did on a traditional problem of poets and profits: "I am enclosing to you the check which was sent to me by the business office. . . . I need the money very much in February, and I do not want it now. You ought to know something about the financial looseness of a man who twangs the lyre, and I simply cannot be trusted with money till the time comes." By the time the money came to him again, large numbers of American troops had joined the battle lines in Europe, and World War I commanded his attention.[27]

Masters himself was far too old for military service, having turned forty-nine in August 1917, but his son, Hardin, caught "the war fever" and "enlisted in the commissary of a negro regiment," after which his father stormed down to the recruiting station to insist (successfully) that his boy was too young to serve. But the war teased Hardin's attention just as it did his father's. Hardin's repeated pleas to join the service finally overcame Masters's repeated efforts to prevent it (he even visited a military camp, bringing back firsthand reports), and nineteen-year-old Hardin was enlisted in the navy by June 21, 1918. As often happened in these and related matters, Helen Masters remembered a different scenario, namely that "Hardin was a senior at the University [of Chicago] High School when war was declared [in 1917] and [that] he enlisted in the Navy and left school. . . . His diploma was given to him later." This would mean that Hardin's service began in April or May 1917; since Masters went east in mid-September 1917 to take his son to Exeter, either Hardin was in a reserve unit or Helen Masters's memory was flawed. (William Marion Reedy remembered seeing Hardin in a military uniform in December 1917.)[28]

In any event, Hardin Masters lived through the war, his most dangerous moments coming when he was ill for three weeks with influenza and unintentionally AWOL in Chicago. Helen Masters told the story thus. Following a stint of sleeping in a damp environment on the Chicago lakefront, Hardin caught "a severe cold," came home on a Sunday pass, and "fainted in the living room": "We had the doctor and he said Hardin had pneumonia, so Lee telephoned the boat and told them Hardin couldn't return for the present. Sick or well they seemed to want him back at once[,] but we had the doctor's authority that he couldn't be moved[,] and we had the joy of keeping him with us and nursing him ourselves." Masters did not talk about his son's wartime experiences in his autobiography except to note in draft chapters that Hardin was on a gunboat moored in the Chicago harbor. Masters did, however, occasionally use factual information about his son and the war in his poems. "God and My Country," for example, recounts the story of Hardin's fainting in the Masters living room:

> And on a day
> When he came home to visit for a while
> He was stricken with the flu. I telephoned
> The officer, who raved and said no trick
> Would go with him. He'd send for him. He did.

Masters would later attribute the onset of Hardin's tuberculosis to his wartime experiences.[29]

In these ways and others, the war made itself felt by Masters. Men who were a generation younger than he, such as his friend Arthur Davison Ficke, another lawyer and poet, routinely left the Midwest for military service or Europe, as did several of his female friends, such as Eunice Tietjens, who traveled to France as a correspondent with the *Chicago Daily News.* Masters was also forced to focus on the war because of his prominence as a writer and the public's preoccupation with the war. A full year before America entered the conflict, for example, Amy Lowell requested "an article on 'Patriotism in the New Poetry'" for *The Craftsman* magazine. This was a difficult task for Masters, for he distrusted the motives of those who advocated war, as he had explained in 1916 to the novelist Hamlin Garland: "But my dear Garland, this talk of honor and dignity is only the dull cliches which the guts of Wall Street and the smaller intestines throughout the country are rumbling for great hunger to get hold of the trough again. And these swine would send your boy or mine into the trenches for honor and dignity, as they'd call it. Let us force them into honest paganism and make them admit it's for spoils. Then I wouldn't care, except that I don't see any sense in getting killed for someone else's pocket book."[30]

In mid-1917, when Masters's work on *Toward the Gulf* was going slowly at Spring Lake, he wondered aloud to Amy Lowell whether the war might account for his writing troubles. Six months later he remarked to Ficke (by then Captain Ficke) that "any bad news from abroad brings its peculiar sorrow"; by March 1918 he announced (again to Ficke) that he was "watching with great anxiety the great German drive." By April Masters was doing nothing of a creative nature: "The fact is I am otiose—I am dreaming, dawdling, waiting," he told Dorothy Harvey. In May he withdrew from *Poetry*'s consideration a poem called "Spoon River Revisited," explaining that it was "out of key—is an affront to the America which is living so heroically." By the summer of 1918, when Hardin was in the service, Masters began to feel a stalemate overtaking all his personal and creative endeavors, as he explained to Monroe:

> We free spirits, spiritual aviators, must take care of ourselves. I find I can live just one day at a time; or, put another way, that I must fight down a [temptation] to devour the days ahead. We wait and wait for an end, for a change . . . , a release. The war has got so thoroughly into me that I can scarcely go on sometimes, complexed as it is with a grief which keeps my imagination at high speed. I have settled down to a grim policy of wearing it out just by the daily grind. . . . I can't write now—have nothing to offer you. Can't see the use most of the time—again see great use. My dreams arrive and fade.[31]

How to slow down an "imagination at high speed" was still on his mind in September 1918 when he wrote a Colonel Wood to thank him for forwarding certain items of information pertinent to the military: "Those extracts are terrific—I am making a file of such things for use, perhaps. But on the other hand I wonder at times how much more of horror we can stand. The trauma in the battle—it must be infinitely terrible; yet the feelings of facing a reality may be worse than brooding over the war—stress racing your machine so to speak." Always, Masters said, he could "hear the spiritual tread of the dead soldiers as they tramped into infinity; something was happening of an occult nature to the tangible air." By October he knew he had accomplished nothing during the summer, as he remarked to John Cowper Powys: "I had a hell of a summer—terrible restlessness and next-place-itis—and a vast sense of blank futility—the war things driving it."[32]

But there were other things driving Masters as well. Intermittent with these activities was his wartime romance with a woman he identified simply as "Rowena" in expurgated chapters of his autobiography. He had met her in Chicago in 1917 not long after his September 13 departure from Spring Lake. She "was looking for a man . . . who would go to France with her" as part of the American war effort; he was drawn to her simply because he was in a mood of "lighthearted sportiveness" (a term meaning that he was upset with Helen Masters again and that almost any woman would do). Rowena's real name was Florence Dugan, and she and Masters had become lovers by December 10 ("she was by no means an easy conquest"), after which she remained available to him through the winter. She was never to be very important to him ("she was not much, but she was all I had"), nor was he very important to her—and would never be unless he were to drop what he was doing and provide her the overseas male companionship she sought. Masters was unable to consider doing so because of his family and other obligations, and so the relationship ground along, doomed from the start by her attraction to the war and by his refusal to be a part of it.[33]

Or maybe it was her attitude that put him off. Florence was "a pretty one," Masters said, but had led an unlucky life (details unspecified) and had made up her mind that "she was going to die in the war." Masters summarized matters thus: "The time had come. She would die with the brave young who were remaking the world. Life had not dealt kindly with her, and now she had the chance to end it gloriously! So she would talk as she drew close to me, and pressed her breasts against me, or as she stood before the mirror of a morning combing her brown silken hair, and flashing her white teeth as her eyes smiled adoration." One evening in March or early April 1918, Florence was with Masters when he finally realized his dream of seeing one of his plays produced "at some place around Hyde Park Boulevard." When he later described the play, however, he could remember none of its details, not even its title, theme, or producer. Perhaps this was because it was one of the plays he regarded as "trash"; perhaps it was because Florence surprised him that same evening by saying she was leaving for New York the next day in preparation for going to France. He was doomed to be lonely again.[34]

One of his few solaces during this time was the tranquility of his farm at Spring Lake. He daydreamed of returning to it as early as February 1918, when he remarked to Dorothy Harvey that he was "preparing to go to Spring Lake with the first breath of spring." He particularly looked forward to the trip because William Marion Reedy was scheduled to arrive in April, as he mentioned to Harvey. "Reedy is coming the 22nd and I'm going to take him to Spring Lake." He subsequently described Reedy's spring 1918 visit in H. L. Mencken's *American Mercury* for April 1935 (at about the same time, oddly, that he was writing in the manuscript of *Across Spoon River* that he himself had left Spring Lake "for good" in the fall of 1917):

> Often [Reedy] stole away from St. Louis to pay me a visit for days at a time. In April of 1918 he came to my farm place at Spring Lake, Michigan, where for two weeks we talked and motored about the country, while he wrote for the *Mirror.* On Tuesday he would go to Grand Haven and telegraph his leader. We always stopped on these trips at Jack's Place in the village where Reedy drank near beer and fellowed with the bartender. We kept late hours, sometimes talking until well into the morning. I never spent a happier two weeks than these; and as for Reedy he went away rested and ready as he could be for the loneliness of St. Louis, and the vexation of his editorship.[35]

Masters had his own set of vexations, of course. He had resumed his law practice after returning to Chicago in 1917, but it was not prospering, in part because he had virtually abandoned it from March through September 1917, when his thoughts were on his summer place. In addition, parts of the summer of 1918 were taken up with concerns about Hardin, who was now in the navy and miserable, and by memories of Florence, who was in New York awaiting passage to France. He could do nothing for Hardin, but he thought that a visit with Florence would do him good, especially if he paused to visit his friend Theodore Roosevelt as well. In mid-July, therefore, Masters traveled to New York.[36]

He would later say that he had enjoyed "visiting with Roosevelt and the fellows" and that he was especially pleased when the advocate of the strenuous life told him he did not look like a poet: "No one would ever take you for a poet with that chin and neck." But Roosevelt's youngest son, Quentin, was killed in the war during Masters's trip to the East, and Florence sailed for France about the same time. The trip signaled the end of both relationships: Theodore Roosevelt was dead within six months, his death hastened by his grief over Quentin; Florence wrote for a time, but her absence caused Masters to review their relation and decide she had no part in his life: "Except for the war, I believe this would never have been. The impatience with which I left Spring Lake would have passed, and in a measure did pass. But the war had left its marks upon me by leading me to Rowena [Florence], who was nothing if she had not had the setting of the war. . . . [Now] I determined to get away both from the war and Rowena."[37]

Like many other women in his life, Florence Dugan provided Masters the sympathetic companionship and diversion he wanted to get him through a troubled time. When the trouble and the times were over—or perhaps a little before (for he hated to feel alone)—he would begin an insistent and successful search for her replacement. As he succinctly phrased it to a friend around the time he decided Florence must pass from his life, "I am alone most of the time. Must get a woman." He later said much the same in an unpublished chapter of his autobiography. After completing the hours he devoted to writing, he had only a handful of options to prevent boredom: the theater, music, reading, drinking, male companions, or a woman. "Best of all for a man of my temperament," he wrote, "is a woman."[38]

News of the war dominated the late summer of 1918. Masters was upset to learn that the American poet Joyce Kilmer had died in battle "because this taking away of the noble spirits, the talent of our country, brings upon all of us a loss that no philosophy in life can alleviate." When Masters submitted two poems to the *Yale Review* in September, each of them, "The Love-Death" and "Epitaph for Us," was tinged with funereal gloom (the former was rejected, and the latter accepted for fifteen dollars). He also managed to squeeze out a handful of prowar publications, asking one hundred dollars for a 1918 poem about airplanes called "The Winged Victory of America." He was not comfortable with this prowar stance, however, and pieces he published in this vein are so dominated by the deadly triumvirate of politics, propaganda, and prayer that there is little room for poetry. The opening stanza of "The World's Peace" and its deification of Allied generals illustrates:

Glory to Joffre, glory to Haig, glory to Foch,
Glory to Diaz, glory to Pershing for strength in battle
For the glory of England, glory of Italy, glory of France,
And the imperishable glory of America!

Published in the *Boston Transcript* for November 23, 1918, "The World's Peace" was dedicated "To the Spirit of F.E.D."—possibly an allusion to his World War I girlfriend, Florence Dugan.[39]

Masters was greatly relieved with the end of the war, describing the armistice celebrations in downtown Chicago as follows:

> One day there was great and sudden clamor in Michigan Avenue, followed by the blowing of whistles and the tooting of automobile horns. [People] rushed to my room yelling that the war was over. And we descended to the avenue to join the mad crowds that were pushing their way along, scattering confetti, and howling like lunatics. The bands came out and the air roared with "How You Goin' to Keep 'Em Down on the Farm" and "Tipperary." We finally edged our way through the dense masses of hysterical people to the Annex where champagne was beginning to flow; and then to the more sedate Blackstone where no attempt was made to preserve decorum. My happiness knew no bounds. The incubus of the war was lifted from me.[40]

A few weeks before the war ended, Masters had begun a very ambitious new book suggested by the world conflict. He called it *Domesday Book,* and when it was finally finished and published in 1920, its 10,000 lines of blank verse exhaustively explored the war's significance to the country and its main character, a woman who does Red Cross work during the war and then returns to Illinois. (William Marion Reedy may have suggested the idea for the book. "I wonder," he had mused to Masters early in 1918, "who'll do the *Iliad* of this war.") Masters relied on many events from his own life for the background of his main character, but some of her overseas experiences might have belonged to any of a thousand women, including, most likely, Florence Dugan or (less likely) Eunice Tietjens, who briefly performed Red Cross work in Europe following her stint with the *Chicago Daily News.* (Masters would later say, however, that his main character was not based on any real woman.) In any event, with the war's end, Masters sat down to a sustained piece of writing that would demonstrate his post–*Spoon River* skills and would by its very subject respond to the critics' claims that he was padding some of his volumes with early writings. Even in this respect, however, *Domesday Book* was not entirely new: "The germ of *Domesday Book*" came, he said, from an unpublished short story he had drafted in 1889. As 1918 came to a close, then, Masters was at work on this major project.[41]

He was still exceptionally well known on both sides of the Atlantic, and his admirers still heaped untempered adulation and acclaim on him. Earlier in the year, when he had gone to St. Louis to deliver a lecture on *Spoon River* to that city's Art League, William Marion Reedy had reminded his readers that *Spoon River Anthology* was "first printed in this city, in this paper. It is the greatest thing for which this city stands in history." The *St. Louis Post-Dispatch* offered a somewhat more objective view of *Spoon River:* "It is said to have a wider immediate circulation than any book of poetry ever published in this country." Certainly, it caught the attention of the prestigious National Institute of Arts and Letters, in Boston, which now extended an invitation to Masters to join its membership. The man from Spoon River himself was simply worn down by the events of 1918. It was not for nothing that his St. Louis speech was entitled "The Rat Trap, and How to Get Out of It." As the *Post-Dispatch* reported, "Masters today said . . . that his anthology contains a true American philosophy of living, which is a doctrine of escaping from one's hindrances." How he himself might escape his own hindrances was not clear. "Really," he wrote Tietjens on December 12, "I have had a splendid hell this last year, and pray—pray for a change."[42]

CHAPTER 7

The Magic Princess of the Sleeping Palace

Pamela, whose story is not recorded in these pages, seemed the magic princess who would put life into the silent, becalmed room of the Sleeping Palace.

—Edgar Lee Masters, *Across Spoon River*

Edgar Lee Masters sometimes blamed World War I for the break-up of his first marriage, ignoring his own intimate role in this personal failure as well as the fact that he had no role at all—not even a small one—in the war itself. But even if the stresses of living through the war and having a boy in the service did contribute to Masters's divorce, his own ongoing values concerning women, marriage, and adultery played a far greater role. These attitudes constituted both a state of mind and a plan of action and were in place well before America went to war. A representative example of this mind-set is to be found in his comments about his first luncheon meeting with Tennessee Mitchell, the woman with whom he fell in love in 1909 and for whom he nearly divorced his wife: "At the luncheon she seemed easy enough to take and to leave in one of those lighthearted adulteries that do no harm, and involve nothing but a technical breach of conjugal fidelity, which not being known are as innocuous as a walk or a talk. . . . I had made up my mind that women in general expect that lighthearted adulteries are carried on behind their backs and that they do not care so long as they do not know about them, so long as their own favored positions as wives are not affected."[1]

Helen Masters fought this attitude, using patience and a smile as counterpoints to her husband's philandering, and won every long-term battle simply by keeping him married to her. Her demeanor following Masters's breakup with Tennessee Mitchell in 1911 illustrates: "At the office I took up heavy tasks which had no interest for me. And every night when I came home, which was by no means always, my wife was sitting on the porch waiting for me, and smiling in weariless friendliness." Between 1911 and the disruptions of World War I, Masters amused himself with a variety of other women (Grace, Adele, Marie, and Virginia—all mentioned by aliases in his autobiography), and so it may have seemed a matter of little consequence when Florence Dugan's role declined and he encountered another pretty face in January 1919.[2]

This pretty face belonged to the woman identified in the closing pages of his autobiography as "Pamela, . . . the magic princess . . . of the Sleeping Palace." Like many of the names in the autobiography, Pamela's was a fabrication designed to protect the real person, but since she has been dead for many years, and because the other protagonists in her story are also gone, she can be identified without hurting anyone: Pamela was Lillian (or "Peggy") Pampell. Born on July 16, 1887, in Maryland, she lived for a time in Kentucky but moved north to attend Indiana University, in Bloomington. She seems not to have graduated from the university (for her name does not appear in alumni association files or commencement books of her era), but she does appear in the school yearbook for 1906–7. She was active as a freshman in Indiana University's artists club and played a sorority girl in a production of *The Match Maker,* as well as being "toastmistress" at "the annual panthygatric dance." By the spring of 1908 she had left the campus and moved north to teach school at Wabash, Indiana, but stayed in touch with friends on the university's student newspaper: "Miss Lillian Pampell . . . of Wabash," the paper noted on April 27, "is a leader in the *Indianapolis Star*'s trip to Europe contest. Miss Pampell was a Pi Phi here."[3]

In the course of trying to sell enough newspaper subscriptions to win the *Star*'s trip to Europe, she traveled from Wabash to nearby Marion, Indiana, where she met J. Woodrow Wilson, a fifty-four-year-old bachelor vice-president of the Marion National Bank and, at various times, the president of the Marion Paper Company, the president of the Indiana Oil Men's Association, and secretary and manager of the Marion Fruit Jar and Bottle Company. He bought a good many of her subscriptions (the story goes) and subsequently made her his wife as well. He built her a new house—a twenty-four-room mansion with a ballroom on the third floor—and indulged her tastes for clothing from New York and Paris. He took her to Europe several times, and then, in 1916, he suddenly died. Lillian (Peggy) Wilson—"Pamela"—was a widow at twenty-nine.[4]

She pursued her cultural interests on an active scale, traveled a great deal, and one night in January 1919, met Masters in Chicago. She was mature, gracious, charming, and, of course, moneyed, and she was also an author, having published a drama collection, *Fruit of Toil and Other One-Act Plays,* in 1916. He was the literary lion of the Midwest, the "Spoon River poet" about whom everyone was talking, and, as usual, was looking for a soft, feminine shoulder. The two soon became lovers, with Masters visiting her in Marion at her mansion, "the Sleeping Palace."[5]

Although Lillian Wilson was exceedingly important to Masters's intellectual and emotional makeup for several years, we have heretofore known little about her. The chief reason for this is that when Masters wrote his autobiography, he did not tell how she had helped cost him his fortune but reduced her story to a few lines in his hazy and deliberately misleading ending to *Across Spoon River:*

> In 1921 I was in Egypt, riding a camel over the sand about the pyramids of Gizeh. From Egypt I went to Athens and saw its wonders; and then to Rome. I was led to this by what happened to me in 1919. One night I wandered out of the iron-dark air of Chicago into a ballroom. And there was Pamela! She led me into meadows of larks, into gardens of robbins [*sic*], into happiness beyond anything I had ever known in my life. I was sure that she was the long-looked-for woman, and I tried every honorable means to free myself to marry her. When I couldn't, I took this trip to Egypt.[6]

In many ways there was not much difference between Lillian and other women in Masters's life (they all resembled her in one way or another), but that was just the point: she was "the long-looked-for woman" in his eyes because she embodied in one person so many different traits he admired. For one thing, he found her very attractive, "a woman whose appearance arrested [his] attention at once": "She was small, but she glimmered from afar. Her hair was golden. . . . At once I was struck with the shimmering laughter in her large yellow gray eyes, at the delicate but voluptuous formation of her mouth, at her dimples which appeared when she smiled, at the sonorous, caressing quality of her voice." In addition, she too was a writer (of poetry as well as drama) and was interested in the arts: "She betrayed by her expression that she knew who I was as soon as I was introduced to her; and at once she told me that she had owned a copy of *Spoon River* since it was published." No less important, she found him attractive: "Then I asked her to dance. . . . She was a compact bundle of firm shoulders and ample waist in my arms; and I held her very tightly, much to her amusement. She was so much shorter than I that she had to look up with her face almost at right angles for her eyes to meet mine. All the while I was making fun as we danced and she was laughing." Finally, she was rich and available, "a widow of considerable wealth" who "lived in a small city about 100 miles from Chicago."[7]

There was, relatedly, Masters's own romantic idealism and unhappy marriage to consider: "I was nearing fifty years of age. . . . If I were ever to realize that hope of a marriage which had romantic and intellectual meaning, it must be soon. And I thought of the long years in which I had given myself dutifully to marital obligations doubtfully assumed, and which time had proven that I should not have entered into." Thus, the man who once said that Americans "were ready for *Spoon River*" because "they'd had their fill of moonlight and silly love stories" now wanted some moonlight and a new love story in his own life.[8]

Masters had met Lillian on the night of January 11 following a Saturday evening outing to the Chicago Symphony with a male companion. During the next two weeks, as Masters worked on a law case and on his World War I poetry epic, *Domesday Book,* he visited Lillian and her friends at her apartment in Chicago's Blackstone Hotel. By the time Lillian's visit to Chicago ended, on January 28, she had invited him to her home in Marion, Indiana; on January 30 he went there, as noted in his diary: "Leave for Peggy's at 10:30 Arrive—3:10 P.M. wonderful evening XX." (The *X*s are code; based on Masters's other comments, each *X* seems to represent one instance of lovemaking.) He stayed for three days at her home at 723 West Fourth Street before leaving for Pittsburgh for a lecture on Sunday, February 2. He took with him some pleasant memories, his dirty shirts, and a diary marked with *X*s. He left behind numerous new acquaintances (for Lillian loved to entertain, as he would learn to his great consternation) and most of the strings to his heart. He had begun what he later described as "the happiest period of [his] life."[9]

Masters was happy because he thought he had at last found the woman of whom he had dreamed since his youth. Lillian's strawberry-blond coloring, welcome smile, and quick, musical laugh were merged with intelligence and a broad understanding of the opposite sex: she seems always to have known what blend of formality and foolishness would make a man feel at ease. Not surprisingly, perhaps, Masters decided after only a few meetings that it was she who might fill the void in his heart and satisfy him intellectually as well. And she was rich, so rich (he began to think) that he might even retire from the law if he established a permanent relation.

What he brought to the relation was in many ways less imposing than Lillian's attractiveness and wealth. He was fifty years old (but looked forty or so) and stood 5' 9¼" in his stocking feet. He was strong in the shoulders, with a trim waist and rather small feet (size 8½; his collar size was 15½). But he was not what fashion mavens of the times would have called "handsome": he was stocky, moonfaced, and balding, a pair of glasses perched on his short nose. His hair was brown, as were his eyes, although he had his own explanation as to their color: "My eyes are olive green, running to hazel and brownish at the rims." His chin was "granite," his friend John Cowper Powys said (but softened by dimples, the ladies said). Surprisingly, he was not a particularly neat dresser. "Edgar Lee Masters never vied for sartorial supremacy with the best dressers on Boul. Mich. [Michigan Avenue] or any other traffic way," one newspaper averred, but the papers sometimes misrepresented him, and he was no doubt fashionable enough. He enjoyed several manly diversions that were part and parcel of his person and character. He liked a drink, enjoyed a cigar, and could go horseback riding, swimming, golfing, and hiking. He was a modest authority on boxing, feeling that it added to his demeanor to be tough. Helen Masters said he did not like parlor games such as cards, although he occasionally played stud poker and would take his turn at diversions such as roulette and chuck-a-luck. He spoke in a soft, midwestern drawl and could tell Illinois stories by the hour.[10]

During his lifetime and afterward, his critics sometimes wondered why a man of such average looks and interests was so attractive to women. The answer lies in his tactics. Early in each acquaintance Masters invariably found some reason to explain his views on love, sex, and morality. If he failed to do this during an introduction, he soon followed it with a letter in which he spoke of such things. He punctuated his comments with references (footnotes, really) to natural laws and great thinkers. The woman was propositioned before she knew it. If she were his intellectual equal, she had to agree with him, for lawyerlike, he had used evidence and argument, both of which were cloaked in the certainty of self-confidence created by precedent: this is what had worked before. If things went as he wished, the battle was over at this point, details of the consummation to be arranged. In the present case none of this was necessary. Lillian was attracted to him because he was famous.[11]

She had entered his life when Masters was near the apex of his fame as an author and traveling a great deal. Some of his travels could be attributed to his efforts to pursue both literature and law simultaneously, and some to the fact that he was restless. In any event, Lillian was attracted to him initially because of his prominence and because many of his literary acquaintances were also well known. For example, when he left her after their Marion get-together, he went to New York, where he talked with the poet Vachel Lindsay, dramatist Percy MacKaye, and novelists Theodore Dreiser and Hamlin Garland. He returned to Chicago, where he addressed the needs of his law office, and was then off to Lillian's for three more days before again traveling east. He lectured on February 24 at the City College of New York, met with his friend Edward Marsh, an editor at Macmillan, and then began a circuit of luncheons and dinners. He also breakfasted with the English author John Galsworthy, had tea with the composer Percy Grainger, and took time out to deliver a poem at the centenary observance for the poet James Russell Lowell. By the time Masters headed back to Chicago on March 2, he had spent twenty-six of the previous thirty-two days on the road and six days with his wife at his home. A crisis was now brewing there.[12]

When Helen Masters's two lawyers later picked a time when Masters deserted his wife, they chose March 1919 as the pivotal month, and this was probably correct, although it needs some explanation. In terms of emotional support, devotion, or expressions of any type meaning love, Masters had abandoned his wife long before; nonetheless, since he began the month at home (on the third and fourth) and ended it there (on the twenty-eighth and twenty-ninth), he had not yet left her in the technical sense. In addition, March 1919 was much the same as that month in other years: Masters paid his income tax ($92.10), worked on legal cases, went on his Sunday walk at the Indiana Dunes, and took off a weekend to see William Marion Reedy in St. Louis. On March 21 he again departed for Lillian's, however, this time without a trip to New York, Pittsburgh, or other "official" designation, and this may have been the turning point. His trip generated diary entries such as "all night till 4:30 XX," a list of cultural activities (classical music on the Victrola), names of several friends they entertained (her Episcopalian clergyman, Father Johnston), and one prayer: "Dear God lead me to my love, like a lamb to its mother." When the final binge of lovemaking was concluded on March 26 at 5:00 A.M., Masters noted in his diary that the "robbins" were singing—faithfully misspelling the word a second time seventeen years later when he ended his autobiography with a reference to Lillian. Then he returned to Chicago for a "long talk with Helen." It was at about this time, too, that Lillian wrote him a letter encouraging his divorce: "Always," she said, "my hand is stretched toward yours; only free it that I may take it." In mid-April he began the process of freeing himself by spending his nights at Chicago's Stratford Hotel.[13]

That done, he decided next to broaden Lillian's intellectual range. She was already a published author, but he wanted to instill in her an artistic drive like his own and make her see him in the light of his collective reading. It was a fine balancing act he asked of her (and every other woman in his life): she had to know enough to admire him; that was nonnegotiable. But she could not know more than he did; that was unforgivable. Since meeting her, he had sprinkled his letters and telegrams with allusions to numerous authors, pausing frequently to correlate the wisdom of other writers with his own passions. His letter of April 10, for example, contained references to Aristotle, Poe, Kant, and Goethe and concluded with the explanation of their significance: "[These] will give you some clue to me." He now showered her with books as well, forgetting that he had tried this same system of reading self-improvement on Helen Masters twenty-two years before ("Oh you shall be the most learned girl in town"). That had not turned out very well, but this spring seemed somehow sweeter ("it has been sweet to me"), and this time things might gel.[14]

He also tried to advance Lillian's career as an author by contacting Houghton Mifflin and encouraging that publisher to read her plays and to "bring them out" in book form: "I have a friend who has written a number of plays about our people here in this country. . . . These are very remarkable dramas from life, poignant, human and humorous, and having a most unusual psychology. . . . You know I wrote to you one time that I would give you a book, and maybe I will; but if I don't do so, and give you a better book by someone else, maybe you will be just as well pleased." When her parcel of plays was forwarded to Houghton Mifflin in May, Masters went a step further, offering to underwrite the success of what he now outlined as two volumes, *The Fruit of Toil* (previously issued) and "a manuscript of plays, never before published": "I will guarantee you against loss, if there be any. But a moderate publicity, I think, will cover them."[15]

Houghton's Ferris Greenslet at first responded in a jocular fashion to Masters's proposal: "By all means, send along your friend's plays," he wrote on May 5, "though don't let him spend the money until he gets it." After Greenslet had "read personally Mrs. Wilson's plays," however, he rejected them, noting "a certain amateurishness" in her work and commenting: "[Her] first volume issued in 1916 did not make any very profound impression on either critics or the public. I question whether a volume issued now even with the most vigorous exploitation would be better." He returned the manuscript "without making any promises for its publication."[16]

Masters also sought to enhance Lillian's career by tying it to the success of *Spoon River* and by mid-May 1919 was letting others know that she was drafting a stage version of the work. The book was already arranged as a series of monologues spoken by the town's 200-plus inhabitants, so that Lillian's subsequent lack of progress could not be traced to an absence of suitable lines. Her problem was in deciding on a plot or incident to tie together these many lines and lives. She had two choices: emphasize some person or incident already in *Spoon River* and make this person or "problem" central to her play or go outside the book and create a new incident or figure that would offer the same dramatic unity. In other words, she had to take 200 unstrung pearls (so to speak) and find a common thread that would tie them together. When she experienced difficulty with this, Masters looked for someone to help. "Won't you call upon Mrs. J. Wood Wilson," he wrote a fellow Illinoisan on May 13, explaining that she was "dramatizing *Spoon River*" for him: "What I wish is that you would tell her something of our common locality in Illinois . . . , to give her a new start with the work. She is resting from it, trying to get a fresh perspective or a story to add in, or take something out—and you might be able to give her just the thing." The gentleman of common locality (a Mr. Morris Bagby) was unable to render appropriate assistance, and this effort to enhance Lillian's career worked no better than Masters's offer to Houghton Mifflin.[17]

Although Lillian valued books ("my books are my salvation"), they were not her chief interest but more a diversion from the isolated splendor of her life in rural Indiana. In fact, viewed retrospectively, it is doubtful that she cared greatly whether she or anyone else ever dramatized *Spoon River*. After she realized her limitations as a dramatist—a process of self-discovery hastened by Masters's intervention with Houghton Mifflin and her own frustration in dramatizing *Spoon River*—she began to deemphasize writing and to look for less taxing activities. One of these was a May 1919 trip to New York City, a trip she needed to make, she said, to say good-bye to an old boyfriend.[18]

Years later, when Masters told his friend Edwin Reese about this trip, he remarked, "The woman I loved disappeared on the 12th day of May 1919"—and perhaps she did. Masters knew that Lillian lived "pretty fast," as he put it, but he had now decided to marry her and prescribed through a friend of hers "some exercise—some care about her diet—some sleep—a life that would reduce her restlessness—her attacks of next-place-itis." He was particularly concerned because he had now burned his bridges at home (or had tried to), and threats to his hopes with Lillian disturbed him more than they should. His reaction to a dream on the night of May 31 illustrates his anxiety: "Vivid dream last night: at Marion I go into a bedroom. Mary [the servant] says: we're closing the house. You folks will have to leave." The next day he sent Lillian a note reassuring her of the steadfastness of their relation and recorded his comments in his diary: "Write Peggy: before this time next year my expectation is you will be my wife." He followed this with a second note on June 4—"You can't marry anyone but me"—but her trip east had made him nervous. He wanted to know whom she was seeing and what she was doing. He dreamed he was spying on her through a hole in the wall of her home in Marion as she sat at her typewriter (and thus became the writer he wanted her to be), but even his dream was flawed: in it, she discovered him and gave him a tongue lashing. To have a record of what he had told her, he now began to keep copies of his handwritten love letters, rewriting them in longhand and identifying them. "Copy of letter for Lillian" reads one. The Spoon River poet was suspicious.[19]

Lillian had gone to New York ostensibly to confront an old boyfriend and to explain to him that she was now committed to another, but her letters to Masters soon showed a certain "irritableness," and then other problems showed up. She spoke of hurting herself. ("You began to write me that you loath yourself, and that you hate yourself, and that you long to kill yourself.") This turned out to be only romantic posturing, but she subsequently disappeared for two weeks (June 5–19). When she finally returned to her Marion home, she made Masters stay away for a week while she entertained "guests." When she at last permitted him to visit, she asked that he return her letters and informed him that he would have to stay at a Marion hotel on future visits. She spoke vaguely, too, of going to China.[20]

Masters was furious, writing her a long letter in which he chided her for causing him to leave his wife: "I am in a position, brought there by you, where I can never again live under the domestic conditions that formerly existed. When I say 'brought there by you,' I only mean that I never should have taken the definite stand that I did, except for the fact that I expected to marry you." He reminded her, too, of all they might still do together: "I am a figure in the world; you are economically independent. We can do anything we wish." Finally, he got tough with her: "This is my letter to you, Lillian Pampell Wilson, and you can go to China or where you will, but you cannot get away from yourself, nor from your part in this history." As to that, however, Masters was absolutely wrong. Lillian could do as she chose.[21]

In the near future she would pursue a relation with a man named Oliver Denton in New York. Whether he was the same man who had been the cause of her May trip to New York is not clear, but in the next year her friendship with Denton blossomed into romance. Matters worsened later in 1919 when Masters several times met Denton at the New York dinners Lillian attended or, just as likely, hosted. Her relation with Denton produced some tense meetings between Lillian and Masters and troubled his mind and his writings in one way or another for years. In a poem called "Peggy," for example (published in *The Overland Monthly* in 1926), Masters publicly described his anguish and anger in discovering that Denton's visits to "the Sleeping Palace" in Marion had been contemporaneous with his own: "I am here and snugly housed / Where you and Oliver caroused / Only two weeks ago." Masters could forecast none of this in the busy postwar spring of 1919, however, and even if he had, there was nothing he could have done as long as he was married to Helen.[22]

It was Masters's opinion that his wife was unmovable on the matter of divorce simply because she did not want to admit that her marriage had failed. Actually, Helen Masters had several reasons for not freeing her husband in 1919. She still had two young daughters at home, Masters's departure from their home had greatly lowered their standard of living, and also important, it had jeopardized her social standing (she was active in The Cordon, the Chicago Woman's Club, and the Chicago College Club, serving as its first vice-president in 1916). Moreover, she had already withstood one earlier divorce request (in 1909, when Tennessee Mitchell threatened), and because Masters had many times been unfaithful to her but had always returned, it was reasonable to assume that this new flame would die down, too. This time, however, it persisted, with Masters taking deliberate and unambiguous steps to be free, as he later explained to his friend Carter Harrison: "By 1919, I was about dissolving my marital relations and marrying again. . . . I had offered my wife the farm, and the town house and alimony and some money in gross to be free." But Helen balked at this offer and all others, and by May 31 she had made plans to go with the children to the farm in Michigan. As he told Dreiser, Masters had no plan for dealing with this impasse and remained in a Chicago hotel, his bank account thinning, his frustrations carrying over to his writings.[23]

In the spring of 1919 Masters was working on, and about to complete, the first draft of his World War I epic, *Domesday Book.* He had already completed four volumes of miscellaneous verses since *Spoon River,* and each had received or was about to receive indifferent reviews. These had not hurt him too greatly, however, for he was still riding the crest of *Spoon River*'s success. If he were to maintain his prominence and compete literarily in the Roaring Twenties, however, his next book needed to be well received. He had in his favor an agreement with Harriet Monroe to publish several prepublication selections from *Domesday Book* in the June 1919 issue of *Poetry;* going against the book's success were matters of haste and domestic stress. During this time Masters experienced money problems: his daughter Marcia's tonsils had to come out, his wife required domestic household expenses, and the house on Kenwood Avenue needed intermittent repairs (it was old, its plumbing was balky, and its heating was uncertain). Masters moved his clothes from his home on May 25 and then had a "long bitter talk" with Helen and mailed Lillian a design for a ring on May 26. Between his moving and the long bitter talk, he "finished and expressed *Domesday* to Macmillan." It was mailed within hours of its drafting; revisions would have to wait.[24]

Such haste was a potentially costly maneuver, for the financial well-being of Masters and his family now rested on this one book. He had spent the better part of most days during the preceding several months writing *Domesday Book* in a rented room of Chicago's Montgomery Ward Building (sometimes referred to as "The Tower"). He could no longer work at home, he said, because his house had developed a "staleness," a large part of which no doubt derived from Helen.

He normally worked through lunch at the Tower ("until 1 o'clock or later"), and it might be midafternoon before he arrived at his law office, which was located in a different building. He had "some cases of a less important sort to attend to," but he did not want to attend to any of them, in part because he wanted to be at Marion or Spring Lake instead of Chicago, and in part because his writing left him spent.[25]

Nevertheless, he was never too tired to go to parties, dinners, or dances with his friends and fellow lawyers Bill Slack and Andrew Sheriff; as Masters said, "I managed to live the hard hours that came on me after the day's writing." Bill Slack was from near Lewistown and had known Masters for nearly twenty years. He was famous in his circle for steak dinners, parties, and girlfriends, and it was probably in his bachelor apartment that Masters had learned the dance steps that later amazed Helen. Andrew Sheriff belonged to that class of men described by Masters as a "soldier of fortune." A native of the East, he had come to Chicago with the intention of marrying into one of Chicago's wealthy families. An interesting footnote to his life is that he was pursuing railroad president Robert Jenkins's daughter Helen when he lost her to Masters. Sheriff had subsequently married well (much better than Masters), but his marriage had not held firm, and now, like Masters, he was wont at the end of the day to see what windfalls evening might bring. It was he who had been with Masters on the night the writer met Lillian. It was natural, then, that he was Masters's first choice for a lawyer in the divorce activities. Remarkably enough, Sheriff's discussions with Helen Masters revealed that she already had numerous details that could be used against her husband in a divorce proceeding, including Lillian's real name.[26]

With *Domesday Book* out of the way (and his love affair tangled), Masters caroused with Sheriff and Slack, made his way to Spring Lake and back, and moped around Chicago. He was miserable. Many of his diary entries for June 1919 read "Nothing." On the evening of June 24, however, he met a green-eyed (and very pretty) twenty-year-old from Kansas City who was studying literature at the University of Chicago. Such a woman would normally have interested him a great deal, but he was so preoccupied with his marital problems that he mistakenly recorded her in his diary as "Helen Coyne" rather than "Ellen." She returned to her studies and he to his problems. He would marry her (after many a winding turn to his life) something over seven years later.[27]

At this point the rumor mill came along to bedevil him. Andrew Sheriff reported that Lillian's clergyman, Father Johnston, had let it slip in Chicago that Lillian and Masters were having an affair. An anonymous letter mailed from Chicago and marked "Confidential" added to his discomfort: "Mr. Masters: In February, March, April and May when you visited for days with Mrs. J. Wood Wilson at Marion Indiana you were watched and from other things everything is known about you. This is to tip off to you that your wife is going to file a bill for divorce and name Mrs. Wilson. Youd better see what you can do to straighten things out before it is too late." But it was already too late. When Masters went to lunch a few days later, two female acquaintances told him it was "all over" Chicago that he was "going to be divorced and marry a rich widow of Indiana."[28]

It had now been nearly two months since Masters had even seen his rich widow of Indiana, and he finally returned to her place in Marion on the evening of July 10. They talked for five days (he spent the nights at a local hotel), and when he returned to Chicago, he mailed all her letters back. Lillian made him feel much worse by writing of a party that ran for days, during which time no one went to bed before 3:00 A.M. (She often joked about the battle between the sexes, sex between the sexes, and the social lubricant of alcohol, telling him on one occasion that she was the "self-elected First Grand Soak . . . of the W. C. D. U.[Women's Christian Drinking Union]"; "I'm glad I'm bad," she told him.) More letters followed, and Masters eventually returned to Marion as her lover.[29]

But fall would bring new tensions. For one thing, he occasionally had disturbing dreams, as noted in his diary: "Dream last night that I shot a deer with a bow and arrow, driving the arrow clear through the animal. Dream of a newspaper spread out—Peggy Wilson is Dead—A flower wreath on top of the newspaper. I kneel and weep." The relation between the death of a deer and an individual "dear" to one has been explored many times in English literature, along with the hunter's relation to the hart (a male deer) and the human "heart" (or love). Whatever else was going on, Masters's subconscious was now clearly projecting a time when his relation with Lillian "Peggy" Wilson (a.k.a. "Pamela") would end, when she would be dead to him. He even wrote a poem in which she died, killed in an accident while society's wagging tongues cheapened their romance; he called the poem "Crayons" (probably for its colors) and likened their love to a flower soiled by its surroundings:

> Anonymous mud is thrown at us. Our flower
> Becomes rain pelted, disked with spattered earth. . . .
> Our April all with crocuses bedecked
> Drifts to July of white reality.
> You ride, I hear, to while away the time,
> And I go on as best I may with rhyme.

Meanwhile, he worked at his law office and fought with Helen over divorce terms affecting the Michigan farm (she wanted it outright; he preferred that it "be deeded in trust for [their] children").[30]

Helen Masters "knew all about Pamela by this time." As Masters remarked to Darrow, "She has accurate and sufficient information with correct names." Darrow was in a position to hear both sides of the Masters family squabble. He would officially become Helen's lawyer in the fall of 1920 when she initiated a court action to get financial support from Masters, but now Darrow listened patiently (and with some self-interest) as Masters talked about Lillian and reviewed his side of the matter. The curious thing about Masters's behavior is that he seems to have known by the fall of 1919 that his wife would be represented by Darrow but confided in him anyway. Consider, for example, Masters's November 8 letter to Darrow in which he asked him on the basis of old friendship to shield Lillian from unnecessary publicity: "In a time of storm rain is likely to fall and flowers can be splotched from the spatter. You will understand that if I should make a second venture I could not bear to have a face before me in which I should read, day by day, a story of regretted remembrance. I therefore ask you in the name of much common understanding to prevent the statement of things, particularly things not well founded but also things unnecessary to state." Darrow, in turn, indicated that Masters could safely place his trust in him and that he would be a friend to both Masters and his wife. Darrow's letter to "Dear Ed" on November 10, 1919, illustrates: "Of course you know me well enough to know that I would never start suit against you or try to make you any trouble in court or out. . . . My relations with both parties might make it possible for me to assist both of you, which[,] of course, I will do, without any thought of compensation, except friendship, if the matter can be worked out." As things "worked out," however, Darrow was to be completely false.[31]

On November 2 Masters left to see Lillian in the Catskills and New York City, but she did not seem happy to see him, and after they had quarreled, he noted in his diary that she was "elusive." The elusiveness might have been traced to the presence of her friend Oliver Denton, who one day had lunch with Masters, Lillian, and several others. Masters subsequently made his usual rounds of New York meetings—breakfasts, lunches, and dinners—and visited with various literary personages and friends, including Corinne Roosevelt Robinson and Percy Grainger. (Grainger soon took a liking to Masters and composed a melody called "Spoon River.") On the evening of November 18, however, Masters went to the Waldorf-Astoria and found Oliver Denton in Lillian's room; although they eventually had dinner together (along with a fourth party), relations were strained. Masters made himself feel better by noting that Lillian was "exquisite" and then much worse by observing that she spoke openly of "luncheon with Oliver." Disgruntled, Masters visited the Macmillan offices and headed back for Chicago.[32]

While in New York Masters had mentioned to Corinne Robinson his interest in writing a novel for boys, and after she encouraged him, he decided to follow up on this idea. The ensuing novel told of Masters's boyhood and that of a Petersburg friend, George Mitchell ("Mitch") Miller, the rowdy son of a father who was a minister and school superintendent and a mother who was all patience. As boys Mitch and Masters had read *Tom Sawyer* together, for Masters's father had given him a copy, but Mitch was more likely to follow action-oriented matters, such as hitching a ride on one of Petersburg's slow-moving trains. One day in 1879 a train lurched while young Miller was riding it, and he fell under the wheels, which amputated his leg at the hip; he died several hours later. Masters had used Mitch Miller's story once before, in the poem "Johnnie Sayre" in *Spoon*

River Anthology, and there it had been successful. In late 1919, however, with Lillian, divorce, and money problems on his mind, he failed to give adequate attention to this prose treatment of Miller's short life. Instead, he simply borrowed outright many elements of the most influential book they had read together (*Tom Sawyer*) and moved its plot across the Mississippi River to Petersburg. His diary shows that the manuscript was completed in only twelve days (between November 27 and December 8) and was soon shipped off to Macmillan.[33]

With his novel done, he allowed Florence Dugan to find him (she had returned unharmed from the war), and he spent some time with her ("I consoled my heart with her"). She was not what he really wanted, however, and he felt worse after seeing her. He closed out 1919 with discussions about his prospective divorce with his eventual chief antagonist, Darrow, and summarized his emotional distress to John Cowper Powys: "My dear friend, I am greatly troubled. . . . Sorrow runs through me, knitting a physical form in the very solar plexus—and tears are close to my eyes all the time." He finally gave in to despair and shortly before Christmas called Lillian while drunk at 2:00 A.M. The joy he had felt on meeting her twelve months before had not translated very well through the rest of the year, but he was now so beguiled by her that even her contradictions appealed to him, as he admitted a few years later in *The New Spoon River:*

> Lillian, with her whims,
> Her tangled complexes,
> And changeable ways;
> And little disharmonies with herself,
> And with me;
> And her teasing charms, and ruddy hair,
> And adorable breasts,
> Was the woman for me in the day of my strength,
> When any lesser woman mystery
> Could not have held me—
> Me the betrayer, and flyer, and deserter![34]

Lillian herself seems not to have taken any of these matters as seriously as Masters. Now thirty-two with an income reportedly in excess of $50,000 per year, she owned or had interests in corporate stocks, real estate in Louisville, and "35 acres of land in . . . Porto Rico," as well as interests in her adopted hometown of Marion. Her late husband ("Daddy," she called him) had left her extremely well off. (She was not, however, as well off as she wished: on the first evening that she and Masters were together in Marion, she got out her husband's will, perhaps to see if there was a way she could own the house outright instead of sharing ownership with one or more of "Daddy's" siblings.) Not surprisingly, the twenty-four-room mansion required a good deal of attention, and Lillian employed several servants. At least one of these, a maid, stayed in the house, and perhaps a cook did as well; others (then or a little later) had living quarters across a driveway on the second floor of the garage, where the chauffeur stayed. The garage also held the furnace for the house, which during cold winters devoured coal at the rate of a railroad car per month. A full-sized basement housed laundry facilities and a central vacuuming system. The third-floor ballroom had a piano and a stage for Lillian's dramatic interests. Lillian herself spent many of her hours in a large living room on the second floor where she read and smoked an occasional cigarette. Lavish carpets, damask walls, and ornately carved ceilings complemented the interior, along with a little fountain in a breakfast room; a tiger skin rested on an oversized divan in the drawing room. Masters's room included "a bottle of gold filigree full of priceless whisky . . . , a box of cigars, books of poetry, a vase of roses, and a rich bed of Japanese embroidery. . . . The walls were done in brocaded silk, the floor covered with a carpet of blue velvet." (In an adjoining room, the insistent gong of a French clock and its whirling pendulum reminded visitors that Lillian's was a world of temporal affairs. "You always talk about a future," she once wrote Masters. "There is no future. It is all today.") The house's exterior was brick and stone. Its portico with six large Corinthian pillars faced a large empty lot once owned by "Daddy."[35]

The hostess of this Indiana pleasure dome met dozens of people in the course of an average year and invited many of these to her home. More than a half-century after Masters left town for the last time, her acquaintances and townspeople still recalled her lavish parties and rock-solid determination "to have a good time and meet people," as one of her friends phrased it in the 1970s. If they were important people, so much the better, a phenomenon on which Masters himself remarked: "She seemed to be a lively, somewhat provincial, young widow, going about in the city. But she has many phases, and that phase was not really herself. As a matter of fact, she is quite adorable; but nevertheless a comique, a strange, restless woman, who leaps chasms to make friends and to find people, evidently to relieve her boredom and her restlessness. And she is very fond of looking up celebrities." When she asked him to introduce her to Dreiser, Masters acquiesced, noting in a letter to Dreiser her motives for seeking out celebrities: "A widow lady, but not in weeds . . . , will shortly be down your way. She is Peggy Wilson, more formally Mrs. J. Wood Wilson, and she wants to meet you. I think rather to hear you, and set her wit against yours, and prove her equality with the best."[36]

Lillian was not, however, fond of the notoriety connecting her with a married celebrity. She sent her letters to Masters's law office or his summer place at Spring Lake. When traveling she sometimes urged him to address his letters care of "Daddy full name," Mrs. J. Woodrow Wilson. At other times she might use a humorous alias, for example, "Addie Pence, L.L.D. (long-legged devil)," or "D.Ph (a maiden's prayers)"—whatever that (or they) was (or were). She was at least once "Daisy Fraser," the town prostitute of Spoon River, as well as "Modesta

Dicker" and occasionally "Mrs. Andrew Winslow" (a name Masters adapted for *The New Spoon River*). He in turn urged her to buy a typewriter to help mask her identity and sometimes sent telegrams under a false name.[37]

When all these precautions failed (as they inevitably did, since the two sometimes appeared in public), Lillian was mentioned as a home wrecker. By February 1920 such whispers had gotten out of hand, and she complained that the Chicago rumors were false. But of course they were not. Masters had experienced marital troubles for years, but Lillian had been the inciting factor in causing him to leave his wife, and the more they were seen together, the more people were going to talk. The gossip mills were also active in Marion. She had inherited a bad situation, and so, it seems, had he.[38]

Lillian's chief problem happened also to be her chief asset: she was just too charming. Numerous male acquaintances showed up at her gatherings in New York, Chicago, and Marion, and although many of these were as harmless as her ubiquitous clergyman, Father Johnston, others were not. Masters was ill at ease. When he remonstrated with her in February 1920, she told him she would always have "men friends," at which point Masters realized he could either like the situation or leave.[39]

Soon after meeting Lillian, Masters himself had provided her with a motive for greater socialization: his efforts with Houghton Mifflin editor Greenslet taught her that her plays were not particularly well done, and she gradually deemphasized her writing, pursuing it only as a hobby. "Did I tell you that two more of my jingles are sold?" she asked Masters indifferently early in 1920. "Pretty soon I can buy eye-droppers for all the guest rooms." Nor did she (as time went on) seem appropriately awed by his talents. In other words, she was unimpressed with her own literary output and did not think much of his either. His celebrity status was in review.[40]

By early 1920 Masters too was reviewing his situation. Although he had not abandoned law for literature (as he suggested he had at the end of *Across Spoon River*), his involvement was sufficiently limited by then as to be part-time and was based on the expedient of making money to augment his earnings as a writer and part-time lecturer. As he knew too well, lecturing was frequently a break-even business, with the expenses of travel, meals, and sometimes hotel accommodations offsetting the honoraria. He sometimes preferred lecturing to reading his verses, for this gave him a forum to air his opinions, and although he could occasionally find a second market for a lecture with the magazines or newspapers, neither paid very well. His motive for turning to fiction with his boyhood reminiscence *Mitch Miller* in late 1919 had been to escape this treadmill for the more lucrative genre of the novel. ("I must do something for money," he had explained to Macmillan's Edward Marsh.) When he traveled to New York to meet with Marsh about *Mitch Miller* in January 1920, he went prepared to strike a hard bargain. His diary shows he spent portions of ten days in dealings with the book—two days less than he had spent in writing it. He came back from New York with a check from Macmillan for $4,000 along with a check for a similar amount for reprint rights in *Romance* magazine: "Sold *Mitch* to *Romance* for $4,000, to Macmillan's for $4,000." Perhaps he really could set aside law for literature.[41]

Meanwhile, he worried about Lillian, Oliver Denton, divorce, deadlines, and occasionally, days in court. He sought counsel from his old friend Reedy, who argued against divorce, perhaps because Helen had already communicated with Reedy privately, urging him to speak positively on her behalf. Reedy told Masters that divorce was a bad idea, that it would be hard on the children, that Helen really loved him, and that divorcing her would be "kicking away a ladder [he] climbed on." The ladder felt more like a millstone at this point, however, and when Andrew Sheriff experienced difficulties in reaching a settlement, he and Masters ended their lawyer-client relation, although they still remained friends.[42]

In the spring of 1920 Masters tried to raise additional cash from the sale of his place at Spring Lake, as he mentioned to his editor at Macmillan, Edward Marsh, who would soon relocate: "Your letter comes just as I'm off to Spring Lake to sell my farm, if I can. I got your announcement with a certain regret as our relations for 5 years have been so pleasant. But change is the wind of life. We can't hold on to anything. I have had so many changes, and losses too, that I am really to the point of not expecting anything—at least of keeping it." Unable to get the price he wanted for the farm, Masters returned to Chicago, where, after a five-day visit at Lillian's, he put the final touches on both *Domesday Book* (June 25) and *Mitch Miller* (July 7). He celebrated the completion of these—his longest poem and first novel—with a visit to Lillian's during July 9–14 (he gave her a watch for her birthday), noting on his way out of town that they were "both very tired."[43]

Lillian then decided to revisit Europe while Masters remained at home—or at least he was supposed to remain at home, for she extracted a promise that he would not go to Europe but would settle his affairs. She asked him to buy her a satchel on July 16; he did so the next day, and a week later she was gone: "Peggy leaves Marion for NY and England" (July 24). Her motives for this trip are not entirely clear. Perhaps she was restive for the bright lights of Europe (given her financial resources, she could travel anywhere). Perhaps she felt Masters's divorce would move more quickly with her out of the way. Or maybe she knew she would be happier overseas than in a Chicago courtroom answering questions as the correspondent in a divorce suit. In any event, Lillian left the Midwest. Florence Dugan had gone away also (destination unknown), and Masters was on his own.[44]

CHAPTER 8

Heart's Desire

Everyone is suffering; no one has found his heart's desire, or having found it is satisfied.

—Edgar Lee Masters to Corinne Robinson, May 22, 1921

The twenty-one-month period from mid-1920 through March 1922 was a particularly trying one for Masters. Death claimed his old friend William Marion Reedy in July 1920. Lillian absented herself on a seven-month trip to Europe beginning in August. The Chicago courts demanded alimony of Masters in October, and his first novel, *Mitch Miller,* generated mixed reviews through the fall. In January 1921 he went to Europe for his first overseas vacation in nearly fifteen years, and his law practice dried up. When he diverted himself with yet another woman young enough to be his daughter, he complicated her life and his, and then his money ran out, and his lawyer missed an important court date. After this, the Chicago press began focusing on his personal affairs.

In some ways Reedy's death was the most damaging event. The St. Louis editor had been covering the 1920 Democratic National Convention in San Francisco when he died suddenly on July 28. The effect on Masters was immediate and devastating, as he explained to a friend named Katharine Jones the day after Reedy's death: "I am so blue today that my physical stomach prolapses—and my heart sinks correspondingly: my friend, my friend Bill Reedy died suddenly yesterday. . . . He is gone—my friend of many years, my understander, my guide, my chum, my mate of long talks and intimate agreements. I shall find no one like him." He said much the same to Harriet Monroe: "A telegram came—I could only think to myself: my friend, my friend, my friend. . . . I shall never know his like again. It is too late for me to build with another so that my [thoughts] and intimacies of feeling shall be known to him in advance of words. . . . I have telegrams from the New York papers, from *The New Republic,* for an estimate, a sketch, etc. I can't do it."[1]

Masters was particularly moved by a story told by Reedy's secretary, Alma Meyer, who said that on the eve of his departure to California, Reedy had thought of his recurrent hope of offering Masters some remuneration for the Spoon River poems. Specifically, he wanted to present Masters with $1,000 as "gift, reward, or pay" for permission to publish the poems. Masters had received no payment from Reedy and wanted none, and although Reedy had mentioned payment before, his secretary's tearful recital of his plans at this time affected Masters greatly. Nor did he feel any better after attending Reedy's funeral in St. Louis on August 4, as he explained to Monroe on the following day: "At the very last I was impelled to look at the dead face of my friend. What a great face! So beautiful, too, in this repose, the like of which is not in any eight hours of our life—every cell locked in breathless sleep. . . . So finally over—no prayers—nothing—the widow tottering back to her auto—a loud wail as she fell into it—'That's all. That's the end'—and for myself I drift, careen, circle on high, far and away, and then back—and don't know where Bill is, or what he is, or what I am." Nor did time heal the wounds, as Masters wrote Witter Bynner more than two years later. "Every day something reminds me of Bill Reedy. I am his memorial stone so far as thought goes." Similar remarks would continue for another decade and a half ("I think of Bill, almost daily," he wrote Bynner in 1935). Reedy had been distressingly right in what appears to be his last correspondence with Masters: "However you go or whatever you do[,] I am with you."[2]

Nor was Lillian any help. She had left Marion to begin her European trip with a girlfriend and servant and was preparing to sail from New York amid a flurry of telegrams, letters, and phone calls from Masters. Whether he asked her to delay her trip for him is unclear. In any event, she did not. "Reedy's death for the time has taken the starch out of me," Masters wrote Eunice Tietjens. "I am more lonely and alone than ever in my life."[3]

The death of Reedy also left Masters without a literary adviser. Reedy had long played this role, letting Masters know what he thought of his pre–*Spoon River* writings and commenting on his post–*Spoon River* creations as well. He was certainly in a better position than anyone else to offer advice, and just as certainly, Masters needed an adviser. In fact, a chief oddity about Masters's career—one of the most intriguing—is that while he valued literature and was contemptuous of the law, he often behaved as if these two attitudes were reversed: he was usually thorough about legal matters (an attitude exemplified by his 4,000-page tort law reference), but he could not find the time to revise or even reflect seriously on some of his literary works, many of which (poems and novels alike) were hastily assembled and fired off to publishers on the day of completion. His son Hilary reported that his father sometimes jotted down the amount of time that a poem required in minutes and seconds and used as an example one that had taken about three minutes. Monroe regarded the matter in a slightly different light, saying of Masters, "He was the worst self-critic I have ever known."[4]

Masters may have been more scrupulous about legal work because he knew he would be held accountable in court by a judge, opposing lawyer, or client and so prepared carefully when he entered that arena. Alternatively, Masters may have felt he could always compete in the literary game through a publisher willing to trade on the fame of *Spoon River.* More likely, however, Monroe was right, as she usually was: Masters really was a terrible self-critic and did not recognize his good writing from his bad. In any event, Masters knew hundreds of people, many of whom were literarily talented, but he felt a kinship with only a few and was willing to accept criticism from fewer still. A review of Masters's associates at the time of Reedy's death shows how "lonely" Reedy's passing left him and how few his potential advisers were.

Among Chicago literati, Monroe was best prepared to offer advice to Masters. She had proofed the galleys of *Spoon River* and offered limited advice on its successor, *Songs and Satires,* but she and Masters were not particularly close, and besides, she was usually occupied with the editorial needs of her magazine. Nor was there anyone else in Chicago in 1920 with whom Masters was close in a useful literary way. In his early days he had relied on the opinions of his former law partner, the minor poet Ernest McGaffey, but Masters had soon outgrown him. Later, Masters and novelist Theodore Dreiser became friends, but Dreiser spent much of his time in New York or Hollywood, while a second friend, John Cowper Powys (who had likened Masters to Chaucer), was often on the lecture circuit. Helen Masters herself could have provided Masters with the quiet writing environment he needed, but she lacked the critical sensibilities to go with her quiet setting, and anyway, he did not want to go home. Lillian offered "the Sleeping Palace," her mansion, but she lacked the critical acumen he needed and had failed in her effort to dramatize *Spoon River.* Carl Sandburg admired the *Spoon River* poems greatly, but as early as 1917 Masters recognized Sandburg as a literary rival likely to do "most injury" to him. Eunice Tietjens understood Masters very well, and she might have helped him, but at about the time he needed her most, she remarried and partially removed herself from his life. Masters was also distant friends with Arthur Davison Ficke and Witter Bynner, but Bynner's status was chiefly that of an acquaintance who was occasionally with Reedy in St. Louis, while Ficke's close friendship with Masters would not develop for several years. Nor did any of the Chicago lawyers with whom Masters worked inhabit the same literary and spiritual plane (indeed, none of them would have wished to do so after witnessing the decline of his once-flourishing legal practice). Masters's contact at Macmillan, Edward Marsh, might have helped, but he had not offered Masters good advice concerning his post–*Spoon River* career, and anyway, Marsh was now relocating and unavailable. So Masters had been left with Reedy as the one literary adviser he knew and trusted and whose company he enjoyed. It was true that they liked to carouse all night over roast beef and beer, and eye the women in saloons in St. Louis and elsewhere, but when morning came, they talked serious literature. Reedy was not always right, but he was respected as a critic and admired by many writers of his generation, and equally important, he was one of the few critics whose opinions Masters valued. So when Masters predicted that he would "never know his like again," he described a significant loss.[5]

Reedy's death and Lillian's departure for Europe closely preceded another important event in Masters's life, the first court action significant to his divorce. Through it, he would learn to dislike his former law partner, Clarence Darrow, more intensely than ever. In 1912 Darrow had returned from California and the McNamara case with his bank account nonexistent and his reputation in tatters. The public thought him guilty of jury tampering, regardless of the verdict of innocence, and his Chicago clientele now shunned him (and correctly so, for he was guilty). He was reduced to accepting cases with a fee as small as $50, according to Masters, who maintained an active interest in Darrow's finances, hoping to secure the $9,000 Darrow owed him from the Haywood case. Curiously, Masters seems never to have considered seeking an in-kind payment from Darrow by having Darrow serve as his lawyer in the litigation he was about to undergo. Masters found Darrow to be an intriguing person ("the most interesting of all the men I knew in Chicago"), but he did not trust him and had already denounced him from coast to coast as "a barrel of slop" in the poem "On a Bust" in *Songs and Satires;* he had flailed Darrow a second time in "Excluded Middle" in *Toward the Gulf* (although both commentaries were so veiled as to be more important to Masters than to Darrow).[6]

Now, however, as Masters's affairs inched toward divorce and as his legal reputation declined while Darrow's slowly recovered, the two men sometimes met in Chicago courts and elsewhere and occasionally exchanged confidences. The following excerpt focuses on a conversation Masters and Darrow had in September 1920, when Masters had, in his words, "been separated from [his] wife eighteen months":

> He often said that he could never forget what I did for him when he was under indictment in California for jury bribing. He knew that I had left home, and at about the time that it happened; and he said to me that he did not wonder. He often expressed the hope that he could do something for me to get my freedom and settle my affairs. But it never entered my head to ask him to act for me as a lawyer. . . . In one way or another Darrow knew about Pamela, for I think he began to watch for a chance to get into this controversy from the time that it arose. Chicago was full of gossip about Pamela and me, and everyone knew that I was no longer living at home.

At some point it became common, when the two met, for Masters to confide in Darrow and to speak of details:

> He talked about my domestic affairs, and about Pamela, not by name, but by way of saying that he had heard that she was a fine woman, and that he would be glad if he could do something to hasten our marriage. These talks did not exactly in-

> volve revelations to him such as I might have made if I had been his client. But he knew so much that it was not easy to talk to him on these subjects without my words merging into details which he may not have known, but seemed to know. There was thus a quality of professional confidence about our communications, though he was not my lawyer, and had no reason to believe that he ever would be.

Any doubt about Darrow's role was erased one day in the fall of 1920 when Masters was summoned to a Chicago judge's chambers to find that his wife had filed a suit for separate maintenance and that Darrow was now her lawyer. As Masters entered the judge's chambers, Darrow remarked that it was a good thing he was in the case so that he could "help"—with which Masters's serious problems began.[7]

The judge's chambers held four people in addition to Masters, and each of them had reason to dislike him. In addition to Darrow, there was Masters's old antagonist Frank Walker, the man who had been trying (and failing) to purchase the farm at Spring Lake, Michigan, when Masters bought it and dispossessed him; Walker would serve as Darrow's assistant in legal proceedings against Masters. Also present was Helen Masters's brother, George, a graduate of Harvard Law School. The judge was one of three who had presided over the 1914 waitress case that Masters had argued while writing *Spoon River Anthology.* At the end of that case, the court had rendered a decision that nobody liked or understood—not the lawyers, not the press, and certainly not Masters's clients, the waitresses, who had "plastered Chicago with bills" denouncing the same judge in whose chambers Masters now sat. After some questions about the likelihood of Masters's leaving the state, the judge remarked that Masters needed legal counsel and adjourned the matter for the following week. At that time "an order for alimony" was issued, and as Masters phrased it, "the money began to fly." (Appearances might also have begun to fly, for one of Masters's first actions was to instruct Macmillan to remove the dedication to Helen Masters in *Spoon River*'s opening pages, but since neither Macmillan nor Masters followed up on the matter, her name remained on the dedication until well into the 1930s.)[8]

Darrow had tried to get the judge to restrict Masters's travel on the assumption that he might flee the country to avoid support payments to his wife. Masters could not have been surprised at being summoned to court to address Helen's financial needs, but he was angered by this attempt to restrict his travel. His diary entry for this day, October 15, records his attitude: "Separate maintenance. . . . I refuse to promise not to go away at all." This refusal notwithstanding, on October 18 the court did impose travel restrictions on Masters: he was to stay within the confines of Illinois or post a bond, a restriction he chose to ignore or possibly had quashed, for he would shortly travel a great deal. His support payments to his wife were set at $150 per month. It was at about this time, too, that Darrow suggested a speedy solution to Masters's search for divorce: all he had to do was give up his interest in his Kenwood Avenue house and the Michigan farm and provide Helen Masters with a cash settlement of $25,000. When Masters replied that he did not have this kind of cash, Darrow suggested that Lillian provide it, with a portion of the sum going to himself as fee. As Masters later summarized the matter to Eunice Tietjens, "[Darrow] proposed to me that Lillian pay $25,000 to the madam to free me." Masters was furious, for he did not like being rescued by a woman, and instead put his hopes in a new novel.[9]

He had spent less than two weeks in drafting his first novel, *Mitch Miller,* and had received $8,000 outright, $4,000 apiece from both Macmillan and *Romance* magazine. *Mitch Miller* had not been a difficult story to write, for it was essentially a summary of Masters's Petersburg years as shared with the title character, a school chum now dead for forty years. Before Masters ended his story, however, he padded it with his own political leanings—rambling invectives telling where the country had gone wrong from Civil War days through World War I. Republicans, churches, and moneyed interests were the chief recipients of these lambastings, along with blacks and anyone responsible for bringing the Philippine Islands under American control. Many of the comments were woefully out of place in a book about boys. Masters had also been injudicious in another way. To maximize sales, he had tried to capture both the juvenile and the adult markets with "a story for grown-ups as well as for children" (as he had explained it to Edward Marsh). Readers noted the inconsistencies between the youthful characters and adult viewpoints, and although some critics glossed over these, others reacted negatively. Even one of Masters's friendliest readers, his son Hardin, described *Mitch Miller* as being "as heavy as middle age," which parts of it were. Masters had little time to enjoy his new status as a novelist, for he had to do something to meet his court-ordered payments to his wife and soon began a sequel to *Mitch Miller,* a longer novel he called *Skeeters Kirby.*[10]

The book was thinly veiled autobiography, telling of a boy from the country who makes his way to the city, where he succeeds as an author and looks for a woman to share his success. It was a big book, and Masters spent much of the late summer and fall of 1920 composing it in longhand and having it typed. He took off ten days between the writing and typing to enjoy his Michigan farm ("worked on trees," "picked apples") and entertained Lillian's rector and friend Father Johnston. During November 16–18 Masters visited Cleveland for a lecture and autograph session and then spent December 12–14 in Indianapolis, where he and the novelist Booth Tarkington were guests at the University Club. Masters concluded 1920 by moving to a new apartment, at 1536 Dearborn, and by signing an agreement in December to publish two books with Macmillan, *Skeeters Kirby* and a new volume of miscellaneous verse, *The Open Sea.*[11]

Lillian's departure for Europe had virtually ensured that Masters would seek out a new woman to serve as his companion, and he soon found one in Dorothy Dow, a twenty-one-year-old free spirit from nearby Lockport, Illinois. She commuted to Chicago two days a week as a student, enjoyed evenings in "dim little speakeasies," wrote passable poetry about love, and would eventually publish several volumes of verse, along with a life of Edgar Allan Poe and other writings. She knew "Masters was by all odds the most famous poet in America, in 1920 . . . , an authentic lion" in literature, and that "he was experiencing the rigors of a public, and not amiable, separation from his first wife." It was inappropriate for Masters now to cavort with her, for he was ostensibly in love with Lillian, but it was entirely in character for him to do so. Masters probably propositioned Dow ("as he seemed to do with every woman," his son Hilary remarked in *Last Stands*), and she may or may not have accepted. When Theodore Dreiser asked her later whether she and Masters had been lovers, she replied that they had not, but Masters sent a letter and poem to Arthur Davison Ficke indicating that they had been. She said they met at the Chicago studio of one John Norton in the Tree Building on Ohio Street; he said they met at Bill Slack's apartment on the South Side. She said he admired her "chiffon nightgown"; he described the nightgown's contents in the letter and poem he sent Ficke. Masters told her he loved her; she was unsure how she felt about him.[12]

Thirty years later—after Masters had died in March 1950 and Dow was about the age he had been when they met—she reread their correspondence and wrote "An Introduction to Some Letters, 1950," an unpaginated document of fifty-five pages that she donated, along with Masters's letters, to Chicago's Newberry Library. (A note among her papers indicates that some of the letters were destroyed.) She was still not entirely clear about Masters's motives in 1920, but she remembered a great deal and left behind an excellent picture of the writer at the start of the Roaring Twenties:

> A trifle above the average in height, he carried himself with authority, which sometimes seemed like truculence. His forehead bulged with wisdom; he had a smallish nose, with somewhat flattened nostrils and a firm mouth. He stood very solidly, and behind that solidity was a granite quality, steadfast and unchanging. His voice was pitched in a low key, with a certain harshness, which deepened when he laughed; his eyes were bluish grey, keen and bright; and he had the bright glow of health in his cheeks, his smile bracketed by two deep dimples.

"With broad shoulders, and a trim waist, and square defiant chin," Masters seemed to Dow much younger than he was, and he often acted it as well, a phenomenon she attributed to the remarkable success of *Spoon River.* But the relationship had not gone on long when Masters made plans to travel overseas in January 1921. He apparently had no plans to see Lillian, for he invited Dow to accompany him ("he advanced the idea that I travel to Europe with him as his secretary"). She turned him down, and Masters sailed for Egypt a few months after their initial meeting.[13]

Masters was never very talkative regarding his motives for this 1921 trip. When he later commented on it, he tied it to his permanent interest in the ancients and to the fact that he happened to have some money: "I had taken this trip because I could then afford it, and perhaps should never be able again to see Egypt and Greece." He had wanted to make such a trip as early as 1913 and began "to think of Rome, of seeing Rome during Easter," while seated beside a Roman Catholic priest named Father John Doody on a December 26, 1920, train trip to the East. He subsequently saw a flyer in New York advertising "a Mediterranean cruise that the *Caronia* was going to make in early January, and . . . went to the ticket office, made further inquiries, and finally deposited part of the price of a ticket to Naples." Masters by this time had apparently addressed the question of travel restrictions imposed by the court and felt he was free to travel anywhere as long as his alimony was paid. How he was going to make such payments in the future, however, was anybody's guess: "The turmoil in which I was living had reduced my earning power at the law, while my books of poetry, though doing well, did not yield a large income, by any means." Perhaps he thought he could always make a living from the law, the hourly wages of which he had recently mentioned to Monroe: "But good Lord, Harriet, after all your striving, think of $30.00 for a poem. I can sit here and talk for an hour with a man about buying a flat building and get $100." In any event, he now took steps to leave, making an elaborate good-bye from New York to Dorothy Dow in Chicago.[14]

The *Caronia* was to sail on January 15, 1921, but before then Masters sent Dow a ring of "gold set with a topaz"; asked for "a little picture" (January 5); explained that he left with "sadness at not seeing" her (January 6); complained that he was lonely (January 9); and on the eve of departure wrote, "Keep yourself for me, dear"—one of two letters he mailed her on January 14. At the end of one of these, Dow noted and initialed the following: "By this time Masters' intentions were matrimonial—as I recall he told me he wanted to marry me as soon as he got his divorce—Masters then asked me if I wanted to marry him. D.D." On January 16, using the Cunard Line stationery of the R.M.S. *Caronia,* Masters noted that he would reach Gibraltar in about a week and wrote Dow that he would "give anything in the world" to have her with him. He was not lonely, however, and soon opted to expand his itinerary to include more European stops, in part because he liked his shipboard companions.[15]

With Masters on the high seas, Dow had time to think. She later recalled that he had suggested "an alliance somewhat less than legitimate," and when she turned him down, "he offered an alternative which included his name as well as his heart." This too she turned down, in part because "he was not quite human, being larger than life," and in part because he was much older: "He was my senior by more than thirty years. . . . Girls of nineteen or twenty [twenty-one] are capable of being dazzled by the sagacity of fifty; but they are also apt to find it somewhat dull." A little more thinking, and his fate was sealed: "It would have been just as reasonable to consider attaching oneself to the ghost of Mr. Robert Browning, or the effigy of Lord Tennyson." Meanwhile, Masters wrote her to say that he had landed at Algiers and was now bound for Egypt.

He sent her a poem entitled "For Dorothy," a sweet nothing ("I wish you were here"), and eventually a scarab.[16]

With Masters in Egypt, Dow in Chicago, Lillian in Europe, and Helen Masters at 4853 Kenwood, it is necessary to pause. Like the author of a good mystery creating a plot, Masters sometimes developed so many threads to his personal life that he alone might keep them straight—but of course he was not a writer of mysteries, which may explain why things became so tangled. He now had three women, each of whom had reason to believe that he might behave as a husband, in part because he had presented each with the traditional symbol of such intentions, a ring. In addition to the gold-and-topaz ring he sent to Dow, there was a ring (or plan for a ring) he had designed for Lillian in May 1919 (he had a duplicate of the design made for himself). And Helen Masters had rings aplenty, for her husband apologized with jewelry. All this made it even stranger when word drifted back to Chicago that Masters had participated in what Dow called "an amorous interlude" with a famous American poetess in Paris.[17]

The only female poet that Masters mentions seeing (and one who was indeed famous) was Edna St. Vincent Millay, whom he mentioned in an unpublished chapter of his autobiography: "Edna Millay was in Paris and I called upon her at her hotel, finding her surrounded by young poets. Later, we dined together and went to the Folies Bergere." Masters's diary shows that he also took "Edna St. Vincent Millay to Savoy dinner—then casino" on February 28. Whether Millay went with Masters to the Luxembourg Gardens on the next day is not clear, but they were certainly together on March 4: "The Louvre. Edna X. Walk. To bed 10." The cryptographic *X* (Masters's shorthand for lovemaking) seems consistent with Dow's description of an "amorous interlude." One of Masters's shipmates from the *Caronia* later volunteered the news that he had let Masters use his hotel room for an afternoon in order for Masters to meet Millay there. In addition, Masters wrote Monroe that he "didn't see anybody in Paris but Edna Millay," which seems to rule out any other candidates for the amorous interlude. H. L. Mencken went a step further in documents he left, saying that Masters and Millay had a brief liaison in Paris and that it was so unsatisfactory to Masters that he never again pursued her. In any event, Masters "phoned Edna" before leaving Paris on March 7 to continue his European tour; they remained cordial but distant friends for much of the rest of his life.[18]

Masters played shuffleboard by day and occasionally danced at night as the *Caronia* moved from port to port. In addition to visiting the places he mentioned in the published portion of his autobiography (Egypt, Athens, Rome), he also saw Monaco, Nice, and London (among other places). His diary shows that he had an audience with the pope in the Vatican on February 18 and visited the graves of Keats and Shelley on the next day before purchasing memorials for the two British poets: "Take wreathes to Shelley's grave and one to Keats' house" (February 23).[19]

Although Masters suggested in his autobiography that he went overseas to forget Lillian ("I tried every honorable means to free myself to marry her. When I couldn't, I took this trip to Egypt"), it is clear that he had not forgotten her. It is just as clear, too, that he did not wish to have her along. If he had been going to see her, he would not have invited Dow to travel with him and would have made clear plans to meet Lillian. Indeed, they could have met. Lillian had been in Paris in October 1920 and February 1921 (she had left for the United States on February 13). Masters either had known her exact itinerary before he left the States or knew her whereabouts from some other means, for he paused at Gibraltar (on his way into the Mediterranean) to write her a letter in Paris, telling her where he was and where he was going. (His overseas letters to Dow seem to have since ceased.) He also wired Lillian a humorous telegram on January 29, saying that he was "opening [a] branch office" in Monaco, and wrote or received letters from her at other times. They even had a long-distance spat as to whether he had promised not to tour Europe without her: "At Rome I had received a letter from Pamela [Lillian], a very angry letter full even of epithets and accusations against my integrity. I had promised her not to come to Europe! Here I had broken my word!" With the guilt of a broken promise nagging him, he now went on to other places, occasionally rereading Lillian's letter, which he kept in his pocket, "taking it out to read too much for [his] peace of mind." He visited his sister, Madeline, and her family in London and then sailed for home in mid-March.[20]

He went on the luxury liner *Aquitania* bound for New York on a voyage on which nothing significant occurred, except that he met one George C. Stokes, a fellow Illinoisan with whom he "drank Scotch and talked books and travel." A great deal would happen because of Stokes eighteen months later, however (for he convinced Masters to return to his wife in September 1922), but on this trip the two drank and talked and tried to forget that they were landlubbers from the Corn Belt "as the *Aquitania* plunged through the stormiest seas [Masters] had ever seen." He was not happy to reach New York harbor, noting in his diary on the afternoon of March 19 that he was "steering toward dock. Infinitely sad—sad—sad."[21]

His homecoming was made worse, he said, by losing the manuscript of his new novel, *Skeeters Kirby,* as he explained in a verbal reminiscence to the writer August Derleth nearly twenty years later:

> When I was coming back from Europe with the manuscript to *Skeeters Kirby*—100,000 words of it—I had it in my suitcase—I lost it. All during the trip I had the suitcase in my cabin—it was always in sight. Well, when we landed, I let the porter carry the bag. The porter went ahead of me and put the bag with others into a taxi. He was out of my sight for only a little while—and that was the last time I saw either the suitcase or the manuscript of *Skeeters Kirby.* I couldn't find the taxi. I think to this day the driver deliberately drove off with the baggage. I telephoned Bob Davis—he was editor of *Cosmopolitan* at that time—and asked his help to find it.

> Davis called the police—he knew the chief well. They grilled the porters and taxi-drivers for hours—but it was no use. I finally put an advertisement in the New York papers, promising a liberal reward and no questions asked for the return of the manuscript, but it never came back. I was heartsick. I went to my farm and I began to rewrite the book.

Derleth repeated this narrative in an easy-to-read memoir involving two other popular authors (Sinclair Lewis and Sherwood Anderson), thus giving rise to an oft-repeated story that Masters's "sole handwritten manuscript of *Skeeters Kirby* [was] lost or stolen in 1921." It would be natural to assume that Masters's diary would corroborate and provide additional details about the manuscript's loss, but this is not the case. In fact, Masters's diary for the day of the purported loss shows no reference to a lost manuscript or police search (or grilling), nor do any of the subsequent entries, so it is probably wise to add to this story.[22]

Masters did indeed misplace the manuscript of *Skeeters Kirby,* but this occurred half a year earlier, at the end of a different trip involving a voyage ending in New York. On the evening of August 29, 1920, while on a trip from Boston to New York, Masters took a ferry from Fall River (south of Boston) and discovered on arriving in New York that he had misplaced a valise containing his writings: "Wrote on *Skeeters.* . . . Leave at 5:05 P.M. for N.Y. by Fall River ferry"; "Lose my satchel and MSS arriving at 6 A.M. at wharf." Twenty years after the loss, when Masters told August Derleth of the trauma of losing his manuscript, he naturally remembered the longer voyage but had entirely forgotten the shorter one on the Fall River ferry.[23]

This is not to say, however, that Masters did not have an abundance of other troubles facing him on his return to New York. He tried to reestablish contact with Lillian and met several times with a woman identified in his diary as "Zueline," possibly the author Marjorie Seiffert. He had learned by March 28 that his father was ill but remained in the East for another ten days, meeting Zueline in Philadelphia before leaving for Michigan on April 7. Because he was accustomed to the luxury of a domestic servant, he asked his family's former cook, Claudia Perry-Wilson, to come from Chicago and join him. Exactly how he would pay Perry-Wilson is not clear, for money was now a recurrent concern, and Masters may have faced creditors in addition to his wife's lawyers. "I ought to be pensioned and left alone," he complained to Tietjens, "instead of being hounded for money." In addition, his son was ill with tuberculosis in Santa Fe, and Masters was restless and lonely. Worse yet, his summer looked as if it was going to be about like his spring, described as follows to Tietjens: "I have a splendid hell most of the time, living like an Arab, and as for association, getting it fugitive and on the run."[24]

Masters would soon have to make a decision about his student girlfriend, Dorothy Dow, and her more mature counterpart, Lillian Wilson. On April 18 he wrote two letters, one to Dorothy Dow ("I do wish I could see you") and a second to

Tietjens to say he had "sat up till midnight" the previous evening exchanging adultery anecdotes with his housekeeper, Claudia. "Then went to bed and had a beautiful dream of Lillian—well—well—ain't this life awful?" On April 20 he again wrote Dow, sending some pressed flowers from Spring Lake and inquiring whether she knew how to type. He wrote Dow two letters on April 25, one of them urging her to live, think, and be free "in order to achieve . . . fullness as an artist" and the other requesting a meeting: "I want some undisturbed time to see you." He wrote again on April 29 and also on May 2, 1921: "Dorothy! For heaven's sake come up here and help me—I need a book typed—I need someone to take my letters. It's [delightful] here. Claudia keeps house wonderfully. You could do all my work and have time to write yourself. I'm going to Maine about July 1st—Do you want to go as my secretary? Answer—E." "This idea was fantastic," Dow later wrote at the bottom of this letter. "I could barely type with two fingers." In summary, she said: "He was not a romantic wooer; hat pulled well over his eyes, he sometimes mixed pictures of a tender future with advice about learning typing so that his manuscripts would be taken care of."[25]

It was about this time (if not before) that Dow realized the complexity of the life Masters was living. "It is my impression that I was not exactly the only string to his bow," she wrote. Plus, there was the matter of the two letters, as she later recalled: "His violent love affair with Tennessee [Mitchell] Anderson had been over years earlier, and something had happened to spoil things between himself and the woman he called, in his autobiography, Pamela. I received two anonymous letters, ugly and obscene, which asked me if I thought he was really in love with me, and advising me to ask about the woman in Indiana . . . [,] whoever she was." Dow never did understand that Pamela and the Indiana woman were one and the same. She certainly did not know that Masters had quietly spent six days with "the woman in Indiana" between May 29 and June 4 and had resumed romantic relations with her. In any event, Dow and Masters eventually got together in Chicago, where they settled their affairs at an unknown location. Masters made a romantic proposition, and Dow turned him down. He tried once more on June 6, this time by letter—"Have you changed your mind?"—at the bottom of which Dow wrote: "'Have you changed your mind' refers to my reluctance to say I would marry him sometime in the future—he was by now growing impatient." They corresponded intermittently through the summer of 1921 (July, August, and September) but on general subjects such as her poetry and his travels rather than personal ones. She felt she knew what he wanted—"he sought the security of that rarest being, a loving heart"—but she also doubted whether she could rely on him for the long term.[26]

Hardin Masters once wrote of his father that "when he once made up his mind that he was through with a friend, philosophy, book, painting, or piece of music, he was really finished with him, her or it": "I have never known a person who could cut a piece of himself, *excise* is the better word, and never even admit a scar." Masters never did excise Dorothy Dow from his life; indeed, the two corresponded intermittently until shortly before his death nearly thirty years later. Nevertheless, he did excise her from both published and unpublished portions of his autobiography, which fail to mention her, even under a pseudonym. The least likely reason for this is that Masters's ego and vanity were wounded when Dow turned him down. A more likely reason is that Dorothy Dow was only a diversion for Masters, his protestations of love notwithstanding. She does not show up in his diaries except in the briefest of ways, and as indicated, Masters had resumed relations with Lillian without Dow's ever knowing it. Hardin Masters was right: his father always knew when a relation was over, which means that he also knew when a relation was not over, which is why he now pursued Lillian again. "Everyone is suffering," he told Corinne Robinson. "No one has found his heart's desire, or having found it is satisfied."[27]

Lillian had known Masters was back at Spring Lake as soon as he arrived in early April, and although they were feuding, they used her minister as a go-between. A diplomatic courier between the wealthy and the prominent, the rector more than once played Cupid when things were tense between them. Masters wrote the minister to say that his father was ill (Masters had at last visited him in Springfield on May 17). This brought a letter of sympathy from Lillian, and this in turn brought a reconciliation on May 29. Hours of talking, happy tears and sad ones, and a picnic all mixed with Masters's steamy diary entries, such as this one for June 3:

> Sweet sweet—all night
> Ends at dawn.
> I want you for mine.
> I can have no one but you.
> I love you so, my husband.

Unfortunately, when he told Lillian of his use of their affair in his new novel, *Skeeters Kirby,* she grew very upset: "I tell her of the chapter in *Skeeters.* She goes to pieces."[28]

He finally gave in to Lillian's reluctance to have her story made public and told Macmillan to "withdraw *Skeeters.*" This magnanimous act had two consequences: it brought Lillian, smiling, back to his side, and it guaranteed that he would remain broke. He did not have to be broke, however, for it was on this visit that Lillian volunteered to buy his divorce by providing Darrow with the requested $25,000: "She went to her room and returned with a package which she flung upon the couch indignantly. 'There,' she said, 'there's the money. Give it to those wolves, satisfy that python Darrow.'" Masters turned down the offer, suggesting that they live together instead, an offer that she turned down; things returned to their usual stasis. A letter to Tietjens summarizes Masters's emotional state at this time: "I spent a week with Lillian about a month ago, and parted with her determined to make a final superhuman effort to be free." What particularly moved him were her bouts of weeping, mingled with concern that he would never be free of his wife, along with some expensive finery she had purchased in anticipation of their wedding: "Lillian's face streaming with dumb tears, her outcries, her prostrate figure on the Victrola, her broken words that she went abroad to stay until I was free, the beautiful things she bought for herself, which she brought forth to show me, saying that all were selected to please me and with a view to the consummation . . . , these things haunt me. . . . I am soon on a new life either with Lillian as my wife or in the discard of unmanageable things."[29]

One significant obstacle stood in the way of his plans to make Lillian his new wife, and that, of course, was his existing wife. Left at home with the children while her husband roamed across three continents, Helen Masters refused to cooperate with any of these plans. In reply to Masters's requests for freedom, she either offered stony silence or momentary acquiescence followed by a change of mind. (She ignored entirely his advice that she should "go to work at something . . . , that economic matters should be treated in relation to what [he] was doing for American literature.") She and her two daughters had undergone genuine privations during the more than two years Masters had been away from home. She had first closed off rooms to cut down heating costs and had subsequently taken in boarders, let the necessary maintenance go undone, and in general experienced a hard time. Marcia Lee Masters mentioned some of their problems in her poem "Wind Around the Moon":

> The house shrank with the cold.
> The radiators, where we used to dry our mittens,
> Had spines as icy as the air
> That swept up from the cellar;
> And mother sold her pearls for coal.

In short, Helen Masters and her daughters experienced all the travails of an unemployed wife and mother whose husband is late in support payments. Money had become a major problem.[30]

There were several reasons for this, the most visible being Masters's just-completed trip overseas. The endless stream of restaurants and hotels in popular tourist areas and return trip on a luxury liner had been expensive, the more so since Masters had been under court order to provide for his wife and children at the same time. Their maintenance in a large fashionable house was expensive, for they had all become accustomed to a lifestyle based on Masters's sometimes excellent earnings as a lawyer. By mid-1921, however, Masters was no longer practicing law. In fact, he later suggested to Harriet Monroe that he had ended his full-time practice in 1919, and his diary indicates that his last legal work prior to his trip abroad had occurred in May 1920. After that time his peripatetic lifestyle involving shuttles from Spring Lake to Marion, New York, and other points had precluded the sustained practice of law, but he had maintained the expense of keeping an office anyway (he had returned to it to pick up manuscripts on April 10 following his return from Europe). "I have closed my law office," he at last informed Tietjens on July 21, 1921. He would now have to live by his pen.[31]

Unfortunately, Masters was not always practical in the use of that pen. His method of composition often generated unnecessarily high production costs; with his major works in particular, he often waited until the text was set in type and ready to be proofed before making revisions. Such changes meant resetting the type, which generated expenses fully chargeable to the author. He phrased matters thus to George Brett at Macmillan:

> My books are produced as follows: they are written in longhand and frequently rewritten. . . . Then they are typed. When typed, they look clearer to my eye. . . . But when the proof sheets come, I see exactly what I have done. . . . Since these proof sheets constitute the text material and visualizing means for getting the exact matter to the reader, shall I throw away a third of my opportunity for doing so because I am scared of being charged for it? I can't do it. . . . I'll go broke before letting a thing come out bad to escape a printer's bill.[32]

Earlier, when he had been working as a lawyer, Masters had been able to afford this type of luxury and had volunteered to pay for it as well. For example, when he was writing his World War I poetry epic *Domesday Book* in mid-1919, he had informed Macmillan's Edward Marsh of this willingness: "I shall revise the work severely in proofs, understanding of course that I stand the expense of it." Later, in 1920, he had complained of these expenses, but in a joking manner: "I have a statement from you for $160.54 for corrections on *Domesday Book*. Gee whiz, is it not possible that you have astigmatism, myopia, or some other infection of the eyes? How do you make these out?" By mid-July 1921, following his trip to Europe, he was no longer joking. Various author-generated expenses of $541.47 along with a large advance royalty for *Mitch Miller* had placed him in the position of owing money to Macmillan rather than vice versa. (As Macmillan's George Brett phrased it, "There is a balance due us on your account of $3,448.02.") Any new royalties from Macmillan would probably be applied to Masters's total indebtedness of $3,989.49 (to which should be added a library fine of $4.09 for a book that Brett had checked out for Masters). He was broke.[33]

Domesday Book was supposed to have saved him from this. Timely, "modern," and especially lengthy, its 10,000 lines of poetry told the story of a member of the "lost generation" who serves as a nurse during the Great War and then returns home to die. The book had a provocative heroine, believable plot, and the sweep of a national epic, and Masters often referred to it as his "finest achievement" and quoted H. L. Mencken, who called it "the longest and most eloquent poem ever written by an American." Masters noted privately, however, that Mencken "often confessed that he is not a judge of poetry," and Masters himself was well aware of the book's shortcomings. "Some of my friends think that I could make it one of the greatest of books by taking more time with it," he told Edward Marsh as he finished drafting it. "I wrote it at great speed" but "came to a point where I lost perspective."[34]

Masters had begun *Domesday Book* on September 23, 1918, and had practically finished it by February 1919, mailing it to Macmillan in May. Harriet Monroe had subsequently published three lengthy excerpts in the June 1919 issue of *Poetry.* These constituted all the space allocated to verse in that issue and reflected Monroe's considerable interest in the volume as his first major work after *Spoon River.* Masters spent portions of the remainder of 1919 with revisions, but his heart (or his patience) was not up to the work, and in mid-spring 1920 he simply called it quits, expressing the manuscript to Macmillan on May 12, along with this explanation: "I suppose if I lived with 'Domesday' three or four years more I might enrich it some; but I believe it is as good as I can make it up to this time."[35]

In its final form the book included material from various sources. The part concerning the discovery of the contents of a diary came from an unknown third party and was "literally true"; another part was from a short story Masters first contemplated in 1889, still other parts were worked-over verses from other times (e.g., the poem that provides the present book's epigraph: "As I shall die"), and much of it—details and names—stemmed from Masters's own past. *Domesday Book* would eventually sell some 15,000 copies during 1920, 1921, and subsequent years, and while this was an excellent sale for a volume of poetry, it did not become the attention-getter Masters was seeking or the "big book" he needed to command additional literary respect. Worse, to the extent that he had tried and failed to produce an equal to *Spoon River,* there was by mid-1921 some justification for referring to him as a "one-book author."[36]

Nor did he have any lucrative new title on the horizon. His autobiographical novel *Skeeters Kirby* was completed but had been recalled to placate Lillian, and after he "wrote 30 pages" on a new work, he abandoned it, dreamed uneasily of the death of Lillian, and made his will. Things were not going well. By mid-July 1921 he was being sustained in part by loans from acquaintances. "The bank of kindness check is here," he wrote Tietjens from Spring Lake, "and helps to cover my dwindling balance." He needed money so badly that he rented his Spring Lake farm to a tenant for $600 and stayed with his parents at their summer home at nearby Saugatuck before settling in at a hotel in Grand Haven. He remained there only two weeks, however, and then went on to Grand Rapids before wearying of it and going to New York, then to Princeton, and at last back to Spring Lake, where he began a new novel.[37]

This, *Children of the Market Place,* was a combination love story and account of the life of Stephen A. Douglas, the political opponent of Abraham Lincoln in 1858 and 1860. Once, in that faraway, misty past Masters often preferred to the present, Squire Davis Masters had stood on the Petersburg square with his young son Hardin (Masters's father) and heard the states' rights Democrat Douglas inveigh against the Republican Lincoln. This moment of family and national history appealed to Masters; in addition, he was slowly developing a dislike of Lincoln. "I have the real intercessor's passion for nailing lies and rescuing obscured Titans," he wrote one publisher concerning his new work. Offsetting Masters's personal interests were his lack of documentation and the haste with which his book was written. He was led to believe that he would not be permitted to read Douglas's correspondence, which he estimated to comprise between ten and twenty thousand letters, and so completed his text without asking to see any of it. The book was written in longhand in September and October 1921 and was then typed and mailed to Macmillan on the day of completion: "Finished typing at 5 minutes of 11. . . . Mail MS to Brett" (November 4).[38]

Children of the Market Place differs from Masters's other major works of fiction in that it is the only one of his seven novels that is not highly autobiographical. Partly a biography of Douglas and partly a social tract focused on the decline of Jeffersonian democracy, *Children of the Market Place* belongs as much to Masters's early years as a pamphleteer as to his mature years as a novelist.

As the title indirectly suggests, the book focuses in part on slavery, an issue that is kept visible in the story through the discovery that the English narrator, James Miles, has a partly black half-sister, Zoe. During Miles's lifetime (from 1815 through 1900), he moves from England to Illinois, where he inherits 5,000 acres and becomes a friend of Douglas. James Miles's fortune allows him the freedom to travel, and his friendship with Douglas provides Masters the means to denounce the individuals and groups he felt were responsible for declines in the country—Republicans and Lincoln, easterners, religious fundamentalists, and non–Anglo Saxons.[39]

Unfortunately, the book displays a weariness at odds with the exciting times it describes. James Miles looks at America through "old eyes," as if the best days were gone, and a weariness also marks his personal life: he makes a dull marriage to a woman who becomes enfeebled, but when he is free to marry the woman he loves, he is too tired to pursue her. "I was the defeated lover of the ideal whom I had found too late," says Miles. As the twentieth century dawns, James Miles is ready for the grave.[40]

Despite its bitterness, *Children of the Market Place* must be accounted a limited success, in part because Masters incorporated his prejudices into the historical fabric of his novel. By telling his tale through the eyes of an impressionable young foreigner and by using a gimmick—presenting campaign rhetoric as truth—Masters achieved a measure of objectivity that is often lacking in his other books. He did not achieve a notably artistic book, however, primarily because it is impossible to say whether it is a life of Stephen Douglas or of James Miles.

Remarkably enough, Macmillan granted Masters a $4,000 advance on the book, primarily because the firm's president, George Brett Sr., thought the volume would be a huge success. Lillian figured in the book as a rich widow, but her story had little to do with that of Douglas, and whether she contributed to the novel's financial failure is hard to say. One of Douglas's grandsons liked the book, but reviews were mixed, and Masters blamed his book's poor sales on a hostile press, which was beginning to notice his marital difficulties: "It was published the day that dreadful creature I was married to took a default decree against me [for tardy support payments]. . . . The publicity concerning the default killed the book in Chicago." Although Masters privately admitted that his book was a potboiler ("for myself, I don't think much of it"), his public plan was to say that he was a victim of financial circumstances: "Naturally, I was running behind on the alimony ordered in the separate maintenance suit. It was impossible that I should not do so under the circumstances, and considering that no book that I wrote made a large sum of money. I was not living extravagantly, but I was not living thriftily. My money went in small bits, without [my] realizing that it is in that way that large sums finally sift from one's pocket."[41]

Instead of accepting responsibility for this state of affairs, Masters chose to blame his wife and her lawyers for dragging out the divorce and his wife's friends for offering her counsel. To get even with Helen, he tried to incite newspaper articles against her. "She hates newspaper publicity like poison," he wrote Eunice Tietjens, previously with the *Chicago Daily News.* "If some newspaper publicity could be started." He trailed off. He also made plans to get even with Clarence Darrow: "There is a curious irony here in the part that Darrow is playing. He is revenging himself for the poems I wrote on him, 'On a Bust' in *Songs and Satires;* and 'Excluded Middle' in *Toward the Gulf.* But these are just Sunday School persiflage compared to what he will get as I go along. I'll make that son of a bitch the most detestable figure in American history." Darrow was meanwhile modifying some of his own plans, explaining to a reporter in late 1921 that he was henceforth "embarked on the laudable business of getting money." A part of that new money would be Masters's.[42]

Masters's relations with others were also worsening, including that with Harriet Moody, the widow of the popular University of Chicago poet William Vaughn Moody. Following her husband's untimely death in 1910, Harriet Moody lived at a fashionable Hyde Park address near the University of Chicago and became known as a patron of the arts who hosted writers from around the world. She and the Masterses knew each other (they lived not far apart), and the two families occasionally visited, although Masters and Moody never met. Harriet Moody had more in common with Helen Masters than with her husband, however, and Masters came to dislike her, perhaps because he had to share his literary prominence with the ghost of her husband at her social gatherings. In any event, he now included Harriet Moody among those who were working against him, as he explained to Tietjens in September 1921: "I have a divining feeling that the madam [Helen Masters] is being coached by Mrs. Moody. I don't know why, except that I hear, every now and then, that Mrs. Moody is very inimical to me in general. . . . I have seen in her the colorless frothings of a deadly envy." Around the same period he wrote: "This woman, Mrs. Moody, has envy against me for her husband's somewhat defeated career. I have long sensed this, and so she would be glad to break my creative life. . . . Wallace Heckman, the attorney of the University of Chicago, is her advisor on the law, and thus we have the widow of that institution's poet laureate and its attorney united with the most perfect specimen of Babbittland [Helen Masters] against me."[43]

Helen's crime was her interference with Masters's long pursuit of happiness begun years before: he had told himself that hard work might lead to success, and success, to the woman of his dreams and contentment, and now Helen was blocking the culmination of these plans. When Masters searched for accomplices, he found them and so let his personal life poison relations with literary patrons such as Harriet Moody, who should have been his friend.

As summer passed to fall, Masters's circle of enemies widened, while the number of friendly acquaintances diminished. Through public lectures and semipublic comments that he knew would be repeated and through his publications and interviews, Masters began to develop a reputation as a "rogue elephant," as one contemporary called him. He was known as a man who could be sharply critical of other authors and the nation and who sometimes suggested the public could be damned as well. An article in *The Bookman* a little after this time summarized his behavior and reputation: "He has that aversion to other successful authors which [the writer] Joe Hergesheimer pronounces distinctive of a first-class man. He has run amock [*sic*] among his fellow poets, lampooning some of them, yea! even Amy Lowell, publicly, and planting drastic opinions on others where they would do the most harm. . . . In revolt against the herd, he despises even his prospective audience, and is continually in contempt of the court of critical opinion." He nursed a particular grudge against the Chicago press, which he felt had failed to give *Spoon River* the prominence it deserved several years earlier: "The daily newspapers [had] seemed to regard my appearance on the stage as the eclipse of favorites who had struggled in vain for years to write books of moment, or as a lessening of the importance of the editors of those papers." Thus, Masters shut himself off from literary acquaintances. He spoke of his "deepening isolation" and "disinclination to meet people" and told Lillian, "The literary people bore me stiff. . . . I'd rather co-fraternize with old Stokesy here [his drinking buddy on the *Aquitania*], or with Bill Slack in Chicago, or with Stover the fisherman in S.L. [Spring Lake]." Certainly, Masters was no longer the "man of the hour" in New York or all "the rage" in Boston. Chicago would decide what it thought of him a little later.[44]

It was under these conditions that Masters completed the fifth volume of miscellaneous poems to follow *Spoon River, The Open Sea.* Its title was meant to suggest an aquatic relation to *Spoon River* and his intervening volumes of verse, the whole to be "artistically related to the progress down the Mississippi River." Although titles of *The Great Valley* (1916), *Toward the Gulf* (1918), and *The Open Sea* (1921) had discernible continuity, their miscellaneous contents did not. In addition, Masters had interrupted the flow of his series with a weak volume of miscellaneous poems, *Starved Rock* (1919). A stone pillar along the Illinois River, Starved Rock was unknown to many readers beyond the state's borders, and many who did know of it knew that it lies upstream from Spoon River instead of toward the gulf. Masters may have guessed that *The Open Sea* would attract no more favorable attention than its predecessors had received, and because he badly needed money and was not getting along with Lillian, he at last allowed Macmillan to publish the novel describing their relation, *Skeeters Kirby:* "Sent proofs of *Open Sea* back. . . . Mailed letter to Brett to print *Skeeters Kirby*."[45]

Masters had high hopes for *Skeeters Kirby;* it was, after all, his story and that of *Spoon River.* Nonetheless, it was probably unwise for him to tell this story at this time: a partial history of his love for Margaret George, his engagement to his wife, and romantic liaisons with women in addition to Lillian, its autobiographical content might be used against him, especially by a lawyer as opportunistic as Darrow, or it could be the source of unwanted questions from reporters. By early 1922 Masters had begun to realize the potential problems of *Skeeters Kirby* and asked for a delay in its publication, even offering at one point to buy the plates from which the book would be printed. "This book will hurt me immeasurably now," Masters wrote George Brett at Macmillan. "A book as frank as *Skeeters Kirby* would have gone all right a while ago. . . . I don't feel that I can weather it now." Even in late 1921, as he reviewed the manuscript for the last time, he examined it less for its artistic flaws than for its potential as a weapon against him. When he at one point deleted certain chapters from the proofs, he did so more from a defensive point of view than from an artistic one.[46]

The stress of these times resulted in the book's oddball dedication. Masters had intended to dedicate the volume to his friend Bill Slack but changed his mind when Slack angered him. In a lighthearted moment, Masters told Macmillan's George Brett Jr. to dedicate the book "TO ELMER CHUBB, L.L.D., Ph.D.," but with the understanding that this be "querried [*sic*] before the book goes to press." Unfortunately, Chubb did not exist. A satiric creation of Masters's imagination, Dr. Chubb was most likely to come to life when Masters was bored, tired, tense, or in the mood to play the buffoon. Chubb, along with several other imaginary brethren, might then spring into existence on broadsides, fake calling cards, and stationery and in occasional verse. Brett was supposed to know this, to realize that Masters was only being satiric, and above all not to print the new dedication. The situation was complicated by the presence of two George Bretts at Macmillan (father and son), but Masters often failed to indicate whether his correspondence was to the junior or senior member of the firm, which provided the potential for botched communications. In any event, Masters discovered how little Brett Jr. knew when a freshly printed copy of *Skeeters Kirby* arrived with the dedication firmly in place. "Take that absurd dedication to Chubb out of *Skeeters Kirby,*" Masters wrote Macmillan, after which he began urging prospective reviewers to "slur over" or try to ignore "this awful joke."

"One of the most ghastly things that has ever happened to me in the literary game" is how Masters described the dedication to Llewellyn Jones, a reviewer with the *Chicago Evening News.* "The book has come and I am sick about this."[47]

Masters could little afford such self-sabotage, and this chance to be regarded as a serious "adult" novelist came to little. From start to finish (or 1920 to 1923, when *Skeeters Kirby* was at last published), Masters was too preoccupied with his personal life to give the book the attention it needed, nor did he do so during the period of intensity when he rewrote its lost or stolen sections (100,000 words or so) in only eighteen days. The final curse on *Skeeters* came when Masters quarreled with Macmillan over printing costs and when, after all was done (but not nearly said), he found the book had generated a $2,000 debit on Macmillan's ledger book. This situation arose partly because *Skeeters* was not a good book and did not sell well and partly because Masters revised some segments of text a remarkable six times after the manuscript was set in pages.[48]

In the fall of 1921 Masters sensed that his relation with Lillian was winding down and returned to his earlier hope of living simply at Spring Lake and letting the world go by; to support himself, he would write a series of novels that traded on his recent experiences: "I pictured myself as a recluse of Spring Lake, gardening, and taking care of a vineyard, and supporting myself by writing books. Why not do that and let everything go? For now the old delight of seeing Pamela [Lillian] was diminished. I had to go there in the utmost secrecy and depart in the same way; and her dignity was affronted by such a proceeding. We could not be happy together as we once had been. I began now to meditate a series of novels, one on the tragedy of hate, one on the tragedy of an aspiration, one on love." The short-term implementation of this plan was not particularly challenging. It was, after all, what he enjoyed most—writing, working with his hands, and enjoying his farm with the help of a housekeeper and handyman. Whether this lifestyle would work over the long term depended on two issues: whether he pursued his divorce (and kept or lost his Spring Lake farm) and whether he could support himself and pay alimony from money derived from his books.[49]

Masters closed Spring Lake in November and returned to Chicago but was restless and spent the holidays in New York City. Christmas 1921 was at least as lonely and unfulfilled as any he had known as a youth. Alone in a New York hotel room, he spent Christmas Eve and Christmas Day reading a copy of D. H. Lawrence's *Sons and Lovers* and posting cynical reflections in his diary: "Smoke, read, lie on the bed. Sleep—A derelict" (December 24); "Lie on the bed, sleep, smoke, a derelict" (December 25). (Whether he discerned the similarities between his domineering mother and Lawrence's is not recorded.) He left for Princeton University and its library the next day. As 1921 came to an end, he was by himself and working: "The bells rang at midnight as I write" (December 31). His total 1921 after-tax income was $2,681.39—about a tenth of the amount he had once made as a lawyer.[50]

By this time Helen Masters's refusal to grant him a divorce had turned his heart against any monetary support for her, even when she had to sublet portions of their home to survive. "Mrs. Stick in the Mud has a house full of roomers," he had written Tietjens in late 1921, swearing at the same time that Helen would receive "not a God damn cent . . . that she doesn't get by the law." The roomers were still there five months later, in part because in February 1922 Masters decided (against all reason) to enlarge his kitchen at Spring Lake, undergoing the expense of carpentry in the dead of winter and making plans to stay there permanently. He financed his new activities with a $7,000 mortgage on the Spring Lake farm. He ignored the fact that the divorce he frequently contemplated would probably cost him the place he was enlarging and that his wife and daughters needed the money he was about to spend. Details appear in an unpublished portion of his autobiography: "It was bitter February of 1922, and loud winds were blowing over my garden. The trees were weighted with snow. I fired the furnace, and finally brought my negro cook from Chicago, whom I had to pay an extravagant wage to secure at this time of year, and under the circumstances." Removing the cook from Chicago to Michigan was absolutely guaranteed to upset Helen, especially since the cook was Claudia Perry-Wilson, an employee of the Masters family for most of twenty-five years and a person of much talent in the kitchen. Masters also hired other workers: "In a week or so, the cold moderated a little, and I hired workmen to build a new kitchen. This was preparatory to settling my life permanently there in the country. They began work when they had to thaw the earth with fire, and then pick the frosted clay. Toward the latter part of March, the kitchen was done."[51]

It was also toward the end of March 1922 that Darrow and Helen Masters grew tired of toying with him. Since separating from his wife three years earlier, in March 1919, Masters had done pretty much as he wished. He had pursued Lillian, amused himself with Dorothy Dow, traveled to Europe (doing as he wished there, too), and returned to his farm at Spring Lake. He had paid only $750 of the more than $2,500 required by the October 1920 court order for separate maintenance. Now he had stolen the cook. Finances permitting, he might have continued in this fashion indefinitely, seeing Lillian, publishing as he could, traveling as he wished, and ignoring the obligations to his wife. "Bargaining for time," his son Hilary once remarked, "was a continuous enterprise for him." It also brought him near-continuous problems. His present problems, for example, had begun twenty-five years earlier when he had thought of ending his engagement to Helen and then married her anyway, as if time might never bring him the complications he clearly foresaw. Judgment Day began with a call from his lawyer.[52]

Actually, Masters had two lawyers at this time, both in Chicago. One was Abraham Meyer; the other was Bill Slack. The former was very competent, and Masters always counted him as an able attorney, mentioning him by name in various places in his writings. Slack was a different story. A native of the Lewistown area, he appears under the name "Fallas" in unpublished portions of Masters's autobiography (named, perhaps, for the lawyer of uneven luck in the town of Spoon River). Masters and Slack had shared an apartment shortly after Masters separated from his wife in 1919, but that was because their bachelor-like lifestyles were congruent and not because Masters admired Slack's legal ability. It was this ability—or inability—of Slack (so aptly named) that now brought Masters a true financial crisis.[53]

Masters's serious financial problems began on March 21, when Slack failed to attend an important court hearing prompted by Masters's refusal to support his wife. On the following day the Chicago press printed accounts of the hearing, the first of several instances of "newspaper publicity" of the type Helen Masters hated and her husband could ill afford. The following is from the *Chicago Tribune*'s March 22 account of the hearing. Masters's old nemesis Frank Walker led the successful attack against him while Darrow remained in the background:

> WIFE OF POET EDGAR MASTERS FREED BY COURT
>
> Mrs. Helen Jenkins Masters, 4853 Kenwood Avenue, wife of Edgar Lee Masters, author and poet, yesterday was granted a decree of separate maintenance by Judge Ira Raynor. Mrs. Masters alleged the author of "Spoon River Anthology" deserted her in March, 1919, and has not supported her and her two daughters.
>
> She declared she had been maintaining her household by taking in boarders. She said Masters had an income of $12,000 a year.
>
> Judge Raynor gave Mrs. Masters judgment for $2,000 back alimony and ordered Masters to pay her $300 a month as alimony and for the support of the daughters. Temporary alimony was ordered in October 1920, but Francis W. Walker, attorney for Mrs. Masters, showed the court that it had not been paid.
>
> Walker said Masters was at his summer home at Spring Lake, Mich. The lawyer said he had been trying to get service on the poet for over a year.

"Another woman" also came up, largely as the result of Masters's blunder in bringing the subject to attention—in writing: "A letter said to have been written to Mrs. Masters by her husband was offered in evidence by Attorney Walker. It said: 'Get a divorce. I'm through. I'm tired. If you don't get a divorce I am going to get another woman in London, where I will be appreciated and where we will be accepted for our talents.'" In a different section of the paper, the *Tribune* printed Masters's picture with the erroneous caption "Spoon River Poet Divorced." The *New York Times* got the story straight, but details there were just as unflattering.[54]

Years later, when Masters wrote about these events in an unpublished chapter of his autobiography, the $2,000 in back alimony had grown to $3,000, but that is less important than the fact that he now had a new adversary with which to deal. The newspapers—one of his best allies in touting *Spoon River* and making him world famous—had now found a chink in his armor. "Bad news," he wrote in his diary for March 22.[55]

CHAPTER 9

The Judas Kiss

There sat my wife smiling. . . . I stepped forward and gave her the Judas kiss.

—Edgar Lee Masters, unpublished autobiographical writings

When Masters published his autobiography, he indicated incorrectly that he had left Helen Masters and his place in Michigan "for good" and "without turning back" in September 1917. When he really did leave her, in March 1919, he vowed to friends that he would never return. Beginning in March 1922, however, a series of events slowly turned him away from his bachelor life at Spring Lake and Lillian's place and redirected his steps to Chicago, his wife, and his children. Money, or its lack, was the foremost cause of this reversal, but it was the successful legal maneuvering of Helen Masters's lawyers, Clarence Darrow and Frank Walker, that made the problem real.

The March 21 court action so costly to Masters was traceable in part to lawyer William Slack's negligence, as Masters said: "Slack overlooked it and the case went by default." But Slack himself was a victim of circumstances, as Masters also remarked: "The case was shifted by design or by accident from the calendar of one judge to the calendar of another, with the result that my lawyer, who was watching it on the calendar where it belonged, didn't see it on the calendar to which it was shifted." In fact, Slack did not learn of the disposition of the case until he read of it in a Chicago newspaper. Regardless, Masters was without legal representation at the hearing, and Helen Masters's petition for a decree of separate maintenance passed without demurral. A second hearing on March 28 was attended by Masters's other attorney, Abraham Meyer, but that hearing simply finalized proceedings of the week before: all Masters's assets, including his house and possessions, were placed in the hands of a court-appointed receiver (one Abraham Link); Masters's annual support payments (or alimony, as he called them) were set at $3,600, about $1,000 more than his total income from the previous year.[1]

His initial solution to his problems was to write his way out of them, to write and publish even more than he was and then lease his place at Spring Lake, as he remarked to Eunice Tietjens on March 25: "I am writing now like a son of a gun. . . . If you hear of or know of any nice couple who would take this place for the summer and let me live with them on a reasonable basis, I wish you would let me know." This plan was still viable two days later when he wrote Tietjens about his financial affairs and progress on a new piece of fiction: "I have 30,000 words done on a new book . . . , a novel. And believe me, no more novels. I have to do this to get money to live on. For living here in Spring Lake is expensive. Why I pay Mrs. Perry-Wilson [the cook] $5,000 a year; and even at that she is restive and about to strike. I can't live on less than $20,000 a year here. I believe I could live as cheap at Nice. So that $12,000 a year isn't a drop in the bucket for me. But poetry is very high now so that I muddle along." But things were much worse than they seemed.[2]

Masters met with Abraham Meyer a day later and found that his copyrights and future royalties were also affected by the court's action. He summarized matters in an unpublished chapter of his autobiography: "All my copyrights and royalties were in the hands of this receiver. My large private library had been confiscated. Everything had been taken from me except 'necessary clothing,' which the decree expressly awarded me. I was hardly earning $300 a month at the time, and of course could not pay any such amount in alimony. I didn't have the cash to pay Winkler [Walker] and Darrow. In sum, the situation was alarming." Masters's efforts to have the decree for separate maintenance set aside "on the ground that he was not present nor represented by counsel" at the first hearing did not bear fruit, nor did a June 2 "codicil to contest decree."[3]

He hired a third lawyer (Daniel Pagelson) to look after his Michigan interests and to assist Slack and Meyer and found that his Spring Lake farm was also in a court-appointed receivership (he had earlier thought of selling his farm to his parents to shield it, but that idea had not worked out): "The Grand Haven lawyer told me one day that a receiver had been appointed for my Spring Lake place, and done there in the Michigan court, all without any notice to me whatever. I was thus homeless and likely at any moment to be turned out of the house, which I liked to think I had bought with the royalties from *Spoon River*."[4]

It was of course absolutely false that *Spoon River*'s royalties had paid for the farm—his fee from the profitable Helen Lee/Bermingham case had done this—but the farm was exceptionally important to him, and its imminent loss to his wife and Frank Walker was galling in the extreme. He had taken the farm from Walker when Walker was experiencing financial difficulties, and now Walker was taking it back. "She is in his hands," Masters wrote Tietjens, "and they are moving to take this little retreat away from me": "This little farm has been my undoing; and I strove for years to have a pretty place where I could work. I earned it with blood. I wanted to share it with someone I loved." He had by this time named his farm and was writing friends on letterhead stationery bearing this new name:

TWELVE ACRES
SPRING LAKE
MICH.

Unfortunately, this personalizing of the place only made its imminent loss more bitter.[5]

Nor did it help that Masters's parents had been drawn into their son's domestic woes. Hardin and Emma Masters now lived in Springfield, at 1401 Holmes Avenue. About six weeks earlier, in February 1922, while Masters was visiting them at their home, Helen Masters had suddenly shown up there. She had wanted to explain her side of the marital disagreement and to reason with Masters's parents, but Masters's father lost his temper, "became spirited," and told her to follow through with whatever she seemed to threaten. "Be divorced," he had told her. "Get things settled." Because Masters had not wished to see his wife at all ("I did not want so disagreeable an experience"), he had removed himself from the house to the lobby of a Springfield hotel for the duration of Helen Masters's one-hour visit; now his wife was following his father's advice.[6]

The impatient treatment Helen received from her father-in-law may have been exacerbated by the family's poor health at this time: Hardin Masters had recently suffered a painful eye disorder and had lost sight in one eye, as well as the active practice of his Springfield law business; Emma Masters had already been diagnosed with the cancer that would kill her in 1926; and Masters's son was ill with tuberculosis in Santa Fe. The poet was on his own.[7]

Trying to salvage at least a part of his assets, Masters sat down on April 10 with his Michigan lawyer, Pagelson, and prepared an affidavit showing his previous year's income. His plan was to convince the Chicago judge in his case, Ira Raynor, that $300-per-month alimony was not only unfair but also impossible to pay. Toward this end Masters had gathered some useful, if negative, facts: he had negotiated a contract with Macmillan calling for him to receive 33¾¢ for each domestic copy of *Spoon River* and half that for foreign sales, but in the six months ending December 31, this best of moneymakers had sold only 771 copies at home and 5 abroad, for a yield of only $261.05. Despite these dismal figures, the court action went against him: "I made an affidavit in which I set down with factual accuracy all my royalties during the past year, and all that I had made in the practice of law. This affidavit was filed; and thus Darrow had possession of my business secrets, and Winkler [Walker] had them, and my wife, and the newspapers, and the whole of Chicago had them. And the word went around, 'Well, well! After all this noise about his books, how shrunk is the actual result!'" The actual result was that Masters owned his "necessary wearing apparel" (as the law defined it) and nothing else.[8]

The judge refused to vacate the alimony unless Masters came to Chicago and took the stand, but he could not do that. As an errant husband behind in his support payments, he was afraid that the court might try to restrict his movements. "They would put me under bond not to leave the state," he told Harriet

Monroe. "Then I'd have to get a friend to stand for that." Worse, testifying on his own behalf would permit Masters to be cross-examined, and that would allow Lillian's name to be introduced (she had already been alluded to as "a notorious woman," or words to that effect). "They would put me on the stand and ask about all my books," he complained to Monroe, "and put before the public all my private affairs. They would bring in the names of people whom I would not have in this case for the world." The result was that "the decree stood," and with it significant damage to Masters's overall reputation: once his revenues were known, it was clear that the "flood" of *Spoon River* had been reduced to a trickle, at least in terms of earnings, and so his reputation as an author was diminished along with his finances and social standing.[9]

Lillian was also slipping away. Masters knew this, of course, and in the spring of 1922 he privately took steps to cover his ego should their once-planned marriage not take place. His letter of April 11 to his friend Mary Aldis illustrates: "You know, if you know anything of my nature, that I would not marry any woman with whom my name has yet been coupled. If I should ever bind myself again, it will be with a woman whose nature and reputation are both clean. . . . Lately, the story has come to me that I followed a woman to Europe, the woman having told the story herself, created of the wish that I would do so." On the next day the perverse Cupid that governed Masters's affair with Lillian caused her to call and say she missed him: "Lillian long distances me at 8:30 P.M. Asks me to come to Marion for Easter." This year, however, Masters was busy tending his grape arbor and fifty apple trees at Twelve Acres; he did not visit her but "sent her [a] satchel of books" instead. As he finished mailing them at the Spring Lake Post Office, he may have wondered why he had not heard from Charmian London.[10]

Charmian London was the widow of the author Jack London, who had died six years earlier. She lived in Oakland, California, and had recently written Masters, sending him her picture as well. Exactly why she had done so is not clear, but Masters replied to her letter on the day he received it (April 4) and indicated a willingness to establish a friendship. He first reviewed his wife's evil nature and its relation to his recent lack of literary work ("I do nothing this spring but telegraph, telephone, and write letters"); then he got around to Charmian: "Your letter of such a different tenor from the others gave me real delight. I am sending you a picture too, by a later mail. I have inscribed it. And thank you for yours. You are a very piquant looking woman, and with dimples, it seems. Are you temperamental, and Puckish? My life here is very hard, because I have no one with me. . . . I may come out your way later." He also gave her his thoughts on romantic love, as he would with any new woman: "It is always passion. . . . It may be profound admiration. . . . It may be congeniality. . . . But it is nothing that has soared away from the physical in the sense that a flame sometimes leaps out and separates itself from the smoke stack. . . . I love to hear from you. You say much that interests me." In the end this flicker of interest in Mrs. London yielded no new relation (although they would correspond periodically), and so his life was spared a new entanglement.[11]

At the same time, however, he was lonely and having trouble sleeping, his mind occupied with his worsening financial condition. He nervously called his lawyers (who had no news) and wandered sorrowfully over his pretty little farm taking pictures, sending copies of these to Tietjens: "I took these pictures the other day, in anticipation of this place being taken away from me. . . . I want you to have these copies." To keep his wife from getting Twelve Acres, he briefly contemplated deeding it to *Poetry*'s Harriet Monroe for "the cause of poetry." "Why not deed it to you," he wrote Monroe, "for the benefit of young and indigent poets as a resting and dreaming place?" This idea went nowhere, as it had nowhere to go (for he no longer had legal control of the farm), and he returned to other musings.[12]

He was afraid to leave Twelve Acres ("I do not know the minute that some one may come and try to lock the door on me"), but now it brought him no joy, and he began to look with jealous eyes on the careers of other writers whose lives were more settled; at other times he blamed the country for the abuse of its poets: "There are no pensions in this country, and I have carried a great burden for nearly 25 years, writing and studying all the while too. Is there no consideration for this? Look at [Robert] Frost: he never earned a tenth of what I have or carried these burdens that I have, nor [Edwin Arlington] Robinson, nor any of them." Masters's own creative work came to a halt. "For the first time in my life, my concentration has slacked," he wrote Alice Corbin Henderson. "I can't do a thing. The days go by with the smoking of a pipe, the writing of a few letters, and a sort of mild looking off into meaningless space." (Perhaps this was simply the look of shock as Masters calculated his legal fees. Helen Masters had no money, so that her legal costs would someday be lumped with his own to pay the five lawyers now in the case: Clarence Darrow, Frank Walker, Abe Meyer, Bill Slack, and Dan Pagelson.)[13]

In April Masters sought to alleviate his financial plight with a loan from his publisher but was summarily turned down. "There is no legal reason," he wrote George Brett at Macmillan, "why you cannot advance me a few thousand dollars." What he wanted in addition to the loan was a means of shielding his royalties by accepting them as advances, his reasoning being that no money could be paid to his wife or a receiver if there was no money in the publisher's account. He also concocted a scheme whereby he would "borrow $5,000 from the Bank of Manhattan" while pledging his contracts as security, with the bank "to receive [his] royalties from [Macmillan] to take care of the interest and the principal." Finally, he asked Macmillan to treat as "trade secrets" all information "surrounding the contracts" and to shield this information from his adversaries: "No information definite or general shall be given them except as it be obtained by regular process." Macmillan's options were limited, however, in part because its Chicago office had been served with papers regarding Masters's property. A trade secret was one thing, but a court order was another, and in the end none of Masters's schemes to guard his royalties worked.[14]

Not that he was in a mood to give in. He would be as stiff and unbending as his wife and her lawyers, he said, and devil take the hindmost, regardless of who got hurt. He explained his position to Slack: "I won't be put down, tied up, for the children, for her, for anything, and they can play on all the sob stuff, and lovely children stuff, and honor stuff, and other stuff that she and my enemies who are advising her can think of. Here I stand. And for God's sake get the reality and the truth of these considerations into your nut. It means a lot to my work." It was for art's sake, then, that he could not go back, as well as his oft-reiterated vow that he would never return to Helen, a remark he made so frequently to so many people that it seemed like a public boast, here addressed to Corinne Roosevelt Robinson: "I can do nothing about my own affairs. [They are] of long standing; and to retrace would be to return to an unlivable condition with the indurated wound of this separation added to it. I never turn back."[15]

Elsewhere, Lillian had finished her satchel of books and one day showed up in Detroit, where she contacted Masters and asked whether he would like to join her. Masters had begun calling her "Robin" in some of his letters and diary entries, perhaps to conceal her identity or perhaps because many of her letters mention the numerous robins in her yard (their early morning chirping sometimes kept her awake after a long night of partying): "Telephone from Robin from Detroit. Write her." Writing was superfluous, however, for Masters had not seen Lillian in eight months, since September 18, and his next diary entry shows he was "off to Detroit." Lillian, he noted on arriving, was "lovely."[16]

So it was not surprising that they soon got together at her home in Marion. Masters's diary shows that he spent the night of May 13 there, but the last full description of a meeting, which appears in an unpublished chapter of his autobiography, combines this May 13 meeting and a longer stay over June 5–8: "We drew up before the great porch and the Corinthian columns. We came to the door, and were admitted by the maid, who smiled and welcomed me when I first crossed the threshold. We went upstairs to Pamela's living room in this my home, as it had come to be. The pendulum of the French clock was still whirling; but the hearth was dark in the summer weather. We paused and looked at each other, Pamela and I." When Masters later described this visit to his boyhood chum Edwin Reese, he highlighted its imperfections, but Masters's diary for the meeting of June 7 shows that he was very satisfied, so much so that when he thought of leaving, he was drawn back: "Start to leave 9:15. Return. Now 12:15. Stay for Lady. Wonderful night."[17]

He presented details of this wonderful night more dramatically in an unpublished chapter of his autobiography. In a movingly written passage that reflects one of the saddest nights of his life, he recalled how the clock marked the hours as his time in the Sleeping Palace ran out:

> Like married persons tired from a long journey we went to bed; and Pamela, grieving but with no tears, pressed her lips against my cheek and throat and after a time fell into sleep. But I did not sleep. I lay there listening to her breathing, and watch-

> ing the shadows from the trees on the lawn wavering across the ceiling. I lay there listening to the street sounds that grew fainter, and to the gong of the French clock in the next room. Neither Pamela nor myself realized that we should never be together again, couched as lovers. But such was Fate. The next morning I was off to Spring Lake, and I was never in her house again.[18]

Pressure on him now mounted anew. Personal resources he had hitherto taken for granted all had questionable utility, and the stress of his situation made it impossible for him to do any new creative work. "Of course I can't write with this on my mind," he wrote Tietjens: "I am excessively nervous at times and can scarcely hold together. I haven't a place to go if ill. I get terrified with the prospects." He felt by now, too, that he could not again practice law in Chicago: "Poetry killed my law business; and when I talk to Slack and Meyer of trying to practice again, they say I can't do it, and I know they are right." Nor could he hope, as he sometimes did, simply to stay on somehow at Spring Lake and write. Helen Masters would not even consider a divorce unless she also received the farm.[19]

He now searched for new ways to wound her, for he thought that this might make her more tractable, while also wondering why she treated him so badly. "They have that house worth $18,000," he said of Helen's chief asset (from which she was making $200 per month by renting its rooms). "I wonder what they want," he asked Tietjens—the *they* being his wife and her numerous allies. "There is no more to be had except my destruction." Nevertheless, he added, "please send me the booklet of The Cordon club." The Cordon was one of his wife's principal social outlets, and he felt that a perusal of its register might yield some leverage he could raise against her.[20]

He never came close. He failed in part because after twenty-four years of marriage, he still did not understand his wife. Worse, he did not understand even when told he did not understand. As early as 1913 Theodore Dreiser had warned Masters that his wife would someday "surprise" him, for Dreiser recognized in Helen a tough and determined side quite different from the meek and compliant personality she showed Hyde Park and her husband. Masters's attitude at the start of the divorce proceedings indicates something of his naïveté in this regard: "I had said to my wife in our talk that I wanted to remain friends with her, and to maintain such relations with her and the daughters that we could meet for dinner or luncheon at times, and that there was no other civilized way to manage this separation." Helen's "capacity for stubborn resistance" (as he called it) had amazed him; plainly speaking, he had not thought she had the character to endure the problems he created. Even when she controlled everything except the shirt he donned on a particular day, Masters still believed that his wife was not very bright, that she could not, in fact, think on her own. "Tell me!" he questioned Eunice Tietjens, "Don't you think some very sinister person, subtle and highly inimical to me, is counseling her?" As he had phrased it to Dreiser in a philosophical letter a few years earlier, "When a man gets down, an erstwhile tractable wife can run over him." "Old Stick in the Mud" ("OSTIM," for short) was turning out to be well named.[21]

By the summer of 1922 Masters was again reduced to tenancy on his own farm, or more accurately, he was seeking a tenant for his farm. He augmented his income with lectures while working as quickly as possible on a new book. In May he appealed to Monroe to help find a tenant who would let him stay on in the status of a poor relation: "Can you think of anyone who would like to come here for the summer and let me board with them? They can have it free for my board and for the room of someone whom I must get to type for me. I have a book about half done. This is a good chance. I'd love to have you come if you can manage it. Think this over please and let me know."[22]

No one wanted his place this year, however, at least not on these terms, and he accelerated his work on his new novel, a family history tentatively entitled "The Houghtons." Diary entries show various days' output at 3,000, 4,900, and nearly 5,300 words. He also lectured and prepared future lectures, soliciting bookings at $150 apiece through the Redpath Bureau. He was paying dearly for the poor artistry of *Skeeters Kirby:* without an above-average book before the public, he had no new source of income. Frustrated, he attacked the Macmillan Company, claiming it had failed to promote *Mitch Miller,* which he now characterized as "the best boy's book that you publish." He chose to ignore the flaws in *Mitch Miller,* and it is clear that these tensions with his publisher came about simply because his need for money outran his royalties. The "unearned advances" on his books ($3,999.83) and author-generated costs for such things as revising proofs now totaled $4,551.65.[23]

And then Helen Masters finally agreed to a divorce. First, however, she or her lawyers decided to extract some of the money due her. The facts regarding this are sketchy because her side of the story is not public and because Masters and his lawyers conducted much of their business by telephone. Nevertheless, the information from Masters's diaries seems helpful: "Abe says he'll endorse note of $2,300." Because Masters owed $2,000 in back alimony and because $300 was one month's support payment, Helen Masters or her lawyers may simply have put these two figures together as an appropriate amount of cash to assuage her immediate needs. Because Masters was broke, Abe Meyer provided this money—after which Masters's other lawyer, Bill Slack, sent a telegraph confirming that the divorce terms had been met: "Wire from Bill saying proposition accepted. Good day." This was followed by news from Meyer that Masters might return to Illinois without being subject to a bond prohibiting his leaving the state: "Phone Abe Meyer who says all right to come back." The return to Chicago was so foreign to Masters's true wishes, however, that he began to speak casually of his death, doing so to Abe Meyer in late June: "In the event of my death, and with that in view, I want you protected. To this end, I am going to make an assignment to you of my royalties, which would soon pay you off with the impetus given them by circumstances then so useless to me." The circumstances failed to materialize, however, and Helen Masters filed for divorce in July, subsequently going to Maine "to be out of Chicago when the divorce was granted." So it was that Masters made plans to return to Chicago and resume the odious practice of law in order to finance the privilege of being sued for divorce by his wife.[24]

He was a portrait of a man divided, to say the least. The only way in which he could afford the divorce terms was to return to the law, but the mere thought of supporting his wife in the manner to which she had been accustomed was revolting to him, and he knew that she and the children would absorb every dollar he made from his much-compromised legal practice. Thus, even if he got his divorce, poetry would again be a part-time affair, and his wife, not he, would control Twelve Acres. Still, he could not live forever on loans and goodwill from his lawyers and others, nor could he exist as a writer with a court order that stymied publication. And what of Lillian? With all these thoughts on his mind, he closed Twelve Acres and returned to Chicago on July 1 to perform some legal work for a friend, Dr. Alexander Burke.[25]

For a day or two Masters seemed to be getting back into his old circle of friends, meeting with a former governor of Illinois: "Talk with Gov. [Charles] Deneen about Burke Case"; "Consultation with Deneen." Masters even invented a public reason to explain to Deneen and others why he was returning to the law: "This consequence is due to many things, but perhaps as much as anything else to the fact that the books upon which I counted most for returns were placed at a price that embarrassed their sale. And that might have been due in part to the state of the labor market and the price of materials."[26]

Masters had barely resumed his practice, however, when he was diverted by one of his own actions from the previous winter. In a moment when he was particularly irate with Helen Masters, he had filed an affidavit indicating that the house at 4853 Kenwood belonged not only to his wife but also to their daughters. One of the lawyers (an understudy to Darrow and Walker) had discovered this cloud on the title and now communicated the fact to Helen. She was in Maine, and although Masters filed a bill to remove the cloud, Helen insisted that nothing take place in her absence. Masters arranged a meeting with one of Helen's lawyers; the lawyer missed the meeting. Divorce proceedings ground to a halt. Masters later described this as "a turning point in [his] fate," and perhaps it was. This last delay, which Masters found especially vexing, may have heightened some of the ugliness that soon followed with Helen. It certainly exhausted the last of Lillian's patience: a lawyer who created legal impediments to his own divorce had problems that she could not address.[27]

In late July or early August Masters took an option on a law office in the same building as Bill Slack and held counsel with his client, Dr. Burke, but he could not keep his mind on the law. He conceived a plan for an American epic to be called "Atlantis" and then left for New York to market his new novel, "The

Houghtons." Unfortunately, Macmillan felt that this new work belonged not to Masters but to the receiver of his property, an opinion shared by two other publishers as well. Attempts to serialize the book were also fruitless.[28]

As his fifty-fourth birthday approached and passed in August, Masters spent two weeks with Lillian (she was in New York for the summer), but they occasionally feuded, and she had other suitors in visible attendance at the dinners she hosted at the Waldorf-Astoria and elsewhere: "She had rights, too, and she was saying that she ought to be married; while as long as I was in her life she could not enter upon any acquaintship [*sic*] that would lead to marriage or had that end in view. At the same time there were other men around her at this time, who seemed likely to me, and whom she treated with amiable comradeship, to say the least." She offered Masters her "friendship" and said he would "never want" (the same terms she might offer an elderly servant), but marriage to her now seemed out of the question.[29]

Worn out, an author without a publisher, a lawyer without clients, and a lover without a beloved, Masters contemplated suicide:

> It was now late August and I had not had a full night's sleep since June, and hardly since March. I was staying at the National Arts Club, and no matter what hour I went to bed I awoke to hear the clocks strike two, and to toss until four or five or later. Then the idea of suicide began to glimmer in my thinking, and grew more definite day by day. I kept thinking of safety razor blades with which to end myself. As I shaved in the morning, I would look at them and half apply them to my throat, even as I despised the cowardice of giving up the fight.

He took no steps to give up the fight, however, although he also considered poison, and as Lillian drifted away, he sought solace from a source without emotional complications, his 1921 drinking companion from the *Aquitania* and trip abroad, George C. Stokes.[30]

Stokes had been in New York City for the past year and a half, ever since the two men had shared some shipboard Scotch to help calm "the stormiest seas" Masters had ever seen. Masters had stayed in touch with Stokes, and now, as the emotional high seas caused by Lillian buffeted his stomach, he telephoned him. Stokes drove Masters around the New York area, listened to his problems, calmed him down, and informed him that he was preparing to drive back to Illinois, offering to take him along. Masters repeatedly declined until August 30, when Stokes suddenly announced that he was leaving the next morning. When Masters mentioned that he had a tentative agreement to rent a law office in Chicago, Stokes offered his encouragement, and Masters suddenly found himself planning to go to Chicago. He had exhausted all his opportunities in New York and required only a meeting with Lillian to explain his imminent departure.[31]

Their last meeting was not marred by emotion:

> She listened to my plans about returning to Chicago, and about trying the law again, for the most part in silence, in weariness too, as though there was nothing

> that she could say that would be of any help to me. When I told her that I was leaving the next morning early by motor with Stokes, she made no return at all that I have any memory of. . . . At midnight I arose to go. We stood by a table facing each other and saying little repetitious words. I took her in my arms and kissed her goodbye. . . . She returned my kiss lightly and without much feeling. I opened the door, and, without looking back, departed.

Masters's diary is equally unemotional: "Good bye to Peggy at 12 midnight."[32]

At 8:20 the next morning he and Stokes set out for Illinois. Stokes was a middle-aged businessman who had made his fortune during World War I and was now returning to northern Illinois to assume management of his wife's large farm near Streator. That fact alone might have generated respect in Masters, for he admired gentlemen farmers, seeing in them a reflection of his grandfather, Squire Davis Masters. No less important, Stokes had a background similar to Masters's and held some of the same opinions: "Like myself, he had been raised in Illinois, he had taught school as I had, he had made his own way without help, as I had, and he knew my life and circumstances from having passed through the same kind himself." He also liked a drink, as Masters did. Stokes was driving what Masters called "his great Cadillac car" to guide his personal stash of alcohol through Prohibition-era America to the farm in Illinois. (His wife had wisely decided to take the train.) Thus, while the interior of the Cadillac was loaded with trunks and personal items, the running boards were covered with suitcases "containing whisky and wine."[33]

The two men talked about Masters's personal problems as they drove and sometime before lunch began sampling the "precious contraband," as Masters referred to the cargo on the running boards. They filled the second day of the trip with "more hours of talking about [Masters's] affairs, and more drinks," and did the same on the third (meanwhile having two near-accidents), the "lawless freight" surviving it all: "Stokes speeded the car as before. We were running sixty miles an hour and more all the time. Crossing Indiana I have never experienced such heat, such blinding glare of a hot sun. The car seemed to cut through swaths of fire, where flames of purple, of red, of blue licked around the wheels. We stopped every now and then to take a drink of whisky, and toward evening, as we approached the Illinois line, we were both well stimulated." It was while they were having a drink with their evening meal in Champaign, Illinois, that Stokes came up with "a solution for everything": Masters should return to his wife. "Give her the Judas kiss," he said. "If you do, she will wipe out the default decree, and you will be a free man again, free for the law, for literature, for anything." Masters was dumbfounded, but he pondered the idea as he parted from Stokes on the next day and took an Illinois Central train to Chicago.[34]

He was met by Dr. Burke and after dinner went to his night's lodgings, probably the Illinois Athletic Club. Before retiring, however, Masters encountered an unidentified "lawyer friend" who informed him that the newspapers now had Lillian's picture and information regarding her relation with Masters and were waiting for an excuse to print a story. Frank Walker, the rumor went, would deal with Lillian as he had dealt with a certain "light" woman in "a notorious case years before." With all this added to his day, Masters went to bed and "woke up with a clear mind: I would give my wife the Judas kiss."[35]

Masters's reunion with Helen took place the next day, Monday, September 4, following phone calls and a meeting with his wife in Abe Meyer's office. Oddly, Masters failed to level with Meyer about his true motives ("I didn't give him my confidence at all as to what was in my mind"): "He telephoned my wife, and she was at his office in a half an hour, and going into consultation with him; I sat in another room waiting to be summoned when he had won her consent to a reconciliation. In a few minutes he called me in. There sat my wife smiling. She had agreed to vacate the decree if I came back to her. I stepped forward and gave her the Judas kiss. . . . Then I went back to that dreadful house. It was Labor Day, 1922." Masters spent the next day preparing to open a law office (his library and furniture were in storage) and saw the hated court decree vacated on September 6, but it was on that day, too, that the Chicago press ran front-page stories of his homecoming.[36]

The *Chicago Daily News* proclaimed, "Masters Are Reunited" and "Wife's Counsel Prepares Papers to Set Aside Divorce Action":

> After three years' separation due to misunderstandings and temperamental outbursts, Edgar Lee Masters, poet, lawyer, and author, and his wife, Helen Jenkins Masters, have decided to accord mutual forgiveness and to live together again at their home, 4853 Kenwood Avenue.
>
> For some days past, rumors that the couple had effected a reconciliation were in circulation, but today, for the first time, a member of the family confirmed the reports.

It fell to Masters's daughter Madeline to affirm that her father had returned, but she could not confirm "the rumor that her parents were about to leave the city on a second honeymoon." Frank Walker was quoted as saying that he was preparing "the necessary papers to set aside the suits for separate maintenance and divorce brought by Mrs. Masters." Masters had returned to his wife and had promised to "be good," according to another newspaper.[37]

The *Chicago Tribune* printed much the same information, according Masters the dubious distinction of appearing three times in its pages: in a "news summary" on page 1, in a headline story on page 1 ("Poet and Wife Drop Divorce"), and in a photograph on the back page. There were actually two pictures: one showed Masters by himself as he looked at the time of *Spoon River;* the other showed Helen Masters in a large overstuffed chair surrounded by her three children. (The two daughters, impishly cute, wore little-girl ribbons and bows; Hardin managed a faint smile and slightly resembled the author F. Scott Fitzgerald.) One of the reporters wondered about "another woman," but he had no definite information, and Lillian's name did not surface. On the other hand, all

Chicago now knew of Masters's marital imbroglio and read details alongside news of President Harding's Teapot Dome affair, the Herrin (Illinois) Massacre, and other state and national scandals surfacing in the summer of 1922. It was on September 6 too that Dr. Burke sent Masters a letter congratulating him on what Burke called "this beautiful reunion . . . , surely, as you so aptly said, the inspiration for a poem." The poem would follow later. Masters wrote "Tears" in his diary that night and the next and sought something to help him sleep.[38]

He now went about his business as Dr. Burke's lawyer and had "books and chairs" in his new office by mid-September, but his heart was not in his work, and several of his diary entries read simply "Bad day." A few days later he noted that he was feeling "dizzy." Perhaps he was simply feeling guilty, as he admitted in an early draft of his autobiography: "I loathed myself for the lie I enacted; I felt covered with nauseating slime for the deception." On the first month's anniversary of his return to Chicago, he received "$30 from *Poetry* for 'Worlds,'" a poem in which he cast himself as an elderly pauper in the charity ward of a hospital, and then spent the next morning (October 4) in court. Life had reverted to what it had been in 1919: he was a Chicago lawyer making less money than he needed, a part-time poet writing less well than he should, and a very unhappy husband. Lillian learned of the reconciliation from friends and newspaper accounts and wrote to say she felt "betrayed"; he had not told her he was returning to his wife.[39]

Masters did not really give his reunion with Helen a chance. For a time he slept in the back of his house with a trunk blocking his door at night; that is, he did not immediately resume conjugal relations. Moreover, he was not truly living at home. He left the house before his wife arose and came home after she retired, not even taking meals there. Some nights he stayed at the Illinois Athletic Club or at hotels. He was also gone on Sundays and saw at various times Dr. Burke (for cocktails) or a Catholic priest he knew, Father John Doody (for cocktails), and between times he sat in his son's room on the third floor and sipped wine and felt out of sorts. He felt a little more out of sorts when he was from time to time dunned the $500 he owed his wife's lawyers for engineering this misery.[40]

He sought to alleviate his unhappiness in the usual way. Although he later wrote that he and Lillian "exchanged no letters" at this time, within three weeks of his homecoming he had received two letters from her and sent her a reply in which he justified his return to his wife while promising Lillian his undying love: "[Helen] had already set going the press against me. . . . Outside of a few elect spirits, nearly everyone was against me. I have seen men crushed by this popular resentment. . . . I haven't the sand to suicide; but with you lost to me I see no use in life at all. It is an immeasurable futility to me now. You will go out of my heart when it ceases to beat." He also lied to her outright: "I came back here expecting to be free. She would not free me."[41]

Nevertheless, his avowed passion did not prevent him from flirting via the mails with another woman, Margery Currey, the former wife of the Chicago novelist Floyd Dell (author of *Moon-Calf*). She was, he wrote her in Seattle, "one of the most enticing women [he] ever knew," "a fine woman," and one for whom he would do "anything": "My dear, I think you have managed your own soul superbly, and I admire you awful much. Among other things, I have a drive now to help people; for I am a large Cask of Amontillado window on all sorts of curious and subtle life problems." In fact, he had helped a woman "just yesterday," he said. Maybe Masters seemed a little too eager; maybe it was the "Cask of Amontillado" metaphor and the view of the tomb of Edgar Allan Poe's famous victim. In any event, Margery Currey did not follow up on this solicitation, thus missing her little glass of amontillado at a Chicago speakeasy, and Masters felt free to look elsewhere.[42]

According to his diary for October 6, he again looked at Ellen Coyne, the woman he would eventually marry in 1926. She was now twenty-three (Masters was fifty-four), and although he had encountered her in 1919 and 1920, she does not show up in his diary for 1921. So their meeting on this day in 1922 may simply have been an accident. She was neither responsible for his present problems nor the solution to them, and they once again parted, she to pursue an acting career, he to go home to his wife—the keeper of the "autumnal morgue," as he was now referring to his home in some sonnets he had begun.[43]

These sonnets became his outlet for describing his feelings about returning to his wife, and because he had much to say and felt intensely, he eventually wrote "fifty" of them, or "nearly fifty" (he cited both figures). Unfortunately, words alone could not relieve the anger he felt, and on the morning of November 15, he struck Helen Masters during one of their arguments. As usual, the couple came away with different accounts of the incident, hers being that he had hit her because she was late for breakfast. The *Chicago Herald and Examiner* said that Masters "slapped" his wife; the *Chicago Tribune* referred to it as "striking" her. Masters said in one account that he had "pushed her about" but admitted in another that he had "slapped" her twice when she suggested he had returned home voluntarily. Regardless, he had now added physical abuse to his list of marital sins.[44]

Except for the sonnets, Masters's writing had pretty well come to a halt after he returned home. For one thing, he found the house cold and uncomfortable; for another, there were strangers lounging about some of the rooms, namely, the tenants to whom his wife had rented rooms to support herself: "The house was partly occupied by second-rate roomers. Every room was in disorder. The furnace did not work, and the first few nights that I was home I sat shivering before a grate fire in the dining room."[45]

To augment his income, he gave lectures and readings. He was asking $100 for a reading, but there were endless minutiae as to exactly what he would do during a reading or lecture and the individuals with whom he would deal, and if travel was involved, there were three expenses to be considered: railroad fare, hotel bill, and possibly sleeper fare. In addition, Masters had to maintain his image as a poet, so it was necessary to settle questions about the program, such as whether he would speak before, during, or after a dinner. Sometimes it was best to give directions, as here for a Mr. Mackoy: "You should announce me as giving a reading, and while I enjoy a banquet where I have nothing to do, I cannot mix one with a part to perform, unless I simply sit and nibble. As far as I can see now, I think that you would better have your program, and then when you are ready for me I shall come in and read. Then after the reading I shall be glad to see and visit with your members as long as I have time before the train back to Chicago. Will you kindly write me about these several matters at once." Finally, if a lecture agency was involved, it would take 20 percent of the fee, sometimes leaving Masters with his labor and not much more (similar rates would prevail through his seventieth year).[46]

As to his legal business, numerous incidents show that Slack and Meyer were correct in saying he could not return to it. He started out anew on September 5 without a desk, secretary, telephone, legal library, or clients (except for Dr. Burke), and although Abe Meyer sent him referrals through the fall, clientele and cash were not what they had once been. Nevertheless, he printed cards showing that he was again at work:

EDGAR L. MASTERS
HAS ENGAGED IN THE PRACTICE OF LAW
AT
1440 AMERICAN BOND & MORTGAGE BUILDING
CHICAGO

He also sent letters to old friends announcing his return to the law, including this one to Monroe on September 12: "Dear Harriet—There ought to be some high class business up your way, requiring finesse and careful consultation, and imaginative management. I am in this office, and I can't call it being yoked because everyone is that, and one has duties; but at least I am flowing, not flying. What can I do for you?"[47]

Such efforts turned out to be essentially worthless, for Masters's return to his wife would ultimately deepen the schism developing between him and Chicago. He looked on his homecoming as a personal humiliation, and this bred in him an exaggerated hostility toward those friendly in any way to Helen—women friends, old acquaintances, nonwriters, and others. It was a stance for which he had been preparing all his life. The world was an adversarial place after all, as he had witnessed in his parents' relations and in his relations with his brother, Tom, and sister, Madeline, and with Darrow and other lawyers and their clients. Two such clients, he and Helen, were adversaries now. Anyone or any institution that seemed friendly to her was against him. Jealous of his fame, anxious to see him get his comeuppance, a densely populated group called "they" had become his enemies: "They hated me for what I had done; they feared me as a voice; they envied the distinction that had come to me. Like the mob at the circus, like the psychology of the crowd that wanted to see the champion dethroned, the leader degraded, they rejoiced in the capitulation to which I had come by the coercion of circumstances."[48]

Masters was especially angered by the newspapers, particularly the *Chicago Daily News,* where Carl Sandburg worked as a reporter to augment his income as a poet. Masters insisted that Sandburg could have lessened the attacks that Chicago newspapers made on him and his works: "The literary pages of Chicago teemed with snipers who shot at me unceasingly from ambush. Many of these were the desk mates of a Chicago poet who could have controlled them as I had softened the criticism of Reedy against him who thought that this poet was nothing but a socialist. These desk mates of his seemed to act on the conviction that my declension was his ascension; but I was not declining and he was not ascending." Masters was wrong, of course: his decline as a poet was well underway, and his decline as a lawyer had gone too far to reverse.[49]

In fact, within a few weeks after returning to his law office, Masters had discovered that most of his old clientele wanted little to do with him. His letter of December 12, 1922, to his Michigan lawyer, Daniel Pagelson, illustrates his situation:

> The picking here is very sparin' as you might guess. To get organized again, to piece one's self together again is a hard thing to do. . . . I oscillate between leaving literature forever, or, on the other hand, making a Herculean effort to reform my lines all anew. . . . I am bending my efforts the meanwhile to pay my debts, which are very many, and I have scraped together since your letter came another $50, which is enclosed. That leaves a balance according to your bill of $50, which I wish you would forgive if you can. I have already paid you $175.

All in all, Masters said he hated the "damn business" of law (to use a polite abridgement of his actual expression). He told an acquaintance he felt like "Apollo cleaning sewers," and his diary for fall 1922 shows few entries related to law cases. His hatred of law is best illustrated by his tardiness in having a telephone installed. Callers to the number he gave out—Central 6083—would have been informed that they had reached the "Chicago Singletax Club," a political group whose secretary had agreed to take messages for him. (He occasionally borrowed the group's stationery as well.)[50]

December 1922 was joyless. Masters's diary for the month is blank, with the exception of one entry showing that he borrowed $2,100 from his friend and client Dr. Burke: "Burke—borrowed 2100." The money was used in part to provide his children with a Christmas. Marcia Lee Masters, then thirteen, later described the occasion in a poem entitled "Childhood Christmas—Before the Divorce," probably making use of some earlier times as well:

The lights upon the tree
Shimmered like a gale of fireflies.

But father sat there in the shadows,
His chair pushed back
From glittering strings
And sleighbell papers, silvery scenes
Of little towns too pretty to be real;
The bright upheaval he disliked
Of angels, Santa Claus, and elves;

While we, impervious as seagulls,
Dived down to get the loot,
Whistling as we brought gifts up—
Games, dolls, and drums, and books;
A beaver hat that father bought for me,
A green purse that we bought for him
To give to mother,
Who stared above our heads
With wounded, Bible eyes.

* * *

Too soon, the gathering over,
The white cloth lifted,
Father gone.
And nothing left but snow
Rattling our casement windows,
And wind—making the branches snap
Like hard-closed gates.

By New Year's or perhaps a little before, Masters and his wife were both ready to end the marriage, and divorce proceedings began anew after he took up residence in Chicago hotels in early February.[51]

Unfortunately, his plan of supporting himself through fiction was not doing well (his gross income for 1922 had been $4,600), and his September 1922 comment to his Michigan lawyer—"I don't write best sellers"—seemed particularly apt at this point. Certainly he was having no luck in placing the manuscript of *The Nuptial Flight* (at this point still called "The Houghtons"). His diary shows he sent a "letter [to] Harcourt offering 'Houghtons,'" but Harcourt turned it down, as did Doubleday. His earlier novel, *Skeeters Kirby,* was at last free of the entanglements of the receivership, but as of February 21 it was neither in Chicago bookstores nor being advertised. Nor did he feel much better when the book finally arrived; despite all his troubles with this autobiographical story, his diary describes "*Skeeters Kirby* [as] a best seller in Chicago" for only one day. Masters would always be convinced that his marital litigation hurt the sales of books from this period (especially *Children of the Market Place*), although there is no objective evidence of this. In any event, his financial distress caused him to work on the only surefire moneymaker at his disposal—a sequel to *Spoon River Anthology.*[52]

More accurately, he began to collect and add to the epitaphs he already had. After the initial publication of *Spoon River*'s 214 poems in the first edition of 1915, Masters had prepared an additional 32 pieces for the augmented (or definitive) edition of 1916. During the next several years, he traded on *Spoon River*'s name with such titles as "Spoon River Revisited" and "More Spoon River Poems" in magazines such as *The New Republic* and *The Literary Digest.* In July 1921 he told Maurice Brown that he had "about 20 epitaphs to add to *Spoon River* some time." Two years later, however, when his money problems were acute, and after encouragement from literary admirers, Masters noted in his diary that he had "146 epitaphs done." He had also developed a plan to market them: he would first publish them serially in a periodical and then collect them in book form, a tactic that had worked well with the original epitaphs. He had 182 epitaphs completed by April 4, 1923, and "sent [some] epitaphs to Hovey of Hearst's *International.*" That failed to yield the interest he was seeking, so he delivered the manuscript to *Vanity Fair* on April 10 and reached an agreement calling for him to receive $1,500 for 150 epitaphs to be published serially beginning in the summer of 1923. He also agreed to a contract with the Bell Syndicate for secondary serialization of the epitaphs in several newspapers. Interestingly, he felt no compunction to pay off his $4,000 debt to the Macmillan Company. George Brett Jr. did not even know of the new epitaphs until well after Masters had signed with *Vanity Fair* (and *Vanity Fair* seems not to have known of Masters's plans with the Bell newspapers until the poems began appearing therein).[53]

His life was made a little more interesting at this time when Whitman Bennett Studios contacted him on April 20 about "film possibilities of some of [his] verses." Masters had been actively hoping for a movie contract for more than a year and daydreaming of one intermittently since 1915. This time he decided to use an agency, as he mentioned to Abe Meyer on April 23: "I am at work with a scenario writer for a movie from *Spoon River.* The Famous Players are the people." The scenario was completed in a week or ten days but then read and rejected in about the same time. Masters blamed the scenario's writer, who Masters felt had not captured the full panorama of *Spoon River,* as he remarked to Famous Players' E. Lloyd Sheldon: "All the way along I was saying that I did not want *Spoon River* reduced to a mere story, and certainly not a conventional or trite story." It was, of course, impossible for any writer to capture the many voices of *Spoon River* in the era of silent films, but as Masters could not have anticipated "talkies," this was just a sour experience for him. It was made a little worse by the fact that he himself contributed to the failure of the script: several of the diary entries for late April show that he wrote on the Spoon River scenario. Still, the experience had planted in his mind the idea that his books were of potential appeal to Hollywood, and this would lead to numerous similar efforts.[54]

During this same time, Masters was lobbying with Liveright's to publish *The Nuptial Flight* and privately circulating some or all of the sonnets he had composed about his September 1922 return to Helen Masters. He also had a feeler out to the British publisher Hodder and Stoughton that resulted in the sale of *Children of the Market Place.* Masters was in New York attending to one or another of these activities on May 3, 1923, when his divorce was at last finalized; a lawyer working both for Darrow and as "general counsel" for the University of Chicago (probably Wallace Heckman) was instrumental at last in removing the cloud on the title of the house.[55]

Masters summarized the news and his feelings to Harriet Monroe on the next day: "Last night at 8:30 I received a telephoned telegram to the effect that I was divorced. It happened yesterday at about one o'clock. So that is that; and I slept wondrously last night. I am getting ready now to write something, and I am looking for a place in which to do it. I have business matters to arrange and then I want to settle and be undisturbed for awhile. . . . I really hope to get into the wilds somewhere in a flannel shirt and walking shoes, etc." He would not get into the wilds at his present location, however, for he was staying with friends at Great Neck, New York, nor would he ever again roam Twelve Acres.[56]

Masters gained his freedom at the expense of his fortune, losing to his wife his beloved farm in Michigan (valued at $10,000) and the Chicago town house (now worth $20,000). He was also assessed a one-time cash settlement of $3,000 and alimony of $150 per month. He was allowed to keep his copyrights, royalties, and library. The *Chicago Tribune* blamed the unraveling of the marriage on the slapping incident of the previous fall, an instance of "breakfast table autocracy":

> WIFE OF POET MASTERS
> TO GET CRUELTY DECREE
>
> Breakfast table autocracy indulged in by Edgar Lee Masters, poet, author, and attorney, wrecked . . . his recent reconciliation with Mrs. Helen Jenkins Masters. . . .
>
> "For a few days our relations were very friendly, after he had begged me to take him back on Sept. 6 last," declared Mrs. Masters. "Then he gradually grew cool and climaxed his cruel attitude by striking me twice on the same day, Nov. 15, 1922, because I was late to breakfast."
>
> Mrs. Masters . . . will be granted a divorce decree which will include provision for cash alimony of $3,000, $150 monthly, and title to the Masters home at 4853 Kenwood Avenue, as well as a summer home at Spring Lake, Mich.

Helen Masters was also awarded custody of their two minor children, Marcia and Madeline, although Masters was granted permission to visit.[57]

In addition, Masters also lost much of what was left of his good name, and this would hurt him in a variety of ways. Some of the most important people in Chicago were "Subscribers to the Fund" of *Poetry* magazine, for example. Those who sympathized with Helen might bring pressure to bear against him through *Poetry.* And what of the larger media? The *Chicago Tribune* (which claimed a weekday circulation of a half-million) had written of him as a "poet, author, and attorney," and although these terms accurately described him, the most lucrative of these avenues of employment suffered from newspaper notoriety. Who would entrust an important legal case to an attorney who was known as a wife beater? And if he did receive an important case, would his reputation prejudice a jury? All this, however, was "just Sunday School persiflage" (as he had once written of Darrow) compared to what Masters would next do to himself.[58]

Masters in 1922, shortly before his divorce. (Courtesy of the Illinois State Historical Library)

Tennessee Mitchell. Masters "contracted madness in her kiss."
(Photo courtesy of the Newberry Library, Chicago)

Lillian Pampell Wilson. Masters felt she was "the magic princess of the sleeping palace" and left his wife to pursue her. (Photography Collection, Harry Ransom Humanities Research Center, the University of Texas at Austin)

Helen Jenkins Masters and her children, Marcia (left), Madeline, and Hardin, in a newspaper photo printed during the divorce. (*Chicago Tribune*)

Clarence Darrow. Masters's former law partner represented Helen Jenkins Masters during the writer's bitter divorce. (Corbis)

Ellen Coyne in 1922. (Photography Collection, Harry Ransom Humanities Research Center, the University of Texas at Austin)

Masters in 1926 shortly before his marriage to Ellen Coyne. (Photography Collection, Harry Ransom Humanities Research Center, the University of Texas at Austin)

Masters with Hilary in 1935. (Photography Collection, Harry Ransom Humanities Research Center, the University of Texas at Austin)

The return of the native. Masters at the Petersburg Centennial, September 1936. (Photography Collection, Harry Ransom Humanities Research Center, the University of Texas at Austin)

Masters and Alice Davis, a quiet evening at the Hotel Chelsea, 1939. (Photography Collection, Harry Ransom Humanities Research Center, the University of Texas at Austin)

Masters in his Hotel Chelsea apartment, April 1940. (Photography Collection, Harry Ransom Humanities Research Center, the University of Texas at Austin)

Ellen, Hilary, and Edgar Lee Masters at Davidson College, spring 1945. (Photography Collection, Harry Ransom Humanities Research Center, the University of Texas at Austin)

On "the hill" in Petersburg. (Photography Collection, Harry Ransom Humanities Research Center, the University of Texas at Austin)

CHAPTER 10

Satin Apples, Sour Grapes

I am tired of fame that can't be eaten—merely satin apples.

—Edgar Lee Masters to H. S. Latham, October 12, 1922

Following his divorce, much of Masters's life reverted to what it had been during his bachelor years ("I live at a hotel and eat at the restaurant, and sew on my own buttons," he explained to Lillian Wilson in June). But much of his life was drastically changed for the worse. He was no longer a young lawyer and part-time poet slowly ascending Chicago's social ladder but was instead unambiguously descending it. He rented from Bill Slack a less-expensive law office at 127 North Dearborn but was seldom in it and seems to have made little money from the law. Whatever money he did make was earmarked by the court for his wife and children. His social decline did not seem likely to change.[1]

Nor did he do anything to invite change. "Chicago," he would say for the next twenty years, was "the most awful hole this side of hell." His divorce represented "a choice between keeping the money and being rid of the woman" ("the woman goes down in the scale as the alimony goes up"). And the newspaper stories were simply venal pieces directed by such people as the McCormicks, who owned the *Chicago Tribune* ("the McCormicks are the source of the cancerous condition of that town"). As for other rumors, well, some of them were traceable directly to Helen Jenkins Masters, he averred, explaining in verse to Eunice Tietjens:

ODE TO FAME

Masters! What are those whispers, whispers,
Whispers about your morals?
Says he that's just the Jenkins tribe
Pissing on my laurels.[2]

Masters sometimes enjoyed the circulation of rumors and racy facts about his personal life, equating them as proof of name recognition, sexual charm, or both. After one of his post–*Spoon River* trips to the East, for example (and talk of him and "a girl in New York"), he had boasted to Harriet Monroe, "There must be a lot of wild stories in circulation about me." By the spring of 1923, however, each new story further distanced him from his legal clientele, or at least the moneyed set, and this further hobbled his career as a lawyer. His problems were exacerbated because his sister, Madeline, was undergoing an unfriendly divorce from her second husband, Neils Gron. (Gron's lawyer read portions of *Spoon River Anthology* in court to show that all the Masterses were "bad and immoral.") Because Madeline's first marriage to Dr. Carl Stone, now deceased, had brought her considerable social prominence, this breakup of her second union seemed newsworthy to the Chicago press. "The Chicago papers ran columns every day," Masters said, "always beginning by saying that she was my sister." Nor did it help that Masters's son was divorced at about this time. Hardin had made a truly bad marriage to a woman who literally had no idea what marriage entailed, and when his divorce was finalized in February 1923, the press as far away as New York City discussed his marital problems alongside those of his father. The entire family, it seemed, was emotionally unstable, cursed with bad judgment, or litigious. The facts were laid out in the papers.[3]

In fact, so much was known of Masters's personal life and attitudes, including his growing contempt for Chicago, that the city had begun to fight back. *Chicago Daily News* reporter Keith Preston had begun the attack a little before Masters and George Stokes set out on the six-state drinkathon that brought Helen Masters her "Judas kiss":

> Edgar Lee Masters doesn't like Chi;
> Furthermore he tells us the why!
> Firstly he finds we are drying as drinkers:
> Second he thinks we are trying as thinkers.
> Edgar Lee Masters doesn't like Chi.
> What'll we do? Lie down and die?
>
> Never, no never! Edgar would laugh,
> Write us a helluvan epitaph.
> Read the *Anthology*, brothers and shiver!
> Shall we be dumb as the dead of Spoon River?
> Lo, those poor hicks that lay under the asters!
> Living at least we annoy Mr. Masters.

When Preston's poem was printed in *The Bookman*, it achieved a national circulation far beyond the *Daily News*'s regional one. *The Bookman* mitigated the sting of Preston's piece by noting that people still admired Masters's "great and permanent achievement" of *Spoon River* (and that he himself represented an "imminent presence"), but with one thing or another, by the spring of 1923 Masters had little left to lose in Chicago. And Chicago was about through with him also. As one critic phrased it, "For Masters[,] that loose federation, the so called Chicago literary school, does not exist. Only Masters exists, a magnificent solitary."[4]

Nor did Masters's fellow poets do him much good. Word of Masters's denigration of Amy Lowell got back to her, and she wrote a suitable response in verse in her much-read book *A Critical Fable:*

> The man whom I next shall bring to the fore
> Is becoming, I fear, an impossible bore.
>
> * * *
>
> But hey, Mr. Masters, how weary and dreary
> You make all your folk! How impossibly smeary
> And sticky they are with old amorous contacts,
> A series of ticketed, sexual facts
> Tucked away, all unwashed, in the ground.

He was, she concluded, a one-book author:

> As it is, his caprice
> Has given us only a great Masters' piece. . . .
> He tries lyrics, and ballads, and novels in verse,
> But lacks always the wit to return to the terse.[5]

Masters was living in these days at 1425 North Dearborn Street but felt this address was so transitory or shabby that he listed the Illinois Athletic Club as his "permanent address." Surprisingly enough, he still had some cash on hand. Within a week of his divorce he had received a $2,500 advance on a manuscript that would become *The Nuptial Flight,* and he had either sold or was about to sell a draft of *Domesday Book* to the University of California for $1,000; he accomplished the latter through an agent, however, and probably gave up 10–15 percent of this amount. (He was unable to discuss selling the far more valuable first draft of the *Spoon River Anthology,* for it no longer existed: "How I would have preserved the originals," his secretary, Jake Prassel, later wrote him, "had I known *Spoon River* was going to cause the stir it did.") In addition, the newspaper serialization of *The New Spoon River* with the Bell Syndicate brought in some cash. More surprisingly, Masters had one piece of real estate that Helen Masters had failed to get, a lot in a Cook County subdivision; unfortunately, he had either forgotten or failed to pay the taxes for so many years that legal encumbrances now exceeded its market value (it was apparently sold for taxes about 1926). Nor is it likely he kept for long the advance on the new book. He owed Abe Meyer more than $3,000 for the loan that helped seal the divorce, and diary entries for May 5 ("send Abe $2,000") and May 10 ("send Abe $1,000") suggest that Masters was soon low on money. Darrow may still have owed him $9,000, but when Masters asked him for a loan of "a few hundred dollars," Darrow arranged for Masters to meet the loan officer of a bank. When Masters's friend Dr. Burke invited him to travel to California, Masters vacillated and then refused, saying that his parents were too ill, but his decision was probably based on his financial condition.[6]

Or maybe some hope with Lillian held him back. Free at last of Helen Masters, he briefly pursued Lillian again, writing (she said) two or three letters a day, such as this one from June 12: "I can imagine no happiness like two winning it together, consciously striving for it together, for the sake of themselves and each other. This kept running through my head yesterday, and last night. I did not sleep well, but only just for a sort of raptness of thought about this possibility. And, too, I was thinking of those prose philosophizings of yours, that you showed me at first, flashes of genius like ore freshly dug." When Lillian indicated that her writing was a thing of the past, as distant as her childhood, Masters remonstrated with her: "Why talk of putting writing away with the toys of childhood in the attic? Be careful! Don't dawdle and then evolve too late. You can do it. . . . Since your thoughts and fancies run to gnomic things, why not poems, just in your own way, thoroughly individual, and cryptic . . . ? Listen, my dear! Before you is the task of working to the best that fine and big self of you, while still retaining the charm of the little girl." Unfortunately, the "girl" for whom Masters had given up so much was no longer interested in being his artistic soul mate but was planning to leave for good.[7]

Perhaps she had been changed by the "severe illness" and operation she had suffered immediately after Masters returned to his wife. He both blamed and flattered himself that the imminent loss of his own company had occasioned this debility, as he wrote in an unpublished chapter of his autobiography: "She . . . fell desperately ill over what had happened, and in a few days was on the operating table." (He decided not to tell his prospective readers that Lillian had simply had a case of appendicitis.) Or maybe she recognized a certain mercantile hesitancy on Masters's part. He had harbored a nagging fear that Lillian's windfall fortune might somehow disappear since, as he said, most of it "consisted of stocks, which were worthless if the business of the corporations fell off. And so if I had married Pamela, she might have turned up poor." Then again, perhaps Lillian did not like the new terms Masters suggested, here in a letter of June 12: "It ought not to be a strangling alliance," he wrote, but "ought to be severable at will": "I have a certain proposition to make to you. I found today the gold ring that my grandmother [Lucinda Masters] wore. . . . It kicks around in my tin box, and will eventually be lost. I want to give it away; for originally I gave it to her. . . . It . . . would be nice to give a FRIEND, meaning FRIENDSHIP

AND NOTHING ELSE!! And I pick you; you can take it or leave it as you choose."[8]

Two weeks later he sweetened this proposition with an offer to marry her, but the offer was too satiric to take seriously:

> Suppose we did get married. It would be no killing matter. And then if we were and after, there would be no [more sensational newspaper] items. You never saw a newspaper print an item like this:
>
> "Mr. and Mrs. Peggy Wilson are living happy this summer."
>
> It's always something like this:
>
> "It is rumored that Mr. Peggy Wilson will seek a divorce charging his wife with having slapped him repeatedly at the golf links last summer."

As Dorothy Dow had tartly observed, "He was not a romantic wooer."[9]

In fact, Masters was again seeing Dow for walks, talks, and luncheons, and one day in June she or someone like her suggested marriage to him, or so he reported to Lillian: "I was proposed to this week by a lovely and loving young poetess, who has the dream of an indissoluble and eternal alliance, one extending even after death. When I told her that there was no marriage in heaven, she said with perfect shamelessness that she didn't care, that she would live with me there just the same. I couldn't see it; and so I say with these limitations and understandings, marriage might do." Although Dow may have made such a proposal, there is something decidedly suspicious about the anonymity of the proposer as well as the moral of this little tale, namely, that it meets exactly Masters's criterion for a relation that is "severable at will," even in that distant haven where permanence is thought to be paramount.[10]

When the newspapers showed an interest in Lillian, Masters prepared for her approval some remarks aimed at misleading nosy reporters. (One reporter had already shown up on her doorstep to ask whether she and Masters would now marry; the reporter had handed her the day's mail with Masters's return address showing on the uppermost letter.) A draft of Masters's planned remarks ("a little statement to be given the press") follows: "I am told by representatives of the press that there are rumors which connect the name of Mrs. Wilson with mine in a contemplated marriage between us. There is no truth in these reports, though I should feel honored if there were. But my circumstances and preoccupations are such that I am compelled to live just as I am living, alone and hard at work. Mrs. Wilson has many interests herself, and I cannot conceive of her marrying anyone." This, Masters suggested, would allow them to continue their relation as they wished, but "without the trammel of a public interpretation which embarrasses social freedom." The statement was apparently never released, principally because there was no need for it: the relation was at last over.[11]

As Masters explained things to his mother on June 30, Lillian was "ill, and tired, and out of humor . . . [and] writes me that she has dismantled her house and is going east": "Her going east consists in getting a room at the Waldorf and just staying there, and entertaining the people that drift around. When I first knew her she was more or less studious and was writing. She seems to have lost all her ambition [and] talks of never writing another line. . . . Perhaps some kind of a wise god is keeping us apart after all. For I never could stand her as she is now."[12]

True to his word, he began an extremely unflattering novel about her the next day and completed it a month later. Published in 1924 as *Mirage* (it had first been called "Love," after its subject, and then "Arthur Kirby," after its autobiographical protagonist), the novel describes Masters's search for a satisfying relation with several women, including Lillian. She had written him but once in July and not at all in August—but by mid-August he was embroiled in a new controversy and had bruited details of the matter from coast to coast and overseas in the pages of *Poetry* magazine.[13]

Things had begun innocently enough on the day before Masters's divorce. After more than a decade of looking after the needs of *Poetry,* Harriet Monroe remarked in the announcements section of the May 1923 issue that she would "sail for Europe on the second of May in pursuit of a real vacation." She indicated that she would meet some of her recent contributors in England and France and asked in a friendly way for the goodwill and cooperation of her magazine's "subscribers and other readers." More important, she left Masters's friend Tietjens in charge of the magazine during her absence:

> The editor *pro tempore,* during the summer and early autumn, will be Eunice Tietjens (Mrs. Cloyd Head), who was associate editor in 1916–17 and will now have a chance to carry out whatever ideas may then have been nipped in the bud. . . . Miss Monroe is convinced that after ten-and-one-half years of her management, during which period she has arranged and carried through the press every number but one, the magazine will benefit by a change. Mrs. Tietjens is to have absolute control, within necessary financial and space limitations, of the next four numbers.

And so it was that *Poetry* became important to the aftermath of Masters's stormy divorce.[14]

Masters sent Tietjens a long poem that the more conservative Monroe would probably have rejected. This, "The Return," chronicled in thirteen sonnets the "return" Masters had made to his wife in the fall of 1922. It was a part of the sonnet sequence of fifty or so poems that he had privately circulated during the winter of 1922–23. He had suffered much, he said, and for a long time as well, and since he believed his sonnets "told a story of spiritual torture and degradation scarcely to be paralleled in the world," he did not now mince words. They turned out to be very sharp words, in part because he had already practiced them: thirteen years earlier, when Helen Masters had prevented him from marrying Tennessee Mitchell, he had concluded *Songs and Sonnets* with twenty-eight sonnets about the complications of love. Buried in that obscure volume, the poems had not made much of an impression, but now Helen had stood in his way a second time, and this time he was going to get even.[15]

The first sonnet told of Masters's doleful approach on a rainy day to his once-attractive house and of the homecoming awaiting him there:

When he returned he saw the porch at first
Where cornices and pillars showed decay.
The entrance door was scaling, seemed accursed;
The water troughs had rusted quite away.
Then it was raining, and the house was cold;
And over wires for lights, the telephone,
A vine hung thick as moss, and the rain tolled
The minutes in a minor monotone.
He stood beside a window and looked out
Into a yard of tangled grass and leaves.
And the rain swished from a half broken spout,
And gusts of wind blew water from the eaves.
She came in and was singing, asked him then:
"Are you not happy to be home again?"[16]

In subsequent sonnets he said that when he viewed his wife, "he knew he hated her" and the "autumnal morgue" she managed, and he went to some lengths to present an unflattering description of her appearance:

He turned to see how yellow was her face
Creased where the collops met along her cheeks;
And see her greasy jacket with torn lace,
And the drab hair that crossed her brow in streaks.

He was careful to insist, too, that it was wrong for his wife to force him home, as he now claimed she had:

His hatred had been raging fire along
These years of separation, now at last
He could feel nothing but a callous wrong,
Except this yard and room that held him fast.

With the matter of guilt established, he felt free to turn to "the other woman."[17]

He did not do this directly, however. To shield Lillian, he transferred the location of his out-of-marriage liaison from Marion, New York, and Chicago to Paris and contrasted Helen Masters's dowdy person and gray surroundings to a sprightly sweetheart he now claimed to have squired about "the Luxembourg," the famous public gardens in Paris. (That he had actually been there—possibly with Edna St. Vincent Millay—merely added a note of authenticity to his story.) Memories of "Chopin and a walk, a slender hand / That held his arm and kept his heart in tune," remind him that his return to Helen was accomplished in part by the threat of blackmail directed at Lillian:

> He must return, or have the one he loved
> Headlined and pictured in the daily press.
> Her [Helen's] hatred was that naked and ungloved,
> And he returned to save that sordidness.[18]

Masters even included information about the October 15 slapping incident of his wife and justified that as well:

> But once at breakfast, as it came to pass,
> He did not speak, because his soul was ill,
> And then she choked him with the poison gas
> That he returned to her of his own will.
> Blinded with fury then he rose and slapped
> Her face and slapped her cowering at the wall.
> He would have throttled her, but something snapped
> In him, he saw that murder might befall.[19]

It was at this point that Eunice Tietjens intervened. Masters had originally sent her fourteen sonnets, but she deleted the seventh in the series, thus creating the "mysterious fourteenth sonnet" later mentioned by some of the Chicago papers. (How the papers found out about the deleted sonnet is not clear.) Tietjens may have removed the sonnet because it showed the Masterses in bed, but more likely she did so because it showed Masters contemplating the murder of his wife. Commenting on the sonnets to Theodore Dreiser years later, Masters told him that "only thirteen were published, one being too much for the editors." There is always the possibility, of course, that Masters himself removed the sonnet. In fact, the Newberry Library houses a galley of sonnet 7 bearing the notation "Not released. Property of E. L. Masters." In any event, the "mysterious" previously unpublished sonnet is with Tietjens's papers in the Newberry Library and reads as follows:

> He lies in darkness like a tranced cocoon
> Awaiting wings, and dreams of life ahead.
> The door creaks and she enters, pauses, soon
> Flings back the coverlet and gets in bed.
> Now shall he strangle her? For there's the scent
> Of banal powder on her; he compares
> Roses and lips and midnight passion blent

With whispers, with these desiccate despairs.
Now shall he strangle her? She yawns and twists
Her lolling flesh, he summons strength to speak:
"You must not stay here." Doubles up his fists—
But instantly she turns the other cheek
And whispers. "Well, good night; tomorrow, dear,
And daily, you'll be better, being here."

He could never be happy in this environment, of course, and when Helen Masters tries to "talk his soul into a lie / Before a public with an outward show" of getting along, her talk infuriates him: "He hates her, she denies him other love. / She has stripped him of other loves but hers, / And severed hands that touched and knew his hand."[20]

Friendless and emotionally scarred, he sees that his fame as a writer is his only lasting ally, and so ends with an appeal to his readers to understand that this public discussion of personal affairs is necessary to him as an artist: "His pain is lessened, being democratized." Of course, he nowhere admitted that his wife's lawyers had been better than his own and that hers had outwitted his simply by tying up his finances; nor did he mention the pertinent fact that his affair with "the one he loved" had pretty well run its course months before.[21]

The sonnets attracted much comment from the Chicago press on the weekend of August 18–19, 1923. The *Chicago Daily News* ran a front-page story telling its Saturday readers that the poems represented "some of the best work ever done by Edgar Lee Masters," but it noted, too, that the sonnet series was "a sensation from other standpoints than a literary one." The *Chicago Tribune* printed a lengthy summary for the 800,000 people it claimed for its Sunday edition: "The poems, his friends say, are likely to cause more than a passing sensation." The *Chicago Herald and Examiner* printed the story on page 3 with this headline: "Reveals Why He Failed to Win Back Wife in His Sonnets"; a secondary headline offered more: "Poet Confesses in His Series of Writings that He Slapped Her." The paper reviewed the facts in the case, along with quotations from the sonnets, and remarked that "the mystery of why Edgar Lee Masters could not effect a reconciliation with Mrs. Masters after three years' separation has been revealed in an unusual manner." The paper also used the story to announce its serialization of *The New Spoon River,* which was scheduled for the *Herald* the next day: "The new series of 'Spoon River' verses by Edgar Lee Masters, in which his own romance is mirrored, will be given first publication in the *Herald and Examiner* starting tomorrow." Except for the poem "Lucius Clute," Masters did not openly discuss his romance with Lillian in *The New Spoon River* (although an insider might have recognized Clarence Darrow as "Louis Raguse" and, less likely, Frank Walker as "Frank Blatt"), but the more important point was this: details of Masters's personal life were now so sensational as to be advertisements for his creations.[22]

The sonnets were his way of evening the score with Helen while explaining his own point of view. They also helped make up for the embarrassment of being laughed at in print by the Chicago press and lampooned nationally by *The Bookman.* Thus, he carefully monitored the newspapers' treatment of the sonnets, recording it in his diary: "Great Spread in all Chicago papers about sonnets"; "More spread about sonnets." Tietjens also followed the outcome of the poems, probably because she had helped create a best-selling issue of *Poetry.* In an undated letter to Monroe, she remarked on the satisfied reaction of the poet, the treatment given the poems by the press, and the Chicago public's eager purchase of over 3,000 copies of the magazine. Masters himself was satisfied with his efforts and spoke in laudatory terms of the sonnets as late as 1938.[23]

One reason for his satisfaction was that their notoriety lent a new and not entirely unwelcome image to Masters. After the publication of "The Return," he was not merely a middle-aged amorist who had cheated on his wife and suffered the complications that naturally ensued; instead, he was revealed as a man of great passions—love, hate, sacrifice, and revenge. He was the stuff of legends, growing more like the great British romantics Lord Byron and Percy Bysshe Shelley, poets whose tempestuous lives had driven them from their native land and wives into glorious exile overseas. (Masters could no longer afford the luxury of foreign exile and would have to settle for New York City instead.) Being "newspapered" by the national press was simply part of the phenomena these men had endured, and now Masters, too, had endured it—and written of it besides. He was finally the Byronic sinner he had aspired to be when he studied under Mary Fisher in Lewistown. Masters would continue to study his relation to the romantic poets, later assimilating the story of their fellow romantic John Keats into his autobiographical works, as is shown in the next chapter.

His new prominence notwithstanding, Masters remained lonely after the sonnets appeared. He had lost many of his male friends during and after the divorce. He lost another when Bill Slack married and began a several weeks' tour of Europe the day before the newspapers discovered the sonnets. But another Lewistown native, Edwin Reese (Masters's college roommate), had also settled in Chicago, and he and Masters spent numerous evenings together in this summer of 1923.[24]

Some of Masters's friends thought he would now marry Lillian; others thought Dorothy Dow and he would marry (they had been seen together in numerous places, including the office of *Poetry*). One of Masters's diary entries the day after the "spread" in the papers confirms this public speculation: "Dorothy phones me. Papers are after her about our engagement." They were after him, too, so much so that they got under his skin, bothering him, he said, through all September. "Damn the newspapers here," Masters wrote a New York friend: "They won't leave me alone. They keep printing stuff about my marital plans; and I have no plans to marry anyone. What good would that do me? . . . They keep connecting my name with that of a young poetess here named Dorothy Dow, whom I have known several years, and have helped with advice and criticism; but that's all." Nevertheless, the newspapers continued to speculate about him and Dow, as in the following item from September 16: "Dorothy Dow, Lockport (Ill.), poetess, refused to deny that she was the dark lady [of the sonnets], nor did she protest when she was informed that she and Mr. Masters were reported engaged." Much later Dow would tell an acquaintance that she and Masters really had been engaged.[25]

By the fall of 1923, however, Dow may have been more interested in the preface Masters had written for her first book of poems, *Black Babylon,* than in marrying him. Six months before, in February 1923, Masters had sent Harcourt Brace a "MS of a book of poems by Dorothy Dow" along with his own "prefatory word for the book." When Harcourt Brace failed to show appropriate interest, Masters made a similar offer to Boni and Liveright and placed the book there; now he withdrew his preface as Dow and he grew apart. He also began telling some of his Chicago friends he had never been interested in Dow (informing some of them as much as a year later). By the fall of 1923, then, Masters was free to pursue other women and did so, having dates with his future wife, Ellen Coyne, on September 24 and 25, shortly before she moved to New York City in late September or early October. By mid-October, however, Masters had discovered yet another woman and felt for a day or two that he had fallen in love with her.[26]

Masters described this woman in an unpublished chapter of his autobiography, where he called her "Idothea" (her real name was Leone), and everything about her suggests he was fortunate in not bringing her to the altar. A thirty-eight-year-old amateur poet, she had sought out Masters through a mutual friend named Janet (probably one Janet Stedman). Idothea/Leone had over a dozen lovers in her past, two of whom had become husbands, and was the mother of a twelve-year-old girl. At the time she met Masters, she was recently divorced and living in a fashionable North Side hotel on an income of $275 per month—$25 from a relative, $100 from alimony, and $150 from blackmail ("a rich man who had been her father's comrade in dissipation had agreed to pay her $150 a month for four years for the return of some letters which he had written her father"). She was thin, with a prominent nose, a pretty smile, and red hair; in other words, she looked somewhat like Masters's 1909–11 flame Tennessee Mitchell. Unlike Mitchell, Leone was the victim of a mysterious lower-back ailment, relief for which caused her to take aspirins by the hour. She wanted to write poetry, and she wanted to marry Masters, or so he decided ("I saw that Idothea wanted to marry me"). He was uncertain about her, however ("in my heart of hearts, I didn't want to marry Idothea"); besides, he said, "she looked too ripe."[27]

He held off lovemaking for several weeks, until November 7, when the romance peaked and declined in one twenty-four-hour period; Masters's diary summarizes the relation in short form: "Luncheon at Leone's. X" (November

7); "Take Leone home. She says she has changed" (November 8). In an unpublished chapter of his autobiography, Masters explained matters in greater (if slightly different) detail: they made love after their association had gone on for "about a month." The next day Leone decided the relationship should end: "It is consummated," she said. "There is nothing further. I cannot enter upon a regular relationship with you." Masters in turn "saw the ghost of Deirdre" (the name he used for Tennessee Mitchell in his autobiography) and soon began to disengage himself. His final involvement was to drive her (with the help of a chauffeur) to a country setting in Wisconsin where she sought relief from her back pain. This trip apparently occurred on November 27, when he gave a lecture in Milwaukee, after which he was through with her. "I never wrote her a line. I never saw her again, and what she did, or where she went, I never knew." Rather, he was almost through with her, for he subsequently described her story in a poem he published in 1936.[28]

He was through with Chicago, too, although he did not know it just yet. He did know, however, that he was ready for a change: "I had plenty now to think of when back in Chicago. I had been stripped, and I was broke. I wanted a change of scene. I wanted a rest." Remarkably enough, he still daydreamed about a judgeship, but the sonnets and newspaper articles had ended all hope of that: "I wish I could be a judge," he mused to Witter Bynner one fall day, "but I can't." He packed his things for New York on November 30, borrowed $2,000 (with the help of Abe Meyer) on December 1, and said good-bye to his Lewistown cronies Bill Slack and Ed Reese. Masters's diary shows he had dinner with an anonymous "Claire" on his final night in Chicago, Saturday, December 1. An "Oh hell!" follows the reference to Claire. Perhaps he would be better off in New York.[29]

Perhaps, too, it is time for suppositions. If Helen Masters had agreed to a divorce when Masters wished it, and if he had married Lillian, his life would have been much different. With his pretty young wife on his arm and a confident scowl on his face (his Parker pen obtruding a bit from his pocket), he would finally have been as he wanted to be, the Spoon River poet at peace, a little past noon of his day (to be sure), but ready for writing with the time he required to produce a book to rival *Spoon River.* The Chicago press would have gone after him, and maybe her, but her charm and wit might have neutralized them (he was unsure about that). Her "Mona Lisa smile," as he called it, shy but knowing, would have offered the press enough to confirm their private suspicions but not enough to condemn the two of them outright (yet more than enough to excite their private envy; he could imagine it in their eyes).[30]

But he had not married Lillian. He was on his way to Union Station, his son Hardin accompanying him, his Thirty Years' War with Chicago concluding, himself both victor and vanquished. He had succeeded beyond his wildest dreams and against great odds in his quest to become a writer. He could not have known three decades before when he stepped off the train from Lewistown and Havana that everything in his early life would lead up to *Spoon River* or that everything that followed it would be colored by its success. Except for *Spoon River,* he might have remained married to Helen. Except for *Spoon River,* he would never have excited Lillian's interest (for he would not have been famous enough). Except for Lillian, he would not have experienced the remarkable years of 1919–23, the most frenetic, bitter, controversial, and unhappy period of his life. He had begun it with two careers, a wife and family, and a girlfriend and ended it alone with barely one career—and it subject to starting over in New York.[31]

It was 1:30 P.M. when Hardin and he, attended by porter no. 13, arrived at car 413 (ominous numbers all, for a man who noticed such things). He was a middle-aged man in a rumpled suit with a gray felt hat and a tie askew, an excellent lawyer who had lost his clients, a father of three without a home, a bachelor in arrears in his alimony, and a man who loved women without a woman. He took with him the change in his pocket, plus $2,000 of borrowed money, a chip on his shoulder, and the need to live by his pen. He did not take with him (time would carefully show him this, although he never quite believed it) the means to succeed in New York City—not after World War I, not with the other writers who were already there, and not with his reputation, education, and attitudes.[32]

CHAPTER 11

Masters at Midcareer

I was a swift runner whom they tripped.

—Edgar Lee Masters, *Toward the Gulf*

By the time Masters left Chicago for New York, he was fifty-five years old and had written twenty-four of his fifty-three books. Because his departure from the Midwest marks the end of a major phase of his artistic life, it will be useful to pause for an assessment of Masters at midcareer.

Although *Spoon River* had enjoyed remarkable success for a book of verse, it had done nothing to rescue Masters's previous dozen books from obscurity. Even with its impetus, none of Masters's pre–*Spoon River* writings ever caught on, not the poems, which were dated; not the plays, which remained unproduced; and certainly not the political publications, which went against the mood of the country.

Nor had any of Masters's post–*Spoon River* writings done particularly well. Poor-to-average reviews had greeted the volumes of miscellaneous verse that followed *Spoon River,* and only *Domesday Book* came close to possessing the imaginative sweep of a major book of verse. Masters's five novels from this period would also experience a checkered reception, but because four of the five are highly autobiographical, they are useful in a biographical study of him and, when analyzed in conjunction with *Domesday Book,* offer unexpected insights into Masters's artistry and character.

When *Domesday Book* appeared in 1920, Masters was in the middle of a very difficult time: the notoriety of *Spoon River* had damaged his law practice, and he wanted to abandon legal work for literature; he had separated from his wife to pursue Lillian; his favorite historical era, "courthouse America"—what he once called "old America"—was being obliterated by the new century; and his career as a writer was on the decline.[1]

For several reasons he badly needed another success, but he knew he could not simply publish another *Spoon River.* His editor at Macmillan, Edward Marsh, had warned him that the critics were "sharpening their pencils" against this, and Masters himself sensed that they would accuse him of having "but one set of strings" if he tried.[2]

But he could not go on as he had. Between *Spoon River*'s appearance in 1915 and *Domesday Book* in 1920, Masters had published four volumes of poems—some of the verses were new, and some were visibly dated—but none of the books excited the critics as *Spoon River* had. He had also written in late 1919 a short autobiographical novel, *Mitch Miller,* but it was completed in only a dozen days, written solely to make money, and secondary to his real interest of poetry. If he were to maintain his position as the literary lion of the Midwest, he would have to produce another major volume. He hoped *Domesday Book* to be such a work, and it is against this backdrop of personal frustration and postwar unsettledness that the book assumes its significance.[3]

In his attempt to repeat the success of *Spoon River* without actually writing a second book of epitaphs, Masters returned selectively to several of the ingredients that had worked well before. He created a large number of characters (over 150) and placed the majority in a small Illinois village in which about 30 of them figured prominently. He gave them unusual names (such as Loveridge Chase, Alma Bell, and Consider Freeland) that were evocative of those in *Spoon River.* And he again took death as a starting point: the occasion of *Domesday Book* is a coroner's inquest into the mysterious death of the heroine who one morning in 1919 is found dead "a mile / Above Starved Rock." Masters also repeated the individual voices of *Spoon River* through the numerous witnesses who testify at the inquest, with the result that he also duplicated that book's objective quality, for the coroner is determined to search out the truth:

> Shall not I as a coroner in America,
> Inquiring of a woman's death, make record
> Of lives which have touched hers, what lives she touched;
> And how her death by surest logic touched
> This life or that, was cause of causes, proved
> The event that made events?

The coroner thus utilizes information from more than two dozen individuals—friends, parents, a minister, a physician, and a governor of the state, as well as others. These provide details on all aspects of the heroine's life and death, from girlhood through postmortem.[4]

But it is not just the story of Elenor Murray that emerges. Masters says early on that *Domesday Book* is a national assessment: "I have made a book / Called Domesday Book, a census spiritual / Taken of our America." The book is not, he hastily adds,

> a book of doom, but a book
> Of houses; domus, house, so domus book.

And this book of the death of Elenor Murray
Is not a book of doom, though showing too
How fate was woven round her, and the souls
That touched her soul; but is a house book too
Of riches, poverty, and weakness, strength
Of this our country.[5]

To take his census, Masters created a heroine whose story must be taken on several different levels. On the two simplest levels, Elenor Murray functions as both a woman and a symbolic "Columbia figure" who behaves generally as does the country from the 1890s to mid-1919. Her exact age is never stated, but during these years she ceases to be a gay charmer and becomes instead a disillusioned veteran of the war. She travels widely, from her home in central Illinois to New York, California, and the Yukon, and like her country, she makes conquests in distant lands and leaves her influence wherever she goes. She establishes numerous liaisons, but she remains single, thereby maintaining her integrity both as a woman and as national symbol.

When World War I comes, she volunteers for Red Cross work and embarks for France. At the same time she encourages her principal lover, an idealistic Chicago professor named Barrett Bays, to join her in the war. A citizen responding to his country's call, he goes to France, where he grows disillusioned with the changes wrought in both Elenor and the national character:

For that day I saw
The war for what it was, and saw myself
An artificial factor, working there
Because of Elenor Murray—what a fool!
I was not really needed, like too many
Was just pretending . . . , saw myself
Swept in this mad procession by a woman;
And through myself I saw the howling mob
Back in America that shouted hate.

Disgusted, he manages to get out of France and returns to the United States, finally realizing the duality of both Elenor and the nation:

Who was this woman?
This Elenor Murray was America;
Corrupt, deceived, deceiving, self-deceived,
Half-disciplined, half-lettered, crude and smart . . . ,
Curious, mediocre, venal, hungry
For money, place, experience, restless, no
Repose, restraint.

Consequently, Barrett Bays determines to have nothing more to do with her.[6]

When Elenor returns to America after the armistice, she begs her lover/citizen to forgive her transgressions and to embrace her again. Her pleas are to no avail, for Barrett Bays will forgive neither the girl nor the nation she symbolizes, and when he refuses her request, she dies. Her heart stops, as does the figurative heart of that "old America" she represents. Her death from syncope in the first week of August 1919 coincides with the emergence of the new feminine symbol of freedom for a "new" America, the flapper.

There is more to *Domesday Book,* however, than just this sentimental, allegorical tale of a vanishing era and a woman who functions as its national symbol. Masters sometimes described *Domesday Book* as his "finest achievement," and this naturally brings up the question of why he felt this way. It is clear that the era in question had an emotional hold on him, but internal evidence shows that he also had another, more personal reason for favoring this book.[7]

He left behind numerous clues that suggest he was burying a part of himself with Elenor Murray. Her initials, the euphonic similarity of the names Edgar Lee Masters and Elenor Murray, the number of syllables, and even the stress on individual syllables suggest that Masters intended at least a portion of Elenor's story to be identified as his. The first hint of this comes with the finding of her body. We should remember that in his previous book Masters had identified readily with the Indians who perished on the crag along the Illinois River known as Starved Rock. Now his heroine dies within "the shadow of Starved Rock." (It is, of course, thematically appropriate that the society she represents follows the Indian culture into oblivion.)[8]

Moreover, although Masters had said that his was "a census spiritual" of the nation, it is only partly that, for *Domesday Book* is also a family census. Elenor's parents and Masters's parents are one and the same. Henry Murray, whose "mind was on the law," is modeled after Hardin Masters, who was a lawyer. Mrs. Murray, who knew "fine things, to be a lady," is mismatched with her husband and is based on Emma Masters, who was more refined than Hardin. Both Emma Masters and Mrs. Murray begin their marriages with two sons, and each loses a son when he is five. Like Masters, Elenor approaches her grandfather for a loan for a second year at college but is forced to leave after only two semesters. Her college costs of $200 per year are the same as Masters's were. Finally, it is significant that the story of Elenor Murray appears under the title of "Domesday Book" and that part of Emma Masters's own family history was preserved in "a Doomesday Book."[9]

There are still other borrowings that might be pointed out: the member of the coroner's jury identified as "Winthrop Marion, learned and mellow, / A journalist in Chicago," is clearly modeled after Masters's St. Louis editor and friend William Marion Reedy, who first published the Spoon River poems; the character of David Borrow may be based on Masters's former law partner Clarence Darrow; the maiden name of Elenor Murray's mother (Fouche) was taken from the married name of a childhood sweetheart of Masters; the last name of Barrett Bays was taken from a Lewistown man of that name; the physician who testifies, Dr. Burke, is no doubt based on Masters's friend Dr. Alexander Burke; and the coroner, Merival, is similar to a poet (Masters himself) questing for the truth. Some of Masters's women friends also make cameo appearances: Tennessee Mitchell is one of the models Masters used to depict Elenor as a mistress; Florence Dugan (the woman Masters called "Rowena" in unpublished portions of his autobiography) provides Elenor with a speech about sacrifice and the war; and Lillian appears in the person of "Arielle," a thirty-year-old widow living in a mansion.[10]

Given these several parallels and autobiographic borrowings, the intriguing question is how Elenor's favored lover, Barrett Bays, figures in all this. Like Elenor, he is obviously meant to be taken as part person and part abstraction. For both characters, their names constitute the keys to their significance. His is an unusual combination of words directing attention to the head: Barrett, or barrette (a clasp), and Bays, the laurel crown for excellence placed on the head to signify recognition. Consciously or unconsciously, Elenor-Edgar's attempt to keep (or clasp) bays shows Masters seeking what poets have always sought and frequently lost: fame.

All this means that *Domesday Book,* in addition to being a political-social allegory about an era, is also a personal narrative. Masters, ever autobiographical, is talking about his own artistic life during and after the Great War, when his hard-won literary eminence began to slip from his grasp. As his books after *Spoon River* drew less-flattering reviews, and as the changing tempo of the postwar period shunted aside the "old America" he preferred, he showed himself dying when critical acclaim (Professor Barrett Bays) was denied him.

Of course, the English language already had one eminently famous example of a poet wounded to death by the critics—namely, John Keats, the British romantic whose death was once thought to have been hastened by savage literary reviews of his creative work. No less an authority than Masters's favorite English author, Percy Bysshe Shelley, had said as much in his memorial poem "Adonais," and Shelley's friend Lord Byron had gone a step further, openly declaring that Keats's life was "snuffed out by an article." These old legends enjoyed wide currency through the time of Masters's literary coming of age and well into the twentieth century, when Masters used them in subtle and artistic ways in *Domesday Book.*[11]

In other words, by 1920 Masters was using the romantic myths surrounding Keats's death and discreetly applying them to himself. We know that he already had an interest in such comparisons, for in *Starved Rock* (1919) an autobiographical character remarks in an aside that he "often . . . pored / On the death mask of Keats." In his trilogy of autobiographical novels completed by 1923, Masters would give this comparison fuller play, but with less artistic subtlety and other intentions in mind.[12]

In the first of these, *Mitch Miller,* Masters told of growing up in Petersburg and of his memories of the title character, a boyhood friend killed in a train mishap. Masters's narrator, Arthur "Skeeters" Kirby, spins an engaging yarn similar to Mark Twain's *Tom Sawyer* until the final parts of the novel, at which point Masters lapses into adult political sermonizing and personal reminiscences of the first time he read the correspondence of John Keats and his girlfriend, Fanny Brawne. The reader has been prepared for the latter through Mitch Miller's recitation of portions of Keats's "La Belle Dame sans Merci" and through Mitch's boyhood crush on a village charmer named Zueline. When Zueline throws him over, Mitch loses his will to live and soon after participates in the dangerous activity that results in his death. Mitch's juvenile longings for Zueline were meant to parallel Keats's frustrated hopes with Fanny Brawne (or the frustrations of Keats's knight in "La Belle Dame"). Masters was no doubt relying on personal experience and his own frustrated hopes to realize himself through women, for by the time he wrote this book, he was suffering from an impossible love affair with Lillian, and while he was moved to draw parallels between his childhood friend and Keats, Masters was really speaking in ways personal to himself—and preparing for the more open identity with Keats that followed in the next book, *Skeeters Kirby.*[13]

Skeeters Kirby is a thinly disguised account of Masters's life from his final months in Petersburg through the time of his removal to Lewistown and subsequent move to Chicago. Like Masters, the title character is a lawyer turned writer who seeks companionship with a variety of women, including Winifred Hervey (based principally on Margaret George); Martha Fisk (based principally on Masters's first wife, Helen); Alicia Adams (Tennessee Mitchell); and Becky Norris (Lillian). Less important girlfriends are also worked into the narrative, for example, Winnie Eichelberger, who lent a portion of her first name to the character Winifred Hervey. "Skeet" (as the hero is called) writes a successful book of verse under the alias of "Willis Aronkeil" (one of Masters's pseudonyms) while getting to know Bob Hayden (William Marion Reedy). After Skeet's marriage fails, his former law partner, Cavette Errant (Clarence Darrow) separates Skeet from his fortune, and as the book ends, Skeet retreats to the safety of male companionship, something Masters occasionally did with male friends such as Reedy and George Stokes.

Those who are familiar with Masters's autobiography will find *Skeeters Kirby* to be an imaginative gloss on the most successful portion of Masters's life. They may also find it curious that Masters drew an open comparison between his writer-hero Skeeters Kirby and John Keats. As Skeet grows up, his facial features come to resemble those of Keats, and a friend who draws Skeet's likeness mentions the resemblance. The character making the comparison has no purpose in the book other than to make this one significant point: "There was a young artist here—a Paul Offield, who sketched me one night as I lay on the bed. . . . Paul said, 'Well, I'll declare! If you'll look at the sketch Severn made of

John Keats at three o'clock in the morning, you will see how close the resemblance is.' I took the sketch and studied it. It filled me with fear. Was I, too, to lapse into a decline?" In *Skeeters Kirby,* then, Masters moved toward the fuller identity with Keats that dominates the final book of the trilogy, *Mirage.*[14]

Before examining this book, however, it will be useful to highlight unpublished information that illustrates Masters's compulsion to let the other poet's life explain his own changes in fortune. One of the most damaging of these changes had come on March 21, 1922, when Helen Masters's lawyers succeeded in tying up Masters's finances. This left him badly shaken and caused him to retreat even further into the subjectively romantic shell he was fashioning. His June 21, 1922, letter to his confidante Eunice Tietjens illustrates his emotional state.

Masters began by saying that he was "in a bad way,"adding, "every day . . . seems like approaching death." He mentioned that "Lord Byron quoted Pope to make the point that the life of an author was warfare upon earth." Masters remembered, however, that Byron was an affluent nobleman, and so he compared himself to Shelley, for Shelley, too, had suffered many disappointments. Nevertheless, Masters sensed that it was really Keats with whom he had the greatest kinship. "Keats had all the woes of an author: poverty, a hostile public, illness, and early death." It is apropos to point out that Masters had expressed worry about his own hostile public and illness in a May 1922 letter to Tietjens. In other words, he was saying in these two letters that he himself had experienced what the great romantics suffered and that his story was like theirs. Hence his decision in the June letter: "I shall venture to write of my own life as an example of an American author, trusting readers to remember all that Byron, Shelley, and Keats enjoyed in the way of cultural influences and [suffered] as victims, in the way of a public, leisure, and opportunity."[15]

This is precisely what Masters did in *Mirage.* He was led to this, one concludes, by his own ego, which insisted that his troubles after *Spoon River*—literary, marital, and financial—were not the result of his own injudicious publications and indiscreet behavior but rather burdens imposed on him by others. To put it another way, misery loves company, and if Masters could convince his readers that his story was like that of the great British romantics, especially Keats, he would be in fine company indeed. This seems to be the only explanation that can account for the quirkier elements of *Mirage.*

Mirage begins with Masters's life story after he lost his fortune, his sweetheart Lillian (here called "Becky"), and much of his remaining reputation. *Mirage* has almost no plot in the usual sense of the word because it is devoted largely to self-justification. For example, Skeet in one instance dreams of his death and of choosing a headstone with a suitable inscription, that is, one that would explain why the quality of his work has fallen off. In seeking such a legend, Masters searched through his previous poems and came up with a line from his 1918 volume *Toward the Gulf:* "What should his epitaph be? In a night of restlessness [Skeet] had thought one out, and he could see how it would look engraved on a white stone. It should be: 'I was a swift runner whom they tripped.' That was true, he had been tripped."[16]

This was important, for with such an explanation—carved on a headstone or expressed through his novels and poems—Masters was holding up as truth what was really only a weak excuse for his refusal to acknowledge responsibility for his failures. He had subtly toyed with the idea that others had "killed" him in the *Domesday* allegory and interjected comments about Keats into both *Mitch Miller* and *Skeeters Kirby.* Now, following his divorce in the spring of 1923, he was ready to go a step further: he likened himself not only to Keats but also to his creations.

In *Mirage* Masters first underscored the idea of his having been destroyed by others by patiently labeling all the enemies who figured in his story and by telling how he felt they hurt him. To end his tale, he had his autobiographical hero return repeatedly to a country churchyard where he quotes Keats and identifies with the knight of "La Belle Dame sans Merci":

> I saw pale kings and warriors, too,
> Pale princes, death pale were they all.
> They said La Belle Dame sans Merci
> Hath thee in thrall.

Masters had prepared all his life for such a comparison, or at least from his days "as a boy on the Masters farm," when he examined his grandmother's embossed paper knight and felt a "thrilling association" simply by contemplating it. In those days the knight had offered him a vision of romance, an entry into myth via the imagination; now it offered him an explanation for his failures.[17]

To describe Skeet's surroundings, Masters borrowed from Keats's poem: on a fall day a lonely individual waits without hope by a body of water with "withered flags at the edge of the shore" ("the sedge is withered from the lake"). Skeet is thus linked with Keats—as he has been all along through his unusual appellation, which seems derived from Keats. Other elements evocative of Keats include Skeet's yearning after a "star" (Keats's "bright star") and his lifelong "search for truth and beauty," two terms indelibly associated with Keats through his most famous poem, "Ode on a Grecian Urn." (Keats's favorable comments on Homer and his depiction of woman as a coiling serpent in "Lamia" no doubt also caught Masters's attention.)[18]

That Masters concluded his trilogy in this fashion is revealing, for he was insisting that his autobiographical hero is really a romantic abused by the world, and now his pilgrimage has destroyed him. Like Keats's knight, he has been hurt by a "belle dame," and in the cemetery he is much like the knight who has also come to "the cold hill side," a place of burial. The belle dame was truly important to Masters, for she (or it) was sufficiently undefined to account for any and all of his difficulties, not only those with his poetry and his public, but also the ones stemming from disputes with his wife and the loss of the woman for whom he had given up nearly everything, Lillian.

All this helps to explain why Masters returned to "the hill" of Spoon River in 1924 to publish his second book of epitaphs: after his setbacks in law, literature, and love, a return to the elegiac writing form that had once brought him international recognition must have looked to be one of the few bright spots of the early 1920s; also, intellectually speaking, he had nowhere else to go, having twice written himself into a graveyard, first through the poetry in *Domesday Book* and then through his prose in his three autobiographical novels concerning Skeeters Kirby.

Masters's identification with Keats also helps to explain a note he published in 1925 in *Poetry* magazine. Here, he defended Keats's reputation—and his own—by highlighting portions of the other poet's life as these applied to himself. Masters began by saying, "Keats' 'La Belle Dame sans Merci' is the greatest lyrical ballad in the English language." He argued that Keats's "ballad goes to the esoteric essence of the soul's search and the soul's betrayal." Not surprisingly, Masters found that betrayal coming at the hands of a woman and from the public at large:

> Some years ago I read a volume of the letters exchanged between Keats and Fanny Brawne, and she seemed to me what Don Juans, learned in the game of woman, would call a teaser. One thing is sure: a woman who prized the adoration that had been given her, and who had any realization of the kind of man who had given it to her, would never have written the letter that Fanny Brawne wrote ten years after Keats' death, in which she said: "Let him rest in the obscurity to which fate has consigned him." This after Shelley's *Adonais,* and after Byron's great tribute to Keats! For a woman with the right heart does not wish obscurity to overtake the man who has loved her; and she will try, when opportunity presents itself, to prevent it. I fancy she was pretty common clay, such as Don Quixotes and others get their fancies heated up over.[19]

Since Masters had in *Mirage* compared himself to Quixote as well as to Keats and had shown how women contributed to his unhappiness, and because he was himself drifting into "obscurity" about "ten years after" his triumph, one cannot say whether he was talking more about Keats or himself. Nevertheless, his note, while not particularly helpful as commentary on Keats, is enlightening in other ways, namely, in showing once again Masters's interest in Keats, his willingness to mingle the facts of the other poet's life with his own, and (most important) his need to publicly remind his peers of the parts of Keats's story that were useful to himself, especially those elements portraying Keats or his characters as victims.

Masters would enlarge on this theme of victimization in a fourth autobiographical novel from this period, *The Nuptial Flight* (1923). This does not continue with the story of "Skeet" Kirby but does draw on some of the same family source materials. The book is an imaginative retelling of the lives of Masters's paternal grandparents, his parents, his brother and sister, and himself. The model for the main character is Masters's paternal grandmother, Lucinda Masters, "Lucinda Matlock" of *Spoon River,* and his use of her guides the details of the novel.

Shortly after Masters became a lawyer, he grew curious about his bloodlines and determined to trace his lineage. This not-unusual interest produced unexpected results when he traced the ancestry of his father's mother, as he mentions in his autobiography: "When I was twenty-eight (and I can be specific about the date from my grandmother's affidavit), I was at the farm with my father, who at the time was the master in chancery of Fulton County. I wanted to get in writing all that my grandmother knew about her people. I questioned her and made notes, and then wrote out an affidavit which my grandmother signed and swore to before my father as a master in chancery."[20]

What Masters discovered was that his grandmother was illegitimate, and this upset him. Masters loved his grandmother—when he died he was buried beside her—but this love, along with his need to search for reasons for his own artistic and domestic failures, left his novel tangled in some very important places. To be faithful to facts, Masters made the fictitious grandmother, Nancy Wilson, a strong character and also illegitimate. To be faithful to his own biases, however, Masters insisted—against all the internal evidence—that the subsequent difficulties that plagued Nancy Wilson's offspring stemmed directly from her "mixed" (not entirely English) blood. A review of the story illustrates.[21]

Nancy Wilson comes to Illinois in the 1840s and marries William Houghton. They settle the land, raise a family, and prosper. They retain their vitality into old age, and most important, Nancy's lifestyle is never hampered in any way by her mixed blood.

Unfortunately, Nancy and William's firstborn is affected by the blood. During his life, Walter Scott Houghton (based on Masters's father) fails in business, makes a bad marriage, has children deficient in judgment, and finally suffers total debility. Although many of Walter's troubles come from his laziness and his choice of loafers for friends, Masters the omniscient author theorized that Walter's difficulties can be traced to the blood of his mother: "Because of his good humor, his ready wit, and his companionable spirit, his store became a loafing place for all the story-telling idlers of the town. Was this the blood of his ancestor cropping out in him; the Irishman, or the Spaniard who was the natural father of old Nancy?" Unlike his namesake, Walter Scott Houghton is never able to free himself from the mistakes of the past; the worst mistake, of course, cannot be rectified, for it involves the blood of his mother. This leaves him too carefree: "Walter Scott derived from somewhere in his stock a desire for happiness. His great vitality did not find its full expression in work."[22]

Compounding Walter's difficulties is his unhappy marriage to an exceedingly strong-willed woman (based on Masters's mother). His wife, Fanny, has been married to Walter for only a brief time when she senses something wrong not only with her husband but with his entire family. She begins to feel "a repugnance for the stock," and the marriage soon begins its figurative "flight" to ruin. Among those affected are their three children.[23]

Their firstborn, Alfred (Masters himself), is an artist and "a dreamer" who gets his impractical nature from his grandmother: "It had augmented itself from some chemical reaction of blood carried over from the veins of old Nancy." This blood costs him his art since it leaves him unprepared to deal with the women who use him. He is first the victim of a wife who manipulates him and ruins him economically. Next his mistress betrays his trust and completes his ruin by destroying him spiritually.[24]

The second child of Walter and Fanny is Elaine (Masters's sister, Madeline). Her blood costs her the fortune she amasses. Elaine invariably chooses male companions who cannot be trusted: "She was drawn to strong males, and these were the young men in town who drank and danced and were addicted to the rural vices." Her mother "was always . . . reminding her that any tendency of that kind was to be watched and restrained, for it was the blood of her father and old Nancy which was to be overcome." When Elaine coquets with the scoundrel who takes her fortune, Masters asks, "Was this the Spanish blood of her which, according to the tradition, flowed in the veins of old Nancy?"[25]

Bertram, the third child of Walter and Fanny, enjoys a more balanced personality and is Masters's practical application of the genetic law that offspring have characteristics of both parents: "Bertram seemed to combine in his nature the aggressiveness and spirit of his mother, her nerve and her cynical vision, with the social gifts of his father, his father's capacity for life and for mingling with people of his own age as he went along." Bertram (Masters's brother, Tom) is free from the curse on the other children and enjoys a successful life.[26]

But all this breaks down in the conclusion. Ironically, the most robust and most energetic member of the family is Nancy, in whose veins the mixed blood runs thickest; it is she who acts as mother and provider when the others weaken. She has always kept her husband strong. In the end she maintains the strength of the others by setting a magnificent feast for her son and his wife, who do not even have food in the house. She also cares for her artist-grandson, Alfred, who is totally defeated by life, and for Elaine, who is a picture of fatigue and despair. Nancy even acts as nurse, putting her son and grandson to bed:

> And when it was time to go to bed, old Nancy, carrying a candle, lighted her son and her grandson to their rooms and tucked them into bed. She helped to undress Walter Scott, helped to straighten him under the covers, patted down his pillow, and kissed him good-night, and went to do the same for Alfred. Then she returned to William who was already in bed, and who said to her with a chuckle: "Well, mother, have you got all your chickens to bed?" "Yes, and very comfortable, too," [she said]. Then she lay down and was soon asleep herself.[27]

Like the "Lucinda Matlock" poem of *Spoon River, The Nuptial Flight* shows that the old pioneers were hardy and that their young heirs suffered from numerous degeneracies. In an effort to justify this belief, however, Masters resorted to an unconvincing and inartistic use of ethnic stereotyping. Masters's numerous comments that the non-English blood of the grandmother caused the Houghton family to decline simply do not make sense, but this explanation afforded Masters an explanation for his own failures, and he pursued it, even at the cost of maligning his beloved grandmother.

What he was really doing in *The Nuptial Flight,* in his three novels involving Skeeters Kirby, and in *Domesday Book* was making use of his wide reading and articulating one of the most basic questions of existence: are individuals shaped most by heredity or environment? In *Domesday Book* the (social) environment is most responsible for the death of the heroine, Elenor Murray (and the figurative death of Masters the artist). In the trilogy of novels regarding Skeeters Kirby, the environment in the form of "la belle dame" dooms Skeet to artistic and spiritual ruin. In *The Nuptial Flight* heredity (bad blood) is the chief cause of the artist Alfred's failure—closely followed by Alfred's hag of a wife and disloyal mistress (Lillian). In no case is the artist (Masters himself) to blame.

This blame shifting harmed Masters to the extent that it furnished him reasons to continue in his undisciplined lifestyle and largely undisciplined writings. The influence of Keats was particularly deleterious. Masters's romantic self-imagings comparing himself to Keats did no good but allowed him to avoid the painful conclusions of more realistic self-appraisal. In hiding behind the life and writings of Keats (and the legends concerning him), Masters failed to face up to the true causes of his post–*Spoon River* literary decline, namely, his own lack of critical judgment about what to publish and his tendency for a bitter self-pity so pronounced that he cluttered his artistic creations with personal complaints. The irony is that despite the numerous allusions to Keats, Masters often lacked what the other poet valued as "negative capability," the ability to judge opposing points of view in a fair and rational manner.

The most subtle result of this lack is manifested in *Domesday Book,* which Masters judged to be his "finest achievement" because it—more than any of his other books—was devoted to his own literary "death," which came too soon for him to handle following his vault to fame with *Spoon River.* The result was that after Masters's several declines began in law, literature, and love, he brooded on these in his published works (the wrong place) and looked for excuses where he could find them (in literature). He settled on Keats's story to explain his own because Keats's life came closest to exciting the pity that Masters felt for himself. Unfortunately, this failure to acknowledge responsibility for his own actions would be partly responsible for some of Masters's future failings in New York City in the next part of his career.

CHAPTER 12

The Literary Lion and the Roaring Twenties

He shall not return
Again to his home, nor stand
Rejoicing by the side
Of wife and brood.
Yet he shall gaze the sea,
And count what he has lost,
And what he did not gain
By landing here.

—Edgar Lee Masters, "The Sirens,"
Invisible Landscapes

One of the most important factors facing Masters as his train drew into New York City was one he could do nothing to control, namely, the fact that times had changed since *Spoon River Anthology* had made him famous in 1914–15. The simple agrarian society from which he had sprung, that he loved, and about which he could at times write so well had ended with World War I. Masters belonged intellectually to this earlier America, to "courthouse America," to the country as it existed during the half-century between the Civil War and the world war. *Spoon River Anthology* had been written out of this era of unindustrialized villages, and when it ended, a part of Masters's life ended also. He knew this, of course, and said as much in his autobiography: "The World War destroyed the era out of which *Spoon River* came."[1]

In its stead was a more urban society and a new generation of American writers. F. Scott Fitzgerald's stories of glittering flappers and jaded young men had already burst on the scene, to be joined shortly by the work of Ernest Hemingway, soon to see his stories of the Great War completed and published with acclaim. In New York a wealth of talented and easy-to-read writers was headquartered informally at the famous "Round Table" of the Algonquin Hotel. Ring Lardner, E. B. White, Alexander Woollcott, Robert Benchley, Dorothy Parker, James Thurber, and others not only enjoyed club status among themselves but would soon have a sophisticated new outlet available to them, *The New Yorker,* founded in 1925.

Masters, a cantankerous conversationalist with a careless tie, unpressed suit, and country drawl, did not fit easily into this urban setting. Raised in the long shadows of the Civil War with many of his values set firmly by his rural grandparents, he seemed a traveler from another time and another place. Divided in thought and manner from his contemporaries, he was a divided personality unto himself as well: he looked younger than his fifty-five years and still hankered for a woman who was youthful, beautiful, and rich, but each succeeding year and each important setback lessened his chances of finding such a being. His one claim to fame, *Spoon River Anthology,* caused related problems. It was still well known—internationally so (it would be translated into several foreign languages during the 1920s)—but its themes were often regarded as country themes, and its author was seen as a country author. (Although one has to wonder: if Petersburg and Lewistown had been located in Vermont and New Hampshire, and "Spoon River" sited in Maine, it is a fair bet that eastern critics would have found Masters's "country" ways much more to their liking, as they did with Robert Frost and Edwin Arlington Robinson.) There was also the overtowering success of *Spoon River* itself to confront: Masters would have to produce a truly great book to avoid being seen as having left his best work behind him. So these were some of the things he faced as he entered New York with too little sleep on the afternoon of December 3, 1923.[2]

On his arrival Masters stayed at the home of two recent acquaintances, Roland and Elsie Farley, a well-to-do couple with a Park Avenue apartment and a country place on Long Island. Roland Farley was a blind musician who was much interested in current creative endeavors (he is discussed under his own name in *The New Spoon River*). He could occasionally hear one of his neighbors playing Percy Grainger's melody "Spoon River," and this led him to put some of Masters's words to music in a song called "Summer Day." (Masters and Grainger had met in 1919, shortly before Grainger composed his work; it was based on a fiddle tune Masters had heard in 1915 from a former soldier named Captain Charles Robinson, who had heard it near the Spoon River in 1857.) Masters and Farley's composition was never to be as successful as Grainger's, but their common interest in the arts had earlier brought them together; in fact, Masters had been staying with the Farleys when his divorce was finalized in May. He was staying with them now simply because two weeks earlier he had asked to: "Can you house me at your place in town? Maybe I'll go to Great Neck if you can't. . . . Oh, I have a new flame who lives way uptown, an actress lady who has taken a notion to me. She writes betimes; and I must see her."[3]

The "actress lady" was Ellen Coyne, a twenty-four-year-old from Masters's Chicago days who was then studying drama at New York's New School of Social Research. He had met her in 1919 and had gone on at least two dates with her after his divorce before she left Chicago in the fall of 1923. She had graduated from a Kansas City high school in 1918, as well as from that city's Dillenbeck School of Oratory, before going to the University of Chicago, where she received a bachelor's degree in English in 1922. Her first love was drama, however, and she was now in New York to see how far she could go with her brains and good looks. She had green eyes, jet-black hair, a killer smile, and very handsome legs. She had already toured with a stock company that visited towns such as Des Moines and places as far west as Montana and had appeared (or would shortly appear) in two movies, one from MGM in Hollywood and the other from Cosmopolitan Studios in New York. She was also a model and posed for artists such as the painter May Mott Smith and the sculptor Joseph Nicolosi. Masters arranged for Ellen to be with him, two midwesterners far from home, at Christmas 1923: "Ellen Coyne at Great Neck." She soon became friends with the Farleys, and as 1923 closed, these three formed the nucleus of Masters's close acquaintances in New York City.[4]

Both Masters and Ellen Coyne later left somewhat misleading accounts concerning their activities at this time, so that their stories should be augmented with information in Masters's diary. The two had become lovers by the first week in January 1924, but because Masters spent much of his time at the Farleys' Long Island house and because Ellen lived across town in the Old Chelsea apartments, at 51 West Sixteenth Street, Manhattan, his courtship involved considerable travel. Wearying of this commute, he moved in September 1924 to the same complex as Ellen and rented an apartment at 53 West Sixteenth Street. (The Old Chelsea comprised three five-story houses made into an apartment system with different numbers for the three original houses.)[5]

At the start of 1924, however, Masters spent much of his time at the Farleys' Great Neck house, where he sought to address his financial plight through several writing activities. The house was a good place for this; Masters had servants to look after his needs, and the Farleys were gone from Monday through Thursday, when they returned from their Park Avenue apartment. Masters spent part of January planning publishing details of his new novel, *Mirage,* a lightly veiled autobiographical story concerning his relations with several women, most notably Lillian Wilson. The manuscript had been completed only two months earlier but was already an item of contention between Masters and his publisher, Boni and Liveright. Masters fussed with the company over the text, the title, and terms of the contract, as well as insisting that he see "the proofs . . . , revised proofs, and later paged proofs in order that the book may be made as perfect as possible." More precisely, he wished to make as perfect as possible the revenge he visited on Lillian, whom he described through the unlikable character of Becky Norris. As he later explained matters to his friend Edwin Reese, this use of his art to punish was well thought out: "I meant to etch Becky in unmercifully; for if ever a woman had a chance to make herself happy and to cultivate the greatness and prosperity of the man who loved her, she had it. She wouldn't. Her only thought was the little things that pertained to her little self."

It was with this insight and motivation, then, that *Mirage,* his fifth novel, went off to meet the public early in 1924.[6]

During this same time, in late 1923 and early 1924, Masters also worked on a play called "New Salem," a drama concerning that Illinois village's best-known inhabitant, young Abraham Lincoln. Unlike all Masters's other plays, "New Salem" had a very auspicious beginning. According to Masters, in mid-1922 the stage and screen star John Barrymore contacted his friend Zoe Akins and instructed her "to wire [Masters] to write a Lincoln play." Masters subsequently did so, visiting Illinois and the site of New Salem in August 1923. He came away with ideas enough to complete a manuscript and with his spirits greatly buoyed by the possibility that his financial problems might be solved if one of his works received treatment by "the Great Profile." Unfortunately, Barrymore's studio obligations forbade the type of free-lance activity he had proposed, but the experience had piqued Masters's interest; he circulated "New Salem" to other markets in 1924 and sent it to the Provincetown Playhouse in November.[7]

Eugene O'Neill, later to be America's first Nobel Prize laureate in drama, was then an associate director with the Provincetown Playhouse. One of O'Neill's associates, Thomas Dickinson, thought Masters's play had potential but felt it needed to be reorganized and presented in more dramatic fashion. Dickinson was willing to make the changes, provided that Masters sign over a portion of the play's potential earnings as payment. Masters balked. He felt he would be overcharged for Dickinson's help, forgetting that his play was worthless without professional assistance. When Masters refused to accept the terms, "New Salem" was returned to him; his one big chance for a break as a playwright was thus nipped in the bud by himself.[8]

This lapse in judgment seems not to have bothered Masters, however, because he had several other manuscripts in the making, including a new story about boys begun in January 1924 and a long poem about Robert E. Lee begun in February. He spent most of his working hours on *Lee* during March and April but was not getting much done. His diary shows he spent enormous amounts of time away from his desk, commuting to see Ellen or having lunch and dinner with literary acquaintances. Nor did he accomplish as much as he wished when he was at his desk. He had tried to pay the Farleys fifty dollars per month for the rent of their place (the same amount he had paid for a one-room apartment in Chicago), but they would accept no rent and preferred to treat him as a house guest, one whom they enjoyed having. In fact, they enjoyed their famous guest so much that they sometimes visited their Long Island house too often for Masters's taste; to work without interruptions, he moved in March to the Nassau Club, in Princeton.[9]

The spring of 1924 was an uneasy one for Masters. He had no permanent address and no permanent plans. He worked on *Lee* and on his new book for boys and reviewed the epitaphs that would shortly be published as *The New Spoon River.* He also contemplated epilogues for both *The New Spoon River* and

Domesday Book, but he was neither happy nor productive, and he certainly was not making money. He faced his first spring in New York City with minimal expectations.[10]

Masters was diluting his unhappiness with drink in these difficult times, and his letters to his boyhood chum Edwin Reese are punctuated with references to alcohol and a sense of despair. "I have tippled gin all day," he wrote Reese one afternoon, adding that he had accomplished nothing that day: "But why do anything? Why? Why? That's what makes me drink gin today. . . . I must either start on a task of writing or start to hoe beans. One thing that ails me is idleness, and somehow I don't want to write. . . . Such disgusting futility has rarely possessed me." Prohibition was in effect, and many of Masters's letters comment on alcohol and its availability. "I can walk a block from here and get good gin," he wrote Reese on May 7, saying that he could also get "beer by the case" for five dollars. Sometimes he drank with others; sometimes he drank alone. Sometimes he reviewed his strange past and the people he had known, and one day he went looking for Lillian—or rather, he asked Reese (still in Chicago) to search for her: "I wish to God you could in some very nice way find out if a certain party is in Marion. The telephone there is 176. I never answered her letter of June 27 last, and her stool pigeon, the rector, ceased to write me in September. So that she may be in India for aught I know. I have felt a strange curiosity about her these last few mornings, hunches and intimations of immorality; and I wondered about her. This is natural, you know."[11]

But Lillian turned out to be closer than he expected. As Masters later explained matters to Reese, he had simply called one of her friends, who told him that Lillian was going to rent an apartment in New York City: "I called the apartment building which I thought she might have located in, and asked for her. The concierge answered that he could not connect me with her apartment without knowing who it was. So I asked for her telephone number in the name of a pianist whom she knows, and the number was given me by the janitor." The new information was duly recorded in his diary: "Locate L. at 30 5th Avenue. Tele. Stuyvesant 5360" (April 21).[12]

He was interested in Lillian again because, as he saw it, his relations with Ellen had grown too serious, and he may have thought of leaving her. His correspondence from this period shows that he remained on the lookout for other women, as he remarked to Elsie Farley a little after this time. "No girls here," he wrote while visiting his sister in Maine. "No widows, flappers, drinkers; but only married ladies who have beaux." He also pondered the appropriate financial assets of a new woman in his life, as he did in a letter to Elsie Farley: "I expect if I went to New York, and just began to live, to dine, to be lionized, I could meet some lady that would fill the bill for a home, and so settle. . . . [But] I'd rather to be free and fain than to be nussed and eventually to lose my glands between eider down and silk." It was not just an easement on wealth that he needed, then. He wanted the freedom of a bachelor in addition to the benefits of consorting with the moneyed set. Frustrated, he flirted through the mails with an old friend named Katharine Jones, asking whether she was "wedded again." Receiving no encouragement, he looked elsewhere.[13]

His dilemma was that a mature lady wealthy enough to support him would soon bore him, he thought, while a woman young enough to interest him would probably not have the collateral goods he desired. Lillian had been unique in this respect, charming, youthful, and wealthy. After speaking with her concierge and janitor, however, he seems to have made no further attempts to talk with her, although he monitored her whereabouts as he could. One day he discovered her name on the passenger list of those making an ocean voyage to the Caribbean, and it was in this mode that she finally sailed out of his life.[14]

It also helped seal his relation with Ellen Coyne. As early as May 1924 they had thought of sharing an apartment ("we are talking of living together"), and he was experiencing pressure to legitimize the relation, as he explained to Reese: "It has about come to the point of marry or quit. . . . But having torn my heart out in running away from Lilly, why take on this one?" "I am expected to marry," he wrote a little later, "but can't bring myself to." In other words, he was not emotionally ready for another serious relation, but he was loath to leave Ellen if it meant being by himself. Since Ellen enjoyed youth, beauty, and intelligence, one suspects that her real problem was that she simply was not rich enough.[15]

The only child of an Irish immigrant and a second-generation Irish mother, Ellen Frances Coyne had been born in Kansas City, Missouri, in 1899. She was raised principally by her mother, Molly, a gentle soul with an interest in the politics of the Democratic Party; Molly's husband, Tom, was often away on trips to Central and South America. A former army sergeant and soldier of fortune, Tom Coyne built railroads and bridges in Latin America during his most successful phase, although he fondly remembered his days with the U.S. Cavalry in Montana and Wyoming and sometimes said he wished he had been with General Custer at the Battle of the Little Big Horn. He was five years too late for that, but not for subsequent actions, during which he was known to ride horses to death. He gravitated naturally to Panama and helped cut the isthmus, even though his engineering training consisted solely of a correspondence course taken as part of his attempt to enter West Point. He had failed in that endeavor but learned enough to build railroads and bridges in lands that had none. He claimed to have rammed miles of track through the jungles of various South American states, including a railroad link across the Andes, and he probably had. The gold coins he brought back proved something, perhaps that. (He used the money to buy Kansas City real estate.)[16]

Wiry and arrogant, and blessed or damned with an immigrant zeal to succeed, Coyne had gone into the Yucatan Peninsula a poor man and had emerged a few years later a richer one. He then returned to Kansas City and married Molly, who had previously turned him down. It was on this trip that he bought a house at 3228 Roberts Street and rebuilt it with walls two feet thick, like a fort. Then he fathered a child, Ellen, and went back to the Latin American jungles, his sharp eyes seeking out another best route for a road, his handlebar mustache masking his emotions. He at some point took his wife and daughter to Panama and then bought a large, isolated spread in the Missouri Ozarks near Galena, moving his family there with the intention of raising sheep. His daughter was unhappy with her schooling, however, and after she threw a fit, the family moved back to Kansas City and the more comfortable house there. Perhaps Coyne built his fortlike house because he was wanted for murder in several Latin American states, perhaps it kept off the chills of his malaria, or maybe he simply wanted something to be left standing when he moved from the house and burned whatever he did not want in a bonfire in his yard—pictures and papers from his past, some of his wife's things, and his daughter's college diploma. When he was through with his Kansas City real estate, he sold it for next to nothing. When he was through with life, he discarded it in suicide—but that was many years after this time in 1924, when Ellen began to write Molly that she was seeing the writer Edgar Lee Masters. Molly was to see him, too, for she had just been chosen as a delegate to the Democratic National Convention, to be held that summer in New York City.[17]

Masters and Molly Coyne got along exceedingly well, a surprising fact given the age difference between her daughter and Masters. In fact, the superficial facts suggest that Molly had more in common with Masters than did her child: each had been married in 1898, each had had a child the following year, and each had spent two decades in what were essentially loveless marriages (like Masters, Tom Coyne was usually a good provider and a terrible husband). Masters charmed Molly with his mixture of dimples, drawl, and midwestern stories. He was much easier to like than Tom Coyne, whose stories of dead Indians, dead horses, and dead Latinos left a gash in Molly's gentle being as deep as the rail cuts Tom carved in the Andes.[18]

Or maybe Masters and Molly found commonality under the hopeful auspices of the Democratic Party. Molly had complimentary tickets to the 1924 convention, and Masters made good use of these, looking down on the convention floor to observe the delegation from Illinois and the passing throng. Masters's political acquaintance William Jennings Bryan was there, still behaving like a presidential candidate but doomed for defeat in 1924, just as he would shortly be defeated by Masters's old nemesis Clarence Darrow in the Scopes Monkey Trial of 1925: "Here was Bryan wandering about the aisles of Madison Square. He was now thin and bent, his hair was stringy and scant, his eyes were burned back in his head like a fire that is winking before going out. . . . I did not get to speak to him, but I watched him critically as he passed from delegation to delegation manufacturing conferences." By the time the convention was over on July 9, Masters and Molly Coyne were friends for life.[19]

Masters was awaiting publication of *The New Spoon River,* which he had proofed in June. He had written epitaphs in addition to those serialized by the Bell Syndicate and had received a $2,000 advance. He used the money to pay off his $2,000 note with Abe Meyer and was again low on funds, asking his publisher Horace Liveright for an additional $1,000 and explaining that the advance "just paid my note and left me nothing for the summer." Masters and Liveright were sometimes drinking companions, and although Liveright could not advance such a sum, he did make Masters a personal loan of $1,000, saying that he had borrowed the money from his wife. On the day of the loan, however, Liveright shifted the debt to the corporation of Boni and Liveright, which promptly reimbursed him. Unfortunately, he apparently failed to tell Masters that he had done this, thus igniting a ten-year feud between Masters and the corporation as to whether Masters owed it $1,000 and whether the money could be taken from Masters's royalties from *The New Spoon River.* Horace Liveright further complicated matters by leaving the company and going to Hollywood. So Masters's relations with the firm of Boni and Liveright were stressed almost before they had begun.[20]

Masters was encouraged to turn back to Spoon River because he needed money, because he had been urged to do so by admirers, and because he knew that the fame of *Spoon River* would generate interest in its sequel. He was originally going to call his new book "The Spoon River Annex," but Horace Liveright disliked that title and convinced Masters to call it *The New Spoon River.* Masters's mother liked the idea of the book so well that she provided him with a list of eighty prospective names to use, the first and last names mixed in such a way that their original owners could not be offended. He used three of the names without changing them and may have borrowed elements of others as well. (He later acknowledged his mother's help by dedicating *The New Spoon River* to her.)[21]

Unfortunately, due to Masters's temperament, personal experiences, and changing times, he could not again journey home as successfully as he had in 1914. The first *Spoon River* had concentrated on a specific part of the national scene, the midwestern village; its subject was the individual in the village, and the objective treatment made the book successful. In contrast, the poems in *The New Spoon River* came across as highly subjective. As Masters explained to Horace Liveright, *The New Spoon River* was "a son of a bitch": "And I want it to be. . . . It gets into the skin and flesh of this, our America, on religion, politics, sex, everything." With his polemics and prejudices clearly showing, Masters seemed to wander in and out of this new book, pausing to tell his readers what to think and making the same points so often that his characters lost their individuality.[22]

Even the artwork for the deluxe and trade editions was designed to suit his biases. Masters had wanted to show "what the age of machinery has done to America" and asked for a drawing showing the old mill or covered bridge at Bernadotte, Illinois, the fishing hamlet on the Spoon River. He wanted these to be shown disappearing under a pall of smoke or obscured by a maze of high-tension electric lines. His request would eventually be honored in a trade edition, and to a degree on the title page of the deluxe edition, on which was printed a rustic view of the bridge.[23]

Nevertheless, the overall effect was not so much that Spoon River had changed but that Masters had failed to change with it. Some of the new poems lamented the ways in which "Spoon River became a ganglion / For the monster brain Chicago." Others attacked foreign elements Masters blamed for contemporary changes:

> I saw that the village names were changed;
> And instead of Churchill, Spears and Rutledge,
> It was Schoenwald and Stefanik,
> And Berkowitz and Garnadello . . . ,
> And then I said with a sinking heart,
> Good-by Republic, old dear!

Overriding all was a sense of loss, mutability, and dislocation, phenomena that Masters had experienced in the extreme by 1924; the epitaph of Martin Venable illustrates these emotions:

> Did you ever destroy a bird's nest,
> So there was not a vestige of it left in the tree?
> Then have you watched the bird when it returned,
> And flew about and about the place where the nest had been,
> Wondering what had become of the nest,
> Or wondering if this be the tree of the nest?
> It was even so with me and Spoon River:
> I returned to find the old town
> And found it not;
> And drifted about wondering
> If Spoon River had ever been my home,
> And if so what had become of Spoon River![24]

Perhaps Masters's views in *The New Spoon River* stemmed from the adverse circumstances under which he drafted the book, doing so during the nadir of his existence, the several months early in 1923 when he and Helen were in the process of ending their marriage but not divorced ("I wrote it in Bill Slack's kitchen in that awful winter of 1923"). Perhaps the critics had sharpened their pencils (as he sometimes insisted) and refused to let him enjoy a second critical success, or perhaps Masters had sharpened his own pencils. The often hostile reception given the first *Spoon River* itself had clearly delineated the differences between Masters and certain groups that felt his book was immoral. After the battle lines between him and these groups were drawn, he seldom chose to lampoon them subtly, as he had in portions of *Spoon River,* but instead attacked directly in inartistic outbursts.[25]

But perhaps he did not know that the outbursts were inartistic. Indeed, Masters's use of hostility was not without example in numerous American locales. During the two decades that preceded World War I, novelists in particular earned success by hurling imprecations at the "robber barons." Henry Blake Fuller, David Graham Phillips, Robert Herrick, Upton Sinclair, and others demonstrated that indignation and success could go together and that anger could be an essential component of art. (One thinks also of those earlier midwestern rebels Mark Twain and Robert Ingersoll, both of whom influenced Masters.) Carl Sandburg also published much in the way of protest literature, free verse damning a host of villains planted firmly in the American grain: tycoons, warmongers, and exploiters of the masses. In addition, several of the people Masters most admired were the era's best-known iconoclasts. Among these was Dreiser, who had been an influence and a friend for a decade, and H. L. Mencken, whom Masters was finally to meet in 1924 and with whom he had been corresponding since 1913. All this had influenced him as he sat at Bill Slack's table and proceeded to prove that even his talent for elegiac verse could be compromised if he cluttered it with an endless stream of angry invectives.[26]

Masters had high hopes for *The New Spoon River.* By 1924 *Spoon River Anthology* had been translated into French, German, and Spanish, and the new book sold very well too, with Masters telling Harriet Monroe at the end of its first ninety days that it "sold better within the same time than the old book did." Reviews were mixed when the book was published in September, however, a few people finding *The New Spoon River* superior but most preferring the old. Some clever critics dusted off their satiric thinking caps and again fashioned commentary in verse, including these lines in *The Saturday Review of Literature:*

> He sees such a ravishing lot of crime,
> Perversion, insanity, slime and grime
> To tell us about, that he has no time
> To put it in meter, much less in rhyme.
> Below him, awaiting their resurrection
> From tombs that no longer afford protection,
> Are acres of subjects for keen dissection,
> That being his jovial predilection.

Even with this send-off, however, *The New Spoon River* was far more successful than many literary sequels, and it is usually considered Masters's second-most important volume of verse, preceding his own favorite, *Domesday Book.* In 1924, however, its chief importance to him was that its advance allowed him to pay off his $2,000 note with Abe Meyer and further shake the dust of Chicago from his heels.[27]

After the Democratic Convention ended in New York in July, Masters wrote intermittently on a play and other works but spent a great deal of time in transit between his room at Princeton's Nassau Club and Ellen's Manhattan apartment. He traveled to Great Neck to visit the Farleys and made other short trips, his days a restless shuttle to friends in and around the New York area. He was doing his own typing these days to save money, and things went slowly. In early August he gave up trying to work, packed his bags at Great Neck, and prepared to visit his sister in Maine. He paused first to say good-bye to Ellen on August 7: "Pack and leave G.N. Meet Ellen at Penn. Hotel. Go to 51 W. 16—X. Autograph *Spoon River*."[28]

Masters's wealthy sister, Madeline, had a summer place on Cushing Island, off the coast of Maine, as well as a home in East Hampton, New York, and a house in Chicago. (The latter was on Prairie Avenue, not long since the most fashionable street in the city.) She soon thereafter sold all three places and purchased three new ones: a house in Washington, D.C.; an apartment in New York City; and a house at Bar Harbor, Maine. Together, they offered her year-round comfort as regards the weather, and if she wearied of all three simultaneously, she could always go to Europe, the largesse from her marriage to the late Dr. Carl Stone (and his father's estate) paying for it all. Her marriage to Neils Gron, a Danish diplomat, had not worked out, but they were now divorced, and she lived the life of the idle wealthy, looking after the child from her second marriage, Edgar Lee Gron. She also looked after the well-being of her three children from her first marriage, Elizabeth, Horatio (or "Buddie"), and Emma Louise. Madeline was selective about how she was known and eventually took back her first married name, Stone. Pretty, unambiguously wealthy, and (according to her family) gifted with excellent taste, she was educated in the arts: she had studied drawing at Knox College, heard lectures on anatomy in Paris, and studied sculpture under Lorado Taft and Gutzon Borglum. This notwithstanding, Masters seldom found much to say to her, possibly because the opulence of her numerous houses contrasted unfavorably with his own quarters, typically a room or two. Now she provided him with new social opportunities, his diary showing that he danced on several occasions during his ten-day visit with her. For one reason or another, however, none of Madeline's friends appealed to him: "Feel depressed and anxious," he wrote in his diary for August 17. He was ready to go back to New York and Ellen.[29]

On his return he found that the Farleys had enjoyed his presence so much that they wanted him to stay permanently. They had thus built him quarters of his own at their Great Neck estate, apparently a renovated outdoor studio or a small house with a study. After trying their new accommodations, however, he found he was still interrupted more than he wished and in mid-September acquired his first permanent address in New York City: "Move to 53." This diary entry was a reference to 53 West Sixteenth Street, the same apartment complex in which Ellen lived. Within a few weeks Masters was using her apartment address as his own, telling the writer and artist Walter Tittle and others to write him at 51 West Sixteenth Street. Masters now began to show signs of staying in New York permanently, letting his Chicago club memberships lapse and saying that he had relocated: "I shall be around this town of New York indefinitely."[30]

One day he and Ellen went to see Joseph Nicolosi, a sculptor for whom Ellen sometimes posed. Parts of *The New Spoon River* decried the arrival of non-English immigrants such as Nicolosi, and Masters's diary for the day reflects his uncertainty: "E. poses for Nicolosi. I am present." He found that he admired the sculptor's artistry, however, and after additional visits to his studio and a dinner or two, Masters found himself the subject of Nicolosi's work: "Nicolosi begins bust of me" (September 18). He would sit for Nicolosi at least ten more times through October 8, his comments to Roland and Elsie Farley mirroring his satisfaction with the emerging work: "Nicolosi is taking infinite pains with the bust, and the end is not yet. He shapes and studies, and stands off and squints, and penetrates with his thought, and pats in and smooths off without weariness; and I shall give him all the time he wants, for this shall be definitive." The bust was more flattering than definitive, however, for Nicolosi sculpted Masters without his glasses and made him appear younger and thinner than he was. Masters approved of the final product, noting in his diary, "I like Nicolosi's sculpture." Nicolosi would also prove to be a friend to Masters on numerous other occasions.[31]

Because Ellen worked as a model only part-time, she was free to pursue her first choice of vocations, the theater. She was working in these days, September and October 1924, with a theater group in Yonkers; Masters's diary for October 9 shows that he traveled to Yonkers "to see Ellen act," but he failed to comment on either the play or the performance, and the quality of her acting is not defined. She was also working with Sue Hastings' Marionettes on New York's Riverside Drive, where she did voices and made costumes.[32]

It was also during the fall of 1924 that Masters began work on what he described as his "magnum opus," a masterwork he hoped would rival *Spoon River* or *Domesday Book*. It was to be called "Atlantis" and would be a verse summary of America from its discovery through the dawn of the twentieth century. He described it as an epic—his "*Aeneid* of the American scene"—and told friends it would be his "long poem, [his] great work," and that it would require "years" to complete. He did not have a contract for such an undertaking but felt that if he researched it thoroughly and made it exhaustive, he could carry it off. He "began to read for 'Atlantis'" on October 20 and by November 21 was "reading as much as possible everyday." He brought Harriet Monroe up to date with his plans at Thanksgiving: "I am now reading for ATLANTIS, my great work. Just finished Prescott's *Conquest of Mexico*—and months of reading yet to do."

Because he wanted to do firsthand reporting on the nation as well as scholarly interpreting, and because he had a chance to make some money from lecturing, late that November he began to make plans for a cross-country tour in 1925: "I felt that I must see America all over again from coast to coast." Related encouragement came from Horace Liveright, who felt that a tour would help sell *The New Spoon River.*[33]

The New York booking agent Colston Leigh subsequently arranged a tour for Masters in conjunction with Armstrong Educational Tours, in Waco. The tour comprised twenty-three speaking engagements across ten weeks of travel, from January 22 to April 1, an itinerary that allowed Masters ample time for reading and local research. In addition to preparing remarks entitled "America and American Poetry," Masters spent several days "committing poems to memory" in preparation for reciting his verse on the road.[34]

He subsequently spoke in Maryland, West Virginia, Missouri, Arkansas, and Texas in January and February. His diary shows that most of his audiences averaged about 600 people, with a high of 1,200 in Waco, and a low of 300 in Dallas. College towns and college lecture halls were his best settings. His most unusual site was a "full" Methodist Church on Friday the thirteenth in Fort Worth. At Austin he visited one of his friendliest admirers, L. W. Payne, a professor of English at the University of Texas.[35]

Another admirer awaited him at the University of Arizona, where Dr. Gerald Sanders, a member of the English faculty (and later cocompiler of *Chief Modern Poets of England and America*), served as Masters's host. (Sanders would several years later begin an ambitious bibliography of Masters's works.) He escorted Masters to the university's large telescope (providing him with a superb view of Orion) and held a reception in his honor. Masters noted in his diary that the desert beer was "better than [that of the] Taylor House at Havana, Ill." He subsequently saw the Grand Canyon and then spoke to audiences in Los Angeles, Sacramento, and Stockton.[36]

At this point the pressure of meeting strangers and speaking began to bother Masters, as he complained to Roland Farley: "This traveling is just killing, and the entertaining makes it worse, and the lecturing: standing for more than an hour and putting all my emotion into it takes all the sap out of me. Lots of drinks everywhere; but I am not doing it much. Gathering material everywhere for 'Atlantis.'" When he arrived in San Francisco, he was glad to relax with the poet George Sterling and his friends. Sterling arrived at Masters's hotel room with "every sort of a drinkable which he could gather up." Indeed, despite Masters's comments about restrained drinking, he also left behind letters before, during, and after his trip that suggest otherwise. He broke his contracts for lectures in Salem and Eugene, Oregon, telling Colston Leigh that he was too ill to travel (in an unpublished chapter of his autobiography he said that the distance was greater than he had originally supposed), but his real reason was probably to relax with Sterling.[37]

Masters pushed on to Reno on March 12 and to Salt Lake City, where he delivered another lecture. He paused to visit Ellen Coyne's aunt and uncle, Albin and Katherine Palm, as well as the governor of Utah, and toured the Mormon Tabernacle and surrounding settlements. The Mormons' earlier settlement at Nauvoo, Illinois, not far from Masters's home of Lewistown, had ended with bloodshed and the martyrdom of the Mormon leader Joseph Smith; the success of the Mormons in Salt Lake City interested Masters, and he stayed there four days, visiting bookstores, buying a ring, and touring a mine. A friendly sheriff presented him with a quart of bootleg corn whisky as a going-away present.[38]

Masters passed through Wyoming and Nebraska, on March 18 reaching Des Moines, Iowa, where he alienated nearly all his audience of 1,200, including the town's ministers and the Des Moines Women's Club. In the course of his lecture (or the interview that followed), Masters was perceived as attacking organized religion: "A man cannot take a drink or fall in love or read a book of his own choosing because the Methodists and Baptists and all the other sects have a stranglehold on happiness." This was printed on page 1 of the *Des Moines Register* ("Poet's Attack on Corn Belt Starts Storm"), along with a notice that Masters had criticized his audience for coughing and wheezing during his lecture and found fault with the town's smoky air: "No wonder you people have colds and ugly bodies and minds." When he was invited to attend a reception, he was too unimpressed with Des Moines to bother: "Flaunting his so-called artistic temperament, the poet refused to be the guest of honor at a dinner which was being held for him last evening. He graciously retracted his original statement that 'Des Moines is the smokiest and dirtiest city I have ever seen' and qualified it by saying, 'This isn't any worse than Salt Lake City.'" At some point Masters decided it would be wise to pour the rest of the corn whisky down the drain: "The auspices in Des Moines indicated a search of my room, after a private talk I had with a newspaper woman was published as an interview, in which I took the culture of Des Moines, and that part of the West, to task. A storm arose about me which followed me to La Crosse, where the Baptist minister tried to prevent my lecturing."[39]

The afflictions of Des Moines carried over to Milwaukee. Masters was not scheduled to speak there, and finding it both "dull" and "dreary," he took a night boat across Lake Michigan, landing at Muskegon, "only a few miles from Spring Lake and [his] lost orchard." The old wound of losing his farm bothered him again, and he pushed on in a sour mood to Toledo, Ohio.[40]

On March 26 he arrived in Cleveland, where Ellen joined him on the morning of the twenty-eighth. They enjoyed three days of relaxation, with trips to bookstores and theaters before his lecture on March 31. He subsequently had a "great audience" of 1,200 in Syracuse on April 1 and returned to New York, his trip completed, on April 2.[41]

His tour had carried him through twenty-two states and to lecture engagements in twenty-one cities. Arrangements had called for at least sixteen of the sites to pay him $200 for his lecture; three sites had generated $150. His total revenue was about $4,000. Railroad charges and hotel expenses shown in his diary and his comments in a letter suggest that his seventy days on the road had netted him about $3,000 (his food expenses were minimized because he had been a guest at numerous locations). The trip had been tiring physically, however, and there were other costs as well: "I sent $1,000 to my former wife out of these hard-earned dollars to pay alimony. I had seen the country and made something for some leisure in which to write 'Atlantis,' but I was spent. I had to rest two weeks before I could work on 'Atlantis.' I had learned that lecturing is a way to make a living, but that it is at the expense of a destroying fatigue which takes one's very life." It also robbed him of his patience and peace of mind when he realized he could have negotiated with his agent for more money.[42]

Because he had not earned as much as he wished, he worked steadily on a variety of writings, including an article with the title "Can an Artist Live in America?" (The question was answered a few weeks later when *The Nation* bought the piece for thirty-six dollars, an amount that Masters considered so paltry that he returned the check to *The Nation,* along with an angry note that "the transaction illustrates . . . the difficulties that surround the life of an artist living in America.") He also approached George Brett Jr. at Macmillan about bringing out his collected poems at this time. This was an attempt both to summarize his career and to make some extra money—for despite having paid Helen Masters some of the money due her, he was still behind in his payments. (Helen always needed the money, not only to live on, but also because the large house on Kenwood Avenue always had maintenance expenses.) Masters could never save enough to satisfy these payments, although he did nothing to economize: in May he moved from the Old Chelsea, where he had been paying sixteen dollars per week, to an apartment at 18 Gramercy Avenue, where his rent was ninety dollars a month.[43]

He was still ambivalent about Ellen and marriage. She had maintained her goal of a theatrical career, but it remained unclear as to how she might achieve this. She had been handicapped by a severe case of eczema, for which she underwent an experimental X-ray treatment that left her face scarred; after that she had to wear heavy makeup. Never one to ignore human drama, Masters may have used the incident in his next novel, *Kit O'Brien,* in which a would-be actress suffers facial disfigurement through a botched skin treatment intended to make her more attractive. Ellen had turned twenty-six on May 18 and was working at the Washington Irving Bookstore. (She had been employed at this bookstore when young Bennett Cerf stopped by and asked her whether she thought it would be a good idea to buy Modern Library from publishers Boni and Liveright; she said it would. Cerf agreed and soon had one of the most successful ventures in American publishing.) Ellen was very able and attracted to Masters, but it remained to be seen whether she had a future with him. She was willing to give him a chance, however, for she was wearing a jade emperor's ring he had given her at Christmas (and would in fact wear it for much of the rest of her life). Her neighbors said she was "starry-eyed" about him; they were not sure how he felt about her.[44]

Ellen was somewhat like Masters's mother, Emma. Never one to take an insult, she was "keen as hell and spunky" (as Masters described her). With her artistic interests, Ellen was also somewhat like the other women who had been important to Masters: his first wife, Helen, who was fond of music; Tennessee Mitchell, who was a music teacher and sculptor; and Lillian, a published playwright and would-be dramatizer of *Spoon River*. In addition to pursuing a dramatic career, Ellen would shortly compose "a little sketch" called "Books," a play submitted to (and rejected by) a New York playhouse. Ellen also looked somewhat like Lillian (some of Lillian's pictures taken in the 1910s and some of Ellen's professional photos taken in the 1920s show women enough alike to be sisters). In addition, Ellen and Lillian (and Helen Masters) had what Masters valued most in a facial profile—a shapely nose, like that of his grandmother, Lucinda Masters. And Ellen, like most of the other women in Masters's life, would eventually find that he was difficult to plan around.[45]

For one thing, he had flirted behind Ellen's back with a pretty young woman named Edwina Stanton Babcock, a would-be author. Masters had encountered her before his 1925 lecture tour and left her with the impression that he led a solitary life ("I am by myself and working"). She had replied to some of his letters while he was on his lecture tour, sending hers to the National Arts Club, as he had directed. (His mail was forwarded from there.) He had tried to win her with his educated primitive approach, offering her a "$100 reward (or the equivalent)" for answering the following:

> [Question:] What words of a celebrated American statesman, when dying, are also the sweetest words that a gentleman can say to a lady?
> [Answer:] I am ready.

Masters mixed such talk with metaphysical matters and overviews of nature's way in the affairs of men and women: "No one knows what nature intends; so we are warranted in following our desires and our reasons, conveniences, tastes, since nature gives us no basis for morality." He had subsequently made himself as agreeable as possible to Edwina Babcock: he kept her apprised of the progress of his 1925 tour, complimented her on her prettiness, let her know when he would return, and told her he looked forward to seeing her ("I hope to see you when I get back to the city—wish it were tomorrow"). When he returned, he arranged for a trip to her hometown of South Nyack and a picnic on the banks of the Hudson: "Edwina at train. Lunch on beach." At some point she saw him with Ellen, however, and no amount of explaining was enough, although he tried: "The girl you saw me with goes about town and sees and knows everything, and then comes and tells me what I should do. . . . I think she is a police dog turned human." But Edwina had recognized immediately that Ellen was too attractive to be anything other than what she was. A little later she departed Masters's life forever.[46]

Meanwhile, Ellen listened to his hopes for "Atlantis" and his new book for boys (called *Kit O'Brien,* after a minor character in *Mitch Miller*). She also helped him prepare his selected poems for Macmillan: "MS of *Selected Poems.* Ellen helps" (May 28). They began the volume with one of his weakest pieces, a lengthy excerpt from a verse play, followed by poems concerning Shakespeare, Voltaire, and the Romans. The first poem of contemporary interest began on page 50. It was not an auspicious beginning, though the volume did have poems of biographical interest, including one called "The Statue," a lengthy narrative concerning several artists who work with a model called "Fayfe" (one of Ellen's nicknames was "Fay-Fay"):

> Rhythm of arms and breasts, rapture of color and curve—
> Where would you get them, you who demand and admire,
> Were there never a form to stay, lest the vision swerve,
> Naked before the sculptor, posing for hire?

A reference to "Nicoli the sculptor" (Nicolosi, of course) was also included. The manuscript for *Selected Poems* took only five days to prepare and was delivered to Macmillan on June 1. The manuscript of *Kit O'Brien* followed, going to Boni and Liveright on June 9.[47]

Masters may have reflected that he could process manuscripts at the rate he wished if he had a helpmate by his side, but before he had time to think this through, Ellen announced that she was going to Ireland. Her father had decided that she was seeing too much of Masters, or as Ellen phrased it a few years later, "My father gave me the . . . trip in '25 to keep me from getting married." England and the Continent were also included in her trip, which she was making with her mother. Tom Coyne did not go (in characteristic fashion, he decided to investigate his roots by himself, doing it later, at eighty-six). By mid-July Ellen and her mother had departed, and Masters was at work on "Atlantis."[48]

"Atlantis" occupies a special place in Masters's list of many books. No other volume cost him so dearly in terms of time and research, for he would spend years working on it, and no other book of poetry was less advised: "Atlantis" was projected to be an epic, but American poetry in the 1920s was slowly moving away from epics—away from the sprawling type of story he was about to tell—and toward more concise verse of the type Masters himself had helped popularize in *Spoon River Anthology.* Remarkably enough, he failed to notice this or chose not to see it.

He had first conceived of "Atlantis" in the summer of 1922 while waiting for Helen Masters to agree to divorce terms. Perhaps some truculence on her behalf reminded him of a god in a feisty mood, or maybe his own sufferings seemed grown to epic proportions. In any event, Masters decided to write a poem as lengthy of line and scope as that of Virgil's *Aeneid.* The story was to be laid down in twelve "books" in 12,000 lines of iambic pentameter and would run to at least 400 pages. He explained his plans to the publisher Horace Liveright:

> It is the epic of America from the discovery of Columbus to the present, treating of the Maya and Mexican civilizations as they existed in 1492; and of the Indian country and cities of New Mexico as they were at that time. It treats of the colonization of the country, and of the contests between France and England and Spain for the continent; of the wars fought here between these peoples and between ourselves; of our notables, our pioneer adventures, our achievements in science and literature and thought; with an invented story to carry the whole running through it from first to last down to the days of Wilson.[49]

"Atlantis" turned out to be as formidable in execution as its planning sounded. Following his 1925 lecture tour, Masters showed his half-finished draft to an unnamed publisher, probably Horace Liveright. The publisher was unimpressed with "the pile of manuscript" (as Masters called it)—it was the middle of the Jazz Age, after all, and no one wanted a new *Aeneid.* On August 6, 1925, three years to the day after conceiving the work, the manuscript of "Atlantis" went to the vault. Masters's magnum opus was stalled, and so were his literary and financial plans for the future.[50]

Another problem also began to affect Masters at about this time. Ten years earlier, when *Spoon River* had been at the peak of its fame, he had been besieged by compilers of anthologies. In his words, he "gave away poems right and left . . . from 1915 to about 1920." In 1921 Harriet Monroe had approached him for selections for an anthology, and he again granted permission: "You have my permission to reprint in *The New Poetry* (revised edition) such poems as you may choose from my various books; the list to be submitted to me for approval." Monroe failed to get his approval before publishing her selections, however, and when Masters looked about, he noticed other things he disliked about other anthologies. For one thing, anthologists chose to reprint the same poems over and over. "There should be a more catholic representation of my work," he told a Macmillan representative in 1922. Worse, Masters complained to William Rose Benet, "people who buy anthologies are too frequently contented with that, and leave [an author's] books as a whole unread." Worse still, anthologists sometimes shaped public opinion against an author and stole the profits as well ("money was being made out of my work, for which I got nothing"). Masters adumbrated the issues to Macmillan's George Brett: "Besides this, anthologies circulate among the thousands who don't buy the books of the author, but content themselves with anthologies, and base their opinions on the judgment of the anthologist." Thus, Masters decided to end the "parasitical activity of anthologists" (a.k.a., "pedantic donkeys" and "ignorant calumniators"); he also took a dim view of publishers who sponsored such things: "There are many stupidities that publishers commit that to me are beyond explanation." So he was understandably upset when he occasionally found one of his poems pirated and angrier still if he found one of his publishers cooperating with anthology makers.[51]

Following his return from his 1925 trip, Masters reminded Brett of his feelings about anthologies: "I want to draw in on the anthologists; but in doing so, friendly teachers and textbook writers must not be slighted." The problem was in deciding which of the prospective editors would write "friendly" appraisals. Marguerite Wilkinson and Ludwig Lewisohn were allowed to use all the poems of their choice, but Conrad Aiken was not allowed to use any. Alfred Kreymborg, Louis Untermeyer, and Mark Van Doren were also turned down, as were John Drinkwater and William S. Braithwaite. Fred Lewis Pattee had already made plans to use some of Masters's poems when Masters returned the sixty dollar check designed to cover their use. Masters's Arizona acquaintance Gerald Sanders suffered a similar reversal ("I withdrew my consent to go in your book"). This must have seemed particularly capricious, for in his discussions regarding Sanders's volume, Masters had already tried to substitute poems of his own choice; demanded that Vachel Lindsay have "an equal representation . . . with Sandburg and Amy Lowell"; insisted that poets Hardy, Robinson, and Frost receive no more pages than himself; and asked to read the proofs of critical and biographical matter for "misstatements." "One important poet," Sanders would later say, "refused us any of his poems." (Masters had a different view, telling the lawyer William Osborne of the Author's League: "[Sanders's] book came out without my being in it, and its back was broken thereby. . . . Without me in it, the anthology is sadly incomplete.") Nor did many other anthologists fare better. A would-be compiler working through Harper Brothers received this note: "I do not regret that you do not find it possible to meet the terms made to you in my letter of the 20th ult for the use of poems mentioned in your first letter. I am pleased not to be included in your book." The remarkable thing was that after seven or eight years of turning down requests from anthologists, Masters in 1929 could tell Henry Seidel Canby that he was still receiving "at least three requests a week from people preparing collections." He continued to receive "an average of three requests a week all the year around" through 1932.[52]

In the end, Masters's withdrawal from anthologies proved to be costly in a variety of ways. He might make only $10 to $20 per poem (the going rate), but if he had permitted only three poems per request, three requests per week at $10 per poem would have netted him over $4,500 in a year—enough to pay Helen her alimony of $1,800 with $2,700 left over. In addition, Masters failed to see that publishing in anthologies would give him the opportunity to work with some of the most important critics and publishers in America and that anthologies represented good advertising for previously published volumes as well as future ones. In fact, after his *Selected Poems* was published in 1925, Masters's sole use for previously published works was in collections of the type he was now shunning. Worst of all, his failure to appear in anthologies gave the impression that his best work was not only over and done but forgotten as well. Fred Lewis Pattee's editor had begged Masters not to take his poems out of Pattee's forthcoming book, reminding him that "all the more important authors and poets" would figure in it, including Frost, Sandburg, Lindsay, Amy Lowell, and Edwin Arlington Robinson. But Masters would not be told. They could take him on his terms or not at all. (It would not be the last time that Masters would waste his energies on projects such as "Atlantis" while ignoring easier and more accessible earnings.) This was his mood, then, as he sat down, alone, lonely, and nearly broke, to think about his autobiography.[53]

CHAPTER 13

Masters Marries Girl!

I said to God, "Don't you know that she is lots younger than I am?"
And God said, "What do you want? Someone your own age?"
"No," says I. "Well?" says God kind of sneery.

—Edgar Lee Masters to Eunice Tietjens, February 6, 1927

An interesting observation about Masters's career is that through the time of his divorce and relocation to New York City, he still had time to redefine himself. He could have taken the easy money that came from anthologies, applied himself to his work, and possibly created a new reputation. But he did not do this. He instead chose paths that provided the greatest potential for problems. For example, he continued to publish with casual indifference to the opinions of his editors, doing so (he would have explained) because he needed the freedom traditionally accorded artists. When his editors gave in to him, as they frequently did, he was free to shape his next book as he chose. The results were disastrous: poor reviews, poor sales, and increased economic stress.

He sought similar freedoms in his private life. He had not felt guilty about pursuing another woman (Edwina Stanton Babcock) while living in close association with Ellen Coyne, but he would not grant Ellen similar freedoms. When she thought of going overseas to pursue a theatrical career and flirted with another man (as she would in the period covered in this chapter), Masters grew upset and used an extreme means to address his concerns: he married her. Thus, instead of using his divorce and relocation to begin a genuinely new life, he soon duplicated some of the situations that had troubled him in Chicago.

Little in Masters's career went as he wished through 1925. *The New Spoon River* sold reasonably well, but his 1924 novel about Lillian, *Mirage,* was far too diffuse and self-serving to satisfy readers (thus vindicating the literary judgment of an editor at Boni and Liveright who had counseled revisions but been ignored). Worse, what might have been the capstone to Masters's career, his *Selected Poems,* appeared in 1925 with various typographical problems, including a line from one poem placed in the text of another. Meanwhile, the manuscript of his new boy's book, *Kit O'Brien,* went from publisher to publisher; "Atlantis" was stalled; and his play about New Salem failed to find a producer. Equally bad, creditors showed up with bills a year or two old and threatened legal action. Fed up with events and distressed with a summer cold, in August Masters and the sculptor Joseph Nicolosi traveled to the New York resort area of Lake George, where the two swam and boated for two weeks.[1]

Perhaps Nicolosi said something that put Masters in a backward frame of reference; perhaps he arrived at the juncture himself. In any event, he now began to plan his autobiography. He felt that the life story of the author of *Spoon River* would generate some badly needed cash, and he also knew that telling his story from his own perspective was preferable to letting the newspapers tell it in pieces. The serious illnesses of Masters's parents may also have played a part. Emma Masters had been diagnosed with cancer in 1921, the same year her husband suffered an eye disorder that left him blind in one eye and unable to pursue his legal career. If Masters were to gather information from his parents, he needed to start before time inflicted further ravages.[2]

He had already gathered a part of his research through a trip to the Jacksonville, Illinois, area in 1917 and through an 1897 deposition he had taken from his paternal grandmother, Lucinda Masters, regarding her roots. As the present moved more and more against him, the past grew more attractive.[3]

One of the first things Masters did as he addressed the past was to ask Nicolosi to make a bronze plate for use as a grave marker for Lucinda and her husband, Squire Davis Masters. The memorial plate bore their names and appropriate dates and the inscription "Illinois Pioneers," along with the notice that the tablet had been "placed by their affectionate grandson Edgar Lee Masters" in 1925. Masters expressed the tablet to his uncle Will in Petersburg and made plans to attach it to a large stone he had had removed from the Rock Creek near Petersburg. Then he traveled to Illinois in September to spend time with his mother and father, gathering from each of them details for his autobiography:

> [My father's] discipline as a lawyer had given his mind tenacity about the facts of anything. He knew dates; he ran back to his boyhood, and then forward to his young manhood, then to Lewistown, then to Petersburg and Springfield, all without hesitation, remembering names of the long ago with no effort at all. It was among the most delightful days I ever spent, listening to his conversation as racy as the soil and with the scent of hickory wood. . . . Meanwhile, my mother lay in bed, occasionally interpolating a correction, which sometimes he accepted. Again, he showed her that she was wrong.[4]

The next day was more difficult. Masters visited the rural church he had sometimes attended with his grandparents and stopped at their nearby farm. He visited the church first, finding it in total disarray:

> Going into the country I took pictures of Concord Church, by that time a ruin, with a great tree grown through one of its walls, with the doors flapping to the wind, and the chandeliers full of swallows' nests, and the carpets rolled up, and

> the pulpit tumbled from the rostrum, and the wallpaper peeled and hanging here and there. I stood by the seat where as a little boy I had sat with my grandfather when he trembled with sorrow and mystical passion to hear Cowper's tragic hymn of the "Fountain Filled with Blood." All the seats now were criss-cross in the room as I looked about, calling to visual memory the pioneers who used to occupy them.

Even less was left of his grandparents' farm, the house having burned, and the landscape itself was changed: "Nothing was left but some remnants of brick walks, and a few trees to identify the place. The orchard was gone. The forest to the south had been cut away, and showed nothing but a bare hill where it had stood. To the north, the Mason County Hills were not hills, but a low rim of gray and purple." He returned to Springfield with the knowledge that the haunts of his boyhood had largely vanished, except as he might capture them in the pages of his autobiography. He said good-bye to his parents, noticing as he did so that his father was growing frail, and with these thoughts on his mind returned to New York City and Ellen.[5]

She had been bitten hard by the theater bug and had kept herself going with a variety of jobs while waiting for her "break" to come. In addition to working in at least one bookstore and with Sue Hastings' Marionettes, she had won several parts with Long Island stock companies. She had not returned to the Midwest or the Far West as a member of any touring company—that was all behind her now, replaced by her hopes with the Abbey Theatre in Ireland and the possibility of a place with that illustrious group (she had met some of the actors and actresses during her trip abroad and had socialized with Sara Allgood). No one knew when the Abbey Theatre's present play would end, however (it was Sean O'Casey's *Juno and the Paycock*), and Ellen had returned home. Not long afterward she had a bit part in a Broadway production of *Julius Caesar,* which again fueled her hopes for a stage career, although Masters did not encourage this. All his theater hopes had ended in disappointment. She was spending as much time looking to the future as he spent on the past.[6]

He was arranging the parts of his autobiography now, gathering his notes and putting into perspective his interviews with his parents. He first thought to capitalize on the historical coincidence that he had spent his childhood in an Illinois town, Petersburg, that lay within two miles of Abraham Lincoln's New Salem. This seemed a marketable idea—the more so as Lincoln's Tomb, in Springfield, was only twenty miles away—and he soon began planning a manuscript with the title of "My Years in the Lincoln Country." By a second accident of history and place, Masters's father, Hardin, had worked in the 1870s as an associate of Lincoln's former law partner, William H. Herndon, whose 1889 *Lincoln* had romanticized the relationship between Lincoln and Ann Rutledge. In 1890, partly as a result of Herndon's writings, Rutledge's remains had been moved from the Old Concord Cemetery, north of Petersburg, to the town's new Oakland Cemetery. In 1921 Petersburg municipal authorities, led by a local historian, had purchased an enormous gravestone and inscribed on it Masters's epitaph for Rutledge in *Spoon River Anthology:*

> Out of me unworthy and unknown
> The vibrations of deathless music;
> "With malice toward none, with charity for all."
> Out of me the forgiveness of millions toward millions,
> And the beneficent face of a nation
> Shining with justice and truth.
> I am Anne Rutledge who sleep beneath these weeds,
> Beloved in life of Abraham Lincoln,
> Wedded to him, not through union,
> But through separation.
> Bloom forever, O Republic,
> From the dust of my bosom![7]

Several people who had known Rutledge and Lincoln during their New Salem years had moved to Petersburg when New Salem failed (and Lincoln left) about 1837. These individuals—the village elders of Masters's youth—interested him greatly, as he had explained to his father: "I have in mind a very thorough portrait of Petersburg. . . . This Petersburg country is among the most famous localities of the world. . . . Tell me about Petersburg as it was in 1872. . . . What was said of Lincoln there at that time? Did I ever see Herndon? If so tell me, and perhaps I can remember it myself. . . . I want you to tell me all you know about Mentor Graham [Lincoln's teacher]. He lived in Petersburg. . . . Of course you can tell me much about [Lincoln's friends] the Armstrongs."[8]

Masters decided to enlarge on this geographic mingling of national culture (*Spoon River,* New Salem, and Lincoln) by involving a fourth pillar of Americana, *The Saturday Evening Post.* He explained his plans to his father: "*The Saturday Evening Post* wants my autobiography, and sent their man here this week to see me after I had written the editor that I should like to use their weekly as my medium. They were greatly interested in the portrait which I said I could draw of Petersburg, and also that I was raised in the Lincoln neighborhood." His work went swiftly, and at the end of a month Masters was able to send a sample third of the manuscript to *The Saturday Evening Post.* Then he read a poem for a New York memorial to the orator and lawyer Robert Ingersoll and left for Springfield to perform additional research.[9]

Meanwhile, his father's frail condition worsened. Although Masters would later claim to have had "no news" of his father's stroke on November 11, his diary suggests that he may have known that his father was gravely ill shortly after arriving in Chicago: "Arrive Chicago 3 P.M. (Father stricken at about noon)" (November 11). Masters remained in Chicago for two more days, talking with friends in the legal profession, Abe Meyer and Bill Slack, and visiting his son, Hardin.

Meyer awoke Masters on the morning of the fourteenth to say that his father was dying, but Meyer was mistaken: the elder Masters had already expired. In fact, there had been quite a search to notify Masters of his father's imminent death, but because Masters was at a hotel and "privately registered to escape the infamous newspapers," a good many people knew about it before he did. Ironically, one of Masters's least favorite newspapers, the *Chicago Tribune,* printed a story describing details of the search: "Hunt for Edgar Lee Masters as His Father Dies."[10]

Masters's stay in Chicago would ultimately cost him considerable peace of mind, for when he arrived in Springfield, he found that his younger brother, Tom, had completed funeral details and that he objected to nearly all of them: the undertaker; the suit, necktie, and footwear for Hardin; the $600 coffin; and especially one of the honorary pallbearers—Clarence S. Darrow. To his credit, Tom had also included the Lincoln scholar Albert J. Beveridge as an honorary pallbearer; Beveridge had been in communication with Hardin regarding the latter's association with William Herndon. Unfortunately, the ghost of Herndon turned out to be a source of irritation between Masters and his brother. Because of Hardin's association with Herndon in the 1870s, Masters thought of burying his father near Herndon's grave: "I thought it would be appropriate to bury him by the side of Herndon in Springfield." (While it might have been "appropriate," it might also have been impossible, since Herndon's two wives were already buried at the site.) But Tom had made plans to place Hardin's coffin temporarily in a mausoleum at Springfield's Oak Ridge Cemetery, thereby ignoring Masters's preferred site, as well as a more logical one, the Petersburg burial ground where Hardin's son Alex was buried. Masters thus had to deal with both a funeral and a burgeoning argument with his brother.[11]

Masters might also have had a disagreement with his mother. In writing what he regarded as a suitable eulogy, Masters sought to describe his father's great joy for living and so made a reference to Hardin's philanderings with other women and to his reputation as a "play-boy" in the villages of Petersburg and Lewistown. Perhaps Emma Masters was too worn down by her fatal disease to object. Perhaps she took the reference in the way that it was intended, as a compliment, or maybe she was simply biding her time. Masters reported that when he assisted her to the coffin, she looked at her late husband as if this last view ended "sixty years of misunderstanding." She seemed remarkably calm.[12]

Or maybe other parts of Masters's eulogy calmed her: "If before coming into the world I could have chosen my father, and chosen him with all the understanding that I have today, he is the man I should have chosen for my father. Whatever I have inherited from him in strength, or health, or gifts, or understanding of life, I count as more precious than all the riches of the world." Masters had liked the words as he wrote them; he liked them better as he watched his mother weep while the minister read them. Perhaps (he wondered privately), "perhaps she wept to hear me pay a tribute that the dead did not deserve."

He did not ask her opinion of that, or of one final act, a death mask he made of his father with the help of a Springfield student of sculpture and a plaster of paris mix: "As I saw my father there in the coffin, I could not bear to have that great brow, that Hawthorne face, that perfect nose and granite chin go into crumbling dust and be lost." Nicolosi subsequently turned the plaster cast into bronze. Hardin Masters's image as well as his influence had now outlived him.[13]

Following his father's death, Masters tried to find his mother a suite in a Springfield hotel, for she now claimed she hated her house, but nothing pleased her, and after placing her with a nurse, Masters returned to New York, where he found that *The Saturday Evening Post* had rejected the sample of his autobiography. He wrote a little, but his mind was on his father, and one day's diary entry reads simply "miss father and grieve." Regardless of whatever else had happened, Hardin Masters's death removed any remaining boyishness Masters felt, as he explained to a friend shortly after the funeral: "Sometimes he seems near me through an inability to realize that he is gone. Again, he seems utterly gone. I feel grown up too, for the first time in my life. In October, I saw him and I felt as always, just like a boy with him. Now I feel old." Hardin Masters had been his most immediate tie to the past and responsible in his way for some of the *Spoon River* pieces, as Masters explained to Harriet Monroe: "My father has been dead a month, but I think of scarcely anything else but him. He was a link with my boyhood; he was a link to the pioneer past, to the American past. . . . *Spoon River Anthology* is his, and I once wrote him that he could have written it better than I. Lots of its material came from his stories."[14]

Another death would also be important to Masters at this time, although the principal was far removed from the Masters family. As Hardin was entering his final summer, two of Masters's former associates were receiving national scrutiny in a legal battle in Dayton, Tennessee. The Scopes Monkey Trial, testing the teaching of evolution in schools, pitted Masters's former law partner Clarence Darrow against William Jennings Bryan, the Democratic Party's three-time-nominee for president (and Masters's friend from his Chicago days). Masters was divided in his feelings about the trial. He disliked Darrow intensely, but he also disliked Bryan's clientele in the Scopes case, religious fundamentalists. But more was involved in the Scopes case than the endless battle between science and religion. At the time of the trial, Bryan had been the champion of country ways and values for more than thirty years. When he defeated Darrow, it must have seemed that the agrarian and populist values of the nineteenth century had prevailed—but Bryan died within a week of the trial's conclusion, offering proof, perhaps, that the old days were waning. As the Roaring Twenties wore on, it was clear that this was the case, that the times were to be dominated by the forces of modernism—urbanization, mechanization, and commercialism—things Masters said he disliked in *The New Spoon River.* The judgment in Dayton had only seemed to validate the values of the old days, but Bryan's death would be a symbolic, pivotal point in Masters's relations with both the age and with others: in the near future he would have either to change his values and beliefs or find himself out of step with the times.[15]

Instead, he became less flexible and more guarded in his relations with others, more hesitant about mixing publicly, even to the point of behaving as a recluse. The newspapers' unwanted attention regarding his divorce had done much to prompt this behavior, the soul weariness and cynicism resulting from his pursuit of Lillian had also worn him down, and the enforced relations with people during his 1925 lecture tour also heightened his desire to spend more time by himself. And certainly the illnesses of his parents cast him in a blue mood and made him unwilling to mingle with others. "I think sometimes that I have a mild case of lycanthropy," he wrote Monroe in mid-1925, referring to his tendencies to behave as a lone wolf; "there are so few I want to see." "I used to think that if I could get out of law, and the politics of the third ward, and get into literature where there are gentlemen that it would be the life. But the politics of literature are viler than any other. . . . The little fry that swim around . . . excite my contempt so that I could stay in one room indefinitely so as not to meet them." Even his relations with his children were carried on at arm's length: his 1925 Christmas presents of fifteen dollars for his daughters were mailed to his son Hardin so that he could forward the money to his sisters. Masters's past and future came together on Christmas Eve 1925, when he received the finished death mask of his father and celebrated Christmas with Ellen: "Get presents. Get death mask of father. Wine and cake. E. X" (December 24).[16]

Masters spent the early spring of 1926 working on his dramatic poem about Robert E. Lee and a biographical study of a prominent Chicago attorney named Levy Mayer. Macmillan's George Brett Jr. planned both trade and deluxe editions of *Lee* and urged Masters to spend additional time with the text, but Masters was anxious to receive the $1,000 advance, and this book, like many others, went to the printer before it should have.[17]

The life of attorney Mayer was done as a work for hire, written solely because Masters needed the money. Mayer (1858–1922) had been a partner in the law firm of Masters's divorce lawyer Abe Meyer (Mayer, Meyer, Austrian, and Platt), so Masters was already somewhat familiar with his subject. (Abe Meyer was a brother of the subject's widow and felt Masters should write the book.) Masters received details about Levy Mayer's life in February and worked on the biography through March and early April, when he completed it. He did not think much of it, later writing that he was "hard at work on a pot-boiler, dictating to a secretary all day." The 1,500 copies of *Levy Mayer and the New Industrial Era* came out in 1927; although the book satisfied Mayer's widow, it made little difference to Masters's career other than to show him that he could write biography, a genre in which he would later produce several other studies.[18]

Hardin Masters's death continued to occupy much of Masters's attention during 1926. In February he published the poem "On the Death Mask of Hardin Masters" (a "prairie Jefferson"), just before the Illinois State Historical Library in Springfield accepted Hardin's death mask (the exchange of letters brought Masters an invitation to publish in the historical society's journal, and yielded the autobiographical essay "Days in the Lincoln Country"). In April Hardin's body was moved from the Springfield mausoleum to its permanent place in Petersburg's Oakland Cemetery. Masters's grief also teased him into trying a sonnet series about Hardin, and he would shortly work on "some reminiscences of [his] father . . . , particularly of his partnership days with William H. Herndon in Petersburg."[19]

Unfortunately, questions about the financial assets of the Masters family led to new tensions. Because Emma Masters had often complained of the house in which she lived, her son Tom and his sister, Madeline, began a successful effort to sell it. Masters felt that nothing should be done with the house until it was clear that his mother was through with it (in other words, until she succumbed to her fatal illness), and he refused to be a party to its sale or to accept his share of the proceeds. As he wrote in an unpublished chapter of his autobiography, "I would not touch a cent until my mother was dead and in no possible need of it." Masters was not as altruistic as he suggested, however, having quietly approached his mother in the spring of 1925 with a request for a $2,000 "advance" on his inheritance. Emma Masters refused the request, saying that she did not know how long she would live and that she might need the money. (Not long afterward she had a nightmare in which she and Masters were in a bookstore; her son told her of a plan for a memorial window for her but would not show her the plan until she gave him $2,000. Perhaps she was afraid of the way Masters would describe her in a future book, itself a memorial "window" holding her up to a critical light.)[20]

It is interesting to note that Masters's creative work, once an unyielding source of friction between him and his parents, had by the time of their deaths so completely captivated them that they themselves were writing. By late 1924 Emma Masters was working three to four hours per day on a novel; her husband had completed an article on longevity and was planning another on his old law associate William Herndon, which he completed in mid-1925 (along with an article against Prohibition). In addition, Masters's brother Tom was keeping a scrapbook about his famous brother (despite ill feelings); his sister, Madeline, was writing verses and had submitted a novel to Liveright's (it was promptly rejected); and "Hardin Wallace Masters" (probably Masters's son) published a poem in *The Literary Digest.* The whole family, it seemed, was scribbling and developing literary sensibilities as well. Emma offered Masters the sound advice that he need not record every influence (read "female") that crossed his path, nor should he feel overly obliged to write about family members: "Each member of your family might have studied your books with more pleasure if you had left them out of them." (Emma was probably referring to the ugly portrait Masters had drawn of her in *The Nuptial Flight,* a novel in which she was pictured as destroying her husband.) In the spring of 1926, however, Masters was most concerned not with literary opinions but with legal ones and the very real possibility that his ex-wife, Helen, might get his inheritance as partial payment on the alimony due her.[21]

In fact, the threat that Helen might seize his share of his father's estate now dominated Masters's thoughts: "My brother had thrown my father's estate of $4,200 into the probate court, in spite of the fact that the Illinois law forbids such a course where the deceased leaves no debts. I could see expenses and litigation looming. The joint estate of my father and mother did not exceed $20,000, and I needed what was coming to me to go on with my literary work. I foresaw that my ex-wife would seize my patrimony if the whole matter were not managed with great care." To handle the matter with such care, he engaged the services of Col. B. M. Chiperfield, a Canton, Illinois, lawyer he had known since his Lewistown days. It was Chiperfield's responsibility to protect Masters's inheritance and also to try to cancel the contract that had sold Emma Masters's Springfield house. With almost predictable perversity, Emma had decided she wanted her house back as soon as it was sold and blamed Tom and Madeline for having influenced her to sell it in the first place. Now she wanted Masters to get it back. Masters had endeavored to do so, threatening the buyer with legal action ("you will surely find that you have bought a lawsuit"), but the house had sold anyway, and Masters was now fed up with the matter. Leaving the able and expensive Chiperfield in charge, Masters cleared his head with a trip to the Southwest.[22]

Masters made this spring 1926 trip ostensibly to research material for his epic "Atlantis" ("I decided that I must see the Indians of New Mexico and their pueblos"), but he also wanted to renew some old acquaintances from "the high and palmy days of 1915." A friend from *Poetry* magazine, Alice Corbin Henderson, was in Santa Fe with her husband. The poet Witter Bynner, a friend from the William Marion Reedy days, was also in Santa Fe. (Masters had just completed an introductory note for Bynner's 1926 edition of *Grenstone Poems.*) Bynner's companion in the Spectra hoax, Arthur Davison Ficke, was also in Santa Fe with his wife, and Masters's friend John Sloan, the artist who had illustrated *Mitch Miller,* was there, too. Masters traveled with several of these people to Puye, Taos, and the ancient settlement of Acoma and thoroughly enjoyed himself in his western surroundings.[23]

After two weeks Masters departed to San Francisco to visit the poet George Sterling. Sterling had offered Masters an uncomplicated haven with beer and whisky during the 1925 tour, and Masters now enlarged his itinerary to see his friend. Masters no doubt anticipated additional good times ("Get out the mandolute and the large cup of . . . wine," he wrote Sterling), or perhaps he felt a comfortable affinity with the other writer because the two had led somewhat similar lives. Like Masters, Sterling had been wedded and divorced, having never accepted the confinements of marriage. He held liberal political opinions, liked to carouse, womanize, and drink, and was something of an athlete. Despite spending a great deal of time with other people, however, Sterling was essentially a loner. Earlier in his career he had made a considerable splash in San Francisco and elsewhere when the authors Jack London and Ambrose Bierce championed his talents and helped him receive national attention. He was never fully accepted in the East, however, and although his followers compared him to Shakespeare, his best work had been completed by the end of World War I. He was fifteen months younger than Masters.[24]

Masters felt that Sterling's poetry was a bit old fashioned but admired him for his devotion to it—for illustrating in his life the artistic beliefs that Masters himself publicly held. The two now amused themselves in San Francisco and then traveled to nearby Carmel, where they spent four days with the poet Robinson Jeffers on his estate. They ended the visit by planting some trees in their own honor (it was Jeffers's idea), and then Masters and Sterling returned to San Francisco. Before they left, however, Sterling began to drink heavily, and he continued to drink in San Francisco. At some point he confided to Masters his plans for dealing with his own uncertain future: "He went to his dresser and brought forth a bottle of cyanide of potassium, saying that one day he would take it, that he would kill himself the moment his sexual power failed him." Sexual dysfunction was not one of Masters's problems, although he certainly understood feeling depressed enough to consider suicide. He encouraged Sterling "to die on his feet fighting," but Sterling was too intoxicated to understand this message, and Masters headed back to New York. Sterling was as much at a loss as Masters when it came to handling the problems of time and change.[25]

On the way east Masters stopped to visit his sick mother, who was undergoing radium treatments in a Springfield hospital. He had not seen her for several months but had informed her that he had arranged for "altar prayers" to be said for her in New York, Baltimore, and Chicago. Perhaps he thought that the prayers would help her peace of mind (perhaps he felt they might also loosen her grip on the "advance" on his inheritance). This July 14 visit seems to have been planned at the last moment, for Masters arrived at the hospital at midnight and talked a nurse into letting him see Emma. She was "a little startled to see me," he wrote later. "She was greatly distressed over the litigation that had ensued from the sale of the house; she was concerned for her son Tom, whom she feared would come to mortifying defeat at the hands of Col. Chiperfield." Of course, Emma herself had helped foment the trouble between her sons by insisting that she hated the house in which she and her husband had lived. Masters sometimes claimed to be nonplussed about Emma's attitude toward both her husband and the house, though he also perceived a possible source for her discontent, as he explained in an unpublished chapter of his autobiography: "I have felt at times that my father did something to her which wounded her incurably, and that her whole nature settled into habitual resentment against him." Masters was being more than a little disingenuous: it was Hardin's philandering through the alleys and saloons of Petersburg and Lewistown that wounded her incurably, and Masters knew this as well as anyone.[26]

This midnight visit in St. John's Hospital would be Masters's final meeting with his mother. When she died three months later, he was still unable to penetrate her moods and finally concluded, "My mother was just herself." He did not return to Illinois for her funeral in October, explaining to Chiperfield, "My complications here just now are many, publishing, proofs, moving, etc. . . . I do not need to go there to grieve." When Masters later recalled his relations with both parents, however, he could find little about which to grieve and left this unexpected account: "I dislike to confess it, but in the interest of truth, I am bound to say that neither my father nor my mother was of any use to me outside of the physical and mental inheritance which they gave me, and that was a gift of involuntary biology."[27]

As things turned out, Emma Masters's concern that Tom would be bullied by Chiperfield was unfounded. The "involuntary biology" of Hardin and Emma Masters apparently included a dominant gene for contentiousness passed along in equal parts to both sons; to put it another way, Tom Masters could be as difficult as his brother. In the end the Masters sons helped turn the settlement of their parents' estates into a thoroughly unpleasant affair, although their parents' mismanagement contributed as well. Emma Masters could have availed herself of at least four attorneys—her husband, two sons, and the family lawyer, George Gillespie (who advised her before and after Hardin's death)—but she had refused to make a will, despite having had five years' notice of her approaching mortality; nor had Hardin prepared a will, despite having assured Masters only three years before his death that he had done so. Things were set for a fight. (In fact, the family had already practiced for such a fight years before when Masters's father had sued his brother Wilbur over Squire Davis Masters's will.)[28]

A review of the facts will be useful. The house that was the subject of so much contention was valued at $10,000 by everyone except Masters, who valued it at $12,000. Masters had resisted the sale of the house through legal means, but a judge had ruled against him, and Masters soon appealed, telling Bill Slack he would take the case all the way to the Illinois Supreme Court. Tom Masters had countered in an incredibly effective way: he or his wife contacted Masters's ex-wife, Helen, and arranged to represent her in a Chicago claim for back alimony, the money to come from Masters's share of his parents' estates. This had two results: it forced Masters to hire a Chicago lawyer to look after this threat to his inheritance (reenter Abe Meyer), and it created a breach between Masters and his brother that would never be healed (Tom now became "that despicable brother of mine"). Tom was in a position to receive a handsome fee from Helen, for he knew the details of her case and knew how much inheritance was due his brother. He may have known, too, that Helen would probably agree to his fee, for she was said to be in need of cash. (It was reported that she had sold the Spring Lake farm for $10,000 and then lost the money in an investment.) Masters looked at the legal fees he was generating and wrote Bill Slack, to whom he also owed money (for rental of a law office at the time of the divorce): "Suppose you look into this and get in somewhere somehow for the rent I owe you." What was a third lawyer, he must have reasoned, when he was already employing two of the best?[29]

So all these matters stemming from the deaths of his parents were unfolding or about to unfold in late 1926 when Masters suddenly remarried. The family story is that Ellen's audition with the Abbey Theatre had borne fruit. She had been promised "some minor parts," and Masters was afraid that she would go abroad and that he would lose her. As a result, he proposed. A second story is that Masters had grown inordinately jealous when Ellen paid the most innocent of attentions to a former suitor. Shortly after his mother's funeral, Masters traveled to central Illinois to visit with his friend George Stokes (he of the contraband whisky on the running boards). Masters then pushed on to the Petersburg-Springfield area to attend to some business. He was gone from New York for about two weeks and on his return was startled (one might say) into marriage. More specifically, he was upset, felt threatened, or was unpleasantly surprised to find that Ellen would even look at another man. Or maybe for the first time in his life he was unsure of his effect on the opposite sex: he had balded a little more, was a little plump, a little gray. In any event, the story goes that he threw Ellen into a cab, and they ended up at city hall, where they were married on Friday, November 5. Ellen had not really wanted to be married ("his pattern was set for trouble," she later remarked), but Masters insisted, and so the thing was done.[30]

Masters left a very different account in an unpublished chapter of his autobiography, where he said that he and his son had traveled to Chicago together after visiting Emma Masters for the last time in Springfield. Hardin had telephoned his sister Madeline to urge her to visit their father at his hotel. She had vacillated, first saying she did not want to see Masters and then saying she would see him and setting a time, after which she failed to come or call to explain her absence. It was then, Masters wrote, that his divorce plan "to be civilized all around" failed and that he knew he should seek "a new life": "I felt that I had no more time to spend on trying to maintain an old life. I had no hopes that there would ever be a fruitful feeling and association between us. I began to think seriously of making a new life for myself, and of establishing a home again for myself. So far as reasoning counts with a marriage, this was what brought me to ask Ellen Coyne to be my wife."[31]

Ellen had moved from her place in the Old Chelsea apartments to the Brevoort Hotel in the summer of 1926 to be close to her work (she was helping to open a bookstore in the Brevoort). Masters left the Old Chelsea a little later, moving to an address on Gramercy Avenue and then to an apartment at number 2 West Sixteenth Street; it was here, in a front apartment, that Mr. and Mrs. Edgar Lee Masters set up housekeeping in the winter of 1926–27. He told his new in-laws in Kansas City that the apartment was "pretty good": "I manage to work." Ellen disliked the apartment, however, finding it noisy and small, and the cramped quarters would eventually contribute to tensions in the new marriage.[32]

The newspapers accentuated the difference in their ages: "Poet Masters, 57, Marries Girl, 27." When the *Kansas City Star* interviewed Molly Coyne, the bride's mother, the paper reported that Masters's new mother-in-law thought he was "between 45 and 50." (That he was already fifty-eight must have offered him a certain satisfaction.) Tom Coyne denied that his daughter had married at all. "She would have told us," he said. (Tom Coyne did not like Masters, whom he thought to be an "old fool," and once told his daughter that she was "wasting time with that guy.") Unfortunately, some newspapers also theorized or declared outright that Ellen Coyne was the cause of Masters's divorce: "No imaginary affair," began one, "inspired Edgar Lee Masters, Chicago lawyer-poet, in his Fourteen Sonnets ["The Return"] against marital infelicity, as was supposed in 1922" [1923]. The paper pointed to the new bride as evidence, proof positive in the eyes of several reporters that Ellen Coyne was the scarlet woman who had wrecked Helen Masters's marriage. One newspaper indicated that Masters had met his new wife while she lived at New York's Brevoort Hotel, where "a romance quickly developed." No one at the paper noticed that Ellen had not moved to the Brevoort until 1926 or that a quickly developing romance begun there would rule out an involvement in Chicago in 1923. The *New York Times* also left the implication that Ellen might have played a part in Masters's divorce: "Masters is said to have met his present bride while writing '14 Sonnets' to his former wife." The *Times*'s wide circulation plus the report that Masters's second wife was much younger played a part in starting the hard-to-tame rumor that he had left his first wife for Ellen. This rumor—entirely untrue—was still being repeated as fact a lifetime later, in 1991.[33]

Masters's inability to fall back on another form of employment more lucrative than writing would play a major part in his standard of living during his second marriage. There is good evidence that he performed limited legal work while in New York, but his major source of income was through books and individual poems and articles. Unfortunately, neither *Selected Poems* nor *Lee* had done as well as he wished. "I feel annoyed," he told George Brett, "that those books did not pay out." The deluxe edition of *The New Spoon River* was also an economic disappointment: he had hoped for about $1,300 from this edition of 360 numbered and signed copies, but it had generated less than $1,000 after two years' sales. Earlier books also showed limited sales, and financial insecurity troubled Masters's marriage from the start.[34]

Nevertheless, he sometimes seemed happy in his new marriage and described his bride in flattering terms to various friends, here writing to Robinson Jeffers: "She is a sweet and honest heart and I am to her what the king was to Liza. She has so felt toward me from her school days, and during her course at the Chicago University, from which she graduated in 1922." Eunice Tietjens received an equally lighthearted message: "Yes'm. I got married. . . . I couldn't help it. God came to me and said that if I didn't marry, He'd get after me. . . . I said to God, 'Don't you know that she is lots younger than I am?' And God said, 'What do you want? Someone your own age?' 'No,' says I. 'Well?' says God kind of sneery." Ellen became "The Kid," his "child-wife," "John" (for one of her relatives), and occasionally "Fay-Fay," a nickname derived from her childhood pronunciation of her middle name, Frances. "I see nothing against her," Masters concluded.[35]

But there was something odd about Masters's marriage. Drinking buddies such as Horace Liveright wondered why Masters had bothered to get married at all, and despite the optimistic-sounding letters Masters wrote to some people, he seemed unhappy or indifferent in others. His diary entries for the day of his marriage and the day after show only that he was in New York, and those for the next two days, that he was writing. Four days after his marriage, he wrote his boyhood friend Edwin Reese that he was weary of searching for a place to repose and tired, too, of searching for a companion. In short, he sounded less like a man happily embarked on a new marriage than a reprise from *The New Spoon River:*

> Like a hawk that circles around the tree where its nest was, but has been destroyed, leaving nothing by which to identify the tree, I have circled over the old haunts; and have gone clear around the country without finding any place that I wanted to stay in, or anyone that I wanted to be with. And dear fool I am so tired; tired of writing, of thinking, of reading, of being famous, of living up to any standard. I wish there was a place where I could go and be with a good man friend, and just sleep and eat and laugh and chew tobacco. And I wish you would come here to see me.[36]

Nor did things improve in the next month, as Masters remarked to Reese just before Christmas. "My stomach is out of order. And I can't see much back of me or ahead." He would also confide to Reese that he had gone to a party and fondled a "light-haired cutie" while on a January 1927 research visit to South Carolina. In this way, too, he would duplicate the tensions that troubled his first marriage. (Some of the correspondence between Masters and Reese is nothing but roguish tall talk between old school chums, but even if these remarks fall into that category, Masters's claim of extramarital gropings this soon after the wedding did not auger well for the new marriage.)[37]

The loneliness visible in Masters's letters at this time may have come from the people who had vanished from his life during the preceding months. On November 9 George Sterling had mailed Masters a congratulatory letter concerning his marriage to Ellen; a week later he drank his bottle of cyanide. Various friends of Masters's father also died around this time, including John Armstrong, a Petersburg-Oakford area fiddler who dated to the days of Lincoln and in whose home Masters and Theodore Dreiser had once spent a night. Even Reedy's death still bothered Masters ("I think of him, with hardly a day passing when I do not"). In addition, Masters had recently published a long poem about one of his unhappy partings from Lillian, and he may have heard that she had remarried in October 1926. (Ever resourceful, she had combined her 1922 loss of Masters with the removal of her inflamed appendix and subsequently married her surgeon, who was younger, wealthier, better looking, and far more fun to be with than Edgar Lee.) In any event, Lillian was now as dead to Masters as were several other people he once counted as friends. Masters's Lewistown friend Grant Hyde, with whom he had set his first poems in print, would die shortly. And the death of Masters's father continued to bother him: "I have passed through several complete changes of friends and environments and don't look for stability; yet every death awakes the same wonder. . . . I have been and am depressed about my father's death. . . . He was really a genius man who got bogled—and that's what hurts me."[38]

Masters's own potential by this time was problematic. In 1926 and 1927 he could still command a $250 lecture fee, but he always wanted more money than he received and disliked traveling to lectures. He was sometimes asked to speak at prestigious dinners, such as those given by *The Nation,* but he disliked the tedium of such affairs. He was occasionally asked, too, to make college addresses and the like (the best schools paid about fifty dollars if he read a poem), but he disliked so many academicians that he never went out of his way to perform at these: "These professors and reviewers are surely a dull set, a crapulous, envious backbiting crowd . . . , as they always have been." Nor would he help himself by agreeing to appear at book fairs or to speak at gatherings promoting books and publishing. As he phrased matters in January 1927, "I won't attend any public dinners, make a speech at any time or place, or be interviewed." Nor would he make himself easy to find (he was not in the phone book). Still, as the new year came on, he had to do something to address his financial needs and worked simultaneously on several writing projects.[39]

The themes and subjects that were occupying him now all had their origins in the past. This was true of the play he was trying to publish, "New Salem," as well as of *Kit O'Brien* (published at last). A 1927 article complimentary to author James Whitcomb Riley also dealt with the old days, and so did an article on the Lincoln and Douglas debates. "Atlantis" was necessarily focused on historical events (indeed, it was planned never to cross into the 1920s), and Masters's autobiography was also firmly rooted in the past.[40]

His April 1927 visit to Tennessee's Overton County was also representative of his interests. He had made the trip to explore Squire Davis Masters's roots and to talk with individuals he had ascertained were relatives. His contact with a distant cousin named Robert Masters in Hilham, Tennessee, proved useful and provided Masters with genealogical information later used in his autobiography. The trip also gave him a chance to meet the Nashville literary group later famous as "The Fugitives" (John Crowe Ransom, Donald Davidson, and Merrill Moore), but the page 1 headline in the *Nashville Tennessean* correctly suggested Masters was more interested in historical figures: "Edgar Lee Masters Pays Visit to Shrine of Andrew Jackson."[41]

A second trip made in mid-1927 also had the past as its inciting factor, but this one ended with seriocomic results. Masters had decided in August to visit his Illinois friend George Stokes and enjoy such rural aesthetics as "the line of the horizon around the orchard." "Such simple delights mend me," he said. This year, however, the simple delights eluded him. For one thing, he was not taken care of as he wished. Stoke's servant girl was being dismissed for the alleged theft of perfumes, powder, and the like, and Masters rode with Stokes as he returned the unhappy girl to her mother. Masters carried the young woman's suitcase ("being a friend of sinners and acquainted with grief"), but there was not much he could do. They left her at her home and returned servantless to Stokes's farm, where Mrs. Stokes announced that she was leaving to look after a sick relative. Masters and Stokes were left to fend for themselves.[42]

Stokes handled the meals—fried potatoes, coffee, preserves, and "likker"—while Masters (and his stomach) slowly grew upset. "I couldn't write," he wrote Robinson Jeffers; "I could only sit and hear talk of broken tractors and raging Methodists." When Masters looked for the horizon around the orchard, he found the romance of the faraway replaced with the reality of the very near: "chickens stalk[ed] meditatively about"; hogs lolled in the mud. "The dullness of mud is in the soul," Masters wrote Jeffers. Of course, it was really his own orchard in Michigan that Masters had been dreaming of, or maybe the vanished orchard of Squire Davis Masters. Masters could not get back to New York quickly enough. This was to be one of several such trips he would make, always nursing the hope of finding in rural places something missing in New York but invariably discovering he was a city dweller rather than a country boy; he could return to Illinois but could not go home again.[43]

Masters's financial prospects at this time were governed by his divorce agreement and his two books published in 1927. He had received a commission rather than royalties for *Levy Mayer,* which paid very well, for when he completed the biography, he deposited a check for $7,500 in the Bank of Manhattan. (Levy Mayer had once been "the richest lawyer in the United States," or was thus described in Masters's book, and his widow could afford this kind of commission.) Her check brought Masters the greatest income he would enjoy in any year after abandoning law, a total of nearly $11,000. Unfortunately, Masters owed much of this to his ex-wife, who had filed a claim for $4,050 in back alimony in January 1927.[44]

Masters's other book published in 1927, *Kit O'Brien,* generated a respectable advance of $1,250 in January along with a contract for a 15 percent royalty rate on the first 5,000 copies and 20 percent thereafter. But the plot was jeopardized by the real-life facts prompting it: two boys from southern Illinois had stolen a pie (just one pie, and possibly their first), for which they were sentenced, circa 1917, to at least two years in the Illinois state reformatory at Pontiac. (In 1922 Masters had used his influence with Illinois governor Len Small to gain access to the Pontiac reformatory, where he studied records of the case.) The character of Kit O'Brien had earlier shown up in *Mitch Miller,* where he was depicted as a village tough, but he had not been developed sufficiently to be a memorable character, nor did many people find him particularly memorable in the novel named for him. Readers and reviewers alike had difficulties in believing that the plot might occur in modern times even though it really had and in spite of Masters changing the incarceration time from years to weeks. Masters added a float trip like Huckleberry Finn's, but *Kit O'Brien,* "a boy's tale . . . for money," as Masters called it, became one of his least successful novels.[45]

Meanwhile, the settlement of the estates of Hardin and Emma Masters grew more complicated. Masters had brought suit against his sister for condoning the sale of the house, and so this case of sibling disharmony took its place alongside two other *Masters v. Masters* suits: his ex-wife's suit for alimony and a "friendly suit" that Tom had persuaded Emma Masters to initiate against Masters in order to put Hardin's estate to rest and pay funeral expenses; Madeline and Tom were copetitioners in the latter suit. Soon afterward Masters authorized Chiperfield to appeal unfavorable court decisions governing either his father's or his mother's estates and then to appeal the decision of any Chicago court that said his inheritance belonged to his ex-wife. As he casually summed up matters to Alice Corbin Henderson, "I am in litigation in Illinois over the little dab that my father and mother left." Masters chose to ignore the fact that he himself had helped set in motion certain of these litigations, refused to let them die (through appellate court actions), or otherwise refused to admit the legitimacy of his adversary's point of view, as with Helen Masters's claim for back alimony.[46]

Masters's strained relations with family members paralleled his relations with other authors. Perhaps Masters guarded his fame jealously because he had achieved it rather late for a poet, or perhaps he was simply unsure of himself, but during the mid-1920s he continued to belittle the name and character of any poet in competition with himself. The lone exception was his fellow Illinois poet Vachel Lindsay; other poets (and schools of poets past and present) frequently bore the brunt of Masters's contempt. By 1927 Masters was routinely maligning the old schools of poetry, but he stubbornly refused to share his fame with new groups, thus exiling himself to a literary limbo in which he was a part of no group. He said, for example, that he could not stand the popular poets of the nineteenth century, and he was equally hostile to those who bridged the nineteenth and twentieth centuries, including the exceedingly popular Dr. Henry Van Dyke and his peers:

> He and Robert Underwood Johnson by a fine psychic onomatopoeia adumbrate the word "horse's ass." I pray you [he was writing to Mencken] send for the collected poems of the aforesaid Johnson and read the verse beginning:
>
> I asked a kiss of a little maid—
> Shyly, sweetly she consented.

> Now that's poetry! It rhymes. It is about a sweet subject. It treats of the beautiful. It is true to life, because the maid consented. It is also poetry because it is as good as Van Dyke's.[47]

But he did not think much of the "modern" writers either: the attention given Robert Frost and the continuing popularity of Edwin Arlington Robinson (three Pulitzer Prizes) stemmed entirely, Masters insisted, from the remarkable success of *Spoon River Anthology.* He told Edward Marsh that "Robinson's revival and Frost's vogue were due to the tidal wave of *Spoon River*": "The truth is that he and Frost were winnowing their gills for water high and dry on the sand bank until the *Spoon River* flood refreshed them with oxygen and enabled them to swim back into the stream." Of course, if Masters had continued the metaphor, he would have been forced to admit that his own career drifted while those of Frost and Robinson fairly sailed along, but such admissions were not a part of Masters's character, and so he said other things.[48]

Robert Frost became "the Calvin Coolidge of American verse," a phrase Masters liked so well that he repeated it for years, along with "the exiguous Robert Frost," meaning that Frost was less than he pretended to be. Frost could be equally ungracious, of course, referring to Masters as "my hated rival," a sobriquet that evolved after *Spoon River* completely overshadowed Frost's first three books: "There is a Masters Mountain and right beside it a Frost Hollow," Frost wrote despairingly to his friend Louis Untermeyer in 1920. "What can be done to bring low the mountain and cast up the hollow?" Untermeyer had pinned his critical hopes on Frost as the new poet of significance and began, somewhat perversely, to write that Masters had "arrived—and left" when he published *Spoon River.* This, of course, meant that Masters would someday have to square off against Untermeyer as well. Female poets also felt Masters's scorn, envy, or wrath. Amy "Barnum" Lowell had received her new middle name when Masters discovered that there was a sucker born every minute who appreciated her verse. No one of these comments did Masters any lasting harm, but their collective impact and repetition and Masters's easy animosity were giving him a growing reputation as a bitter and cantankerous man.[49]

All these matters were still on his mind as he returned to work on his autobiography in late 1927. Masters had drafted a variety of short pieces in July and August and resumed work on the ill-fated manuscript of "New Salem" in September. He and Ellen moved to 451 West Twenty-third Street in October, and it was there, following a two-year hiatus, that he at last returned to his life story. This draft of his autobiography carried his life through his time with Lillian and divorce from Helen but tapered off quickly after he told of his 1923 departure from Chicago. He wrote briefly of his parents' old age (but not their deaths), the 1925 lecture tour, and his work on "Atlantis" but failed to say that he had remarried. Indeed, it might have been clumsy if he had: he had built his biography so that it led up to his several years' relation with one woman (Lillian)—after which he had rather quickly married a different one. He teased the reader away from these personal facts by concentrating on some potentially controversial political opinions in his manuscript's final pages, after which he closed his book with the observation that the United States abuses its poets. He typed the date "November 4th 1927" on the manuscript's last page, gave it the title of "My Youth in the Spoon River Country," and spent five days revising it before making an appointment with Macmillan's George Brett Jr. to discuss marketing.[50]

He probably did not tell Brett that he had already failed to sell the manuscript to the magazines. *The Saturday Evening Post* and *The Century* had turned down a draft of it in 1925, and Oscar Liveright had approached both *Harper's Bazaar* and *Cosmopolitan* on Masters's behalf in February 1927. Masters himself had tried out a sample of the text with the *Pictorial Review* in October 1927. All these had decided it was not for them, but magazines were always iffy, and besides, his old friend George Brett would surely publish it, intertwined as it was with *Spoon River* and his other books. Instead, what happened next postponed the publication of Masters's autobiography until years later.[51]

Masters had known for some time that several of his books were losing money. As early as mid-July 1921, for example, Macmillan had informed him that his account was in arrears. He knew, too, that *Skeeters Kirby* had lost about $2,000 after its initial advertising and sales and that Macmillan's board of directors had made some ominous remarks about books for which "advances were not yet earned." He also knew that Horace Liveright had shown no interest in "Atlantis." Nor had Otto Liveright seemed especially keen about the autobiography when the two men spoke of it in January 1927. Nevertheless, Masters was totally unprepared for the news George Brett now delivered: "Long talk with Brett, Jr., at Arts [Club]. Wouldn't say there was loss on my books as a whole. Put autobiography in vault. Drunk." But Brett soon indicated that all Masters's books published by Macmillan had lost money except for *Spoon River Anthology* and its 1916 successor, *Songs and Satires*. Not surprisingly, Brett did not seem much interested in Masters's autobiography.[52]

This had a remarkable impact on Masters. He had for years told himself and others that he had made tremendous sacrifices for his art, for poetry. He had endured a thousand distractions and hardships resulting from an injudicious first marriage and the practice of law and had always believed that these had prevented him from scaling the literary heights he might have achieved, as he had once explained in detail to Alice Corbin Henderson:

> I have done nothing in my life that was not a service in the devotion to Apollo [the Greek god of poetry] since I was seventeen years of age. Through poverty, toil of other sorts, distractions, even in disgusts, and darkness, I have held to this faith, and all my wanderings were wanderings in the quest. . . . I fought my own family for an education, such as I have; I fought to establish myself in the law; I fought to progress while supporting a family. I fought against the enervation of dullness and

> inertia with a woman in matrimony; I published for 17 years under a pseudonym in order not to disturb my earning career as a lawyer, because I had those children at stake. Yet all of it has been for Apollo.

Now George Brett had shown him that this thinking was flawed, that none of his recent books fulfilled the promise of earlier work. In fact, the only books that had earned sufficient public acceptance to yield a profit had been those completed while he was still laboring at the law and was unambiguously married to Helen.[53]

His crisis now, in the fall of 1927, at age fifty-nine, was that nobody seemed interested in this remarkable story. And so if there was a definite time when Masters knew that his fame as the author of *Spoon River* had slacked, it was then. He was at last forced to undergo a sobering "morning after" to the intoxication of being famous—but he did not want to, as his final diary entry for November 10 shows: "Put autobiography in vault. Drunk."[54]

He had once before been caught off guard like this—a decade earlier, in 1917, when he was spending his first summer at his place in Spring Lake, Michigan, and working on *Toward the Gulf.* He had left his place in a hurry that summer, blaming a domestic disturbance for his abrupt departure, but he was also upset by the realization that he did not have in him another book as good as *Spoon River.* Masters had then hastened back to Chicago and used his legal practice to try to forget this important moment of self-discovery, but he could no longer fall back on that, and rather than admit the flaws in his life story, he spent the evening in drink.

CHAPTER 14

Life as an Empty Bucket

If poetry were something remembered in tranquility, I should never write any.

—Edgar Lee Masters to Alice Corbin Henderson, February 6, 1927

After the newspapers had calmed down about Masters's marriage, and after he had sued his sister and been sued by her, his ex-wife, his mother, and his brother—after the family had demonstrated that it was one of the most disputatious in Illinois, and after all the lawyers in the story except Masters had profited—he was left with the same set of problems he had faced before, except that he was a little older and his financial prospects were slightly dimmed. His artistic life became a patchwork of old manuscripts and recent ones. Sequels and lengthy new works mixed with poetry, plays, and short stories and latent hopes for Hollywood until he thought his stomach might act up. There were also other problems.

The Masterses' marriage had proceeded without serious tensions during its first several months. He continued to write, and Ellen took odd jobs and small parts in stock companies while waiting for her break to come, but Broadway never beckoned again, and someone else got the part with Dublin's Abbey Theatre. (She was newly married, after all, and could not go traipsing overseas.) Unfortunately, the theater had been her primary hope for a significant income, and this became a problem when Masters's own income fell short of providing for his obligations. He was supposed to send $150 per month to Helen, but he was not doing so and feared that she would find a judge who would say that his inheritance belonged to her. He had to worry, too, about what he would do if Helen again tied up his book royalties or compromised his ability to pay rent on the apartment.

It was a furnished apartment to which neither had brought much. "He lived very modestly," Ellen would say of his life before their marriage. His clothes, manuscripts, a jade Buddha (a gift from the Farleys), and (surprisingly enough) a gun were about all he had. His personal library of 1,000 volumes had remained in Chicago with Helen, a pawn in her efforts to get the alimony due her. Ellen and Masters each had pictures of family members, however, and these now hung in the apartment. Ellen had painted the walls a light cream punctuated with bright spots of blue. The bathroom was yellow. It was in these surroundings that she left him on many days. He would be at the kitchen table writing, or about to write, pictures of Tom and Molly Coyne looking at him from one wall and those of Squire Davis and Lucinda Masters from another. The Spoon River poet at work: he tried to put himself in the mood.[1]

With his plans for his autobiography scuttled, he needed some new work on which to pin his hopes. Through the fall of 1927, "Atlantis" languished on an agent's desk, and his play "New Salem" made the rounds of prospective producers along with two other plays, "The House in the Wood" and "Wood Alcohol," but none received encouragement, and Masters sought a new subject, one that would require a minimum of research. He finally decided on a dramatic poem concerning the Illinois folk character of Jack Kelso, a New Salem fisherman and reader of Shakespeare reputed to have removed some of Abraham Lincoln's rough edges during the 1830s. Masters had a good many other things on his mind as well, however, and one of these lent a particular urgency to his financial situation: he was going to be a father again.[2]

The Masterses' tiny apartment did not seem a good place for a child to be born, so Ellen returned to her parents' Kansas City home in August 1927. Masters tried through the fall to get away to visit her, but one thing or another prevented it, and it was mid-December before he saw her and met his new father-in-law. He liked Tom Coyne and the warmth of his unusual house and spent ten days loafing about Kansas City and the Coynes' living room before opening holiday presents on Christmas Eve. Ellen remained in Kansas City to await the birth of their child when Masters left on December 26.[3]

The arrival of a child would probably end her theater career. Her various jobs had all been on the periphery of the theatrical mainstream and, except for the bit part on Broadway, had not seemed likely to lead to stardom. In mid-August 1926 she had been the victim of an automobile mishap serious enough to send her to the hospital for four days; she seems to have done little in the theater after this, and even less after her November 1926 marriage. She had learned that she could not count on the theater to provide her a living, although she continued to practice her art in other ways. Onstage or off, her jewelry and makeup remained ample, her mascara, heavy lipstick, hearty laugh, and strong voice adding to life a little more than she would otherwise have enjoyed. Perhaps she wanted a child at this time, perhaps not.[4]

The birth of a child would complicate Masters's life, add to his financial burdens, and create other responsibilities as well; nevertheless, he had occasionally daydreamed about a new family, as he did in a 1924 letter to Roland Farley: "I like to see life come to being, whatever it is, chickens or dogs; and sometimes I feel like I'd like to procreate a child again with the right mother, just to play with it, and to see her nuss it." It was this ambivalence that brought Masters to fatherhood again. In fact, he was still trying to make up his mind about it when his son Hilary Thomas Masters entered the world on February 3, 1928, in Kansas City: "Hillory born 4:15 A.M. Get stewed—in P.M." (The name on the birth certificate, "Hillory," evolved into "Hilary" and remained thus after Masters communicated with Tennessee relatives about the spelling; the new baby's middle name came from his grandfather, Thomas Coyne, and from some early members of the Masters clan, not from Masters's "despicable brother," Tom.)[5]

Masters spent the next day trying to decide what he really thought of fatherhood at fifty-nine, writing three different correspondents three very different evaluations. Harriet Monroe received a lighthearted one: "Yesterday at 4:15 A.M. my child-wife gave birth to a boy weighing 8 pounds. He will be named Hillory after his great-great-great grandfather who went to the Revolution from Virginia." The birth, Masters said, "demonstrated my virility again beyond a reasonable doubt." He even wrote a mock-heroic poem for the occasion, comparing himself to ancient Greeks and toasting himself with "synthetic nectar" (it was synthetic because Prohibition was in effect). John Cowper Powys received a quite different summary: "I am much alone just in these rooms, reading, writing, and wondering what things are about. . . . To take this on with what I am now, and what I have been, and what I have gone through of change whirls me as in a maze and with vertiginous effects." He also wrote Ellen on February 4, distancing himself so much that he sounded more like a grandparent than a father: "I hope the boy will be a great comfort and help to you always; and while I think of it, I send some advice." He then counseled Ellen against a too-liberal upbringing of their son in favor of a regimen of "truthfulness," "industry," "good manners," "economy," "and all those fundamental things a la Franklin." He sounded as if he might not be nearby to raise Hilary, and indeed, he would not be. He had decided not to get too close to this situation.[6]

He was in fact well practiced in this removal of himself from family distractions. He had sacrificed his first family to pursue intellectual interests while working behind the closed door of his second-floor study on Chicago's Kenwood Avenue. He had left to Helen much of the management of the three children. Then he had walked away from all of them and moved several miles away. He was miles away now. He would entrust Ellen with the management of this new child; she and her parents could probably work things out. In fact, the Coynes wanted things to be thus, as he explained in an unpublished chapter of his autobiography: "Hilary was born in Kansas City whither his mother Ellen had gone in a choice of the place of his nativity. Tom Coyne and Molly Coyne, his grandparents, seized upon him as their own; and then there were the many difficulties of raising him in New York City, in a hotel or an apartment. A writer pays everything for his art." In fact, the costs were so high that he sometimes worried about them: "Whether it is worth it or not, I can very often entertain doubts. For at times I feel that I would rather be with Hilary than to write out the greatest conceptions that I have had. But I have been going on completing work that was imagined or begun before Hilary was born, and with the propulsion of years back of it." He thus inflicted on Hilary some of the same parental disregard that had been visited on himself. That Hilary might someday have a point of view on this or grow up emotionally undernourished seems not to have occurred to Masters.[7]

Or maybe such thoughts did occur to him and were brushed away as impractical. He could not possibly work if he were constantly interrupted by the clamor of an infant, not in a small apartment with age sixty on the horizon, his poetic powers in question, and his books doing none too well. He could not, it was clear, shoulder the responsibilities of fatherhood. They would all starve. And so an arrangement was made. The Coynes would look after Hilary; Ellen would balance motherhood with the need to work and would at some point rejoin her husband in New York City.[8]

It was the spring of 1928, and he was now in a desperate race to prove himself, to show the Coynes that he could support a wife and family and to show literary America that his creative powers had not soured. "Dear Kid," he wrote Ellen in March (she was still in Kansas City), "You can't imagine how alone I am": "I write all the time, when not sleeping or walking. Wondering betimes what it is about, and how it can be possible that my life has come to this pass."[9]

He was working a great deal, but only a few of his labors bore fruit. The manuscript of *Jack Kelso* was accepted, and *The Nuptial Flight* was translated into German, yielding him fifty British pounds and 10 percent on the published price, but work on a new play (*Ácoma*) generated no immediate profits, and *Spoon River Anthology* was stolen outright in northern Europe. While publishing negotiations were underway in Sweden and Denmark, a publisher pirated the book in Finland, a country with which the United States had no copyright agreement. When actor Lionel Barrymore showed an interest in "New Salem," it looked for a time as if a second Barrymore might contemplate the role of Lincoln, but then he too backed out, and for the same reason as his more famous relative, an existing studio contract. "New Salem" again went begging. Masters was particularly bothered by this disappointment because his friend Percy Grainger had recently enlarged his piano composition of "Spoon River," rescoring it for twenty instruments, and could now offer a choice of scores for the movie's background music.[10]

Masters's daily life reflected his straitened circumstances. He was living in a small furnished apartment at 451 West Twenty-third Street, a quiet address at which he accumulated a few books and lived amid Spartan surroundings. He had a stove on which he prepared his breakfast and lunch before going to the Players Club to pick up his mail or have a drink. He could always get a drink at the Players, even during Prohibition, and since he thought Prohibition was a foolish law, he enjoyed breaking it. The Players Club was his one daily luxury, a brief chance to socialize as his life grew more insular.[11]

The season's only bright spot came in mid-June when he took a vacation and visited Ellen and Hilary in Kansas City. Everything was livelier there. He played with Hilary, drank too much, and wore himself out, as his diary entries indicate: "Much wine—X" (June 12); "Pretty tired from no sleep and wine" (June 13); "Playing with Hilary. . . . Hoover nominated" (June 14). He looked after his boy, talked politics with Molly, and listened to Tom Coyne explain that he needed a hotel-sized boiler in the basement to ease the chills of his malaria. Masters left after nine days, the bright Kansas City spring and his son's good spirits revitalizing his own. Maybe this arrangement would work after all. He arrived back in New York just as his book about Jack Kelso was being distributed.[12]

Jack Kelso: A Dramatic Poem had a historical impulse that nobody could fault. During the 1830s, when young Abraham Lincoln lived in New Salem, someone—perhaps it was Kelso—had spent some afternoons introducing him to the plays of Shakespeare and the poetry of Robert Burns. Someone had done this and lent Lincoln a wonderful literary style and then wandered off into myth, his fate unknown, his place in American literature and folklore ensured. There were paintings and stories of Kelso and Lincoln in a fishing boat on the Sangamon, a volume of Shakespeare being read aloud by one of them while the other listened, the float on a fishing line begging for attention while the taller of the two sat with his chin on his hand in thought. Or maybe this moment took place on shore, under a tree by Rutledge's Tavern. Or maybe none of this happened. Nobody knew. But Masters knew there was a story here and developed it as a dramatic poem, something that could be presented by theater groups or read over the radio and deliver some badly needed royalty checks to his mailbox at the Players.

Perhaps it was the ongoing curse of the drama that made *Kelso* unpresentable. More likely it was Masters's text, which wandered far afield from New Salem. In fact, it wandered all over, though not into myth, as the real Kelso had, but onto the well-burnished pathways Masters reserved for his enemies: Methodists, Baptists, prohibitionists, expansionists—the country gone to hell under Republicans. By the time Masters was done, Lincoln was on his way to becoming an American ogre, and Jack Kelso had tried to throw himself down a well. "Charming lyrics," the critics would say, had been replaced by "turgid ranting." *Jack Kelso* was a failure.[13]

During this same time in 1928, Masters was publishing an occasional short story (e.g., in *The New Yorker* in July) and a few poems (the *Ladies Home Journal* paid $250 for one), making an occasional lecture (e.g., at Columbia University), and performing some long-distance legal work, apparently for Chiperfield, the Canton, Illinois, lawyer. None of these activities was regular, however, and each seemed attended by special problems: Masters sold very few poems for as much as the one to the *Ladies Home Journal,* he never published another item in *The New Yorker,* his lucrative lectures were few and far between, and his legal work was sporadic and sometimes specially cursed as well (the job for Chiperfield, for example, concluded when a mail plane went down over Pennsylvania and sent Masters's work to the bottom of the Monongahela). When he dusted off "Atlantis" for Appleton's consideration, four successive readers told the company that the manuscript was too long. Masters was in the process of asking Appleton for advance royalties on "Atlantis" when the poor reviews for *Jack Kelso* began to come in, and the company lost interest entirely.[14]

Disgruntled, Masters worked on a sequel to his lengthy World War I epic, the volume he called his "finest achievement," *Domesday Book.* The "Epilogue to *Domesday,*" as he called it in his notes, was completed in September 1928 (although it had been planned since 1922) and mailed to Appleton in October. Masters recalled the manuscript in December, gave it a new title, and returned it to Appleton in time to sign a contract the day after Christmas. *The Fate of the Jury: An Epilogue to Domesday Book* followed the lives and deaths of the men on the coroner's jury in *Domesday Book,* but at a point that should have been halfway through this new tale, Masters suddenly broke off his account and gave only hasty synopses for some of the jury members. The sequel to his "finest achievement" did not interest him enough to complete it. When one of Appleton's editors told him that the book seemed unfinished, Masters told him that life itself is fragmentary, and the remark was relevant in some respects: the plot dealt with the main character's pursuit of, and marriage to, "Arielle," a woman based on Lillian Wilson, but since Masters could not know how such a real-life union might have turned out, he did the easy thing and got rid of Arielle by having her go insane, which effectively ended the story. He was in a very bleak mood as the winter of 1928 came on. "No news," he told John Cowper Powys as the year ended: "I never see Dreiser or anyone. Just work and to the club for my mail. Once in a while I meet someone I like to talk to there."[15]

Still, things were not as bleak as they might have been. A New York City literary club had named itself after Masters during the year, the New York artist Gordon Stevenson was slowly painting his portrait, and the New York Author's League had invited him to serve as one of only twenty people on its Literary Council. He accepted, joining ranks with some of the most important writers in the nation: Eugene O'Neill, Sinclair Lewis, Edith Wharton, Robert Frost, Ring Lardner, Booth Tarkington, Edna Ferber, John Dewey, and Edna St. Vincent Millay, among others. The Author's League had recently been instrumental in influencing some magazines to pay for contributions on acceptance rather than publication, and it often interceded for authors in other ways as well. (For example, it would give grants to financially stressed authors, one of whom would be Masters himself several years later.)[16]

During the first six months of 1929, Masters worked on various titles and lectured. In addition to proofing *The Fate of the Jury,* he researched and wrote much of a dramatic poem to be called *Manila;* he also contemplated selections for a future book to be called *Poems of People,* worked on the plays "Love and the Law" and "Wood Alcohol," and met with drama agents Richard Madden and Harold

Hendee to promote his plays. When he had his picture taken at the beginning of this period, he looked as if he had been interrupted at some difficult task, appearing ill, worried, and a little grumpy. Maybe he was beginning to look his age. Maybe there were other things on his mind.[17]

Maybe it was the cooking. Ellen had returned to New York in February 1929, a year after Hilary's birth. Bored to the brim with Kansas City and the stifling atmosphere of her parents' house, she was ready to resume the New York life, and she and Masters sometimes went out together, as his diary entries show: "Over to Hoboken to dinner. E and I." There are only a few references to joint activities, however, all of which concern dining out. Ellen was not then a good cook, and there is ample evidence that Masters was not satisfied with her culinary skills ("she puts on the coffee and proceeds to cosmetics"). They moved to a new apartment at 321 West Twenty-fourth Street in April, but things failed to improve. Some of Masters's letters to friends are spotted with references to the poor cooking of his "child-wife" and related disappointments from the kitchen. Certainly, his meals did not improve his disposition, as a March 13, 1929, letter to Powys indicates: "I am pretty tired; and all the electricity is about oozed from my flesh through these sterile pavements. I must get my feet in the soil, or become a tin marionette. Meanwhile, I hate all the course of events in America, nearly all the people, all the customs, standards, the religions." Some days he washed away his disgust and disappointments with alcohol ("cannot get along without likker"). At other times he daydreamed about making a great deal of money. Perhaps it was time to follow the path of a good many other impoverished and morally bushed authors and see what Hollywood had to offer.[18]

The story of Masters and the movies would make a tale in itself. Across parts of three decades, Masters and an unknown number of his agents promoted at least nineteen of his books in at least fifty-two unsuccessful attempts to break into Hollywood; every one of the major studios turned him down, including MGM, Paramount, Universal, Warner Brothers, RKO, and finally, Disney. "The big money" appealed to him, as did Hollywood success stories (his cousin Norma Rankin, a.k.a. "Mignon Callish," was an actress in Hollywood), and Masters had a good deal of encouragement from acquaintances. Everyone agreed that any one of the *Spoon River* poems might make a movie—"Rosie Roberts," for example, was turned into a twenty-two-page scenario called "The Power of the Night"—but despite this general agreement, not one of Masters's poems or books ever came close to being filmed. Only Jean Renoir, the son of the painter, thought seriously of filming *Spoon River, Domesday Book,* or a combination of both, but this too fell through. Perhaps it was this ongoing frustration that led Masters in 1929 to make the claim that Hollywood's first Academy Award–winning film, *Wings,* had been illegally derived from one of his poems.[19]

In January of that year, Masters alleged through the Author's League that the makers of *Wings* had used his poem "In the Philippines" as the basis for their film. Masters had read this poem "to thousands" in Los Angeles during his 1925 tour, and it was then, he alleged, that the "story was stolen." He was in the mood to believe such things, having just completed a decade in which anthology makers all over the country had tried to appropriate his poems for nothing. Now he filed a complaint with the Author's League, which set up a committee to analyze the similarities between *Wings* and "In the Philippines." The Author's League did him no good, however, probably because its committee observed that much of *Wings* takes place over France during World War I, whereas "In the Philippines" is set in the Pacific during the preflight days of 1900. Masters was no doubt grasping at straws, his exposure to this famous movie capping almost a decade and a half in which he had hoped to see one of his works filmed but had no real encouragement.[20]

He had first shown an interest in the movies as early as 1915 when he told Theodore Dreiser about a movie scenario he wanted to pursue. Several years later Paramount got as far as a scenario for *Spoon River:* "When I came on here [New York City] in 1923, the Paramount people took an interest in *Spoon River.* I had several sessions with their head man . . . and went over to their studios where I talked with their writers; they made a trial at making a scenario, and I tried my hand at it. All came to nothing."[21]

It is interesting to note that in the one scenario in which Masters's hand is visibly dominant, he chose to identify the village of Spoon River with the Illinois settlement of Bernadotte, the diminutive fishing hamlet on the Spoon River. This scenario, "Spoon River: Suggestions for a Film," has no definite plot but consists of only six scenes from the 1830s through "the age of bathtub gin." Its chief problem was that Masters had no idea how to enliven his *Spoon River* characters in ways appropriate for the screen. At the end of *Spoon River*'s epilogue (which Masters had added to the 1916 edition), he had placed a satanic figure who convened the dead of Spoon River by blowing on a trumpet. Masters decided to use this figure in his movie scenario, but the effect was simply to create some zombies with speaking parts, as suggested by his note from the scenario: "I thought that the plot of the epilogue might be used, namely to have that satanic character there portrayed stand up as he does and blow a horn and thereby summon the dead to arise. They could crawl forth from under heaving leaves. Such of them as might make the play could then stand forth and take their parts. The film could end by having them returned to their graves." Unfortunately, Masters had no technical knowledge of the cinema and only limited talent for traditional dramatic exchanges (as witnessed by his string of failed plays), so that most of his advice about the cinema was not worth much. It might have been worth more if he had routinely gone to the movies and studied them, but he hated movies. "I dislike the movie theater intensely," he told an interviewer in 1928. "I hardly ever see a film."[22]

Meanwhile, Ellen decided that one of them should become more practical. She too had had dreams, but unlike her husband, she knew when it was time to change strategies and carried few illusions about his abilities to support them.

In the fall of 1929, therefore, she entered Columbia University to begin work on a master's degree in English. "Poets often go hungry," she said of the decision. "One of us had to have a steady job." She was aided in her determination to pursue graduate work by an April 1929 court judgment awarding her $2,000 as a result of her 1926 auto accident.[23]

Her plans for graduate school had reverberations that altered the shape of her marriage. Masters was often jealous of, and felt threatened by, anyone who had a better education than he did. Perhaps this was a form of guilt, a silent recognition that he himself was partially responsible for the deficiencies of his college education, for he knew by now that he could have worked his way through Knox College, as many other students had. Perhaps the thought came to him, too, that his writing lacked the discipline that a sound education might have provided. This absence of a college degree was behind many of Masters's feuds with members of the eastern intellectual establishment. They did not all look down their New England noses at him because he was from the Midwest and thus beneath contempt, as he so often felt, but he regarded them with suspicion because many of them had passed a course of higher study and he had not. No matter that he was self-educated; no matter that he had read and remembered everything, as Eunice Tietjens said. What mattered was that those eastern men had degrees and he did not. How would he handle them at a social gathering when the talk turned to schooling? And how would he deal with polite razzing about his wife having more education than he did?[24]

Ellen's undergraduate work at the University of Chicago had not been a threat to Masters, but now she was pursuing graduate studies in American literature at Columbia, and one of these days she might know more than he did. He could not stand the thought of that, for none of his women ever knew more than he did; that was the "agreement" (call it that). But this is not what he told himself. Rather, he told himself that the table by the window of their tiny apartment was not big enough for two people with books, notes, and manuscripts. And who got the use of the typewriter? And whose work was cleared off when the table was needed for other things? He was critical of her academic work from the start.[25]

Ellen did not want to change her college plans, not only because her economic situation demanded she do something, but also because the examples of her husband and her father told her she was doing the right thing: each man had achieved a measure of success by doggedly pursuing goals. When Ellen had gone to the University of Chicago, her father had told her to study law or medicine (since she had been born hopelessly female and could not aspire to West Point), but she had ignored him, and now she wanted to ignore her husband too. She could be as stubborn as both Tom Coyne and Edgar Lee Masters. Needless to say, she wanted above all things to be admired by them.[26]

Circumstances would briefly favor her new plans. One day in mid-1929, Masters's lawyer Chiperfield discerned a softening on behalf of Helen Masters regarding Masters's alimony payments. Perhaps the attritions of time had worn

Helen down. Perhaps she had wearied of seeing her name dragged through the mud. Perhaps the arrival of young Hilary in Kansas City had softened her heart. Or maybe it was the appellate court judgment that went against her. In any event, something caused Helen at last to agree to a settlement regarding alimony. She had largely controlled Masters's financial well-being for seven and a half years, since March 1922, when Bill Slack had missed the hearing that sent Masters's assets into receivership. Now she forgave Masters's years of missed alimony in exchange for a one-time payment of $1,500 from his parents' estates. In other words, Helen's Chicago lawsuit bore fruit, but only a fraction of the funds due her, as Masters summarized things to Chiperfield: "Now in consideration of giving her $1,500 of the money there at Springfield, she has satisfied the Chicago decree in toto, and has released me from all future liability for alimony, etc." This did not, however, mean that Masters was much better off financially.[27]

His parents' estates had once been reckoned at $18,000, but Emma Masters's doctor bills had come to $4,200, and legal and funeral expenses had further depleted the estate. Masters's share of the estate had earlier been $4,120, but after paying Helen her $1,500 and Chiperfield his fee of $1,150 and after deducting "many little expenses" (they are not itemized but may have included the costs of tombstones, court fees, and payments to Abe Meyer), Masters's share of Emma Masters's estate was only $425.31, with an additional $417.25 from his father's estate. These constituted the nest egg (along with the $2,000 court settlement) with which Ellen began her master's program in the fall of 1929.[28]

Masters was not in good health during the fall. As Ellen went to classes, he was bothered with toothaches, a prolonged bout with the flu, and intermittent neuralgia in one arm. A cough kept him awake as winter came on. After Ellen's classes concluded in December, his illnesses cleared up (interestingly enough), and he and Ellen journeyed to Kansas City to spend the holidays with her parents and Hilary: "Hilary walked long blocks with me in the cold, holding my hand with a tight grip and sending into my nerves the intimate feeling that I was his father, though not so much seen by him during his life." He and Hilary sat on the porch steps of Tom Coyne's house on Roberts Street and watched the afternoon shadows lengthen in the cold winter air. Hilary, he noted, was "in perfect content" while with him. Masters stayed in Kansas City for a week and then left Hilary and Ellen with her parents while he visited his uncle Will in Petersburg.[29]

Masters retained a fondness for Wilbur Masters (his father's brother) for much of his life and extended the cordiality to Will's daughter Edith, an unmarried schoolteacher and administrator in the Petersburg schools. Will was like a brother to Masters, far more brotherly, in fact, than his real brother, the estate-snarling lawyer in Springfield. It was doubtful that Masters would see Tom on this trip, for Tom had cost him a great deal of money through legal fees in the settlement of their parents' affairs. That litigation had also been costly to Tom, however; he had suffered from a dangerous stomach ulcer since at least 1924, and the settlement of Emma's estate had aggravated it. On the night of December 31, as Masters sat up with Edith to see in the new year of 1930, Tom grew very ill. A little after midnight, at about the time Masters was going to sleep in Petersburg, Tom died twenty miles away in Springfield. Meanwhile, Ellen proceeded to Springfield with no knowledge of her brother-in-law's death. Masters met her at the Springfield train station, a broad smile covering his face. And what, she wanted to know, what was so very funny? "Tom's dead!" he said, his smile broadening. Tom was buried in Petersburg's Oakland Cemetery, and Masters and Ellen returned to New York. Hilary remained in Kansas City.[30]

Following the funeral Ellen returned to her studies at Columbia, and Masters, to his writing. In February he agreed with Horace Liveright to publish three dramatic poems in a volume to be entitled *Gettysburg, Manila, Ácoma*. Each of the three offered a revisionist view of history, but none was likely to prove popular. *Gettysburg* was not an account of the pivotal battle of the Civil War but a sympathetic portrayal of Abraham Lincoln's assassin, John Wilkes Booth. The other two plays offered viewpoints nearly as unpalatable. *Manila* focused on a Spanish-American War battle for the Philippine Islands but ignored the popular American hero Admiral Dewey in favor of a native view of American domination of the islands. In *Ácoma* the Indians of the "City in the Sky" were presented in a favorable light while all whites were shown in unflattering ways. Long-winded political preachments marred all three plays. Reviews of *Gettysburg, Manila, Ácoma* were few, in part because the volume was issued only in a limited, autographed edition of 375 copies and in part because it was a toss-up as to which of the three poems was most unreadable. The book was published in the spring of 1930 but sold only 250 copies during the next five years. In 1936 Liveright's invited Masters to purchase the remaining 125 copies himself.[31]

The firm of Horace Liveright also published a second title from Masters in 1930, a thin volume of verse entitled *Lichee Nuts* concerning the inhabitants of a metropolitan Chinatown. The Chinese Americans commented on the domestic scene, thus giving Masters a chance to vent his own views. Masters's interest in the Chinese dated back to his Lewistown days, when he had become interested in eastern philosophies through Emerson. Later the character of "Yee Bow" had shown up in *Spoon River Anthology*, having been modeled after a man of the same name in Petersburg. Poems with Chinese characters had also figured in Masters's 1921 volume *The Open Sea* and in *The New Spoon River* in 1924. Masters may also have been led to literature with an oriental impulse because several of his friends had published poems in this vein, including Vachel Lindsay, Witter Bynner, Arthur Davison Ficke, and Eunice Tietjens; Masters's acquaintance with a Chinese Chicagoan named Hip Lung also played a part. H. L. Mencken liked the lichee nut poems well enough to publish several in the *American Mercury*, and publisher Horace Liveright admired the poems outright, offering Masters a $500 advance on the volume.[32]

Some of the poems were reminiscent of *Spoon River Anthology*'s terse commentaries, including this one, in which Masters spoke of his Chicago acquaintance Hip Lung:

> When Hip Lung wanted to own the earth
> He smoked the opium pipe and curled up in dreams
> Behind his screen of tortoise shell.
> But coming out of the dream he would sit for hours
> On his chest of inlaid pearl saying nothing;
> Or if anyone entered he said, How is business?
> As China he was a happy man;
> As America a worried man,
> And America killed him at last
> When they took him to court on a debt.

Other poems reflected Masters's own experiences, including a rephrasing of a thought he had once confided to Edwina Stanton Babcock:

> Yesterday Yang Chung was talking of ascetics and drunkards,
> And arguing that ascetics live as fully as drunkards.
> "Denial," said Yang Chung, "has as much sensation
> As indulgence."

But too many of the poems were simply Masters's own biases recast in pidgin English:

> America is little boy yet.
> What America needs is to lose war,
> To have great humiliation—
> More than once.

And some poems lacked all objectifying influences:

> Someone tell Hip Lung
> About old Whig party in America
> Which was so hated and distrusted
> That it took the name republican. . . .

Overall, *Lichee Nuts* is a teaser among Masters's many books. With better editing its succinct form and ironic vignettes might have been coaxed into a volume that would have rekindled his career. Instead, reading the 100-plus short poems in one sitting is a little like opening and reading the messages of so many politicized fortune cookies. Within a year or two the book had ceased to command attention.[33]

In the spring of 1930 the Masterses moved to a colorful if seedy hotel where he would remain for the next thirteen years. The Hotel Chelsea, 222 West Twenty-third Street, was a home for New York creative types and celebrated for its short parade of the famous and a much longer parade of the near-famous, eccentric, and weird—poets, painters, playwrights, novelists, and their spouses, friends, and hangers-on. A few of those who passed through the Chelsea's imposing lobby were on their way "up"; a far greater number would never succeed, had reached a plateau in their lives, or were faced with the knowledge that their best work was behind them. The Chelsea's eleven stories had once made the hotel New York City's tallest building, but by the time Masters arrived, it was simply large, tolerant of idiosyncrasies, and affordable. The Masterses' first apartment consisted of only one room and a bath, although later apartments had a living area, bedroom, and bath. None was large enough for a family, however, and Ellen would dislike them all.[34]

Gathering the family was now a 2,600-mile round trip, the distance Ellen traveled by train when she went to Kansas City in the spring of 1930 to get Hilary, returning with him in July for their vacation in rural Harlemville, New York. Harlemville consisted of a gas station, a grocery, and a cluster of old houses and barns on nameless township roads amid creeks and woods. Masters was busy writing but took time out from work to enjoy the rural area. John Cowper Powys was a quarter-mile away in the shadow of Phudd's Mountain, and Arthur Davison Ficke and his wife were nearby too. When Ellen and Hilary arrived in July, Masters enjoyed his most relaxing vacation since divorce problems and Lillian had sent him to Europe nearly a decade before. He busied himself with Hilary and introduced him to the beauties of rural life: "That little boy walked every day with me to Steurewald's grocery story at Harlemville and back, the total distance being a mile, along a dirt road, with innumerable crows perched on the fences as we passed, and flying as they saw us to the rooky woods at the top of Phudd's Mountain. I loved this old house, particularly the kitchen where I did what writing came to mind this summer." For the most part, however, he occupied himself with Hilary and the country roads, enjoying with Ellen their daily visits to the Powys and Ficke residences.[35]

September ended this family idyll. Ellen and Hilary returned to Kansas City, and she stayed for a time to visit her parents and look after Hilary. This separation seems to have bothered Masters more than others. Combined with the growing loneliness he sometimes felt, it made him despondent, as he suggested to Ellen: "The club bores me to extinction. I go over there only for mail—once a day, late. The fountains of life seem completely dry. . . . Have nothing to write just now; and I realize that I have no friends that I care for. . . . Life for the time has turned upside down, and there's nothing in the bucket to spill." His bad mood would shortly poison his relations with Ellen as well.[36]

She returned to New York for fall semester classes at Columbia, taking fifteen semester hours in what was a busy autumn. By Christmas 1930 she needed only to complete one more class, write her thesis, and take exams to have her master's degree. On January 16 she began this final course, but something went wrong, and within three weeks she returned to Kansas City, as Masters's diary indicates: "Ellen leaves for Washington, Chicago, Petersburg, K.C."[37]

It was at this point that the couple began slowly to separate, Ellen spending more time with her parents, and Masters remaining at the Chelsea. They would get together at various times during 1931 through 1935, but they would not resume a year-round marital arrangement until well into the 1940s. Hilary came down with several childhood illnesses, and Ellen would experience ill health in the autumns of 1932, 1933, and 1934, and these illnesses served to keep them separated and to delay the completion of her graduate work. Nonetheless, Masters himself constituted the real reason for her slowness in completing her graduate degree. If Ellen had wished to be only a "schoolmarm"—a teacher at the high-school or grade-school levels—he might not have felt threatened, but she was training to be a college English teacher, and Masters almost always felt uncomfortable around the "professors." He fought her at every turn. Later on, Hilary would consistently infer that their separation was precipitated by Masters's hostile attitude toward Ellen's studies. She could not succeed, she felt, if she had a constant critic hounding her in the two small rooms of the Chelsea. The same critic controlled the table by the window. After she left, Masters noted in a front page of his diary that "in case of accident" a responsible party should contact "Mrs. E. L. Masters" at the Kansas City address of her parents. The change of address, he discerned, was semipermanent.[38]

CHAPTER 15

What Abe Lincoln Said

Lo! He babbles of the fish-frys of long ago,
Of the horse-races of long ago at Clary's Grove,
Of what Abe Lincoln said
One time at Springfield.

—Edgar Lee Masters, "The Hill," *Spoon River Anthology*

The Masterses' separation had a number of consequences, the most far-reaching of which would be Masters's affair with another woman several years later in the mid-1930s—which had a pronounced effect on Ellen. Later on she would discourage anyone from exploring the nuances of her marriage; indeed, much later on, after Edgar Lee had died, she would patiently refuse and sometimes confuse researchers seeking information concerning her, her husband, or his friends. "There will be time to delve into personal matters when more is known and when no one is hurt or made unhappy," she wrote one scholar seeking biographical materials. "All studies should concentrate on the writings of Mr. Masters." She delayed would-be fact-finders until she approached her ninetieth year in 1988 and passed power of attorney to her son, Hilary. By that time most of Masters's old friends were dead, along with many of hers, and their letters had passed to the University of Texas at Austin.[1]

But these letters reveal few details about the Masterses' marriage. Except for commenting on the economic grimness of the 1930s, their correspondence in the first half of the decade says little about them except that they lived apart, she with her parents in Kansas City, where she was said to be "visiting," and he in his rooms in the Hotel Chelsea in New York. She waited patiently for life to get better while Hilary grew to school age; Masters published as much as he could and hoped somehow to escape the Great Depression's grip on the writing game.[2]

His life at the Chelsea took on a bachelor simplicity after Ellen left. He ate at the automat, walked daily to 15 Gramercy to get his mail at the Players Club, and lived as cheaply as possible. He had a permanent, unquenchable faith that he might somehow grow rich, despite having no plans as to how this might be accomplished. ("I have been thinking all along that I'd make a fortune out of something," he told his uncle Will.) A library across the street from the Chelsea aided him in his various endeavors, and he may have relied on it as he wrote a book that for a season or two attracted almost as much attention as *Spoon River Anthology,* his 1931 biography *Lincoln: The Man.*[3]

In many ways Masters was especially well suited to write a life of the sixteenth president. Masters had grown up within two miles of Lincoln's New Salem and had played among its foundation stones and along the nearby Sangamon River: "In my boyhood New Salem Hill was nothing but a cow pasture. Not a building of the old village remained. The foundations, which were uncovered about 1918 and built upon again in a restoration of the village, were then overgrown with weeds. When we went fishing by the dam, which was the same one which spanned the river in Lincoln's day, and by the water mill built around 1840, we often climbed up to this pasture to look at the very spot where Lincoln had pitched horse-shoes and acted as a judge of foot-races." In addition, Masters's father, Hardin, had worked for a time beginning in 1872 as an associate of William H. Herndon, Lincoln's former law partner. Herndon became a close family associate (one of Masters's aunts went along as a friend of Herndon's bride on the couple's honeymoon to Washington), and Herndon was along on the outing to the Sangamon on the day Masters nearly drowned. Other members of the Masters family had personally encountered Lincoln. In 1847 Squire Davis Masters had hired Lincoln to represent him in a dispute over a promissory note. Although Lincoln had been a "good intercessor" in a second dispute, which never came to trial, he had refused a fee in both instances (he had lost the first case and done nothing in the second). Lincoln and Masters's grandfather met a third time when Squire Davis Masters was elected justice of the peace in 1849 and heard one of Lincoln's cases at the Masters farmhouse north of Petersburg: "Lincoln tried a case before my grandfather under the maple trees in front of the Masters' homestead, for my grandfather was a Justice of the Peace for a time." The case was tried under the trees instead of inside at the behest of Lucinda Masters, who noted that both the court and its spectators included tobacco chewers.[4]

These associations notwithstanding, it was a Masters family tradition to be suspicious of Lincoln. Masters's Petersburg grandparents both had southern roots, to which Masters credited their virtues and strengths, and these roots made them doubt Lincoln. Moreover, Squire Davis Masters had fought in the Blackhawk War and disliked it, and he feared that Lincoln's ascension might mean war. He also disliked "Black Republicans" who might try "to abolish all distinction between the Negro and the white race" (as he put it in a letter dated 1855). Masters explained the old man's position thus: "In 1854 he was elected to the Illinois legislature, where he voted against Lincoln for United States senator because he thought Lincoln's politics would bring on war between the states. He was a peace man."[5]

Not surprisingly, Squire Davis's son Hardin was an amalgam of both North and South: he had first attempted to join the Union army at the opening of the

Civil War and then decided he was pro-South and became involved in a botched plan to free some men who had been jailed for resisting the Northern draft. Hardin had certainly made up his mind about his political sympathies by the time his first son was born, however, as Masters explained in a discarded draft of his autobiography: "I came into the world early on Sunday morning, August 23, 1868, and was named for Gen. Robert E. Lee, for whom my father had the greatest admiration." So from the first (it might be said), Lee Masters was cast in an adversarial mode with Lincoln, who had left an indelible imprint on Petersburg not only through his life but also by virtue of having surveyed Petersburg when he lived two miles south at New Salem.[6]

Lincoln had visited later as well. Abraham Lincoln was a familiar sight in Petersburg until he was elected to the presidency and left behind scores of acquaintances, many of whom figured in stories that Masters heard as he grew up, individuals such as Bowling Green, the New Salem justice of the peace before whom young Lincoln practiced law, and Jack Kelso, the unambitious New Salem intellectual thought to have shared his knowledge of books with Lincoln. Masters also saw some of Lincoln's other associates, including Mentor Graham, the schoolmaster who straightened out Lincoln's grammar and taught him surveying. Masters was an acquaintance, too, of the Armstrong clan (leaders of the roistering Clary's Grove Boys of New Salem fame), at least three of whom were significant to Lincoln's story. And Masters also knew John McNamar, the man who may have jilted Ann Rutledge before her story became entwined with Lincoln's.[7]

Between 1835, when Ann Rutledge died, and 1930, when Masters was composing his story of Lincoln, Rutledge's story also became linked with Masters. As the nineteenth century closed, the gravesite of Ann (or Anne or Anna) Rutledge in the Old Concord Cemetery, near Petersburg, came to be well off the road in a field (the old roads having been fenced in and new roads created), and as more people began to visit her grave, it was felt that it would be appropriate to move her remains to the Oakland Cemetery, in Petersburg; in 1890 this was done. In 1906, when newspaper publisher William Randolph Hearst visited Petersburg to deliver a lecture, he saw the wisdom of preserving the nearby site of New Salem and purchased it. Having stimulated local interest in it, he then agreed to let a civic group manage the site before it was turned over to the state as a park. During these same years there was a local movement to create a more impressive headstone for Ann Rutledge (a tiny stone having served until then). A large stone was subsequently purchased and placed on her Petersburg grave in 1921, and after the appropriate permission was granted, Masters's *Spoon River* epitaph concerning her was chiseled into the stone. It was perhaps the second-most enduring event of his career—the first being the writing of *Spoon River*—but Masters did not go to the ceremony because in 1921 he was busy with his long-term problems with Lillian Wilson.[8]

But perhaps he should have observed this moment of emergent Americana or more closely monitored how his work was handled. When the poem was chiseled into the granite, the title was omitted and two of the lines were altered. One might assume these changes were accidental, or a matter of making the poem fit the stone, but the explanation was much simpler than that (as anyone who has lived in a village would know): the chairman of the group in charge of the activity made the changes, the "better," Masters said, "to conform to that man's ideas of the use of words." (The same individual, local historian Henry B. Rankin, later altered another of Masters's poems, "William H. Herndon," and reprinted it.)[9]

So Masters had all of this as incentive—his family background, the proximity of New Salem to Petersburg, and the placing of his poem on Ann Rutledge's tombstone—when he sat down to write his life of Lincoln. Masters also had some incentives from American historical scholarship. By 1930 Masters had read William Herndon and Jesse Weik's 1889 *Lincoln,* as well as "other lives of Lincoln," including that of Albert J. Beveridge. Beveridge had corresponded with Masters's father and communicated with Masters by telephone and letter but was able to carry his life of Lincoln up to only 1858 before dying in 1927. When Beveridge's work was published posthumously in 1928, Masters said it "blew up" the Lincoln story. It also left it incomplete. When Masters sent condolences to Beveridge's widow, he received in return a note in which Mrs. Beveridge lamented her husband's unfinished work. It would be too much to say that her comments planted the seed for Masters's biography of Lincoln, but it is accurate to say that Beveridge's incomplete work and untimely death cleared the way for someone to draft an accurate account of Lincoln's life, one that viewed him as a man rather than a creature of myth. As Masters later summarized things to Theodore Dreiser, "It was Beveridge's book that stirred me to my performance." All these matters may have motivated Masters to write his biography of Lincoln, but there was still one other matter, perhaps the most important: Carl Sandburg had recently published a life of Lincoln that was proving so popular that it was making people think of Sandburg rather than Masters when they spoke of the New Salem–Petersburg area.[10]

In December 1922, at about the time Masters was settling in for a miserable Christmas with Helen Masters (following his abortive return to her), Sandburg was exploring the possibilities of a simple one-volume biography of Lincoln. The idea grew, and in 1926 Sandburg's *Abraham Lincoln: The Prairie Years* appeared in two volumes and provided the American people with exactly the image they desired of the president. The book was an easy-to-read blend of fact and fiction, the whole presented as truth. It would call for a sequel and would also heighten and maintain a long and lasting enmity between Sandburg and Masters. Who (the books seemed to ask), who had the literary rights to describe the New Salem–Petersburg area to the American people? Masters, who was raised there, or Sandburg?[11]

Masters and Sandburg had been friends during their early days as poets in

Chicago. Masters had carried a manuscript copy of Sandburg's *Chicago Poems* to New York in 1915 and had tried unsuccessfully to market it ("the publishers said that it was just imitation of me"). Later Masters had provided a blurb for the advertising of *Chicago Poems,* and Sandburg had returned the favor by writing a promotional statement for Masters's 1923 novel *The Nuptial Flight.* On the surface, at least, the two had much in common: in the early 1920s, they were both making about the same amounts of money, they both used the same lecture bureau, they both griped about publishers and payments, they both distrusted anthology makers, and they were both judged by their peers to be crude and lacking in critical judgment. In addition, they had both published in *Poetry* and received that magazine's Levinson Prize. Moreover, both Masters and Sandburg were critical of many of society's leading citizens, including contemporary politicians and religionists such as Billy Sunday. To protect themselves, each had relied on pseudonyms. The problem was that they came from villages only seventy miles apart. Sandburg did not feel that his license to tell central Illinois stories should expire at Galesburg's city limits; Masters felt that it should.[12]

In fact, the two men had been growing apart even before the success of Sandburg's Lincoln biography. Although Masters had tried to help Sandburg publish his *Chicago Poems,* he soon realized that Sandburg was a chief competitor when the critics began to compare their works. By 1917 Masters regarded Sandburg as the literary rival likely to do "most injury" to him, and not long after this the injuries began to sprout. Sandburg worked on the *Daily News* with Keith Preston, the satirist who had lampooned Masters in a piece circulated nationally ("Edgar Lee Masters doesn't like Chi"); worse, Sandburg was a sometimes friend of Clarence Darrow; worse still, Sandburg had a way (Masters thought) of going behind his back and accomplishing things that never came to Masters or that came only slowly. An early example was the 1923 doctor of letters degree awarded to Sandburg by tiny Lombard College in Galesburg. (Galesburg was also the home of Knox College, where Masters had attended classes for a year.) Sandburg had dropped out of both high school and college, so Masters wondered why his own college had not contacted him about an honorary doctorate. How did Sandburg do these things? Accompanying it all was what Masters regarded as Sandburg's overtowering debt to him. "Chances are," Masters told Ellen, "Sandburg would never have been heard of except for the popularity of *Spoon River,* which brought to shore all treasure trove as well as brush and refuse."[13]

When news of Sandburg's forthcoming biography of Lincoln reached Masters, he felt as if Sandburg were trespassing on his territory, that his rival was making unfair use of the region he had popularized in *Spoon River Anthology.* He would repeat this claim in one form or another for the rest of his life, goaded to it by circumstance as Sandburg's public acceptance slowly grew while Masters's reputation slowly declined. Masters's 1924 comments to Agnes Lee Freer, shortly after Sandburg began his biography, are representative:

> Amy Lowell bracketed me with Sandburg in her book, though I have no part with him in any way. Others have done the same thing. It helped him; it hurt me, so far as such an absurdity could hurt. Then little things occurred, trifles: the *News* published that Sandburg was Reedy's most intimate friend; then I found Sandburg's footprints in Petersburg, Illinois, among my intimates, and almost everywhere I had lived; and I always found him following me to pick up the same advantage that came to me or the crumbs of it, altogether a sort of stealthy following, and watching, and undermining where possible.
>
> The truth is that he has no country; he is not attached to Galesburg, where he was born, while I have the Lincoln country as mine, by right of birth, because of the affection of the people, and because I have portrayed it. I understand that he is now writing a life of Lincoln. Why!

The situation was worsened because several other people said that the Spoon River region was Masters's. Harriet Monroe herself had said so in a 1917 *Poetry* article in which she discussed the work of Masters, Sandburg, Vachel Lindsay, and others. She concluded that "none of these has got this particular region into his blood and bones so deeply as Mr. Masters, who was 'raised' in one of its typical villages."[14]

Thus, when Sandburg's biography of Lincoln appeared early in 1926, it was extremely upsetting to Masters:

> The most brazen piece of publishers lying that I have seen in an age is being pulled this week anent Sandburg's *Prairie Years*—his work on Lincoln. In March 1922, I published *Children of the Market Place,* a novel on Douglas and at the last treating of Lincoln too. So Sandburg, who has been tracking and aping me, set to write a biography.
>
> The joke of all this is that my grandfather lived within 7 miles of New Salem and within 5 miles of Petersburg from 1847 to 1904; and my father lived there from 1847 to 1880, and I lived with him there until the latter date, from the time I was a year old. All my people are buried there. It is my one home in all this world. And along comes this Swede and says it's his home—or tries to make it the same thing as Galesburg.

In fact, Sandburg had known exactly how Masters felt about the area in question, having written about Masters's article "Days in the Lincoln Country" when it appeared in the journal of the state's historical society.[15]

Masters would have been even more upset if he had known that moviemaker D. W. Griffith, who had ignored Masters's *Children of the Market Place,* would shortly offer Sandburg $10,000 for a week's work on a movie script about Lincoln and that profits from the Lincoln biography would help Sandburg settle for several years in a comfortable Michigan estate not far from Masters's lost farm at Spring Lake. At the same time, Masters was eminently aware of the overall commercial value of Sandburg's Lincoln book: "That slick Swede Sandburg, who started as a socialist wanting to assassinate anyone with a tuxedo, has ridden Abe Linkern to prosperity."[16]

When the press and public began praising Sandburg for his biography, Masters could respond only by saying over and over, "His Lincoln book derives from me," and "Sandburg began to hang around me about 1914, and heard me tell about Lincoln." Masters never did read *Abraham Lincoln: The Prairie Years*, telling some of his friends that he had tried it and been put off by its "bad style." (His remarks have some merit to the extent that Sandburg has often been regarded as a poor historian.) When Mark Van Doren invited Masters to review Sandburg's biography in *The Nation*, Masters refused, speaking of a future "biography that will really count."[17]

Masters began his life of Lincoln on April 29, 1930, just a day after moving to the Hotel Chelsea and four days after he had signed a contract with Dodd, Mead and Company and received an advance of $1,000 for the book. He worked on the manuscript for forty-seven consecutive days and completed it on June 14, after which he took a rest and revised it for an additional ten days in June and July. He apparently did not review the manuscript during his 1930 vacation with Hilary and Ellen at Harlemville, New York. When his family returned to Kansas City on September 2, he returned to New York City and delivered the manuscript to Dodd, Mead on the following day.[18]

It should be remembered that Masters had at his disposal a battery of facts and a privileged position that few other authors could then command: his father's legal work and conversations with William Herndon gave Masters the opportunity to help set straight the Lincoln record. If he needed to document an item regarding Lincoln, Masters had only to say that Herndon had imparted this information to his father during a conversation under the trees of the Menard County Courthouse, during a buggy ride to the Sangamon River, or whatever seemed appropriate. And Hardin Masters did impart such information to his son, remarking at the beginning of one of his letters, for instance, that he was about to tell Masters a previously unpublished story about Lincoln. Because Hardin Masters's memory was excellent up to the time of his death, Masters could repeat his stories with some authority. Moreover, others recognized Hardin's authority. When citizens in the Springfield area raised a monument to William Herndon in Springfield's Oak Ridge Cemetery in May 1918, Hardin Masters was chosen to deliver the principal address. (The works of two poets also figured in the ceremony: Vachel Lindsay recited his popular "Abraham Lincoln Walks at Midnight," and Masters's *Spoon River* epitaph on "William H. Herndon" closed the proceedings.)[19]

The remarkable thing about Masters's *Lincoln* is that he chose not to inform his readers that he had intimate information but instead gave the impression that he was relying on the works of previous Lincoln scholars, principally Beveridge and Herndon. There is only the briefest reference to the Masters family in the text and none at all in the footnotes; Herndon's association is objectified, most typically with expressions such as "Herndon wrote." Masters's motive, of course, was the desire that his text appear to be an objectively written biography, not just a series of family biases made public. But the biases were evident to all and sundry: Masters blamed Lincoln for most of the nation's crises from the creation of the Republican Party in the 1850s through the dawn of the twentieth century. It should be recalled that Masters was an ardent Democrat and that the Democrats placed only one man in the White House between 1860 and 1912. Masters regarded this period as a half-century of Republican misrule, as he once explained to southern writer Allen Tate. "The Republican Party started the [Civil] War to entrench themselves politically, so they lifted up Lincoln to keep themselves entrenched; and they did it and have done it." If Masters discredited Lincoln's politics and character, the Republicans would also be discredited, and with them the Lincoln mythmakers—the chief and most popular one now being Masters's competitor for public hearts and minds, Carl Sandburg. Masters would discredit Sandburg by discrediting Lincoln, by showing the American people that Sandburg had been wrong, and in the process reclaim his homeland, "the Lincoln country" that was his by birth.[20]

Masters began his story of Lincoln by saying he hoped to present the first wholly truthful portrait of the president, noting, "The time has arrived when his apotheosis can be touched with the hand of rational analysis." That was on page 1. By page 4 Lincoln was described as having been "against liberty . . . from his first days in 1832 at New Salem, Illinois, to the end of his life"; no less important, "the motley forces who had joined the Republican Party" had "raped the Philippines" (taken by U.S. forces during the Spanish-American War of 1898). If at times the "hand of rational analysis" seemed to be moving rapidly, it was probably because there were so many myths that needed exploding: "It is not for lack of facts that the myths have grown up about Lincoln. The facts have been disregarded in order that the portrait of him might be drawn which America wanted. This of itself is a spiritual fact." A closely related "spiritual fact" was that all Republicans were "impostors and hypocrites." "The purpose has been to bring together the testimony in full," Masters the lawyer wrote, after which he spared neither facts nor their long-term interpretations where these would do the most damage to Lincoln and his party.[21]

Masters's Lincoln was "cold," "cunning," "devious and censurable." He was "not over scrupulous" about the legal cases he accepted but was ever "an aid to monopoly and privilege" and in favor of the industrialized East over the agrarian West. As president, Lincoln had provoked South Carolina into starting the Civil War. Even his best moments were flawed. The Gettysburg Address was a sham, a "refusal of the truth which is written all over the American character." The frontier athleticism associated with Lincoln had something wrong with it too: "What he learned in wrestling undoubtedly had its influence upon his debating mind. To elude, to dodge under, to get away, to come to, to grip, to get the best hold short of a foul, and even to foul, when it can be safely done, all these tactics of wrestling entered into Lincoln's forensic performances."[22]

Moreover, Lincoln was sexually odd: "Lincoln was an under sexed [*sic*] man.

That is the simplest way to express it." (Lincoln made up for this, in part, by telling "sex stories . . . of the filthy variety.") Lincoln was disrespectful of his mother, denying her a tombstone after her death, and mean to his father—although this might be forgiven since Lincoln's father was "unmoral," "shiftless," "worthless," and "less than second grade." *Lincoln: The Man* had two textual illustrations in its opening chapters. The first was a reproduction of "lines written by Lincoln in his fourteenth year":

> Abraham Lincoln
> his hand and pen.
> He will be good but
> god knows When.

The second showed Lincoln's license to sell liquor from the days when Lincoln and William Berry owned a New Salem store. The book ended (or nearly so) with the remark that assassin John Wilkes Booth's bullet "was the last one fired for States' Rights." The volume was dedicated to Thomas Jefferson, our "greatest president."[23]

An interesting component of this assessment was the way Masters imputed to Lincoln certain elements of his own behavior, in the course of which he faulted Lincoln for doing things he himself had done. For example, Lincoln had married his wife for money and position: "Her father was a man of wealth; and it is possible that the ambitious Lincoln conceived that her father's means would be a help to his ambition. It is possible and probable too." In other words, Lincoln's motives had been almost the same as Masters's had been when the young lawyer and would-be writer was courting Helen Jenkins, a response to the fact that there were too many lawyers and too few good cases: "When a man is ambitious in a field in which there is no money for a living, he must marry it." Lincoln, like Masters, had tried to back out of his engagement, going one night to visit his fiancée to tell her that they must part, but the poor woman "burst into tears," and the marriage eventually took place. And it yielded the same results as Masters's marriage would later yield: "Lincoln paid a thousand fold [*sic*] in suffering and in torture of mind, in humiliation of soul and in bitter self-reproach for any benefit that he ever derived from his marriage with Mary Todd." In the end Masters was to perform an excellent job in dissecting Lincoln's marriage; more precisely, Lincoln was made as amorally ambitious as his biographer. To put it all another way, Masters's Lincoln was a traitorous demagogue whose turbulent times and up-from-dirt ambitions only partially masked the facts that he was a poorly educated social climber, an egomaniacal poser of low intelligence—unmannerly, unkempt, unwashed, and untrustworthy.[24]

Despite Lincoln's undesirable traits, however, Masters felt that the book about him would "always sell for years to come." He did not worry about the costs involved in revising its galley proofs and urged his publisher, Dodd, Mead and

Company, to hurry and complete the volume in time for Lincoln's birthday in February, a time for "great publicity." (He chose not to worry about adverse reactions, telling Mencken that he would simply "take to the woods" if bad publicity followed.) Ellen Masters designed the jacket art, plans were made for a five-dollar trade edition and a ten-dollar deluxe edition of 150 copies, and ads were placed in the best magazines. Interviews were arranged with the Associated Press, United Press Association, and International News Service. On February 6, 1931, *Lincoln: The Man* went forth to meet the public.[25]

The public's reaction to the new biography was spontaneous, immediate, and lasting: most people hated it. Perhaps the timing was wrong. In 1931 the country was in the depths of the Great Depression. The present was terrible; the future, doubtful. The past was the only certainty. Then Masters entered to tell people that part of their most valued past was a sham, that the Great Emancipator—the most mourned, most idealized, and most respected figure in American history—was a fake. What they wanted (as Harriet Monroe once put it) was a picture of Lincoln "growing greater . . . through the mists of time." What they wanted, in other words, was what Sandburg had already given them in *Abraham Lincoln: The Prairie Years.* What they got was something else.[26]

Reviewers everywhere found something to dislike about Masters's new book. *Time* magazine coined the word "Lincolnoclast" to describe it and said that it would make Lincoln turn in his grave, adding that admirers of Lincoln might borrow from a once-popular song and wish that Masters were in "de cold, cold, ground." The *New York Times Book Review* found almost no redeeming values in *Lincoln: The Man:* "Charles Dickens was kinder to Bill Sikes," wrote the reviewer, remembering the murderous villain of *Oliver Twist,* who was accidentally but properly hanged from a chimney in a London slum (an event closely followed by the death of his dog, also bad). "Lincoln Killed Our Freedom, says Masters," wrote the *New York Telegram:* "Sitting in the skyscraper offices of his publishers, his mouth a grim, austere slit, only his battered hat to show him a poet, Masters confessed he had little hope. A major poet of the Republic, he tilted his chair back and stared through shelled spectacles and blamed Lincoln for all of it."[27]

There was talk of getting even with Masters. A bill was introduced in Congress to bar *Lincoln: The Man* from the mails. The proposed bill, sponsored by Congressman Crail of California, read in part: "The book entitled 'Lincoln, the Man,' edited by Edgar Lee Masters, is hereby declared to be obscene, lewd, lascivious, filthy, and indecent, and a scurrulous [*sic*] and unprincipled attack on a good man." The Board of Trade of Boston Book Merchants banned *Lincoln: The Man,* as did a large bookseller in Philadelphia. Hate mail came addressed to "Mr. Traitor Edgar Lee Masters," and the Knights of the Ku Klux Klan sent him a card: "We have our [drawing of an eye] on you! K K K K." (It was probably just as well that the Klan did not know of Masters's satirical poster on the president: "The Virgin Birth of Abraham Lincoln.")[28]

A New Salem civic group accepted a bust of Lincoln by Masters's sister, Madeline, and placed it in the interpretative center devoted to Lincoln. Since Masters was convinced that his sister had no ability, he was absolutely sure this was an insult aimed at him, and it probably was. The situation was made a little more galling because Masters had recently given the center a copy of a book owned and signed in 1798 by his great-great-grandfather John Wasson (the grandfather of Lucinda Masters).[29]

Two miles away in Petersburg, the people who had placed Ann Rutledge's *Spoon River* epitaph on her headstone in Oakland Cemetery now met and spoke of chiseling it off. Their initial motive was revenge, but they soon had another motive as well: historical accuracy. Masters had repudiated the Lincoln–Ann Rutledge love affair in *Lincoln: The Man.* He said it was hogwash, and a related claim soon provided a motive to remove his epitaph. Masters's critics found a source saying that Ann Rutledge was not really buried beneath the Petersburg stone with Masters's epitaph but instead rested elsewhere. An elderly relative of Ann Rutledge said it was a "greedy undertaker" who in 1890 first concocted the scheme of moving Ann's remains from the Old Concord Cemetery, north of town, to the new cemetery on the south edge of Petersburg. More precisely, Oakland Cemetery promoter D. M. Bone and his friend the undertaker Samual Montgomery decided it would be financially advantageous to move Rutledge's remains. Petersburg already had a nice cemetery (Rose Hill), where the founder of the Grand Army of the Republic, B. F. Stephenson, was buried along with many of the town's first citizens, but Montgomery and Bone seemed to feel that the new cemetery could not compete unless it also had a famous person interred therein. So on May 15, 1890, the undertaker and one of Ann's relatives went to her grave in the Old Concord Cemetery (the same that Masters had visited as a boy). They opened the grave, dug down, and found nothing except "four pearl buttons," which they moved along with some dirt to the new cemetery. Masters's epitaph was thus a fraud, for Ann Rutledge's body was not really "beneath these weeds" in Petersburg, as the epitaph claimed, but had already become a part of the meadow, a part of America in the Old Concord Cemetery miles away. Masters's poem should therefore come off; perhaps the whole stone should come down. In the end nothing was done, although for a time parts of the community were as worked up as they had been when *Spoon River* arrived.[30]

Lincoln: The Man was to be much like *Spoon River* in one other way as well: ordinary citizens who read it and hated it were perfectly willing to engage in heated discourse with those who had read it and admired it or to tell the author how they felt about the book. Some readers were speechless with admiration, and others were speechless with indignation. Some read the book several times, and others swore they could not stand to read it once. They read it and wept—because the book was true, and because the book was false. It was said to be both "the greatest book ever written," excluding the Bible, and the worst book. People said Masters should be publicly "slapped"; some challenged him to debates. Men in prison wrote Masters, and children sent him letters. The

History Committee of the Sons of Confederate Veterans met to endorse the book. The Jersey City Lions Club publicly denounced it. Masters received pictures of himself with his face viciously mutilated, and he received requests for autographs. Complaints and compliments arrived in approximately equal numbers at Masters's address, at that of his publishers, and in the offices of newspapers, but the responses of those who did most to shape public opinion were decidedly negative. Cartoons on both coasts showed Masters sticking out his tongue at the Lincoln memorial and slinging mud at it. In the end *Lincoln: The Man* did far more damage to Masters's reputation than to Abraham Lincoln's and served in one more way to alienate Masters from his public. Sandburg, of course, remained untouched.[31]

Not surprisingly the book sold reasonably well in the United States, and Masters said it went into six printings (the publisher claimed 7,100 copies were sold), but the facts were grimmer overseas. Masters's London publisher wrote him about a year after the publication of *Lincoln* to say that the book had been "an absolute failure." The company (Cassell) had printed 1,500 copies, given away 70 for review, and still had over 1,200 on hand in mid-1932. Cassell regretted paying Masters his £100 advance, for the book had brought in only £22, and ended by saying that it wished it had not published the book at all.[32]

Other costs were less calculable. Masters's splenetic vehemence against Lincoln and the one-sided interpretations of facts hurt Masters immeasurably with his public. *Lincoln: The Man* became one of the most unpopular books of the decade and was a liability for Masters as long as he wrote and published. Dorothy Dow phrased the phenomenon thus: "I believe it took him half a dozen years to realize that, after the Lincoln book, nothing else of his would ever be a great financial success. . . . The publication of *Lincoln* marked Masters's downfall in public esteem. Almost at once, nearly as much condemnation as he had had adulation was showered upon him." The final curse on *Lincoln* came years later when Masters looked for the manuscript of the book to sell it and found that it had been misplaced.[33]

By the spring of 1931 Masters had heard enough complaints about his Lincoln biography and decided to clear out of New York City for his 1931 vacation with Ellen and three-year-old Hilary. He looked at a vacation site in rural Hillsdale, New York, and thought of purchasing it, but he did not have enough money and did not know what he should do about the future. He complained to Ellen (then in Kansas City) in May 1931:

> I am perplexed with a thousand things, and they get worse. I have to think of going on with this writing, or else returning to the law, or getting a job. That isn't all: just what I should set my hand to now bothers me so that I can't sleep. That "Atlantis" matter just will not work. . . . It won't work.
>
> Meanwhile the book market is horrible. . . . Nothing is selling. My book [about Lincoln] is stopped. . . . I spend my evenings in this room, staring. I hate the club; and I have no friends.

He would, he said, "be glad to get under a tree and stay drunk for months to come."[34]

He decided instead to do battle once more with the Civil War and his hometowns of Petersburg and Lewistown, this time in a novel. He thought seriously about returning to Petersburg to live while writing the book; as Ellen later phrased it, "He wanted . . . some place where the customs might still be the same as they were in the time of Lincoln and Douglas." When he found Petersburg too changed, he, Ellen, and Hilary went instead to Galena, Missouri, near the area where Ellen's father had once planned a sheep ranch and where Masters found the old America he was seeking "pristine and unchanged." He had arrived in Galena by June 11 and was soon drafting a novel with the working title of "Leonard Westerfield," later renamed *The Tide of Time.*[35]

In addition to relying on local rural impressions to get in the mood for this new book, Masters was aided by notes he had gathered from his college friend Ed Reese regarding nineteenth-century Lewistown (Reese had worked for a time on the *Lewistown News*). Masters also relied on notes concerning nineteenth-century Petersburg from an attorney who was a friend of his, Frank Blane, and from Fern Nance Pond; the latter combed the *Menard Index* and *Menard Axis* for news of nineteenth-century Petersburg. (Fern Pond's great-grandfather, Sevigne Houghton, had lived on a farm across the road from Masters's grandfather and is mentioned in the opening poem of *Spoon River Anthology.*)[36]

Masters was also aided by Galena's Leverett family, self-reliant farm folk with two sociable sons, Homer and Wilbur, who played the fiddle and guitar, respectively. (Their father had once worked for Ellen's father when Tom Coyne was trying to establish his sheep ranch.) They played for Masters and Hilary, rendering some of the nineteenth-century fiddle tunes Masters had heard while growing up, so that he had "The Arkansas Traveler" and "Turkey in the Straw" as backdrop to his work, along with "The Missouri Harmony" and "Good Morning, Uncle Johnny, I've Fetched Your Wagon Home." One of the sons created a tune in honor of Hilary, "The Mr. Ittie March" (for Masters referred to both his sons as "Mr. It" or "Ittie"); Masters in turn drafted a poem called "Fiddling by the Moon," a September 1931 composition showing "Homer Leverett fiddling by the moon, / With Wilbur Leverett strumming by the moon." Masters's summer was made complete when one of the Leveretts recalled a variant of the old fiddle tune Percy Grainger had used as the basis for his "Spoon River." The tune was related to the one Masters had learned from his 1915 acquaintance Captain Robinson, which Masters had not long since described in the opening epitaph of *The New Spoon River:*

CAPTAIN ROBINSON

If the tune "Spoon River," played by the nameless fiddler,
Heard by me as a youth in the evenings of fifty-seven,
By the cabin door on the banks of the little stream,

May under the genius hands of Percy Grainger
Become a symphony utterable to the baton
Of great conductors, and only thus, in brasses,
Viols, violins, flutes, and strings of the harp,
The boom of the drum, the thunder tubes of the organ—
If this may be, may not my dream of the sixties
Flower to a drama of song, a great Republic?
Till the smoke of the cabin, the smell of honey and corn,
And days of labor, and evenings of neighborly talk,
And nights of peaceful sleep under friendly stars,
And courage, and singing nerves, and honest hope,
And freedom for men to live as men, and laughter,
And all sweet things that ripple the tune of the fiddler,
Become a symphony rich and deep as the sea!

This pastoral experience in the Ozarks ended in mid-August when Masters expressed the manuscript of *The Tide of Time* to Dodd, Mead. Ellen and Hilary returned to Kansas City, and Masters went on to New York. Once there, everything went wrong.[37]

Masters was asking for a $3,000 advance on *The Tide of Time* and felt certain he would receive it after an employee of Dodd, Mead told him that the new book was "one of the greatest novels ever written in America." (More precisely, the manuscript of *The Tide of Time* had found its way into the hands of a secretary at Dodd, Mead; she had read the book and liked it, and Masters chose to believe her when she told him it was "the greatest.") When Dodd, Mead asked him to cut or change portions of the book, he refused (for all his other publishers had given in to him), but this time the Great Depression was on, and the economics of publishing were different. Dodd, Mead rejected the manuscript outright and suggested he try another publisher, perhaps because of the hostile critical reception recently given its volume *Lincoln: The Man*.[38]

Masters was livid with rage ("I haven't been more furious in years," he told Ellen). Nor did the times help him any. His son Hardin had recently lost his job as a stockbroker, Masters's club was "full of brokes," and his friends Oliver Herford (who had illustrated the 1916 *Spoon River*) and Joseph Nicolosi were both out of work. Masters decided that the nation was again abusing its artists. "You see where literature gets off," he wrote Ellen, "how material things control it, as Marx contended." The reference to Karl Marx did Masters little good in this context, and similar statements, some of them in his published works, would several years later help put the FBI onto Masters's trail.[39]

Because he was friendless, broke, and in debt to Macmillan and Liveright, Masters at last seriously contemplated going home to live in Petersburg, where his uncle Will resided. In November he wrote Wilbur that he was thinking about "coming to the Illinois country to live for the rest of [his] life": "I am tired of the city; and life has become so confused and hard that I want to get where there are trees and sky and air. I must confess that my mind is puzzled." He asked to stay at Wilbur's small house, but Wilbur's wife was not well, and their daughter, Edith, lived with them, so Masters asked Will to look for other rooms around Petersburg: "I could take a couple of rooms in some business block like over Frackleton's bank or somewhere and make them into living quarters. I saw good rooms one time in the rear of Pond's office." Masters seemed not to notice that he now resembled two of his less enviable *Spoon River* characters: Lucius Atherton, the village heartbreaker, who in his later years "lived at Mayer's restaurant, / Partaking of short-orders, a gray, untidy, / Toothless, discarded, rural Don Juan"; and Benjamin Pantier, attorney at law, who lost his friends and lived by himself "in a room back of a dingy office."[40]

Before Masters could pack his things, however, he came to a different realization: he could not return to the village of his boyhood, for it no longer existed. He explained to Uncle Will: "The kind of civilization that is there [now] depresses and tires me. The old land that I knew has vanished; has rolled up like a scroll and been put away." So while he was tired of the city, there was nothing left for him in the country, as he remarked to Ellen in November 1931: "My western country is gone, and . . . it is not there to return to. . . . I am really more perplexed than I ever expected to be." The only thing that kept him going, he said, was his work: "Then I turn about in my thinking and reflect that I have some more books to write." He also reflected that he would probably make even less money if he left New York: "What little I make, I pick up by being here."[41]

He would not, however, pick up much from his next book. In 1928 Masters had published a drama about one of Lincoln's New Salem associates, Jack Kelso. At the end of Kelso's story, Masters had provided the means for yet another story in the person of a young boy named "Godbey," whose story he worked on in mid-1928. He had subsequently placed the manuscript for *Godbey: A Dramatic Poem* in a vault, where it remained until 1931, when, with the *Lincoln* furor at its height, he offered it to Dodd, Mead. The American editions of *Lincoln* had sold satisfactorily, and Masters and Dodd, Mead reached an agreement to publish a signed, limited edition of 347 copies of *Godbey* in November 1931.[42]

Unfortunately, what might have been a simple poetic drama of the New Salem frontier emerged as a terrifically confusing book. Godbey, now middle-aged, passes from the reality of this world to another, wanders in caves, and ends by agreeing to serve as a caretaker for a village idiot from the Petersburg area. Along the way Godbey encounters a singing tree, some gastropods, "The Temple of Five and Four," and the philosopher Jean-Jacques Rousseau, as well as a cracker-barrel character called "Pappy Taylor." (Also included are two monkeys, a spider, a grasshopper, and a cricket meant, Masters said, to represent literary critics Paul Elmer More and Irving Babbitt, the Church, John D. Rockefeller, and Rockefeller's son, respectively.) Masters later averred that *Godbey* "covered the whole field of life"—by which he meant politics, religion, law, and learning—

but most readers must have shaken their heads and wondered whether his nineteenth-century protagonist had been smoking too many corn silks.[43]

Whatever his readers thought, there were not many of them, nor were there many buyers: ninety days after publication, Dodd, Mead reported that only 100 copies had sold and that the company would incur a loss. Masters was in no mood to hear such news, for his limited edition of *Gettysburg, Manila, Ácoma* had already suffered a similar fate. He promptly engaged a lawyer and sued Dodd, Mead for breach of contract. *Godbey* was supposed to have been issued in a trade edition, Masters now said. He asked that his contract be canceled and that copies of *Godbey* be given to him free and demanded his royalties plus $500 (to make the plates for a trade edition). He also threatened a suit for damages. In reply, Dodd, Mead told Masters and his lawyer to read the terms of the contract that governed *Godbey* and reminded them, too, that Masters had already waived a trade edition. The company offered to sell all its remaining copies of *Godbey* to Masters at $1 per copy, an offer Masters declined. (He had only one copy himself but was too stubborn to buy others, preferring to make Dodd, Mead keep them all.) Relations were poor on both sides even before Masters sent Dodd, Mead a letter that effectively ended the relationship: "A lawyer that would betray his client's interests, as you have betrayed mine with *Godbey,* and at last with *Lincoln,* could be disbarred." It was on this note that Masters's relations with yet another New York publisher came to an end.[44]

He still owed Macmillan about $4,000 in unearned royalties, and he still owed Liveright $1,000 (from Horace Liveright's loan). He had alienated Macmillan by taking *The New Spoon River* to Liveright and then alienated Liveright by finding fault with the promotion of *Lichee Nuts* and by telling company representatives "they could go to hell." Now he had tried to sue Dodd, Mead. Maybe this was the reason he would publish no books in 1932; he was on poor terms with all his publishers.[45]

Then again, maybe it was his poor treatment of material in the area he claimed "by right of birth." It was poor writing about the New Salem–Petersburg area that hurt Masters more than anything else as the Great Depression settled in. Masters's *Lincoln* had been a public relations disaster, *Godbey* a psychedelic dream, and *The Tide of Time* too diffuse and wandering for a publisher to risk. Masters's poor treatment of indigenous material actually strengthened Carl Sandburg's claim on the Lincoln country. Even the minor footnote that might have come to Masters and his father for their help on Albert Beveridge's Lincoln biography was obscured and lost. When Beveridge's *Lincoln* was published posthumously in 1928, neither Masters nor his father was mentioned in the book's preface, although another member of the Masters family was: "Mr. Thomas D. Masters, of Springfield," Masters's hated brother, who had made himself helpful and pleasant enough to be named along with university professors and the like as one of those contributing to Beveridge's landmark life of Lincoln. (One of the things Tom had done was to send Beveridge a copy of Masters's Civil War novel *Children of the Market Place,* thus using Masters's own work as a means of ingratiating himself with Beveridge.)[46]

Masters closed out 1931 by grasping at straws. Frazzled, pulled in too many directions, with none of them leading to a steady income or a reunion with his family, he tried to market a handwritten version of *Spoon River Anthology;* to sell some of his manuscripts; to secure a salaried position on the *New York World-Telegram;* and to attract a new publisher, Alfred A. Knopf (which was not interested). Characteristically, Masters also did things that hurt him: he resigned from the National Institute of Arts and Letters in 1931 because he did not like the membership, he spread ugly tales about the mentalities and characters of his publishers, he got drunk, and he never forgave those with whom he had quarreled or who had picked a quarrel with him. (His father had been known to hold onto old grudges in much the same way.)[47]

At least a portion of Masters's ill humor might be traced to his ongoing inability to fashion a volume to rival *Spoon River.* His acquaintances Dreiser and Sandburg had managed to gain growing recognition, but Masters by now seemed more like certain other "one-book" authors from the Midwest, Ben Hecht, Floyd Dell, and Glenway Wescott. Over the years Masters was sometimes relegated to this group, but *Spoon River*'s fame kept him among the better-known personalities as well. It was an uneasy position to occupy. Financial disappointments made the sting of his predicament a little sharper.

Masters's worldly goods at this time (excluding food and utensils, clothing, bedding, and a little money) consisted of manuscripts, a trunk of books, "one electric radiator" (or space heater), a suitcase, and a "large Webster's Dictionary," as well as a gun, a jade sculpture of the Buddha, and pictures of people he admired from the old days. Back in Illinois Masters's friend Vachel Lindsay measured his own personal assets against the debilitating effects of the Great Depression and committed suicide. It was Lindsay's unhappy tale that would next occupy Masters.[48]

CHAPTER 16

A Poet in America

I see him now, trudging the lonely highway of eternity.

—Edgar Lee Masters to John Cowper Powys, December 16, 1931

Early in 1932 the widow of the Illinois poet Vachel Lindsay (1879–1931) invited Masters to write a biography of her late husband by using Lindsay's letters and diaries and Masters's own personal memories. Masters was not eager to write such a book, for he felt that she herself should do so, and at first offered to write only a preface. Elizabeth Lindsay insisted, however, and after she and Masters exchanged letters, he began to gather his information and prepared to write. His research time would amount only to two months, with an additional one month for writing, but the result was the authorized biography of Lindsay that would mark the beginning for much future scholarship. Unfortunately, due to the Great Depression and changing tastes in literature (in the course of which Lindsay's literary reputation declined), the Lindsay biography never yielded Masters the economic or literary gains he might otherwise have received.[1]

At first glance Masters and Lindsay seem to be so unlike as to make Masters an inappropriate biographer. At the turn of the century, as Masters dueled with Chicago's gamy political system, fought its judges, and cheated on his wife, Lindsay was making serious plans to study art and keep himself pure until marriage. In 1904, as Masters worked with Clarence Darrow in the Supreme Court defense of an anarchist, Lindsay was laying the foundations to walk through the country preaching a "Gospel of Beauty." Later, as the firm of Darrow, Masters, and Wilson defended clients who settled their differences with dynamite and murder (and while Masters was making and spending $30,000 a year), Lindsay was preparing to recite his verses in America's tiny towns and support himself through sales of a pamphlet called *Rhymes to Be Traded for Bread.* And surprisingly, in the early 1910s, as Masters wondered whether poetry was worth pursuing at all, Lindsay suddenly succeeded in attracting national and international attention with two major volumes of verse, *General William Booth Enters into Heaven* (1913) and *The Congo and Other Poems* (1914). Still later, as *Spoon River Anthology* vaulted Masters to fame and led him to Lillian, frustration, and despair, Lindsay published *The Golden Book of Springfield* (1920), an account of the ways in which the town of his nativity might reach utopian perfection in the year 2018 (the year of Illinois's bicentennial).[2]

As different as these characteristics might seem, Lindsay and Masters shared a number of common experiences and values that became the bases for Masters's book. Both had southern roots and a reverence for the Illinois past embodied in the values of the pioneers and people of their grandparents' generation. The two also had fathers who were professional men and mothers who were not particularly good for their sons or easy to get along with (although the two women knew and liked each other). In addition, Masters and Lindsay had lived in the same region—they spent their boyhoods only twenty miles apart—and held similar opinions of the region, namely, that it had been corrupted by greed, industrialism, and urban values (Masters), or that it was thus corrupted but might yet be redeemed (Lindsay). Lindsay and Masters also had common literary and economic sensibilities: neither knew his good writing from his bad, neither spent adequate time in revising, neither could ever hold onto a dollar, and each knew for a certainty that the United States abused its poets. Moreover, each sat to the left in politics, and each had married a woman approximately half his age in the mid-1920s. Of course, there was one more reason for Masters to write Lindsay's biography, and it was the most important of all: Lindsay exemplified in his life the devotion to art that Masters could only claim to practice. So these were some of the salient facts regarding the two when Masters commiserated with Lindsay's wife, Elizabeth, two days after her husband's death on December 5, 1931.[3]

Lindsay had died a painful and puzzling death, a suicide in the Springfield house in which he had been born, next to the governor's mansion. After drinking a quantity of liquid disinfectant, he had awakened his wife and delivered his last significant words: "They tried to get me; I got them first." A sympathetic doctor had subsequently indicated that Lindsay died of heart failure, and so the first thing Masters needed to do in writing a biography was to establish the facts of Lindsay's death. The first thing he did, however, was to offer consolation and aid to Elizabeth Conner Lindsay, the mother of two and a widow although barely in her thirties:

> It is strange that I got vibrations that were somehow disturbing. We didn't see much of each other; but I loved him as a man and as a poet, with a heart all gold, a spirit all goodness, and generosity toward all men. He will always be to me the pilgrim boy, trudging along the highway of the endless years. Truly, my heart is hurt.
>
> The Players Club displayed the flag at half mast, and men have been gathered

> about talking in sorrow of him. . . . If there is anything I can do for you here, let me know. If there are poems to be brought out, and I can help you about them in any way, I shall be happy to do it for the sake of my friend who is gone, and for you.[4]

The offer was not an empty gesture. Masters gave Elizabeth Lindsay a $50 check he had received for a poem written in Lindsay's memory and solicited money in her name from his friend Corinne Roosevelt Robinson, Mrs. Andrew Carnegie, John D. Rockefeller Jr., and others. Rockefeller declined to help, but Mrs. Carnegie was responsible for a $500 donation to Lindsay's widow, and Mrs. Robinson also responded favorably, as did the Players Club and the Authors Club. Masters was eventually able to gather about $900 for the widow. He also assisted Elizabeth Lindsay with financial and legal advice and helped her interpret the guidelines of beneficent organizations that might be of use to her.[5]

With Elizabeth Lindsay's financial needs assuaged, Masters turned next to the biography. He had first met Lindsay on a trip to Springfield about 1914 and had later seen much of him at the office of *Poetry* and at the Chicago home of Harriet Moody, William Vaughn Moody's widow. The two also got together in New York before and after Masters moved there in 1923. Masters's first and last impressions of Lindsay were that he was so "gullible" that he needed someone to look after him. Masters was struck with Lindsay's "apostolic manner" (he "looked like a pastor") and by his abstention from alcohol and sex, two traits that the libertine Masters found amusing. (He once told Mencken that Lindsay wore "a chastity belt with spikes.") Masters eventually decided that Lindsay was "America's greatest lyric poet" ("because his only rival, Poe, had less poetical ideas and a more limited gamut"), but for several years preceding Lindsay's death, Masters had not seen Lindsay at all. In fact, Masters's last significant relation with him occurred in 1926, when Masters nominated him for membership in New York's Players Club (the vote carried). A little later Masters had quietly interceded on Lindsay's behalf to urge George Brett at Macmillan to "do everything" he could for him "in a money way"—in other words, to publish Lindsay and provide him with generous contracts. He knew that Lindsay would need such help. "Lindsay can't think any better than a child," Masters explained to Harriet Monroe.[6]

Surprisingly, Masters would write his life of Lindsay without examining all available research material. Monroe offered Masters the use of her correspondence with Lindsay, but he refused it. He also declined to read Lindsay's correspondence with Sara Teasdale, a St. Louis poet whom Lindsay once wished to marry. Masters also ignored other documents he could have seen, focusing instead on Lindsay's diaries and information from Elizabeth Lindsay, as well as limited information from third parties, such as the college that Lindsay had attended in Hiram, Ohio. As Masters later explained to Corinne Roosevelt Robinson, he had to be highly selective to impose order on Lindsay's often orderless environment: "Lindsay wrote tons of letters. . . . His letters would make volumes; and it was rare that he wrote a good letter. He amplified, diffused, expanded, stretched, and recapitulated his ideas. And this is a way of saying that his letters cannot be greatly used for biographical purposes."[7]

Because Masters had spoken and dealt with Lindsay and had seen how his mind worked, it is probably best that Masters ignored Lindsay's more diffuse documents, many of which are incomprehensible, and trusted instead to experience and his own subjective understandings. Masters told Powys about ten days after Lindsay's death: "I can't quit thinking of Vachel Lindsay's sudden death. It quite shocked me. Strange, too, I had been thinking of him for a month forebodingly. My rugged body and lawyer-like exterior, not to say my merchant look, hide all kinds of antennae and nerves which pick messages out of the air." One of the messages he picked out of the air was translated to Ellen Masters only two weeks after Lindsay's death: "I have a hunch somehow that Lindsay suicided."[8]

Elizabeth Lindsay respected Masters's discernment and may have recognized in him a grief over Lindsay's passing that paralleled her own. She knew of her husband's respect for Masters, that he had named "the Truth Tower" in *The Golden Book of Springfield* after Masters, and that Masters had encouraged Lindsay in his writings and been his friend in social situations, such as that involving the membership in the Players Club. (Lindsay needed such friends: "I am delighted you stand by me, dear boy," he wrote Masters.) She knew, too, that Lindsay and Masters had a fierce, proprietary devotion to their respective Illinois towns, as Lindsay had written Masters in 1927 when Masters felt threatened by Sandburg's new book on Lincoln: "Springfield is still *mine*. . . . Be sure I am like you. I am not going to be robbed of Central Illinois by anyone. . . . I am profoundly moved by your own loyalty to this whole Central Illinois land." Elizabeth Lindsay wrote Masters that her husband "was always in agreement" with him, especially about matters of poetry and Illinois's and America's indifferent relations with their poets.[9]

She had not, however, decided how much of Lindsay's life should be told. Masters soon confirmed the fact that Lindsay had taken his life (based, he said, on the discrepancy in reports concerning Lindsay's final hours); he now offered to omit these details and to ignore the letter in which Elizabeth Lindsay affirmed them: "I won't put it in the book, of course. It is not necessary. And I'll return to you the letter in which you disclose the details." Elizabeth Lindsay had finally approved the essential information and provided all the facts, indicating that Lindsay's death had come by "drinking a teaglass full of Lysol at about one o'clock in the morning." What she wanted above all was for Masters to make it absolutely clear that Lindsay had lived as long as he could, that his debts, disappointments, uncertainties about himself, and the economic realities of the Great Depression had made life unbearable: "His life on any terms . . . had become utterly unendurable and an unthinkable ordeal to him." Masters well understood such feelings, having experienced some of them himself, and proceeded to write a biography that was sensitive to Lindsay's various moods and to several of his own.[10]

It took a considerable amount of courage for Elizabeth Lindsay to work as she did with Masters. Admitting that Lindsay had killed himself could have endangered the $4,000–$5,000 insurance payment she had received. Retelling Lindsay's story was also an emotionally wrenching experience for her, especially since she was on her own with two small children and was changing jobs to maintain her self-sufficiency. Her comments to Masters after the biography was drafted show something of the pressures on her: "I shall never work with anyone again as I did with you—in the first place, because you are special; in the second place, because it is too utterly excruciating to be compelled to live over and over again a cumulative tragedy which it is right and necessary for me to forget."[11]

With the research preliminaries out of the way, Masters searched for a proper location to write his book and finally decided to rent a small place in rural Colebrook, Connecticut. Ellen and Hilary joined him there in May in "a tumbled down house" on a parcel of land large enough for an ample garden. Masters's letter to Elizabeth Lindsay after settling in summarizes both his literary and family interests: "We are about established here. Ellen came Monday night. The house is in fair order. We are cooking in a funny old kitchen on a fine old wood stove and sleeping mightily. Hilary is playing all day long in the garden newly plowed, digging, and drinking quantities of milk. The summer looks propitious; and I am having the greatest delight getting the material analyzed for composition."[12]

After Hilary had caught a morning's worth of toads and crickets and put them in glass jars for observation, and after the garden had ceased to amuse him, he might go in and see "Pop." Masters would be typing at the kitchen table on a small portable typewriter, or writing in longhand, generating pages of text in his "neat, nearly indecipherable script" (as Hilary later described it). In the evening Masters would rest from his labors on the front porch, sitting on the steps or in one of the rockers and smoking his pipe. He would occasionally relight his pipe and look out across the grass and watch his corn grow in the twilight.[13]

They remained in Colebrook for two months, until late July, Masters working on the biography of Lindsay for several hours each day before playing with Hilary in the afternoons and evenings. Nonetheless, the long summer days were not long enough for all of Masters's garden to reach maturity before Ellen and Hilary left, this time for a trip to the West. Masters explained to Elizabeth Lindsay: "My little boy is so beautiful and wonderful. . . . He talks much, with a large vocabulary, and is so strong and lusty. Ellen is taking him in about two weeks to Kansas City to start for the Yellowstone."[14]

Ellen's father, Tom Coyne, wanted to revisit the scenes of his young manhood in the West while stationed with the U.S. Army's cavalry in the 1880s. He planned to take his wife, Molly, as well as Ellen and Hilary, and they would all visit a variety of places of historical or scenic interest. It was to be an educational trip for Hilary. Masters told friends that he was happy about the "wonderful motor trip" Hilary would make to Yellowstone Park and other points, but the early morning parting in Colebrook left Masters desolate: "They left in [a friend's] car at about 3:30 in the morning, while it was yet dark. I stood at the dining room window and watched the car as it went down through the yard to the highway—and then suddenly gone. I crept upstairs and tried to sleep. Then I had days of terrible loneliness—terrible." His problem was that everything reminded him of his boy, as he related to Elizabeth Lindsay:

> Everything here speaks of Hilary, who is the most beautiful and wisest and gifted child of my production—that I know about at least. He wore a path across the lawn to play with a little boy here. He scrawled his name on the door and the mantle. His harmonica and ship were on the mantle yesterday afternoon, coming suddenly into my observation. I took a walk to the brook last night at dusk where he used to throw stones in the water. I never in my life was lonesomer than I was yesterday toward nightfall.

It was a relief in some ways to return to New York.[15]

Things were not much easier for Ellen. Traveling (or doing anything else) with Tom Coyne was usually an adventure in itself. He was not only a bad driver in the usual sense of that term but an exceptionally unpredictable one who might (his wife once surmised) grab his Colt .44 army revolver and shoot the car. In the summer of 1932 his previous experience behind the wheel consisted of a driving lesson or two in the four-door Buick in which they were now traveling west. (Molly did not drive, and Ellen had not yet learned.) Tom Coyne wanted to sleep under the stars on this trip, but his wife refused, and so they settled for a series of musty cabins that grew more primitive as they approached their destinations, the prairie near the Seventh Cavalry's debacle at Custer's Last Stand and some mountains around Yellowstone. As things turned out, Tom Coyne had only one minor accident with the car ("I was steering it correctly but it turned right into the Goddamn bridge"). He flirted with disaster at every turn, however, one of which yielded a near head-on collision that left them dangling on the edge of a cliff. Hilary could still remember the scene vividly over forty years later:

> The sudden maneuver has put us on the shoulder of the mountain highway. The wheels scramble and spin on the crumbling earth. There is no fence, no tree or rock to spoil the magnificent panorama or to hamper the drop down into a gorge several thousand feet below.
>
> "Look at that lovely view," my grandmother observes as the car rocks and moves crablike on the edge of the canyon. "Look down there," she tells my mother, who does not look but falls back into the seat beside me to press her face into the em-

> broidery of a souvenir pillow. It says GREETINGS FROM CHEYENNE, WYOMING.
>
> "Go. Get up," my grandfather commands the Buick. "Get on there. Hi-yah!" Slowly, one by one, the rear tires find solid purchase and the heavy car gradually pulls itself back onto the highway pavement.

A day or two later Tom Coyne led a good-natured Yellowstone Park bear into the family's sleeping quarters. "By God," he said then (or a little before or afterward, or perhaps all three times), "By God, Hilary, sometimes I wish I had been with the Seventh Cavalry in '76." Ellen waited until she was in the privacy of her own bedroom in Kansas City to have a nervous breakdown.[16]

She had tried to strike out on her own by pursuing graduate studies in English but still had one course and a thesis to write. She had not done what her father wanted her to do regarding her education, nor had she done what her husband wanted. She had cut short her summer with Masters to go on the trip with Tom Coyne, and now she was back in Kansas City in the rooms in which she had been raised as a girl. And what should she do about Hilary? He could not be with his father on a full-time basis, but she did not wish to stay in Kansas City until Hilary was of age. Where was there a place for her? Disconsolate, she finally took a secretarial course and learned to type in preparation for the time she might complete her master's thesis. Hilary would later remember that she spent much of that fall in bed.[17]

Meanwhile, Masters was experiencing his own set of problems and creating some as well. Elizabeth Lindsay had decided she did not want the biography dedicated to her, nor did she want Masters to use all the information she had provided. Then, too, Masters sometimes provided her with information she would sooner not have learned. After a discussion of Lindsay's sexuality, for example, Masters one day informed her that her late husband had "needed a lusty hired girl now and then to make him healthy and sane on the subject." (Masters was no doubt thinking of his mother's hired girls, all but one of whom had been unusually "sane" on this subject.) Exactly when Lindsay would have availed himself of such a servant is not clear: he had remained a virgin by choice through age forty-six, when he married.[18]

Sexual blandness notwithstanding, much of Lindsay's life lent itself to an interesting story. His idealism, his several rambles on foot through various sections of the United States, and his devotion to writing made him a colorful character. He had met and addressed thousands of people in hundreds of lectures. (He must certainly be one of the few American poets to have sold poems for two cents apiece after midnight in New York City.) Masters caught the unusualness of Lindsay's life, and by judicious use of Lindsay's diaries, he completed a well-constructed and easy-to-read text with the title of *Vachel Lindsay: A Poet in America.*[19]

Finding a publisher was another story. The Macmillan Company's George

Brett had encouraged Masters to do the Lindsay biography but offered only a $250 advance and a 10 percent royalty, figures that Masters considered so paltry that he told his old friend to "go to hell." Indeed, the money was paltry in contrast to the advances Masters had received from Macmillan for books such as *Toward the Gulf* ($2,500) and *Mitch Miller* ($4,000). Alfred A. Knopf was next to reject the book (in late 1932), followed by Houghton Mifflin, Appleton-Century, Sheldon Dick, and perhaps others. All of them wanted a manuscript with more mercantile appeal than one focused on a prematurely dead poet. Masters would finally despair of placing his manuscript anywhere and told Elizabeth Lindsay he would "eliminate" himself as Lindsay's biographer: "It may be that someone else can write a biography which will find a publisher; but as for me, I have exhausted the publishing market." Through 1933 and 1934 the manuscript of *Lindsay* would join several other manuscripts of Masters that were completed but unpublished.[20]

He now had an unhealthy backlog of such manuscripts (some of which he kept in a warehouse) and was growing frustrated with the times. The manuscript of his autobiography and his epic poem "Atlantis" both remained without publishers, as did his novel *The Tide of Time. Gettysburg, Manila, Ácoma* was available only in a limited edition, as was *Godbey* (an attempt to reissue the latter through Appleton-Century failed in mid-1932). He was still circulating two of his plays ("The House in the Wood" and "Wood Alcohol"), but there was no interest in these. Plans for foreign translations were all tentative. The Great Depression was making itself felt everywhere.[21]

Equally disturbing, Masters knew that if he experienced a crisis and needed money, there was no one to whom he could turn. His parents' estates had yielded next to nothing, his cranky but financially able brother Tom was dead, and his uncle Will was as bad off as Masters. A Tennessee cousin named Robert Masters had written recently to beg clothing, so that avenue was also shut off. Moreover, Masters's children from his first marriage had all drifted out of his life: Madeline to marry, without her father's consent or consultation; Hardin to try a career in business; and Marcia to go to college and marry (she subsequently divorced, remarried the same man three weeks later, and then divorced him again). Masters's children from his first family all had their own concerns. In addition, Masters had fallen out with George Stokes following one too many fried meals and tractor anecdotes. Many of Masters's literary friends were also broke or hard-pressed by the depression. It would have been a good time, in other words, for Masters to have asked his wealthy sister for a loan, but Madeline underwent an operation for a heart disorder in September 1932 and suddenly died, although not before financial mismanagement and the Great Depression largely destroyed her fortune. Masters was left with his thoughts, expressed here to Uncle Will: "Just look at this panorama and try to think what it means. It can't be done. . . . Life is so vast, so deep, so cruel, so mysterious that it shuts our mouths. We cannot say anything worthwhile; and for all these reasons the old are silent—they have no words for all that they know."[22]

It was the collective effect of these events that early in 1933 caused Masters to make a claim for money that should have been made years earlier. In 1921, before he had decided he was philosophically opposed to anthologies, *Poetry*'s Harriet Monroe had approached Masters for permission to reprint several of his poems in an enlargement of a poetry anthology that Monroe and her friend Alice Corbin Henderson had compiled for the Macmillan Company. Masters had acquiesced, letting his old friends use his poems for the asking and making but one stipulation: "You have my permission to reprint in *The New Poetry* (revised edition) such poems as you may choose from my various books; the list to be submitted to me for approval." Monroe had not submitted a list for Masters's approval, however, but had published twenty-one poems anyway, and as she and Henderson collected royalties from the book, Masters observed that his works were being published without remuneration to himself ("their heirs and assigns profit forever off my work"). Now—a dozen years later—he and his lawyer at the Author's League, William Osborne, claimed Masters was the victim of breach of contract and that he deserved royalties. He said he would settle for $1,000.[23]

Neither Macmillan nor Monroe was happy about the claim. Monroe felt that Masters should have requested payment earlier, or perhaps Macmillan should have seen to this, for Masters had notified George Brett of his agreement with Monroe and had made it clear that approval must precede publication. To avoid litigation, Macmillan gave in, and Masters received $500 (minus his lawyer's 10 percent). It was about the same amount he would have received for the use of his poems in 1921. Macmillan, in turn, received the right to continue using the poems in future editions of the Monroe-Henderson anthology. Surprisingly, Masters and Monroe remained on speaking terms after this. Her letters to him remained friendly and businesslike; Masters, in turn, allowed some of his letters to be used in Monroe's autobiography.[24]

The $500 from the Monroe-Macmillan feud was one of the few financial bright spots for Masters in 1933, for although he brought out two new books, neither performed well in the marketplace. *The Serpent in the Wilderness* was published in May 1933 but in only 400 copies (with 365 for sale). All 400 volumes were numbered and signed. The first 84 were bound with a page of Masters's handwritten manuscript and retailed for $12.50; another 281 copies retailed at $8.50. The book's publisher, Sheldon Dick, indicated that *The Serpent in the Wilderness* was his "first book," and although the volume was nicely printed and bound, minor glitches troubled the work. One of the first 84 copies had a manuscript page from *The Fate of the Jury* mistakenly bound into it. The publisher's promotional announcement of the book contained a printed sample of Masters's text, but that sample seemed to have been picked at random. It began with a sentence fragment in which Masters was discussing "poisonous sewage" and ended with a sentence fragment concerning "interminable wrangles about property." Overall, the promotional copy seemed a blend of autobiography (Masters's) and bad judgment (the publisher's).[25]

Nor did the book enjoy a favorable reception in its finished form. The six long poems in *The Serpent in the Wilderness* constituted a miscellany of Masters's thinking from various years and moods. One of the poems ("Beethoven's Ninth Symphony and the King Cobra") would attract favorable attention, but the others were an undistinguished mélange, rambling verse essays on the nature of primeval mud mixed with anti-Americanisms and "the meretricious morals of the Bible and Jesus"; unrestricted praise for the Greek way of life highlighted American shortcomings. Sales of the ninety-one-page book were minimal. A month after its promotion and publication, it was selling about one copy per week. A review in the *New York Times Book Review* generated a "dozen sales," but several months after its publication, there was still "no profit" on *The Serpent in the Wilderness.* Nor could the book be saved by a lower-priced trade edition. Although Masters and Sheldon Dick had agreed that a trade edition would follow the limited edition in about eighteen months, Dick's prospectus had accidentally reported that there would be "no trade edition," so that avenue was out. In the end *The Serpent in the Wilderness* failed to sell "to the extent of the total printing."[26]

Nor would Masters's second book of 1933 do well. *The Tale of Chicago* was a historical account of a city Masters knew well, and its release in 1933—the year of the Chicago World's Fair—must have seemed a good idea, especially since the book would have both trade and deluxe editions. Masters received an advance of at least $1,000 but marred his story by hasty research (relying on memory in many cases), parenthetical remarks against twentieth-century life, and editorials against the city in favor of the country: "There are two strains of blood in America, one that stayed close to the soil and developed character and originality, the other that struggled for riches in the cities and became parasitical. . . . The megalopolis at bottom was avarice and hate."[27]

Unhappy with sales, Masters quibbled with the publisher, Putnam's, over the printing costs charged to him, the amount of ad space, the price of the book (too high at $3.75), the amount of his royalties (too low), the reporting time for royalties (too slow), and the firm's bookkeeping ("dubious"). Later, when the book sold only seventy-six copies in the entire United States during a six-month period, Masters enlisted the aid of the Author's League and prompted that body to begin an investigation. His book was a financial failure, and somebody (not he) was to blame. He told Putnam's that "twenty million" people would have bought the book if it had been handled properly. (Of course, if it had been "handled properly" through more ads, even more of Masters's Chicago creditors would have written Putnam's seeking payment for Masters's old debts, as some of these eventually did.)[28]

In the end Putnam's was left with 1,700 copies of *Chicago* and offered to let Masters buy them at 50 percent of the manufacturing cost; he countered by suggesting that the company sell *Chicago* at its minimal (or "remainder") price and give him 50 percent of the proceeds. This would be an act of "compensatory decency," he said, one that would make up for the company's mishandling of the book's sales. Putnam's seems not to have considered this proposal, but the cumulative effect of Masters's various comments and a demand for a large advance on a new manuscript settled the corporate mind about other matters: Putnam's decided it did not want his new manuscript (*The Tide of Time*) and wished him good luck in placing it elsewhere; Putnam's never published anything else by Masters.[29]

Masters's work had more urgency than usual in 1933, not only because the previous year had been a terrible one financially, but also because he was toying with the idea of buying one of the inexpensive farmhouses around Hillsdale, New York, where he and his family spent the summer. He told Ellen he was "more vital" in the country; she seems to have been neutral to the idea but was willing to explore it when she arrived in her father's Buick with Hilary and her mother in June. Ellen had learned how to drive during the previous year (Tom Coyne's driving had frightened her into it), and she and Masters now went about Columbia County in the Buick to investigate places to purchase. They at last settled on a small and somewhat run-down house that had some land with it and a hand pump on a well. A broken-down sofa on the front porch went with the house. Masters intended to offer $1,350 for the property but was never able to mend his financial affairs enough to do so. Ellen was relieved, for she felt her husband was essentially a "city person" anyway.[30]

In September 1933, after Ellen and Hilary returned to Kansas City, Masters began work on a project that looked for a time as if it might yield a third anthology, one to sit alongside *Spoon River* and *The New Spoon River.* The idea was the invention of Raymond Moley, who had served in President Franklin Roosevelt's "Brain Trust" as an adviser and speechwriter before resigning to take charge of a new weekly called *Today.* Moley had approached Masters with the idea, urging him to consider "a new *Spoon River,* embodying a revisiting of the old scene." Masters liked the concept but suggested he expand it from a village view to a review of the entire United States. He summed up his plans as follows: "I have thought often of taking stock of the whole country, the past and the present, epitaphically. 'American Anthology' might be the title. . . . How I'd love to put Andrew Jackson into 14 lines, and his Rachel, and Webster . . . , Lee, Poe—and maybe Mencken of today—anybody and everybody as my fancy led me." He thought he might write three hundred epitaphs or so, much as he had done with the poems of the two *Spoon Rivers,* drafting several a week and submitting them for immediate publication. Moley liked the idea, and Masters sat down to work.[31]

He was teased from the start, however, with the fact that his files were "full of American stuff," not the least of which was the dormant manuscript of America's past, "Atlantis." At some point Masters moved the name "American Anthology" onto the manuscript of "Atlantis," and at about the same time he began to be suspicious of Moley—although suspicion should have run in the opposite direction, for Masters was now contemplating the sale of old material as new. It was the same thing he had done years before when he packaged old poems as new ones in the wake of *Spoon River*'s success, and it was entirely in character that he do so again. "What do you know of Raymond Moley?" Masters asked his friend H. L. Mencken in October. "He isn't altogether a straight shooter who knows his stuff," he warned Ellen a little later.[32]

For reasons that are not clear, Masters failed when he tried to draft a new anthology with short pieces about historical personages. Perhaps he never tried too hard; perhaps he did not try at all. More likely he tried to substitute the already composed pieces and found them inappropriate. His letter of November 12, 1933, to Moley reviews the matter: "I tried to cast my material into the [epitaph] form which I partly outlined to you; and I have to confess that the result was not happy. On October 27, I abandoned it, and took another way. Hence it is that I cannot give you the 'American Anthology.'" Nor did he have other epitaphs to substitute for the planned work: "What I am writing in its stead would not be suitable for a weekly journal, I fear. The cantos are too long, too long for a single issue; and if they were cut in two, they would be spoiled as poetry." He suggested instead a miscellany of pieces, but none with the brevity, pungency, or ironies of *Spoon River Anthology:* "I should feel that with poems on [poet] Philip Frenau, Washington, Van Buren, George Rogers Clark, etc., that a gallery would be hung with portraits which Americans might delight to stroll through to their own good and to the inspiration of the American cultus." In other words, he proposed a collection no different from something his nineteenth-century forebears would have assembled, one that would be laudatory, uncontroversial, and forgettable.[33]

Moley's reaction to this was predictable. An "idea" man, he saw his plans for "a new *Spoon River*" turn into some conventional verses on American heroes. He accepted (for fifty dollars apiece) poems on Andrew Jackson, Stonewall Jackson, and Martin Van Buren but just as often rejected Masters's poems, articles, and stories. Masters's third "anthology" had dried up at its source.[34]

Masters and his family thus continued to feel the pinch of tough economic times and to live apart through 1933, although earlier in the year he had advised Ellen that he wanted to be reunited with her and Hilary if he could handle it financially: "If I make the arrangements, I want you to bring Hilary. I want him with me, and, as you say, he can go to school here. Don't get fussed; don't worry yourself down. If I fell flat here, you could go back to Kansas City, couldn't you? In these days, all people are doing everything, and things that they never dreamed they'd have to do." As things turned out, his expectations did "fall flat." Ellen was ill in the fall of 1933 and remained in Kansas City, coming to the Hotel Chelsea in December. Hilary had to remain in Kansas City. Perhaps the Coynes were right: they were better able to care for Hilary in the Midwest than Masters was in New York. Or perhaps Masters was more like Vachel Lindsay than he knew. He too was "a poet in America" and, like Lindsay, often found himself trudging a lonely highway, encumbered by debt, family responsibilities, and a diminishing market for creative work.[35]

CHAPTER 17

Life at the Chelsea

Tell me how souls can be
Such flames of suffering and of ecstasy,
Then fare as the winds fare.

—Edgar Lee Masters, "The Hotel Chelsea"

During the mid-1930s Masters would realize a long-deferred dream of having two of his plays produced, but the limited proceeds were not nearly enough to allow him to reunite his family. Masters and Ellen had hoped to live together after Hilary came of school age (the plan was for him to remain in Kansas City while she and Masters lived in New York), but Hilary's childhood illnesses delayed this. This separation and other stresses finally sent Masters in search of other women, one of whom briefly threatened his marriage.

Like many other Americans in the 1930s, Masters was barely making ends meet. He could plan on small annual royalties from *Spoon River*, but these covered only about half the cost of his lodging, so he had to continue producing new works. Unfortunately, he had a backlog of books he had completed but not yet published, including "Atlantis," his autobiography *Across Spoon River*, *Vachel Lindsay*, and the novel *The Tide of Time*. These languished in trunks or made brief trips to agents, all of whom responded with the same sad tale: no one wanted these books, not with the Great Depression and all, not with the belt-tightening going on in American publishing, and not with Masters's track record since *Spoon River*. Masters's diaries for two years from the mid-1930s (1934 and 1936) are missing, but even without them, it is possible to piece together a fairly detailed picture of his life.[1]

At every point in his career when he felt particularly pressed for money, Masters would begin a serious attempt to generate revenue from drama. He had first done this during his turn-of-the-century Chicago years; although he often earned an adequate wage then, he was not setting much aside, so he began self-publishing plays with the hope of making enough money to retire from the law. He turned to drama again in 1916 after his post–*Spoon River* bout with pneumonia exhausted his bank account (he added a play called "The Epilogue" to the augmented edition of *Spoon River*). He tried his hand at drama again after depleting his funds at Spring Lake, Michigan, in 1917. He tried drama once more in 1920–21, as he ended his law career, providing *The Open Sea* with a dramatic introduction. He turned to drama again with "New Salem" in 1923 as his divorce paupered him and yet again in 1926 (with *Lee*) as he grew serious about Ellen. He prepared his dramatic poem *Jack Kelso* as he waited for Hilary to be born in 1928 and published *Godbey* in 1931 after the biography of Lincoln damaged his literary reputation. His three plays of *Gettysburg, Manila, Ácoma* might also be linked to economic concerns, for he published them during the first year of the Great Depression, so it was perfectly in keeping with a thirty-year pattern when Masters again turned to the stage as he felt the pinch of his worst economic times.[2]

During the 1920s the only dramatic effort from Masters that had reached the stage was a sixty-line prologue he drafted for a 1928 presentation of George Farquhar's eighteenth-century comedy *The Beaux' Stratagem* for New York's Hampden Theater. Details are sketchy as to how this responsibility came his way. The reviews concerning Masters's contribution were not unfriendly, but the occasion was not nearly important enough to ignite his tardy dramatic career.[3]

He nevertheless persisted, and by early 1934 the Samuel French company was showing an interest in publishing a collection tentatively called "Duologues of Fortune's Mood," a title that underscored the use of only two actors in each of the plays: *Henry VIII and Ann Boleyn, Andrew Jackson and Peggy Eaton, Aaron Burr and Madam Jumel,* and *Rabelais and the Queen of Whims.* These were published as *Dramatic Duologues: Four Short Plays in Verse* in the summer of 1934 in a paperback trade edition plus a deluxe edition of 120 copies. (The title was somewhat misleading, for one of the "plays in verse" was actually a mixture of prose and verse.) Of the four, only *Andrew Jackson* attracted attention. Perhaps Masters felt closer to Jackson than to the other people of whom he had written (his grandmother may have heard Jackson speak during her Tennessee girlhood), or perhaps Jackson's country ways and those of Masters were complementary. In any event, the University of Chicago's Frank O'Hara produced an edited version of *Jackson* for three nights in December 1934, but after a great deal of labor and many manuscripts to Samuel French, Masters's second play to be produced netted him royalties of only $36.67. He did not see the play performed and later told *Poetry*'s Amy Bonner that "the duologues published by Samuel French [had] never been produced at all."[4]

Masters's *Richmond: A Dramatic Poem,* set in the closing days of the Civil War, would also find an outlet with Samuel French in 1934. Masters grafted a plot involving adultery, murder, and early death onto a war setting, along with a heroine meant to symbolize the Old South. She was really just a mouthpiece for his own parochial views, however, and characterization lagged behind political points, as Masters admitted to Robinson Jeffers: "I have been striving for many years to get all the things set down that I have brooded on through the years. There are so many of them, and so many of them involve such creative concentration that amid this life of many distractions I shall do well to merely outline what was in my mind." *Richmond: A Dramatic Poem* sold for only 50¢ in paperback, but it seems never to have been produced, a fate shared by most of Masters's plays.[5]

Nor did Masters's nondramatic works yield the attention he wished. A group of vocational high school students at Cleveland's John Huntington Polytechnic Institute admired Masters's poem "The Seven Cities of America" (in *The Serpent in the Wilderness*) and asked permission to reprint it as a printing-class project. Masters acquiesced, stipulating that none of the new copies be sold (for copyright reasons). The students' original plan seems to have called for numerous copies, but by the time the 2,200-word poem was printed, *The Seven Cities of America* had shrunk to only eight copies. Masters put a smiling face on the matter to Gerald Sanders: "In 1934, some young fellows at John Huntington Polytechnic Institute brought out a fine edition of *The Seven Cities of America,* originally appearing in *The Serpent in the Wilderness.*" This private printing had no impact on Masters's career.[6]

Masters's other publication plans in 1934 involved a constantly shifting portfolio of different genres with far differing requirements. *Esquire* paid $150 for two pieces, and Ray Moley occasionally purchased articles and poems for *Today,* but much of Masters's work went begging in endless cycles of queries, submissions, and rejections. He wanted to write a biography of Thomas Jefferson, but no one was interested; perhaps publishers familiar with the Lincoln biography feared he would try to destroy yet another American icon. At various times college students and amateur actors read portions of *Spoon River* in public for an evening or two, but no one wanted Masters's unpublished works, and his trunks remained full.[7]

The movies were still a possibility, but one that faced a major problem: Masters told his agent that no scenario should be sent to Hollywood without his personal approval, which practically speaking meant that he would have the opportunity to ruin an otherwise sound script. His hardheadedness and complete absence of talent in this regard virtually ensured this outcome. If negotiations proceeded as far as specifics with the movie powers that be, Masters could still alienate potential producers with his own intractable personality. Being his agent was a hopeless case as far as the movies were concerned.[8]

In addition to confronting these ongoing frustrations, Masters found himself once more dunned for the $1,000 loan made a decade earlier by Horace Liveright. By 1934 Liveright's company had changed hands, and when the debt was transferred to the new company, Masters found himself again called on to pay. Because he thought the old company owed him nearly $900 for earnings on *Gettysburg, Manila, Ácoma,* he ignored the new owners' request to pay and also went a step further; he lied outright and said that no loan had ever been made: "The old corporation went into bankruptcy owing me about $900 on *Gettysburg, Manila, Ácoma,* which you didn't assume, I take it, while bringing forward what . . . is called a loan to me of $1,000, which neither the old corporation nor Liveright nor anyone for either of them ever made to me." The net effect of this move was to alienate a little further a major publisher and diminish by one the number of places that might handle his works.[9]

Despite troubled relations with publishers, Masters's relations with his family remained relatively good through early 1934. Hilary had begun kindergarten in Kansas City in January 1933 and was now in first grade, and this allowed Ellen and Masters to contemplate spending more time together. Ellen had come to New York in December 1933 and remained through the winter, helping Masters with his typing and enjoying the city before being called home in late April when Hilary was overtaken by several childhood illnesses ("chicken pox and a fast accumulation of child maladies of that sort"). The maladies advanced to an operation for the removal of Hilary's tonsils and adenoids, and the resulting medical bills prevented the Masters family from having its customary summer vacation in 1934.[10]

Masters had felt overwhelmed when Ellen left; his creative work suddenly seeming too much for him, as he explained to John Cowper Powys's friend Phyllis Playter: "Ellen went away yesterday leaving piled up emotions about a thousand things. These imaginative, dramatic towers grow bigger with every year, and loom above me until my shrunk self looks up in vain." He wrote a play about the Mormons ("Moroni") during the summer but felt a keen disappointment about not spending the summer with his family, as he expressed to Powys in August: "Ellen is still west. . . . She got dust in her eyes and has had an irritation which has caused her suffering. Her father is experiencing weakness of heart. . . . It has been a cruel deprivation to me not to have them with me. I feel like a criminal to be separated from Hilary; but I haven't been able to manage them being here."[11]

The effects of Hilary's illnesses, broken education plans, and a commuter marriage were too much for Ellen, and she experienced an undiagnosed illness in the fall of 1934. She would later remark on the stress she experienced during these times, and Masters told acquaintances that she was ill. Her debility probably resulted from the cumulative effects of family tensions and the Great Depression.[12]

This 1934 illness may have played a part in the information Masters chose to include in his autobiography. If stress was partially responsible for Ellen's illness, then it would have been reasonable for Masters to try to minimize this, which he could do by omitting parts of his autobiography that would upset her. Ellen had by now read a draft of the autobiography and commented on Masters's relations with his 1909–11 girlfriend Tennessee Mitchell. Masters's remarks to Ellen in December 1934 show that he was willing to let her decide what to publish—and whether to publish the autobiography at all: "It is all so shameful that it makes me hesitate about publishing the book; and if you don't want it published, it shall not be. . . . However, out of all this filth, folly, absurdity, madness, vulgarity, and wandering about, I think anyone will perceive in me a flame that didn't go out and was aspiring to something fine and beautiful. That's the way I look to myself." Ellen did not insist that the passages about Tennessee Mitchell be removed (Ellen had been only ten when Masters began that romance), but she was less comfortable about the descriptions of Lillian Wilson from 1919 to 1923, when she herself was on the periphery of his life. In the end, as Masters put the finishing touches on his life story, he decided to delete the final third of his autobiography, thus guaranteeing that "the feelings of many [were] saved." In his personal life, however, Masters continued to be reckless where the feelings of others were concerned, as a series of events beginning in late 1934 illustrates.[13]

A decade and a half earlier, in 1919, while Masters was in the process of leaving Helen Masters for Lillian, he had been interviewed by a young female reporter with whom he had been very candid. Masters had encouraged violation of the new Prohibition law by saying that poets would "make their own" illegal alcohol. He also encouraged violation of the marriage vows for those who were "mismated." This combination of subjects gave the interview its title: "Poetry, Prohibition and Polygamy (Luncheon Conversation between Edgar Lee Masters and Madame X)." Madame X chose not to be identified, but she was Constance Murray (Constance Greene following her marriage), who became a friend of both Masters and Ellen. Constance and Masters had remained friends, and as the Great Depression wore on, Masters corresponded with her, waggishly addressing her as "Daisy Fraser," the town prostitute in *Spoon River.* She in turn maintained an interest in him because he was a famous author and because she occasionally gave lectures entitled "Personal Recollections of Poets" and "Intimate Talk on Authors I Have Known." She was well-connected literarily, for she was the adopted daughter of Henry Mills Alden, the editor of *Harper's,* as well as the daughter of the poet Ada Alden, the sister of the poet Aline Kilmer, and the sister-in-law of the poet Joyce Kilmer. Her promotional brochure for speaking engagements emphasized her literary connections: "No one . . . knows more about the figures in American poetry than she does."[14]

Masters had barely renewed this relation, however, when he began another. Dorothy Worthington Butts Gardner Batcheller was a twice-divorced thirty-seven-year-old mother and part-time poet living at the Chelsea when she and Masters met late in 1934. Like Lillian, she was a "celebrity hunter" (a real "bug house for publicity," Masters said) and was visibly well off (she was prepping her son for Harvard). She pursued Masters and established a relation by asking him to autograph copies of his books and by offering to serve as his agent to market *The Nuptial Flight* to Hollywood. Round-faced, thick-lipped, and a trifle heavy, she attracted Masters chiefly by making herself readily available to him during the late winter and spring of 1935; his nickname for her was "Dodo." He left a written record of their activities as well as several poems concerning her and was confident enough of her by March 1935 to take her with him to meet America's foremost woman novelist of the 1930s, Pearl Buck: "Dinner with Pearl Buck & [Richard] Walsh. D. Along." Dodo might have enjoyed a more permanent place in Masters's record, but she moved to Vermont for the summer of 1935. So Dodo the poet was in his life and Constance the journalist on its flirtational margins as Masters prepared to receive Ellen and Hilary at the Hotel Chelsea in the summer of 1935.[15]

Masters's financial condition at this time was relatively good, but he remained busy. He was putting the finishing touches on a new book of miscellaneous poems, *Invisible Landscapes,* which Macmillan was going to publish. (Macmillan had not published anything by Masters in nearly a decade, perhaps because in 1926 he had threatened to paint a poor image of the company in his autobiography if it failed to accept the manuscript that became *The Fate of the Jury;* that ruse had failed, and the publisher and author now got together again.) In addition, Masters finally found a publisher for the *Lindsay* biography when Scribner's agreed to print 3,000 copies and provide a $500 advance. The two new books would be published a day or two apart in September 1935. Masters was also working on his autobiography, which Ellen was going to retype when she arrived. This would give him the opportunity to make good on his earlier promise to let her excise material she found objectionable.[16]

Hilary would remember this summer of 1935 as the only summer that the entire family spent at the Hotel Chelsea, the three of them crammed into one small suite consisting of two rooms and a bath. On most mornings seven-year-old Hilary would awaken on the apartment's pull-out couch to find his father already at work at the table by the bay window. The writer's thinning hair against the light produced a halo over his head:

> He would be freshly shaved and pink and smelling of witch hazel, and though the windows behind him would be open and the curtains billowed with a steady river breeze, it would already be quite warm; he would wear only the tops of old-fashioned BVDs and a pair of trousers. . . . I would lie there, breathing as quietly as possible, and watch him. Usually, when he paused to relight his pipe or take aim at the cuspidor, he would notice me. His smile was dimpled, like that of an elderly cherub, and the eyes would lighten.
>
> "Morning, Mr. It."[17]

While Ellen retyped the autobiography, Masters worked on his other manuscripts, and Hilary perused the pictures in his father's numerous books, investigated the Chelsea's stairwells, or roller skated across the hotel lobby, out to the sidewalks, and down Twenty-third Street to wherever he wished to go: the Bronx Zoo, Fifth Avenue, Broadway, or the Staten Island Ferry. On other days he rode the subway all day or visited the automat or restaurant off the hotel lobby. Meals were irregular at the Chelsea, unless there was a check in the mail for a poem or other writing. A check meant a meal at Cavanaugh's, Pappa's Restaurant, or Lüchow's. On some afternoons the Brown Knight might materialize, provided that he had finished his nap—sweating into his underwear in the too-warm living room as his parents did the real napping in the bedroom. They could be a family after all, even in New York City.[18]

But they could not do this indefinitely. It was now established that Hilary should be raised in a real house with a real yard rather than in the confines of a New York apartment where his juvenile high spirits would sooner or later collide with a novel, poem, or play. Nonetheless, during this summer they went to museums and to Coney Island, took trips to the country, and enjoyed themselves, the parents showing young Hilary the sights of New York City and vicinity until September, when they had to part again. Masters described this parting from Hilary and the resulting introspection to his father-in-law, Tom Coyne: "For days, I could not get at anything, or compose my mind. . . . He has grown into a big boy, but with the same amiable and reasonable mind that he had as a little boy. If I have ever seemed unfeeling, it was in order to control myself, and adjust myself to circumstances that I could not control. For all the time I had to concentrate my mind on this writing for the sake of a living and to finish up my career, whatever it is, or may chance to be."[19]

In 1935 that career would involve sales of poems to magazines and textbooks and early receipts from *Invisible Landscapes* and *Vachel Lindsay. Invisible Landscapes* had some sentimental poems that were attractive enough to win a Gold Emblem of Honor from the National Poetry Center of New York State, but the book sold fewer than 900 copies in 1935 and netted only $416; sales of *Lindsay* were brisker, with 1,300 selling between September and the first week in December. (The Lindsay biography brought Masters the Mark Twain Medal "for preeminence in literature," although Masters refused to travel to Missouri to receive it; he also refused to travel across town to the National Poetry Center's award ceremony for *Invisible Landscapes.*) It was at this time, too, that he explored the possibility of a trade edition of *Godbey,* but that came to nothing. Sometimes he felt that his new books were being compared unfairly to *Spoon River,* as he remarked to Arthur Ficke in the fall of 1935: "*Spoon River* has always been in my way; and yet I think every book I wrote since then had pieces in it as good or better than anything in *Spoon River.*" Yet it was *Spoon River* that kept him going: each new book was somewhere advertised as coming from "the author of *Spoon River,*" and *Spoon River* provided him with annual royalties and brought him more attention than did some of his new books.[20]

There were other tensions, too. He had found that being the father of a young child and living apart from his wife produced some bewildering strains, especially when he felt the years beginning to show, as he related to his friend Mary Bell Sloan in the fall of 1935: "My own case is so difficult: here I have the responsibilities of a man of twenty or so; I have the same feelings and energies (when I don't stay up too late) that I ever had; my head is full of plans and dreams for writing—and yet I have all the disturbances and complexities of life of a man of my age. This double existence in which I dart from twenty years of age to sixty-six [sixty-seven] bewilders me at times. And meantime my emotional life is equally perplexed." That emotional life would soon grow even more perplexing when he found himself strongly attracted to women other than his wife. As he summed up things to Powys at about this time, "Far from falling off, I was never more aware of woman's fascination."[21]

When Ellen and Hilary left New York for Kansas City, Masters immediately got in touch with Constance ("Madame X"), urging her, "Come here and take care of me" (his wife, he explained, was gone). It is not clear whether she accepted his offer, but the signed love poems he soon sent her suggest an intimacy: "you unveiled / Your flesh to me . . . my bride / In passion." A poem called "Your Hands" is also suggestive of a relationship:

> Along my loins, too, did the touches given
> Of your lambent fingers soothe
> The flesh, whose evocated truth
> Expresses dreams afar, of heaven.

Heaven remained elusive, however, and Masters was soon sending Constance poems about dead lovers, followed by a note that their relationship was simply a "friendship." He may have anticipated that Constance would not work out, for he was also receptive to another woman.[22]

Alice Elizabeth Davis was employed intermittently as a typist when her path crossed that of Masters in September 1935. She had moved to the Chelsea in June of that year and took up residence on the tenth floor (Masters lived on the second). They went on an outing to Palisades Park the day after they met and soon became good friends. Davis was thirty-four, young enough to inspire numerous poems (wherein she appeared as "Anita"). She had dark hair, a toothy grin, a boyish chest, and thin legs. She looked nothing like Masters's other important girlfriends except that her prominent nose and thinness suggested a slight resemblance to Tennessee Mitchell.[23]

Alice soon began typing for Masters, and although she also typed for others, she seems never to have had enough work to make a living. But she dressed stylishly, had a good sense of humor, and was fun to be with. She also had a history of allying herself with men who were married or otherwise emotionally unavailable and had a number of gentleman callers at the Chelsea. Originally from St. Louis, she spent her time in New York with women much like herself, her gentlemen callers, and Masters.[24]

She and Masters soon found that they had somewhat similar backgrounds, for Alice too had been born in Kansas and had been raised in part by a favorite grandmother. In addition, she also wrote verse. She promoted herself as a specialist in public relations (research, advertising, and copywriting) and was soon making minor editorial changes in Masters's manuscripts. (They would agree jointly later about the phraseology of poems concerning her.) He provided her life with a new sense of drama, for he was a famous man, and she gave him what he had always wanted, a girlfriend who was a whiz on the typewriter. It did not hurt that she could look attractive at important outings. (She was, unaccountably, an acquaintance of the ambassador from Latvia, and no less an authority than the *Washington Post* once indicated that the dress she had worn to an embassy function had made her a "stunning figure.") By Christmas 1935 she and Masters were well on their way to falling in love, as one of Masters's letters made clear:

> In all my life I never received such a letter as you wrote me then. I stood here in this room 214 and shed full flowing tears to think that another human being, a dear woman, would have such thoughtfulness for me. At the time you were troubled by money affairs, and yet you just showered me with gifts. I have received more costly remembrances in my time, but never any as precious as these were, considering the thought and sacrifices that you had to give them. . . . Gradually, like the oncoming of spring . . . , love entered my heart; and when . . . I came to you and told you that I loved you it was wholly and deeply true.[25]

This May-September relationship failed to raise any eyebrows at the Chelsea, which was accustomed to such things. Perhaps Alice was looking for a father figure for guidance; perhaps Masters was looking for a daughter to ease his old age; or perhaps the two had something common in their past, something out of their youths. Alice had lost her mother when she was just a few months old, and in this respect was somewhat similar to two other important girlfriends from Masters's mature years: Lillian, whose mother had died when she was a little girl, and Tennessee Mitchell, who lost her mother at a comparatively early age. (All three women had made their way in the world after battling adversity and had little memory of a mother's love, being like Masters in this regard.) So perhaps he had a ghost or two from the past pointing the way to his easy understanding of Alice Davis. In any event, the two now began a romantic relation.[26]

He became her "Dearest Edgar Lee Bunny Buster Punkin and Cookie," and she became his "Hen." He gave her copies of his books, and she arranged them on a shelf in her room, glancing at them from time to time to reassure herself of his presence. She began a journal to record their relations, which he encouraged her to do, and he went a step further and jotted down details of their intimacies in his diary ("X" and "O to" show up frequently, the former indicating sexual intercourse and the latter, fellatio). He might have been sidetracked from Alice by finding that Lillian was living nearby in late 1935, but she was now happily remarried, and Masters was more interested in Alice. The return of Dorothy "Dodo" Gardner in the fall of 1935 did not diminish that interest, although he did see Dodo several times in late 1935 and early 1936.[27]

Perhaps he needed a comforting companion such as Alice because his circle of acquaintances had recently been thinned by death. *Spoon River* illustrator and friend Oliver Herford had died, along with his wife; other friends and acquaintances also passed on, and Masters dutifully recorded each of their deaths in his diary. Such losses sometimes led him to seek more out of life or consolidate his position, as he had done in 1926 when he married soon after the deaths of both parents. In any event, the loss of former friends made existing ones more important. Perhaps that is why he took Alice to dinner so frequently and loaned her money, for he had adequate money in 1935. Various sources—book royalties, lectures, and magazine payments—earned him at least $2,700, and he made an additional $2,000 from the sale of a handwritten copy of *Spoon River Anthology*.[28]

By the spring of 1936 Alice was typing for Masters at $25 per week. When not working, they made trips to Chinatown, Washington, D.C., or other points. She introduced him to her friends at Sunday gatherings of a gourmet society of which she was secretary, and she met his literary friends. He told people she was his "secretary," a designation she was happy to have, although many people knew her simply as "Hen." (The nickname was a private joke, a reference to the similarities between the motions of a hen's head in pecking at grain and Alice's head in administering fellatio.) In the evenings in her room or his, he would read her the day's newly composed poem as she sewed, or they would plan the next evening's outing. She especially enjoyed a small German tavern in Hoboken. One night he told people that they had just been married, and in many ways they were, except that they lacked a license and lived at different addresses. "No law, no ceremony, no ritual can so firmly bind hearts," Masters wrote in a note. They both agreed that they were in love.[29]

As time went by he composed a number of sonnets and other poems to and about Alice, some of which had literary merit:

> There is but one [way] to make the swift sands gleam:
> Love me for life, and let me fill your cup
> With love, then let us drink it up,
> Our lips together at the brim.

But his poems to Hen were all doggerel at its worst: "I think I never shall have a yen / For any chicken but my Hen." She was, he told his friends, his "angel chicken," a term she took as a compliment. There is no record of her reaction to another poem, a love poem in which he looked at their future and correctly predicted its outcome:

> All this will be but currents of the air
> Veering and lost. Tell me how souls can be
> Such flames of suffering and of ecstasy,
> Then fare as the winds fare.

Alice Davis's presence by mid-1936 may have been a factor in preventing Ellen and Hilary from traveling east for the family's annual summer get-together; in any event, they remained in Kansas City.[30]

Nevertheless, there was a special reason for Ellen and Hilary to visit Masters in 1936, for his play about the Mormons was to be presented in mid-August. Masters had struck an agreement with actor-director Charles Coburn for the presentation of "Moroni" at the Mohawk Drama Festival at Union College in Schenectady. Coburn would pay no fee for the use of the play and would receive 5 percent of the net if "Moroni" were picked up by a New York theater or generated a movie contract within six weeks after it played. Some 1,200 people saw "Moroni" one night, and Masters appeared on stage to compliment Coburn and the actors, but no major backers appeared. In the end Masters had only the satisfaction of seeing his play produced. And of course it provided an interesting outing for Alice, who accompanied him to Union College, where she took pictures and collected press notices.[31]

Alice did not, however, accompany him to Illinois a few weeks later when Masters spoke at the Petersburg Centennial in what was to be a turning point in his slow process of mellowing. The town fathers had at least partially forgiven him for the things he had written of their relatives in *Spoon River* and had invited him to be one of the featured speakers at the village's one-hundredth anniversary. (By 1936 parts of Spoon River country had an "*Anthology* aristocracy," people who felt a sense of pride in having their forebears mentioned in Masters's famous book.) A timid speaker, Masters initially had not wanted to go, as he told Mencken: "I'm off to Petersburg, Illinois, tomorrow for the centennial there, and dread it like hell—but must go." He sometimes missed the little town, however, and the occasion would give him the chance to show Hilary the countryside of his boyhood, as he explained to Charles Coburn: "I want my little boy Hilary to be there to see this, so also that I can take him over the country, pointing out the places where I caught fish, camped out, shot squirrels, played terrible pranks, flew kites, and gathered blackberries with my dear old grandmother." The occasion also gave Masters's hometown a chance to see his new wife (she spoke on the third and final day of the celebration, the only woman thus honored).[32]

More important, the centennial gave Masters a chance to make his peace with the community. After he, Ellen, and Hilary were given VIP treatment, Masters made a particularly conciliatory speech:

> To be here among you during these centennial festivities has given me a happiness that I have no words for. I have said many times that no matter where life has taken me my heart has remained here. . . . There is no prettier town of its size in our country than Petersburg. And that isn't all. I have known of no town that has been founded and governed by a people more genial, more progressive, better bred, above all, more American. . . . Just multiply towns like Petersburg over America and this country will right itself. I am one of you. I am prouder that I am sprung from this land than of anything else in my life.

The little village would remember and reprint his words for years. Masters was so mellowed by the experience that he sent a letter to Alice saying that the "sweet village of kind people" had treated him extraordinarily well. The rest of his family would remember the day also, for Ellen, Hilary, and Masters would not again gather for any length of time for eight more years, not until after Hilary graduated from high school in 1944.[33]

Alice Davis was in part responsible for this. She allowed Masters to continue what was essentially a bachelor lifestyle, while Ellen and Hilary brought responsibilities. Ellen regarded Alice's sexual specialty of fellatio as a "therapeutic" exercise required by some men and administered by some women—but not herself; she thus removed the concept of romance from the practice and placed it in the category of medical procedure, thereby shielding herself and her feelings but possibly prolonging the time that her husband spent with Alice. Of course, Ellen would have found this approach much more difficult if Masters had followed up on his impulse to tell the world that he and Alice were lovers in his series of verses about her, "the Anita poems."[34]

Some of these alluded directly to "Anita" or Alice, some of them spoke of their romance without identifying tags, but all of them were casually frank. Masters's initial plan was to put them in a book to be called "Love's Philosophy" (named for Shelley's poem) to preserve Alice's image for future generations. She herself could admire her image as she typed the poems and typed herself into the margins of American literary history, for he had told her he would someday submit his manuscripts to the Library of Congress. ("If he is remembered at all," she wrote in her journal, "my name will be linked with his.") Masters eventually drafted at least twenty-nine Anita poems recorded across some fifty pages of Alice's journal—and then changed his mind about publishing them in a single volume in favor of marketing only a few. He and Alice would ultimately be together as lovers or friends through 1943, during which time his writing slowly became less caustic.[35]

The first sustained indication of a mellowing in his poetry had come in 1935 with several sentimental poems in *Invisible Landscapes,* among which were rhymed verses about the ruins of Concord Church, which he had once attended with his grandmother:

> And never a hill by midnights still
> Grew lonelier or more weird,
> When the door creaked on the broken sill,
> And the vacant windows peered;
> When the stars kept watch on the graves until
> The moon from the prairie neared.

The surrounding landscape had changed as well, as he explained in a poem named for the township of his grandparents' habitation, "Sandridge": "Those who survive for many years outlive / The landscape that they knew, which fades and flies. / Time makes a landscape ashes when it dies." These losses notwithstanding, Masters felt that the landscapes of the past might somehow manifest themselves in the present, as his title poem suggested:

> The invisible landscape brushes
> Your idle cheek as you speed;
> For here where sunlight hushes
> Is the place of a vanished breed,
> Who loved and suffered and fell
> As leaves, and entered the peace
> Of the land, and became the spell
> Of whispering wind in trees.

So perhaps the past was not lost as long as the poet's memory functioned, or readers of his verse remained. In any event, new poems he composed from this time on frequently focused on a mellow past.[36]

In August 1936 Masters continued with this gentler mode in several of the verses in *Poems of People.* He had since 1922 worked intermittently on this collection of miscellaneous poems, the title of which he had liked well enough to make application to register it with the Copyright Office in 1923. (He was probably happy with the title's emphasis on everyday people and the nuances of Whitman.) *Poems of People* has a unity that most of Masters's other miscellaneous volumes lack, in part because many of the subjects have been "caught in the tangle of life's circumstances" (as Masters phrased it) and in part because Masters's intrusive author's voice was partially held in check. When he did speak in personal tones, it was often through the hushed tones of such poems as "Peace in Loneliness":

> I seek retirement and to be alone,
> Where I, though lonelier grown,
> Find peace in loneliness.
>
> * * *
>
> Hence if you wonder how my days pass whom
> Our youth's days passed, the simple secret is:
> Sometimes I read Euripides,
> Sometimes I walk the room;
>
> Sometimes I munch a biscuit; or I stare
> The silence of my walls, or count the dead,
> While wooing sleep upon my bed,
> And wonder where they are.

Poems of People drew only average reviews, but readers liked it better than many of Masters's previous volumes, and it went into a second printing. He was happy with the book through the time of its publication and sent a copy to President Roosevelt in September.[37]

Unfortunately, in his second volume of 1936, *The Golden Fleece of California,* Masters returned to several of the themes and blunt statements of his earlier works. In fact, *The Golden Fleece* was an earlier work, having been hastily written over the last ten days of December 1930. Issued in a signed edition of 550 copies, this book tells a story of the California Gold Rush, following the lives of several Illinoisans who make their way west to what they suppose will be riches and adventure. One of those making the trip is an Illinois college student "immersed in Greek / There at McKendree College." Masters might have used Knox College as his point of departure, since he had attended that institution, or Illinois College in Jacksonville (which his father and brother had attended and which Squire Davis Masters had helped construct), but in this new story, Masters relied on two other family tales: Lucinda Masters's son Henry had died in the Platte River in Kansas as a young man, thus ending parental intentions to send him to McKendree, and a second relative had died among the icy floes of the Missouri River. Masters used these two family tragedies to bring his narrator into an on-the-trail romance that lasts across the Great Basin to California. When the narrator's sweetheart dies, he makes an opportunistic but unhappy marriage to a wealthy woman (the Widow Chase) modeled after Lillian. His companions also come to unhappy ends, the result of pursuing "the Golden Fleece," the materialistic impulse that Masters felt was ruining the country. Didacticism dominated much of *The Golden Fleece,* and some reviewers felt Masters's sociological and political points overshadowed his verse.[38]

He may have had some of the same misgivings, or felt the book was too short to publish commercially, for he had earlier offered its 11,000 words as a project to the printing class of a technical high school. When that fell through, the manuscript was accepted by the Countryman Press of Weston, Vermont. (There was always a small press willing to consider a book by the author of *Spoon River.*) Masters candidly explained to the press's owner why he was working with his company: "I keep producing faster than one publisher can take care of me." *The Golden Fleece* was later issued in a trade edition, but general readers liked the story no better than did those of the limited edition, and Masters's total receipts a year after the initial publication were less than $400.[39]

Considerably greater attention was caused by his autobiography, *Across Spoon River,* published by Farrar and Rinehart late in 1936. There is no documented discussion of the influence that Ellen exercised over its outcome as she retyped it, but her potential influence was considerable. She was, after all, the final arbiter as to whether the book would be published during Masters's lifetime, although Masters himself apparently made the final decision as to where to end the document, as he explained to his friend John Hall Wheelock: "It is about

200,000 words long. By cutting it off with the period which saw the publication of *Spoon River* . . . , it would be about 150,000 words long, or less. I am advised by friends to publish it this way: with this ending, leaving the rest of it for a later time, after my death perhaps. In that way the feelings of many are saved, I escape hacking, and the publisher is advantaged. This morning I set to work to perform this dichotomy."[40]

In the end Masters said he was "pleased" with the final version of the manuscript, and except for omitting certain items that his publisher felt might be libelous, *Across Spoon River* told the story that Masters and Ellen wanted told. By ending his story with events of 1917 (at a time when *Spoon River* was sweeping the nation), Masters could leave readers with a picture of himself at the top of his fame and avoid relating the disastrous effects of his divorce or facing unwanted questions regarding his second marriage. He also reminded readers one last time that they should think of poet John Keats when they thought of him, that at one point in his younger years he had appeared "exactly as Keats" and that an artist had captured this image. The chief shortcomings of his book were its fragmentary nature (which would trouble scholars for years) and its vagueness as to the identities of those being discussed: Clarence Darrow is "the famous criminal lawyer," Frank Walker (Helen Masters's second lawyer) is "Frank Winkler," and Lillian Pampell Wilson is "Pamela"; other people, notably girlfriends, are also disguised.[41]

The book's illustrations were also carefully screened: in one way or another, they all focused on the old days, when Masters was younger or when *Spoon River* was "in flood." The dust jacket showed the book's essentials—author, title, and publisher—and an artist's view of a bridge across Spoon River. More specifically, it showed a view of the covered bridge at Bernadotte, Illinois, as it had appeared between 1883 and February 1915. Masters had used the scene before, on the title page of the deluxe edition of *The New Spoon River,* but the rustic view was equally appropriate here.[42]

In the final analysis, *Across Spoon River* is useful not only in describing Masters's character but also in illustrating it. He fibbed to his readers about his date of birth on the first line of the book, saying he was born in 1869 instead of 1868. This opens up a host of other questions, all of them related to his credibility, and one wonders why he jeopardized it in such a prominent way. Ellen Masters explained a chief reason for the bogus birth date to Masters's cousin Edith in 1970: "About 1917 [1918], when he was a sought-after poet—especially sought after by women—*Who's Who* [*in America*] made the mistake of one year. By then, his secretary, I presume, took care of such things. You know how he wanted to stay young. So he went along with the mistake, except to those who knew better and the federal government for official papers."[43]

But that is not the full story. Numerous reference books have shown Masters's birth date in its inaccurate form, but it was also about 1917 when Masters filled out an information form for *The National Cyclopedia of American Biography* and showed his "exact date of birth" as "August 23, 1869." (The form was completed and signed by Masters himself, not a secretary, after the publication of *The Great Valley* in 1916 but before *Toward the Gulf* in 1918.) In other words, Masters took an active hand in the misrepresentation of his age, so why he did so needs to be explained.[44]

One reason, of course, was simply to seem more attractive to women. In addition, he wanted to be able to say, as he sometimes did, that "he published his first book of verse before he was thirty," but this statement was untrue. His first "book was printed, bound, and ready to publish in early 1898," according to his own words on the subject, but a delay ensued, and the book was "never published" in the formal sense of the word but only given to the author. (This is why Masters sometimes referred to his 1902 volume *Maximilian* as his "first published book," accomplished at about age thirty-four.) His 1898 book was reviewed in Chicago and Lewistown in late November 1898, three months after Masters's thirtieth birthday. Perhaps he felt that the only way he could achieve his goal of being noticed as a poet before he was thirty was to have been "born" later—in 1869.[45]

Hilary Masters reported that his father preferred the birth date of 1869 because the architect Frank Lloyd Wright and the writers Edwin Arlington Robinson and William Vaughn Moody were thought to have been born in that year. It pleased Masters to be placed among them. Like Masters, each was something of a pioneer in his artistic work, and although Masters was sometimes critical of the poetry of both Robinson and Moody, he was willing to borrow on their fame if it strengthened his own literary position.[46]

Finally, Masters himself may have begun the confusion about his birth date as early as December 1916 when he mailed Amy Lowell a six-page biographical sketch that showed 1869 as his birth date. Masters may not have written this sketch, however, for in a letter dated December 20, 1916, he says he "asked a man here [Chicago] to write something" about himself. So the misrepresentation of Masters's birth date may have had several sources.[47]

Not surprisingly, this kind of confusion sometimes led to problems. For one thing, there was the already-circulated birth date of 1868, which was known to a wide variety of people, including the compilers of certain popular vest-pocket calendars, which linked each day of the year with a famous item of Americana. In fact, Masters had used one of these vest-pocket organizers as his diary for the year 1930: April 18 showed that "Paul Revere started on midnight ride, 1775"; August 17 showed "Davy Crockett, Indian scout, born 1786"; and August 23 showed "Edgar Lee Masters, American poet, born 1868." How could he explain that?[48]

With this much potential for trouble emanating from the first line of *Across Spoon River,* it is not surprising that subsequent pages also offered problems. The children from Masters's first marriage were upset by his treatment of Helen Masters ("my autobiography made my daughters very indignant"), and his son

Hardin was so distressed that he could not sleep. Helen Masters was no doubt upset also.[49]

Reviewers and critics also found controversial sections. Even with the excision of Lillian's story and no mention of Florence Dugan, Leone, his second marriage, or the arrangement with Alice Davis, *Across Spoon River* emerged as a controversial book. Some reviewers described it as an excellent background book necessary for understanding *Spoon River* ("it is, after all, the autobiography of a man who wrote one of the decisive books of our time"). Others saw it as "a life of appalling conflict." Some wondered about the book's unfinished status and guessed that it would someday be completed: "Toward the end it comes to a hushed place, the only part of his life about which he does not tell everything, and we may suppose that 'Across Spoon River' will have a sequel some day."[50]

This cumulative evaluation of Masters began to paint a broader story: he was described as grim and troubled, as an imperfectly educated and sometimes baffled man who aspired to literary greatness and found fame and acceptance with *Spoon River Anthology.* He had spent the rest of his life writing without learning to write well, however, and this problem extended to his autobiography, which was poorly edited and ill proportioned. Some critics felt Masters spent too much time on love affairs (he would have listed more, he said, but felt it would be "wearisome"); others said he spent too much time on self-justification and too little on self-understanding. One reviewer (Robert Spiller) noticed some of the similarities between Masters and his father but failed to notice Hardin Masters's shaping influence on his son's morality, the backbone of much of his being—the same influence (it might be noted) that was largely responsible for Masters spending his evenings with Alice Davis instead of trying to reunite his family.[51]

Masters had expected that his biography would produce a lot of money, and there was talk of a movie, but nothing came of this, nor did the book sell particularly well. It had not earned its advance profits at the end of its first season (although it did sell well enough for its publisher to undertake another Masters book in the following year).[52]

In the end *Across Spoon River* generated little sympathy for Masters. Indeed, the public impression of Masters in 1936 was of a cynical, iconoclastic, and bitter man. The bitterness of *Across Spoon River* was such that some reviews of the book had shown photographs and drawings of a grim-faced Masters without an ounce of humor in his expression. (One drawing showed him standing on a pedestal with his arms folded and looking down his nose into a valley of ashes spawned by the gray, ugly flower of smokestack America, a familiar stance.) People seemed to forget that he occasionally served as a poetry judge or sold some mild and very average verses for average prices (fifteen dollars or so) and that at least a part of his time was unexcitingly peaceful.[53]

What fed the public's overall bad impression of Masters was his tendency to get the worst from any image-making process. Dorothy Dow reported that he once began a lecture to a woman's club with these words: "When I look out at your dull, empty, and unenlightened faces." (Alice Davis explained that Masters looked to Mencken for approval, so it should not be wondered that Masters sometimes resembled "The Great Iconoclast.") Many people thus came to regard Masters as hating humanity too much to be a part of it. He would leave behind numerous impressions of this: "I always refuse to be a guest of honor . . . , to sit at the speaker's table . . . , to be entertained . . . , [or] to attend poetry meetings," he told a correspondent with New York's National Poetry Center in mid-1936.[54]

Those who missed such remarks as these were likely to remember his blunt comments about other writers: many of the young poets were dismissed as "communist mathematicians"; T. S. Eliot was a "quack"; Louis Untermeyer was a cheap imitator who deserved the nickname "Nosey"; and anything by Carl Sandburg was "hogwash," even though the "eastern iota-subscripts" might like it. Masters nursed a special hatred for what might have been one of his readiest outlets, the magazines. He especially disliked those that "catered to the moron interested in prize fighters, movie queens, gunmen, sadists, buggerers, thieves, bull fighters, lion tamers, etc." Most poetry magazines were flawed as well. At the last, even Harriet Monroe had things "all mixed up" with "Yeats and insane furriers and handsome curly-haired fairies and aspiring friends." Surprisingly, literary agents did not get condemned, probably because they allowed Masters to avoid talking directly to "the swine who run the publishing business."[55]

Interestingly, Masters did not consider himself a bitter man: "To call me 'bitter' is to turn the good and the pure from me. And it is an awful lie. I have denounced things. Why don't they denounce the things that I denounce?" "They" (a large and growing group) simply did not understand him, eventually steered a wide path around him, and finally ignored him entirely. Predictably, there were always those who would publish or otherwise circulate Masters's harshest comments. When that happened, he would either glory in creating a new hornet's nest about himself or say simply that he had been misquoted and that he had not been so harsh and hasty as all that.[56]

He could have partially offset his printed and typed comments if he had been a more skilled public speaker, but as he admitted late in life, he was seized with a sense of timidity when asked to speak to large groups. He had undergone an exceptionally trying time and made a bad impression while campaigning for Bryan on the Petersburg square in 1896, and this outing as a speechmaker haunted him for years. As he summed up things in his autobiography, "It was as impossible for me to speak well as it was for me to waltz, or play the violin." This is why he found so many gatherings so tiresome: "Dining, shaking hands, standing up at places of audience, making speeches (for they want speeches always and everywhere) is the most wearisome thing in the world." Unfortunately, from age forty-six on, it was often hard for Masters to enter a public room without someone wanting to formalize the occasion, and so he was in a bad way indeed. The fame of *Spoon River* thus alienated its creator from his fellow humans and made him a victim of his own success. The pity is that Masters might genuinely have enjoyed certain outings, such as Knox College's celebration of its one-hundredth anniversary, but he saw that a trip to Galesburg would cost him money and would require a speech, and so he informed the college that he did not "'go in' for this kind of thing." (His trip to Petersburg for its centennial celebration might not have been made had it not offered him a chance to show his boyhood haunts to Hilary.)[57]

Alice Davis observed this behavior, saw him behave as a "spoiled child" (as she put it), but she knew how to handle him. Buttermilk would soothe his upset stomach, and a little later she would have him "purring with contentment." It was all a matter of showing him "friendliness." That was it, of course, and the fact that she was not in competition with him and gave him exactly what he wanted: companionship without commitment.[58]

CHAPTER 18

A Strip of Faded Carpet and an Old Clipping

It gets more and more down to a strip of faded carpet, and an old clipping.

—Edgar Lee Masters to Constance Greene, March 6, 1939

By 1937 Masters had come to be one of the most prolific writers in the country, a fact that was sometimes called to his attention by his acquaintances, who differed in the implications of this productivity. Dreiser described his output as "outstanding," and Mencken marveled at his "extraordinary fecundity," but Witter Bynner warned Masters to "forget the verbiaginous manners" and try to "recapture the *Spoon River* idiom." Masters himself was well aware of his remarkable output. "I turned out at last the most voluminous of American poets."[1]

His headquarters for this activity was his bachelor apartment at the Hotel Chelsea. Located on the second floor, in room 214, the apartment was a boar's nest of bookshelves and reading materials, old clothes, rocking chairs, frayed carpets, and tipsy lampshades, the whole overlooking a grimy courtyard and a struggling ailanthus tree. These were all he had of nature, except the sky, which was visible if he looked up from his plain writing desk at the bay window. Pictures of Goethe, Whitman, H. L. Mencken, and Thomas Jefferson hung crookedly on the walls; a squeaky phonograph stood beside them, along with a record of "Spoon River" and other tunes. The room was ugly, drab, and depressing, some said, but Masters was comfortable in these surroundings, all of it thoroughly fumigated with his Prince Albert pipe tobacco. Even when his rent was raised to $17.50 a week in mid-1937, he made no plans to seek a less expensive address, for this was home. It was "quiet as a village," he said.[2]

And he himself seemed of the village, according to a reporter who interviewed him at this time: "In appearance, dress, and manner, he looks . . . like an elderly small-town lawyer. . . . He is sturdy, round-faced and baldish, and gives at first an impression of unbending gruffness." Another reporter came away with a similar impression: "Since he dresses carelessly, wears heavy spectacles and a characteristic expression of thin-lipped disapproval, he looks not unlike some midwestern deacon described in *Spoon River Anthology.*" His favorite words, another visitor noted, were "pish," "pshaw," and "bah."[3]

One of those who visited him during these years was a girlfriend of two decades earlier, Dorothy Dow. She had since married and had no romantic interest in Masters, but she was interested in him as a writer and as a part of her own past. By this time, she observed, the first impression that Masters offered a visitor was not a favorable one: "His hat brim drooped, his dollar necktie was merely a string, and his suit needed pressing." Nevertheless, Dow noticed that in many ways, Masters was essentially the same as he had been in the 1920s: "He continued to feel fit and eager; he had the same chuckle, and if the pipe he smoked was not the same, it smelled like it. He was still dogged, slightly suspicious, essentially devoid of masculine charm; but somehow appealing. The tremendous ups and downs, the vituperation and misunderstanding, the adulation, or jealousy, which had attended the rise and fall of his fame, seemed to have mellowed, rather than hardened him. He had always been a rock." Perhaps he had remained a rock because he swam fairly often at the YMCA pool across the street or because his days on his grandparents' farm had toughened him, or maybe he was still a rock because he thought it might impress the next woman to follow Alice.[4]

Or maybe not. Dorothy Dow felt that Alice had Masters well in hand. Alice was "young enough to be his daughter," Dow noticed, and let it be known that she and "Buster" (her favorite nickname for him) "shared the apartment." (This may or may not have been true, for most of the time Alice maintained her address eight floors up in room 1010.) Dow observed that Alice not only typed, cleaned, and waited on Masters "in all possible ways" but also could do something many other people could not: she could always make him smile. After viewing Alice and Masters on several occasions, Dow concluded that he was in "an autumnal romance . . . , his last, and perhaps his most satisfactory."[5]

Masters's diaries tend to affirm the Septembral nature of the romance and his general satisfaction with it. Masters's diary for 1937, for example, shows that Alice made herself handy: "Took poem to D. to copy"; "D. comes to write letters and straighten out closet"; "D. comes down at 3. Wraps books, draws checks, putters around." It was true, too, that she served him in all possible ways, as she did on January 20: "D. comes to my room. Great X." And on January 11: "'OOX.'" In fact, a day without Alice was a day without sunshine: "Alone all day. Terrible bore."[6]

Alice in turn was accepted by prominent people in social situations in which she otherwise would not have figured. There is, for example, a picture of Alice Davis standing between Theodore Dreiser and Masters at a rural vacation spot. All three are smiling; she is smiling the most. The same observation might be made of the dinners she and Masters enjoyed with H. L. Mencken, then the nation's most important commentator on American letters. She also received an occasional night at the theater, an endless string of dinners and lunches, and once in a while an egg sandwich and chocolate drink made by Masters and brought to her room. So she got something out of the relationship too, including numerous sweet nothings addressed to her or her alias: "I love you, Anita," or "Love me and be my friend."[7]

Alice also joined a long line of women "educated" by Masters (some evenings he read Schopenhauer to her; sometimes he read his own things). Some of the writings came from an envelope labeled "Obscenia and Foolishness." Masters had already sent or read the contents of the envelope to Eunice Tietjens, Lillian Wilson, Constance Greene, and a bedful of other women, as well as male acquaintances, and now he shared this side of his personality with Alice. Some of the best pieces featured an imaginary battle of words between a fictitious busybody named "Dr. Elmer Chubb, DD, LLD, Ph.D.," and a rake named "Lute Puckett." Dr. Chubb was a smut hound based on the traveling evangelist Billy Sunday, the later William Jennings Bryan, a St. Louis moralist named Percival Chubb, and the allegorical character of Prudence. Lute Puckett was based on Masters himself, although named after a Lewistown acquaintance; "Pieces by Puckett" (filthy poems) formed the basis for some of the discussions.[8]

Other satiric creations that came to life under Masters's pen included "Harley Prowler," a detective, and "Lucius Atherton," late of the Spoon River cemetery but now resurrected as the inventor of "Fem Vigoro" (an elixir for women) and "Atherton's Burglar Proof Gland Protectors." Fem Vigoro was an open spoof of Lydia Pinkham's famous vegetable compound; the gland protectors seem to have been original with Masters. Both inventions were advertised on printed broadsides. The advertisement for the gland protectors featured fake testimonials from several of Masters's least favorite people, including the poet Dr. Henry Van Dyke. "I was recently attacked," he witnessed. "Save for Atherton's Burglar Proof Gland Protectors I would not be the man I am today." Atherton was also the proud author of a pamphlet entitled *The Story of the Good Little Girl and the Bad Little Girl,* a satire on village morality in which sin leads to the governor's mansion while virtue is punished. Meanwhile, Dr. Chubb printed a broadside entitled "Sinful Sensations," a copy of which Masters sent to Harriet Monroe, a spinster. "File with Masters," she wrote at the top of the sheet, consigning its interpretation to a future era.[9]

George Brett at Macmillan wanted to publish a volume of such satiric writings, but Masters felt that this would detract from his role as a serious poet and refused. At the same time, he himself frequently jeopardized this standing. One evening when he and Alice were on an outing, Masters introduced himself as "Lute Puckett" and produced a business card with Puckett's name on it. Masters and Alice also attended a reading of Masters's poetry at which he signed the guest book as "Lute Puckett" before being seated in the audience and learning that the guest of honor (Edgar Lee Masters) would be unable to attend. Alice felt that Masters's involvement with such personae was good in that it helped save him from complete embitterment, and she was no doubt correct.[10]

Unfortunately, Alice wanted more than juvenile humor, thin sandwiches, and the tender ministrations of a sixty-eight-year-old and not very well off poet. Masters's diary for July 1937 shows that he was only one of several men with whom she was keeping company: on July 3, for example, she went to dinner with the Chelsea artist Joe Chase, a Mr. Vorhees took her to dinner the next evening, Masters followed on the fifth, "Garth" took her to dinner on the sixth, and the writer Frank Condon did so on the seventh. A Mr. Mosher came looking for her while she was with Vorhees, and Masters took her to dinner on the eighth. With only a slight extension, she could have dined with a different man every night of the week.[11]

Nothing in Masters's past (not even Lillian) prepared him for a level of social activity this great, especially when it was carried on right under his nose. His diaries reflect his uncertainty. He frequently noted the hours of the day when he would call Alice's room and find her out or the line busy or when he would meet her at the elevator in the company of another man. In fact, much of Masters's diary for 1937 deals less with his literary activities than with Alice's comings and goings. He monitored the places she went, her companions, what time she returned, what entertainments she followed, and so on. He could derive a part of this information from her telephone ("not back at 15 of 1 A.M.; phone doesn't answer"). The remainder he drew from questionings. She did not seem to mind the questions and volunteered much information, which only piqued his interest.[12]

In August Masters and Alice took a trip that would constitute his vacation for the year, a two-week ramble through New Hampshire to Weston, Vermont, where he met with publisher Vrest Orton. Orton had published Masters's 1936 book *The Golden Fleece of California* and, living in a town of three hundred, was glad to welcome one of his most significant visitors. Masters composed several *Spoon River*–like verses he called "Vignettes from Vermont" and observed his sixty-ninth birthday on the road in Manchester, as he recorded in his diary: "Birthday presents. . . . Birthday dinner. Fail with D. at night. Gas and heartburn" (August 23). He was beginning to feel the years even if he had let guests believe he was only sixty-eight.[13]

Unaware of Masters's Vermont trip, Ellen had returned to New York to continue her education, preparing for and passing an examination for her master's degree. She still had one more course to take and a thesis to finish, but an important exam was now behind her, and she went to the Hotel Chelsea with Hilary to surprise her husband with the news. Masters was supposed to be in his room at his desk, puffing on his pipe and working on a book. He was supposed to be genuinely amazed that she would soon receive her degree, and then he was supposed to break into a smile and say, "My God, kid, you've done it": "He was supposed to say [that] and cackle like some old country character who's been outfoxed and then [they] would all go downstairs and outside and around the corner to Pappa's Restaurant for a big meal." Instead he was gone somewhere with a woman. Ellen threw herself onto her husband's bed and sobbed for the rest of the afternoon. Hilary made her some tea and examined his father's books.[14]

"I don't know where my husband is," Ellen confided to Mencken. "I should like to know." She decided to stay at his apartment and discover what was going on—but Masters found she was there and on his return checked into a different hotel. (He had recently told Mencken that it was "impossible" to live with her.) Then a friend of Masters told him that Hilary had said that Ellen might stay all winter. (Infantile paralysis was raging that summer in Kansas City, and this may have contributed to Ellen's decision to linger at the Chelsea.) In any event, Masters now found himself in a stressful situation with Ellen, as his September 4 diary entry indicates: "She's in Chelsea and going to stay."[15]

Details on what happened next are skimpy, but Masters made no great effort to reestablish relations with Ellen. Nor did Hilary's letters seem to have much effect: "So sorry to have not seen you. Because I came here to see you. Wish you were here to see me. But I know you are busy. Momie will write you soon." A little later Ellen and Hilary were back in Kansas City and weighing Christmas 1937 as the best time to see Masters. Hilary's letter explains the matter from a boy's point of view:

> My Dear Pa:
>
> This thing of just settin and lookin at your picture on the mantle there ain't much to. When pictures can't talk to a feller there ain't no use.
>
> You was mighty close to me once but I guess you thought I was just a little shrimp that wasn't worth coming to see. Well I ain't forgot that but if you come to see me at Xmas time I'll see about maken up.
>
> Yours
>
> Hil[16]

Masters was not in the mood for reconciliations in 1937, and even if he had been, the books he published in that year could not have provided the financial impetus. Each of these—a biography of poet Walt Whitman, the novel *The Tide of Time,* and the epic of "Atlantis"—all had significant potential, and yet for one reason or another, all missed their mark. Masters had long been compared to Whitman (Powys had described Masters as "the natural child of Walt Whitman"). When John Hall Wheelock at Scribner's suggested the biography, Masters jumped at the opportunity. "No one would ever need to write about Whitman again," he said. "There might be egoists along the way who would think they could do a better [job]. Outside of that, my book would close the case." Masters had admired Whitman for years (he had first read the other author at eighteen and had made his first pilgrimage to Whitman's house in the 1920s).

When Wheelock offered a $1,000 advance and a 15 percent royalty, Masters was ready to begin.[17]

He had done preliminary work on the book the previous year, pausing to examine an esoteric question regarding a postmortem analysis of Whitman. "The Good Gray Poet" had been a phrenology buff, and Masters did his best to discover the whereabouts of Whitman's brain, its weight, and so on. Because Masters wanted to confer with the doctor who had treated Whitman in his final illness, and because Alice had not seen Whitman's house, they traveled to New Jersey and to Whitman's home in Camden. The caretakers of the house greeted them with a brandy cordial, which put Alice to sleep, so while Masters did research, Alice took a nap in the bedroom where Whitman died. She awoke in time to take a picture of Masters standing on the doorstep of the Whitman house, the same image that was later used on the biography's dust jacket, along with a previously unpublished picture of Whitman. Alice was also involved in the research for the book and its final shape, as Masters remarked to John Hall Wheelock. "She did research for me on the Whitman book, and then edited and typed my script."[18]

Masters's *Whitman* was published in 3,000 copies in March 1937 but relied heavily on other biographies, and Masters's insights were often buried under extensive quotations of earlier interpreters. When Masters spoke in his own voice, he often used tones that offered insight into his own values as much as into Whitman's. Masters again took up the cudgel against Republicans, and he made sure that readers knew Whitman was for free trade (not a Republican tariff) and state sovereignty (not a strong central government). At the same time, Masters seemed too eager to show that Whitman, like himself, preferred isolation to working with "the literary gang." Negative comments about American churches and the poets Robinson and Frost also muddied the waters. There were, however, several insightful passages regarding literary influences. Masters felt he divined the influence of Spinoza in Whitman's understanding of nature and remarked that Robert Ingersoll had been the only contemporary of Whitman to rely on "prose poems." Nevertheless, much of Masters's book was characterized by an abundance of facts and a minimum of artistry; in the end, "the natural child of Walt Whitman" failed to catch the essence of his literary godfather. The most visibly new items in the book were the previously unpublished photograph of Whitman and Alice Davis's picture of Masters. At the end of six months, *Whitman* had sold 1,500 copies, but it had generated only $830 in royalties after eighteen months. In other words, it had not earned its $1,000 advance. Masters noted that "Whitman didn't sell" but blamed the reading public as "tricky and unpredictable."[19]

Masters would also publish his long-deferred novel *The Tide of Time* in 1937. It had been refused by several publishers, including Dodd, Mead and Company, Harper and Brothers, and Simon and Schuster, so that Masters was understandably delighted when Farrar and Rinehart at last agreed to publish the book and provide an advance of $1,250. Unfortunately, the manuscript had grown by 30,000 words since Masters had composed it in the Missouri Ozarks in the summer of 1931. The book's editors now felt that it was too lengthy; it ran from the War of 1812 through World War I and beyond. The editors also complained about the book's contradictory sections and its poor punctuation. Masters responded in predictable ways: "I can punctuate according to my own meaning," he said, "whether according to rules or not." As to the contradictions, Masters replied that no one would care if the dates in the manuscript "did not square exactly with other dates." He later attempted to placate the editors but waited until the galleys to do so, again generating author expenses that would eat into his profits. The book was published in September but had only sluggish sales through the fall of 1937.[20]

The Tide of Time is Masters's last and longest novel, his final sustained effort to approach his family from an artistic standpoint and deal with both its satisfying and troublesome parts. The book focuses on the character of Leonard Westerfield Atterberry, who comes to adulthood during the American Civil War and practices law in his native Ferrisburg, a blend of Masters's two hometowns. The novel is not a sequel to the better-known trilogy on Skeeters Kirby or any of Masters's other novels but forms an amalgam of Masters's life and that of his father (whose victory in the Ferris case in Lewistown was a turning point in his career, hence the fictive town of "Ferrisburg"). The novel may have been Masters's means of speculating on the turns his life might have taken had he remained in the village. Or perhaps Masters felt compelled to write this history and that of his father to see whether a satisfying life might be fashioned Frankenstein-like from several of the parts thereof. The answer is both yes and no.

Leonard Westerfield is more southern than northern (he goes by both his given names), attends an academy near his hometown (as Hardin did), and graduates from college (as Masters had wished to do). He is helped in all he does by the love and good reputations of his parents, Captain Squire Atterberry and his wife, Dorcas, based on Masters's esteemed grandparents. (In this way Masters at last became what he always was in spirit, his grandmother's son.) Leonard Westerfield is elected to a judgeship and to Congress (two honors that eluded Hardin) and is also elected mayor of his village (as Hardin was). Leonard Westerfield is displeased with the nation's foreign and domestic policies but spends much of his time on village-level disputes, for example, fencing with a prohibitionist editor named "William T. Davis," a pale version of Hardin and Edgar Lee's newspaper nemesis William T. Davidson of Lewistown. When Leonard Westerfield dies at an advanced age, he is remembered as one who met the exigencies of his times. He had done his "duty," Masters says, quoting Goethe, by meeting "the claims of the day."[21]

Leonard Westerfield has not really accomplished much, however, nor has his personal life been all it might have been. Following a youthful affair with a free-thinking Chicago woman named Sophronia (based in part on the autobiography's "Honoria"), Leonard Westerfield marries his village sweetheart, Adele. Adele is a blend of Masters's two most significant Lewistown loves, Margaret George and Winnogene Eichelberger (she has some of the former's mental gifts and the latter's attractiveness). There is no great passion in this union, however, and no great meeting of minds. The marriage is notable for its blandness, much like the rest of Leonard Westerfield's life. There are allusions to the poets Byron, Shelley, and Keats but no efforts to live as a poet and no vicarious excitements.[22]

In fact, most of the domestic "excitement" was carefully excised from this story of Masters and his father. Hardin's quarrelsome wife, Emma, had no place in the book, and Masters's wife Helen had only the most fleeting of influences: Leonard Westerfield takes Adele as his bride in part because the parents and the community expect the marriage to take place. (It was under such circumstances that Masters had taken his marital misstep with Helen.) Leonard Westerfield occasionally "imagine[s] that men had wives who were creatures of constant delight and inspiration," but he attracts no such woman for himself and finally gives up looking: "Somehow it crept into his mind that there was no wonder woman, but only women of character and good sense, at their best, like Adele and his mother Dorcas." It is interesting that the marriage of Leonard Westerfield and Adele takes place in haste after he comes to believe that he might be losing her, a mirror of the circumstances under which Masters entered into his second marriage.[23]

Perhaps it is the era that shapes and defeats these characters. The historical focus of *The Tide of Time* is mostly on the half-century following the Civil War, years in which, Masters felt, the nation had lost its way by abandoning Jeffersonian democracy: "Of one thing Leonard Westerfield was very certain, and that was that the country was changed, and was changing, and that his life could not escape the multitudinous effects of the war. He mourned unspeakably the passing of the old era; he would have given anything in the world if his years had been destined to have been passed in an extension of the age in which the Captain had spent the greater part of his life." One of these changes results in the death of Leonard Westerfield's son during the Spanish-American War, the nationalistic endeavor that Masters regarded as the advent of American imperialism and the last nail in the coffin of Jeffersonian democracy.[24]

Ultimately, *The Tide of Time* shows that Masters was fascinated with the pivotal events of these years but was too much the realist to imbue the life of Leonard Westerfield with more than a modicum of success and about the same helping of happiness. At the same time, he was too much the romantic to sunder completely his boyhood ties with the past: "The time never came when the sounding board of his own imagination ceased to call out of the past a world that existed in a kind of youthfulness which did not die." Faced with two extremes—the sense that "something was profoundly wrong with life" and the memory of an earlier time when things were better—Masters's village characters live in a landscape where the individual achieves small victories but is constantly hindered by great naturalistic forces, "the tide of time." This same tide had affected numerous lives in *Spoon River Anthology,* where it reflected one of many points of view. In *The Tide of Time* this is the dominant point of view and resonates through the book as an apology for lives half lived.[25]

Masters's long-delayed epic of America, "Atlantis," would also prove disappointing. Published by Appleton-Century in the fall of 1937 and now titled *The New World,* Masters's poetic "summation of the USA," as he called it, was nominated by its publisher for the Pulitzer Prize. Masters went over the galleys carefully, making many changes—and creating a formidable bill for author's alterations. The reading and research for *The New World* had turned out to be far more extensive than for any of Masters's other books (he had rewritten it entirely in 1933), but he would not receive commensurate compensation. Many readers soon tired of this sprawling history liberally laced with opinions, and reviews were uniquely unkind: *Time* referred to it as "Disappointment No. 33" (it was actually Masters's thirty-fourth book since *Spoon River*), and *The Saturday Review of Literature* said *The New World* was "one of the most long-winded books of our day." The Pulitzer committee agreed. Masters was not surprised by that committee's decision: he had long ago decided that the "dishonest donkeys" in charge of Pulitzers were too provincial to treat him fairly. It was in this fashion, then, that Masters's self-styled "great work" was summarily dismissed by the critics.[26]

During 1937 Masters also circulated a piece that he later published as a pamphlet entitled *Hymn to the Unknown God.* A pantheistic verse essay in 154 lines, the work is complemented by a foreword, an addendum, a prayer, and a statement of intent by the publisher, the New Age Ministry of Religious Research, of Brown City, Michigan. Masters thought highly of the piece in mid-1937 (when it was published in the *University Review*) but a year or so later was commenting to friends, "It fails." Because the poem is similar to dozens of Masters's other works, the significance of *Hymn to the Unknown God* is as much bibliographic as critical: the pamphlet is a rare item of Mastersiana of interest primarily to collectors.[27]

In addition to writing or publishing these works, Masters continued to pursue outlets for his plays, short stories, and possible new poetry collections as well as a possible work about Petersburg. He also continued his feud with poetry anthologists and considered lawsuits against companies he felt had made inappropriate use of his work. Some of that work was simply politics expressed in verse, "America in 1937," for example:

> The banks, the bourses, and the Bible Belts
> Howled for the conquest of the Philippines;
> Then Wilson warred to free the world's desmesnes,
> Then once again the noisy Roosevelts.

Masters had learned from Shelley that the purpose of poetry is political and that poets are the "unacknowledged legislators of the world," but the country had heard enough of Masters's politicized grumblings by this time and ignored such writings.[28]

Much of the remainder of Masters's verse from 1937 was considerably pleasanter, tending toward a sentimental view of his youth. In the following the subject is again the Bible Belt, but here his subjects can do no harm, for these are the people of his grandparents' generation, the pioneers who helped settle Illinois:

> I never shall forget the eyes of old grandmothers
> Who looked at me so tenderly
> In their faded hats and cloaks;
> Or Greenberry Atterberry whose voice with feeling trembled
> When calling me a good lad
> Because he loved my folks.
> I still can hear their voices as they sang of love excelling,
> Of rocks and hills and valleys where milk and honey flowed;
> And how beyond the Jordan was a fair eternal dwelling
> Where the heart would find its happiness,
> And the soul an abode.
>
> * * *
>
> And now amid the hammer's blow, the squawking of the radio,
> The rattle of the trucks on the walls along the street,
> I hear their singing voices above the iron noises,
> I see the grove of oak trees, and endless fields of wheat.[29]

Perhaps it was writings about the elders of his youth that caused Masters to pause and evaluate his own prospective old age. His diary for 1937 suggests that he made $5,500 in that year, two-thirds of it from Farrar and Rinehart for *The Tide of Time* and *Across Spoon River,* although his federal income tax return shows only about $3,800. Since Masters lacked the capacity to save money (he was "a son of the Democratic Party," his son Hardin explained), and since most of Masters's books earned royalties for only about a year, it was clear that he would face genuine deprivation when he grew too old or ill to continue in his present mode. His response to this was to write letters to newspaper editors and members of Congress to propose "legislation to take care of America's creative men and women." What he urged was "pensions for America's children of the light, who through devotion to their art, or for other reasons, find themselves at last crippled in the means of life." It sounded wonderful (England had such a system, he said), but the idea failed to gain momentum. As Masters contemplated his seventieth year, then, he had no long-term means of providing for himself, Ellen, or Hilary.[30]

The impact of this loomed largest for Hilary, who may have noticed that it was not easy being the son of Edgar Lee Masters. Since his birth in 1928, Hilary had seldom seen his father except at Christmas and during summer get-togethers. What personal attention he received usually came through the mail. He received the usual childhood toys, holiday gifts, and playful messages ("Mr. Ittie, I love de") and plenty of long-distance hugs (or "duds") and kisses, shown on Masters's letters as *X*s and *O*s. Hilary was just as likely to get a dollar bill or a telegram as a stuffed animal, however, and he certainly got more airmail than most children (the next-day delivery allowed Masters to feel closer). When Hilary was still a little boy and Ellen was working on her master's at Columbia, he sometimes received updates on his mother's academic progress: "Your ma is studying at the university and becoming very smart"; in addition, Masters occasionally offered Hilary political advice (the Republicans were "bad people") or invited him east for a "beah" (beer).[31]

Despite Hilary's hopes to see his father for Christmas 1937, the Masterses remained apart for the holidays. At this time or a little before, Ellen realized that if she were to make anything of her life, she would have to go it alone. Her work in Kansas City with her parents had been minimal—lecturing on poetry now and then and making costumes for plays—but now she decided to finish her master's thesis and her one remaining course at Columbia. Masters knew little about her plans, as his diary for January 31, 1938, shows: "Ellen blows in at 3:30 unannounced. What a surprise!" They apparently stayed in separate rooms that night, for his diary shows Ellen "check[ed] out" on the next day and left no local address. They may have feuded about his 1937 vacation with Alice or possibly about the way he had obstructed her efforts to obtain a master's degree, which she would complete in 1938.[32]

It was at about this time, too, that Ellen offered Masters a divorce. She had finally been made to see that her husband's affair with Alice was the extension of a larger problem, namely, that she had a limited place in his life. He refused her offer, not only because he was afraid of losing contact with Hilary, who remained in Kansas City, but also because Masters simply did not have the energy or will to undergo a second divorce. There were also other reasons. Despite family tensions, Ellen occasionally saw her husband to talk over Hilary's wellbeing, and Masters had come to rely on her in the same way that he relied on Alice: the get-togethers gave him a chance to get off his chest whatever was bothering him, be it the poor respect accorded the artist in America, low-paying magazines, or the snobbish and malicious members of the eastern publishing establishment.[33]

Meanwhile, Ellen became a partner in a New York bookstore and slowly began to achieve a measure of economic freedom, independent of both her parents and her husband. But she paid a price. Her living quarters during the closing years of the depression consisted of tiny apartments, including one she had at a place called the Altora Club. At the time of her bookstore partnership, she slept on a bed in a back corner of the store. She did, however, have a vacation, of sorts. In the summer of 1938 she worked at an outdoor children's camp called Lutherland (in Pennsylvania's Pocono Hills) and was employed there several summers thereafter. Hilary spent the summers with her, getting free tuition at a boy's camp across the lake.[34]

Thus, as Ellen gradually battled her way to economic independence, Masters's financial condition worsened. The beginning of 1938 was complicated by a lover's spat with Alice Davis, and he refrained from seeing her for a time, in order (he wrote in his diary) to "give D [a] chance to get married—though no one will marry her." Masters and Alice slowly ended the physical part of their relation at this time, and one day he dreamed the relation was over. Alice herself had earlier confided to her journal that the relationship would "probably taper off into a nice friendship . . . robbed of all the throbs" they then felt, and that was to be the case.[35]

Masters would publish only one book in 1938, a biography entitled *Mark Twain: A Portrait.* Like his biographies on Vachel Lindsay and Walt Whitman, this book was assembled in short order, across a space of about seven weeks. His advance on the book was tied to the Whitman book's performance, and when that turned out to be disappointing, Masters received an advance of only $500. Like the biographies of Lindsay and Whitman, the Twain book was printed by Scribner's in 3,000 copies. The Twain biography would also be like the Whitman book in that Masters relied heavily on previous biographies.[36]

Masters's father had once given him a copy of *Tom Sawyer,* which Masters said he "read to tatters" at about the time he was getting to know a Lewistown youth named Hare Hummer, who was much like Twain's Huckleberry Finn. Twain and Masters also shared a dozen or more fundamental similarities: each had southern roots and a lawyer father who had made a bad marriage, each lost a brother to death and spent considerable portions of his boyhood at the farm of a relative, each worked as a printer and was filled with midwestern stories, and each had friends about whom he later wrote. Each left the village of his youth while never forgetting it and then married a genteel wife and traveled much. In addition, they were both indelibly associated with rivers—and neither could manage money.[37]

Despite these similarities, Masters's book was unflattering to its subject; the final 20 percent or so is simply ranting about Twain's political views. Twain's worst sin was that he had become "de-Southernized," giving up his rural, agrarian values and aligning himself with the industrialized and corrupt East. Masters explained to John Hall Wheelock: "I attacked Twain not for the thinness of his culture, but for the thinness of his character, for the desertion of the culture that he knew, for his apostasy politically, turning in favor of the robbers of his day when he should have stood by Jeffersonian Democracy." Thus, Twain had wasted his time satirizing such characters as the King and the Duke in *Huckleberry Finn* when he should have been lambasting the boodle politics of presidents such as Ulysses Grant. Twain also had a tin ear for dialect, Masters said, and turned himself into a literary machine who published poorly done books simply because he knew they would sell. Twain also had disastrous taste in women, his wife having "emasculated" him. "I have combed that clown to the best of my ability," Masters told Mencken, "and I suppose I will get hell for it."[38]

This time there was not a public outcry against Masters but something nearly as humiliating: *Mark Twain: A Portrait* was read in the light of earlier and better biographies and failed to attract attention. The book was published in February 1938 but had failed to earn its $500 advance a dozen years later. Scribner's turned down Masters's next manuscript and never published anything else by him.[39]

Masters was particularly hard pressed for money in the summer of 1938 and observed the completion of his seventieth year as a virtual cliché of the American poet: aged, alone, and nearly destitute, his health compromised by arthritis and neuritis. "Of all the human problems," he mused to Jack Powys, "I know of none tougher than the one that concerns itself with the use of life after a man's principal work is done." Masters sold a piece or two to major markets such as *Esquire* but spent much of his time struggling to raise money. He tried to undertake a lecture tour but had only one significant lecture; his agent reported that some places had never heard of him and that others refused to consider him. Masters also thought of writing a textbook, submitted a grant application or two, tried to sell his manuscripts, lobbied unsuccessfully for a twenty-fifth anniversary edition of *Spoon River,* and submitted plays to drama contests. In desperation he added his name to a chain letter and finally wrung $250 from the Carnegie Fund of the Authors Club of New York.[40]

"My anxiety about money is just crippling me," he told Hardin in November. Actually, his anxiety had been crippling for most of the year, which makes it even more remarkable that he now turned down honorary faculty status and an honorary degree from Knox College. (Masters's friend H. L. Mencken was also scornful of honorary activities and may have provided Masters with a model for refusing such things.) The honorary degree might have attracted attention to Masters's name or his books or resulted in a teaching stipend somewhere, but Masters was out of the mood for such things unless he was sure significant cash was attached. Money was a real problem, and he would hereafter depend more and more on friends and beneficent organizations.[41]

At some point those friends had grown younger. By the late 1930s Masters was meeting and corresponding with the Wisconsin writer August Derleth (who would dedicate a book to Masters) and the Kentucky writer Jesse Stuart, both of whom esteemed the rural lifestyles Masters held dear. Masters had also met the novelist Thomas Wolfe and talked him into moving into the Hotel Chelsea: "He used to come to this room of mine and set and talk volubly, spluttering and jammed with his own words. I saw Dreiser when he was about the same age, and [Wolfe] was not the steady, powerful mind that Dreiser was, not the thinker perhaps, but maybe the better artist." Wolfe was then working on the manuscript of *You Can't Go Home Again* (with a theme that Masters well understood); Wolfe's sudden death in September 1938 deprived Masters of a friend he would have valued.[42]

Masters now admitted to associates that he felt very much alone and had few means to take his mind off his loneliness. "Man's journey on this earth is hell," he told Powys: "When I think of all that I have been through, when I think that the storm still beats about me as hard as ever, I am sure of this. Then [comes] this awful loneliness that nothing ever eased and blotted except the wonder of sex!" But even this was denied him as his physical powers began to fail. He sentimentalized about the women in his life to Hardin: "I believe that I have spent thousands of dollars along the way, just to have a companion at dinner, this in Chicago and here, generally a woman." Now he opened his wallet again, to count the bills, making sure that he had enough to purchase Alice's companionship for another meal at the automat.[43]

During the holidays of 1938 Alice reprinted the *Spoon River* epitaph of "Edmund Pollard" on her Christmas cards. Pollard had urged readers of his epitaph to live life to the hilt: "You will die, no doubt, but die while living / In depths of azure, rapt and mated, / Kissing the queen-bee, Life!" Such ecstasies were hopelessly distant to Masters by this time, as he explained to Constance Greene, herself only a bittersweet memory: "There was a day . . . when any dull afternoon could be brightened by a loose woman and a drink. No more, no more. . . . Life grows more unexplainable all the time. It gets more and more down to a strip of faded carpet, and an old clipping, and a little brass icon." These were what he had as the winter of 1938–39 came on—the frayed carpets of the Hotel Chelsea, some yellowed clippings attesting that his was a famous name, and the cause of that fame, the "little brass icon," *Spoon River Anthology*.[44]

Not far away Ellen signed a contract to spend the spring semester of 1939 teaching ninth-grade English at the Lincoln School of Columbia Teachers College. The prestige of the position was considerably greater than the pay, but the job marked another milestone on her way to self-sufficiency and anticipated the time when her earnings would be greater than her husband's.[45]

CHAPTER 19

A Lonely Old Man in New York

Something in the Eternal Will
Makes the heart companionless,
Dooms the soul to take its way
Grieving for its loneliness.

—Edgar Lee Masters, "Fellow to the North Star"

The author of forty-eight books, Masters had now worked industriously on the major genres of creative writing (poetry, fiction, and drama), as well as with several types of factual writing (history, biography, and autobiography), but he had not exhausted his store of ideas and would publish five more volumes before his writing career came to a halt. His personal life was more problematic. He continued to see Ellen and Hilary from time to time but did nothing to effect a permanent reconciliation. He also continued to see Alice Davis, although without the old intimacies. Masters's relation with the rest of humanity was also tentative, as Arthur Davison Ficke noted in his unpublished manuscript "Notes on Edgar Lee Masters, 1938–39."[1]

Ficke found Masters so utterly consumed by personal disappointments that "he had not a spark of humor in his make-up. He was bitter, bitter, bitter. . . . All life had lost its savor for him, and he remained alive out of mere stubbornness." Masters had a special contempt for anyone who had adversely altered the period of his life that brought him the most attention—1914, when *Spoon River* came into being, through mid-1917, when America entered World War I. When he was thinking of these days, Ficke noted, Masters might end a period of silence with the observation that "[President] Wilson was just a horse's ass" or move from that pronouncement to assail one of the political systems he blamed for contemporary ills: "It was impossible to say which he despised most—German Nazi-ism, Russian Communism, English Imperialism, or American Capitalistic Democracy." As the Great Depression wore on and World War II threatened, Masters became more despondent. "I never knew anyone," wrote Ficke, "who gave up quite as completely as Masters did in 1938–39." Above all there was always an overriding sense that life had failed him: "Once, in the period around 1914, he had been the most discussed poet in America if not in the whole world; and now he was completely forgotten."[2]

That is why he became so difficult: "He felt that people had done very little for him, and he wasn't going to do very much for them. Any form of cooperation was anathema to him." He was, for example, utterly indifferent to the effect he created, dropping tobacco ashes and matchsticks wherever he was while ignoring niceties that might have created a good impression: "He was always neatly dressed," Ficke wrote, "yet his clothes somehow had the air of having just emerged from a night spent on a train. . . . He was very self-absorbed."[3]

He was also a virtual prisoner on the block where the Chelsea stood. As Masters grew older, he became afraid of the cars that sped by and insisted on taking Ficke's arm when they ventured into traffic; a product of the previous century, Masters was now afraid to cross the streets of the century in which he at last found himself. He longed for the places and states of mind that characterized the old days, including an idealized image of the American village, which he liked to think had existed during his grandparents' generation and which, paradoxically, he had done much to destroy through his bitter epitaphs in *Spoon River Anthology.* Perhaps the old bromide was true (he may have mused) that each man kills the thing he loves.[4]

As 1938 ended, however, he was faced with the more prosaic metaphor of keeping the wolf from the door. He apparently made only about $1,200 in 1938, enough to survive but with nothing extra to begin the new year. Alice was no help in this regard. She had so little money that she was sometimes unable to pay her hotel bill. Masters occasionally gave her simple foods (such as shredded wheat and grapefruit) or loaned her money. At one point she sold a well-written article about Masters to *Kansas* magazine, but it is doubtful that she received significant remuneration, nor is it likely that she made much from a similar article printed in the newsletter of the firm that owned the Chelsea.[5]

Nor could Ellen have been much help. She was now teaching, but her salary was minuscule, and any extra cash would have been consumed by Hilary's bout with erysipelas in Kansas City during that year. She had been forced to leave her teaching position for nearly a month and return to her parents' house to look after Hilary and was far too financially strapped to consider helping her husband.[6]

It was at this juncture that Masters's long hoped for government sinecure finally materialized. Since at least 1934 he had been trying to secure a position that would recognize his prior service to the Democratic Party while not demanding much work. When his old friend Carter Harrison was named to a high-ranking government office in Chicago, Harrison was able to use his influence with Secretary of the Interior Harold Ickes. After surprisingly little red tape, the honorary job of "government secretary" of the Virgin Islands was offered to Masters.

Tourism was then a chief staple of the islands' economy, and Masters's job would have been to function as a "greeter" in addition to looking after the well-being of the natives. His salary would have been $5,200 to $6,000, four to five times what he had made in 1938. He did not immediately accept the position, however. Instead, he began finding things wrong with it, commenting negatively on prospective expenses of moving and entertaining and on the lack of job security—not to mention the weather ("I have nerves," he explained to Harrison, "and I can't tell how constant warm weather will affect me"). In the end Masters remained in New York. Ellen's career was at last taking off, and she had refused to go with him (she was also concerned about Hilary's education). Nor could Alice go with him. "I couldn't take a sweetie for a housekeeper," he explained to Mencken, "on account of the dignified position that I would be in."[7]

Instead of undertaking a change in his affairs, then, Masters continued with business as usual through the winter of 1939: he sold articles to *Esquire,* published a nostalgic piece on Lincoln's village of New Salem, agreed to a CBS radio show on *Spoon River,* and sold an occasional poem. Masters was "scratching for money" in 1939, however, and had to beg loans from friends as well as sift through unpublished manuscripts in search of overlooked sources of cash. He also appealed to the Authors Club for more money, tried to sell his manuscripts, and drafted part of a play entitled "Spoon River." He had only limited success getting speaking engagements and again daydreamed about Hollywood, with no success whatsoever (one contact said *Spoon River* was "lacking in mush"). Alice also tried to interest Hollywood in *Spoon River,* but this, too, came to nothing.[8]

It was in the midst of these discouraging affairs that Masters became convinced that his work had been plagiarized by two of the most successful writers of the times, Thornton Wilder and Robert Sherwood. Wilder's 1938 stage play *Our Town* contained an oblique reference to *Spoon River Anthology,* and this convinced Masters that Wilder had stolen the idea of *Our Town* from his work. (The ensuing movie made him a little more certain.) When Masters read Wilder's other works, he found traces of *Domesday Book* in Wilder's 1927 novel *The Bridge of San Luis Rey.* Masters had barely gotten his temper under control over these presumed piracies when Robert Sherwood's 1939 play *Abe Lincoln in Illinois* appeared and convinced him that Sherwood had illegally used his play "New Salem." (The alleged theft had occurred, he said, while "New Salem" was circulating with one of the Barrymores.) Masters did nothing about the Lincoln "theft," but he had lawyer Sidney Fleisher investigate the possibility of "proceedings against Thornton Wilder and the movie company for appropriating . . . *Spoon River Anthology* for *Our Town.*" Fleisher did not have much to go on, for the worst that Wilder had done had been to include in *Our Town* a reference to Masters's poem "Lucinda Matlock": "It's like what one of those Middle West poets said. You've got to love life to have life, and you've got to have life to love life." After the potential lawsuit was abandoned for lack of evidence, Masters simply told his acquaintances over and over that Wilder and Sherwood had stolen from him: "I am robbed all the time. Thornton Wilder used *Domesday Book* for his *Bridge of San Luis Rey,* and my *Spoon River* for his play *Our Town.* Sherwood wrote his play *Lincoln* around one that I wrote, and even used an episode almost ad literam. The use of *Spoon River* for *Our Town* damaged me on a sale to Hollywood."[9]

Masters spent part of the spring of 1939 working on the galleys of his only volume for that year, *More People,* an underrated book of verse that added to his 1936 *Poems of People.* Published in August 1939, the book had several pieces of biographical interest, including some describing the failing powers of an aging man and the romantic desires of a young woman. The final poem, "Lands End," was drafted on Masters's seventieth birthday and reviewed the limited options of a man who has gone as far as he can:

> Year after year imagination gathered
> Into itself the roar of Time, the madness,
> The tumult of humanity, the world of grief.
> Now these must counterpoint this sea and listen,
> As to a shell, the burdens of stilled music,
> And match them with the dirges of the deep.
>
> Not wishing to return to a traveled country,
> Unable to go farther, this coast must be
> Paced back and forth, where there are muffled voices
> Of waves that beat upon the stones below;
> And sea winds whispering from the echoing grots,
> Saying "Endure," saying "Endure," "Endure."[10]

Masters's later years might have been easier if his three grown children could have helped, but while he had mellowed sufficiently to attempt reconciliations, none of his children was likely to be much use to him. Hardin had been "worth $200,000 in 1929," Masters said, but he had lost all his money in the depression and had next to nothing by 1939. Masters's elder daughter, Madeline, was much better off (Masters said she was "well-fixed") and by 1936 was willing to meet with her father, but he was not ready to accept her help. As he told John Cowper Powys, "I'd rather mount a cow and ride into the desert than to put myself in her hands." Both father and daughter were still on uneasy terms regarding her 1928 marriage (Masters had not approved of the marriage, which turned out to be successful and long-lasting). Masters was on better terms with his younger daughter, Marcia, who despite the family's tangled finances had managed to attend the University of Chicago for two years before dropping out to pursue a career in journalism, but Marcia had no more money than most other journalists working at the end of the Great Depression.[11]

Thus it was fortunate that Ellen began to achieve more economic security during 1939. She worked during the summer at her seasonal job in the children's camp in the Pocono Mountains (Hilary was again with her) and stopped on the way back to give Masters some good news: she had been hired by the Bentley School in New York. The latter was a well-regarded private institution, and if not the finest of its type, it was sufficiently respected for employment there to be a sign of success: "Ellen comes. Has got a job at Bentley School at $1,000 for 8 months." She found a room near her school and soon moved in, for there was no talk of a reconciliation with Masters. (She occasionally supplemented her salary with evening work as a hat-check girl.) Eleven-year-old Hilary was returned to Kansas City and his grandparents, producing the usual pangs of separation on Masters's behalf: "His face just tears the heart out of me," Masters wrote Powys. "I am such a poor father under the circumstances, and find it impossible to be with him."[12]

At the same time Masters did little to alleviate his loneliness. When the Poetry Society of America notified him in December 1939 that he might receive its annual award, he immediately found reasons to avoid the ceremony, as he explained to the society's president, A. M. Sullivan: "While pleased to accept the medal . . . , I could not bring myself to go to the meeting. It did not seem fitting. I would be obliged to stay there while speeches were being made, and poems read; and I could not very successfully avoid making some remarks myself. I just could not bring myself to go through this ordeal." Perhaps he did not go because he would be required to speak, or perhaps it was because he thought that this dinner (and others like it) might remind him of the time when he was "the most discussed poet in America," as Ficke described those days.[13]

To the extent that Masters did shun gatherings because they might remind him of his former prominence, his behavior followed inexorably from his situation and attitudes. Public gatherings such as that of the Poetry Society were not intended to highlight the discrepancies between Masters's past and present, but he saw that as the inevitable result and thus tended to stay home. His comments to Theodore Dreiser bear this out: "On Thursday, the Poetry Society had a dinner . . . , and Hen was wild to go, never having been to one. She raged because I wouldn't go. But I know the crowd, and the game, and can't stand it. After all, she didn't have a time that could be called 'hot.'" But he had, of course, having once been the "hottest" poet in America. Thus he could not go to the Poetry Society dinner, because it would have been too humbling. The medal he might have received went instead to his friend and fellow poet Padraic Colum—and Masters again seemed an antisocial grump for failing to attend.[14]

One of those who thought he was wrong to shun the Poetry Society gathering was Masters's friend Gerald Sanders. Masters had met the professor in 1925 while visiting the University of Arizona on his lecture tour through the West and had communicated again when Sanders was considering an anthology of contemporary poems. Sanders had since moved to Ypsilanti and Michigan State, where he began an ambitious bibliography of Masters's works, a project that would occupy him for seven years between 1935 and 1942. He was always candid with Masters, as he was on this occasion, telling Masters he was "crazy" for turning down the Poetry Society award. Masters brushed aside his comments, choosing to focus instead on the terribleness of the times. "Altogether a negligible year," he wrote in his diary for the last day of December. "Little money, anxiety, loneliness."[15]

His despair was reflected in a brief work from 1940, a pamphlet entitled *The Triumph of Earth;* a poem of some 250 lines, it portrayed life as a dank cistern in which humans and their good intentions are lost in impenetrable, existential gloom. Only a few optimistic words at the end saved the poem from complete despair. The title and contents played on Shelley's "Triumph of Life," one of Masters's favorite poems, but *The Triumph of Earth* seems never to have circulated beyond a few copies. Hand-corrected printing errors are shown on many (and perhaps all) copies and suggest that Masters never issued it in perfect form.[16]

He found a more congenial subject in an edited collection of Emerson's prose and poetry, *The Living Thoughts of Emerson,* published in March 1940. Theodore Dreiser used his influence to win Masters a contract for the book, along with an advance of $350, and Masters "enjoyed immensely" his work on the book, telling Mencken that Emerson "was a radical after [his] own heart. . . . Off and on to the end he combed America for lice and crabs and got them."[17]

The Emerson book is important in understanding Masters, for he used his introduction and selections to affirm one last time that many of his own values had evolved from Emerson. He began with his youth:

> I was ready for Emerson at about fifteen years of age, ready in the sense that I was fallow soil. I had no preconceptions, I had never joined a church or experienced conversion. . . . At the same time I felt the cramping influence of the village, I could see what the local preaching and proselyting were doing to the community: how they interfered with rational enjoyments, with mental advancement, with intelligent investigation and conviction. I bought Emerson's essays for a few cents from a Boston publisher and read every one of them.

Like Masters, Emerson had rejected organized religion in favor of a higher humanism—of the Greeks, Thomas Jefferson, and Goethe—and discovered that an individual's subjective truths can be as meaningful as those accepted by society at large.[18]

Such subjectivity came at a price, however, and during his middle and later years Masters experienced some of the same ups and downs that Emerson did. Neither sought popularity, yet each achieved a measure of fame by liberating his country from old norms and ways, Emerson through what Masters called his "declarations of intellectual independence for his countrymen" and Masters through the use of new forms and viewpoints in *Spoon River.* In the course of their activities, both men took their country to task in uncompromising ways, with the predictable result that each experienced periods of financial hardship. Each was essentially a truth-teller and skeptic, and each endured the loneliness that often comes with that calling.[19]

The loneliness in turn heightened their sensitivity toward friendships that would obviate such aloneness. Except for the differences in literary style, Emerson's comments on love and sex might also have been Masters's: "Ever the instinct of affection revives the hope of union with our mates. . . . Thus every man passes his life in the search after friendship." "The heart has its sabbaths and jubilees, in which the world appears as a hymeneal feast, and all natural sounds and the circle of the seasons are erotic odes and dances. Love is omnipresent in nature as motive and reward. Love is our highest word, and the synonym of God." Masters was more direct, saying that "sex . . . lifts human beings out of their soul loneliness" and that "earth love is only a symbol of its diviner being . . . , a forecast of a higher sphere." To the extent that both men saw humanity as a part of nature, the influence of Spinoza might be detected. In several ways, then, Masters's book of Emerson's writings serves as a gloss on Masters's own values, from his teenage years in Lewistown through the time of the book's compilation, when Masters was in his seventies and seeking an antidote to loneliness through Alice Davis.[20]

In the summer of 1940 Masters signed a contract to write a history of the Sangamon River for Farrar and Rinehart's Rivers of America series. His advance was small—$225—but it enabled him to return to Petersburg to research the book and to make what would be his last trip home. Except for his uncle Will, now in his eighties, little remained from the days of Masters's boyhood. Many of the roads had been fenced or had disappeared; also gone were small farms, woods, and individual landmarks such as trees, ponds, and buildings, including Concord Church, where his grandparents had worshiped, and his grandparents' house, which had burned. (The site itself was forever lost to Masters, for Squire Davis Masters had willed it to his son Will, who would bequeath it to his daughter, Edith.) On the Spoon River at Bernadotte, time and the river had leveled the old mill that Masters remembered from his youth; at New Salem the deserted village was now restored to its state during Lincoln's day and was connected to Petersburg by a "hard road." And Bowman's Lane—the dirt road north of Petersburg over which Masters had traveled in choking dust and hub-deep mud—Bowman's Lane was now a blacktop. Masters drove around his boyhood haunts until he was lost, a phenomenon he once likened to "looking back at paradise lost." He was accompanied by Hardin, who was with him for part of this trip, and Thomas Masters, a son of Masters's brother, Tom. One or another of them drove him to Rose Hill Cemetery in Petersburg, where Masters priced a lot not far from the grave of the founder of the Grand Army of the Republic, B. F. Stephenson. The seventy-five-dollar lot was apparently too expensive, for Masters also visited Oakland Cemetery and inspected a burial plot not far from his grandparents' graves. It was time to think of such things.[21]

After visits with a boyhood friend named Frank Blane and a member of the Rutledge family, Masters and Hardin headed to Chicago, where they visited Madeline and Marcia. "Sad parting," he wrote in his diary. He was feeling more tender toward his daughters as changing times deprived him of many other things that had once brought him pleasure.[22]

Back in New York Alice Davis's problems continued unabated. She had earlier antagonized the hotel's management regarding her room bill and had moved her things from apartment 1010 to Masters's apartment in room 214 in June 1940. (One day in late summer she answered the telephone in Masters's apartment and found herself talking to Ellen; Masters had not told Ellen he was going to Illinois.) Alice routinely secured and lost jobs and had no luck in finding permanent employment. She sometimes stayed with Masters during the last half of 1940, although she was not at his place every night. She continued her part-time typing in his room and worked for some of the best-known writers of the day (including John Dewey and poet George Sylvester Viereck, as well as the poet and dramatist Percy MacKaye and possibly Thomas Wolfe). She could never generate enough money to live on, however, and Masters's diary for 1940 shows that she often relied on him for a daily meal—and he in turn relied on her for company. By the end of the year her situation had improved enough for her to move her things out of Masters's room and into another room at the Chelsea.[23]

The changing nature of his relations with Alice also brought a change in her long-term responsibilities. Masters had once toyed with the idea of making Alice and Gerald Sanders coexecutors of his literary effects but discarded the idea when he saw that Alice's presence would create an unnecessary strain on Ellen. For some time thereafter, Sanders was Masters's only literary executor, in part because Sanders's bibliography would make him familiar with Masters's works and in part because Masters was unsure what his relations would be with Ellen at the time of his death.[24]

He was forced to think of such eventualities not only because of the 1940 trip home but also because many of his friends were growing old and infirm: the Chicago lawyer Abe Meyer had already died; his college chum E. P. Reese would die in 1940, as would B. M. Chiperfield, the Canton, Illinois, lawyer; Masters's school chum Frank Blane would die in 1941, and so too would the poet and lawyer Ernest McGaffey and the Streator, Illinois, farmer George Stokes. Old friends at the Chelsea also went to their rewards, as Masters's diary shows.[25]

Perhaps it was the mortality of old acquaintances that caused Masters once more to consider completing his life story, even if it meant letting someone else tell it. The person Masters had really wanted to write his biography had been William Marion Reedy, the editor of *Reedy's Mirror,* in which many of the Spoon River poems had been first published. After Reedy died in 1920, Masters seems to have considered John Cowper Powys, a novelist and lecturer. As early as 1919 Masters had asked Powys to write an "appraisal" of him and his books ("I have been extravagantly praised and personally attacked but never valued"); in fact,

Masters said that Powys understood him better than did Reedy: "I think you have done more for me in telling me what I am than anybody else. Reedy tells me pretty well when I succeed, but I think he is so near to me that he does not know what I am, as you do." As time went on, however, Masters had second thoughts about Powys, as he had explained to Lillian Wilson in 1923:

> Before I went to New York in March, I was getting ready biographical material for Jack Powys, dictating some of it, and writing some of it. . . . I think my case is one of the most interesting in America, of a man threading his way through obstacles, discouragements and delays to the thing he wished to do, and with few helping him. When I lost Reedy, I lost the voice that would have spoken for me, and made everything so much easier. Powys is sympathetic, but has never been a voice; and as a biographer he will be sympathetic; but how much he will understand . . . I don't know.

As things turned out, Masters's concerns about Powys were well placed. Powys completed a typed manuscript called "The Real Edgar Lee Masters," but it was only thirty-five pages in length and focused principally on Masters's writings. Although Masters had initially suggested an "article," he seems not to have told Powys that he had his hopes set on a far lengthier "appraisal." Powys's work remains unpublished, possibly because Masters said he was "not satisfied with it." Because Masters wanted to guide the content of his life story ("I have an inexpressible horror about being misrepresented"), and because not just any biographer would do (an occupational hazard of feuding with people, as Masters did), it was 1940 before he again trusted a third party to tell his story.[26]

Kimball Flaccus was a rising young poet when he met Masters in January of that year. He interviewed Masters for two articles during the spring of 1940 and soon offered to write "a book about him." Masters must have felt he had the right person for his biography when Flaccus completed his articles and saw them published later in the year, one in the summer issue of *Voices,* the other in a fall issue of *Common Sense.* Flaccus took time to visit the New York World's Fair with Masters in the fall of 1940 and began the process of getting to know Masters personally while gathering information about him.[27]

Meanwhile Masters had his Sangamon River book to occupy him. He had a financial need to publish a new book in 1941, but his chances for a successful book were not particularly good, and even old friends could not imagine Masters attaching his name to any volume that would be a commercial success. Interest in Masters's verse had become so scant by 1941 that he was giving his poems to "the hometown papers in Illinois"—which, of course, is how he had begun his career. This may be how he came to the attention of James A. Decker, a press owner at Prairie City, Illinois, a village of 500 inhabitants a few miles northwest of Masters's boyhood home of Lewistown. (Masters may also have heard of the press through his friend A. M. Sullivan, who had published two books with Decker.) Decker had examined a new collection of Masters's poems by April 1941 and soon offered a contract resulting in the June publication of

Illinois Poems, a thin volume offered in 500 copies at two dollars; a deluxe edition of fifty autographed copies sold at five dollars.[28]

Masters had a large number of central Illinois themes with which to work, not only because this was his favored area and because he had a number of images he had not fully explored, but also because Uncle Will's letters kept reminding him of his boyhood days. Will was an endless source of old stories about Masters's beloved grandparents, boyhood hunting and fishing trips to the Sangamon River, and the neighbors of Masters's boyhood. Will remembered exactly what happened the day Sevigne Houghton let his hogs run in the road next to Squire Davis's farm—or any other event, it seemed, from sixty-five years before. And Will had a measure of eloquence as well. He was never anything but a country farmer, but he had a poet's soul and could describe as clearly as he wished incidents that had occurred decades earlier: "I see you yet; as Dear Old Grandpa and Grandma pulled along in the Bowman Lane; dust hoof deep, a cloud that fell and followed on the wake of the team of plugs that drug their hind feet until their hoofs were worn square." Masters said he was "kept in the mood" to write of old times "by constant letters from . . . Uncle Wilbur."[29]

Masters included a poem about Will at the end of *Illinois Poems,* so perhaps Will was responsible for the nostalgia of the verses, or maybe it was simply the advancing years that now caused Masters to adopt a mellow tone in this new book. In any event, he published a volume of verse that was attractively autobiographical and lacking entirely in the rancor that characterized *Spoon River*'s discussion of the same geographical area; one example is "Petersburg" and its depiction of the village square and cemeteries of Rose Hill and Oakland:

> Petersburg is my heart's home. There
> I knew at first earth's sun and air;
> Still I can see the hills around it,
> The people that walked its business square.
>
> Still I can smell the coal mine's smoke
> Beside the railroad, see the oak
> Upon that hill of Horace Wood's,
> One of the best of gentle folk.
>
> * * *
>
> Nestled near where the river creeps
> Petersburg like an old man sleeps;
> The pioneers are gone, but others
> Walk the square where memory keeps
>
> Thought of the farmers, the Saturdays
> When Benjamin Short and Tilford Hays
> Stood by the stores and talked of cattle,
> Corn and clover and country ways.

* * *

Rose Hill is over the river and
South of the houses there is Oakland;
Many a bright eye there is hidden
That once this square by the river scanned.

And why they came and why they went,
Why we were into their places sent
Brings wonder that daily overcomes us
For what we mean and what they meant.

Masters's second Illinois home of Lewistown also received attention as he left behind a not-so-subtle reminder that he had already recorded the doings of this town in a document likely to be permanent:

Gone is the court house, in the long ago
By Newton Walker built; gone houses, churches,
Gone streets, however the looker searches;
Gone Proctor's Grove, gone Spudaway below
The village hills, gone with the populace
That walked about, and vanished like a vapor.
For at last a story printed on fragile paper
Outlasts all bronze, all stone that chisels chase.

Twenty-four other poems appeared in the book, several of them combining a questing spirit with the calmness of acceptance.[30]

When the Poetry Society of America this year offered him its annual medal, Masters accepted. "Poet Breaks Old Rule," said one newspaper; "Edgar Lee Masters Accepts Medal from Society": "Edgar Lee Masters, 72, Kansas-born poet whose 'Spoon River Anthology' has run through seventy editions, broke his long-standing rule against accepting literary or academic honors last night by receiving the 1941 medal of the Poetry Society of America." He read several poems, "all of which were well received and applauded," and made a brief speech, after which he went home and assumed a more familiar stance: he wrote a letter to Poetry Society president A. M. Sullivan to carp about press coverage, denounce the inclusion of certain names he felt should have been omitted from the program, and kick himself for agreeing to attend at all. If he had not been a sometimes friend of Sullivan, Masters might have refused this meeting outright, although he may have been influenced to attend by three members of the Poetry Society's executive board: Amy Bonner of *Poetry,* with whom he corresponded; Gertrude Claytor, a minor poet and friend of Alice's; and his would-be biographer, Kimball Flaccus.[31]

Masters's acceptance of the 1941 Poetry Society medal was nearly simultaneous with the outbreak of World War II, and steps leading to the war would result in new tensions, namely, an FBI file on Masters. Masters had criticized American culture and politics in numerous books and articles, finding fault with capitalist moneyed interests, especially as they manifested themselves from the 1860s through the 1920s. In 1938 he had responded to a poll concerning the Spanish Civil War and to a question by polltaker Donald Stewart of the League of American Writers: "Are you for, or are you against Franco and fascism? Are you for, or are you against the legal Government and the people of Republican Spain? Edgar Lee Masters, author of 'Spoon River Anthology,' answered this letter by stating: 'I am for Republican Spain, of course.'" He also wrote a poem—"The War in Spain"—supporting this point of view. Virtually every page of Masters's FBI file still had large blocks of text blacked out as late as the mid-1990s (several pages are said to be too sensitive to release), so it is difficult to determine exactly what the FBI suspected of Masters (on some pages only Masters's name and words such as "the informant said" are left free of the censor's pen). Nevertheless, given the security measures of World War II and J. Edgar Hoover's concern with communists, it is possible to come up with some reasonably good guesses.[32]

The immediate cause for FBI suspicion was Masters's siding with "Republican Spain" and thus inadvertently with the communists and socialists who supported that side of the Spanish Civil War. In fact, Masters, Alice, and Dreiser had gone to a League of American Writers meeting concerning Spain in September 1938, and the FBI troubles probably began there. But Masters was also an acquaintance of one of the most partisan German sympathizers among American literati, George Sylvester Viereck. Viereck's pro-German sympathies had led the Poetry Society of America to expel him at the time of World War I and would result in his incarceration during World War II. Masters had met him through Alice Davis in 1936 and saw him at various times after that, including June 21, 1940, when Masters lost his diary while attending a social gathering at Viereck's. About a year later, in the spring of 1941, an "FBI investigator" had asked one of Masters's acquaintances about Masters and Alice, and six months after that another agent had contacted Alice to ask her "about typing she did for V" (Viereck): "She tells him she and I met V. at Gourmet [Society]. He doesn't mention my name." In addition, Alice Davis once mentioned that she occasionally went to "Trotsky meetings," and while she thought of herself as a Republican, the Trotsky meetings would certainly have drawn FBI attention to her.[33]

These would have been reasons enough to begin an FBI file on Masters; several other activities would have offered reasons to continue it. In addition to Masters's relations with Dreiser (a socialist sympathizer) and acquaintance with Sandburg (a socialist reporter in his early days), it should be recalled that during his "radical" lawyer years Masters had known the socialist poet John Reed, thought to be among the first American writers to have an FBI file. (There was also the 1904 John Turner case, in which Masters and Darrow had defended an anarchist in the halls of the United States Supreme Court.) Relatedly, Masters occasionally corresponded with other "revolutionaries," including Emma Goldman (Goldman had reviewed Masters's 1905 book *The Blood of the Prophets* in her radical journal *Mother Earth*) and the socialist Eugene Debs, about whom Masters had written a poem. Nor did it help any during World War II when an interned Japanese named Takeshi Haga (a friend of Alice's) used Masters's name as an FBI reference, which the FBI would have considered "in the event that [Haga was] paroled under rules and regulations governing the treatment of alien enemies." In addition, Masters's nephew Dexter Masters might have appeared suspicious to the FBI. Dexter, a son of Masters's brother, Tom, headed the Consumers Union (and the magazine *Consumer Reports*), and because J. Edgar Hoover may have seen this organization as an anticapitalist group, Dexter's involvement could have focused FBI attention on Masters, who was friendly to him. Dexter was reputed to be a Marxist, although there is a story, too, that he was at Los Alamos during the building of the atomic bomb. (In any event, he was an authority on atomic energy and eventually wrote a novel called *The Accident*, which hinted darkly of American misdeeds or mistakes at Los Alamos and elsewhere.)[34]

All of this means that the FBI might have traced suspicious associations of Masters from the turn of the century (the Turner case and Emma Goldman's review) through the 1910s (John Reed) and 1920s (Debs) and into the 1930s and 1940s (Alice Davis, Viereck, Spain, Dreiser, and the Japanese internee). Dexter Masters and his knowledge of atomic energy seem to offer the only contemporary reason for keeping portions of Masters's FBI file closed, but Dexter Masters's death makes this difficult to verify.

Nonetheless, all available evidence suggests that the FBI file on Masters was as fruitless as were the bureau's files on many other American authors. Masters's politics were exactly as described by Arthur Davison Ficke: at one time or another, Masters disliked intensely all forms of modern government. But he also saw (and said) that the United States had to defeat Germany and Japan in World War II, and he discerned the evil in communist Russia as well. As early as 1938 Masters had approached Scribner's about a book he wanted to write: "It would be a book which would stand for America against Communism, Fascism, and every other alien plan." The communists themselves were unprincipled scum as far as Masters was concerned: "There is no respect, no capacity for honoring fine things in these vulgar radicals, these atheists, and wreckers." To put it another way, Masters's intellectual interests might lead him into any number of relations and exchanges of letters with people of every type, but when all was said and done, Masters was never a threat to the republic.[35]

Nevertheless, the FBI might have brought pressure to bear on the organizations friendly to Masters, such as the American Academy of Arts and Letters. Masters had been elected to an early version of this organization in 1918 on the wave of *Spoon River*'s nationwide acclaim, but he encountered several individuals he disliked on his way to his first meeting (about 1920), so he turned around at the door and never went back. He refused to pay his dues of five dollars per year and resigned in 1931, becoming one of the few people to quit the organization.[36]

Despite these tensions, when *Illinois Poems* yielded next to nothing, Masters applied in the fall of 1941 for a loan of $500 from the American Academy but then failed to repay it. Surprisingly, in May 1942 the academy awarded him a gift of $1,000 in recognition of his place in American literature, as a certificate signed by the academy's Stephen Benet shows: "To Edgar Lee Masters, born in Kansas, in recognition of his long and distinguished services to American letters and the timeless verse in which his people are remembered." Perhaps Benet had done something to upset Masters, or perhaps Masters was embarrassed by his failure to repay his earlier loan; in any event, he refused to go to the ceremony. He explained matters thus to Dreiser: "I refused to attend the meeting where the money was bestowed. I told Benet that I wouldn't go, so they sent it to me, and I took it, for the reason that just then I needed it." Despite the snub, Masters would negotiate at least one more unreimbursed loan from the American Academy (in 1943), after which the group would have no more to do with him.[37]

In the spring of 1942 Masters published *The Sangamon*, his last book to be handled by a major publisher. An amalgam of personal and third-party information, the book included material from Masters's bittersweet trip home in 1940, along with his family's history; Rev. R. D. Miller's *Past and Present of Menard County* (the author was the father of Masters's friend Mitch Miller); and the local research of two of Masters's Petersburg acquaintances, boyhood friend Frank Blane and local historian Fern Nance Pond, who had helped Masters with the background for his novel *The Tide of Time*. Masters had contemplated a river book for some time. His initial plan had been to combine the histories of the Sangamon and Spoon Rivers and create a volume for Farrar and Rinehart's Rivers of America series or a title for Erskine Caldwell's American Folkway series. Caldwell wanted a broader geographic emphasis and Farrar a lesser one, with the result that Masters chose Farrar and Rinehart and concentrated on only the Sangamon. He completed most of a draft during October and November 1940, agreed to its revisions (the original last chapter was dropped), and saw the book published in May 1942.[38]

The Sangamon is vintage Masters, the writer at his mellowest. It is as if the angry fires that had fueled *Spoon River* and many other books had at last died down and allowed him to write calmly and gracefully about an area he knew and loved. In fact, he did this so well that it is easy not to notice that *The Sangamon* is neither good history nor good geography: for one thing, it fails to describe all the geographic assets of the Sangamon River valley; for another, it is clearly subjective in many places and ends in a mystical trance. And so the charm that *The Sangamon* has exercised on readers comes from matters other than its completeness and objectivity.

To the extent that *The Sangamon* focuses on some of the same people who appear in *Spoon River*, it serves as a gloss on Masters's most famous book. To the extent that it serves as a late-in-life self-portrait of Masters and his values, *The Sangamon* partially offsets Masters's failure to complete his autobiography. (The use of the first person "I" lends authority to both matters.) And the book is easy to read as well: a combination of local color and Americana, *The Sangamon* meanders through a countryside that is partly fact and partly state of mind: "The Sangamon River! Not navigable, not noted for its commercial activity, not distinguished for majestic scenery, nor for a battle, . . . distinguished for nothing but for good and useful lives lived along its shores, and for the beauty of its prairies that sleep and bloom and wave their grasses to the passing winds. It flows along where fiddlers lived, where little villages slept, mesmerized by time."[39]

If *The Sangamon* seems sometimes to have a mythic element, it is because we are in the land of myth, exploring through Masters's memories ("magical," he called them) the landscape he had given a new dimension through the pages of *Spoon River Anthology:* "The country possessed my imagination, and it does so to this day. It may be that I idealize it, but at any rate it has a magical appeal to me quite beyond my power to describe. . . . The silence and the pastoral beauty of the country there bring one into a trance."[40]

More precisely, the best parts of *The Sangamon* focus on the countryside contained in, contiguous to, or very close to Menard County, Masters's boyhood home. In fact, Masters's vision was more sharply focused than this: "The most beautiful, as well as the most historic, part of the Sangamon River is in Menard County, along the boundary of New Salem village and at Petersburg." ("I know of no town in Illinois more attractive than Petersburg.") And of all the residents of the Petersburg area, the one who seemed most representative of the region's good people was one of Masters's own relatives, Squire Davis Masters: "My grandfather was so typical of the people of Menard County along the Sangamon River that I can describe them as temperaments, as American influences, as exemplars of Americanism by a few touches concerning his life and ways, his political and social faith."[41]

For this reason the dozen square miles or so of Squire Davis Masters's world make up much of *The Sangamon.* It is a world of nineteenth-century agrarian, Jeffersonian values, the values that shaped Masters in his youth and against whose loss he reacted for much of his adult life. His treatment of this society in *The Sangamon* was done with just enough detail to explain to the reader why this account is worth reading, and several reviewers liked the book very much, although reviews were limited, probably because Masters's books preceding *The Sangamon* had not been very popular.

Masters's second volume of 1942, *Along the Illinois,* would be his last collection of poems published during his lifetime. Although James A. Decker's press owed royalties on his 1941 volume *Illinois Poems* (the book had sold only about one hundred copies in its first ninety days), Masters returned to that Illinois press to publish *Along the Illinois.* (The owner-publisher advertised his press as "the largest publishing house in America devoted exclusively to poetry," but details were less grandiose: the printer was in his twenties and had but one employee—his sister—and his "publishing house" consisted of the rear of the village drugstore in Prairie City.) The new volume was for a time called "Sandridge to Spring

Lake" (a title that would have nodded to Masters's two favorite rural locales, the Menard County township where his grandfather's farm had been located and Masters's twelve-acre farm in Michigan, lost during his divorce). Like *Illinois Poems, Along the Illinois* focused primarily on the countryside of Masters's youth; his uncle Will had helped prompt some of the contents of both books, as had two Petersburg women who corresponded with Masters during his later years, Emily Marbold (the sister of Mitch Miller) and Dell Fouche (an early childhood girlfriend).[42]

The best poems caught the essence of rural areas that had been important to Masters during his early years, especially places along the Illinois, Sangamon, and Spoon Rivers. His affinity for these locales is clearly evident in poems such as "River Towns." After commenting on the physical similarities between Illinois villages and the settlement of Grand Haven (near his Michigan estate of Spring Lake), Masters concluded the poem with the observation that the towns of his early days had achieved a meaning that went beyond their mere geographies:

> As at Petersburg the town communes
> With the earth, and by the earth is quieted here
> And voices on the streets are like the sound
> Of fainting wind in autumn hollows:
> The town is memory longing for the places
> Far up the river, never found
> By the river's winding spaces
> Which the heart forever follows.
>
> Those who have reached the sea return
> To Bernadotte no more,
> Or Petersburg. They yearn
> For Miller's Ford in vain,
> For Havana and Grand Haven too.
> The sea is as the years which chain
> Their steps as Time which never
> Frees them to live their youth again.
> Youth is the river towns they knew
> By the enduring river.

Along the Illinois was published in 340 copies in August 1942 and retailed at two dollars. It received attention from only one major reviewing source, *The Saturday Review of Literature.* Masters's hopes to reissue *Along the Illinois* and *Illinois Poems* as one book with a New York publisher eventually came to nothing.[43]

Much of the remainder of 1942 also resulted in disappointments. Gerald Sanders abandoned his plans for a bibliography when he had trouble finding copies of Masters's early publications, and the war forced Kimball Flaccus, shortly to enter the navy, to delay his plans for a biography. The war also ruined any likelihood of a standard edition of Masters's works when the Macmillan Company notified him that the plates for ten of his books would be melted to form "the core of bullets." (The list included one of his favorites, *Domesday Book.*) The war nearly sent Masters back to Illinois, not only because he feared that New York City would be bombed, but also because he was briefly slated to write a history of the Illinois Supreme Court (where a former law partner in the Darrow firm, Francis S. Wilson, was then a justice). But that fell through, and Masters remained in New York.[44]

It was also at this time that Masters went through one of the most bizarre experiences of his old age, his September 1942 effort to adopt Alice Davis. In Masters's words, she had "to get up at 6 in order to be to work at 8, and then [endure] grilling work till 6, then [return] to her dark room" at the Chelsea. He sought to lighten her load by making her his "adopted daughter," as he explained to Gertrude Claytor: "I got a lawyer and the blanks for adopting her, and then ran into a snag, which is that I have to have the consent of the woman who happens to be my wife. I am trying now to overcome or circumvent that, and maybe I can. If she were my adopted daughter, I could do things for her that I can't now; for one, we might live together and be undisturbed. Her lot and my own difficulties keep me upset." There is, of course, a legitimate question of Masters's sincerity in this attempt (Ellen said he was not serious at all, and Hilary guessed it might be a joke), but by the fall of 1942 Masters's daily life was a very lonely one, and as he looked at the years ahead, he may have decided that he needed Alice to take care of him. (Alice pointed out that an "adopted relative" could get wartime ration books for him.) In fact, she already acted much as a relative would: on one or more of her trips to St. Louis, she stopped in Petersburg to examine the countryside Masters had known as a boy. Uncle Wilbur had treated her as if she were a family member and had shown her around.[45]

Perhaps it was World War II and the times that were making things so topsy-turvy. A contingent of merchant marines had been quartered on the second floor of the Hotel Chelsea early in 1943, and their high spirits, loud radios, and girlfriends grated heavily on Masters, who was relocated to the third floor. Still, even with the war and the sailors, his life was essentially as it had been in the late 1930s. He still saw Ellen from time to time (she had managed to get Hilary a scholarship to attend Brewster Academy in New Hampshire), and he saw Alice on an almost daily basis, but he had an overwhelming sense that the times were changing, as he remarked to Gerald Sanders: "My morale is so low that I am limber as a stalk of spaghetti. Still, I write poems, when I am not worrying about money. Every now and then the world ends for some generation. It is ending now for lots of us." When he wrote a poem for the anniversary of a time capsule buried at the New York World's Fair, he could see only a "meaningless" future.[46]

The tumultuous times also made themselves felt on his first family. In the summer of 1943 his daughter Marcia was engaged to August Derleth, the Wisconsin writer whose rural-oriented works Masters very much approved. Masters had by then come to be on good terms with Marcia, who had been married previously and now had a daughter called "Little Marcia," and she and her daughter had visited Masters and Alice in New York in the summer of 1942. The prospective marriage would thus bring together three people of whom Masters thought a great deal. The engagement was called off suddenly in November 1943, however, and Marcia and her daughter left Chicago for California. The end of the engagement was doubly important, for Masters had also approached Derleth about serving as his biographer in lieu of Kimball Flaccus, then in the navy. In the end Marcia was further away than ever, and although Masters was now getting along with Madeline, she remained in the Chicago area and was far from the Chelsea, as was Hardin, then in the service.[47]

Masters spent much of 1943 looking futilely for money. He made about $2,200 during the year but had no new book contract. He wanted to write a book about the famous people he had known, a "book of biographical gossip" tentatively titled "American Book of Portraits." When that idea failed, he tried to graft the biographical gossip onto the remaining one-third of his autobiography, but that was also turned down. In June he finally admitted that the final part of his autobiography was not going to find a publisher during his lifetime: "I suppose this ends the matter, and now my manuscript lies unrevised and locked up till some better day, if any ever comes."[48]

Masters kept on writing, however, because that was the only thing he could do, because it was the one hope he had, and because, he said, "[It] eases my loneliness." He offered to write a history of the Spoon River for the Rivers of America series but was turned down; he tried and failed to get a college lectureship; and he accepted charity from those who were well off, asking for and receiving $100 from a New York patron of the arts and $75 from the Relief Committee of the Poetry Society of America. In December 1943 his luck ran out.[49]

Masters had suffered poor teeth for years but had deferred dental work, so that he was not eating properly during several of his later years at the Chelsea. His poor eating habits and seasonal colds led to what he thought was the flu in the second week of December. He lay in his room at the Chelsea struggling for breath while Alice hovered near, convinced that he would soon recover. But when Nicolosi visited, the sculptor immediately grew alarmed and decided to contact Ellen. She came and "took over," in Alice's words. Ellen or Nicolosi called an ambulance and made arrangements for Masters to be removed to medical facilities. The nearest hospital was Bellevue, a traditional pauper's hospital, and it was to this institution that Masters was taken, his life in danger from pneumonia and malnutrition. His Hotel Chelsea days were over.[50]

CHAPTER 20

Last Chapter

The soul of the river had entered my soul,
And the gathered power of my soul was moving
So swiftly it seemed to be at rest.

—Edgar Lee Masters, "Isaiah Beethoven," *Spoon River Anthology*

Masters would never fully recover from his December 1943 bout with malnutrition and pneumonia. He had always been weak in the lungs, the result of a boyhood case of pneumonia and the 1915 pneumonia that nearly killed him at the time of *Spoon River.* Although he claimed he could "cook famously," he seldom did so, and poor diet and bad teeth now broke his health and ended his career as a writer. He would publish a few more things, but these would be insignificant.[1]

Because he had no money with him when he arrived at Bellevue, he was placed near a ward with indigent patients, thus starting the rumor that he was "ill and penniless" and "without funds." That rumor and Bellevue's reputation as a hospital for the impoverished and insane would give rise to countless newspaper and radio stories, all of which would have been more sensational if reporters had known that Masters's bed was not in a room but in a hallway.[2]

Life magazine tried to get a picture of him in his sickbed, a neon sign in Times Square indicated "POET EDGAR LEE MASTERS VERY ILL," and news of his penury and impending death reached friend and foe alike, although not everyone heard this at once. Because Ellen had not wanted to disturb Hilary during his exams at Brewster Academy, it had fallen to one of his roommates to tell him that his father was "starving" and "near death." The children of Masters's first family were also contacted and again found themselves in the papers: "Poet Masters Not Destitute, Says Daughter." Masters himself would spend a part of the next year telling people he was not broke. He finally asked Harriet Monroe to publish in *Poetry* a notice that his poverty had been greatly exaggerated; she obliged in the May 1944 issue: "poet plus Bellevue equals 'human interest story.'"[3]

Masters was in Bellevue only briefly before Ellen moved him to New York's

Park East Hospital and then to a New York nursing home called Hillcrest Mansion. In the spring he was moved to a boardinghouse where he gradually recovered some of his strength and received the dental work he needed. By May 1944 he was well enough to accompany Theodore Dreiser to the American Academy of Arts and Letters to see Dreiser receive the academy's gold medal. In the summer Masters went with Ellen to the Pocono Mountains, where she assumed the summer directorship of the children's camp at which she had worked for several summers. When sixteen-year-old Hilary joined them as a counselor at the adjoining camp for boys, the family was reunited and living at the same address for the first time since the summer of 1935. At the end of the summer, Ellen and Masters moved to Charlotte, North Carolina, where Ellen had been hired to organize an English department for Charlotte's Country Day School. Hilary, now a high-school graduate, was sent to nearby Davidson College.[4]

For most of 1944 Masters did "literally nothing" in the way of writing. He wanted to write more poems, but his typing table was "tippy," and he had trouble staying awake after meals, including breakfast; as late as November 1944 he described himself as being "in complete convalescence." (When H. L. Mencken saw him in July, he described Masters as having the gait of "a man 275 years old.") "I couldn't write a poem to save my life," Masters told his Hollywood acquaintance Dudley Nichols near the anniversary of his trip to Bellevue. One day he gave up, or nearly so, as he explained to Arthur Ficke: "A doctor here has prescribed a tonic for me, and I believe it will work. What's the use of kidding: the time comes for all of us to lie down. I have some more poems to write, but maybe I can't do it. And if I don't, what of it? It is now more than 25 years since *Spoon River*. . . ."[5]

His gloomy comments notwithstanding, Masters did write a little in 1944, but he was severely handicapped in being separated from his manuscripts. "His papers had to be dumped into trunks . . . when his things were moved from the Chelsea," Ellen explained, and because the trunks were now in storage, he had no means of accessing his work in progress. He was especially upset that a new manuscript of "about a hundred poems" had been misplaced when Ellen closed his apartment at the Chelsea. Except for this mishap, he would have brought out a new volume of verse in the fall of 1944, he said; Macmillan was already interested in the manuscript.[6]

Despite not having a new book before the public, Masters did have some income in 1944. John Hall Wheelock had placed Masters's name in nomination for the Shelley Memorial Award in October 1943, and news of Masters's illness resulted in his name being placed before several other groups, which now came forth with cash awards. The Poetry Society of America formalized the Shelley Memorial Award of over $550 in January 1944, the Carnegie Fund of the Authors Club of New York provided a check for $375 in May (with a pledge for a similar amount in the fall), the Author's League volunteered money, and the Episcopal Actors Guild of America forwarded a check for $200. (Masters was especially happy with the Shelley Award. "I can think of nothing more appropriate," he wrote Wheelock, "than for the Shelley Award to come to me because of the great love I bear for the poet.") In addition, Dudley Nichols helped Masters get $500 for screen options on *Spoon River* and *Domesday Book,* with a promise of an additional $500 in 1945 for *Spoon River* only. Complete strangers sent money to Masters, and so did old acquaintances, such as Dr. Alexander Burke (from the Chicago days) and the poet Edna St. Vincent Millay (her check for $50 remained uncashed, however, for Masters knew that Millay herself had experienced problems).[7]

Ellen accepted her husband's new condition, along with his past wanderings, present gripes, and expensive medicines (the cost for the latter sometimes equaled a week of her income). Perhaps she accepted things because he had called for her instead of someone else when he was close to dying. "Call Ellen," he had whispered into Nicolosi's bristly ear. And she had come and saved him when Alice Davis might have let him perish. Ellen thus triumphed over husband and mistress simultaneously, and having taken control of his life, she never relinquished it.[8]

Alice Davis did not at first think that Masters's life would change following his illness. She informed him that she was trying to compile a volume of his poetry for publication and showed every willingness to continue as his secretary as well as act as his editor. She and Mencken visited Masters while he was convalescing, and she wrote numerous times, but her influence was ended. After she and two friends brought Masters some roses at the Hillcrest home, he rechristened them "The Three Roses," the name of a cheap whisky. A little later she realized that their shared experiences were over. In May 1944 she wrote to say that she had recently met a member of the merchant marine named Anthony Clover and had decided to marry him; the marriage lasted about a year.[9]

Meanwhile, the Masters family was going through the awkward motions of readjustment at the Selwyn Hotel in Charlotte, North Carolina. Hilary had been only seven during the family's last summer together in 1935. Now he was a sixteen-year-old graduate of Brewster Academy, attending Davidson College, and showing an interest in the navy. Masters seems not to have tried too hard to bridge the lost years; it was all he could do to deal with the present. "We have everything we need here," he dictated to Ellen (for his hands had become unsteady, and she handled much of his correspondence): "There's good food in the hotel restaurant downstairs. I spend the day reading or working. Ellen is busy with her English classes and can bring me any book I want from the library. Hilary is attending a college nearby. The beds are fine, and we have good sleeps." He dictated the same letter to everybody.[10]

His acquiescence to domesticity had not come easily. He had mutinied at the last minute in New York's Pennsylvania Station. They were waiting to board the train for North Carolina when he announced that he would not be leaving New York. "Of course you can," Ellen had said. (He had nowhere to live, his furniture was stored, and he could barely walk.) "What I am saying," he replied, "is that I cannot make this trip. Nor will I make this trip. . . . You can go, but I am not leaving." When Ellen had endured this kind of talk for as long as she could, she suddenly grabbed him by the shoulders, shook him, and gave him a tongue lashing so severe that train station drunks and a small army of waiting soldiers all gave her their undivided attention. When she told him, "Stand up," he stood up, and that was that. Earlier, she had known that she had assumed control of his life; after this, he knew it too.[11]

Now there was little argument over such things as anthology requests; whatever would bring in revenue was usually placed on the literary auction block. He tried to sell his manuscripts and agreed to reprint requests when these were offered, but as he and Ellen marketed his writings, he still clung tenaciously to old ways and friends: he published a piece called "Fiddlers of the Ozarks" (its story of itinerant fiddlers in the Illinois hills of Johnson County was based on his 1931 visit to the Missouri Ozarks); he wrote a preface for August Derleth's *Selected Poems,* doing so because he approved of Derleth's reverence for rural things; and he memorialized departed friends. Between these activities he groused about better days: "Some years ago . . . sonnets were at $20," he complained to an acquaintance. "Now they are fifteen cents a ton."[12]

He had virtually given up on his biography being completed while he was alive. August Derleth had shown no interest in becoming Masters's biographer after he and Marcia Masters broke up, and Kimball Flaccus was at a military outpost in the Aleutian Islands 4,000 miles away, on active duty with the navy. Flaccus and Masters had agreed on an outline for the biography in 1942, and Flaccus saw Masters briefly in 1943 on his way to the Aleutians. The physical distance between Masters and his planned biographer seemed to bother Masters, however, and he slowly grew disenchanted with the young poet. "I like Flaccus," Masters wrote John Hall Wheelock in 1944, "but I doubt if he is qualified to write a book about me. There are fine understandings to be observed." These probably concerned Masters and women other than Ellen, but it is impossible to say. By the time Flaccus was out of the military and again focused on the biography, Masters would be dead.[13]

Life at the Selwyn Hotel in Charlotte was much easier on Masters than the ragged ends of his Chelsea days had been. As Ellen worked, he read and spent a portion of most days thinking about writing, but he did very little and was as likely to sit in the room and doze as anything. (Continued support from the New York Author's League made his time a little easier.) Their quarters were so small that Hilary had to stay in another room when he came "home" on weekends. Still, the winter of 1944–45 was satisfying to Masters and seems to have been satisfactory to Ellen and Hilary, as Masters summarized to a friend: "Ellen is well and busy. She is a wonderful girl, and her devotion to me has carried me along. Maybe I am going to be completely well after a time. . . . Hilary is deep in Greek. He comes here on Saturdays and stays over Sunday."[14]

To formalize his satisfaction with the new arrangement, Masters had his will remade in North Carolina. He also completed arrangements to have it made again with New York witnesses when he and Ellen returned to that city for a visit in the summer of 1945. He explained his motivation to John Hall Wheelock: "The will that I made here [North Carolina] devised all my copyrights, manuscripts, and whatever money I have to my wife Ellen; except for the matter of witnesses, the will that I made is all right." Because Masters felt that legal challenges were more likely to arise in New York City than elsewhere, he insisted on New York witnesses, so as to make it easier for Ellen to handle his manuscripts after his death: "I want to protect my wife against all troublemakers. . . . I want her to manage the publications of the writings that I leave."[15]

There were also other objective indicators that it was time for Masters to be thinking of such things. Old friends continued to die or suffer severe incapacitations. His former girlfriend and confidante Eunice Tietjens had died in 1944. Dreiser would die in 1945. John Cowper Powys had a serious ulcer, and Arthur Davison Ficke had throat cancer. Mencken would be overtaken by a stroke in the near future. Old friends in Petersburg and Lewistown also passed on.[16]

News of Masters's severe illness had a positive effect on his relations with other parts of Illinois, especially the University of Chicago. Following the collection of $1,000 among Masters's acquaintances, Joseph Nicolosi's bust of Masters was cast in bronze, and plans were made for its installation in the university library. Wartime metal shortages delayed the casting, but shortly after the end of the war, the bust was in place. University of Chicago president Robert Hutchins was writing Masters about its presentation as early as February 1945, but Masters felt the distance was too far to travel and remained in the East. (Dedication ceremonies were finally held in April 1947, with Ellen in attendance.)[17]

Masters and Ellen returned to Charlotte for the fall of 1945. His writings were not numerous, but he drafted "three articles" and explored the possibility of letting the Trovillion Press in rural Herrin, Illinois, publish his next volume of verse. Hal Trovillion had published a variety of books by authors on both sides of the Atlantic and was extremely cordial to Masters, sending him sample copies of his attractively done volumes and mentioning several of their mutual friends, including William Marion Reedy and the Masters family lawyer George Gillespie. (He might also have mentioned John Cowper Powys.) But Masters had had only so-so results with his last small press (that of James A. Decker), and this relation came to an end without any book being issued.[18]

Early in 1946 Hilary simplified the family's finances by quitting Davidson College and joining the navy shortly before turning eighteen. He would serve a two-year hitch as a naval correspondent in Chicago and Washington, D.C., and on the carrier *Midway.*[19]

Masters and Ellen spent the spring of 1946 in Charlotte. They were still staying at the Selwyn Hotel, but he seems to have done little or no writing ("I am doing nothing"). He had no desk in the Selwyn, and his literary work may have been confined to fulfilling a promise to Mark Twain's cousin Cyril Clemens to provide an introduction to Clemens's book about the humorist Benjamin Shillaber. Clemens had asked for the introduction well before Masters's illness, and Masters's 1,500-word contribution may have been drafted prior to 1946.[20]

Masters continued to authorize reprints of his poems, usually those from *Spoon River,* and had occasional requests for permission to use his poems in radio broadcasts, but the proceeds from such activities were small, and he was fortunate in having support from beneficent organizations aimed at helping authors. He received checks from the Authors Club of New York, received "a Bryher Award" of $250, and was elected a fellow of the Academy of American Poets, which yielded a remarkable $5,000. (Old friends Witter Bynner and Robinson Jeffers were on the academy's board at the time.) The Masterses were in New York City for the summer of 1946, perhaps because he hungered for news of the New York literary scene and because the trip would make him feel as if he were still actively involved. He would shortly have "a book ready," he said (he had found the misplaced manuscript), and may have hoped he could speed its marketing while there.[21]

In the fall of 1946 Ellen accepted a better-paying job at Ogontz Junior College for women in the Philadelphia suburb of Rydal, Pennsylvania. Tom Coyne, Ellen's father, was now in a home for old soldiers, and Ellen's mother came to live with her daughter and son-in-law in a small faculty apartment on the campus. Masters's share of the apartment consisted of his Hotel Chelsea writing table (retrieved from storage) and a metal lawn chair. He had hardening of the arteries and Parkinson's disease, which caused his hands to tremble, and by winter had grown more dependent on Ellen, as his December 1946 letter to Dr. Burke shows:

> Ellen with her college teaching, keeping this house, and taking care of me is much burdened. You perhaps do not know that I am an invalid, and I'm pretty helpless. I can do very little for myself. She is the best wife in the world. How she manages to do everything, I do not know. And it grieves me a good deal. I must be given shots every other night, and on Saturday Ellen takes me to a doctor . . . for a shot in my hip. Thanks to much work on Ellen's part, we have very comfortable living quarters. Our windows look on one side into a golf course, and on the other side into wooded hills.[22]

Despite his physical problems Masters continued to make plans to publish a new volume of verse, now with the title of "Far Horizons," but he was ambivalent about who should publish it. "The trouble with most of the publishers," he told August Derleth, "is they're venal, and some of them are downright crooked." When Derleth expressed hope that the new manuscript would someday be printed, Masters assured him it would not be lost. In the meantime, with reprint requests, iffy health, and one thing or another, the new manuscript languished.[23]

During the summer of 1947 the Masters family moved from its cramped quarters in the college's faculty apartments into temporary but spacious housing in a college mansion that served as a dormitory during the school year. They had the place to themselves during the summer months, and Ellen saw to it that most of their visitors were delayed until then. Master had several interviews with journalists and scholars during the summer. "We have everything we need here," he told them. "It all comes with her job," he would say, pointing at the expanse of property surrounding the empty college. "She's a marvelous woman." That was what Ellen wanted to hear and what he wanted to say. He had finally conceded that it was her education that was keeping them going.[24]

Unfortunately, the strain of being a teacher as well as nurse and secretary to Masters would shortly take its toll on Ellen. Added to the strain were new duties as department head at her junior college in the fall of 1947. Ellen had begun experiencing arthritic discomfort earlier that year and saw a chiropractor for spinal pain before undergoing three operations in New York at Christmastime of 1947. Masters commiserated with her while she was in the hospital: "I am doing pretty well and hope you are. I have an Xmas present for you, but Hilary thinks I should keep it till you come home, and I will. You are the dearest woman in the world."[25]

She had barely returned to their home, however, when Masters collapsed from an unknown cause and went first to a hospital for two weeks and then to a convalescent home in Melrose Park, Pennsylvania. Ellen subsequently moved him back to college housing for the summer of 1948, but Masters's condition was such that he required "a trained nurse" for eight hours a day. By September 1948 Ellen had returned him to the Melrose Park nursing home. It was done reluctantly, but she herself was some days nearly crippled with arthritis and in "great pain" much of the time.[26]

Masters would do very little writing after this, and it is doubtful that anyone except Ellen could have read his handwriting, although he maintained an interest in creative work and continued to attract modest attention: the press of James A. Decker sought (without success) to publish his new manuscript in November 1948; the Carnegie Fund checks continued to arrive until they totaled more than $5,000; and an Italian composer made plans to present *Spoon River* through an opera entitled *La Collina*—"The Hill." It would be presented slightly over a year later at La Scala Opera House in Milan.[27]

The attention and money were welcome, for Masters's maintenance costs at the nursing home were $3,000 a year, an amount that Ellen bore largely by herself, with occasional help from Hardin. Masters still had poems he wanted typed but let Ellen determine how and where they might be published. She was no doubt largely responsible for the last article to appear under his name during his lifetime, a one-page effort in *Cosmopolitan* telling of his decision to become a writer. Marketing the manuscript of poems called "Far Horizons" had also become Ellen's responsibility, and she worked on the project in mid-1949 with

Masters's friend Gerald Sanders, who was supposed to provide the manuscript with a final edit. The professor had already given up on his bibliography of Masters's works and been dismissed as Masters's literary executor, and this new involvement would also come to nothing. (When Sanders finally retired from the professoriate, he occupied his time with the less demanding task of running a rural newspaper in Georgia.) Ellen continued the book project into the fall of 1949.[28]

She had been teased with several questions as she went through some of her husband's many papers during the summer of 1949. For one thing, "nearly all" her letters to Masters were missing, as were those from Tennessee Mitchell. She may have suspected that Alice Davis had destroyed the letters (a natural suspicion from Ellen's point of view), or the letters could have been lost during one of the family's several moves. "Someday," Ellen wrote their friend Amy Bonner, "I have to get down to writing out more fully than I have already done a long, long story."[29]

But she would not do this right away. Teaching, marking student essays, and going to college functions all had to come first, and some days her arthritis hurt her. In addition, some days she visited Masters at the nursing home, checked out books for him at the library, or typed poems for the new manuscript. There simply was no time to write her "long story." She might have begun it during the Christmas holidays of 1949 but failed to do so, and everything would change after that.

Masters's Chicago friend Dorothy Dow had sent him a new book of Lord Byron's letters, and Masters was enjoying these, punctuating his comments with news about Byron's "quarrels." (All great authors have great quarrels.) Being treated fairly was a hard thing to come by in this world, and as he grew older, he sometimes wondered about his treatment in the next world—though he did not say this outright, preferring the indirect approach and the philosophy of Spinoza: "As to God, after thinking it over all my life, I have come to the conclusion that there is a mind as large as the universe that is in everything, but why He seems so unconcerned of this planet, save to keep it going, I'll have to go and inquire." Such an inquiry may have crossed his mind when he was diagnosed with bronchitis and pneumonia early in March 1950, but as he did with many other things, he probably thought he would sleep on it.[30]

He sometimes prepared himself for sleep by thinking of the rural landscape near his grandfather's farm in Petersburg. He had found that by concentrating on each remembered detail of a field, hill, or woods, he could move without knowing it from the beauty of that location to the next morning. He had been thinking recently of a long-gone road in the Sangamon River bottoms and of an old river crossing known as Sheep Ford. He and his uncle Will used to go fishing there. They would ride double on Old Pepperdog or Molly, the horse stopping automatically to let him slide off and open a gate into the bottoms. (Will remained on the horse, the reins in one hand, their fishing poles in the other.) The gate would open easily, and he could imagine himself walking back to the side of the horse to swing up. The rocking gait of the old horse would carry them slowly through a long, shady tunnel of sycamore trees and into a clearing filled with bright light. Ahead, the soft dust of the road merged silently with the river at Sheep Ford.[31]

AFTERWORD

The hills are half asleep and how can it be an ill
To be asleep thereunder, asleep with the hill?

—Edgar Lee Masters, "In Praise of Sleep,"
Along the Illinois

Edgar Lee Masters died in his sleep at the age of eighty-one far from Spoon River and other places of his youth in a Pennsylvania nursing home on the night of March 5, 1950. He left nothing of value except his papers and his copyright to *Spoon River Anthology*. He had said for years that he had given up everything for poetry, and whether this was true or not, it was all he had left at the end.[1]

He had known as early as 1925 that he wanted to be buried next to his grandmother Lucinda Masters in Petersburg, his "heart's home." "It remains my spiritual home," he told a friend, "and I want to be taken back there when I die and be buried by the side of my old grandmother." "[She] used to love me so as a boy, and did so much for me," he explained to Harriet Monroe. "I gave her more love than I ever gave anyone else." Masters's uncle Wilbur, a friend to the end, provided Ellen with two grave sites so that Masters could be buried by his grandmother and Ellen in turn could be buried by her husband.[2]

Now he returned home in a modest casket in a railway baggage car, with Ellen on the train and comforted by her friend Constance Greene, the woman with whom Masters had flirted vigorously in 1935. Twenty-two-year-old Hilary Masters flew on to Springfield, charged with completing details for his father's funeral. It would not be an easy funeral. Masters's two marriages had each yielded families that psychologists of a future era would call dysfunctional; neither family knew much or cared to know much about the other.[3]

Certain other matters were also strained. The Poetry Society of America spoke through poet Padraic Colum and asked Ellen to bring Masters's remains to New York City for a final showing of respect from his "old friends." She refused. His old friends had been few and far between when he was elderly and nearly broke.

She also refused the photographer from *Life* magazine who came to Petersburg and sought an open-casket picture. She would not have it. It was "just a family funeral."[4]

Masters's first and second families remained apart in Petersburg. His former wife, Helen, was there with her son, Hardin, and her daughters, Madeline and Marcia. Ellen was there with Hilary. They were all welcome at the home of Uncle Will, now in his nineties, a spry vestige of the old days whose wife and daughter served generous pieces of angel food cake heaped high with coconut frosting. The two families, first and second, would have to be together at the funeral home.[5]

The funeral home. Masters had written of it in *Spoon River Anthology,* faulting its former owner for selling his vote in the state legislature and polluting an Illinois waterway, as well as poisoning relations with his children. The house was a monument operating under a curse in *Spoon River,* but the present generation of owners, the Lanings, did not seem to mind. One of them, the artist Edward, would live to publish a piece about Masters and Petersburg in a respected publication, *American Heritage.* Masters himself had once thought of living in the Laning house in the late 1920s while researching a prospective story about Petersburg. Later on, he and Ellen had visited there; now it served his final needs.[6]

Instead of asking for a funeral sermon, Masters had decided mourners should hear phonograph records of his favorite musical selections, works by Beethoven, Chopin, Dvorak, Sibelius, and others. The boy in charge of the record player forgot his directions, however, and also played flip sides of the records, letting unplanned pieces into the funeral service. At the end of the music a sad-appearing bearded man who looked curiously like Abraham Lincoln read Masters's poem "Silence," and the room wept:

> I have known the silence of the stars and of the sea,
> And the silence of the city when it pauses,
> And the silence of a man and a maid,
> And the silence for which music alone finds the word,
> And the silence of the woods before the winds of spring begin,
> And the silence of the sick
> When their eyes roam about the room.
> And I ask: For the depths
> Of what use is language?
>
> * * *
>
> If we who are in life cannot speak
> Of profound experiences,
> Why do you marvel that the dead
> Do not tell you of death?
> Their silence shall be interpreted
> As we approach them.[7]

Perhaps that is why they wept. They had all approached him at some point during his time at the funeral home, and now he had left them with the assignment of interpreting his silence. "For the depths / Of what use is language?" The old school chums he had outrun in races seventy years earlier did not know; their elderly wives did not know either. Masters had once tried to steal kisses from them. There were no answers in that high-ceilinged Victorian home with its profusion of flowers. These had been supplied by "girls," Ellen would report, "girls—all around 80—who had gone to school with Lee in Petersburg." It was, the community agreed, a very unorthodox ceremony.[8]

The funeral cortege moved from the funeral home along silent streets (it was a Friday, but village businesses were closed out of respect for the dead) and along sidewalks where youngsters released from school watched the hearse. About 250 high-school students attended the graveside rites in Oakland Cemetery. A brief prayer of Masters's grandfather was read, as was one of Masters's favorite creations, "Howard Lamson," a poem from *The New Spoon River;* it shows nature dealing wisely with the troubled affairs of humankind: "The rolling earth rolls on and on / With trees and stones and winding streams— / My dream is what the hill-side dreams!"[9]

Masters was buried on "the hill" among the pioneer dead, some of whose stories he had made famous in *Spoon River Anthology.* That fame notwithstanding, there were few literary persons at his funeral, unless one counts Mark Twain's cousin Cyril Clemens and two who were to be successful later, Masters's daughter Marcia, a poet, and Masters's son Hilary, a future novelist and short-story writer. There was also one unidentified graduate student, the photographer from *Life,* and several reporters from metropolitan newspapers. In an irony that might have come from *Spoon River,* Masters the poet was laid to rest by four lawyers and two judges, representatives of the legal profession he claimed he had learned to hate. But there were always more lawyers than poets in villages such as "Spoon River" (a condition that persists to this day), and an aged man has to rely on whoever is available. (A less philosophical reason is that Ellen had called on an Illinois lawyer and legislator to choose the pallbearers, and he had simply called friends from Illinois bar associations.)[10]

Masters's burial next to his grandmother meant that he would not be buried next to his father, mother, brother, or sister, all of whom lie in a family plot elsewhere in the cemetery. Each of these had angered Masters a great deal over one thing or another (in the matter of his college education, for example), so it is probably appropriate that Masters was separated from them in death, for that was often his position in life.

The epitaph of the Western world's best-known epitaph maker came from one of his poems and was selected and lightly edited by his wife, Ellen. The poem, "To-morrow Is My Birthday," was first published in *Reedy's Mirror* and then reprinted in *Toward the Gulf* in 1918. Masters spoke of it as his "high water mark in blank verse," in addition to several times describing it as one of his best. The inscription reads as follows:

EDGAR LEE MASTERS
(1868–1950)

Good friends, let's to the fields . . .
After a little walk, and by your pardon,
I think I'll sleep. There is no sweeter thing,
Nor fate more blessed than to sleep.
I am a dream out of a blessed sleep—
Let's walk and hear the lark.

When Reedy had first published the poem in 1917, he had told Masters it offered proof that he "hadn't shot [his] wad in *Spoon River.*" The poem was "the Big Thing," Reedy said. To the extent that it became Masters's final word on himself, it might appear to be his most important poem, but it is not. One of his most important poems is reproduced nearby, however, just forty paces away on the stone over the grave of Ann Rutledge. It is this poem that people were most likely to read during Masters's lifetime, and it will no doubt remain popular.[11]

And so things came to an end for Masters and his troubled relations with his contemporaries. His most important contemporary in many ways had turned out to be his first wife, Helen Jenkins Masters. She never remarried, in part because she remained in love with Masters (or so her son, Hardin, said). After the 1923 divorce and appearance of Masters's vicious sonnet sequence, "The Return," she lived with as much dignity as she could and went on with a social life that included friends on Chicago's Lake Shore Drive and other fashionable addresses. She lived with her daughter Marcia for many of her final years and died in the Chicago suburb of Highland Park in 1958 at the age of eighty-four.[12]

Of the three children from Masters's first family, Marcia Lee Masters became the best known. She was a successful writer for much of her adult life and gathered her best poems in three volumes: *Intent on Earth* (1965), *Wind Around the Moon* (1986), and *Looking Across* (1990). Some of her verse was written with a backward glance at her parents' divorce, and no study of that domestic trauma can be complete without consulting her poems. Marcia Lee Masters was also a successful newspaper reporter and editor during her working life, which included appointments with the *Los Angeles Times, Chicago Tribune,* and other newspapers. She died in 1994.[13]

Her elder sister, Madeline Masters Gebhart, chose to live a private life and seldom appeared at activities concerning her famous father. An exception was the late 1960s centenary of the birth of Masters observed by the Society of Midland Authors and attended by all three of Masters's children from his first marriage. The centenary was held in the wrong year—1969—the result of Masters's lying about his birth date. (A commemorative medal struck by the Franklin Mint suffered the same fate.) Madeline Masters died in 1996.[14]

Masters's son Hardin spent the bulk of his life in the banking business and the military. He served in World War II and the Korean War and retired with the rank of colonel in the U.S. Air Force. He was active in the arts in his later years and prior to his death in 1979 published two short books concerning his father, *Edgar Lee Masters: A Centenary Memoir-Anthology* (1972) and *Edgar Lee Masters: A Biographical Sketchbook about a Famous American Author* (1978). The latter describes what appears to have been a chance meeting with Lillian Wilson, whom he called a "lovely lady" but one he never forgave for having destroyed the family of his young adulthood.[15]

Lillian Wilson would meet her second husband, the explorer and physician John Colin Vaughan, in 1922. (Dr. Vaughan had performed her appendectomy that year, when Masters left her to return to his wife.) Lillian and Vaughan were married in 1926 and lived for a time in her Marion, Indiana, mansion until the Great Depression destroyed her fortune; true to her nature, however, and the destiny appointed her, she managed to live quite nicely on her husband's income. As the 1930s came to a close, she and Vaughan were living in a Park Avenue hotel apartment in New York City, and she died there about 1950. Her Indiana mansion is now on the National Register of Historic Places (although not for the literary history enacted there but for its unusual architecture).[16]

Dorothy Dow, the young poet with whom Masters diverted himself in the 1920s, married and published several volumes of verse, along with a biography of Edgar Allan Poe and other writings. Nevertheless, her unpublished memoir of Masters, called "An Introduction to Some Letters, 1950," may bring her more lasting attention than her other pieces. She died in 1989.[17]

Masters's principal girlfriend from the Hotel Chelsea years, Alice Davis, made what seemed an unlikely second marriage to an East Coast minister, the Reverend Charles Tibbetts. Nothing else in her life ever brought her the prominence she enjoyed as Edgar Lee Masters's girlfriend, however, and her most enduring act was to follow the advice of H. L. Mencken and deposit Masters's letters along with a 528-page journal called "Evenings with Edgar" in the New York Public Library. She also completed a fourteen-page photo memoir concerning her relationship with Masters; a copy of the latter is at the University of Virginia Library. Alice Davis died in 1988.[18]

It fell to Masters's second family, particularly Ellen Masters, to tie up the many strands of Masters's life and to organize his papers with an eye toward placing them in a permanent repository. After her husband's death Ellen occasionally consented to interviews or spoke about her husband and his career, but her more typical stance was to guard her husband's memory and her place in his life. She did not want a biography completed while anyone (including herself) might be hurt by it. Unfortunately, Masters had already helped set in motion a biography to be prepared by the poet and scholar Kimball Flaccus.[19]

Flaccus and Masters had agreed in 1940 and 1942 that he would write the official biography, but Masters later grew cool to the idea, saying, "Flaccus was not the man to do the book, being an easterner and not in key with the material or with me." There is no indication, however, that Masters communicated this to Flaccus, who served several years in the navy with the long-term thoughts that he might someday write a biography of Masters. Following his navy time he completed doctoral coursework and a 1952 dissertation on Masters, after which he turned to the biography. Unfortunately, Ellen, too, was ambivalent about Flaccus serving as her husband's biographer, although she sometimes encouraged him in his work ("you are the best equipped") and wanted him present at certain functions, such as the Petersburg Post Office's issue of the Masters stamp ("I expect you to be there"). Nevertheless, she refused to name him as the authorized biographer and steadfastly refused to let him quote information or see letters in her possession. These impediments notwithstanding, Flaccus worked intermittently on his biography from the early 1940s through the early 1970s. He had developed plans for a two-volume work by the time Ellen transferred her husband's papers to the University of Texas at Austin. (She apparently did this without informing Flaccus.) "My position," she once told him, "is that of doing for my husband to the best of my ability." He chose to interpret that as meaning a biography; she in turn was always half-afraid of what such a book might reveal. (She twice tried to gain access to Alice Davis's materials at the New York Public Library, but Davis had the materials sealed until after she and Masters had died.) Ellen no doubt wanted Flaccus to write a "critical" biography, one that would focus on Masters's books and touch only lightly on the man, instead of a "straight" biography, that is, one that would focus on his life. In any event, Flaccus and Ellen constituted one of American literature's stranger "odd couples" for more than twenty years as he jockeyed to gain her goodwill and she just as consistently denied him. Flaccus died in 1972, his book incomplete.[20]

Ellen Masters continued with her teaching career after her husband died, spending several of her retirement years in the borough of State College, Pennsylvania. She kept a tight rein on biographical information but cooperated with scholars who focused on Masters's creative works. She died just short of her ninety-eighth birthday in 1997, having outlived her husband by nearly half a century. Hilary placed her ashes next to his father's stone in Petersburg's Oakland Cemetery and on her mother's grave in Washington, D.C.

One of the projects that Ellen approved during her later years was completed during the 1970s when the scholar Frank Robinson combined some of the poems from Masters's last manuscript ("Far Horizons") with others to form a volume called *The Harmony of Deeper Music: Posthumous Poems of Edgar Lee Masters.* Some of the best poems give voice to Masters's lifelong search for love and beauty, as does "I Have So Loved This Earth":

> Unconsciousness alone will save
> My heart from heartache in the grave—
> I have so loved this earth, I must

Be nothing but insensate dust
Not to be tortured when Cherryplain
Grows red and green with April rain,
And when the hills of Harlemville
Echo bird voices, when the shrill
Cry of the jay is in the pines,
And when the sun at dawning shines;
When summer clouds are white and high,
When waste gold streaks the evening sky.

* * *

If I must give them up 't will be
Painless, if without memory.
To prize a beauty, find a worth
I missed in life were agony—
I have so loved this wonder earth.

But what if in grave-dreams should come
Beautiful things your eyes ignored,
Something for which your lips were dumb?
What if you lay and ached with love
For earth you had not loved enough,
Or ached for eyes, or for a breast
To which your heart had half confessed,
Because of flesh that could not speak
Full utterance—how the flesh is weak,
Doomed to inadequate words, mistrust,
Then doomed to darkness, silence, dust![21]

Other poems show an acceptance of the human condition, as is illustrated in this excerpt concerning three elderly men:

They are wise, but their wisdom is unavailing;
They know their state, and they remember
What life was, and what it is in their December.

* * *

They are not terrified but calm,
Quiet of desire and will;
Epithalamium and psalm
Take their reflection as a water still
With ice, and what they failed to live,
Or lived, has now no qualm.

Yet other poems reflect Masters's long-term interest in Grecian culture, which still held his heart at the end:

> The leaves whisper finalities,
> The grass gestures, asking what is loss?
> The clouds sum mortalities,
> The mountains look afar, over the Atlantic deep.
> They say a poet is asleep
> At Skyros.

The pity of such poems—written during the 1920s, 1930s, and 1940s—is that most or all remained unpublished during Masters's life, affirming once more that what he needed most during his post–*Spoon River* career was a competent editor whose judgment he trusted.[22]

In 1988 Ellen had passed power of attorney to Hilary, and it was left to him to decide whether to make public his father's personal papers and writings, such as diaries. Hilary Masters worked as a newsman, press agent, and political aide in Robert Kennedy's presidential campaign before deciding on a career as a writer. He subsequently taught creative writing at several universities, was a Fulbright lecturer on American literature in Finland, and served as the chair of the creative writing unit of Carnegie Mellon University. He published eight novels, two collections of stories, a book of essays, and a family biography and saw his work published in some of the finest outlets in the country, in addition to winning various writing awards. One of his short stories, "Ohm's Law," dealt with the question of how to handle the papers of a famous father. His family biography, *Last Stands: Notes from Memory,* put into artistic order a part of his life and the lives of his parents and maternal grandparents. In 1990 he decided it was time for a biography.[23]

Hilary Masters's decision was the immediate occasion for this biography, along with the biographer's fascination with Masters and his many books. Edgar Lee Masters caught the essence of the American village better than anyone else did, and few authors have suffered such a long literary decline after such remarkable success. In the end Masters was the victim of his one enduring achievement, *Spoon River Anthology:* no matter what he published after it, he could never produce a rival to it, and so each ensuing volume represented a decline. *Spoon River Anthology* made him famous, but it also contributed to some of the sadness in his life and is (to borrow from it) his "true epitaph, more lasting than stone."[24]

APPENDIX: A CHRONOLOGICAL LIST OF MASTERS'S BOOKS AND PAMPHLETS

BOOKS

A Book of Verses (Chicago: Way and Williams, 1898).
Maximilian: A Play in Five Acts (Boston: Richard G. Badger, 1902).
The New Star Chamber and Other Essays (Chicago: Hammersmark, 1904).
[Dexter Wallace,] *The Blood of the Prophets* (Chicago: Rooks, 1905).
Althea: A Play in Four Acts (Chicago: Rooks, 1907).
The Trifler: A Play (Chicago: Rooks, 1908).
The Leaves of the Tree: A Play (Chicago: Rooks, 1909).
Eileen: A Play in Three Acts (Chicago: Rooks, 1910).
[Webster Ford,] *Songs and Sonnets* (Chicago: Rooks, 1910).
The Locket: A Play in Three Acts (Chicago: Rooks, 1910).
The Bread of Idleness: A Play in Four Acts (Chicago: Rooks, 1911).
[Webster Ford,] *Songs and Sonnets: Second Series* (Chicago: Rooks, 1912).
Spoon River Anthology (New York: Macmillan, 1915; augmented ed., 1916).
Songs and Satires (New York: Macmillan, 1916).
The Great Valley (New York: Macmillan, 1916).
Toward the Gulf (New York: Macmillan, 1918).
Starved Rock (New York: Macmillan, 1919).
Mitch Miller (New York: Macmillan, 1920).
Domesday Book (New York: Macmillan, 1920).
The Open Sea (New York: Macmillan, 1921).
Children of the Market Place (New York: Macmillan, 1922).
Skeeters Kirby (New York: Macmillan, 1923).
The Nuptial Flight (New York: Boni and Liveright, 1923).
Mirage (New York: Boni and Liveright, 1924).
The New Spoon River (New York: Boni and Liveright, 1924).
Selected Poems (New York: Macmillan, 1925).
Lee: A Dramatic Poem (New York: Macmillan, 1926).
Kit O'Brien ([New York]: Boni and Liveright, 1927).
Levy Mayer and the New Industrial Era (New Haven, Conn.: "under direction of Yale University Press," 1927).
Jack Kelso: A Dramatic Poem (New York: D. Appleton, 1928).

The Fate of the Jury: An Epilogue to Domesday Book (New York: D. Appleton, 1929).
Gettysburg, Manila, Ácoma (New York: Horace Liveright, 1930).
Lichee Nuts (New York: Horace Liveright, 1930).
Lincoln: The Man (New York: Dodd, Mead, 1931).
Godbey: A Dramatic Poem (New York: Dodd, Mead, 1931).
The Serpent in the Wilderness (New York: Sheldon Dick, 1933).
The Tale of Chicago (New York: Putnam's, 1933).
Dramatic Duologues: Four Short Plays in Verse (New York: Samuel French, 1934).
Richmond: A Dramatic Poem (New York: Samuel French, 1934).
Invisible Landscapes (New York: Macmillan, 1935).
Vachel Lindsay: A Poet in America (New York: Scribner's, 1935).
Poems of People (New York: Appleton-Century, 1936).
The Golden Fleece of California (Weston, Vt.: Countryman, 1936).
Across Spoon River: An Autobiography (New York: Farrar and Rinehart, 1936).
Whitman (New York: Scribner's, 1937).
The Tide of Time (New York: Farrar and Rinehart, 1937).
The New World (New York: Appleton-Century, 1937).
Mark Twain: A Portrait (New York: Scribner's, 1938).
More People (New York: Appleton-Century, 1939).
The Living Thoughts of Emerson, selected and with an introduction (New York: Longmans, Green, 1940).
Illinois Poems (Prairie City, Ill.: James A. Decker, 1941).
The Sangamon (New York: Farrar and Rinehart, 1942).
Along the Illinois (Prairie City, Ill.: James A. Decker, 1942).
The Harmony of Deeper Music: Posthumous Poems of Edgar Lee Masters, selected and edited and with an introduction by Frank K. Robinson (Austin: Humanities Research Center, University of Texas, 1976).

PAMPHLETS

Bimetallism ([Lewistown, Ill.]: Lewistown News, [1896]).
The Constitution and Our Insular Possessions (N.p. [Chicago?], n.d. [1900?]).
Samson and Delilah (N.p. [Chicago?], n.d. [1903?]). No copy located.
United States ex rel. John Turner vs. William Williams, Commissioner of Immigration (N.p. [Chicago?], n.d. [1904?]). No copy located; possible copies extant as *United States versus John Turner* (Chicago: Gunthorp-Warren, 1904).
The New Star Chamber (New York: Committee of Forty-Eight, n.d. [1904?]).
Browning as a Philosopher (N.p. [Chicago?], n.d. [1912?]).
[Lucius Atherton,] *The Story of the Good Little Girl and the Bad Little Girl* (N.p., 1923).
The Seven Cities of America ([Cleveland]: John Huntington Polytechnic Institute, 1934).
Hymn to the Unknown God (Brown City, Mich.: New Age Ministry of Religious Research, n.d. [1937?]).
The Triumph of Earth (N.p., April 18, 1940).

NOTES

A GUIDE TO CITATIONS AND ABBREVIATIONS

Masters and His Books

ELM	Edgar Lee Masters
ASR	*Across Spoon River: An Autobiography*
SRA	*Spoon River Anthology*

Libraries and Repositories

American Academy of Arts and Letters	American Academy of Arts and Letters, New York City
Amherst	Amherst College Library
Arkansas	University of Arkansas Libraries, Fayetteville
Berkeley	Bancroft Library, University of California, Berkeley
Bobst Library	Bobst Library, New York University, New York City
Brown University	John Hay Library, Brown University
Chicago	Regenstein Library, University of Chicago
Cornell	Olin Library, Cornell University
Dartmouth	Dartmouth College Library
Denison Library	Denison Library, Claremont College, Claremont, California
Federal Bureau of Investigation	Federal Bureau of Investigation, Washington, D.C.
Georgetown	Lauinger Library, Georgetown University
Harvard	Houghton Library, Harvard University
Hoover Institution on War, Revolution and Peace	Hoover Institution on War, Revolution and Peace, Stanford, California
HRC	Harry Ransom Humanities Research Center, University of Texas at Austin
Illinois College	Schewe Library, Illinois College, Jacksonville

Illinois State Historical Library	Illinois State Historical Library, Springfield
Iowa	University of Iowa Libraries, Iowa City
Kentucky	King Library, University of Kentucky, Lexington
Knox College	Seymour Library, Knox College, Galesburg, Illinois
Library of Congress	Library of Congress, Washington, D.C.
Lilly Library	Lilly Library, Indiana University, Bloomington
Masters Museum	Masters Museum, Petersburg, Illinois
Michigan	University of Michigan Libraries, Ann Arbor
Middlebury College	Starr Library, Middlebury College, Middlebury, Vermont
Minnesota	Walter Library, University of Minnesota, Minneapolis
Newberry	Newberry Library, Chicago
NY Public	New York Public Library, New York City
Pennsylvania State University	University Libraries, Pennsylvania State University, University Park
Princeton	Princeton University Libraries
Rochester	Rhees Library, University of Rochester
Southern California	University Library, University of Southern California, Los Angeles
Southern Illinois University	Morris Library, Southern Illinois University, Carbondale
Stanford	Stanford University Libraries
State Historical Society of Wisconsin	State Historical Society of Wisconsin, Madison
SUNY Buffalo	University Libraries, State University of New York at Buffalo
UCLA	University Research Library, University of California at Los Angeles
University of Pennsylvania	Van Pelt Library, University of Pennsylvania, Philadelphia
Virginia	University of Virginia Library, Charlottesville
Wellesley	Clapp Library, Wellesley College
Western Illinois University	University Library, Western Illinois University, Macomb
Williams College	Chapin Library, Williams College, Williamstown, Massachusetts
Yale	Beinecke Library, Yale University

Manuscripts and Files

"ELM: MSR"	"Edgar Lee Masters: Man of Spoon River," unpublished life study by Kimball Flaccus (1911–1972), Dartmouth College
"Flaccus file"	Numbered research files of Kimball Flaccus, HRC
"My Youth in the Spoon River Country"	early draft of *ASR*, HRC
"Unpub. chapter"	Unpublished chapter of *ASR*, HRC

Diaries

1884–1891	Housed at the HRC
1906–1943	Property of Hilary Masters

INTRODUCTION

1. Percy Boynton, *Some Contemporary Americans* (Chicago: University of Chicago Press, 1924), 52 ("the most read").

2. "Bitter Poet on Sad Poet," *Time*, October 7, 1935, p. 67 (80,000 copies); Mrs. Sylvia F. Frank, Customer Service Department, Macmillan Publishing Company, Inc., to Herbert Russell, March 8, 1977 (never out of print); translations are discussed in Frank K. Robinson, *Edgar Lee Masters: An Exhibition in Commemoration of the Centenary of His Birth* (Austin: University of Texas, 1970), 15; Rumanian, Serbo-Croatian, and Slovak translations are at HRC; Herb Russell, "Imitations of *Spoon River:* An Overview," *Western Illinois Regional Studies* 2 (Fall 1979): 173–82.

3. Louis Untermeyer, *American Poetry since 1900* (New York: Henry Holt, 1923), 123.

4. ELM, *ASR*, 396.

5. ELM to Gerald Sanders, April 26, 1935 ("no decent sketch"), HRC; ELM to [David] Karsner, October 15, 1926 ("I am"), HRC; Diary 1924, September 18 (wants to revise interview).

6. Herbert Russell, "Edgar Lee Masters' Final Years in the Midwest," *Essays in Literature* (Macomb) 4 (Fall 1977): 212–20.

7. John T. Flanagan, *Edgar Lee Masters: The Spoon River Poet and His Critics* (Metuchen, N.J.: Scarecrow, 1974), 8.

8. See articles by Charles E. Burgess concerning Masters's paternal ancestry: "Some Family Source Material for *Spoon River Anthology,*" *Western Illinois Regional Studies* 13 (Spring 1990): 80–89; "Edgar Lee Masters' Paternal Ancestry: A Pioneer Heritage and Influence," *Western Illinois Regional Studies* 7 (Spring 1984): 32–60; "Ancestral Lore in *Spoon River Anthology:* Fact and Fancy," *Papers on Language and Literature* 20 (Spring 1984): 185–204; "*Spoon River:* Politics and Poetry," *Papers on Language and Literature* 23 (Summer 1987): 347–63; and "Maryland-Carolina Ancestry of Edgar Lee Masters," *Great Lakes Review* 8–9 (Fall 1982–Spring 1983): 51–80. For Masters's maternal ancestry, see Kimball Flaccus, *The Vermont Background of Edgar Lee Masters* (New York: Vermont Historical Society, 1955). For cameos of Masters's later years, see Gertrude Claytor, "Edgar Lee Masters in the Chelsea Years," *Princeton University Library Chronicle* 14 (Autumn 1952): 1–29; August Derleth, *Three Literary Men: A Memoir of Sinclair Lewis, Sherwood Anderson, Edgar Lee Masters* (New York: Candlelight, 1963), 37–56; Hardin W. Masters, *Edgar Lee Masters: A Centenary Memoir-Anthology* (South Brunswick, N.J.: A. S. Barnes, 1972); Hardin Wallace Masters, *Edgar Lee Masters: A Biographical Sketchbook about a Famous American Author* (Rutherford, N.J.: Farleigh Dickinson University Press, 1978); Hilary Masters, *Last Stands: Notes from Memory* (Boston: David R. Godine, 1982); John H. Wrenn and Margaret Wrenn, *Edgar Lee Masters* (Boston: Twayne, 1983).

9. *ASR*, 383 ($27,000), 393 ("haven"), 381 ("I decided"), 394, (September 13).

10. Ibid., 406 ("I have written"); Claytor, "Masters in the Chelsea Years," 5 ("Most biographies").

11. Masters's claim in his autobiography that he was born "on August 23, 1869," is contradicted not only by the 1910–11 *Who's Who in America* (Chicago: Marquis, 1910), 1283, but also by his death certificate on file in the Pennsylvania Department of Health, Bureau of Vital Statistics, which shows his date of birth as "8-23-1868." The date of August 23, 1868, is also reported in two of the Masters family Bibles, those of his father, Hardin, and grandfather, Squire Davis Masters, with the pertinent handwriting in both Bibles reportedly being that of Masters's mother, Emma; see Burgess, "Some Family Source Material," 89. Masters's uncle, Wilbur Masters, noted, "Our family record Bible" showed "Edgar Lee born Aug 23 1868"; see Wilbur Masters to "Dear Gig" [ELM], September 4, 1949, HRC. Masters also told his first father-in-law, Robert E. Jenkins, that he was born August 23, 1868, and Jenkins used the information in his *Jenkins Family Book* ([Chicago,] 1904), 63, 185, 186. The birth year of 1868

also appears on Masters's tombstone in Petersburg, Illinois, and his second wife, Ellen, also affirmed 1868 as the correct date; Masters's passport (in the possession of his son Hilary) also shows 1868. In addition, Masters himself used the 1868 date in an early draft of his autobiography: "I came into the world early on Sunday morning, August 23, 1868, and was named for Gen. Robert E. Lee, for whom my father had the greatest admiration"; see page 1 of an *ASR* draft of 313 pages, dated November 4, 1927, on page 305, HRC. The frequently reported but erroneous date of 1869 was printed by a biographical dictionary, and Masters let the error stand because he did not mind being thought of as a year younger; see William Kimball Flaccus, "Edgar Lee Masters: A Biographical and Critical Study" (Ph.D. diss., New York University, 1952), 63. Finally, not even the previously cited *Who's Who* entry is perfect: it incorrectly shows the month of Masters's birth as April. *ASR*, 395 ("as it turned out"); correct details about ELM's Michigan place are in the unpublished chapters omitted from *ASR*, HRC, and in following chapters of the present volume.

12. For Masters's use of diaries in composing his autobiography, see *ASR*, 400–402.

13. See *ASR*, 400, where Masters mentions a diary dating from his "fifteenth year"; the earliest boyhood diary at the HRC is from 1884. Information concerning diaries used in this study comes from the diaries themselves and from Masters's son Hilary.

14. Masters to Tietjens, May 7, 1922 ("poetry killed" law), Newberry; *ASR*, 377 ("law business"); unpub. chapter 20, pp. 415–16 (Masters's three children from his first marriage drifting away from him), HRC; Diary 1919, February 14 (dinner with children).

15. *ASR* (details of Masters's life); ELM, *Skeeters Kirby* (New York: Macmillan, 1923), 97 (too weak to work and go to college).

16. See chapters 1–3 of the present volume.

17. See chapters 7–10 of the present volume.

18. See chapter 11 of the present volume.

19. Hilary Masters to Herb Russell, December 31, 1992 (writer of poetry or a famous poet).

20. See chapter 12 and following chapters of the present volume.

21. Hilary Masters to Herb Russell, conversation, June 19, 1997 ("Sad"); Marcia Cavell to Herb Russell, May 6, 1994 ("One pities him"); "Edgar Lee Masters, Famed Poet, Convalescing Near City Line," unid. news clipping (malnutrition and pneumonia), Virginia.

22. ELM to John [Hall Wheelock], March 2, 1944 ("fine understandings"), Princeton; unpub. chapter 24, p. 481 ("It is pertinent"), HRC.

23. ELM to Alfred Kreymborg, October 6, 1921 ("particular and expert"), Princeton; ELM to George Brett, August 1, 1921 ("I punctuate"), HRC; ELM to Rinehart, August 6, 1936 ("I appreciate"), HRC; ELM to Gerald Sanders, February 24, 1942 ("Do you realize"), HRC.

CHAPTER 1: ROAD TO SPOON RIVER

1. *ASR*, 34 (sports and dances), 8 (horses, education, businesses), 9 (meets wife); Illinois College Office of the President to ELM, September 3, 1926 (preparatory work at Illinois College), HRC; ELM handwriting on reverse of picture P217 (Hardin engaged to Kate Gardner before meeting Emma), photo archives, HRC; R. W. Cowden to ELM, November 4, 1935 (no record of Hardin at Ann Arbor), Michigan; Charles E. Burgess, "Some Family Source Material for *Spoon River Anthology*," *Western Illinois Regional Studies* 13 (Spring 1990): 87 (birth and death dates of Hardin and Emma Masters); ELM, "My Youth in the Spoon River Country," 22–23 (Hardin's early vocations, law), HRC; "ELM: MSR," ch. 1, p. 14 (McNeely), Dartmouth.

2. ELM to Robert Morss Lovett, January 29, 1930 ("about sixteen"), HRC; Emma's marriage book, *Bridal Greetings* (marriage date of September 10, 1867), HRC; *ASR*, 10 ("temper"),

36 (Emma's background), 61–62 (Emma's qualities and meeting with Hardin), 11–13, 21–27 (housing and Hardin's work); Charles E. Burgess, "The Use of Local Lore in *Spoon River Anthology*" (M.A. thesis, Southern Illinois University, 1969), 11 (meet in Petersburg); Burgess, "Some Family Source Material," 87 (September 10 marriage date, ages at marriage); "ELM: MSR," ch. 1, pp. 14–15 (marriage might have taken place on August 10, 1867), ch. 1, p. 15 (stayed with Hardin's parents until May 1868), ch. 1, p. 18 (Abram Bergen), ch. 2, p. 3 (log cabin), Dartmouth; ELM, "My Youth," 21–22 (Hardin and Civil War, "releasing from jail"), HRC.

3. *ASR,* 11 (hatred of Midwest), 62 (housekeeping skills); ELM, "My Youth," 45 ("When she was happy"), HRC.

4. *ASR,* 10 ("Her will was unconquerable," Methodists), 55 (New Hampshire); Emma Masters to ELM, April 14, 1926 (Emma unforgiving as young wife), April 19, 1925 (Vermont influence), both HRC.

5. *ASR,* 21 (state's attorney), 27 (help from father), 29 ("away much"), 34 ("much away," "out late," "revels"); Hardin Wallace Masters, *Edgar Lee Masters: A Biographical Sketchbook about a Famous American Author* (Rutherford, N.J.: Farleigh Dickinson University Press, 1978), 99 (play-boy); "Edgar Lee Masters' Impressive Tribute to Father Read Today at Funeral of Veteran Lawyer," [Springfield] *Illinois State Register,* November 16, 1925, pp. 1, 8 ("play-boy"); *Funeral Service . . . for the Late Hardin Wallace Masters* ([Springfield]: Illinois State Register, 1925) (pamphlet regarding Hardin's funeral, Knox College); Emma Masters to Madeline Masters, November 27, 1925 (Hardin's "waywardness"), HRC; Burgess, "Some Family Source Material," 89 (Hardin's extramarital affairs), 87 (Madeline Masters's year of birth as 1870); Madeline Masters's tombstone (birth date of 1875); Burgess, "Some Family Source Material," 87 (Masters family Bible of Squire Davis Masters shows 1870); *ASR,* 26 (Madeline born before their brother Alexander [b. 1873]); Ellen Masters to Kimball Flaccus, May 3, 1970 (Madeline born 1870), HRC; information on the births of Masters's brothers is from Burgess, "Some Family Source Material," 87; Thomas Davis Masters's tombstone (birth date of 1878); Diary 1884, December 5 and 26 ("Mat"), genealogy notes ("Mattie").

6. *ASR,* 4 (devout, land holdings), 15, 33, 58 (farm's appearance), 6 (death), 5 ("He never," Irving), 4, 44 (Virginia, Tennessee); ELM, *The Sangamon* (Urbana: University of Illinois Press, 1988), intro. Charles E. Burgess, 142 ("Cartwright"), 29 (animals bred); plat books in the County Clerk's Office, Menard County (information on Squire Masters's real estate holdings); ELM, "Days in the Lincoln Country," *Journal of the Illinois State Historical Society* 18 (Jan. 1926): 785 (acreage); papers filed with the will of Squire D. Masters, County Clerk's Office, Menard County (total value of chattel goods at death in 1904 was $80).

7. Burgess, "Some Family Source Material," 82 (eight children, Lucinda dies at 95); *ASR,* 3, 8 (Lucinda), 6, 7 ("a wonderful"), 8, 33 ("What a"), 41 ("Often I went"), 15 ("There was such"); *ASR* draft dated November 4, 1927, p. 4 (New England grandparents "never visited"), HRC; ELM to Mr. Baldwin, May 10, 1924 ("My grandmother"), HRC.

8. *ASR,* 3–4; ELM, "My Youth," 51 ("farmer"), HRC; Charles E. Burgess, "Maryland-Carolina Ancestry of Edgar Lee Masters," *Great Lakes Review* 8–9 (Fall 1982–Spring 1983): 51–80 (revised paternal ancestry and related details).

9. Herbert K. Russell, *The Enduring River: Edgar Lee Masters' Uncollected Spoon River Poems* (Carbondale: Southern Illinois University Press, 1991), 14 (Petersburg area place names and locations); ELM, "My Youth," 57 (Rock), HRC; ELM, *The Sangamon,* 71 (Estill Hill); "ELM: MSR," ch. 2, p. 21 (Shipley's Hill Cemetery), Dartmouth.

10. Russell, *The Enduring River,* 15, 25 (Petersburg); *ASR,* 23, 24, 44 (Petersburg); ELM to Frank [W. Allan], August 13, 1937 (the Hill Gang), HRC; Hardin Masters to ELM, September 16, 1925 (brewery, saloons, tailors, coal mines, bootmakers, 3,000 people), HRC; ELM, *The Sangamon,* 65 (circus), 168–69 (New Salem); ELM, "My Youth," 30 (flour, wool, and tile busi-

nesses), HRC; Charles E. Burgess, "Sandridge: A Masters Landscape Revisited," *Western Illinois Regional Studies* 14 (Fall 1991): 7 (map of Petersburg).

11. *ASR,* 25–29 (river, brother Alex), 26 ("a boy as beautiful"); ELM to Mr. Hansen, July 20, 1926 ("about ten," "pool," "had sunk," "You were clean"), HRC; ELM, *The Sangamon,* 72–73 (near drowning).

12. *ASR,* 25–31 (illnesses, "Lee," Mitch, lightning); ELM to Dan [Henderson], September 30, 1945 (not knocked down by lightning but shocked while digging with a spade under a tree during a drizzle), HRC; ELM to Christian [Gauss], February 27, 1937 (kicked), HRC; Emma Masters to Madeline [Stone], November 30, 1925 (nursed grievance), HRC.

13. *ASR,* 31–32 (storms, feather bed, grandfather's place safe); ELM, "My Youth," 50½ (Queen), HRC; "ELM: MSR," ch. 2, p. 10 (Gyp), Dartmouth; ELM to Mrs. Harmon Marbold, July 20, 1942 (storm, "Depths," coughing), HRC.

14. ELM, "My Youth," 76 ("My grandmother"), 78 (religious activities, "I would bend my head"), HRC; ELM, *The Sangamon,* 134–35 (Old Concord).

15. Wilburne Masters's Petersburg tombstone (age and spelling of name); ELM, "My Youth," 80½ ("famous fiddler," "Perhaps the next night," "Arkansas Traveler," hunter-gatherer, duck hunting, fishing, pecans), 80½A ("Paddy"), HRC.

16. ELM, "My Youth," 80½B ("scudding," Mother Goose), HRC; Wilbur Masters to ELM, n.d. (horse racing, camping, swimming), September 23, 1945 (existence of mules), December 17, 1943 (Old Pepperdog and Molly), September 19, 1931, May 21, 1932, March 1, 2, and 10, 1947 ("Giggle"; many other letters begin "Dear Gig"), all HRC; *ASR,* 58 (kite).

17. *ASR,* 26 ("nothing but loathing"), 39 ("particle of charm"), 40 (German school, "school order"); "ELM: MSR," ch. 2, p. 7 (apple), ch. 2, p. 20 ("They opened"), Dartmouth; Kimball Flaccus, "Notes on Edgar Lee Masters," June 12, 1942, Flaccus file 24 (McDougal), HRC; "ELM: MSR," ch. 2, p. 10 (shows "McDougall"), Dartmouth.

18. *ASR,* 4 (loved Burns's poetry), 17 ("the Dark Ages"), 19, 29, 34, 36, 38, 41, 44, 60 ("few books"); ELM, "My Youth," 46 (mother read Burns), HRC.

19. ELM, "My Youth," 48 (Hardin's enemies, pistol), HRC; *ASR,* 46–48, 53 ("It was July").

20. *ASR,* 47–48, 54–55, 56 ("and prevented"), 57, 61, 65, 68–69, 81–82; ELM to [Dean] McCumber, March 11, 1936 (five houses), Masters Museum.

21. *ASR,* 54 (shadeless lot), 55 (visits mother); "ELM: MSR," ch. 2, p. 12 (Emma's social activities in Petersburg), ch. 3, p. 7 (Emma refuses to sign bill of sale), Dartmouth.

22. "ELM: MSR," ch. 1, pp. 7–11 (Dexter family history), Dartmouth.

23. ELM to Mr. Mamer, February 7, 1927 ("I spent happy days"), HRC; ELM to "Frank," March 29, 1939 (boxing, parallel bars), HRC; ELM, "My Youth," 96 (Walker), 98 (baseball, wrestling, running), HRC; "ELM: MSR," ch. 3, p. 8 (ice skating, roller skating), ch. 3, p. 16 (sewing), Dartmouth; Diary 1885, March 22 (blood poisoning); *ASR,* 74 ("real labor"), 63.

24. *ASR,* 67–69, 80–82, 129–30; ELM, *The Sangamon,* 207 (Hardin works without compensation); "ELM: MSR," ch. 3, p. 30 (cites 1888 as the year pivotal to Hardin's fortunes in the law), Dartmouth; [Edwin P. Reese,] unid. ms. regarding ELM, misc. file, 45 (sketch of Hardin's womanizing), HRC; Howard Wilson, "Trip to Lewistown," unpub. ms., October 18, 1983 (Hardin and venereal disease), Knox College; "ELM: MSR," ch. 9, p. 24 (horse racing and gambling), Dartmouth; Mrs. Charles MacDowell to Kimball Flaccus, September 30, 1955 (Hardin drank often), Georgetown; Kimball Flaccus to George Proctor, February 1, 1955 (Presbyterian Church fashionable), Georgetown; Charles E. Burgess, "*Spoon River:* Politics and Poetry," *Papers on Language and Literature* 23 (Summer 1987): 354 (Emma joins church).

25. ELM to Edwin Reese, December 19, 1931 ("Christmas"), HRC; Diary 1884, December 26 ("Christmas morning"), November 30 (Thanksgiving feast); Earnest Elmo Calkins, *They Broke the Prairie* (New York: Scribner's, 1937), 88 (New England Christians).

26. *ASR*, 86 ("I made"); ELM to Mother, August 18, 1910 ("indifferent"), Knox College.

27. ELM, "My Youth," 101 ("It was"), HRC; *ASR*, 48, 70–71 ("first verses," "I set them"); ELM to Gerald Sanders, October 26, 1935 ("The Minotaur"), April 19, 1935 ("My first printed"), June 3, 1935 (Grant Hyde), all HRC; Flaccus, "Notes on Edgar Lee Masters," June 12, 1942, Flaccus file 24 (thirty-forty copies), HRC.

28. ELM to Lowell, December 20, 1916 ("music"), Harvard; ELM to Lewis Chase, July 16, 1917 ("I began to write verses"), Library of Congress; *ASR*, 59 (Mary Fisher), 60 ("Byronic despair," "All this was"), 66, 74, 77; "ELM: MSR," ch. 3, p. 8 (Sparks), ch. 4, p. 3 (Tennyson book), Dartmouth; ELM to Mr. Gimbel, January 18, 1934 (Poe), HRC; ELM, Commonplace Book and Diary 1889–90 (Crabbe quotation), HRC; Diary 1885, March 22 (Adam Casebolt); ELM to [Clarence] Decker, November 28, 1936 (Greeks and Romans), Dartmouth; ELM, *Skeeters Kirby*, 70 (highly autobiographical novel whose character "Will Morley" affects a Byronic mien); George Proctor to Kimball Flaccus, June 23, 1955 (Will Worley was model for Morley), Georgetown.

29. ELM to Miss Tankersley, May 12, 1926 ("I began to write"), HRC; *ASR*, 41–43.

30. *ASR*, 59, 69 ("a riot"), 69–70 ("Boys arose"), 70 ("the time was past"), 71 ("casual," "intermittent," "interrupted," "When I was taking"), 72 ("pandemonium"); ms. attributed to E. P. Reese, n.d., n.p. (Masters expelled), Illinois State Historical Library; Diary 1884, November 23 (Miss Fisher gone), December 19 ("We stomped," "laughed at"); graduation program, Flaccus file 1886 (class of four, Hardin speaks, "A Tribute . . . "), HRC; report card, Lewistown Public Schools, for term beginning December 10, 1883, misc. file D–I (absences), HRC.

31. *ASR*, 66–67 ("She kept up"), 70 ("I was reading").

32. Ibid., 74 (son of physician); "ELM: MSR," ch. 3, p. 15 (tipples), ch. 3, p. 28 (social column and other writing), Dartmouth; "Spoon River Poet Called Great," *New York Times* (magazine section), April 4, 1915, p. 7 (Chicago and St. Louis papers).

33. *ASR*, 76, 81, 84–85, 99–101; ELM, "My Youth," 134 ("stories"), HRC; "ELM: MSR," ch. 3, p. 18 (Judge Winter), ch. 4, p. 2 (Scientific Association meets monthly, fifteen to twenty members, 1887 membership), ch. 4, p. 7 (science and religion), Dartmouth; Flaccus file 1888 (clairvoyance), HRC; ELM to Kimball Flaccus, October 21, 1941, Flaccus file 1885 (Whitman paper, met monthly), HRC.

34. *ASR*, 76–77 ("My grandmother," "to more").

35. ELM, "My Youth," 139 ("engagement" to Margaret George), HRC; "ELM: MSR," ch. 4, p. 10 (townspeople expect ELM to marry Margaret), ch. 4, p. 9, and ch. 5, p. 1 (Greek), Dartmouth (Masters's Greek lessons were very limited, for he later said he had "no start" in Greek until he got to Knox College; see *ASR*, 110); *ASR*, 89 (Wordsworth, George Eliot), 90 (reads with Margaret, Big Creek), 100 ("friendship," Marlowe, Webster, Latin); George Proctor to Kimball Flaccus, April 12, 1955 (information on Winnogene Eichelberger), March 31, 1956 (Winnogene Eichelberger was "Alfreda" in *ASR*), May 18, 1956 ("Winks" spelled as "Winx"), all Georgetown; Kimball Flaccus to George Proctor, May 11, 1956 (Winnogene Eichelberger was "Alfreda"), Georgetown; Diary 1889, April 10, [April 12] ("Winks," "Winks" as "Winnie").

36. *ASR*, 100 (Eugene Field, "I had about"); Diary 1889, April 30 (Chautauqua); ELM, "My Youth," 134 ("mostly under"), HRC; Gerald Sanders to ELM, May 8, 1938 (sixty-plus poems in *Inter-Ocean*), HRC; Parlin Public Library, Canton, Illinois, to Gerald Sanders, March 25, 1936 (Bilge), HRC; undated list by Ellen Masters with Gerald Sanders papers (pseudonyms—"Aronkeil" spelled "Aaronkeil"), HRC; ELM, *Spoon River Anthology: An Annotated Edition*, ed. John E. Hallwas (Urbana: University of Illinois, 1992), n.p., picture caption (Brown); "Lorens Ahrenkeil Dead," *Petersburg Observer*, June 18, 1954, p. 1; "ELM: MSR," ch. 3, p. 21 (Brown and Proctor), Dartmouth.

37. ELM to Harriet [Monroe], September 2, 1924 ("It was a rough"), Chicago; Diary 1889, April 8 ("Arose at 7"); Diary 1891, May 4 ("Fame").

38. Editorial Offices, *The Atlantic Monthly,* to ELM, August 22, 1889 ("I return"), HRC; *The Writer* to ELM, October 22, 1889 ("Try to be"), HRC; *Waverly Magazine* to ELM, January 18, 1889 ("Why waste," "Give to literature"), HRC; ELM, "Learning to Write," *The Writer* 3 (Jan. 1889): 11 ("It is"), 13 ("I have"); "ELM: MSR," ch. 3, p. 29 (publishes two short stories in *Waverly*), Dartmouth.

39. "ELM: MSR," ch. 4, pp. 15–16 (breaks up with Margaret in summer 1889, lonely, writing for father, *News,* Canton paper, *Inter-Ocean,* nervous breakdown, travels with Ed Reese), Dartmouth; *ASR,* 113 (Louise); ELM to Widdle [Wilbur Masters], February 24, 1940 (information on Havana's May Heberling), letter property of Hilary Masters.

40. *ASR,* 109 ("mortification," "I could not"), 110 ("just across the street"), 115 ("atheist"), 116 ("everything was"), 117–20; Earnest Calkins to ELM, April 24, 1941 (poetry accepted and room location), HRC; Knox College President's Office to ELM, July 1, 1889 ("college building," "attainments"), HRC; W. E. Simonds to Hanno Hannibal, July 16, 1937 (Knox Academy), HRC; "ELM: MSR," ch. 5, p. 1 (Latin and Greek deficiencies), ch. 5, p. 3 ("Old Soph"), ch. 5, p. 11 (plays), ch. 5, p. 13 (poetry accepted), Dartmouth; Herman Muelder, "Edgar Lee Masters and Knox College," unpub. ms., 1975, pp. 18 (K.E.K.), 13 (E.O.D.), 7 (five buildings), 11 (middle preparatory school), Knox College; *Catalogue of Knox College* (Galesburg: Galesburg Printing and Publishing, 1890), 73 (E.O.D); *The Gale,* vol. 3 (Galesburg, Ill., 1890), 137 (the Knox yearbook describes ELM as "a mighty wonder"; the phrase is partially repeated in *ASR,* 118).

41. ELM, "My Youth," 140 ("all scribbling," "idling"), HRC; *ASR,* 89, 90, 113 (ELM "engaged"), 124 ("to relieve"), 208; Emma Masters to ELM, October 27, 1924 (whisky, "dig right into," "glamour of writing"), HRC; Illinois College Office of the President to ELM, September 3, 1926 (Hardin and "Preparatory Department"), HRC; Illinois College Registrar to Herb Russell, August 23, 1993 (Preparatory Department); Muelder, "Edgar Lee Masters and Knox College," 6 (costs of tuition, room, board), Knox College; ELM, "Edgar Lee Masters '89–90," in "Writings at Knox," unpub. document, n.d. (father hated college's conservatism), Knox College.

42. [E. P. Reese, memoir of college days], Flaccus file 1888, HRC.

43. Ibid., (parents doubt worth of college); ELM to Earnest Calkins, December 28, 1932, Flaccus file 1932 ("constriction," asks to be sent elsewhere), HRC; *ASR,* 112 ("My father looked," "and looked as if," no high school), 128 ("a hundred"), 127 (Madeline to Knox).

44. ELM, *Skeeters Kirby,* 97 ("in your state").

45. "ELM: MSR," ch. 5, p. 15 (book salesman), Dartmouth; *ASR,* 125 ("During the school hours"); E. W. Mureen, *A History of the Fulton County Narrow Gauge Railway: The Spoon River "Peavine,"* Bulletin 61A (Boston: Railway and Locomotive Historical Society, 1943), facing title page (map of railway).

46. "ELM: MSR," ch. 3, p. 18 (Will Winter), ch. 5, p. 19 (studies law with Will), Dartmouth; ELM, "My Youth," 152 (French, Italian, Greek), HRC; Diary 1891, May 4 (Italian, Knox nostalgia, "I never can"), May 5 (*News,* law with Will), May 7 (own writing), May 8 (Greeks), May 19 (law; many other similar entries for May 1891).

47. *ASR,* 129–32; ELM to Mary Kellam, December 21, 1925 (licensed in law in 1891), HRC; Diary 1891, May 23 (twenty-six passed); ELM to Dear Folks at Home, July 11, 1891 (Minneapolis work details and address), HRC; *Chicago Inter-Ocean* to ELM, June 26, 1891 (no jobs), HRC; ELM, "My Youth," 150–51 (Minneapolis work), HRC.

48. "ELM: MSR," ch. 5, p. 20 (Dyckes), ch. 5, pp. 20–21 (loses case), Dartmouth; Flaccus, "Notes on Edgar Lee Masters," October 22, 1941, Flaccus file 24 (second floor, *East Lynne, Uncle Tom's Cabin*), HRC; [Edwin P. Reese], unid. ms. regarding ELM, misc. file, 31–32 (ELM's law

activities with father), HRC; ELM to Rupert Hughes, January 31, 1939 ("incapable of systematic work"), HRC; *ASR*, 79 ("My father's office").

49. "ELM: MSR," ch. 5, pp. 22–23 (Emma's stories, window shade, domineering nature), Dartmouth; *ASR*, 134 ("to go to Chicago"), 133 ("ribbon clerk"); Diary 1891, May 23, ("If I were").

50. ELM, "Introduction to Chicago," *American Mercury* 31 (Jan. 1934): 49 (date ELM left Lewistown); ELM to Robert Morss Lovett, January 29, 1930 ("about 400 poems"), HRC; ELM, "A Peavine Railroad of the Spoon River Country," ms., n.d. ("it twisted"), HRC; *ASR*, 135–38 (twelve dollars, Havana).

51. *ASR*, 86 ("largely wasted").

52. Ibid., 81, 84, 85, 89, 120, 121, 160, 197; Flaccus, "Notes on Edgar Lee Masters," October 15, 1941, Flaccus file 24 (Plutarch), October 19, 1941, Flaccus file 24 (Tennyson), both HRC; "ELM: MSR," ch. 4, p. 4 (Homer Roberts taught in Fulton County), Dartmouth.

53. Flaccus, "Notes on Edgar Lee Masters," October 21, 1941, Flaccus file 24 (books read between 17 and 21), HRC.

54. Diary 1891, May 6 ("I look").

55. Ibid., June 4 ("I have been").

56. *ASR*, 139 ("to see").

CHAPTER 2: A DARK, POETIC HAMLET

1. Hilary Masters, *Last Stands: Notes from Memory* (Boston: Godine, 1982), 91 ("round-faced," "There were"); *ASR*, 136, 140.

2. Bernard Duffey, *The Chicago Renaissance in American Letters: A Critical History* ([East Lansing]: Michigan State College Press, 1954), 27 (people), 45 (money); Louis Untermeyer, ed., *Modern American Poetry* (New York: Harcourt, 1964), 3–4 (New England, old England).

3. Duffey, *The Chicago Renaissance*, 51–55, 66–69, 71–74.

4. *ASR*, 140–50 (uncle, newsman, nurse, attorney, millionaires), 146 ("Before us"); Flaccus file 1892 (Augustus Ladd), HRC; "ELM: MSR," ch. 6, p. 2 (Augustus Ladd), ch. 6, p. 3 (Busbey), Dartmouth.

5. *ASR*, 150, 151 ("galling"), 157, 163, 164, 166–67; ELM, "Tennyson," *Coup D'Etat* 12 (Nov. 1892): 29–30.

6. ELM to Van Vechten, February 7, 1898 (Kickham Scanlan), Princeton; ELM, "My Youth in the Spoon River Country," 158 (opens law office), 163 ("I was . . . writing verses"), HRC; *ASR*, 167 (fifty dollars, "pick up"), 168.

7. *ASR*, 168–69 (fair, Corbett), 217 (prostitutes, married woman), 193–94 (possible allusion to syphilis scare); Arthur Davison Ficke, "Notes on Edgar Lee Masters, 1938–39" ("most beautiful"), Yale; *ASR* draft dated September 17, 1934, pp. 115–16 (syphilis, "wanted to see"), HRC.

8. *ASR*, 87 ("an older girl," "explained the technique," "emotions became," "Wherever my idealism"), 88 (Zueline at eleven), 88–89 (learns to harden heart), 89 ("natural gratification"); Kimball Flaccus, "Notes on Edgar Lee Masters," June 6, 1942, Flaccus file 24 (Nettie, age seven), June 12, 1942, Flaccus file 24 (Cora), both HRC; George Proctor to Kimball Flaccus, December 8, 1953, June 23, 1955 (father broke up Lewistown relationship with Delia Proctor), Georgetown; "ELM: MSR," ch. 3, p. 20 (Zueline Wallace), Dartmouth; unpub. chapter (epilogue), 568 ("Few can"), HRC; ELM to Mencken, February 17, 1937 (serving maid), December 3, 1934 (graveyard), both NY Public.

9. Flaccus, "Notes on Edgar Lee Masters," July 3, 1942, Flaccus file 24 ("angling"), HRC; "ELM: MSR," ch. 7, p. 149 ("angling," 1895 marriage of Margaret, Margaret's death in 1897), Dartmouth; *ASR*, 193 ("one of the most"), 195–207.

10. *ASR*, 166–67 (name), 174 ("intercessor spirit," "Shelley"), 177; ELM, "Helen of Troy," *Coup D'Etat* (Feb. 1893): 25 (a rare instance of ELM signing his full name to a poem during early years), Knox College.

11. *ASR*, 183, 184 ("He read"); "ELM: MSR," ch. 7, p. 145 (Rachelle), Dartmouth.

12. ELM to Mrs. [Ernest] McGaffey, February 10, 1941 (1896 law partnership with McGaffey, "He lived"), HRC; Flaccus file 1896 (McGaffey with law firm for a year), HRC; Max Putzel, "Masters's 'Maltravers': Ernest McGaffey," *American Literature* 31 (Jan. 1960): 491–93; "ELM: MSR," ch. 6, p. 4 ("Petit" based on McGaffey), Dartmouth; *ASR*, 153 (Press Club, Opie Read).

13. *ASR*, 185 ("affinityship"), 207 ("get married"), 209 and 214 (1896, reference to 1896 political campaign), 214 ("you never," "It was"), 215, 223–24, 423 (various women); "ELM: MSR," ch. 7, p. 147 (Runyon), Dartmouth.

14. *ASR*, 161–62; ELM, "My Youth," 158 (wedding), 163 ("My winning it"), HRC.

15. ELM, "My Youth," 163–64, HRC.

16. ELM, "My Youth," 8–9 ("wonderful," "a large"), HRC.

17. *ASR*, 229 ("impressed by"), 230 ("I imagined"); Helen Masters, "Mrs. Edgar Lee Masters," typescript, April 10, 1950 (engagement date), HRC; Robert E. Jenkins, *Jenkins Family Book* ([Chicago:] 1904), 63 (Jenkins data).

18. "Edgar Lee Masters—Super Antagonist," *Boston Evening Transcript*, November 14, 1936, pt. 7, p. 1 ("He made").

19. ELM, "My Youth," 175 ("The lady did nothing"), HRC; *ASR*, 228–29, 230 ("I never"), 242 ("She really was").

20. *ASR*, 235–45; ELM to August [Derleth], October 25, 1943 ("If I had walked"), State Historical Society of Wisconsin.

21. *ASR*, 230 (all quotations).

22. Wedding announcement, Masters Papers (marriage details), Knox College; *ASR*, 246 ("like a man"), 247 ("everything I did"), 248, 253.

23. *ASR*, 261 (all quotations).

24. Helen Masters, "Mrs. Edgar Lee Masters" (the document focuses primarily on the period 1896–1915; some pages show duplicate information, and there are a few inserts by a third party), HRC.

25. ELM to Helen Jenkins, September 6, 1897 ("My dearest love"), May 18, 1897 ("My Dearest Love"), September 4, 9, 1897 ("Lamb"), September 22, 1897 ("My Dearest Dolly"), April 18, 1898 ("hubby to be"), June 19, 1899 ("Darling Child"), May 13, 1897 ("It is reported"), all HRC.

26. ELM to Helen Jenkins, May 18, 1897 ("What you are," meeting to avoid church), HRC; Helen Masters, "Mrs. Edgar Lee Masters" (president), HRC; Earnest Calkins to ELM, December 24, 1932 (tobacco use at Knox), HRC.

27. ELM to Helen Jenkins, August 25, 1897 ("It is evident"), September 4, 1897 ("I am glad"), both HRC.

28. ELM to Helen Jenkins, August 25, 1897 ("I think"), September 6, 1897 ("I don't think"), September 22, 1897 ("I have been"), February 19, 1898 ("I love"), all HRC; ELM to "Susan," February 17, 1898 ("Helen is"), HRC.

29. Helen Masters, "Mrs. Edgar Lee Masters" (family details, "Mother Goose," bazaar), HRC; ELM, "My Youth," 171 (home adjacent to bazaar), HRC; Jenkins, *Jenkins Family Book*, 50 (Helen Mary Jenkins born August 5, 1874).

30. Helen Masters, "Mrs. Edgar Lee Masters" ("budding," Groveland, judge's wife, opera, proposal, deacon, superintendent), HRC; *ASR*, 218–30.

31. Helen Masters, "Mrs. Edgar Lee Masters" ("His frequent letters"), HRC; Helen Jenkins to ELM, February 22, 1898 ("I think"), HRC; "Edgar Lee Masters the Bridegroom," unid. newspaper clipping, [Spring 1898], vertical file 97 (pictures and text discussing ELM's marriage to Helen and their common ancestor), HRC; *ASR*, 9 (Putnam).

32. Helen Jenkins to ELM, February 22, 1898 ("You are," "I have you"), February 14, 1898 ("Fate"), both HRC; Helen Masters, "Mrs. Edgar Lee Masters" (pictures), HRC; warranty deed, ELM to Helen, June 22, 1898 (lots in Browne's Addition and Cochran's Second Addition, Cook County), HRC.

33. Helen Masters, "Mrs. Edgar Lee Masters" (Hardin's birth), HRC; ELM to Helen, June 19, 1899 ("I want"), August 14, 1899 ("Ittie Boy," "I am"), April 20, 1904 ("Bug"), March 2, 1900 ("Life"), April 16, 1900 ("we will"), all HRC.

34. ELM to Helen, May 31, 1901 ("We are"), n.d. [probably about 1901] ("You are Queen"), April 11, 1903 (love letter), April 20, 1904 (love letter), all HRC.

35. ELM to "Dear Kid" [Ellen Masters], December 20, 1934 (Jingle), letter property of Hilary Masters; Hilary Masters to Herb Russell, April 26, 1993 (Helen was "Jingle"); ELM, "So We Grew Together," *Songs and Satires* (New York: Macmillan, 1916), 21–30; rpt. in ELM, *Selected Poems* (New York: Macmillan, 1925), 75–81; ELM to Rupert Hughes, January 31, 1939 (Hardin is model for subject in "So We Grew Together"), HRC; "ELM: MSR," ch. 6, p. 12 (ELM much like father), Dartmouth.

36. ELM, "Mars Has Descended," *Poetry* 10 (May 1917): 90 ("boredom"); "The Ladies Everleigh," *Chicago Tribune*, January 21, 1979, sec. 9, pp. 34–36 (2131, ten to fifty dollars, "to pleasure," 1900 to 1911); ELM to Carter Harrison, September 8, 1936 ("Next to"), HRC; ELM, "The Everleigh Club," *Town and Country* 99 (Apr. 1944): 111 (ELM tells of his visits to the house).

37. ELM, "The Everleigh Club," 109–11; ELM to Carter Harrison, November 15, 1938 ("loafing," "just to"), HRC.

38. ELM, "My Youth," 203 ("not finding"), HRC; Flaccus, "Notes on Edgar Lee Masters," June 11, 1942, Flaccus file 24 (Cook County Democracy), HRC; "ELM: MSR," ch. 11, p. 10 (Masters makes trip several times, Cook County Democrats), Dartmouth; ELM, "Bobby Burke," *Poems of People* (New York: Appleton-Century, 1936), 134–35 (Cook County Democracy).

39. *ASR*, 189 ("observation"), 191 (4,000 pages), 249 ("consoling"); ELM to Hewitt [Howland], April 20, 1928 (summarizes legal work), HRC; ELM, "My Youth," 163 (1894, Supreme Court), HRC; ELM to Lovett, January 29, 1930 ("I plunged"), HRC; ELM to Alice Corbin Henderson, January 29, 1918 (about 10,000 pages), HRC; "ELM: MSR," ch. 7, p. 157 (gun), Dartmouth.

40. *ASR*, 81 (delegate), 209 ("It was," "I sat").

41. Ibid., 210–12; ELM, *Bimetallism* ([Lewistown, Ill.]: Lewistown News, [1896]).

42. *ASR*, 237–38, 239 ("I begin to see").

43. Kevin Tierney, *Darrow: A Biography* (New York: Crowell, 1979), 162–63; *ASR*, 268 ("very poor"), 270 (Altgeld, "was not"); ELM to Carter Harrison, March 21, 1938 (met in 1897), HRC; "ELM: MSR," ch. 7, p. 147 (first Masters-Darrow meeting in 1896), unid. chapter, p. 1 (Cook County Bar Association), Dartmouth.

44. *ASR*, 236–37, 256–58, 272; ELM, "My Youth," 187½ (rents mansion), HRC; see two warranty deeds for lots in Chicago and Vinemont, Alabama, misc. file O–R, HRC.

45. Tierney, *Darrow*, 177 ("an alliance"), 192, 193 (eloquence, inspiration), 194–200; ELM to Rupert Hughes, n.d. (Wilson on Supreme Court), HRC; *ASR*, 273 ("He seemed").

46. *ASR*, 273–74 ("a brief," "government by injunction").

47. Ibid., 274 ("anarchist"), 275 ("wings wobbled," "all my," brief sold as free speech tract); Flaccus file 1901 (Turner brief sold as free speech pamphlet), HRC; [Ellen Masters,] "Bibliography of the Works of Edgar Lee Masters," *United States versus John Turner* (Chicago: Gunthorp-Warren, 1904), HRC; details of the case are in U.S. ex rel. *John Turner v Williams*, 194 U.S. 279 (1904); the brief shows "United States ex rel. John Turner vs. William Williams, Commissioner of Immigration," HRC; the title used by Ellen Masters has not been found.

48. "Spoon River Poet Called Great," *New York Times* (magazine section), April 4, 1915, p.

9 ("I am keenly interested"); *ASR,* 221 (radical), 274 (Scanlan tried criminal cases); ELM, "My Youth," 209½ (Jefferson), HRC; ELM to Elizabeth Lindsay, March 31, 1936 ("I was never a criminal lawyer"), HRC.

49. Masters's annual earnings are set at $25,000–$35,000 in Irving Stone, *Clarence Darrow for the Defense* (Garden City, N.Y.: Garden City Publishing, 1943), 162; Masters says "as much as $20,000" annually in ELM, "My Youth," 229, HRC, where he mentions pampering family members; Dale Kramer uses "$25,000 to $35,000" in *Chicago Renaissance: The Literary Life in the Midwest, 1900–1930* (New York: Appleton-Century, 1966), 79; *ASR,* 291 ($10,000); Tierney, *Darrow,* 194 ("never kept strict account"); ELM to Arthur [Ficke], July 3, 1932 ("Frank Wilson"), Yale.

50. Herman Muelder, "Edgar Lee Masters and Knox College," unpub. ms., 1975, p. 34 (founds Knox prize in 1903), Knox College; Helen Masters, "Mrs. Edgar Lee Masters" (apartment locations, European travels, and the birth dates of Masters's children), HRC; *Knox Student* 13 (Jan. 11, 1906): 228 (ongoing essay contest, alumni president); *Knox Student* 14 (Nov. 8, 1906): 139 (name of contest).

51. ELM, "The Two Annie Oakleys," ms., HRC; Tierney, *Darrow,* 194, 195, 199, 206, 231, 232, 237; *ASR,* 291; ELM, "My Youth," 196 (banking scheme [Masters apparently entered into the banking scheme without any pressure from Darrow or Darrow's son]), HRC.

52. Helen Masters, "Mrs. Edgar Lee Masters" ("Lee was"), HRC; ELM to Treasurer, Western Federation of Miners, January 28, 1908 ("done business"), HRC; Darrow to ELM, November 29, 1907 ("If the firm," "I would feel"), HRC.

53. *ASR,* 249, 251, 261–66, 289 ("were not mated"), 295, 298, 300 ("contracted madness"), 301, 305; ELM, "Ballade of Ultimate Shame: T. M., August 20, 1909–May 23, 1911," *Songs and Sonnets: Second Series* (Chicago: Rooks, 1912), 32–33 (dates of Masters's relation with Tennessee Mitchell).

54. *ASR,* 301; Helen Masters, "Mrs. Edgar Lee Masters" (details on house), HRC; Hardin Wallace Masters, *Edgar Lee Masters: A Biographical Sketchbook about a Famous American Author* (Rutherford, N.J.: Farleigh Dickinson University Press, 1978), 33–35 (details on house); copy of deed to Helen Masters, house conveyed August 1909, misc. file O–R, HRC.

55. *ASR,* 305, 311 ("knelt in penitence"); ELM, *Althea: A Play in Four Acts* (Chicago: Rooks, 1907), 3, 44, 127, 155 ("dropping down"); Diary 1912, end paper ("a lonely home").

56. *ASR,* 276, 308, 331, 336, 338 ("the ideas"), 340 ("books that I"), 342 ("the prose poems"), 343 ("all the English"), 400.

57. *ASR,* 282, 291, 317; ELM to Carter Harrison, March 21, 1938 ($9,000, "deep in literature," "didn't want it known"), HRC; William Holly to Kimball Flaccus, n.d., Additions to be Added to Main Collection (Darrow owes ELM nothing), Georgetown.

58. *ASR* draft of 582 pages, 313 ("made an $8,000"), 310 ("Ultimately, there was"), HRC; ELM to Carter Harrison, March 21, 1938 (in practice for himself), HRC; 182 Ill. App. 194 and 180 Ill. App. 199 link names of Masters and Darrow in appellate cases heard in 1913 and 1916.

59. *ASR,* 317, 385, 396; ELM to Carter Harrison, March 21, 1938 ("It is a fact"), HRC; Darrow to "Dear Ed" [ELM], February 3, 1912 ("As you know"), HRC; Tierney, *Darrow,* 253 (guilty plea).

60. *ASR,* 385 ("all the while," money from bank), 396 ("that lawyer"); Hilary Masters to Herb Russell, August 19, 1992 ("had gone around Chicago"), December 31, 1992 (depositions as IOUs); ELM to Carter Harrison, March 21, 1938 ("I got him $1,000"), HRC; ELM to Mr. Barnard, May 22, 1938 (loans seem to be to Darrow rather than to Masters), HRC.

61. Fremont Older to ELM, February 2, 1912 (asks help for Darrow and encloses Mrs. Darrow's undated request for help and names of possible helpers), HRC.

62. *ASR,* 326 (judgeship), 327 ("I secured"), 282 ("gave many banquets," Greenwood Ave-

nue apartment, Democratic Party work), 209 (1896 campaign); Flaccus file 1899 (met Bryan at Hardin's), HRC; Bryan to ELM, December 1, 1900 (friendly letter), June 28, 1904 ("I had the pleasure"), July 10, 1906 (London), March 29, 1905 (help with 1908 campaign), all HRC; ELM to Alice Corbin Henderson, January 29, 1918 ("devoted to the radical," active politically from 1896–1908), HRC; Flaccus file 1906 (home on same ship), HRC; *ASR* draft of 582 pages, 318 ("wanted a radical above him"), HRC; ELM, "My Youth," 212 ("In the spring"), HRC; ELM to Woodrow Wilson, February 19, 1913, March 5, 1913, both HRC; ELM to Dreiser, March 16, 1939 (active politically until 1908, when he gave up on Bryan), University of Pennsylvania.

63. *ASR,* 326 ("write opinions"), 327, 332, 333; ELM, "And So I Threw Away $20,000 a Year," *Cosmopolitan,* July 1925, p. 81 ($20,000); Carter Harrison to James A. Farley, November 30, 1938 (same man in judgeship to 1937), HRC.

64. ELM, "My Youth," 213–14 ("I was living," "former senior partner," "I was known"), 210 ("ugly publicity," "society paper"), HRC; Gerald Sanders note, misc. file, n.d. (Wilson discovered writings), HRC; ELM to Carter Harrison, November 28, 1938 (Wilson disliked his writings), HRC; Diary 1939, March 21 ("What beat me"); *ASR,* 333 ("it would have been").

CHAPTER 3: WHITE STONES IN A SUMMER SUN

1. May Swenson, "Introduction," *Spoon River Anthology* (New York: Collier, 1977), 13 ("world"). Quotations are from this edition.

2. Cyril Clemens, "A Chat with Edgar Lee Masters," *Hobbies* 55 (Aug. 1950): 123 ("read to tatters"); ELM to Mencken, October 5, 1937 ("We all"), NY Public.

3. *ASR,* 100 (Field published Masters), 260 (never met Moody); ELM, document regarding Moody, June 3, 1935 ("I read"), HRC.

4. *ASR,* 255 ("I determined"), 271 (*The Constitution,* Tom Watson), 271–72 ("thought the Democratic Party," legislature); ELM, *The Constitution and Our Insular Possessions* (N.p. [Chicago?], n.d. [1900?]); ELM, *Samson and Delilah* (N.p. [Chicago?], n.d. [1903?]); ELM to C.D. Abbott, December 11, 1936 (*Samson* pre-1904), SUNY-Buffalo; Kimball Flaccus to Judith Bond, April 25, 1953 (*Samson* published in 1903), Georgetown; ELM, "My Youth in the Spoon River Country," 121 ("the notes to"), HRC.

5. ELM to Miss [Marcia] Patrick, June 18, 1896, UCLA; Kimball Flaccus, "Notes on Edgar Lee Masters," June 28, 1942, Flaccus file 24 (Marcia Patrick is Marcella), HRC.

6. *ASR,* 187–92 (a few poems written in Chicago), 251 (problems with first book); "ELM: MSR," ch. 4, p. 4 (*Khayyam*), Dartmouth; ELM to August [Derleth], September 8, 1943 ("That book was written"), State Historical Society of Wisconsin; ELM to Robert Morss Lovett, January 29, 1930 (400 poems, discusses McGaffey and *A Book of Verses,* "genuinely admired"), HRC; Flaccus, "Notes on Edgar Lee Masters," September 5, 1940, Flaccus file 24 (contract for $450), November 11, 1941, Flaccus file 24 (*Inter-Ocean,* "Under the Pines"), both HRC; ELM, *A Book of Verses* (Chicago: Way and Williams, 1898), 23 ("In our rough clime").

7. ELM, *The New Star Chamber and Other Essays* (Chicago: Hammersmark, 1904); ELM, *The Blood of the Prophets* (Chicago: Rooks, 1905); *ASR,* 255 ("protestor"), 268, 271, 276; ELM, *The New Star Chamber* (New York: Committee of Forty-Eight, n.d. [1904?]) (pamphlet).

8. *ASR,* 184 (Benedict Arnold), 259, 285 (Mr. Fiske); ELM, *Maximilian: A Play in Five Acts* (Boston: Richard G. Badger, 1902); ELM, *The Trifler: A Play* (Chicago: Rooks, 1908); ELM, *The Leaves of the Tree: A Play* (Chicago: Rooks, 1909); ELM, *Eileen: A Play in Three Acts* (Chicago: Rooks, 1910); ELM, *The Locket: A Play in Three Acts* (Chicago: Rooks, 1910); ELM, *The Bread of Idleness: A Play in Four Acts* (Chicago: Rooks, 1911); ELM to Gerald Sanders, April 2, 1935, note with letter (printed "30 copies" of plays), October 26, 1935 ("The Rooks Press"), both HRC (all books printed by the Rooks Press were printed at Gunthorp-Warren Printing

Company, Chicago [Flaccus, "Notes on Edgar Lee Masters," ca. September 1942, Flaccus file 24, HRC]); a play as early as 1890 is reported by [Frank] Kee Robinson, "The Edgar Lee Masters Collection: Sixty Years of Literary History," *Library Chronicle of the University of Texas* 8 [Spring 1968]: 45; ELM to Harriet Monroe, September 2, 1924 (plays "all trash" and "for money"), HRC; ELM to [Barrett] Clark, February 15, 1934 ("I do not"), HRC; Helen Masters, "Mrs. Edgar Lee Masters" (Mrs. Fiske), HRC; in ELM to [Barrett] Clark, February 15, 1934, Masters says that *The Trifler* was also considered by "Wagenalls and Kemper," Yale; ELM, "The Genesis of *Spoon River,*" *American Mercury* 28 (Jan. 1933): 47 ("Fate had cornered me"); according to Flaccus, "Notes on Edgar Lee Masters," October 21, 1941, Flaccus file 24, Masters also said that he published "about 80 copies" of each play, HRC.

9. ELM, *Songs and Sonnets* (Chicago: Rooks, 1910); Flaccus, "Notes on Edgar Lee Masters," May 25, 1942, Flaccus file 24(thirty-forty copies), HRC; ELM to Amy Bonner, March 11, 1938 ("books of verse"), Pennsylvania State University; Dale Kramer, *Chicago Renaissance: The Literary Life in the Midwest, 1900–1930* (New York: Appleton-Century, 1966), 179 (indicates that all of Masters's pre–*Spoon River* volumes were self-published); ELM to [Barrett] Clark, February 15, 1934 ("*Maximilian* was not"), Yale (Masters was probably fibbing about *Maximilian* not being subsidized; the publisher, Richard G. Badger, was well known as a subsidy publisher, as reported by H. L. Mencken in *My Life as Author and Editor,* ed. Jonathan Yardley [New York: Knopf, 1993], 8); Judith Bond to [Kimball] Flaccus, April 17, 1953, Georgetown (ELM gave a lecture entitled *Browning as a Philosopher* [N.p. (Chicago?), n.d. (1912?)] to the Chicago Literary Club on November 18, 1912; copies of the lecture with printed title, name of audience, and date are at the Newberry and HRC); ELM to Dreiser, October 22, 1913 (1913 play), University of Pennsylvania; ELM, "In Memory of Professor Newcomer," *The Dial* 55 (Oct. 16, 1913): 299.

10. Bernard Duffey, *The Chicago Renaissance in American Letters: A Critical History* ([East Lansing]: Michigan State College Press, 1954), 137, 171–73, 184 ("We shall"), 239; Harriet Monroe, *A Poet's Life* (New York: Macmillan, 1938), 252 ("We shall").

11. *ASR,* 102 (ELM's boyhood aspirations to be a writer), 286 ("I told him," "germ"); ELM, "Genesis of *Spoon River,*" 44 (ELM's aspirations as writer).

12. ELM to Robert Morss Lovett, January 29, 1930 (poems to Reedy in 1904), HRC; ELM to Gerald Sanders, May 10, 1938 ("From about 1904," sent copy of *Maximilian*), HRC; ELM to Miss Dondore, July 6, 1928 (suggests 1907 meeting), HRC (Masters sometimes said he met Reedy in 1906, but in the letter to Dondore, Masters said, "I planned a novel about the small Illinois town I grew up in . . . long before I knew Reedy"; since Masters's plans for this novel are clearly set in 1906, this suggests 1907 as the meeting date); Harry Hansen, *Midwest Portraits: A Book of Memories and Friendships* (New York: Harcourt, Brace, 1923), 223 (Reedy encouraged McGaffey by 1900); ELM, *Toward the Gulf* (New York: Macmillan, 1918), vii ("It was you").

13. ELM to Dreiser, November 27, 1912 (*Financier,* "I believe"), December 3, 1912 ("some facts," "labor question," "look me up"), December 9, 1912 (shows imminent meeting of ELM and Dreiser), August 13, 1913, August 18, 1913, and August 20, 1913 (provides research and legal details), December 1, 1913 (admires frankness), all University of Pennsylvania; ELM to Carter Harrison, January 7, 1913 (introduces Dreiser), University of Pennsylvania. Many years after their first meeting, ELM would believe that he first met Dreiser in 1911; see ELM to Dreiser, January 27, 1940, and May 5, 1943 (where Masters mentions writing Dreiser as early as 1907), both University of Pennsylvania.

14. ELM to Dreiser, September 23, 1913, December 22, 1915 ("I remember"), January 14, 1915 (*The Girl in the Coffin*), January 28, 1914 (*The Titan*), December 1, 1913 ("frankness"), March 30, 1914 ("aeroplanist," "It has added much"), n.d. [1914] ("names," "Do you"), all University of Pennsylvania.

15. ELM to Dreiser, September 21, 1913 ("heavy drain"), October 22, 1913 ("heavy as hell"), October 29, 1913 ("loaded to the gunnels"), March 30, 1914 ("one or two" poems per week, "The poems"), all University of Pennsylvania.

16. ELM to Dreiser, September 21, 1913 ("wealth of material"), April 13, 1914 ("I am trying," "Spring strikes me"), April 20, 1914 (shows poem composed by April 20, 1914), all University of Pennsylvania; ELM, "The Oakford Derby," Dreiser Collection, University of Pennsylvania; Frank K. Robinson, *Edgar Lee Masters: An Exhibition in Commemoration of the Centenary of His Birth* (Austin: University of Texas, 1970), 18 (first poem).

17. ELM to Dreiser, April 20, 1914 ("Drop in"), May 31, 1914 ("I am including"), February 25, 1913 (shows Armstrong-Dreiser meeting), all University of Pennsylvania; see note in Flaccus file 1912 (shows ELM and Dreiser meeting Armstrong in late 1912 or early 1913) and ELM to Jack [Powys], April 15, 1939 (shows Armstrong-Dreiser meeting took place in 1911), both HRC; *ASR*, 330–31 (Dreiser to Petersburg area in 1914); Charles E. Burgess, "The Use of Local Lore in *Spoon River Anthology*" (M.A. thesis, Southern Illinois University, 1969), 135*n*28 (Dreiser to Petersburg area in 1913); Thomas P. Riggio, ed., *Dreiser-Mencken Letters: The Correspondence of Theodore Dreiser and H. L. Mencken, 1907–1945* (Philadelphia: University of Pennsylvania Press, 1986), 2:524–25 ("It was I").

18. ELM to Alice Corbin Henderson, March 27, 1916 ("annoyed," "shallow," "injurious," "fat nervous type"), December 4, 1917 ("tad-poles"), both HRC.

19. "ELM: MSR," chap. 9, p. 2 (Monroe proofed), Dartmouth; *ASR*, 337 ("one of the").

20. *ASR*, 335 (meets Sandburg), 340 ("Sandburg generally"); ELM to Dreiser, April 13, 1914 ("tramp to the sand dunes"), University of Pennsylvania; Diary 1914, April (shows numerous conversations and get-togethers involving Sandburg and Masters), May 4 (swim); ELM to Henderson, August 20, 1914 ("consorting," "old man Sandburg"), HRC; Carl Sandburg, "Notes for a Review of 'The Spoon River Anthology,'" *The Little Review* 2 (May 1915): 42 ("I saw Masters"); Monroe, *A Poet's Life*, 370 (February meeting); Harriet Monroe, "Comments and Reviews," *Poetry* 5 (Mar. 1915): 280 ("editors night").

21. ELM, "My Youth," 215 ("This getting"), HRC.

22. *ASR*, 349 (mothers of two men friends); Harriet Monroe, "Too Far from Paris," *Poetry* 4 (June 1914): 110 ("Mr. Lindsay"); ELM to Sherwood Anderson, December 21, 1935 (Lindsay "led the way"), HRC.

23. *ASR*, 180 ("fascinated"), 284 (McGaffey to Lewistown to live); "Questions for George P. Proctor, Submitted by Kimball Flaccus," February 25, 1953 ("literary material"), Georgetown; Clarence Darrow, *Farmington* (Chicago: McClurg, 1904), 128 ("stones," "the hill"), 276 ("white stones," "the hill").

24. *ASR*, 338–39 ("We went").

25. Diary 1914, April 2–3, May 24; Kimball Flaccus, "Edgar Lee Masters: A Biographical and Critical Study" (Ph.D. diss., New York University, 1952), v (memory); ELM to Dreiser, May 25, 1914 (may go to Europe), University of Pennsylvania.

26. ELM to Alice Corbin Henderson, August 20, 1914 ("Let me tell you"), HRC.

27. Eunice Tietjens, *The World at My Shoulder* (New York: Macmillan, 1938), 44; ELM to Dreiser, August 20, 1914 ("pickled"), University of Pennsylvania.

28. ELM to Mrs. Andrew Carnegie, January 21, 1941 (*Spoon River* composed on paper scraps), HRC; ELM to Robert M. Hutchins, February 21, 1941 (*Spoon River* composed on paper scraps), HRC; ELM to Alice Corbin Henderson, September 29, 1914 ("We aeroplanists," "on business"), August 11, 1916 ("Spoon River came from nowhere"), both HRC; ELM to Miss Dondore, July 6, 1928 ("When I sent"), HRC; ELM to Abraham Rosenbach, January 24, 1934 ("rewritten"), HRC; ELM to Dreiser, July 11, 1914 ("Spoon River stuff"), University of Pennsylvania; Jake Prassel to Kimball Flaccus, May 12, 1953 (ELM revised little), Georgetown (Pras-

sel's ambitions are shown in unpub. chapter 18, p. 389, HRC); Diary 1914, July 28 ("Simon Peter"), August 4 ("The Moon Rises").

29. *Record of Appointment of Postmasters 1832–September 30, 1971,* microcopy 841 (Washington, D.C.: National Archives Microfilm Publications, 1973), roll 28, Illinois, DuPage-Johnson Counties (shows Fulton County post office of Spoon River); Rita L. Maroney, research administrator/historian, Office of the Postmaster General, Washington, D.C., to Herb Russell, January 16, 1990 (confirms post office from 1838–1847); Graydon W. Regenos and Ada Y. Regenos, eds., *Historic Fulton County: Sites and Scenes—Past and Present* (Lewistown, Ill.: Mid-County, 1973), 136 (location of village of Spoon River); ELM, "Genesis of *Spoon River,*" 48–49 ("When I wrote," Pleasant Plains and Reedy).

30. Helen Masters, "Mrs. Edgar Lee Masters," HRC.

31. *ASR,* 327 ("splendid neutrality"); ELM to Dreiser, January 17, 1914 (has a girlfriend), University of Pennsylvania; Diary 1914, March-July (acquaintance with E. A.), August 17, 31, September 22, October 12 (sexual relations with E. A.), October 28, November 13, 20, December 18 (sexual relations with Eunice Tietjens) (diary entries for October 28 and 29 establish Masters's relations with Tietjens: he saw her twice during the day of the twenty-eighth and had breakfast with her on the twenty-ninth; he was with "ET all night" on the twenty-eighth and left behind his diary notation for lovemaking, the letter *X;* Masters would later tell friends that he and Tietjens had shared only "friendship" [see ELM to Constance (Greene), August 13, 1936, Flaccus file 1936, HRC], but he was merely protecting Tietjens's reputation, just as he later protected Lillian Wilson); ELM, *Children of the Market Place* (New York: Macmillan, 1922), 465 ("old America").

32. ELM, "My Youth," 219 ("Into it"), HRC; for background on the real people whose stories went into Masters's book, see *Spoon River Anthology: An Annotated Edition,* 1–79, 363–436, and picture captions.

33. ELM, "Recipe for Fame," *Songs and Sonnets: Second Series,* 81 ("Thus be"), 65 ("The cock").

34. ELM, "What is Poetry?" *Poetry* 6 (Sept. 1915): 307 ("a question of form"); ELM to Henderson, October 26, 1914 ("I am for"), HRC.

35. Harry B. Kennon, "Spoon River Cemetery," *Reedy's Mirror* 23 (July 3, 1914): 6–7.

36. ELM, "My Youth," 227 ("In the summer"), HRC; *ASR,* 341 ("Every week").

37. *ASR,* 362 ("My law"); ELM to Gerald Sanders, May 10, 1938 ("A man was"), HRC.

38. ELM to Mr. Woodruff, August 7, 1914, Cornell.

39. ELM to Witter Bynner, August 14, 1914, Harvard.

40. ELM to Witter Bynner, August 24, 1914, Harvard.

41. *ASR,* 346 ("first magazine"); "Voices of the Living Poets," *Current Opinion* 57 (Sept. 1914): 204.

42. [Alice Corbin Henderson], "Our Contemporaries," *Poetry* 5 (Oct. 1914): 42–44.

43. ELM to Monroe, November 21, 1914 ("I'm going"), December 23, 1914 (dictionary, "old myths"), January 11, 1915 ("Oh no"), February 2, 1915 ("You see"), all Chicago; Ezra Pound, "Status Rerum—the Second," *Poetry* 8 (Apr. 1916): 39 ("The St. Louis"); ELM to Robert Morss Lovett, January 29, 1930 ("It almost broke"), HRC.

44. William Marion Reedy, "The Writer of Spoon River," *Reedy's Mirror* 23 (Nov. 20, 1914), 1–2; Diary 1914, November 20 (lovemaking with "E.T.").

45. ELM to Dreiser, October 20, 1914 (Reedy sends copies to Dreiser), University of Pennsylvania; Robert Elias, *Theodore Dreiser: Apostle of Nature* (New York: Knopf, 1949), 182 (John Lane rejects); Richard Lingeman, *Theodore Dreiser: An American Journey, 1908–1945* (New York: Putnam's, 1990), 105 (Macmillan approached Masters through Reedy); Kramer, *Chicago Renaissance,* 272 (Macmillan approached Masters via Reedy); ELM to Robert Morss

Lovett, January 29, 1930 (Macmillan "chased" ELM), HRC; ELM to Lew Sarrett, October 6, 1941 ("My life was"), HRC; Max Putzel, *The Man in the Mirror: William Marion Reedy and His Magazine* (Cambridge, Mass.: Harvard, 1963), 207 (regarding copyrighting); Riggio, ed., *Dreiser-Mencken Letters,* 2:391 (Lane rejects ms.); Diary 1914, August 28 (letter from Macmillan reaches Masters), September 4 (need to copyright poems), December 31 (signs contract with Macmillan).

46. William Marion Reedy, "Spoon River in Flood," *Reedy's Mirror* 24 (Aug. 20, 1915): 1.

CHAPTER 4: WHEN SPOON RIVER WAS IN FLOOD

1. William Marion Reedy, "End of Spoon River," *Reedy's Mirror* 23 (Jan. 15, 1915): 4; *ASR,* 353 ("In the January"), 354–58 (illness); Diary 1914, November 5 (poetry, law work, and reading).

2. *ASR,* 353–58 (illness); ELM to Elizabeth Lindsay, April 20, 1932 (law office relocated to Springfield in 1906, Tom a partner), HRC; ELM to Ridgely Torrence, March 18, 1915 ("charming nurse," "gale," "the expected arrival," "stepping off"), Princeton; "ELM: MSR," ch. 9, p. 12 (Bauman), Dartmouth; ELM to Dreiser, March 12, 1915 (falls ill on January 25, 1915), March 19, 1915 (proof sheets to Dreiser), both University of Pennsylvania; ELM, "And So I Threw Away $20,000 a Year," *Cosmopolitan,* July 1925, p. 191 (Monroe proofed).

3. ELM to Harold Rugg, March 9, 1915 (publication date), Dartmouth; ELM to Hamlin Garland, March 15, 1915 ("I appreciate," "I may say"), Southern California; ELM to Dreiser, March 5, 1940 (Masters tells the story of Garland and *Collier's*), University of Pennsylvania ("ELM: MSR," ch. 9, p. 19, shows Henry Fuller instead of Garland [Dartmouth]).

4. ELM to Amy Lowell, March 29, 1915 ("to further," "variety of"), Harvard; ELM to Torrence, March 18, 1915 ("Truly, I"), Princeton; ELM to Dreiser, April 8, 1915 (mentions Pound letter, "back from visiting"), University of Pennsylvania.

5. ELM to Ridgely Torrence, March 24, 1915 (Masters returns to law office in mid-March), Princeton; ELM to Harriet Monroe, March 11, 1915 ("head swims"), April 19, 1915 (Sam Morgan), both Chicago (in a letter to Harriet Monroe on February 2, 1915, housed at Chicago, Masters said he was "getting ready to go into court tomorrow," but other comments suggest he did not return to his law office until March); ELM to George Brett, January 20, 1940 (date of publication of *SRA*), HRC; ELM to Mr. Rinehart, January 16, 1937 (activities at French Lick), HRC; ELM to Dreiser, April 30, 1915 (ten days at French Lick), University of Pennsylvania; *ASR,* 360 ("reading *Spoon River*").

6. *ASR,* 360 ("the Great Dane"), 362 ("In these days," "I sat"); "Poet Masters, 57, Marries Girl, 27," unid. news clipping, n.d., n.p. (Danish diplomat), Illinois State Historical Library.

7. ELM to [Witter] Bynner, July 6, 1915 ("beach"), Harvard; *ASR,* 365–66 ("the author").

8. ELM to Joseph Warren Beach, August 3, 1915 (in New York City by August 3), Minnesota; ELM to Witter Bynner, September 11, 1915 (stayed in New York for ten days), Harvard; ELM to unknown addressee, [January 1947?] ("He entertained"), University of Pennsylvania; Penelope Niven, *Carl Sandburg: A Biography* (New York: Scribner's, 1991), 268 (Masters attempts to market Sandburg's *Chicago Poems*); *ASR,* 368 (in New York, "the new man"), 369 (attempts to market Sandburg's ms.), 373 ("the reincarnation," "to sustain"); ELM to Helen Masters, August 15, 1915 ("I gave," "I seem"), HRC; ELM to Harriet Monroe, September 17, 1915 (three weeks in Michigan, Monroe), Chicago.

9. Dorothy Dow, "An Introduction to Some Letters, 1950" ("It was"), Newberry; ELM to Dreiser, April 2, 1915 ("I am"), University of Pennsylvania; Reedy to ELM, September 28, 1915 (Masters and novel), HRC.

10. ELM to Joseph Warren Beach, August 11, 1915, Minnesota; ELM to Arthur Davison Ficke,

November 9, 1915, Yale; ELM to Lowell, November 3, 1915 (Monroe's visit), November 9, 1915 ("These days"), both Harvard; Amy Lowell to ELM, December 18, 1915 ("The Executive"), Harvard; ELM to Monroe, November 7, 1915 (regarding Lindsay), Chicago.

11. ELM to Garland, December 21, 1915 ("One of the"), Southern California; ELM to Beach, December 22, 1915 ("I only wish," "I saw"), Minnesota; *ASR,* 366 (new poems and epilogue).

12. ELM, "The Genesis of *Spoon River,*" *American Mercury* 28 (Jan. 1933): 48 ("I was astonished"); ELM to Dreiser, April 2, 1915 ("Who the 'ell," "I don't"), July 3, 1915 ("But *S.R.*"), both University of Pennsylvania; Eunice Tietjens, *The World at My Shoulder* (New York: Macmillan, 1938), 45 ("He used"); Reedy to Dreiser, September 16, 1915, as quoted in Max Putzel, *The Man in the Mirror: William Marion Reedy and His Magazine* (Cambridge, Mass.: Harvard, 1963), 215 ("I don't think").

13. ELM to Monroe, April 17, 1915, Chicago.

14. ELM to Wilbur Cross, September 28, 1915, Yale; Cross to ELM, October 5, 1915, Yale; ELM to Ficke, November 9, 1915 ("You and the rest"), Yale.

15. Jake Prassel to Kimball Flaccus, May 12, 1953 (ELM not a mixer), Georgetown; ELM to Dreiser, July 3, 1915 (antisocial), University of Pennsylvania; ELM, "And So I Threw Away $20,000," 190 (antisocial).

16. ELM to George Brett, January 20, 1940 (date of publication), HRC; for printings and editions, see [Edward J. Wheeler], "Voices of the Living Poets," *Current Opinion* 59 (Nov. 1915): 349; Putzel, *Man in the Mirror,* 211 (nineteen printings); "Edgar Lee Masters," *Book Review Digest* 11 (1915): 318 (price of book); Percy Boynton, *Some Contemporary Americans* (Chicago: University of Chicago Press, 1924), 52 ("Mr. Masters'").

17. W[illiam] D[ean] Howells, "Editor's Easy Chair," *Harper's Magazine* 131 (Sept. 1915): 634–35; Amy Lowell, *Tendencies in Modern American Poetry* (Boston: Houghton Mifflin, 1921), 175 ("Spoon River is"), 174 ("One wonders").

18. Pound, "Webster Ford," *The Egoist* 2 (Jan. 1915): 11 ("AT LAST"), 12 ("The silly"); Harriet Monroe, *A Poet's Life* (New York: Macmillan, 1938), 368 (repeats Pound's comment, "He and Masters"); Carl Sandburg, "Notes for a Review of 'The Spoon River Anthology,'" *The Little Review* 2 (May 1915): 42 ("the people"), 43 ("other books").

19. Raymond M. Alden, "Recent Poetry," *The Dial* 59 (June 24, 1915): 28 ("A really"); "Edgar Lee Masters," *Book Review Digest* 11 (1915): 318 ("Spoon River is"); "A Human Anthology of Spoon River," *New York Times Book Review,* July 18, 1915, p. 261 ("The village"); "Notes," *The Nation* 100 (May 27, 1915): 604 ("A grave"); Willard Huntington Wright, "Mr. Masters' 'Spoon River Anthology': A Criticism," *The Forum* 55 (Jan. 1916): 113 ("The Anglo-Saxon"); William Stanley Braithwaite, "Spoon River Anthology," *The Forum* 55 (Jan. 1916): 120 ("It is indeed"); William Stanley Braithwaite, "The Soul of Spoon River," *Boston Transcript,* May 1, 1915, pt. 3, p. 8 ("It is"); Lawrence Gilman, "Moving-Picture Poetry," *North American Review* 202 (Aug. 1915): 274 ("What Mr. Masters"); Shaemas O'Sheel, "Where Great Vision Is," *The Forum* 55 (Jan. 1916): 121 ("What then"); ELM, "Genesis of *Spoon River,*" 54 ("fotograph album"); Reedy to ELM, February 23, 1916 ("*Spoon River*"), HRC.

20. "Books and History," *New York Times Book Review,* January 2, 1916, p. 4 (references *The Forum* 55 [Jan. 1916]: 109–23).

21. ELM to William Stanley Braithwaite, January 3, 1916 ("I want"), Harvard; ELM to Dreiser, January 21, 1916 ("up to"), University of Pennsylvania.

22. Tietjens, *World at My Shoulder,* 45 ("Masters proved"); Hardin Wallace Masters, *Edgar Lee Masters: A Biographical Sketchbook about a Famous American Author* (Rutherford, N.J.: Farleigh Dickinson University Press, 1978), 63 ("The animals"); Helen Masters, "Mrs. Edgar Lee Masters," typescript, April 10, 1950 (children's plays and music), HRC.

23. Marcia Lee Masters, *Wind Around the Moon* (Georgetown, Calif.: Dragon's Teeth, 1986), 16–17, 20–21.

24. Hardin Masters, *ELM: A Biographical Sketchbook,* 34 ("silence"), 27–28 ("I always"); *ASR,* 277.

25. Hardin Masters, *ELM: A Biographical Sketchbook,* 52–53 (servants, "Every man's"), 57 (clothing), 113 ("Going to the").

26. Helen Masters, "Mrs. Edgar Lee Masters" (Cuba and other travels, friends, spiritualist, "Lee always"), HRC; ELM, "My Youth in the Spoon River Country," 222 (trips west), HRC; ELM to Dreiser, March 17, 1939 (Jefferson Club, 1905), University of Pennsylvania; *ASR,* 267, 277, 282; ELM to Father, February 22, 1905 (home from Cuba), Knox College.

27. *ASR,* 29–30 (Masters's mother had maids); Charles E. Burgess, "Some Family Source Material for *Spoon River Anthology,*" *Western Illinois Regional Studies* 13 (Spring 1990): 82 (grandparents' servants).

28. Helen Masters, "Mrs. Edgar Lee Masters" (music, reading, walks), HRC; note filed with "Rough Sketch for Setup of Spoon River Fiddle Tune," n.d., misc. file (Helen and ELM collaborate on "The Lark"), HRC; Hardin Masters, *ELM: A Biographical Sketchbook,* 43 (walks, Landis, Morgan), 108–9 (Morgan), 118 (Dawes); ELM, "My Youth," 235 (Morgan to house in 1914), HRC.

29. Helen Masters, "Mrs. Edgar Lee Masters" ("Lee used," "Lee always," "In the evenings," "Lee told me," various house guests), HRC; ELM, "My Youth," 239 (Reedy told ELM to dedicate *SRA* to Helen), HRC; Helen Masters did not move all copies of *A Book of Verses,* for the Chicago bookseller Ben Abramson (of the Argus Bookshop) later told Masters he had found "about 40" unbound copies of the book at a different location in 1926 (see Abramson to ELM, March 21, 1931, HRC); ELM to Dreiser, May 12, 1915 (Helen's scrapbook), University of Pennsylvania.

30. Helen Masters, "Mrs. Edgar Lee Masters" (Cordon, Kenwood, driving), HRC; ELM to Alice Corbin Henderson, June 19, 1916 ("madam has"), HRC; Hilary Masters, *Last Stands: Notes from Memory* (Boston: Godine, 1982), 66 (mentions the accident). The date of the accident is not clear, but ELM stopped driving in 1917; see *ASR* draft dated September 17, 1934, pp. 305–6, HRC.

31. Helen Masters, "Mrs. Edgar Lee Masters" ("He had never"), HRC; unpub. chapter 20, p. 410 (shows ELM learning to dance), chapter 19, pp. 402–4 (parties and dance music at Fallas's [Slack's] apartment), HRC; Selig Greenberg, "Edgar Lee Masters . . . ," *Providence Evening Bulletin,* May 4, 1936, p. 9 (club members can't pay); *ASR,* 283 ("back to Aeschylus").

32. Orvis Irwin, "More about 'Spoon River,'" *The Dial* 60 (May 25, 1916): 498; William Stanley Braithwaite, "More Hot News from *Spoon River,*" *Boston Transcript,* March 29, 1916 (last ed.), p. 21; "Another Walt Whitman," *Literary Digest* 52 (Mar. 4, 1916): 564; ELM to Louis Untermeyer, April 30, 1916, Middlebury College; ELM to Corinne [Roosevelt] Robinson, June 29, 1916 ("most cordial," "invites me"), Harvard; ELM to Hamlin Garland, February 9, 1916, Southern California; Mrs. A. L. Danielson to Kimball Flaccus, December 5, 1952, Flaccus file 1915 (smooch), HRC.

33. ELM to Mrs. Cody, March 9, 1916 ("I have been," "I have no"), Amherst; ELM to Alice Corbin Henderson, March 27, 1916 ("I've been so busy"), HRC.

34. ELM, "My Youth," 229 ("from lawyers"), HRC; ELM to Amy Lowell, May 23, 1916 ("I begin," "I've been"), Harvard.

35. ELM to Harriet Monroe, August 3, 1916, Chicago.

36. *ASR,* 396 ("long-looked for"); ELM to Harriet Monroe, August 3, 1916 ("I want for nothing"), Chicago; ELM, "Sterling Sucher," *The New Spoon River* (New York: Boni and Liveright, 1924).

37. ELM to Mr. Barrett, August 31, 1916 ("I'm pressed"), Virginia; ELM to Mrs. Chase, October 23, 1916 ("I am booked"), Wellesley; ELM to Amy Lowell, November 22, 1916 ("It is hard"), Harvard.

38. "Announcement of Awards," *Poetry* 9 (Nov. 1916): 106 (Levinson); Amy Lowell to ELM, December 11, 1916 ("a series"), Harvard; see nine letters between Masters and *Yale Review* editor Wilbur Cross, October 25–November 25, 1916, Yale.

39. ELM to Lowell, December 20, 1916, Harvard.

40. ELM to Harriet Monroe, December 1, 1916 (*Spectra,* "Have you seen"), November 4, 1916 ("paid the coal bill"), both Chicago; William Jay Smith, *The Spectra Hoax* (Middletown, Conn.: Wesleyan University Press, 1961), 24 ("at the core of things," dice); ELM to Dreiser, April 8, 1915 ("very domestic"), University of Pennsylvania.

41. Tietjens, *World at My Shoulder,* 42; Robert E. Spiller et al., eds., *Literary History of the United States: History* (New York: Macmillan, 1974), 1180 ("Several planets").

42. *ASR,* 370 ("I could fill"); ELM, "Genesis of *Spoon River,*" 53–55 ("received a room full," "It was," "Some said").

43. ELM, "Genesis of *Spoon River,*" 49 ("parodied"); William Marion Reedy, "About Some Poets," *Reedy's Mirror* 26 (July 13, 1917): 454 ("Everybody").

44. Bliss Carman, "Spoon River Anthology," *The Forum* 55 (Jan. 1916), 116 ("His Anthology").

45. See Franklin P. Adams's "Conning Tower" column, the *New York Tribune,* June 17–November 11, 1915.

46. Untermeyer's poem appeared in the *New York Tribune* on October 11, 1915, p. 7; Masters to Untermeyer, November 8, 1915, "Edgar Lee Masters Portfolio," Lilly Library.

47. Herb Russell, "Imitations of *Spoon River:* An Overview," *Western Illinois Regional Studies* 2 (Fall 1979): 173–82.

48. J[ohn] C[ollings] Squire, "If Gray Had Had to Write His Elegy in the Cemetery of Spoon River Instead of in That of Stoke Poges," *Tricks of the Trade* (New York: Putnam's, 1917), 62–65; rpt., "Gray in Spoon River," *Reedy's Mirror* 27 (Mar. 29, 1918): 197.

CHAPTER 5: REFLECTIONS ON SPOON RIVER

1. James Hurt, "The Sources of the Spoon: Edgar Lee Masters and the *Spoon River Anthology,*" *The Centennial Review* 24 (Fall 1980): 403–31 (analyzes adversarial relations).

2. *ASR,* 244, 246, 248 ("prison"), 293 ("drop"), 342.

3. Ibid., 403 (Virginia stock), 405 ("the foundation"); Robert Van Gelder, "An Interview with Mr. Edgar Lee Masters," *New York Times Book Review,* February 15, 1942, p. 2 (related intellectually to Jefferson); ELM, *Spoon River Anthology: An Annotated Edition,* ed. John E. Hallwas (Urbana: University of Illinois Press, 1992), 51 ("those who labour"), 39 ("the Democratic ideal"); Herbert E. Childs, "Agrarianism and Sex: Edgar Lee Masters and the Modern Spirit," *Sewanee Review* 41 (1933): 333–34 (Jeffersonian influence).

4. ELM, *Spoon River Anthology: An Annotated Edition,* 7 ("In one sense").

5. *ASR,* 336 (studies Whitman, "What had enthralled").

6. ELM, *Spoon River Anthology: An Annotated Edition,* 34–35 ("single poem").

7. ELM, "Raphael and Fornarina," December 1–2, 1943 ("Man's genius"), Ficke Collection, Yale; ELM, *Skeeters Kirby* (New York: Macmillan, 1923), 321 ("The union," "Psychologically considered"); ELM, *Whitman* (New York: Scribner's, 1937), 104–5 ("irrepressible yearning"), 148–49 ("cosmic longing," "secret of the mystery"); ELM to Jack [Powys], June 26, 1938 ("Then [comes]"), HRC; "ELM: MSR," ch. 14, pp. 10–11 (glad he wrote of sex), Dartmouth.

8. Ronald Primeau, *Beyond Spoon River: The Legacy of Edgar Lee Masters* (Austin: University of Texas Press, 1981), 101 ("In the kind").

9. *ASR,* 74 (Emerson in high school); Primeau, *Beyond Spoon River,* 74 (no condescension), 69 (ELM and "Circles"); Ralph Waldo Emerson, *The Living Thoughts of Emerson,* selected and

with an introduction by ELM (New York: Longmans, Green, 1940), epigraph ("Life travels"), 2 ("Out in middle Illinois").

10. *ASR,* 77 ("new world"), 284–85 ("As a boy").

11. John H. Wrenn and Margaret Wrenn, *Edgar Lee Masters* (Boston: Twayne, 1983), 92–93 (inadequate mother love caused ELM to pursue women); *ASR,* 170–71 ("the pursuit").

12. *ASR,* 250 ("There is").

13. Ibid., 87 ("there grew up"); my discussion of Shelley's influence on Masters comes largely from Primeau's *Beyond Spoon River,* 116–38, 120 ("the Secret Power"); "ELM: MSR," ch. 11, p. 5 ("the union"), Dartmouth.

14. *ASR,* 403 ("it is distant"), 407 ("I do not"), 408 ("I dwell").

15. Primeau, *Beyond Spoon River,* 129–30 (Shelleyan visions).

16. *ASR,* 97 ("enthrallment"), 402; ELM to August [Derleth], September 7, 1943 ("lifelong delight"), State Historical Society of Wisconsin; ELM, "The Genesis of *Spoon River,*" *American Mercury* 28 (Jan. 1933): 43 ("studied constantly"); Van Gelder, "Interview with Mr. Edgar Lee Masters," 28 (read *Faust* while writing *SRA*).

17. *ASR,* 398 ("two personalities"), 399 ("two persons," "Hittite city"); ELM, *Spoon River Anthology: An Annotated Edition,* 60–61 (*Faust*'s influence).

18. *ASR,* 407 (love), 408 ("Goethe declares").

19. ELM to Dreiser, May 5, 1943 ("As to God"), University of Pennsylvania; unpub. chapter 28, p. 555 ("all we see"), HRC; my discussion of Spinoza's influence on Masters comes largely from ELM, *Spoon River Anthology: An Annotated Edition,* 20–27; ELM to "Robin! Darling!" [Lillian Wilson], June 12, 1923 ("Immortality is something," "Years ago," and quotation from "The Village Atheist"), HRC.

20. In David Karsner, "Sifting Out the Hearts of Men," *New York Herald-Tribune,* December 12, 1926, p. 28 ("I have been") (rpt., ELM, *Spoon River Anthology: An Annotated Edition,* 21); ELM, "My Youth in the Spoon River Country," 57 (never baptized), HRC (but see also "Washington Day by Day," *Trenton Evening Times,* September 10, 1929, p. 6, a news filler in which ELM says he was "sprinkled" as an infant); "ELM: MSR," ch. 2, p. 19 (no church member), Dartmouth; unpub. chapter 19, p. 399 ("In these days"), HRC.

21. *ASR,* 400 ("As a boy"), 323 (Browning and Tennyson); ELM, *Browning as a Philosopher.*

22. Primeau, *Beyond Spoon River,* 139–67 (Browning's overall influence).

23. Ibid., 145 ("Masters' experience").

24. Ibid., 157 ("In the eternal").

25. Willis Barnstone, "Introduction," *The New Spoon River* (New York: Collier, 1971), xx ("microbiographies"); "ELM: MSR," ch. 4, p. 9, and ch. 5, p. 1 (Flaccus regarding Greek), Dartmouth; *ASR,* 74, 77, 84, 110 ("no start"), 111 ("Greek fascinated"), 112 ("My Greek"), 118; ELM, *Toward the Gulf,* xi (Masters says he reread Homer each spring until 1914).

26. Primeau, *Beyond Spoon River,* 12 (religion a problem), 150 ("wholeness"); *ASR,* 413 ("its purest").

27. *ASR,* 80 ("For myself"), 401 ("In a word").

28. ELM, *The Harmony of Deeper Music: Posthumous Poems of Edgar Lee Masters,* selected and edited with an introduction by Frank K. Robinson (Austin: Humanities Research Center, University of Texas, 1976), 15 ("I am a Hellenist").

29. A sample magazine reprint is "A New *Spoon River Anthology,*" *McClure's Magazine,* Dec. 1915, p. 7.

30. ELM to Amy Lowell, June 20, 1917 ("I published"), July 15, 1917 ("several others"), both Harvard; *ASR,* 166, 373 ("most of it"); ELM, "Helen of Troy," *Songs and Satires,* 70; ELM to Alice Corbin Henderson, January 29, 1918 (sketch showing "Helen of Troy" printed in 1893), HRC.

31. Herbert K. Russell, "Edgar Lee Masters' Literary Decline: From *Spoon River* to *The New Spoon River* (1915–1924)" (Ph.D. diss., Southern Illinois University, 1977), 39 (idealistic achievement); T. S. E[liot], "Mr. Lee Masters," *The Manchester Guardian,* October 9, 1916, p. 3.

32. "An English Parnassian—and Some Others," *The Athenaeum,* no. 4611 (Nov. 1916): 529.

33. *ASR,* 374 ("I was pretty"); ELM to Amy Lowell, July 15, 1917 ("I mention"), Harvard.

34. Reedy to ELM, n.d. [probably October 1, 1915] ("one hell," "need not"), October 9, 1915 (best work in free verse), January 3, 1916 ("It isn't"), n.d. [after "the Spoon River experience"] (encourages ELM in drama), December 8, 1916 (praises later work [*The Great Valley*] as "deeper" than *Spoon River*), January 11, 1917 (pronounces "Widow LaRue" as best of all of ELM's work), March 13, 1918 ("foxy"), all HRC.

35. ELM to Henderson, April 13, 1916 ("What gratifies me"), HRC.

36. ELM, *The Great Valley* (New York: Macmillan, 1916); ELM to Alice Corbin Henderson, August 11, 1916 ("rented the loveliest cottage," "My boy"), HRC; ELM to Dreiser, August 21, 1916 ("Little House"), University of Pennsylvania.

37. *ASR,* 375–76 ("appeared at," "snapped," "disturbed," "without tranquility," "In the fall").

38. William Aspenwall Bradley, "Four American Poets," *The Dial* 61 (Dec. 14, 1916): 528; ELM to Macmillan [Company], (Latham), n.d. (75 and 250 copies), HRC.

39. *ASR,* 377 ("My books"); ELM to Dole, July 10, 1915 ("I am occupied"), Princeton.

40. *ASR,* 302 and 304 (grandmother in 1909).

41. Edward Laning, "Spoon River Revisited," *American Heritage* 22 (June 1971): 105.

42. Amy Lowell, *Tendencies in Modern American Poetry* (Boston: Houghton Mifflin, 1921), 162.

CHAPTER 6: A COUNTRY PLACE

1. *ASR,* 381, 341; Helen Masters, "Mrs. Edgar Lee Masters," typescript, April 10, 1950 (rented summer places), HRC; ELM to Witter Bynner, August 24, 1914 ("The Oaks"), Harvard; ELM to Mr. Woodruff, August 7, 1914 ("The Oaks"), Cornell; unpub. chapter 22, p. 445, chapter 23, pp. 462–71 (Stokes), HRC; William Merival, in ELM, *Domesday Book* (New York: Macmillan, 1920), 13, is a well-educated, large landowner; unpub. chapter 24, p. 489 (shows ELM's admiration of large country places), HRC.

2. ELM to [Lewis] Chase, July 16, 1917 ("Industry and concentration"), Library of Congress.

3. *ASR,* 374, 380 ("he had"); Theodore Roosevelt to ELM, June 16, 1916 (invitation), HRC; ELM to Corinne Robinson, January 8, 1917 ("tangled"), Harvard; Kimball Flaccus to Dorothy Dow, April 9, 1953 (ELM's hate turns to friendship), Georgetown.

4. Flaccus file 1917 (ELM and Reedy met Roosevelt on day of Poetry Society of America dinner at the National Arts Club), HRC; Diary 1917, January 25 ("Poetry dinner"); Masters is confused in his autobiography when he suggests this January 1917 meeting took place in March or April 1917 (*ASR,* 379–81); ELM to Henderson, January 30, 1917 ("Oh I have"), HRC.

5. ELM to Mrs. [Dorothy] Harvey, February 12, 1917, Rochester.

6. *ASR,* 378–83; ELM to Mrs. [Dorothy] Harvey, February 23, 1917 ("I'm off"), Rochester.

7. *ASR,* 383 ("I had").

8. Hugh Duncan, *The Rise of Chicago as a Literary Center from 1885 to 1920* (Totowa, N.J.: Bedminster, 1964), 56 (few Chicago writers live well); ELM to Edward Marsh, December 24, 1917 (limited overseas royalties), HRC; ELM to [H. S.] Latham, n.d. [ca. 1916] (limited overseas royalties), HRC; H. S. Latham to ELM, October 19, 1922 (few American authors sell in England), HRC; Edward Marsh to ELM, November 22, 1917 (wartime shipping hinders sales), HRC; ELM to Mr. Kennedy, February 3, 1927 ("sale of the book"), HRC; "Bitter Poet on Sad

Poet," *Time,* October 7, 1935, p. 67 (80,000 copies in one year); Alice P. Hackett, *60 Years of Best Sellers, 1895–1955* (New York: Bowker, 1956), 74–75, 120–122 (best-sellers).

9. Hilary Masters to Herb Russell, conversation, July 25, 1998 (10 percent on first 3,000, 15 percent afterward); ELM to George Brett, August 1, 1921 (usually makes revisions), December 15, 1927 (15 percent royalties after the first 3,000 copies), both HRC; Macmillan [Company] to ELM, December 19, 1947 (15 percent usual royalty rate), HRC; ELM, "The Genesis of *Spoon River,*" *American Mercury* 28 (Jan. 1933): 53 (Monroe marks galley); ELM to Dreiser, October 12, 1915 ("If I could"), University of Pennsylvania; *ASR,* 278 (insurance).

10. *ASR,* 381 ("I decided"); ELM to Monroe, May 4, 1917 ("hatched out"), Chicago.

11. ELM to Henderson, May 14, 1917 ("Everything seems"), HRC; Dale Kramer, *Chicago Renaissance: The Literary Life in the Midwest, 1900–1930* (New York: Appleton-Century, 1966), 320 (places chickens in dining room); Mary Margaret Weeg, "The Prose of Edgar Lee Masters: Its Revelation of His Views and Its Significance in His Canon" (Ph.D. diss., Indiana University, 1964), 6 (quilting patterns, as reported by Masters's cousin Edith).

12. *ASR,* 386–88; ELM to August [Derleth], May 16, 1940 (Oregon, Illinois), State Historical Society of Wisconsin; ELM, "My Youth in the Spoon River Country," 227–30 ("beautifully situated," property adjacent to 1914 rental site), HRC; ELM to Mrs. Charles Shippey, June 3, 1938 (1903 Spring Lake visit), HRC; sales agreement, May 24, 1917, misc. file O–R, HRC; ELM to Emma Masters, n.d. (Walker family and farm), HRC; ELM to Paul Carus, August 7, 1917 (arrival date at farm), Southern Illinois University; Diary 1914, June 6, July 26, August 2, 19, 26 (Masters and Walker families visit).

13. Helen Masters, "Mrs. Edgar Lee Masters" (purchase price and related information), HRC; land survey and diagram, misc. file O–R (adjacent ten-acre tract and two-acre tract), HRC; *ASR,* 388 ("And so I," "There was glorious"), 388–89 ("I had a contractor"), 392 (tennis court); ELM to August Derleth, October 8, 1939 ("I had a good bank"), State Historical Society of Wisconsin.

14. ELM to Harriet Monroe, June 1, 1917 ("What is poetry"), July 29, 1917 (house nearly done), both Chicago; ELM to Lowell, July 11, 1917 (absence of ink and table), June 20, 1917 (bibliography), both Harvard; Lowell to ELM, June 8, 1917 ("I found"), July 6, 1917 (handwriting), both Harvard; *ASR,* 389 ("I set to work").

15. Lowell to ELM, July 20, 1917 ("we have," "As to 'Spoon River'"), Harvard; ELM to Monroe, March 29, 1917 ("Old Bill"), Chicago; [William Marion Reedy?], "American Poetry," *Reedy's Mirror* 26 (Sept. 7, 1917): 574–75 (poet laureate).

16. ELM to [Amy] Bonner, March 11, 1938 ("a long visit"), Pennsylvania State University; Paul Carus to ELM, August 2, 1917, August 23, 1917, both Southern Illinois University; ELM to Carus, August 7, 1917, August 26, 1917 ("Do you know"), both Southern Illinois University.

17. ELM to Harriet Monroe, September 8, 1917 ("I wish"), July 14, 1918 ("It would be"), both Chicago.

18. *ASR,* 395 ("the script," "there were," "My book"), 389 ("by July").

19. ELM, *Toward the Gulf,* vii ("To William"), [295] (advertisement); ELM to Gerald Sanders, January 29, 1941 ($2,500), HRC; Publication Department, Macmillan Company, to ELM, December 20, 1917 ($2,500), HRC.

20. *ASR,* 389–93, 393 ("For myself"), 390 ("rented a house," "rather friendly"); ELM to Emma Masters, n.d. ("Walker's Point"), HRC.

21. ELM, "My Youth," 234–35 (Hardin's relations), HRC; Hardin's relations and the water system are discussed by the character of "Mitford" in ELM's *Mirage* (New York: Boni and Liveright, 1924), 214–20.

22. *ASR,* 394 ("One day"), 395 ("I returned"); see ELM, "Spring Lake," *Starved Rock* (New York: Macmillan, 1919), 128; ELM to Dreiser, April 18, 1938 (no one incident caused ELM to

leave Spring Lake, but rather four matters: expenses, "routine," loneliness, and the war), University of Pennsylvania.

23. ELM to Harriet Monroe, October 2, 1917 (at Spring Lake), October 6, 1917 (at Spring Lake), both Chicago; "Wife of Poet Masters to Get Cruelty Decree," *Chicago Tribune,* May 4, 1923, p. 19 (loss of Spring Lake farm); ELM to Helen Masters, May 5, 1918 (plans for Spring Lake), HRC; *ASR,* 396 ("Leaving Spring Lake").

24. ELM to Dorothy Harvey, September 21, 1917 ("I have been"), Rochester.

25. ELM to Monroe, September 8, 1917 (well), Chicago; Hardin Wallace Masters, *Edgar Lee Masters: A Biographical Sketchbook about a Famous American Author* (Rutherford, N.J.: Farleigh Dickinson University Press, 1978), dust jacket (Exeter); unpub. chapter 18, p. 386 (Hardin leaves Exeter), HRC; ELM to Theodore Roosevelt, October 31, 1917 ("last night"), HRC; ELM to Helen Masters, May 5, 1918 ("I'm wondering"), HRC; "Wife of Poet Edgar Masters Freed by Court," *Chicago Tribune,* March 22, 1922, p. 3 (leaves wife in 1919).

26. ELM, "My Youth," 256 (hard to heat), HRC.

27. ELM to Hewitt Howland, April 20, 1928 ("The last year"), HRC; ELM to Edward Marsh, December 24, 1917 ("I am"), HRC; Publication Department, Macmillan Company, to ELM, December 20, 1917 (check was for $2,500), HRC.

28. *ASR,* 393 ("war fever"); unpub. chapter 18, pp. 394 (visit to camp), 395 ("enlisted in"), HRC; Hardin Masters, *ELM: A Biographical Sketchbook,* 41 (June 21, 1918); Helen Masters, "Mrs. Edgar Lee Masters" ("Hardin was a senior"), HRC; Reedy to ELM, December 27, 1917 (Hardin in uniform), HRC.

29. Helen Masters, "Mrs. Edgar Lee Masters" ("a severe cold," "We had"), HRC; ELM to Alice Corbin Henderson, October 23, 1918 (Hardin ill with flu for three weeks), HRC; unpub. chapter 19, p. 397 (Hardin on a gunboat), HRC; ELM, "My Youth," 234 (gunboat in Chicago harbor), HRC; ELM, "God and My Country," *The Open Sea* (New York: Macmillan, 1921), 292.

30. ELM to Ficke, December 11, 1917 (Tietjens and *Daily News*), March 26, 1918 (Ficke in service), both Yale; Lowell to ELM, April 20, 1916 ("an article"), Harvard; ELM to Garland, October 3, 1916 ("But my dear"), Southern California.

31. ELM to Lowell, June 5, 1917 (writing troubles), Harvard; ELM to Ficke, December 11, 1917 ("any bad news"), March 26, 1918 ("watching"), both Yale; ELM to Dorothy Harvey, n.d. [April 1918] ("The fact is"), Rochester; ELM to Harriet Monroe, May 29, 1918 ("out of key"), June 4, 1918 ("We free spirits"), both Chicago.

32. ELM to Colonel Wood, September 12, 1918, Denison Library (Masters's correspondent may have been the soldier-poet Charles Erskine Scott Wood); unpub. chapter 19, p. 399 ("spiritual tread"), HRC; ELM to John Cowper Powys, October 4, 1918 ("I had"), University of Pennsylvania.

33. Diary 1917, September 18 (Florence Dugan; referred to as "F.D." on September 17, 23, November 4, 11, 13, and December 14, 24); Diary 1917, December 10, 11, 28, 29 (sexual relations with F.D.); unpub. chapter 18, p. 385 ("looking for a man," "lighthearted," "she was by"), chapter 19, p. 399 ("she was not"), both HRC.

34. ELM to Monroe, July 14, 1918 ("a pretty one"), Chicago; unpub. chapter 18, p. 387 ("she was," "The time," Florence leaving), HRC; ELM to [Barrett H.] Clark, October 16, 1934 ("at some place"), HRC.

35. ELM to Dorothy Harvey, February 9, 1918 ("preparing to"), n.d. [April 1918] ("Reedy is"), both Rochester; ELM, "Literary Boss of the Midwest," *American Mercury* 34 (Apr. 1935): 453 ("Often [Reedy]").

36. Unpub. chapter 18, pp. 389 (law business poor), 396 (Hardin unhappy, Florence on mind), HRC; ELM to Harriet Monroe, July 14, 1918 (in New York), Chicago.

37. ELM to Monroe, July 14, 1918 ("visiting with Roosevelt"), Chicago; unpub. chapter 19, pp. 398–99 ("No one," Quentin killed, Florence sails), chapter 20, p. 415 ("Except for the war"), both HRC; ELM to Tietjens, August 26, 1918 (girlfriend to France), Newberry.

38. ELM to Alice Corbin Henderson, November 8, 1918 ("I am alone"), HRC; unpub. chapter 19, p. 406 ("Best of all"), HRC.

39. ELM to Mrs. [Henry Mills] Alden, August 23, 1918 ("because this taking"), Library of Congress; ELM to "Editor, *Yale Review*," September 16, 1918, Yale; editor of *Yale Review* to ELM, November 25, 1918 ($15), Yale; ELM to Monroe, January 14, 1918 (asks $100 for "Winged Victory of America"), Chicago; "The World's Peace," *Boston Transcript*, November 23, 1918, pt. 3, p. 4.

40. Unpub. chapter 19, pp. 403–4 ("One day"), HRC.

41. ELM, "My Youth," 236 (began *Domesday* in September 1918), HRC; Reedy to ELM, January 7, 1918 ("I wonder"), HRC; Kimball Flaccus to Ellen Masters, September 8, 1954 (*Domesday*'s main character not based on a real person), HRC; Eunice Tietjens, *The World at My Shoulder* (New York: Macmillan, 1938), 158 (Red Cross); *ASR*, 369 ("germ").

42. William Marion Reedy, "The Man from Spoon River Comes," *Reedy's Mirror* 27 (Mar. 29, 1918): 1 ("first printed"); "Edgar Lee Masters, Poet, to Lecture before Art League," *St. Louis Post-Dispatch*, March 29, 1918, p. 21 ("It is said," "Rat Trap," "Masters today said"); ELM to Robert Grant, November 15, 1918, November 20, 1918 (National Institute), both Harvard; ELM to Tietjens, December 12, 1918 ("splendid hell"), Newberry.

CHAPTER 7: THE MAGIC PRINCESS OF THE SLEEPING PALACE

1. Unpub. chapter 20, p. 415 (blames war for divorce), HRC; *ASR*, 298 ("At the luncheon"), 299 ("I had made up my mind").

2. *ASR*, 311 ("At the office"), 315 (Grace, Adele, etc.).

3. Ibid., 405 ("Pamela . . . the magic princess"); Lillian Pampell's date and place of birth are on her marriage license for her second marriage, County Clerk's Office, Grant County, Indiana, repeated in a letter from Jerry Miller, *Marion Chronicle-Tribune*, Marion, Indiana, to Herbert Russell, January 31, 1978; Lillian told ELM that her birth date was July 16, 1888, but that her father chose 1886, so she apparently used 1887 as a compromise (see Lillian [Pampell] Wilson to ELM, August 8, 1919, HRC); *Daily Student*, Indiana University, Bloomington, Indiana, November 16, 1906, p. 1, February 27, 1907, p. 1, March 4, 1907, p. 1, April 27, 1908, p. 4; Frank B. Jones, alumni secretary, Indiana University Alumni Association, to Herbert Russell, July 8, 1977; data on Lillian Pampell is also to be found in the 1906–7 Indiana University yearbook.

4. J. Woodrow Wilson's biographical data is in a letter to Herbert Russell from Ida Mae Good Miller, cataloger, Indiana Historical Society Library, Indianapolis, June 20, 1977; information about Lillian P. Wilson's Marion, Indiana, years is in two newspaper accounts from the *Marion* [Indiana] *Chronicle-Tribune*, "Hostess House: Home with a History," February 29, 1976, sec. A, [p. 1], and "Peggy and Edgar's Literary Love Affair," February 12, 1978, sec. 2, p. 9; see also Betty Drook Shutt, *The Hostess House Story* (Marion, Ind.: Chronicle-Tribune, 1989), a pamphlet describing Lillian Wilson and her house.

5. Lillian P. Wilson, *Fruit of Toil and Other One-Act Plays* (Indianapolis: Bobbs-Merrill, 1916); R. E. Banta, *Indiana Authors and Their Books, 1816–1916* (Crawfordsville, Ind.: Wabash College, 1949), 343 (biographical sketch).

6. *ASR*, 396 ("In 1921").

7. Unpub. chapter 20, pp. 412 ("a woman," "She was," "She betrayed"), 413 ("Then I," "a widow," "lived in"), HRC; ELM, "After Thought," to August Derleth, n.d. (Lillian writes

poetry), State Historical Society of Wisconsin; *Mirage* shows that Lillian "dyed and blondined her hair" (119) and that its natural color was "ruddy" (51, 265).

8. Unpub. chapter 20, p. 416 ("I was"), HRC; August Derleth, *Three Literary Men: A Memoir of Sinclair Lewis, Sherwood Anderson, Edgar Lee Masters* (New York: Candlelight, 1963), 40 ("were ready," "they'd had").

9. Diary 1919, January 11, 14, 21, 22, 24 (Blackstone), 25, 28, 30, 31, February 1, 2; "Hostess House," sec. A, [p. 1] (address); unpub. chapter 21, p. 422 ("happiest period"), HRC.

10. Diary 1921, page facing January 1 (Masters's various measurements); ELM's passport (ELM's height slightly over 5'9"), property of Hilary Masters; Dale Kramer, *Chicago Renaissance: The Literary Life in the Midwest, 1900–1930* (New York: Appleton-Century, 1966), 68 (hair color); John Cowper Powys, *Autobiography* (London: Lane, 1934), 549 ("granite" chin); Dorothy Dow, "An Introduction to Some Letters, 1950" (dimples), Newberry; *ASR*, 187 (boxing); ELM to Mr. Butler, April 15, 1936 ("My eyes"), HRC; ELM, "My Youth in the Spoon River Country," 217 (golf), HRC; Helen Masters, "Mrs. Edgar Lee Masters," typescript, April 10, 1950 (cards), HRC; ELM to Mr. Rinehart, January 16, 1937 (stud poker, etc.), HRC; "Poet Masters, 57, Marries Girl, 27," unid. news clipping, n.d., n.p. ("Edgar Lee Masters never"), Illinois State Historical Library; Hilary Masters, *Last Stands: Notes from Memory* (Boston: Godine, 1982), 97 (looks younger than is), 177 (drawl); Hardin Wallace Masters, *Edgar Lee Masters: A Biographical Sketchbook about a Famous American Author* (Rutherford, N.J.: Farleigh Dickinson University Press, 1978), 121 (soft voice).

11. Masters's attitude toward women is illustrated repeatedly in subsequent chapters of the present volume.

12. Diary 1919, February 4–27, March 1, 2; ELM to John Cowper Powys, March 19, 1919 (Lowell centenary), University of Pennsylvania.

13. Diary 1919, March 3, 4, 5 ($92.10), 12–14, 15–17, 21, 22 ("all night"), 23 ("Dear God"), 26, 28, 29, April 4 ("long talk"); *ASR*, 396 ("robbins"); ELM to Lillian Wilson, July 7, 1919 (quotes her suggestion that he be divorced), HRC; unpub. chapter 21, p. 428 (quotes divorce suggestion), HRC; Lillian Wilson to Edwin Reese, August 15, 1925 (Episcopalian), HRC.

14. ELM to Lillian Wilson, telegram, March 20, 1919 (speaks of Sophocles), April 10, 1919 ("will give"), both HRC; ELM to Dreiser, April 28, 1919 (spring "sweet"), University of Pennsylvania.

15. ELM to Ferris Greenslet, April 23, 1919 ("bring them out," "I have"), May 20, 1919 ("a manuscript"), both Harvard.

16. Ferris Greenslet to ELM, May 5, 1919, June 20, 1919 ("read personally"), both Harvard.

17. ELM to Mr. [Morris] Bagby, May 13, 1919 ("Won't you," "What I"), Virginia; ELM to John Cowper Powys, March 19, 1919 (Bagby's first name), University of Pennsylvania.

18. Lillian Wilson to ELM, March 27, 1920 (books are "salvation"), HRC; ELM to Lillian Wilson, July 7, 1919 (old boyfriend), HRC.

19. ELM to Edwin Reese, n.d. ("The woman"), Illinois State Historical Library; ELM to Lillian Wilson, July 7, 1919 ("pretty fast"), July 3, 1919 ("copy of letter"), both HRC; ELM to Louise Van Dyke, June 25, 1919 ("some exercise," copy of letter), HRC; Diary 1919, May 31, June 1 ("Vivid dream"; "Write Peggy"), 4 ("You can't"), 6 (dream).

20. ELM to Lillian Wilson, July 7, 1919, HRC.

21. Ibid.

22. Oliver Denton is mentioned in diary entries for November 12 and November 18, 1919, and May 1 and May 5, 1920; Denton's relation with Lillian is discussed under her real nickname in Masters's poem "Peggy," *The Overland Monthly* 84 (Sept. 1926): 291 (rpt., ELM, *More People* [New York: Appleton, 1939], 166–69).

23. Masters to Eunice Tietjens, July 26, 1921 (marriage failed), Newberry; ELM to Carter

Harrison, March 21, 1938 ("By 1919"), Newberry; ELM to Harriet Monroe, August 3, 1916 (letterhead stationery shows Helen Masters's position with the College Club), Chicago; Eunice Tietjens to ELM, March 27, 1922 (Helen is acting president of The Cordon by 1922), HRC; "Masters Tells Divorce Scrap in 13 Sonnets," *Chicago Daily Journal,* August 18, 1923, p. 1 (Chicago Woman's Club); ELM to Dreiser, May 31, 1919 (no plan), University of Pennsylvania.

24. Diary 1919, May 30 (tonsils), 19–21, 25 (money to Helen), 26 ("long bitter talk," "finished and expressed"); ELM to Monroe, n.d. (arrangements for *Domesday Book* selections in *Poetry;* Masters asks for his payment of "$100 at once"), Chicago; Emma Masters to ELM, September 10, 1925 (plumbing and heating of house), HRC.

25. ELM to Dreiser, January 9, 1919 (Montgomery Ward Building), University of Pennsylvania; ELM, "My Youth," 236 ("The Tower" is the Montgomery Ward Building), HRC; unpub. chapter 19, pp. 401 ("staleness," "until 1 o'clock"), 402 ("some cases"), 401–2 (physically tired), HRC.

26. Unpub. chapter 19, pp. 402 (near Lewistown), 403 ("I managed"), 402–3 (details on Sheriff), HRC; ELM, "My Youth," 164 (soldiers of fortune), HRC; ELM to Carter Harrison, March 21, 1938 (Sheriff a lawyer), HRC; Andrew Sheriff to ELM, telegram, November 8, 1919 (Sheriff represents ELM), HRC; ELM to Clarence [Darrow], November 6, 1919 (Helen has information concerning Lillian), HRC; ELM, *Mirage,* 131, 167, suggests that Helen received her information about Lillian from a detective who followed Masters.

27. Diary 1919, June 9–24; Retired Professors Registry form, American Association of University Professors (Ellen's major was in English), property of Hilary Masters; other information on Ellen Masters is from her son, Hilary.

28. Diary 1919, June 28 (Sheriff and Johnston), July 6, 7 ("all over," "going to be"), 8, 10–14, 15 (letters), 17, 30. The anonymous letter, which is postmarked June 16, 1919, and housed in the HRC, no doubt came from a person friendly to Helen Masters and was intended to frighten Masters into quietly returning to his wife. One candidate for its author is a detective who may have followed Masters (see note 26); another is Helen Masters's brother, George, a lawyer who was knowledgeable of his sister's marital problems (see unpub. chapter 22, p. 439, HRC).

29. Lillian Wilson to ELM, July 20, 1919, July 27, 1919 (parties), December 27, 1930 [1920] (joke about sex), December 22, 1920 ("Grand Soak"), September 1, 1921 ("glad"), all HRC.

30. Diary 1919, October 15 ("dream"), 17, 20 (work), 19 ("be deeded"), 21 (feuds with Helen); the poem "Crayons" ("Anonymous mud . . .") is with ELM's letters to Alice Corbin Henderson, HRC.

31. Unpub. chapter 21, p. 425 ("knew all about"), HRC; ELM to Darrow, November 8, 1919 ("She has," "In a time"), HRC; Darrow to ELM, November 10, 1919 ("Of course"), HRC.

32. Diary 1919, November 2–6 ("elusive"), 10, 11, 12 (lunch), 13, 18 ("exquisite," "luncheon"), 19. See chapter 12, note 3, of the present volume, for details about Grainger and his music.

33. Unpub. chapter 21, pp. 430–31 (Corinne Robinson's influence on ELM's *Mitch Miller* [New York: Macmillan, 1920]), HRC; "ELM: MSR," chap. 1, p. 9 (Mitch's father a minister and school superintendent), Dartmouth; Julie Scott, "Oakland Cemetery in Petersburg," *Western Illinois Regional Studies* 14 (Fall 1991): 52 (Mitch dies in 1879); Diary 1919, November 27, December 8 (*Mitch*); Kimball Flaccus, "Notes on Edgar Lee Masters," June 12, 1942, Flaccus file 24 (father gives ELM copy of *Tom Sawyer,* details of death), HRC; *ASR,* 38.

34. Unpub. chapter 21, p. 431 ("I consoled"), HRC; Diary 1919, December 5–6 (Darrow), 21 (calls Lillian); ELM to John Cowper Powys, December 22, 1919 ("My dear friend"), University of Pennsylvania; ELM, "Lucius Clute," *The New Spoon River* ("Lillian, with her whims"); ELM, *Mirage,* 51, 265 (Lillian Wilson's hair naturally "ruddy").

35. Unpub. chapter 22, p. 438 ($50,000), HRC; ELM to Lillian Wilson, telegram, Novem-

ber 7, 1919 (Louisville), HRC; ELM to Arthur Yager, July 20, 1920 ("35 acres" in "Porto Rico"), HRC; Lillian Wilson to ELM, April 7, 1920 ("Daddy"), December 3, 1919 ("You always," "all today"), July 19, 1920 (Puerto Rico), all HRC; reverse of picture P229, of J. Woodrow Wilson, shows "Daddy," photo archives, HRC; ELM, *Mirage,* 91, 122, 190 (J. Woodrow Wilson as "Daddy"); "Hostess House," sec. A, [p. 1] (Lillian's domestic setting); unpub. chapter 21 (husband's will, house, servants, and finances), HRC; ELM, "My Youth," 242 ("a bottle," Masters's room), 244 and 259 (cigarettes), HRC; Mrs. Merrill Davis to Herb Russell, telephone conversation, August 1977 (empty lot).

36. "Peggy and Edgar's Literary Love Affair," sec. 2, p. 9 ("to have a good time"); ELM to "Dear Old Top" [Mrs. William Van Dyke?], September 22, 1919 ("She seemed to be"), HRC; ELM to Dreiser, August 29, 1919 ("A widow"), University of Pennsylvania.

37. Lillian Wilson to ELM, April 7, 1920 ("Daddy full name"), May 1, 1920 ("Addie," "D. Ph"), June 4, 1921 (Winslow), June 24, 1921 ("Modesta"), telegram, May 2, 1919 ("Daisy"), all HRC; "James Dowder" [ELM] to Lillian Wilson, telegram, November 7, 1919 (false name), July 7, 1919 (typewriter), both HRC.

38. Lillian Wilson to ELM, February 29, 1920 (rumors false), September 12, 1921 (gossip in Marion), both HRC.

39. Lillian Wilson to ELM, February 29, 1920 ("men friends"), HRC.

40. Lillian Wilson to ELM, March 19, 1920 ("Did I"), March 3, 1920 (questions ELM's talent), both HRC.

41. Diary 1920, January 10–30; ELM to Edward Marsh, August 21, 1919 ("I must"), HRC; Diary 1920, January 27 (sold *Mitch*); ELM to Brett, December 15, 1927 ($4,000 advance), HRC.

42. Reedy to Helen Masters, January 12, 1920 (will speak for Helen), HRC; Reedy to ELM, February 27, 1920 ("kicking away a ladder"), HRC; Andrew Sheriff to ELM, telegram, November 8, 1919 (promises speedy divorce settlement), HRC. Sheriff subsequently became the character of Roger Farnsworth in *Skeeters Kirby* (see, e.g., 175–79).

43. Masters to [Edward] Marsh, May 26, 1920 ("Your letter"), Virginia; Diary 1920, June 10–15, 25, July 7, 9–14 ("both very tired").

44. Unpub. chapter 21, pp. 432–33, HRC; Diary 1920, July 16, 17, 24.

CHAPTER 8: HEART'S DESIRE

1. ELM to Katharine Jones, July 29, 1920 ("I am so blue"), Additions to be Added to Main Collection, Georgetown; ELM to Monroe, July 31, 1920 ("A telegram"), Chicago. Little is known of Katharine Jones, except that she was a divorced friend of Masters and that her niece typed *Domesday Book.* See Kimball Flaccus, "Notes on Edgar Lee Masters," June 20, 1942, Flaccus file 24, HRC; ELM to "Dear Kath," July 17, 1920, November 20, 1923, in Additions to be Added to Main Collection, Georgetown.

2. ELM to Mencken, November 30, 1924 ("gift, reward"), HRC; ELM to Mr. Baldwin, May 10, 1924 (misses Reedy), HRC; Reedy to ELM, June 20, 1920 ("However you go"), HRC; ELM to Harriet [Monroe], August 5, 1920 ("At the . . . last"), Chicago; ELM to Bynner, November 20, 1922 ("Every day"), June 17, 1935 ("I think"), both Harvard; Diary 1923, July 28 (misses Reedy).

3. Diary 1920, July 27–29; ELM to Tietjens, August 10, 1920 ("Reedy's death"), Newberry; Lillian Wilson to ELM, n.d. [ca. September 1920] (to Europe with girlfriend), HRC.

4. ELM to Monroe, March 29, 1917 (Reedy on Masters's post–*Spoon River* works), Chicago; Connie Lauerman, "A Poet's Surprise Son is Master of His Own Past at Last," *Chicago Tribune,* November 25, 1982, sec. 7, pp. [1], 7 (Hilary describes his father's hasty habits of composition); an exception to ELM's usually thorough legal work is mentioned in *ASR,* 292; Harriet Monroe, *A Poet's Life* (New York: Macmillan, 1938), 378 ("He was the worst").

5. Hilary Masters, *Last Stands: Notes from Memory* (Boston: Godine, 1982), 98 (Monroe proofed galleys); Monroe, *A Poet's Life*, 378–79 (influences *Songs and Satires*); Max Putzel, "Masters's 'Maltravers': Ernest McGaffey," *American Literature* 31 (Jan. 1960): 491–93; Carl Sandburg, "To Webster Ford," *Reedy's Mirror* 23 (Nov. 27, 1914): 7 (poetic admiration for Masters); ELM to Harriet Monroe, December 3, 1917 ("most injury"), Chicago; Witter Bynner, *Grenstone Poems* (New York: Knopf, 1926), ix–xii (Masters-Bynner meeting in 1916); Edward Marsh to ELM, August 14, 1919 (tells Masters his post–*Spoon River* poems are "growing in depth and beauty"), HRC.

6. Unpub. chapter 22, pp. 436 ($9,000), 437 ("most interesting," $50 fee), HRC; Geoffrey Cowan, *The People v. Clarence Darrow: The Bribery Trial of America's Greatest Lawyer* (New York: Times Books, 1993), 434 (Darrow guilty); ELM to Tietjens, July 26, 1921 ("On a Bust," "Excluded Middle"), Newberry.

7. Unpub. chapter 22, pp. 436 ("been separated"), 437 ("He often said"), 437–38 ("He talked"), 438 (the fall of 1920), 439 ("help"), HRC.

8. Ibid., 439 ("plastered Chicago"), 441 ("order for alimony," "the money"), HRC; Robert Jenkins, *Jenkins Family Book* ([Chicago,] 1904), 49 (George Jenkins a graduate of Harvard Law School); *ASR*, 334 (waitress case); George Brett to ELM, November 10, 1920 (acknowledges request to delete Helen's name from dedication of *SRA*), October 21, 1931 (again acknowledges request to delete Helen's name from dedication), both HRC.

9. Diary 1920, October 15 and 18 (Darrow tries to restrict travel); "Poet and Wife Drop Divorce," *Chicago Tribune*, September 6, 1922, p. 1 (reviews marriage problems, describes support payments of $150 per month); unpub. chapter 22, p. 442 (Darrow's suggestion regarding the $25,000), HRC; ELM to Eunice Tietjens, July 21, 1921 ("proposed to me"), Newberry; "Summary of a Legal Document in Cook County Courthouse," Flaccus file 1922 (travel restrictions set on October 18, 1920), HRC; ELM to "Dear Mother," n.d. (mentions bond), HRC.

10. ELM to Edward Marsh, August 21, 1919 ("a story"), HRC; Hardin Wallace Masters, *Edgar Lee Masters: A Biographical Sketchbook about a Famous American Author* (Rutherford, N.J.: Farleigh Dickinson University Press, 1978), 85 ("as heavy"); unpub. chapter 21, p. 431 (*Romance*), HRC; ELM, *Mitch Miller*, 231–62 (various invectives).

11. Diary 1920, August 10–October 4 (writes), October 5 ("worked on trees"), 6 (Johnston), 8 ("picked apples"), 14, November 5, 16, 18, December 3, 12–14, 29 (book contracts).

12. Unless otherwise indicated, information concerning Dorothy Dow is from her "Introduction to Some Letters, 1950," an unpublished and unpaginated document of fifty-five pages at the Newberry Library; Hilary Masters, *Last Stands*, 95 ("as he seemed"); ELM letter and poem ("To Dorothy") to Arthur [Ficke], October 12, 1937 (clearly suggest a physical intimacy with Dow), Yale; ELM to Dow, April 26, 1945 (shows they met at the apartment of Bill Slack), Newberry; ELM to Edwin Reese, November 2, 1925 (suggests a close physical intimacy with Dow: "I thought this Dow stuff was dead for good. Maybe it is now when she gets in bed with another man"), Illinois State Historical Library.

13. Dow, "Introduction to Some Letters," Newberry.

14. Unpub. chapter 22, pp. 442 ("to think of Rome"), 443 ("a Mediterranean cruise"), 444 ("I had taken"), 438 ("The turmoil"), HRC; Diary 1920, December 26 (Doody); ELM to Monroe, n.d. [ca. 1920] ("But good Lord"), Chicago; ELM to Dreiser, October 22, 1913 (wants to see Greece and Rome), University of Pennsylvania.

15. Letters from Masters to Dow are in the Newberry Library; Masters's letters of January 14 show the sailing date and the "gold" ring he sent; the ring is also mentioned in Diary 1920, December 27; unpub. chapter 22, p. 444 (likes passengers, extends trip), HRC.

16. Dow, "Introduction to Some Letters," Newberry; Masters to Dow, January 27, 1921 (Algiers, poem, "I wish"), Newberry.

17. Dow, "Introduction to Some Letters" ("amorous"), Newberry. Lillian's ring is mentioned in Diary 1919, May 14, and Diary 1920, July 26, as well as in ELM to Lillian Wilson, July 23, 1920, HRC (there is no name or address on this letter, but the recipient is clearly Lillian).

18. Unpub. chapter 22, p. 444 ("Edna Millay was"), HRC; Jean Gould, *The Poet and Her Book: A Biography of Edna St. Vincent Millay* (New York: Dodd, 1969), 130 (Masters was in Paris in early 1921); Mrs. Bigelow Crocker to Kimball Flaccus, October 14, 1957 (her father gave up hotel room for afternoon), Georgetown; ELM to Monroe, April 21, 1921 ("didn't see"), Chicago; H. L. Mencken, documents dated January 6, 1939, and March 29, 1944, both in "Manuscripts by H. L. Mencken" (Millay and unsatisfactory meeting), NY Public; Diary 1921, March 7 ("phoned Edna").

19. Diary 1921, February 12–23.

20. *ASR*, 396 ("I tried"); ELM to Mary Aldis, April 11, 1922 (indicates that Lillian had been in Paris in February 1921 and "had sailed for America on February 13"), Newberry, with the Tietjens papers; Diary 1920, October 9 (Lillian in Paris on October 1); Diary 1921, January 29 ("opening branch") (Masters may have briefly stopped writing Dow at this time or his letters may have been lost; a note among Dow's papers at the Newberry indicates that some letters were destroyed); unpub. chapter 22, p. 444 ("At Rome"), HRC.

21. Unpub. chapter 22, p. 445 ("drank Scotch," "as the *Aquitania*"), chapter 23, pp. 466–71 (return to Helen), HRC; Diary 1921, March 19 ("steering").

22. August Derleth, *Three Literary Men: A Memoir of Sinclair Lewis, Sherwood Anderson, Edgar Lee Masters* (New York: Candlelight, 1963), 40–41 ("When I was"); Frank K. Robinson, *Edgar Lee Masters: An Exhibition in Commemoration of the Centenary of His Birth* (Austin: University of Texas, 1970), 21 ("sole handwritten").

23. Diary 1920, August 29 ("Wrote on"), 30 ("Lose").

24. Diary 1921, March 20 (Lillian), 28 (father), April 1–4, 30, May 1 (Zueline; the woman named "Zueline" is identified as author Marjorie Seiffert in a card catalogue of the HRC), April 14 (Claudia Perry-Wilson), November 30 (mentions Zueline and Marjorie Seiffert); ELM to Tietjens, April 8, 1921 ("I ought," "I have," Hardin's tuberculosis), Newberry.

25. Masters to Dow, April 18, 1921, April 20, 1921, April 25, 1921, April 29, 1921, May 2, 1921, all Newberry; Masters to Tietjens, April 18, 1921, Newberry; Dow, "Introduction to Some Letters" ("He was not"), Newberry.

26. Dow, note on Masters's letter of April 29, 1921 (indicates the two saw each other in Chicago after Masters returned from Europe), Newberry; Dow, "Introduction to Some Letters" ("It is my impression," "His violent love," "he sought"), Newberry; Masters to Dow, June 6, 1921, Newberry; Diary 1921, May 29–June 4 (at Lillian's).

27. Hardin Masters, *ELM: A Biographical Sketchbook,* 115 ("When he once," "I have"); ELM to Corinne Robinson, May 22, 1921 ("Everyone is"), Harvard.

28. Unpub. chapter 22, p. 446 (Lillian knew ELM was home, minister as go-between), HRC; ELM to Edwin Reese, April 14, 1924 (minister as go-between), Illinois State Historical Library; Diary 1921, May 29–June 5 (reconciliation and distress over *Skeeters*).

29. Diary 1921, June 5 ("withdraw *Skeeters*"); unpub. chapter 22, p. 447 ("She went," Lillian's offer of $25,000), HRC; ELM to Tietjens, July 21, 1921 ("I spent," "Lillian's face"), Newberry.

30. ELM, "My Youth in the Spoon River Country," 257 ("go to work"), HRC; for two artistic descriptions of Helen Masters's financial problems, see her daughter Marcia's poem "Wind Around the Moon," in *Wind Around the Moon* (Georgetown, Calif.: Dragon's Teeth, 1986), 20–21, and Masters's poem "The Return," *Poetry* 22 (Sept. 1923): 291; ELM to Tietjens, October 29, 1921 (Helen Masters accepts boarders), Newberry.

31. Diary 1920, May 10, 24 (law work); Diary 1921, April 10 (mss. at office); ELM to Tietjens,

July 21, 1921 ("I have closed"), Newberry; ELM to Harriet Monroe, June 9, 1925 (ends law practice in 1919), Chicago.

32. ELM to Brett, August 1, 1921, HRC.

33. ELM to Edward Marsh, June 24, 1919 ("I shall"), HRC; ELM to Macmillan Company, November 6, 1920 ("I have"), HRC; George Brett to ELM, July 21, 1921 (Masters owes $541.47 for various expenses and $3,448.02 as "balance due" on his account, a total of $3,989.49), October 15, 1921 ($4.09), both HRC.

34. Kimball Flaccus, "Edgar Lee Masters: A Biographical and Critical Study" (Ph.D. diss., New York University, 1952), 217 ("finest achievement"); Hardin Masters, *ELM: A Biographical Sketchbook,* 85 (remembers his father's good opinion of the book); ELM to Hewitt Howland, December 7, 1934 (quotes Mencken's "most eloquent" expression), HRC; ELM to Mr. Kennedy, February 3, 1927 (quotes Mencken's "most eloquent" expression), HRC; ELM to Mr. Towson, October 5, 1926 ("often confessed"), HRC; ELM to Edward Marsh, June 24, 1919 ("Some of my friends"), HRC.

35. Diary 1919, May 26 (first mailing); ELM to Edward Marsh, June 24, 1919 (dates of composition), HRC; ELM to George Brett, May 12, 1920 ("I suppose," mails *Domesday*), HRC.

36. ELM to Edward Marsh, June 24, 1919 (use of diary, "literally true"), HRC; ELM to John Williams, February 19, 1936 (15,000), HRC; *ASR,* 368–69 (1889 story). For another use of these ideas, see ELM's "Recessional, in Time of War, Medical Unit," published in *Reedy's Mirror* in 1918 and reprinted in W.S. Braithwaite's *Anthology of Magazine Verse for 1918 and Year Book of American Poetry* (Boston: Small, Maynard, 1918), 96–97.

37. Diary 1921, July 1 ("wrote 30 pages"), 26 (Lillian's death), 29 (will); unpub. chapter 22, pp. 448–52 (describes Masters's wanderings during the summer of 1921), HRC; ELM to Tietjens, July 21, 1921 (will, "kindness check"), Newberry; ELM to Bill Slack, May 6, 1922 ($600), HRC.

38. ELM to R. D. Douglas, February 19, 1931 (Stephen A. Douglas at Petersburg, Hardin hears), HRC; ELM, "My Youth," 51 (Hardin hears Douglas), HRC; ELM to *Haldeman-Julius Weekly,* March 1, 1923 ("I have"), HRC; ELM to Mencken, February 19, 1931 (10,000 letters, inaccessibility to letters), HRC; ELM to Mencken, April 1, 1931 (10,000 letters), April 26, 1931 (20,000 letters), both NY Public; Diary 1921, September 2–October 22 and October 25–November 4 (writing, typing, and mailing).

39. ELM, *Children of the Market Place,* 1, 7, 35, 44, 143–44, 329, 414, 454; ELM, *Spoon River Anthology: An Annotated Edition,* 427 (a man named James Miles lived in Petersburg and was a friend of ELM's grandfather).

40. ELM, *Children of the Market Place,* 211–12, 332, 349, 354–55, 382 ("I was the defeated").

41. George Brett to ELM, November 23, 1921 ($4,000, Brett Sr. admires), June 2, 1922 (*Children* a financial failure), both HRC; R. D. Douglas to ELM, February 16, 1931 (Douglas relative likes book), HRC; ELM to Gerald Sanders, January 29, 1941 ("It was published," "for myself"), HRC; unpub. chapter 22, p. 452 ("Naturally I was running"), HRC; the character of "Mrs. Winchell" is based on Lillian.

42. ELM to Tietjens, July 27, 1921 ("She hates"), July 26, 1921 ("There is a"), both Newberry; Kevin Tierney, *Darrow: A Biography* (New York: Crowell, 1979), 304 ("embarked on").

43. For Masters family visits to the home of Mrs. William Vaughn Moody, see Marcia Lee Masters's "One Evening at Mrs. William Vaughan [*sic*] Moody's," *Wind Around the Moon,* 50–52; ELM to Robert Morss Lovett, January 29, 1930 (Masters never met Moody), HRC; ELM to Tietjens, n.d. ("This woman"), HRC; ELM to Tietjens, September 1, 1921 ("I have"), Newberry.

44. "The Literary Spotlight," *The Bookman* 55 (Aug. 1922): 576 ("rogue elephant," "He has that aversion"); unpub. chapter 20, pp. 409–10 ("The daily newspapers"), HRC; ELM to Mrs.

[Corinne] Robinson, May 22, 1921 ("isolation"), Harvard; ELM to Monroe, December 12, 1921 ("disinclination to meet people"), Chicago; ELM to Lillian Wilson, September 11, 1921 ("The literary"), HRC.

45. Diary 1921, October 6, 7 ("Sent proofs"); ELM to Edward Marsh, December 24, 1917 ("artistically related"), HRC.

46. ELM to Brett, May 20, 1922 (delay printing), June 11, 1921 (purchase plates), June 24, 1922 ("This book"), June 25, 1922 ("A book as frank"), all HRC; galley proofs and paged proofs are at the HRC.

47. George Brett to ELM, March 28, 1922 (refers to ELM's letter of March 24 to remove dedication to Bill Slack, add Chubb, query), HRC; ELM holograph on reverse of telegram from Emma Masters to ELM, March 22, 1922 ("remove dedication to Slack from *Skeeters Kirby*"), HRC; ELM to Macmillan, February 17, 1923 ("Take that"), HRC; ELM to Llewellyn [Jones], February 17, 1923 (original dedication plans, new dedication to Chubb, "slur over," "One of the most"), HRC.

48. ELM to George Brett Sr., n.d. (rewrites in eighteen days), HRC; ELM to Brett, n.d. (owes $2,000 on *Skeeters*), HRC; Macmillan to ELM, November 22, 1922 (six revisions), HRC.

49. Unpub. chapter 22, p. 452 ("I pictured myself"), HRC.

50. Diary 1921, November 24–December 31; ELM to Maurice [Brown], December 25, 1921 (in New York's Hotel Pennsylvania), University of Michigan; ELM to Harriet Monroe, April 17, 1922 (1921 income), HRC.

51. ELM to Tietjens, October 29, 1921 ("Stick in the Mud"), March 27, 1922 (roomers), both Newberry; unpub. chapter 23, p. 454 ("It was bitter," "In a week"), HRC; ELM to Harriet [Monroe], February 27, 1922 (enlarges kitchen), Chicago; ELM mortgage and promissory note, loan from Horatio O. Stone, March 1, 1922, misc. file O–R ($7,000), HRC; Hardin Masters, *ELM: A Biographical Sketchbook,* 76–79 (Claudia Perry-Wilson).

52. Harriet Moody to "Harriet," April 23, 1922 (only $750), HRC; Hilary Masters to Herb Russell, December 31, 1992 ("Bargaining for time").

53. Abraham Meyer appears in *ASR,* 409, and in unpublished chapters of ELM's autobiography; Masters's sharing an apartment with Bill Slack is mentioned in Dow's "Introduction to Some Letters," Newberry.

54. "Wife of Poet Masters Freed by Court," *Chicago Tribune,* March 22, 1922, pp. 3, 36; "General News," *New York Times,* March 23, 1922, p. 12; Kimball Flaccus to Dorothy Dow, April 9, 1953, April 21, 1953 (Darrow behind the scenes in legal dispute), both Georgetown.

55. Unpub. chapter 23, p. 454 ($3,000), HRC; Diary 1922, March 22.

CHAPTER 9: THE JUDAS KISS

1. ELM to Tietjens, March 29, 1922 ("Slack overlooked"), Newberry; ELM to George Brett, n.d. ("The case"), April 2, 1922 (identifies Link), both HRC; note, Flaccus file 1922 (Slack reads of receivership), HRC; Diary 1922, March 22, 28, April 7 (court receivership); "Wife of Poet Masters Freed by Court," *Chicago Tribune,* March 22, 1922, p. 3 ($3,600 per year).

2. ELM to Tietjens, March 25, 1922, March 27, 1922, both Newberry.

3. Diary 1922, March 23 (meets with lawyer), June 2 ("codicil"); unpub. chapter 23, p. 454 ("All my copyrights"), HRC; "Poet and Wife Drop Divorce," *Chicago Tribune,* September 6, 1922, p. 1 ("on the ground").

4. Diary 1922, April 7 (Spring Lake receivership); Emma Masters to ELM, telegram, March 22, 1922 (offers to buy Michigan farm to help save it), HRC; unpub. chapter 23, p. 455 ("The Grand Haven lawyer"), HRC.

5. ELM to Tietjens, March 29, 1922 ("She is," "This little farm"), April 18, 1921 (letterhead stationery), both Newberry; ELM to Monroe, April 21, 1921 (letterhead stationery), Chicago.

6. ELM to Mother, February 8, 1926 (February 1922 as date of visit), HRC; unpub. chapter 22, p. 453 (all quotations), HRC; "Edgar Lee Masters' Impressive Tribute to Father . . . ," *Illinois State Register,* November 16, 1925, p. 1 (1401 Holmes Avenue, Springfield).

7. ELM to Mary Aldis, June 9, 1922 (illness of mother and father), Newberry; ELM to Tietjens, April 8, 1921 (son's tuberculosis), Newberry.

8. Diary 1922, April 10 (affidavit); unpub. chapter 23, p. 456 ("I made an affidavit"), HRC; "Poet and Wife Drop Divorce," 1 (Judge Raynor); George Brett to ELM, March 22, 1922 (royalty rate of 33 ¾¢ per copy and sales of $261.05), HRC; ELM to Carter Harrison, March 21, 1938 ("wearing apparel"), HRC.

9. ELM to Monroe, April 6, 1922 ("They would put me under," "They would put me on"), HRC; unpub. chapter 23, pp. 456 ("a notorious woman"), 457 ("decree stood"), HRC.

10. ELM to Mrs. [Mary] Aldis, April 11, 1922 ("You know"), Newberry; Diary 1922, April 1, 8, 12 ("Lillian long"), 14, 26 ("satchel of books"); ELM, "My Youth in the Spoon River Country," 231 (fifty trees), HRC.

11. ELM to Charmian London, April 4, 1922 ("I do," "Your letter"), June 27, 1924 (shows correspondence), both HRC; ELM to Roland Farley, May 6, 1924 (shows correspondence), HRC.

12. ELM to Tietjens, April 11, 1922 ("I took"), Newberry; ELM to Harriet Monroe, April 18, 1922 ("the cause"), Chicago.

13. ELM to Tietjens, April 3, 1922 ("I do not know," "There are no pensions"), Newberry; ELM to Henderson, April 20, 1922 ("For the first"), HRC.

14. ELM to Brett, April 2, 1922 (loan), April 26, 1922 ("There is no"), April 15, 1922 ("borrow $5,000"), April 12, 1922 ("trade secrets," "No information"), all HRC; Brett to ELM, April 10, 1922 (Chicago office served), HRC.

15. ELM to Bill [Slack], March 26, 1922 ("I won't be"), HRC; ELM to Mrs. [Corinne] Robinson, May 22, 1921 ("I can do"), Harvard.

16. Lillian Wilson to ELM, March 30, 1920 (robins), HRC; ELM to "Robin! Darling!" June 12, 1923 (addresses Lillian as "Robin"), HRC; ELM to Mother, February 8, 1926 (did not see Lillian between September 1921 and May 1922), HRC; Diary 1922, May 9 ("Telephone"), 10 ("off to," "lovely").

17. Diary 1922, May 13, June 5–8; unpub. chapter 23, p. 458 ("We drew up"), HRC; ELM to Edwin Reese, May 7, 1924, Illinois State Historical Library.

18. Unpub. chapter 23, p. 459, HRC.

19. Masters to Tietjens, May 7, 1922 ("Of course," "I am excessively," "Poetry killed"), Newberry; ELM to Abe Meyer, May 1, 1922 (Helen will receive the farm), HRC.

20. ELM to Tietjens, May 7, 1922 (all details and quotations), Newberry.

21. *ASR,* 288 (Dreiser warning); unpub. chapter 21, pp. 425–26 ("I had said"), HRC; ELM, "My Youth," 257 ("stubborn resistance"), HRC; ELM to Tietjens, May 30, 1922 ("Tell me"), Newberry; ELM to Dreiser, April 2, 1915 ("When a man"), University of Pennsylvania; ELM to Lillian Wilson, July 15, 1921 ("OSTIM"), HRC.

22. ELM to Monroe, May 20, 1922, Chicago.

23. Diary 1922, May 21 (3,000 words), 23 (4,900 words), 25 (nearly 5,300 words, work on *The Nuptial Flight* ["The Houghtons"]), June 18, 27 (lectures); ELM to William A. Colledge (Redpath Bureau), June 21, 1922, Iowa; ELM to Brett, July 30, 1922 ("best boy's book"), May 19, 1922 ("unearned advances," $4,551.65), both HRC.

24. Diary 1922, June 20 ("Abe says"), 22 ("Wire from Bill"), 29 ("Phone Abe"); ELM to Abe [Meyer], June 24, 1922 ("In the event of my death"), HRC; unpub. chapter 23, p. 460 ("to be out of"), HRC; "Poet and Wife Drop Divorce," 1 (Helen Masters files for divorce in July 1922).

25. ELM to Bill Slack, March 26, 1922 (shows dislike of supporting wife), HRC; Diary 1922, July 1 (goes to Chicago).

26. Diary 1922, July 6 ("Talk"), 12 ("Consultation"); ELM to Governor [Charles Deneen], September 19, 1922 ("This consequence"), HRC.

27. Diary 1922, July 19–24 (cloud, lawyer misses meeting); unpub. chapter 23, p. 460 (understudy, cloud on the title and related problems with Helen Masters, "turning point"—although the chapter mistakenly suggests the key events transpired in August rather than July), HRC.

28. Diary 1922, July 31 (looks for office), August 6 ("Atlantis"); unpub. chapter 23, pp. 460–61, 463 (office, receivership, New York publishers), HRC; *Pictorial Review* to ELM, August 17, 1922 (turns down serialization), HRC.

29. Diary 1922, August 16–30 (Lillian); unpub. chapter 23, pp. 464 ("She had rights"), 461 ("friendship," "never want"), HRC.

30. Unpub. chapter 23, p. 462 ("It was now"), HRC; ELM, "My Youth," 268 (poison), HRC; Diary 1922, August 19–31 (shows Stokes's intermittent presence).

31. Unpub. chapter 23, pp. 462–65, HRC; Diary 1922, August 30 (prepares to leave).

32. Unpub. chapter 23, pp. 465–66 ("She listened"), HRC; Diary 1922, August 30.

33. Unpub. chapter 23, pp. 463 (farm and fortune, "his great Cadillac," Mrs. Stokes), 466 ("containing"), 467 ("Like myself"), HRC; Diary 1922, August 31 (departure for Illinois).

34. Unpub. chapter 23, pp. 467 ("precious contraband," "more hours"), 468 ("lawless freight," "Stokes speeded"), 469 ("a solution"), 470 ("Give her the Judas kiss," "If you do"), 467–69 (near accidents), HRC; Diary 1922, September 3 (shows departure to Chicago).

35. Unpub. chapter 23, p. 472 ("lawyer friend," "light" woman, "notorious case," "woke up"), HRC.

36. Diary 1922, September 4, 5; unpub. chapter 23, p. 472 ("I didn't," "He telephoned"), HRC; ELM, "My Youth," 271 (law materials in storage), HRC.

37. "Masters Are Reunited," *Chicago Daily News,* September 6, 1922, p. 1 ("After three," "the rumor," "the necessary papers"); "Masters Tells Divorce Scrap in 13 Sonnets," *Chicago Daily Journal,* August 18, 1923, p. 1 ("be good").

38. *Chicago Tribune,* September 6, 1922, p. 1 ("another woman"), 34 (pictures); Burke to ELM, September 6, 1922 ("this beautiful"), HRC; Diary 1922, September 6–7 ("Tears"); unpub. chapter 23, p. 475 (aid to sleep), HRC.

39. Diary 1922, September 13 ("books"), 8–17 ("Bad day"), 20 ("dizzy"), October 3 ("$30 from *Poetry*"), 4 (court); ELM, "My Youth," 269 ("I loathed"), HRC; Lillian Wilson to ELM, September 13, 1922 (friends and newspapers), HRC; unpub. chapter 23, p. 473 (Lillian feels "betrayed"), HRC.

40. Unpub. chapter 23, p. 475 (trunk against the door), HRC; ELM, "My Youth," 274 (club and hotels), HRC; unpub. chapter 24, esp. pp. 477 ($500), 478, 479, 482, HRC.

41. Unpub. chapter 24, p. 479 ("no letters"), HRC; ELM to Lillian Wilson, September 27, 1922 (two letters, "[Helen] had," "I came"), HRC.

42. ELM to Margery Currey, September 21 ("one of"), October 11 ("fine woman"), October 30, 1922 ("My dear," "just yesterday," "anything"), all Virginia.

43. Diary 1922, October 6; Ellen Coyne is alluded to in Diary 1919, June 24 (where her name erroneously appears as "Helen"), and Diary 1920, December 23, and an "Ellen" shows up infrequently on other dates, e.g., June 15, 1920, but the use of the first name only is inconclusive; ELM, "The Return," *Poetry* 22 (Sept. 1923): 292 ("autumnal morgue"); the sonnets are also mentioned in unpub. chapter 24, pp. 478 and 481, HRC.

44. Masters's two accounts of the slapping incident are in unpub. chapter 24, pp. 483–84 ("pushed her"), HRC, and "The Return," 296 ("slapped"); Helen Masters's account is in "Wife of Poet Masters to Get Cruelty Decree," *Chicago Tribune,* May 4, 1923, p. 19 ("striking," late for breakfast on November 15); "Reveals Why He Failed to Win Back Wife in His Sonnets,"

Chicago Herald and Examiner, August 19, 1923, pt. 1, p. 3 ("slapped"); unpub. chapter 24, pp. 481 ("fifty" sonnets), 478 ("nearly fifty" sonnets), HRC. The correct number of sonnets appears to be forty-nine: thirteen of the sonnets were published in the September 1923 issue of *Poetry;* "thirty-six of them were never published," according to ELM in unpub. chapter 24, p. 481, HRC; one of the sonnets forwarded to *Poetry* for publication was omitted, as is discussed in the next chapter.

45. Unpub. chapter 24, p. 481, HRC.

46. Ibid., 480 (lecture), HRC; ELM to [Harry Brent] Mackoy, October 18, 1922 ($100, "You should"), Kentucky; ELM to Bill [Slack], January 8, 1918 (agency fee 20 percent), HRC; Ernest Briggs to ELM, October 31, 1938 (agency fee 20 percent), HRC.

47. Unpub. chapter 24 (obstacles Masters faced when he resumed his law business), HRC; ELM to Monroe, September 12, 1922 (printed cards, "Dear Harriet"), Chicago.

48. ELM, "My Youth," 270 ("They hated me"), HRC.

49. Ibid., 279 ("The literary pages"), HRC.

50. ELM to Pagelson, December 12, 1922 ("The picking"), September 26, 1922 ("damn business"), both HRC; unpub. chapter 24, p. 478 ("Apollo"), HRC; ELM to Brett, September 22, 1922 (shows the telephone number of the Chicago Singletax Club on Masters's letterhead stationery), HRC.

51. Diary 1922, December 9; Marcia Lee Masters, *Wind Around the Moon* (Georgetown, Calif.: Dragon's Teeth, 1986), 14 ("The lights"); unpub. chapter 24, pp. 483–84 (realization that marriage is ruined), HRC; Diary 1923, February 2–5 (hotels); "Summary of a Legal Document in Cook County Courthouse," Flaccus file 1923 (Masters left his house for the last time on February 7, 1923), HRC.

52. ELM, federal tax return for 1922 (shows a gross income of $4,602), property of Hilary Masters; Diary 1923, February 5 ("letter [to] Harcourt"), April 6 (ELM "mailed 'Houghtons' to Doubleday"), February 21 (status of *Skeeters*), April 22 ("*Skeeters Kirby* a best seller"); ELM to Dan [Pagelson], September 28, 1922 ("I don't write"), HRC; ELM to Brett, May 5, 1922 (litigation hurts sales), HRC; ELM to Gerald [Sanders], January 29, 1941 (litigation hurts sales), HRC.

53. "Spoon River Revisited," *The New Republic* 17 (Nov. 23, 1918): 105; "More Spoon River Poems," *The Literary Digest* 64 (Feb. 21, 1920): 40; ELM to Maurice [Brown], July 11, 1921 ("20 epitaphs"), Michigan; Diary 1923, March 2 ("146 epitaphs"), April 4 (182 epitaphs), 6 ("sent [some]"), 10 (manuscript to *Vanity Fair*—serial publication began in July 1923); ELM to John N. Wheeler, April 10, 1923 (secondary serialization), HRC; Bell Syndicate to ELM, April 11, 1923 (plans to serialize), HRC; *Vanity Fair* to ELM, April 9, 1923 ($1,500), October 15, 1923 (*Vanity Fair* unhappy about newspaper use of poems), both HRC; Brett Jr. to ELM, April 24, 1923 (Brett unaware of new Spoon River poems), HRC; ELM, "My Youth," 279 (newspaper use of epitaphs), HRC; unpub. chapter 24, p. 480 (encouraged to write additional epitaphs), HRC.

54. Whitman Bennett Studios to ELM, April 20, 1923 ("film possibilities"), HRC; ELM to George Brett Jr., March 19, 1922 (hopes for movie contract), HRC; ELM to Meyer, April 23, 1923 ("I am"), HRC; ELM to Lloyd Sheldon, May 10, 1923 ("All the way"), HRC; ELM to Dreiser, December 22, 1915 (movie hopes), University of Pennsylvania; Diary 1923, April 26–30 (wrote on Spoon River scenario), April 30 (mailed scenario to Sheldon).

55. Diary 1923, April 25–May 10 (Liveright's), March 17 and April 25 (sonnets to friends), April 13 (sells *Children*); unpub. chapter 24, p. 485 ("counsel" for university), HRC.

56. ELM to Monroe, May 4, 1923 ("Last night"), Chicago; ELM to Abe Meyer, May 2, 1923 (Great Neck), HRC.

57. "Wife of Poet Masters to Get Cruelty Decree," 19 ("Breakfast table autocracy"); ELM

to George Brett, April 2, 1922 ($20,000), HRC; ELM to Samuel Falls, October 17, 1922 ($10,000), HRC; Abe Meyer to ELM, May 2, 1923 (right to visit children), HRC; unpub. chapter 24, p. 486 (copyrights, royalties, and library), HRC.

58. Financial supporters of *Poetry* were routinely identified in the front pages of each issue; the *Tribune*'s circulation was periodically printed on page 1; ELM to Tietjens, July 26, 1921 ("Sunday School persiflage"), Newberry.

CHAPTER 10: SATIN APPLES, SOUR GRAPES

1. ELM to Lillian Wilson, June 23, 1923 ("live at a hotel"), HRC; unpub. chapter 24, p. 476 (rents room), HRC; ELM to Roland Farley, June 2, 1923 (127 North Dearborn on letterhead stationery), NY Public.

2. ELM to Carter Harrison, September 13, 1936 ("most awful hell," "the McCormicks"), HRC; ELM to Ficke, September 19, 1930 ("a choice," "the woman goes"), Yale; ELM to Tietjens, n.d. ("Ode to Fame"), Newberry.

3. ELM to Monroe, March 29, 1917 ("girl," "There must"), Chicago; Hardin Masters to ELM, December 15, 1922 (*SRA* read in court, "bad and immoral"), HRC; unpub. chapter 24, p. 486 ("The Chicago papers"), HRC; "H. W. Masters Gets Decree," *New York Times,* February 10, 1923, p. 18 (Hardin's marriage problems—his second marriage would be more felicitous); unpub. chapter 28, p. 548 (Carl Stone's death in 1907), HRC.

4. "The Literary Spotlight," *The Bookman* 55 (Aug. 1922): 576 ("Edgar Lee Masters doesn't like Chi"), 572 ("great and permanent," "imminence," "For Masters").

5. Amy Lowell, *A Critical Fable* (Boston: Houghton Mifflin, 1922), 33, 35, 37.

6. ELM to Monroe, June 21, 1923 (Dearborn address, California plans, parents' health), Chicago; ELM to Mr. Bridges, May 4, 1923 (Illinois Athletic Club), Princeton; ELM to Abe Meyer, May 10, 1923 ($2,500), HRC; ELM to Elsie Farley, March 3, 1941 (sold draft of *Domesday Book* for $1,000), HRC; ELM to Ben Abramson, n.d. (sold *Domesday* through agent), HRC; Abramson (Argus Book Shop) to ELM, February 8, 1939 (commission on manuscript sales is 20 percent), February 20, 1939 (agrees to manuscript sales commission of 15 percent), both HRC; Jake Prassel to ELM, September 25, 1930 ("How I would have"), HRC; ELM to Bill Slack, March 20, 1926 (Chicago lot), HRC; ELM to Carter Harrison, March 21, 1938 (loan officer, "few hundred"; the date of this request to Darrow is unclear but is apparently 1923 and apparently after Masters's divorce), HRC; ELM to Mr. Decker, September 12, 1938 (draft of *Domesday*), Dartmouth; unpub. chapter 24, p. 488 (Burke and California), HRC; Diary 1923, May 5, 10.

7. Lillian Wilson to ELM, June 30, 1923 (two-three letters per day), HRC; ELM to [Lillian Wilson], June 12, 1923 ("I can imagine"), June 25, 1923 ("Why talk of putting"), both HRC.

8. ELM to Lillian Wilson, June 25, 1923 ("severe illness"), June 12, 1923 ("It ought not," "I have a certain"), both HRC; unpub. chapter 23, p. 473 ("She . . . fell"), chapter 21, p. 424 ("consisted of stocks"), both HRC; ELM, "My Youth in the Spoon River Country," 267½A, 268, 271 (Lillian's appendectomy), HRC; Lillian Wilson to ELM, September 24, 1922 (suggests "adhesions" from a previous surgery), HRC.

9. ELM to Lillian Wilson, June 23, 1923 ("Suppose we," "Mr. and Mrs. Peggy Wilson," "It is rumored"), HRC; Dorothy Dow, "An Introduction to Some Letters" ("He was"), Newberry.

10. Diary 1923, May 26–27 (sees Dow), June 27–28 (sees Dow), July 24 (sees Dow), August 3 (sees Dow); ELM to [Lillian Wilson], June 12, 1923 ("I was proposed to"), HRC. Masters's diary for the time of his "proposal" shows he was with a Rockford, Illinois, businessman and philanthropist named Fay Lewis on June 2–8, 1923 but makes no reference to a proposal; John Molyneux to Herb Russell, November 8, 1993 (information on Fay Lewis).

11. ELM to Lillian Wilson, June 26, 1923 ("a little statement," "I am told," "without the trammel"), HRC; Lillian Wilson to ELM, June 22, 1923 (reporter), HRC.

12. ELM to Emma Masters, June 30, 1923, HRC.

13. Diary 1923, July 1–August 3 (works on novel), October 3–6 (title of "Arthur Kirby"); ELM to George Brett, January 14, 1922 (manuscript that became *Mirage* once called "Love"), HRC; ELM to Roland Farley, October 6, 1923 (*Mirage* once called "Arthur Kirby"), NY Public; *Mitch Miller,* 7 (Skeeters Kirby's real name is "Arthur").

14. "News Notes," *Poetry* 22 (May 1923): 112.

15. ELM, "The Return," *Poetry* 22 (Sept. 1923): 291–303; unpub. chapter 24, p. 481 ("a story of spiritual torture"), HRC; ELM, *Songs and Sonnets,* 72–90.

16. ELM, "The Return."

17. Ibid.

18. Ibid.

19. Ibid.

20. "Reveals Why He Failed to Win Back Wife in His Sonnets," *Chicago Herald and Examiner,* August 19, 1923, pt. 1, p. 3 ("mysterious fourteenth sonnet"); ELM to Dreiser, March 23, 1938 ("only thirteen"), HRC; the galley of sonnet 7 is filed with a letter from ELM to Tietjens, May 18, 1923, Newberry; ELM, "The Return" ("talk his soul," etc.).

21. "The Return."

22. "Masters Poems Tell of Truce with Wife," *Chicago Daily News,* August 18, 1923, p. 1 ("some of," "a sensation"); "Masters Weighs His Divorce to Find New Poem," *Chicago Sunday Tribune,* August 19, 1923, pt. 1, p. 4 ("The poems"), p. 1 ("News Summary"); circulation of the *Tribune* was set at 773,485 on September 2, 1922, p. 1; *Chicago Herald and Examiner,* August 19, 1923, pt. 1, p. 3 ("the mystery," "The new"); ELM to Samuel P. McConnell, April 27, 1934 ("Frank Blatt" is modeled after Frank Walker), HRC.

23. Diary 1923, August 18 ("Great Spread"), 19 ("More spread"); Tietjens to Monroe, n.d., "*Poetry Magazine* Papers," Chicago; ELM to Arthur Davison Ficke, October 22, 1938 (still likes sonnets), Yale.

24. ELM to Roland Farley, January 22, 1925 (loses male friends), September 2, 1923 (Slack marries and sails), both NY Public; ELM, "My Youth," 278 (Reese in Chicago), HRC.

25. Unpub. chapter 24, p. 488 (possible marriage to Lillian), HRC; Dow, "Introduction to Some Letters" (at office of *Poetry*), Newberry; Diary 1923, August 20 ("Dorothy phones"); ELM to Roland Farley, October 2, 1923 ("Damn the newspapers"), NY Public; "Spoon River Poet Rumored Engaged to Woman Writer," unid. newspaper clipping stamped September 16, 1923 ("Dorothy Dow, Lockport"), NY Public; Alice Davis to H. L. Mencken, August 6, 1946 (Dow says she and Masters once engaged), NY Public.

26. ELM to Harcourt Brace, February 26, 1923 ("MS. of a book," ELM's "prefatory word"), HRC; Horace Liveright to ELM, December 27, 1923 (ELM will not do introduction), HRC; Dale Kramer, *Chicago Renaissance: The Literary Life in the Midwest, 1900–1930* (New York: Appleton-Century, 1966), 323 (book introduction for Dow canceled); in a letter dated April 30, 1924, and housed at the University of Chicago, Masters told Harriet Monroe he was "not getting married" and that "that Dorothy Dow matter is finally killed"; Diary 1923, September 24–25 (sees Ellen Coyne); unpub. chapter 26, p. 517 (Ellen Coyne moved to New York "about two months" before Masters did), HRC; unpub. chapter 25, pp. 504–5 (Masters's "love" for "Idothea"), HRC.

27. Diary 1923, November 3 (Janet Stedman), 4–11 (Leone); unpub. chapter 25, pp. 494 ("Idothea"), 503 ("A rich man"), 507 ("I saw that," "in my heart"), 495 ("she looked"), 504–5 (other details), HRC.

28. Diary 1923, November 7, 8, 27 (Milwaukee); unpub. chapter 25, pp. 504 ("about a

month"), 505 ("It is consummated," "saw the ghost"), 512 ("I never wrote"), HRC; all other details are in unpub. chapter 25, HRC; "Letter to De Mussett," *Delta Kappa Epsilon Quarterly* 54 (May 1936): 51–53 (part of Idothea's story in verse).

29. Unpub. chapter 25, p. 512 ("I had plenty"), HRC; Diary 1923, November 30, December 1–2 (money, Reese, Slack); ELM to Witter Bynner, October 15, 1923 ("I wish"), Harvard.

30. ELM, "Bridget Calypso," *The Harmony of Deeper Music,* 26 ("Mona Lisa"); ELM, *Mirage,* 413 (Lillian's nickname is "Bridget Calypso"), 139 (character based on Lillian has a "Mona Lisa . . . smile").

31. Hardin Wallace Masters, *Edgar Lee Masters: A Biographical Sketchbook about a Famous American Author* (Rutherford, N.J.: Farleigh Dickinson University Press, 1978), 82–83 (Hardin and ELM to train station on December 2, 1923).

32. Diary 1923, December 2 (car 413, porter 13, at 1:30).

CHAPTER 11: MASTERS AT MIDCAREER

1. ELM, *Children of the Market Place,* 465 ("old America").

2. *ASR,* 366 ("pencils"), 373 ("strings").

3. Diary 1919 (*Mitch* drafted between November 27 and December 8).

4. ELM, *Domesday Book,* 9 ("a mile"), 20–21 ("Shall not I").

5. Ibid., 3–4.

6. Ibid., 349 ("For that day"), 354–55 ("Who was this woman").

7. William Kimball Flaccus, "Edgar Lee Masters: A Biographical and Critical Study" (Ph.D. diss., New York University, 1952), 217 ("finest achievement").

8. ELM, *Starved Rock,* 1–4; ELM, *Domesday Book,* 9 ("the shadow of Starved Rock").

9. ELM, *Domesday Book,* 41 ("mind was on the law"), 39 ("fine things"), 42 (loses son), 161 (college costs), 162 (two semesters); *ASR,* 10 ("in a Doomesday Book").

10. ELM, *Domesday Book,* 21 ("Winthrop Marion"), 28 (Fouche), 324–26 (Tennessee Mitchell as mistress), 55 (Florence Dugan speech), 370–74 (Lillian as Arielle); John H. Wrenn and Margaret Wrenn, *Edgar Lee Masters* (Boston: Twayne, 1983), 77 (Darrow as Borrow); "Circuit Court," unid. news clipping, n.d., n.p. (Bays), Georgetown; *ASR,* 409 (Burke).

11. M. H. Abrams et al., eds., *The Norton Anthology of English Literature* (New York: Norton, 1962), 2:345 ("snuffed").

12. ELM, *Starved Rock,* 101.

13. ELM, *Mitch Miller,* 241, 243–44, 250, 259–61.

14. ELM, *Skeeters Kirby,* 118.

15. ELM to Tietjens, June 21, 1922 ("in a bad way," "every day . . . seems"), May 7, 1922 (worries about health, public), both Newberry.

16. ELM, *Mirage,* 203 ("What should his epitaph be?"); ELM, *Toward the Gulf,* 195 ("I was a swift runner").

17. ELM, *Mirage,* 416 ("I saw"); *ASR,* 400 ("as a boy," paper knight).

18. ELM, *Mirage,* 427 ("withered flags"), 26 ("star"), 416 ("search for truth and beauty"); ELM, *Skeeters Kirby,* 297 (mentions "Lamia").

19. ELM, "What Is Great Poetry?" *Poetry* 26 (Sept. 1925): 350–51.

20. *ASR,* 6 ("When I was").

21. Ibid., 7 (illegitimate).

22. ELM, *The Nuptial Flight* (New York: Boni and Liveright, 1923), 112 ("Because of his"), 142 ("Walter Scott derived").

23. Ibid., 98.

24. Ibid., 163 ("dreamer," "It had augmented").

25. Ibid., 158 ("She was drawn"), 159 ("was always . . . reminding"), 343 ("Was this the Spanish blood").

26. Ibid., 159.

27. Ibid., 374.

CHAPTER 12: THE LITERARY LION AND THE ROARING TWENTIES

1. *ASR*, 342 ("The World War").

2. Hardin Wallace Masters, *Edgar Lee Masters: A Biographical Sketchbook about a Famous American Author* (Rutherford, N.J.: Farleigh Dickinson University Press, 1978), 110 (ELM careless in his dress); Hilary Masters, *Last Stands: Notes from Memory* (Boston: Godine, 1982), 97 (ELM appeared younger than his age); Frank Wing, *Yesterdays* (Chicago: Reilly and Lee, 1930), n.p. (picture and text suggesting *Spoon River* focuses on country types); Diary 1923, December 3 (to New York).

3. Biographical note on Farley, ELM-Farley correspondence, NY Public; Elsie Farley to ELM, n.d. (Farleys at 435 Park Avenue), May 19, 1924 (Long Island home), both NY Public; ELM to Roland Farley, November 17, 1923 ("Can you house"), NY Public; unpub. chapter 24, p. 487 (at Great Neck when divorce finalized), HRC; ELM to Dear Fool [Edwin Reese], February 2, 1926 (Farley set some of Masters's words to music), Illinois State Historical Library; G. Schirmer, Inc., to ELM, June 11, 1930 ("Summer Day"), HRC; Roland Farley to ELM, July 15, 1923 (hears "Spoon River"), HRC; ELM to Percy Grainger, January 14, 1938 (Robinson's fiddle tune), HRC; ELM to Mr. Dickinson, November 22, 1924 (Robinson a soldier, heard song near Spoon River in 1857, ELM heard in 1915), HRC; Diary 1919, February 25 (meets Grainger); "Biographical Information" folder (Captain Charles Robinson heard fiddle tune known as "Spoon River" in 1857 at Bradford, Illinois), Knox College; unpub. chapter 26 (other details), HRC.

4. Retired Professors Registry form, American Association of University Professors (drama, New School of Social Research), property of Hilary Masters; Diary 1923, September 24–25 (two dates), December 25 ("Ellen Coyne"); unpub. chapter 26, p. 517 (Ellen preceded ELM to NY by "about two months"), HRC; "Kansas City Girl Is the Bride of Edgar Lee Masters," *Kansas City Star,* November 6, 1926, p. 3 (high school, Dillenbeck); Hilary Masters, *Last Stands,* 94–95 (Des Moines and travels); Hilary Masters to Herb Russell, conversation, 1992 (modeling activities, tour in Montana), May 9, 1993 (model for Smith); "Teacher at Ogontz," *Campuscope* (Pennsylvania State University's Ogontz Center), February 1956, p. 7 (two movies); "Famous Poet's Wife and Son Are Visiting in Kansas City," *Kansas City Star,* November 24, 1936, p. 13 (movies).

5. Diary 1924, January 6 (lovers), September 15 (Masters moves to Old Chelsea); Ellen Masters, "Days and Nights at the Old Chelsea," *New York* 12 (Nov. 26, 1979): 94, 96 (describes her life in the Old Chelsea).

6. Diary 1923, October 31 (*Mirage* [then called "Arthur Kirby"] to publisher); Diary 1924, March 27 (*Mirage* published); ELM to Mr. Smith (Boni and Liveright), December 12, 1923 (text), December 20, 1923 (title), January 23, 1924 (terms of contract), all HRC; ELM to Boni and Liveright, January 25, 1924 ("the proofs"), HRC; ELM to Edwin Reese, August 6, 1924 ("I meant to etch"), Illinois State Historical Library; unpub. chapter 26 (other details), p. 515 (servants), HRC.

7. Diary 1923, September 13 (works on "New Salem"); ELM to [Barrett] Clark, October 26, 1934 (drafts "New Salem" in fall 1923), Yale; ELM to Roland Farley, October 2, 1923 ("to wire," Barrymore, visited New Salem in August), November 21, 1924 (Provincetown Playhouse), both NY Public; Diary 1924, January 3 (circulates "New Salem").

8. Provincetown Playhouse to ELM, December 9, 1924, December 12, 1924, both HRC.

9. Diary 1924, January 8 ("began *Kit O'Brien,*" a story for boys), February 4 ("begin to work on *Lee*"), March 19 (begins to spend nights at Princeton); ELM to Elsie Farley, April 2, 1924 (works on *Lee* in spring of 1924), January 7, 1924 ($50 rent), both NY Public; Elsie Farley to ELM, n.d. (likes famous house guest), HRC.

10. Diary 1924, April 2–17 (*Lee*), May 28 (boy book), March 6 (reviews *The New Spoon River* poems); ELM to Horace Liveright, May 6, 1924 (has begun epilogue to *Domesday Book,* wants to write epilogue for *The New Spoon River*), HRC.

11. ELM to Edwin Reese, June 28, 1924 ("I have tippled gin"), May 7, 1924 ("I can walk"), April 14, 1924 ("I wish to God"), all Illinois State Historical Library.

12. ELM to Dear Fool [Edwin Reese], n.d. [Spring 1924] ("I called"), Illinois State Historical Library; Diary 1924, April 21.

13. ELM to Elsie Farley, August 19, 1924 ("No girls here"), May 9, 1924 ("I expect"), both NY Public; ELM to Katharine Jones, n.d. [1924], Flaccus file 1924 ("wedded again"), HRC.

14. ELM to Dear Fool [Edwin Reese], n.d. [Spring 1924] (ocean voyage), Illinois State Historical Library.

15. ELM to Edwin Reese, May 7, 1924 ("we are talking"), June 28, 1924 ("It has about come"), July 24, 1924 ("I am expected to marry"), all Illinois State Historical Library.

16. Hilary Masters, *Last Stands,* 3–88.

17. Ibid., 3–88, 78 (murder), 116 (address), 120, 142 (bonfire), 177 (sells property); Hilary Masters to Herb Russell, conversation, November 1996 (Ozarks land), conversation, June 19, 1997 (to Panama).

18. Hilary Masters, *Last Stands,* 79 (married 1898).

19. Unpub. chapter 26, p. 518 ("Here was Bryan"), HRC; Diary 1924, June 16 (Molly in town), July 9 (convention ends).

20. Diary 1924, May 20 (wrote two epitaphs), June 3–5 ($2,000, delivers *The New Spoon River* to Liveright, pays Abe Meyer), June 18 (proofs); Diary 1925, January 12 (drinks with Liveright); ELM to Horace Liveright, May 18, 1924 ("just paid my note"), HRC; Horace Liveright to ELM, June 11, 1924 (gives check for $1,000), June 23, 1924 (borrowed the $1,000 in question from his wife), September 27, 1930 (in Hollywood), all HRC; T. Smith (Boni and Liveright) to ELM, n.d. (Liveright received $1,000 reimbursement from company), HRC; Boni and Liveright to ELM, October 21, 1932 (says he owes company $1,000), HRC; ELM to Boni and Liveright, December 28, 1934 (repayment should not come from royalties of *The New Spoon River*), HRC.

21. ELM to Mary [Bell Sloan], September 30, 1924 (ELM began *The New Spoon River* following encouragement from a Mrs. Merwin in Bloomington, Illinois, one of many admirers of *SRA* who encouraged a sequel), Dartmouth; ELM to Jack [Powys], April 25, 1939, Flaccus file 1939 (*The New Spoon River* and "Spoon River Annex"), HRC; Emma Masters to ELM, n.d. (list of eighty names, including three that were used in the book: Priam Finish, Stella Sturgis, Watson Watt), HRC.

22. ELM to Horace Liveright, May 6, 1924 ("a son of a bitch"), HRC.

23. ELM to John Cowper Powys, February 6, 1928 ("what the age of machinery"), University of Pennsylvania; ELM to Horace Liveright, June 11, 1924, June 30, 1924, and July 13, 1924 (cover designs), all HRC.

24. Quotations are from the epitaphs of "Martin Venable," "McDowell Young," and "Marx the Sign Painter," ELM, *The New Spoon River.*

25. ELM to Harriet Monroe, September 2, 1924 ("I wrote it"), Chicago; *ASR,* 366 (critics sharpening pencils).

26. ELM to Agnes Lee Freer, September 25, 1924 (meets Mencken), Chicago; ELM to Dreiser, March 20, 1913 (mentions "a letter from Mencken"), University of Pennsylvania.

27. ELM to Horace Liveright, May 6, 1924 (translations of *SRA*), HRC; ELM to Harriet Monroe, December 23, 1924 ("sold better"), HRC; ELM to Mary [Bell Sloan], September 30, 1924 (*The New Spoon River* published in September), Dartmouth; "Edgar Lee Masters," *The Saturday Review of Literature* 2 (July 3, 1926): 903.

28. Diary 1924, July 8–August 7; ELM to Elsie Farley, April 14, 1924 (does own typing), NY Public.

29. Diary 1924, August 11–21 (at house in Portland, Maine), 17 ("Feel depressed"); ELM to Elsie Farley, May 9, 1924 (Madeline's homes on Cushing Island, East Hampton, New York), NY Public; unpub. chapter 28, pp. 546–48 (Edgar Lee Gron, Elizabeth, Emma Louise, other houses, apartments of Madeline), HRC; *ASR*, 376 (Buddie); ELM to Dear Fool [Edwin Reese], February 2, 1926 (Prairie Avenue), Illinois State Historical Library; "Poet Masters, 57, Marries Girl, 27," unid. news clipping, n.d., n.p. (Gron a diplomat), Illinois State Historical Library; Wilbur Masters to ELM, April 17, 1927 (good taste), HRC; ELM to Dear Kid [Ellen], December 20, 1934 (good taste), HRC; Hardin Masters to ELM, May 1, 1924 (Stone name), HRC; ELM to Madeline [Masters Stone], January 30, 1926 (Madeline's studies, Taft), HRC; Madeline [Stone] to ELM, January 28, [1926?] (Taft, Borglum), HRC; ELM to Father, February 22, 1905 (Horatio), Knox College.

30. Unpub. chapter 26, p. 516 (housing at Farleys), HRC; Elsie Farley to ELM, n.d. (housing), HRC; Roland Farley to ELM, July 15, 1923 (mentions an outdoor studio), HRC; ELM to Charmian London, June 27, 1924 (Farleys wish ELM to stay permanently), HRC; ELM to Walter Tittle, December 11, 1924 (at 51 W. 16th St.), HRC; ELM to Edwina Stanton Babcock, October 26, 1924 ("I shall be"), HRC; ELM to Illinois Athletic Club, September 13, 1924 (ends membership), HRC; Diary 1924, September 15 ("Move"); ELM to Norman Foerster, January 7, 1925 (at 51 W. 16th St.), Stanford.

31. Diary 1924, August 24 ("E. poses"), August 24–October 8; ELM to Roland and Elsie Farley, October 4, 1924 ("Nicolosi is taking"), NY Public; Diary 1925, January 17 ("I like"); ELM to Madeline [Masters Stone], January 30, 1926 (Nicolosi an immigrant), HRC.

32. Diary 1924, September 30, October 6, 9 (Ellen's dramatic activities); ELM to Hardin Masters, November 21, 1924 (on letterhead stationery of Sue Hastings' Marionettes, 596 Riverside Drive), HRC; Hilary Masters to Herb Russell, conversation, 1992 (Sue Hastings).

33. ELM to Edwin Reese, June 2, 1925 ("magnum opus"), Illinois State Historical Library; ELM to Horace [Liveright], May 16, 1927 (from 1492 to World War I), HRC; ELM to Frank [W. Allan], December 15, 1926 ("Aeneid"), HRC; ELM to George [Gillespie], November 22, 1925 ("years" to complete), HRC; Horace Liveright to ELM, October 21, 1924 (tour would help *The New Spoon River*), HRC; ELM to Roland and Elsie Farley, August 10, 1923 ("long poem"), NY Public; ELM to Roland Farley, November 21, 1924 ("reading as much as possible," lecture tour), NY Public; ELM to Harriet [Monroe], Thanksgiving Day, 1924 ("I am now reading"), Chicago; Diary 1924, October 20 ("began to read for 'Atlantis'"); unpub. chapter 26, p. 519 ("I felt that I must"), HRC.

34. Ellen Masters, "Days and Nights at the Old Chelsea," 94 (Colston Leigh); A. J. Armstrong to ELM, January 31, 1925, February 5, 1925 (Armstrong agency arranges most of tour), both HRC; Colston Leigh to ELM, January 9, 1925 (ELM's preferred "lecture" consisted of introductory remarks followed by the recitation of his poems, with the emphasis on the poems), HRC; ELM to Joseph Wood Krutch, July 30, 1925 (ELM's preferred "lecture" format), HRC; ELM to Colston Leigh, December 9, 1924 (lecture on America and poetry), HRC; Leigh Lecture Bureau to University of Arkansas, n.d., misc. file C–Cz ("America . . ."), HRC; ELM to Roland Farley, January 22, 1925 ("committing poems"), NY Public.

35. Diary 1925, January 22–February 20 (itinerary); ELM to [Colston] Leigh, January 31, 1925 (West Virginia lecture), Pennsylvania State University.

36. Diary 1925, February 23–March 11, February 27 ("better than").

37. ELM to Roland Farley, March 10, 1925 ("This traveling"), NY Public; unpub. chapter 26, p. 520 (Sterling, "every sort of a drinkable," Eugene, Salem), HRC; ELM to Edwina Stanton Babcock, January 22, 1925, March 23, 1925, and April 25, 1925 (drinking remarks), all Princeton; Leigh to ELM, March 21, 1925 (ELM says he is too ill to go up coast), HRC.

38. Diary 1925, March 12–16; unpub. chapter 26, p. 520, HRC.

39. Diary 1925, March 17–20; "Poet's Attack on Corn Belt Starts Storm," *Des Moines Register,* March 20, 1925, p. 1 ("A man cannot," "No wonder you people"); Sara Toubes, "Iowa Can Rest Easy . . . ," *Des Moines Register,* March 19, 1925, p. 2 ("Flaunting his so-called"); unpub. chapter 26, p. 520 ("The auspices"), HRC.

40. Diary 1925, March 25–26; unpub. chapter 26, p. 521 ("dull" and "dreary," "only a few miles"), HRC.

41. Diary 1925, March 26–April 2, April 1 ("great audience"); unpub. chapter 26, p. 521, HRC.

42. Diary 1925, end papers (towns and most speaker's fees of $200); end papers of the 1925 diary also show some (but not all) of Masters's hotel bills, railroad costs, and food expenses; ELM to Abe [Meyer], January 8, 1927 (about $3,000), HRC; unpub. chapter 26, p. 521 ("I sent $1,000"), HRC; ELM to [Colston] Leigh, February 20, 1925 (could have made more money on tour), Virginia.

43. Diary 1925, April 11 (article on artist in America), 13 (collected poems), May 14 (to 18 Gramercy); ELM to [Mark] Van Doren, September 2, 1925 (returns check to *The Nation,* "the transaction"), HRC; ELM to Miss Rosebrook, May 11, 1925 ($90), HRC; Sidney Colestock to ELM, September 24, 1924 ($16), HRC; Emma Masters to ELM, September 10, 1925 (maintenance on house), HRC; unpub. chapter 26, p. 521 (apartment on Gramercy), HRC.

44. Hilary Masters to Herb Russell, conversation, November 1996 (X ray and scars), June 11, 1997 (eczema, Irving Bookstore), conversation, May 9, 1993 (Cerf anecdote, ring); Diary 1924, May 18 (Ellen's twenty-fifth birthday), December 24 (ring); Charles E. Burgess, "The Use of Local Lore in *Spoon River Anthology*" (M.A. thesis, Southern Illinois University, 1969), 152–53 (shows a scarred actress in Lewistown); ELM, *Kit O'Brien* ([New York]: Boni and Liveright, 1927), 57, 286 (scarred actress); Anne Kimball to Kimball Flaccus, n.d. [March 10, 1956] ("starry-eyed"), Georgetown.

45. ELM to Elizabeth Lindsay, May 11, 1932 ("keen as hell"), HRC; The Neighborhood Playhouse to Ellen Masters, April 17, 1927 ("Books"), HRC; *ASR,* 225 (Helen's nose); ELM, "I Call Her Dorcas," *The Rotarian* 62 (May 1943): 8 (Lucinda's profile).

46. ELM to Miss Babcock, December 16, 1924, October 26, 1924 ("I am by myself"), both Princeton; ELM to "Irish" [Edwina Stanton Babcock] March 1, 1925 (alludes to her correspondence via the Arts Club and her interest in writing), March 23, 1925 (her prettiness, "I hope to see"), both Princeton; ELM to "Virgin" [Edwina Stanton Babcock], December 23, 1924 ("$100 reward"), Princeton; ELM to Edwina Stanton Babcock, n.d. ("What words"), Princeton; "Hittite" [ELM to Edwina Stanton Babcock], January 7, 1925 ("No one knows"), Princeton; [ELM to Edwina Stanton Babcock], n.d. [Spring 1925] ("The girl you saw"), Princeton; Diary 1925, April 23 ("Edwina at train"). The answer to Masters's riddle is not given in letters to Babcock but is repeated in numerous letters to male acquaintances and also to Elsie Farley, October 21, 1924, NY Public; the statesman in question is Woodrow Wilson.

47. Diary 1925, May 26–30, June 1, 9; ELM, *Mitch Miller,* 38–39; ELM, "The Statue," *Selected Poems,* 151–55 ("Fayfe," "Rhythm of arms"); Hilary Masters to Herb Russell, June 11, 1997 (Fay-Fay).

48. Unpub. chapter 26, p. 521 (Ellen and Molly Coyne to Ireland), HRC; Ellen Masters to Kimball Flaccus, November 1, 1953 ("My father gave me"), HRC; Tom Coyne to ELM, May 31, 1946 (Coyne's trip planned), HRC; Hilary Masters to Herb Russell, May 9, 1993 (Tom Coyne to Ireland by himself as old man).

49. Diary 1922, August 6 (conceives "Atlantis"); ELM to Horace [Liveright], May 16, 1927 ("It is the epic of America," meter, lines, "books," and pages), HRC.

50. Unpub. chapter 26, p. 521 (publisher, "pile of manuscript"), HRC; Diary 1925, August 6 (puts manuscript in vault).

51. ELM to Ludwig Lewisohn, October 28, 1932 ("gave away poems"), HRC; ELM to Monroe, November 29, 1921 ("You have my permission"), HRC; ELM to Mr. Latham, January 13, 1922 (ELM must approve Monroe's selections, "There should be"), HRC; ELM to William Rose Benet, June 11, 1922 ("people who buy"), HRC; ELM to George Brett, December 7, 1921 (ELM must approve selections), January 19, 1922 ("Besides this, anthologies"), both HRC; ELM to T. R. Smith, May 26, 1926 ("money was being made," "parasitical activity," "pedantic donkeys," "ignorant calumniators," "There are many"), HRC; ELM to Mark Van Doren, May 16, 1928 (pirated poem), HRC; ELM to Mr. Thomas, May 19, 1926 (angry at Macmillan Company for cooperating with anthology maker), HRC.

52. ELM to George Brett, August 12, 1925 ("I want to draw in"), HRC; ELM to Alice Corbin Henderson, April 20, 1922 (Aiken turned down), HRC; ELM to Ludwig Lewisohn, October 28, 1932 (turns down Aiken, Drinkwater, Van Doren, Kreymborg but approves Lewisohn), HRC; John L. B. Williams to ELM, November 7, 1941 (ELM refuses Untermeyer), HRC; ELM to William S. Braithwaite, July 28, 1928 (turns down request), HRC; ELM to Horace Liveright, May 14, 1926 (returns check for Pattee book), HRC; ELM to Gerald Sanders, February 22, 1928 ("I withdrew"), December 14, 1927 (tries to shape Sanders book by substituting poems, "equal representation," Hardy, Robinson, Frost, "misstatements"), both HRC; ELM to [William] Osborne, April 2, 1933 ("book came out"), May 20, 1933 ("Without me"), both HRC; ELM to R. M. Pearson, October 7, 1930 (Harper Brothers, "I do not regret"), HRC; ELM to Henry Seidel Canby, February 15, 1929 ("at least three requests per week"), HRC; ELM to J. H. Nelson, April 18, 1932 ("an average of three requests"), HRC; ELM to Marguerite Wilkinson, August 16, 1922 (Wilkinson allowed to reprint), Middlebury College; Gerald Sanders and John H. Nelson, eds., *Chief Modern Poets of England and America* (New York: Macmillan, 1929), v–vi ("One important poet").

53. ELM to Gerald Sanders, February 22, 1928 ("$10 or $20" per poem), HRC; William Rose Benet to ELM, June 12, 1924 ($10 per poem), HRC; ELM to George Brett, December 14, 1927 (just under $20 per poem), HRC; Dana Ferrin to ELM, June 15, 1926 ("all the more"), HRC.

CHAPTER 13: MASTERS MARRIES GIRL!

1. T. Smith to ELM, February 8, 1924 (*Mirage* needs revisions), HRC; Final Notice before Legal Procedure (Loftis Brothers) to ELM, October 3, 1925 (old debt), HRC; the errors in *Selected Poems* include the following: "The Death of Sir Launcelot," 197 (a poem about the British Middle Ages, it includes a line from "Achilles Deatheridge," a poem about the American Civil War), "The Mourner's Bench," 203 (typographical error in line 16), "Nature," 312 (typographical error in its penultimate line), and several instances of broken type; Diary 1925, June 9, 17, July 6, August 7, September 16 (unsuccessful attempts to market *Kit O'Brien*), August 10 (play rejected), August 14–31 (with Nicolosi at Lake George).

2. Unpub. chapter 22, pp. 445, 448 (mother's and father's illnesses), HRC.

3. Record of the Trip to Morgan County, Illinois, October 15, 1917 (genealogical research in Jacksonville area), HRC; Lucinda Masters Deposition, September 9, 1897, HRC.

4. Unpub. chapter 26, pp. 522 (Nicolosi, memorial boulder from Rock Creek), 524–25 (sees mother and father, "discipline as a lawyer"), HRC; Diary 1925, September 14 (expressed the tablet); Wilbur Masters to ELM, September 5, 1925 (Wilbur seems to have moved the boulder), HRC.

5. Unpub. chapter 26, pp. 525–26 ("Going into the country," "Nothing was left"), 527 (father frail), HRC; Diary 1925, September 29 (to church and farm).

6. Hilary Masters to Herb Russell, June 17, 1993 (Sue Hastings, Allgood); "Teacher at Ogontz," *Campuscope* (Pennsylvania State University's Ogontz Center), February 1956, p. 7 (Abbey Theatre, *Julius Caesar*); Diary 1925, September 21 (Ellen returns from Europe); Elisabeth Earley, interview with Ellen Masters, December 2, 1970, p. 25 (bookstore mentioned, ELM did not support Ellen's theater hopes), property of Hilary Masters.

7. ELM to Mr. Lorimer, November 7, 1925 ("My Years in the Lincoln Country"), HRC; ELM to Mr. Mamer, February 7, 1927 (Hardin worked with Herndon from 1872–80), HRC; Charles E. Burgess, "Sandridge: A Masters Landscape Revisited," *Western Illinois Regional Studies* 14 (Fall 1991): 14 (Rutledge's remains moved); Herbert K. Russell, *The Enduring River: Edgar Lee Masters' Uncollected Spoon River Poems* (Carbondale: Southern Illinois University Press: 1991), 16 (1921 gravestone); Charles E. Burgess, "Masters and Some Mentors," *Papers on Language and Literature* 10 (Spring 1974): 178*n* (Hardin Masters–Herndon relation), 184 (Herndon's influence in moving of Rutledge remains); ELM, *The Sangamon*, 135–36 (local historian).

8. ELM to Mr. Mamer, February 7, 1927 (memory of village elders), HRC; ELM to Hardin Masters, September 14, 1925 ("I have in mind"), HRC.

9. ELM to Hardin Masters, September 19, 1925 ("*The Saturday Evening Post*"), HRC; ELM to Mr. Lorimer, November 7, 1925 (sends autobiography to *Post*), HRC; Diary 1925, September 27–October 7 (research), November 9 (Ingersoll), 10 (trip).

10. Diary 1925, November 11–14 (father's illness and death); unpub. chapter 26, p. 527 ("no news"), HRC; ELM to Harriet [Monroe], December 16, 1925 ("privately registered"), Chicago; "Hunt for Edgar Lee Masters as His Father Dies," *Chicago Tribune*, November 15, 1925, pt. 1, p. 10.

11. Unpub. chapter 26, pp. 528–29 (funeral details), HRC; "H. W. Masters Funeral Rites Are Expected to be Held at Residence Monday Afternoon," *Illinois State Register*, November 15, 1925, p. 5 (Darrow, Beveridge as honorary pallbearers); ELM to "Dear Fool" [Edwin Reese], November 23, 1925 ($600 coffin, mausoleum, Hardin owns burial lot in Petersburg, "I thought it would be"), HRC; Emma Masters to ELM, April 23, 1926 (Oak Ridge mausoleum), HRC; ELM to Albert J. Beveridge, February 26, 1926 (shows Beveridge corresponding with Hardin Masters regarding Herndon), HRC.

12. "Edgar Lee Masters' Impressive Tribute to Father Read Today at Funeral of Veteran Lawyer," *Illinois State Register*, November 16, 1925, pp. 1, 8 ("play-boy"); Hardin Wallace Masters, *Edgar Lee Masters: A Biographical Sketchbook about a Famous American Author* (Rutherford, N.J.: Farleigh Dickinson University Press, 1978), 99 ("play-boy"); unpub. chapter 26, p. 529 ("sixty years of misunderstanding"), HRC.

13. Unpub. chapter 26, pp. 529 ("If before coming"), 530 ("Perhaps she wept"), 531 ("As I saw," Nicolosi), HRC.

14. Ibid., 530–31 (mother), HRC; Diary 1925, November 21 (autobiography returned), November 30–December 15 (writing), November 26 ("miss father and grieve"); ELM to "Herbert," November 23, 1925 ("Sometimes he seems"), HRC; ELM to Monroe, December 16, 1925 ("My father"), Chicago.

15. ELM to Mencken, July 21, 1925 (Masters's dislike for Bryan's clients, religious fundamentalists), HRC.

16. ELM to Monroe, June 9, 1925 ("I think," "there are so few," "I used to think"), Chicago; ELM to Hardin Masters, December 20, 1925 (Christmas 1925), HRC; Diary 1925, December 24.

17. Diary 1926, January 13–27, February 23 (*Lee*), 5, 12–20, 25–27, March, April 1–21 (*Levy Mayer*); ELM, *Lee: A Dramatic Poem* (New York: Macmillan, 1926); ELM to Art [Ficke], January 19, 1940 ($1,000 advance on *Lee*), Yale; Frank K. Robinson, *Edgar Lee Masters: An Exhi-*

bition in Commemoration of the Centenary of His Birth (Austin: University of Texas, 1970), 24 (*Lee* editions); George Brett Jr. to ELM, October 17, 1925 (spend time on *Lee*), January 19, 1926 (time on *Lee*), both HRC.

18. Abe Meyer to ELM, June 16, 1921 (letterhead shows members of law firm), HRC; ELM to Abe [Meyer], January 8, 1927 (Meyer proposed book on Mayer), HRC; Rachel Mayer to ELM, June 13, 1927 (likes husband's biography), HRC; ELM to Edwin Reese, November 9, 1926 (biography done for a fee), Illinois State Historical Library; unpub. chapter 27, p. 532 ("hard at work"), HRC; ELM, *Levy Mayer and the New Industrial Era* (New Haven, Conn.: "under direction of Yale University Press," 1927), [p. 306] (1,500 copies); John H. Wrenn and Margaret Wrenn, *Edgar Lee Masters* (Boston: Twayne, 1983), 103 (Meyer a brother to Mayer's wife).

19. ELM, "On the Death Mask of Hardin Masters," *Illinois State Register,* February 7, 1926, pt. 2, p. 8 ("prairie Jefferson"); Jessee Palmer Weber, secretary, Illinois State Historical Society, and librarian, Illinois State Historical Library, to ELM, March 17, 1926 (receives death mask of Hardin Masters), February 25, 1926 (solicits article ["Days in the Lincoln Country"]), both HRC; ELM to Miss Flashmer, August 18, 1926 ("some reminiscences"), HRC; Diary 1926, April 17 (father's body), January 11 (sonnets); August Derleth, "Masters and the Revolt from the Village," *The Colorado Quarterly* 8 (Autumn 1959): 167 (shows ELM had copy of the death mask in his apartment in New York in 1940, but whether this was the bronze version or the plaster cast is not clear; no death mask of Hardin Masters was in the Illinois State Historical Library in 1993).

20. Unpub. chapter 27, p. 533 ("I would not touch"), HRC; ELM to Mother, September 6, 1925 ($2,000 advance), HRC; Emma Masters to ELM, September 10, 1925 (refuses $2,000 advance), June 1, 1925 (has nightmare over request for $2,000, shows ELM asked for the advance at least twice), both HRC.

21. Emma Masters to ELM, December 14, 1924, December 17, 1924, October 18, 1926 (Emma's writing), January 8, 1925, April 14, 1926 (Tom's scrapbook), September 10, 1925 (influences), May 19, 1925 ("Each member"), all HRC; Hardin Masters to ELM, December 5, 1924 (article done), November 14, 1924 (longevity, Herndon), August 10, 1925 (Herndon done), all HRC; Madeline Masters, poems, n.d., HRC; Horace Liveright to Madeline Masters Stone, August 2, 1923 (rejects novel), HRC; ELM to Mencken, December 29, 1925 (article against Prohibition), NY Public; Hardin Wallace Masters, "Chicago," *The Literary Digest* 75 (Nov. 25, 1922): 36.

22. Unpub. chapter 27, pp. 532 ("My brother"), 533–34 (Chiperfield), HRC; ELM to Mr. Thayer, May 11, 1926 ("you will surely find"), HRC.

23. Unpub. chapter 27, p. 534 ("I decided that," "high and palmy days," friends, research), HRC; Diary 1926, June 11 (leaves New York); Witter Bynner, *Grenstone Poems* (New York: Knopf, 1926), ix–xii.

24. Unpub. chapter 27, pp. 535–37 (Sterling), HRC; ELM to Dear George [Sterling], June 18, 1926 ("Get out the mandolute"), Berkeley.

25. Unpub. chapter 27, pp. 536–37 ("He went," "to die"), HRC.

26. Diary 1926, July 13–14 (visits mother); Emma Masters to ELM, May 19, 1926 (radium), HRC; ELM to Emma Masters, telegram, February 9, 1926 ("altar prayers"), HRC; unpub. chapter 27, pp. 537 ("a little startled"), 538 ("She was greatly," "I have felt"), 534 (disliked house), HRC.

27. Unpub. chapter 27, p. 539 ("My mother," "I dislike to confess"), HRC; Diary 1926, October 7–10 (does not attend mother's funeral); ELM to Chiperfield, October 8, 1926 ("My complications"), HRC.

28. George Gillespie to ELM, January 2, 1926 (Emma will not make a will), HRC; ELM to Alice Corbin Henderson, February 6, 1927 (no wills), HRC; Diary 1925, November 19 (mother advised by Gillespie after Hardin's death); *ASR,* 303 (Hardin sues Wilbur).

29. ELM to Chiperfield, March 31, 1926 (house worth $12,000), HRC; ELM to Bill [Slack], February 13, 1927 (Supreme Court, Abe Meyer, "Suppose you look," Helen's claim), HRC (Helen Masters is discussed under the pseudonym of "Willa Carvallo," also the title of a poem in *Poems of People*); ELM to Frank [W. Allan], May 2, 1927 ("despicable brother"), HRC; ELM to Dreiser, October 20, 1944 (Helen's $10,000 lost), HRC; unpub. chapter 27, pp. 541–42 (Helen Masters, Tom represents Helen, Spring Lake loss), HRC.

30. Hilary Masters to Herb Russell, May 9, 1993 ("some minor parts"), conversations, 1992–93 (marriage details); Diary 1926, October 18–November 1 (trip to Illinois, Stokes, Petersburg); Rose C. Feld, "Spoon Rivers with the Full Quality of America," *New York Times Book Review,* September 7, 1924, p. 2 (plump, balding, gray); Elisabeth Earley, interview with Ellen Masters, December 2, 1970, p. 61 ("his pattern," Ellen does not really want to marry), property of Hilary Masters.

31. Unpub. chapter 27, p. 541 (all quotations), HRC.

32. Ellen Masters, "Days and Nights at the Old Chelsea," *New York* 12 (Nov. 26, 1979): 96 (Brevoort bookstore, No. 2 West 16th St.); Diary 1926, September 30–October 10 (moves to No. 2 West 16th St.); ELM to Tom and Molly Coyne, December 8, 1926 ("pretty good"), HRC; Ellen to Kimball Flaccus, April 21, 1951 (did not like apartment), HRC.

33. "Poet Masters, 57, Marries Girl, 27," unid. news clipping, n.d., n.p. ("No imaginary affair," "a romance"), Illinois State Historical Library; "Kansas City Girl Is the Bride of Edgar Lee Masters," *Kansas City Star,* November 6, 1926, p. 3 ("between 45 and 50"); "To Wed 'Spoon River' Poet," unid. news clipping, Flaccus file 1926 ("She would have told"), HRC; Gee Gee [Tom Coyne] to Fay-Fay [Ellen], March 21, 1939 ("old fool," "wasting time"), letter property of Hilary Masters; "Edgar Lee Masters, Poet-Lawyer, Weds," *New York Times,* November 7, 1926, p. 10 ("Masters is said"); Elizabeth Hardwick, "Wind from the Prairie," *New York Review of Books* 38 (Sept. 26, 1991): 9–16 (incorrectly describes Ellen as homewrecker).

34. Diary 1926, January 13 (legal work); Diary 1927, January 31, February 4 (legal work); ELM to Arthur Ross, July 7, 1937 (offers legal advice in 1930s), Virginia (Mary Margaret Weeg, who consulted Masters's cousin Edith Masters, also reported limited law work by Masters while in New York; see Weeg, "The Prose of Edgar Lee Masters: Its Revelation of His Views and Its Significance in His Canon" [Ph.D. diss., University of Indiana, 1964], acknowledgments and 152); ELM to George Brett, April 30, 1935 ("I feel annoyed"), HRC; ELM to Horace [Liveright], March 26, 1926 (hopes for $1,260 from deluxe edition), HRC; ELM to Gerald Sanders, October 26, 1935 (360 copies), HRC; Boni and Liveright to ELM, October 21, 1926 (receives $976.50 for deluxe edition of *The New Spoon River*), HRC; proof page, *The New Spoon River,* misc. file M–N, n.d. (details for deluxe edition), HRC.

35. ELM to Robinson Jeffers, January 11, 1927 ("She is a sweet"), July 20, 1927 ("John"), both HRC; ELM to H. L. Mencken, November 5, 1930 ("child-wife"), HRC; ELM to Tietjens, February 6, 1927 ("Yes'm. I got married," "The Kid," "I see nothing"), Newberry; Hilary Masters to Herb Russell, conversation, 1993 ("Fay-Fay" and Frances).

36. Horace Liveright to ELM, November 11, 1926 (wonders why ELM married), HRC; Diary 1926, November 5–8; ELM to "Dear Fool" [Edwin Reese], November 9, 1926 ("Like a hawk"), Illinois State Historical Library.

37. ELM to Edwin Reese, December 15, 1926 ("My stomach"), n.d. [early 1927] ("light-haired cutie"), both Illinois State Historical Library.

38. Unpub. chapter 27, p. 537 (Sterling congratulations), HRC; Diary 1926, November 17 (Sterling's death); ELM to [Fremont] Older, November 19, 1926 (Sterling suicide), Berkeley; *ASR,* 330 (Armstrong and Dreiser); ELM to Mrs. [Corinne Roosevelt] Robinson, January 10, 1926 (Armstrong's death), Harvard; ELM to Witter Bynner, January 11, 1926 ("I think of him"), Harvard; ELM, "Peggy," *The Overland Monthly* 84 (Sept. 1926): 291 (poem about Lillian); Jerry

Miller to Herb Russell, January 31, 1978 (Lillian's Grant County, Indiana, marriage license issued on October 2, 1926); Betty Drook Shutt, *The Hostess House Story* (Marion, Ind.: Chronicle-Tribune, 1989), [p. 5] (Lillian married her surgeon, Dr. John Colin Vaughan, date of marriage license); Diary 1927, June 13 (Hyde death); ELM to Mary [Bell Sloan], March 31, 1926 ("I have passed"), Dartmouth.

39. ELM to Harold Rugg, February 4, 1926 ($250), Dartmouth; [O.G. Villard?] to ELM, February 6, 1926 (*The Nation*), Harvard; Diary 1926, April 16 (addresses college group); Mark Van Doren to ELM, January 13, 1926, January 18, 1926 (to read poem at Columbia for $50), both HRC; ELM to Horace Liveright, October 5, 1924 ("Those professors and reviewers"), HRC; Horace Liveright to ELM, October 22, 1924, October 27, 1924, and October 29, 1924 (ELM refuses to speak at bookseller's annual book week), all HRC; ELM to Daniel Reed, January 10, 1927 ("I won't attend"), HRC; ELM to New York Telephone Co., October 20, 1927 (refuses to be in directory), HRC.

40. Diary 1927, March 2–6 (Riley), 7–14 (Lincoln and Douglas debates).

41. Diary 1927, April 1 (Tennessee), 5 (The Fugitives); ELM to Robert Masters, April 16, 1927 (Masters family genealogy), HRC; Merrill Moore to Kimball Flaccus, n.d., but with letter dated April 5, 1954, Flaccus file 1927 (Masters stayed at young Moore's father's house), HRC; *Nashville Tennessean,* April 3, 1927, p. 1.

42. ELM to Robinson Jeffers, July 20, 1927 ("the line," "Such simple delights"), HRC; ELM to Robinson Jeffers, August 31, 1927 ("being a friend of sinners," servant), SUNY Buffalo; Diary 1927, August 9–28 (Illinois visit); Masters also discussed the dismissed servant girl in the poem "In Illinois," in *Poems of People.*

43. ELM to Robinson Jeffers, August 31, 1927 ("likker," "I couldn't," "the horizon," other quotations), SUNY Buffalo.

44. Bank of Manhattan deposit slip, August 17, 1926, misc. file D–I ($7,500), HRC; "Summary of a Legal Document in Cook County Courthouse," Flaccus file 1927, January 11, 1927 (owes Helen $4,050), HRC; ELM, *Levy Mayer,* 190 ("richest"); Masters's federal tax return for 1926 (shows a gross income of $10,838), property of Hilary Masters.

45. Memorandum of Agreement between ELM and Boni and Liveright, November 22, 1926 (terms of *Kit*), HRC; ELM to Horace [Liveright], December 26, 1926 (*Kit* based on fact, Governor Small), HRC; ELM to Governor Small, February 22, 1927 (southern Illinois thieves), HRC; ELM to Mary Aldis, April 8, 1924 ("a boy's tale"), HRC; unpub. chapter 26, p. 515 (1922 trip to reformatory), HRC; ELM, *Kit O'Brien,* 135 ("several weeks" of incarceration).

46. ELM to Chiperfield, January 15, 1927 (sues sister), June 7, 1927 (appeal settlements of estates of father and mother), June 16, 1927 (appeal any court decision giving inheritance to Helen Masters), all HRC; ELM to Henderson, February 6, 1927 ("I am in litigation"), HRC; Emma Masters to ELM, February 16, 1926 (need to settle estate to pay funeral expenses), HRC; "Edgar Lee Masters Named Defendant in Friendly Suit Here," unid. news clipping, n.d., n.p. (Masters is sued by his mother, brother, and sister), HRC; "Lee Masters in Legal Tilt with Brother," *Chicago Tribune,* October 4, 1927, p. 5 (appellate court action, ELM contests court charge of $59).

47. ELM to Elizabeth Lindsay, May 18, 1932 (dislikes nineteenth-century poets), HRC; ELM to Mencken, December 24, 1926 ("He and Robert"), HRC.

48. ELM to Edwin Marsh, December 17, 1917 ("Robinson's revival"), HRC; ELM to George Brett, January 5, 1928 ("The truth is"), HRC.

49. ELM to John Gould Fletcher, May 15, 1939 ("Calvin Coolidge of American verse"), HRC; ELM to "Dear Kid" [Ellen], September 19, 1931 ("exiguous"), HRC; ELM to Elizabeth Lindsay, January 15, 1932 (Frost as Coolidge), HRC; ELM to Harriet [Monroe], March 28, 1927 (Frost is the "Coolidge of poetry"), June 23, 1925 ("Barnum"), both Chicago; Louis Unter-

meyer, ed., *The Letters of Robert Frost to Louis Untermeyer* (New York: Holt, 1963), 29 ("my hated rival"), 96 ("There is a Masters Mountain").

50. Diary 1927, July, August, September 18–30 ("New Salem"), October 20 (moves), 23 (autobiography), November 5–9 (revising); ELM, "My Youth in the Spoon River Country," title page, 305½A (date), HRC.

51. Diary 1925, November 7 and November 21 (*Saturday Evening Post*); ELM to Mr. [Paul] Reynolds, December 18, 1925 (*Century*), HRC; Oscar Liveright to ELM, February 2, 1927 (*Harper's*), February 16, 1927 (*Cosmopolitan*), both HRC; *Pictorial Review* to ELM, November 2, 1927, HRC.

52. ELM to Macmillan, July 26, 1921 (owes money), HRC; ELM to Brett, n.d. (*Skeeters* loses $2,000), HRC; ELM, "My Youth," 267½ ("advances were not yet earned"), HRC; Horace Liveright to ELM, June 2, 1927 (no interest in "Atlantis"), HRC; George Brett to ELM, December 9, 1927 (only *SRA* and *Songs and Satires* made money), HRC; Diary 1927, January 31 (sees Otto Liveright regarding autobiography), November 10 ("Long talk").

53. ELM to Henderson, April 14, 1922 ("I have done"), HRC.

54. Diary 1927, November 10.

CHAPTER 14: LIFE AS AN EMPTY BUCKET

1. Hilary Masters to Herb Russell, conversation, August 1993 (furnished apartment), July 20, 1993 ("very modestly"), August 19, 1996 (library remained with first family), June 17, 1993 (pictures of Squire Davis and Lucinda Masters, Ellen's pictures, her favorite room colors); Dale Kramer, *Chicago Renaissance: The Literary Life in the Midwest, 1900–1930* (New York: Appleton-Century, 1966), 187 (gun at office); Hilary Masters, *Last Stands: Notes from Memory* (Boston: Godine, 1982), 102 (jade Buddha, gun at home); ELM to Roland and Elsie Farley, October 4, 1924 (acknowledges gift of a statuette of Buddha), NY Public; unpub. chapter 23, p. 456 (library of 1,000 volumes), HRC.

2. Diary 1927, October 18, November 12 ("Atlantis" with agent Briggs), 28 ("New Salem" circulates), December 3 ("The House in the Wood," "Wood Alcohol"); Diary 1928, January 16 (*Jack Kelso* far enough along to show).

3. Diary 1927, August 3 (Ellen to Kansas City), November 15 (ELM cannot go to Kansas City), December 17 (arrives in Kansas City), 26 (leaves).

4. Diary 1926, August 11–15 (auto accident); Hilary Masters to Herb Russell, October 18, 1993 (accident); Hilary Masters, *Last Stands,* 121, 158 (looks and laughter), 187 (lipstick), photo inside book cover (mascara).

5. ELM to Roland [Farley], May 6, 1924 ("I like"), HRC; Diary 1928, February 3; Hilary Masters to Herb Russell, conversation July 8, 2000 (spelling of his first name).

6. ELM to Harriet Monroe, February 4, 1928 ("Yesterday at 4:15," "demonstrated my virility," "synthetic nectar," mock-epic), Chicago; ELM to John Cowper Powys, February 4, 1928 ("I am much"), University of Pennsylvania; ELM to Ellen Masters, February 4, 1928 ("I hope," advice), HRC.

7. Unpub. chapter 28, p. 544 ("Hilary was," "Whether it"), HRC.

8. Hilary Masters, *Last Stands,* 10, 36 (Hilary comes under care of Coynes).

9. Ibid., 36 (ELM's hard work); ELM to "Dear Kid" [Ellen], March 18, 1928 ("You can't"), HRC.

10. Diary 1928, March 14–15 (*Jack Kelso*), 15–25 (*Ácoma*); ELM to Horace Liveright, July 15, 1928 (*Nuptial Flight*), HRC; Brandt and Brandt to ELM, April 11, 1927 (Sweden and Denmark), November 17, 1927 (Finland), both HRC; ELM to Miss Sillcox, November 18, 1927 (Finnish theft), HRC; ELM to Mr. Madden, September 26, 1929 (Lionel Barrymore, two "Spoon Riv-

er" versions), HRC; Percy Grainger to ELM, March 14, 1928, February 5, 1929, and January 5, 1930 (Grainger's use of *Spoon River*), all HRC; unpub. chapter 24, p. 492 (Lionel Barrymore), HRC.

11. Diary 1927, October 20 (address); Hilary Masters to Herb Russell, conversation, August 1993 (furnished apartment); ELM to Jack [Powys], December 20, 1928 (apartment, breakfast, lunch, club for dinner), HRC; Hardin Wallace Masters, *Edgar Lee Masters: A Biographical Sketchbook about a Famous American Author* (Rutherford, N.J.: Farleigh Dickinson University Press, 1978), 88–90 (drinks at Players).

12. Diary 1928, June 12–20, 29 (*Kelso*); Hilary Masters, *Last Stands,* 11 (boiler).

13. ELM, *Jack Kelso: A Dramatic Poem* (New York: Appleton, 1928); John T. Flanagan, *Edgar Lee Masters: The Spoon River Poet and His Critics* (Metuchen, N.J.: Scarecrow, 1974), 83 ("lyrics," "ranting").

14. ELM, "Conversation," *The New Yorker,* July 14, 1928, p. 21; *Ladies Home Journal* to ELM, October 26, 1928 ($250), HRC; ELM to Chiperfield, February 23, 1928 (mail plane), HRC; Appleton (Rutger Jewett) to ELM, June 2, 1928, June 14, 1928 ("Atlantis" too long), both HRC; Diary 1928, July 18 (Columbia); ELM to William Carlton, June 21, 1934 (advance royalties—Appleton's is referred to as "The Century Company"), Williams College.

15. Diary 1928, September 4–22 ("epilogue to *Domesday*"), October 26 (mails), December 1 (recalls), 8–9 (works on, new title), 26 (contract); ELM, *The Fate of the Jury: An Epilogue to Domesday Book* (New York: Appleton, 1929); ELM to Roland [Farley], May 6, 1924 (works on "Epilogue to *Domesday*"), HRC; ELM to Latham (Macmillan), March 5, 1922 (contemplates "additions" to *Domesday*), HRC; ELM to Mr. Jewett, December 9, 1928 ("life" incomplete), HRC; ELM to Jack [Powys], December 30, 1928 (says he worked on *Fate* in 1923, "No news"), HRC.

16. ELM to Arnold Rubin, March 7, 1928 (literary club named for ELM), HRC; Arthur Train to ELM, January 4, 1929 (Literary Council), HRC; ELM to Arthur Train, January 10, 1929 (agrees to Literary Council), HRC; ELM to Harriet [Monroe], April 14, 1928 (payment for contributors), Chicago; Diary 1928, October 18–December 18 (sits for artist Stevenson).

17. Diary 1929, January 11 (lecture), 20–24 and February 2 (proofs *Fate*), January 31, February 1, and May 3–14 (*Manila*), February 2 and 18–20 (*Poems of People*), March 14 (Madden, Hendee, promoted plays "The House in the Wood" and "New Salem"), 15–22 ("Wood Alcohol"), April 2 (Madden, "Wood Alcohol"), 6–18 ("Love and the Law," Madden); the picture is with Diary 1929 and is dated October 1928.

18. Diary 1929, February 7 (Ellen back), February 23 and March 24 (dine out), April 29 (move); Hilary Masters, *Last Stands,* 123 (Kansas City bored Ellen); ELM to Eva [Wakefield], February 22, 1929 ("she puts," "child-wife," poor cooking, "cannot get"), Western Illinois University; ELM to John Cowper Powys, March 13, 1929 ("I am pretty tired"), University of Pennsylvania.

19. Documentation of ELM's attempts to break into Hollywood is with the author and in HRC files involving every major studio; ELM, Diary of a Lecture Tour, 1925, March 4 (Norma Rankin is Mignon Callish), HRC; Mignon [Callish] to ELM, December 30, 1936 ("the big money"), HRC; Hilary Masters, *Last Stands,* 53 (Mignon Callish); Dreiser to "Fairest Edgar" [ELM], July 9, 1943, in *Letters of Theodore Dreiser,* ed. Robert Elias (Philadelphia: University of Pennsylvania, 1959), 3:988 (nearly every epitaph a movie); [Frank] Kee Robinson, "The Edgar Lee Masters Collection: Sixty Years of Literary History," *Library Chronicle of the University of Texas* 8 (Spring 1968): 45 ("The Power of the Night"); Dudley Nichols to Kimball Flaccus, April 2, 1952 (Jean Renoir), Georgetown.

20. ELM to Miss Sillcox (Author's League), January 24, 1929 (*Wings* taken from ELM poem, "to thousands," "stolen"), HRC; Luise Sillcox to ELM, January 28, 1929 (sets up committee), HRC.

21. ELM to Dreiser, December 22, 1915 (scenario), University of Pennsylvania; ELM to Jim Tully, July 27, 1937 ("When I"), HRC.

22. ELM, "Spoon River: Suggestions for a Film" (some copies have date of April 15, 1941), HRC; David Karsner, *Sixteen Authors to One* (Freeport, N.Y.: Books for Libraries Press, 1968), 140 ("I dislike"); ELM to Mr. Clark, October 31, 1934 ("hardly ever see a film"), Yale.

23. Hilary Masters to Herb Russell, June 17, 1993 ("Poets often go hungry"), October 18, 1993 (money from auto accident); ELM to Edith Masters, October 2, 1929 (Ellen to Columbia), HRC; Diary 1929, April 4 (receives $2,000 settlement for auto accident); Ellen's work at Columbia is shown on her transcript.

24. Eunice Tietjens, *The World at My Shoulder* (New York: Macmillan, 1938), 45.

25. The questions and conclusion are suggested by Hilary Masters, *Last Stands,* 137–39.

26. Hilary Masters, *Last Stands,* 94 (law or medicine), 138, 140–42, 162.

27. Unpub. chapter 27, p. 542 (Helen loses claim on inheritance in appellate court), HRC; Mencken note, "Manuscripts by H. L. Mencken," folder 13, n.d. (indicates that a judge decided in 1928 that Helen's divorce decree did not constitute a lien on ELM's inheritance), NY Public; "Summary of a Document in Cook County Courthouse, Chicago, Illinois" (Chiperfield accomplished settlement), Georgetown; ELM to Abe [Meyer], September 12, 1929 ("Now in consideration"), HRC.

28. ELM to Bill [Slack], February 13, 1927 ($18,000), HRC; ELM to Chiperfield, September 17, 1929 ($4,120, $425.31, Chiperfield's $1,150, "many little expenses"), HRC; Diary 1929, end papers, September 23 (father's estate and costs, $417.25); unpub. chapter 27, p. 542 ($4,200 in medical bills—ELM here estimates that he received $1,500 from his parents' estates), HRC.

29. Diary 1929, October 25–December 12 (intermittent health problems), December 22–28 (in Kansas City), 28 (to Petersburg); unpub. chapter 28, p. 545 ("Hilary walked," "perfect content"), HRC.

30. Diary 1929, December 31, and end pages that continue through January 8, 1930 (Uncle Will and Edith, Tom dies); Emma Masters to "Geigy" [ELM], January 8, 1925 (Tom has serious stomach trouble), HRC; ELM to Roland Farley, April 13, 1924 (Tom has ulcer), NY Public; unpub. chapter 28, p. 545 (Tom dies after illness), HRC; Hilary Masters to Herb Russell, conversation, May 1993 ("Tom's dead"); Diary 1930, January 9 (return to New York).

31. *Gettysburg, Manila, Ácoma* (New York: Liveright, 1930); Diary 1930, February 10 (contract for *Gettysburg*); slip case and front material show deluxe edition of 375 copies; Liveright Publishing (Arthur Pell) to ELM, January 31, 1936 (125 copies remain), HRC.

32. "ELM: MSR," ch. 6, p. 16 (Lewistown and Emerson influence), Dartmouth; *ASR,* 138 (Yee Bow); ELM, "Hip Lung on Yuan Chang," *The Open Sea,* 220–24; ELM, "Yet Sing Low," *The New Spoon River;* ELM to Carter Harrison, April 14, 1939 (Hip Lung a friend), HRC; ELM to Horace Liveright, January, 16, 1930 (Liveright admires poems), HRC; ELM, *The Tale of Chicago* (New York: Putnam's, 1933), 236–37 (Hip Lung in Chicago); *American Mercury* 4 (Jan. 1925): 61–62, and *American Mercury* 5 (June 1925): 238–39; ELM to Art [Ficke], January 19, 1940 ($500 advance), Yale.

33. ELM, "Hip Lung," "Ascetics and Drunkards," "America Little Boy Yet," "Republican Party and Turtle Shell," *Lichee Nuts* (New York: Liveright, 1930), 11, 31, 103, 128; "Hittite" [ELM to Edwina Stanton Babcock], January 7, 1925 (denial and indulgence), Princeton.

34. Diary 1930, April 27–28 (to Chelsea); Hilary Masters, *Last Stands,* 35 (the Chelsea); Hardin Masters, *ELM: A Biographical Sketchbook,* 110 (interior of Chelsea); Ellen to Kimball Flaccus, April 21, 1951 (dislikes Chelsea rooms), HRC.

35. Diary 1930, May 3 (to Kansas City), May 1–June 14 (writing); unpub. chapter 28, pp. 550–52 (Harlemville, "That little boy"), HRC.

36. ELM to "Dear Kid" [Ellen], September 11, 1930 ("The club bores"), HRC.

37. Transcript of Ellen Masters, Columbia University (shows fifteen hours); Diary 1931, January 16, February 4 ("Ellen leaves").

38. Elisabeth Earley, interview with Ellen Masters, December 2, 1970, pp. 27 (ELM fights Ellen's master's), 84 (Ellen prepared for career in college teaching), property of Hilary Masters; Hilary Masters, *Last Stands,* 139 (ELM critical of Ellen's classes); Diary 1931, front page ("accident").

CHAPTER 15: WHAT ABE LINCOLN SAID

1. Ellen Masters to Herb Russell, April 27, 1977 ("There will be time," "All studies"); Hilary Masters to Herb Russell, conversation, November 1996 (1988 power of attorney).

2. Hilary Masters to Herb Russell, conversation, 1994 ("visiting").

3. Hilary Masters to Herb Russell, conversation, November 1996 (automat); ELM to Mencken, November 5, 1930 (mail at Players), HRC; ELM to "Widdle" [Wilbur Masters], September 28, 1931 ("I have been thinking"), HRC; ELM to Elizabeth Lindsay, April 30, 1932 (library), HRC.

4. ELM, "The Genesis of *Spoon River,*" *American Mercury* 28 (Jan. 1933): 41 (played at New Salem, "In my boyhood"); ELM, "Days in the Lincoln Country," *Journal of the Illinois State Historical Society* 18 (Jan. 1926): 782–86 (law association of Herndon and Hardin, 1847 court case, "good intercessor," "Lincoln tried a case"); *ASR,* 5 (justice of the peace), 18 (Lincoln as lawyer), 45 (Herndon's and Hardin's law association); Charles E. Burgess, "Masters and Some Mentors," *Papers on Language and Literature* 10 (Spring 1974): 178–179*n* (Herndon and Hardin's law association); ELM, *The Sangamon,* 71 (Herndon and Hardin's law association), 73 (near-drowning); ELM, "My Youth in the Spoon River Country," 25 (ELM's Aunt Minerva on honeymoon), HRC; ELM to "Widdle" [Wilbur Masters], September 19, 1926 (tobacco chewers), HRC.

5. Squire Davis Masters to [A. K.] Riggin, January 16, 1855 ("to abolish"), HRC; *ASR,* 5 ("In 1854"), 4–8.

6. ELM, "My Youth," 21–22 (Hardin and Civil War), HRC; *ASR* draft, November 4, 1927, p. 1 ("I came into"), HRC; "Washington Day by Day," *Trenton Evening Times,* September 10, 1929, p. 6 (named for Lee); ELM to Mr. Wilson, March 27, 1925 (named for Lee), Virginia; ELM, *The Sangamon,* 53 (surveyed).

7. *ASR,* 25, 45 (Mentor Graham); ELM, *The Sangamon,* 102 (Bowling Green), [50–51] (Kelso), 92–93 (Armstrong family), 119 (John McNamar); ELM, "Genesis of *Spoon River,*" 41, 52 (various New Salem figures).

8. The spelling of Ann Rutledge's name is discussed by Charles E. Burgess in "Illinois Newspaperman Disputes Recent *Spoon River* Legends," *Tri-State Trader* [Knightstown, Indiana], June 6, 1970, p. 24; ELM, "Genesis of *Spoon River,*" 52 (moved 1890, 1921 inscription); Josephine Craven Chandler, "The Spoon River Country," *Journal of the Illinois State Historical Society* 14 (Oct. 1921): 267–68 (Hearst, park, remains moved); ELM, *The Sangamon,* 136 (1921 permission and inscription); ELM to Mr. [Henry] Rankin, July 31, 1920 (grants permission), Illinois College.

9. ELM, "Genesis of *Spoon River,*" 52 ("better to conform"); see also "Ann Rutledge Monument," *Petersburg Observer,* January 14, 1921, [p. 4], regarding monument; ELM to Mr. [Henry] Rankin, July 31, 1920 (grants permission for use of poem), Illinois College. Rankin's authority for changing the Rutledge poem was based on the four years he spent while a law student working in the Springfield office of Lincoln and Herndon and his apparent belief that he had a better feel for Lincoln material than Masters did. Rankin was never shy about telling others what he knew of Lincoln—or about rewriting other people's poems. Three years

after changing Masters's poem on Rutledge, Rankin published *Intimate Character Sketches of Abraham Lincoln* (Lippincott, 1924) and appropriated Masters's poem "William H. Herndon" from *Spoon River Anthology*. Although Rankin mentioned Masters in this book, it is doubtful that Masters knew in advance how Rankin would use the poem; Rankin removed words and lines from "William H. Herndon" in addition to rearranging lines and adding new words, new punctuation, and a new format (see 12, 21, 22, 24, 26).

10. ELM to Dreiser, March 19, 1915 (reads Herndon's *Lincoln*), April 30, 1940 ("It was"), both University of Pennsylvania; ELM, *Lincoln: The Man* (New York: Dodd, Mead, 1931), 2 ("other lives"); ELM to Albert J. Beveridge, February 26, 1926 (references Masters's father helping Beveridge), HRC; Albert J. Beveridge to ELM, March 1, 1926 (Hardin's help), HRC; ELM to Mencken, February 8, 1931 ("blew up"), HRC; Catherine Beveridge to ELM, n.d. (late husband's work unfinished), HRC; ELM to [Ferris] Greenslet, July 23, 1928 (Beveridge and ELM corresponded, as did Beveridge and Hardin Masters), Harvard.

11. Penelope Niven, *Sandburg: A Biography* (New York: Scribner's, 1991), 407 (Sandburg's 1922 plans).

12. ELM to "Dear Kid" [Ellen], September 19, 1931 ("the publishers"), HRC; ELM to Ben Abramson, n.d. (blurb for *Chicago*), HRC; ELM to [Horace?] Liveright, August 18, 1923 (blurb for *Nuptial*), HRC; ELM to [Clarence] Decker, November 28, 1936 (blurb for *Chicago*), Dartmouth; Niven, *Sandburg*, 370 (Sandburg's income), 377 (Armstrong lecture bureau), 351 (payments), 350 (anthologies), 352 (no critical judgment), 335 (Levinson), 265 (Sunday), 262 (pseudonym).

13. ELM to Harriet Monroe, December 3, 1917 ("most injury"), Chicago; Niven, *Sandburg*, 454 (Preston), 476 (Darrow), 410 (doctorate); ELM to "Dear Kid" [Ellen], September 19, 1931 ("Chances are"), HRC.

14. ELM to Agnes Lee Freer, September 17, 1924, Newberry; Harriet Monroe, "Frost and Masters," *Poetry* 9 (Jan. 1917): 203.

15. ELM to "George" [Stokes?], February 1, 1926 ("The most brazen piece," "The joke of all"), HRC; Carl Sandburg, "Lincoln Days," unid. newspaper clipping, n.d., n.p. (discusses Masters's affinity with the Lincoln country), HRC.

16. ELM to D. W. Griffith, March 8, 1924 (offers *Children* as a movie), HRC; ELM to Harriet Monroe, February 4, 1928 ("That slick Swede"), HRC; Niven, *Sandburg*, 476 (Griffith), 515 (Michigan).

17. ELM to Eunice Tietjens, June 27, 1938 ("his Lincoln book"), Newberry; ELM to Dreiser, April 30, 1940 ("Sandburg began to"), University of Pennsylvania; ELM to Wilbur Hatfield, December 26, 1939 (never read book, "bad style"), HRC; ELM to Mark Van Doren, February 1, 1926 ("biography that will really count"), HRC; Victor Hicken, "Sandburg and the Lincoln Biography: A Personal View," in *The Vision of This Land: Studies of Vachel Lindsay, Edgar Lee Masters, and Carl Sandburg*, ed. John E. Hallwas and Dennis J. Reader ([Macomb]: Western Illinois University, 1976), 105 (poor historian).

18. Diary 1930, April 25–June 14 (signed contract, moved to Chelsea, drafted *Lincoln* in forty-seven days), diary front pages ($1,000 from Dodd in April), June 30–July 9 (revises *Lincoln*), September 2–3 (Hilary and Ellen leave, ELM to New York, delivers manuscript); Dodd, Mead, and Company to ELM, April 10, 1930 (offers $1,000), HRC; ELM to Elizabeth Lindsay, May 18, 1932 (says he wrote *Lincoln* in only forty-five days), HRC.

19. ELM, "My Youth," 51 (courthouse lawn a favorite place to meet), HRC; Hardin Masters to ELM, September 23, 1925 (unpublished story), HRC; unpub. chapter 26, p. 524 (Hardin's memory), HRC; *Ceremonies at the Unveiling of Monument to William H. Herndon, Abraham Lincoln's Last Law Partner* [Springfield, Ill.?: Sangamon County Bar Association?, 1918?] (Hardin speaks, two poems); "Unveil Shaft in Memory of W. H. Herndon," *Illinois State*

Register, May 31, 1918, [p. 2] (Hardin Masters and text, Masters's poem, Lindsay recited "Abraham Lincoln . . .").

20. ELM to Widdle [Wilbur Masters], February 10, 1931 (book principally from Beveridge and Herndon), HRC; ELM, *Lincoln: The Man,* 118 (briefly references Masters's father); ELM to Allen Tate, April 24, 1931 ("The Republican Party"), Princeton.

21. ELM, *Lincoln: The Man,* 1–4, 124 ("It is not"), 116 ("impostors"), 2 ("The purpose").

22. Ibid., 139 ("cold"), 42 ("cunning"), 116 ("devious and censurable"), 508 ("not over scrupulous"), 509 ("an aid"), 391 (provokes war), 479 ("refusal of the truth"), 32–33 ("What he learned").

23. Ibid., 145 ("under sexed"), 87 ("sex stories"), 9 ("unmoral," "shiftless," "worthless," "less than"), facing 16, 30 (illustrations regarding "lines written" and liquor), 477 ("Booth's bullet").

24. Ibid., 59–65 (all quotations).

25. ELM to Mr. Bond, May 6, 1931 ("always sell"), HRC; Dodd, Mead to ELM, October 27, 1930 (galley proofs), January 23, 1931 (Associated Press, etc.), January 17, 1931 (deluxe edition of 150 copies at $10), October 29, 1931 (ads), all HRC; ELM to Mr. Lewis, December 28, 1930 (birthday publicity), May 27, 1931 (plans next edition), both HRC; ELM to Ellen, October 14, 1933 (jacket art), HRC; ELM to Mr. Dodd, September 13, 1931 ("great publicity," February 6 publication), HRC; ELM to Mencken, January 8, 1931 ("take to the woods"), NY Public; Frank K. Robinson, *Edgar Lee Masters: An Exhibition in Commemoration of the Centenary of His Birth* (Austin: University of Texas, 1970), 27 (Ellen designed jacket); "Lincoln Killed Our Freedom, says Masters," *New York Telegram,* February 6, 1931, p. 6 (published February 6).

26. Monroe, "Frost and Masters," 206.

27. "Lincolnoclast," *Time,* February 16, 1931, p. 15; Charles W. Thompson, "A Belittling Life of Lincoln by Edgar Lee Masters," *New York Times Book Review,* February 8, 1931, p. 5 ("Charles Dickens"); "Lincoln Killed Our Freedom," 6 ("Sitting in").

28. "Defending Honest Abe against Debunkers," *The Literary Digest* 108 (Feb. 28, 1931): 34 (Congress); HR 17036, Flaccus file 1931 ("the book"), HRC; ELM to Harry Hansen, n.d. (Boston ban), HRC; ELM to "Dear Kid" [Ellen], March 8, 1931 (barred from store in Philadelphia), HRC; anonymous to ELM, February 8, 1931 ("Mr. Traitor"), HRC; KKKK to ELM, n.d., HRC; ELM, "The Virgin Birth of Abraham Lincoln," misc. file L–Lz, HRC.

29. Unpub. chapter 28, p. 549 (sister's bust), HRC; ELM to Edith Masters, February 10, 1926 (Wasson's signed book to New Salem center), HRC.

30. "Deny Masters Picture of 'Unkempt' Lincoln," *New York Times,* February 9, 1931, p. 8 (Illinoisans think of removing Rutledge epitaph); ELM, *Lincoln: The Man,* 49 (Rutledge story a myth); Dale Carnegie, *Lincoln the Unknown* (New York: Century Company, 1932), 43–44 (Ann's relative, "greedy undertaker," "four pearl buttons"); Harry Hansen, "The First Reader," *New York World-Telegram,* February 10, 1932, p. 23 (repeats Carnegie's story); Charles E. Burgess, "Some Family Source Material for *Spoon River Anthology,*" *Western Illinois Regional Studies* 13 (Spring 1990): 88 (Bone and Montgomery).

31. See "Letters re *Lincoln: The Man,*" misc. file (shows individual and public responses to the book, including Murray Clark to ELM, March 11, 1931 ["slapped"], and E. S. Crothers to ELM, March 16, 1931 ["the greatest book"]), HRC.

32. ELM to [John Hall] Wheelock, February 11, 1937, Flaccus file 1937 (six printings), HRC; Kimball Flaccus, conversation with Frank Dodd, June 30, 1953, Flaccus file 1931 (7,100 copies), HRC; Cassell and Company to ELM, April 7, 1932, HRC; Masters also said the book "sold to 8 editions" in ELM to Arthur [Ficke], June 1, 1939, Yale.

33. Dorothy Dow, "An Introduction to Some Letters" (*Lincoln* hurt Masters with his public), Newberry; Dodd, Mead to ELM, January 19, 1938 (manuscript lost), HRC; Mr. Brown to

ELM, November 15, 1938 (suggests Lincoln ms. may have been found), HRC. The status of the manuscript is difficult to ascertain since Masters sometimes used the word *script* to mean not "manuscript" but "marked galley" (see ELM to Mr. Decker, September 8, 1938, HRC).

34. ELM to "Dear Kid" [Ellen], May 6, 1931 (Hillsdale, possible purchase, "I am perplexed," "be glad to get"), HRC.

35. ELM to Mrs. [Corinne Roosevelt] Robinson, January 30, 1931 (considers Petersburg), Harvard; Hilary Masters, *Last Stands: Notes from Memory* (Boston: Godine, 1982), 46 ("he wanted"); ELM to John Farrar, December 24, 1936 ("pristine"), HRC; Diary 1931, June 11 (arrives Galena).

36. *ASR*, 83 (Reese on Lewistown newspaper); Frank Blane to ELM, November 14, 1930, misc. file C–Cz (research), HRC; Fern Nance Pond to ELM, September 4, 1948 (great-granddaughter of Sevigne Houghton), January 22, 1929 (*Axis, Index*), both HRC; ELM to John Farrar, December 24, 1936 (help from Ed Reese, Pond), HRC.

37. Elisabeth Earley, interview with Ellen Masters, December 2, 1970, pp. 30–31 (Mr. Leverett worked for Tom Coyne), property of Hilary Masters; ELM to Percy Grainger, January 14, 1938 (Galena, Missouri, variant on "Spoon River," Captain Robinson), HRC; ELM to Mr. Dickinson, November 22, 1924 (soldier, 1915), HRC; ELM to "Dear Kid" [Ellen], September 19, 1931 (Hilary nicknamed "Mr. Ittie"), HRC; ELM, typescript, September 11, 1931 ("Fiddling by the Moon"), HRC; ELM, "Fiddling by the Moon," *The Harmony of Deeper Music,* 72 (September 11, 1931, composition); unpub. chapter 28, p. 552 (Leverett family), HRC; Hilary Masters, *Last Stands,* 47 (Homer and Wilbur Leverett, "Mr. Ittie March"); ELM, *The Sangamon,* 102 (representative fiddle tunes); Diary 1931, August 10 (mails ms.), 24 (Ellen and Hilary to Kansas City).

38. ELM to "Dear Kid" [Ellen], October 11, 1931 ("one of the greatest," $3,000, *Tide* refused, ELM intractable regarding changing *Tide*), HRC.

39. Ibid. ("I haven't been more furious," Hardin, "full of brokes," Herford, Nicolosi, "You see where literature gets off"), HRC; ELM to Ellen, November 20, 1931 (Hardin out of broker's business), HRC; Robinson, *ELM: An Exhibition,* 59 (Herford illustrations); ELM, *The New World* (New York: Appleton, 1937), 124 (Marx).

40. ELM to Widdle [Wilbur Masters], November 9, 1931 ("coming to the Illinois country," "I am tired," asks to stay with Wilbur), November 20, 1931 ("I could take a couple of rooms"), both HRC; Wilbur Masters to ELM, November 17, 1931 (wife ill, daughter lives with), HRC.

41. ELM to Widdle [Wilbur Masters], September 15, 1931 ("The kind"), HRC; ELM to Ellen, November 20, 1931 ("My western country," "Then I turn"), HRC; ELM to Dreiser, August 19, 1939 ("What little"), University of Pennsylvania.

42. ELM, *Kelso,* 260–64 (Godbey); Diary 1928, July 5–August 6 (researches and writes much of *Godbey*); Diary 1930, November 21 (vault); Diary 1931, April 13 (*Godbey* to publisher); ELM to Frank [Rosenberger], November 20, 1931 (signed, limited edition published November 14, 1931), HRC; Dodd, Mead to ELM, September 15, 1931 (347 copies), HRC.

43. ELM, *Godbey: A Dramatic Poem* (New York: Dodd, Mead, 1931); ELM to Howard Lewis, September 16, 1931 (plot and characters, "covered the whole"), HRC; ELM to Mencken, November 9, 1931 (characters and allegory), HRC; ELM to Agnes Lee Freer, January 5, 1932 (characters and allegory), Newberry; John T. Flanagan, *Edgar Lee Masters: The Spoon River Poet and His Critics* (Metuchen, N.J.: Scarecrow, 1974), 84 (politics, religion, law, and learning).

44. Dodd, Mead to ELM, January 13, 1932 (100 copies), HRC; Dodd, Mead to William Osborne (Masters's lawyer), February 12, 1932 (breach of contract disputed), February 23, 1932 (all done per contract), both HRC; William Osborne to ELM, January 20, 1932 (contract, free copies, royalties, $500, damages), February 8, 1932 (ELM waived trade edition, $1 per copy), both HRC; ELM to Frank Dodd, January 26, 1932 ("A lawyer that"), HRC; ELM to August

[Derleth], October 13, 1939 (ELM has one copy, Dodd, Mead keeps rest), State Historical Society of Wisconsin.

45. ELM to "Dear Kid" [Ellen], March 8, 1931 ("they could"), HRC.

46. Albert J. Beveridge, *Abraham Lincoln (1809–1858)* (Boston: Houghton Mifflin, 1928), 1:viii (notice of Tom); Beveridge to ELM, March 1, 1926 (receives copy of *Children* from Tom), HRC.

47. ELM to Brett, December 13, 1931 (tries to market handwritten draft of *SRA*), HRC; ELM to Lee Wood, November 27, 1931 (newspaper job), HRC; ELM to Alfred A. Knopf, December 19, 1931 (book idea), HRC; ELM to "Dear Kid" [Ellen], March 8, 1931 (faults of publishers), HRC; ELM to Horace Liveright, December 9, 1831 [1931] (drunk), HRC; ELM to Nathan Wallack, December 7, 1931 (tries to sell mss. of *The New Spoon River* and *Mitch*), Western Illinois University; Nancy Johnson to Herb Russell, July 30, 1990 (resigns from National Institute of Arts and Letters); unpub. chapter 26, p. 523 (Hardin unforgiving), HRC.

48. Diary 1931, December 5 (Lindsay dies), end paper (Masters's personal effects at Hotel Chelsea in 1931).

CHAPTER 16: A POET IN AMERICA

1. ELM to Elizabeth Lindsay, January 30, 1932 (she should write biography, ELM will do preface), April 23, 1934 (book took only ninety days), both HRC; ELM to Harriet Monroe, February 24, 1936 (two months' research, one month's writing), HRC.

2. ELM, *Vachel Lindsay: A Poet in America* (New York: Scribner's, 1935), 226 ("Gospel of Beauty"), 229 (*Rhymes*).

3. ELM to John D. Rockefeller Jr., January 6, 1932 (mothers of Lindsay and ELM were friends), HRC; ELM to Elizabeth Lindsay, December 7, 1931 (commiserates with), HRC; *ASR*, 349 (mothers were friends).

4. ELM, *Lindsay*, 361 ("They tried to get me"); Elizabeth Lindsay to ELM, May 14, 1935 (heart failure), July 30, 1932 (confirms suicide by Lysol), June 29, 1933 (Elizabeth was twenty-one in January 1922 when she met Lindsay), all HRC; ELM to Elizabeth Lindsay, December 7, 1931 ("It is strange," "The Players"), HRC.

5. Diary 1931, end paper (sells Lindsay poem to *Herald-Tribune* for $50); ELM to Irita Van Doren (*Herald-Tribune*), December 30, 1931 (asks that above $50 check be made out to Elizabeth Lindsay), Princeton; Corinne [Roosevelt] Robinson to ELM, January 6, 1931 [1932] (sends check for $50), n.d. (Mrs. Carnegie sends $500), both HRC; ELM to Rockefeller, January 16, 1932 (solicits money from Rockefeller), January 6, 1932 (money from Authors Club and Players), both HRC; ELM to Carter Harrison, November 16, 1938 ($900), HRC; ELM to Elizabeth Lindsay, January 2, 1932 (other organizations and aid), HRC; ELM to Corinne [Roosevelt] Robinson, January 15, 1932 (Mrs. Carnegie's check, Rockefeller refuses), January 10, 1932 (Mrs. Carnegie's check), both Harvard.

6. *ASR*, 344 (saw much of Lindsay at time of *SRA*), 349–51 ("gullible," "apostolic manner," "looked like," "America's greatest," "his only rival," sex and alcohol); ELM to Mencken, December 3, 1934 ("chastity belt"), NY Public; Diary 1919, February 4 (sees Lindsay in New York); Diary 1924, May 2 (sees Lindsay in New York); Diary 1928, November 27, December 5 (sees Lindsay); Lindsay to ELM, June 16, 1926 (Players), HRC; ELM to George Brett, March 9, 1928 ("do everything"), HRC; ELM to Harriet [Monroe], September 16, 1925 ("Lindsay can't think"), Chicago.

7. ELM to Harriet Monroe, February 24, 1936 (declined to see Lindsay's correspondence with Monroe, Teasdale, and others in preference for selected letters and Lindsay's diaries), Chicago; ELM to Elizabeth Lindsay, April 20, 1932 (asks for selected documents), HRC; ELM

to Lawrence Underwood, June 27, 1932 (Hiram), HRC; ELM to Mrs. Robinson, July 12, 1932 ("Lindsay wrote tons of letters"), Harvard.

8. ELM to Jack [Powys], December 16, 1931 ("I can't quit"), HRC; ELM to "Kid" [Ellen], December 19, 1931 ("I have a hunch"), HRC.

9. Elizabeth Lindsay to ELM, n.d. [ca. 1932] ("Truth Tower," "was always in agreement"), HRC; "E." [Elizabeth Lindsay] to ELM, June 29, 1933 (Illinois ignored Lindsay's needs), HRC; ELM to Lindsay, May 1, 1927 (encourages his writing), HRC; Lindsay to ELM, June 16, 1926 ("I am delighted," Players), June 8, 1927 ("Springfield is still"), both HRC.

10. ELM to Elizabeth Lindsay, July 23, 1932 (discrepancy in reports, "I won't"), HRC; Elizabeth Lindsay to ELM, July 30, 1932 ("drinking a teaglass full," "His life"), HRC.

11. Elizabeth Lindsay to ELM, May 14, 1935 (heart failure versus suicide), January 10, 1932 ($4,000–$5,000 in insurance), May 27, 1933 ("I shall never work"), all HRC.

12. ELM to Dreiser, March 13, 1940 ("tumbled down house"), University of Pennsylvania; ELM to Elizabeth Lindsay, May 25, 1932 ("We are about established"), HRC.

13. Unpub. chapter 28, p. 553 (toads and crickets), HRC; Hilary Masters, *Last Stands: Notes from Memory* (Boston: Godine, 1982), 89 ("indecipherable script"), 89–94 (porch, rockers), 32, 90, and 153 ("Pop").

14. ELM to Elizabeth Lindsay, July 16, 1932 ("My little boy"), HRC; [Elizabeth Lindsay], n.d. [summer 1932] (garden not mature), HRC.

15. ELM to [Elizabeth Lindsay], n.d. [Summer 1932] ("wonderful motor trip," "Everything here speaks of Hilary"), HRC; ELM to Tom [Coyne], October 1, 1942 ("They left in the car"), HRC; Hilary Masters, *Last Stands,* 90 (friend drives to train).

16. Hilary Masters, *Last Stands,* 5, 65–66, 69–70 ("I was steering"), 73, 74 ("The sudden maneuver"), 75, 76 ("By God"); Hilary Masters to Herb Russell, conversation, November 1997 (Ellen's breakdown).

17. Hilary Masters, *Last Stands,* 65 (tries to please husband and father); ELM to Jack Powys, September 21, 1933, Flaccus file 1933 (Ellen ill in September 1932), HRC; Hilary Masters to Herb Russell, conversation, November 1996 (secretarial course), October 18, 1993 (breakdown, bed), conversation, November 1997 (Ellen's breakdown).

18. Elizabeth Lindsay to ELM, May 14, 1932 (dedication), September 7, 1932, May 27, 1933 (cannot use all information), all HRC; ELM to Elizabeth Lindsay, May 11, 1932 ("needed a lusty hired girl"), HRC; *ASR,* 31, 89 (Emma's maids).

19. ELM, *Lindsay,* 124–31 (sells poems), 124–27 (2¢, midnight).

20. Elizabeth Lindsay to ELM, November 28, 1933 (Brett encouraged), HRC; ELM to Gerald [Sanders], January 29, 1941 ($250, 10 percent, "hell," $2,500, $4,000), HRC; Alfred A. Knopf to ELM, November 1, 1932 (rejects ms.), HRC; Sheldon Dick to ELM, June 27, 1933 (Houghton Mifflin has rejected), October 12, 1933 (Sheldon Dick rejects ms.), both HRC; Appleton-Century (John Williams) to agent G. Anne Brooks, March 23, 1934 (rejects ms.), HRC; ELM to Elizabeth [Lindsay], April 23, 1934 ("eliminate," "It may be"), HRC.

21. ELM to Jack [Powys], May 20, 1931, Flaccus file 1931 (warehouse), HRC; Appleton-Century (John Williams) to ELM, August 10, 1932 (rejects *Godbey*), HRC; ELM to Richard Madden, April 15, 1931 ("Wood Alcohol" and "The House in the Wood"), HRC; Leavitt Ashley to ELM, October 12, 1931 (ELM wants to sell translation rights to *The Nuptial Flight* and *Skeeters*), HRC.

22. Wilbur Masters to ELM, September 25, 1931 (Wilbur cannot pay bills on farm and house in town), HRC; Robert S. Masters to ELM, January 6, 1932 (asks for clothing), HRC; ELM to George Stokes, September 20, 1931 (falling out with Stokes), HRC; ELM to "Dear Kid" [Ellen], October 11, 1931 (falling out with Stokes), September 14, 1933 (Powys "broke"), both HRC; ELM to "Widdle" [Wilbur Masters], September 26, 1932 ("Just look"), HRC; ELM to Agnes

Lee Freer, April 23, 1928 (daughter Madeline marries without consent, son Hardin in business), June 1, 1928 (daughter Madeline says ELM should not have sent her a wedding gift), March 23, 1933 (sister Madeline's death), all Newberry; "Divorced Couple to Rewed," *Kansas City Times,* January 3, 1931, p. 8 (Marcia's marital problems); Gary Panetta, "The Poet and His Daughter Connect through Verse," *Peoria Journal Star,* December 13, 1992, pp. B-1, B-2 (Marcia to college); ELM to Harriet [Monroe], September 7, 1925 (bad heart), Chicago; unpub. chapter 28, pp. 547–48 (sister Madeline's loss of money), HRC.

23. ELM to Harriet Monroe, November 29, 1921 ("You have my permission"), Chicago; George Brett to Monroe, May 11, 1933 ($1,000, Author's League), Chicago; William H. Osborne to ELM, March 6, 1933 (details of Monroe feud), July 24, 1933 (royalties and breach of contract), both HRC; ELM to George Brett, December 7, 1921 (ELM must approve Monroe's selections), October 28, 1932 ("heirs and assigns"), both HRC.

24. [George Brett Jr.] to William Hamilton Osborne, May 11, 1933 (ELM should have requested payment at time of use), Chicago; ELM to George Brett, December 7, 1921 (publication contingent upon ELM's approval), HRC; William Osborne to ELM, November 25, 1933 (gets $500, $50 to lawyer), HRC; ELM to [William] Osborne, November 28, 1933 (10 percent to lawyer), HRC; Macmillan Company to William Osborne, [1933] (Macmillan pays $500), HRC; Monroe to ELM, February 27, 1936, March 16, 1936 (friendly to ELM), both HRC; ELM to Geraldine Udell, December 28, 1936 (allows use of letters in Monroe autobiography), HRC.

25. Sheldon Dick to Harriet Monroe, April 20, 1933 (*Serpent* to come out May 13, first book), Chicago; ELM, *The Serpent in the Wilderness* (New York: Sheldon Dick, 1933), end paper (400 copies); publisher's announcement, "Mr. Sheldon Dick Announces the Publication of *The Serpent in the Wilderness*" (365 copies, 84 at $12.50, 281 at $8.50, "first book," "sewage," "wrangles"), HRC; Frank K. Robinson, *Edgar Lee Masters: An Exhibition in Commemoration of the Centenary of His Birth* (Austin: University of Texas, 1970), 29 (*Fate of the Jury*).

26. ELM to Jack [Powys], March 10, 1933 ("the meretricious"), HRC; Sheldon Dick to ELM, June 19, 1933 (sells about one copy per week), April 7, 1934 ("no profit"), August 23, 1933 ("dozen sales," "no profit," "no trade edition"), all HRC; ELM to Mr. Wakefield, July 17, 1942 ("to the extent"), Western Illinois University.

27. Putnam's to ELM, August 2, 1933 (limited edition), HRC; ELM to Elizabeth Lindsay, June 1, 1934 ($1,000 advance—Masters's letter says $10,000, but this is no doubt a typographical error), HRC; John T. Flanagan, *Edgar Lee Masters: The Spoon River Poet and His Critics* (Metuchen, N.J.: Scarecrow, 1974), 129 (memory); ELM, *The Tale of Chicago* (New York: Putnam's, 1933), 66 ("There are two"), 336 ("The megalopolis").

28. ELM to Carrick (Putnam's), August 1, 1933 (printing costs), September 8, 1933, September 12, 1933 (ad space), September 14, 1933 (price too high), October 20, 1933 (royalties, "twenty million"), April 13, 1934 (timeliness of royalty statement), May 15, 1935 ("dubious" bookkeeping), all HRC; G. P. Putnam's to Author's League, May 2, 1934 (seventy-six copies in six months), HRC; Callaghan and Co. to Putnam's, n.d., misc. file A–B (seeks payment of old debt), HRC.

29. Putnam's to ELM, September 21, 1936 (1,700 copies at 50 percent), September 19, 1933 (refuses *The Tide of Time* [then called "Leonard Westerfield"]), both HRC; ELM to Putnam's, September 23, 1936 ("compensatory decency"), HRC.

30. ELM to Miss Damarel, August 6, 1933, August 17, 1933, September 7, 1933 ($1,350, contemplates purchase of rural place), all HRC; ELM to Ellen, September 20, 1933 ("more vital"), HRC; ELM to Carrick (Putnam's), June 8, 1933 (June 9 arrival), HRC; Hilary Masters, *Last Stands,* 93 (run-down house, "city person"), 108 (Ellen drives, Molly).

31. Raymond Moley to ELM, September 13, 1933 ("a new *Spoon River*"), September 25, 1933 ("American Anthology" approved), both HRC; ELM to Raymond Moley, September 15, 1933 ("I have thought"), HRC; ELM to Ellen, October 14, 1933 (300 pieces), HRC.

32. ELM to Moley, September 15, 1933 (files "full"), HRC; ms. of "American Anthology," October 27, 1933 (name of ms. marked out and replaced with the title of "Atlantis"—later *The New World*—showing that Masters had earlier moved title of "American Anthology" to ms. of "Atlantis"), HRC; ELM to Mencken, October 5, 1933 ("What do you know"), HRC; ELM to Ellen, October 14, 1933 ("He isn't altogether"), HRC; Robinson, *ELM: An Exhibition,* 52–53 ("American Anthology" as new name for "Atlantis").

33. ELM to Raymond Moley, November 12, 1933 (all quotations), HRC.

34. Moley to ELM, January 20, 1934 (Van Buren and two Jacksons), February 28, 1934, May 10, 1934 (turns down poems), March 13, 1934 (turns down story and article), all HRC; ELM to Moley, April 13, 1934 (proposes an idea for a story on Illinois—Moley seems not to have responded), HRC.

35. ELM to Ellen, September 20, 1933 ("If I make"), HRC; ELM to Jack Powys, September 21, 1933, Flaccus file 1933 (Ellen ill in fall 1933), HRC; Thomas Coyne to ELM, July 4, 1938 (Hilary better off in Kansas City), HRC; ELM to Percy [MacKaye], May 3, 1934 (Ellen to New York in December 1933), Dartmouth.

CHAPTER 17: LIFE AT THE CHELSEA

1. End papers of Masters's diary for 1935 show he received about $800 from his *Spoon River* publisher, Macmillan, in 1935—but this figure also includes one-time translation rights to *SRA* in Denmark and royalties from his new book of poems, *Invisible Landscapes;* Dorothy Dow, "An Introduction to Some Letters" (quotes Masters's secretary Alice Davis as saying that *SRA*'s royalties would pay one-half the costs of his lodging at the Chelsea), Newberry.

2. ELM to Dreiser, February 1, 1918 (1917 plays), University of Pennsylvania.

3. Edward Cushing, "The Theaters," *Brooklyn Eagle,* June 5, 1928, p. 14A (prologue for *The Beaux'*).

4. ELM, *Dramatic Duologues: Four Short Plays in Verse* (New York: French, 1934); ELM to [Barrett] Clark, May 23, 1934 ("Duologues of Fortune's Mood"), February 24, 1936 (O'Hara edited *Jackson*), both Yale; ELM to French, July 16, 1934 (proofs completed by ELM, which suggests imminent publication of the book), Yale; ELM to Gerald Sanders, October 26, 1935 (120 copies of "deluxe" edition), HRC; Frank O'Hara to ELM, November 12, 1934 (plans *Jackson*), HRC; Samuel French to ELM, February 21, 1935 ($36.67), HRC; F. H. O'H [Frank O'Hara] to "Judith," April 29, 1947, Flaccus file 1934 (*Jackson* performed December 6, 7, 8, 1934), HRC; ELM to Charley [Coburn], August 4, 1936 (does not see play), HRC; unpub. chapter 24, p. 493 (December 1934 production), HRC; Hilary Masters, *Last Stands: Notes from Memory* (Boston: Godine, 1982), 92 (ELM's grandmother heard Jackson [but see *ASR,* 304, which lacks a reference to hearing Jackson]); ELM, *Skeeters Kirby,* 274 (grandmother saw Jackson); ELM to [Amy] Bonner, January 9, 1939 ("the duologues"), Pennsylvania State University.

5. Frank K. Robinson, *Edgar Lee Masters: An Exhibition in Commemoration of the Centenary of His Birth* (Austin: University of Texas, 1970), 31 ("I have been striving"); ELM, *Richmond: A Dramatic Poem* (New York: French, 1934) (cover of paperback shows 50¢).

6. ELM, *The Seven Cities of America* ([Cleveland]: John Huntington Polytechnic Institute, 1934); Richard Minch to ELM, August 12, 1934 (eight copies, had wanted more copies, Cleveland publishing address), April 24, 1934 (high school printing-class project, no copies to be sold), both HRC; ELM to Gerald Sanders, April 2, 1935 ("In 1934, some young fellows"), HRC; Robinson, *ELM: An Exhibition,* 31 (describes *Seven Cities*).

7. *Esquire* to ELM, March 23, 1934 ($150), HRC; ELM, "The Yahoos Came to Town," *Today,* June 30, 1934, pp. 10–11, 24; ELM, "The Machine Age Comes to Spoon River," *Today,* April 14, 1934, pp. 8–9; Raymond Moley to ELM, January 20, 1934 (five poems for *Today*), Hoover

Institution on War, Revolution and Peace; ELM to Jack [Powys], August 14, 1934, Flaccus file 1934 (Jefferson), HRC; ELM to Harry Staton, May 3, 1934 (dramatic presentation of *SRA*), HRC; ELM to Barrett Clark, October 11, 1934 (trunks are full), Yale.

8. ELM to G. Anne Brooks, September 11, 1933 (must approve scenarios), HRC; G. Anne Brooks to ELM, September 15, 1933 (agrees that ELM see movie scenarios), HRC; ELM to Jacob Wilk, December 17, 1931 (ELM intractable with Warner Brothers), HRC.

9. ELM to Liveright Publishing Company, May 21, 1934 ("The old corporation"), HRC.

10. ELM to Jack [Powys], March 10, 1933, Flaccus file 1933 (kindergarten), August 14, 1934, Flaccus file 1934 (tonsils), both HRC; ELM to Elizabeth [Lindsay], April 23, 1934 (typing, Ellen to Kansas City), HRC; ELM to Percy [MacKaye], May 3, 1934 ("chicken pox"), Dartmouth.

11. ELM to Phyllis [Playter], April 26, 1934, Flaccus file 1934 ("Ellen went away"), HRC; ELM to Jack [Powys], August 14, 1934, Flaccus file 1934 ("Ellen is still west"), HRC; ELM to Mary [Bell Sloan], August 16, 1935 ("Moroni"), Dartmouth.

12. Mencken to ELM, October 11, 1934 (remarks that "Mrs. Masters is ill"), HRC; Ellen Masters to Gerald Sanders, September 16, 1949 (recalls the stress and tensions of "about fifteen years ago"), HRC.

13. "Lewd" [ELM] to "Dear Kid" [Ellen], December 20, 1934 ("It is all"), letter property of Hilary Masters; ELM to Wheelock, November 7, 1935 ("the feelings"), HRC.

14. "Poetry, Prohibition and Polygamy (Luncheon Conversation between Edgar Lee Masters and Madame X)," *New York Sun,* March 9, 1919, sec. 5, p. 4, Flaccus file 1919 ("make their own," "mismated," handwritten note on clipping shows interview is by Constance Murray Greene), HRC; ELM to Constance Greene, April 6, 1932, Flaccus file 1932 (stays in touch), April 30, 1932, Flaccus file 1932 (suggests an intimacy), both HRC; ELM to Constance Greene, Thanksgiving Day 1934, Flaccus file 1934 ("Daisy Fraser"), HRC; Diary 1917, end paper (shows ELM had met Constance Murray by 1917); Hilary Masters to Herb Russell, September 24, 1995 (Murray is maiden name); Constance Greene to Kimball Flaccus, letter postmarked July 10, 1951 (promotional brochure shows her speech subjects and family members), Georgetown.

15. Dorothy Gardner to ELM, July 28, 1935 (poet, Vermont, letterhead shows she had lived at the Chelsea), April 21, 1936 (as agent), February 26, 1937 (prepping son for Harvard), all HRC; ELM to Dorothy Gardner, December 31, 1935 ("Dodo"), April 22, 1936 ("Dodo," submitted synopsis of *Nuptial Flight* to Hollywood), both HRC; biographical note on Dorothy Gardner in ELM's hand, n.d. (Dodo's age, child, marriages to Gardner and Batcheller, divorces, Vermont), HRC; picture of ELM, Dorothy, and Dorothy's son dated March 24, 1935 (Dodo's appearance [picture is in folder labeled "Letters to E. L. Masters from Dorothy Gardner Butts," among ELM papers]), HRC; ELM's typed notes on Dorothy Gardner, April 24, 1936 (books to autograph, "celebrity hunter," "bug house," to Windsor, Vermont), HRC; poems about her are in folder labeled "Letters to E. L. Masters from Dorothy Gardner Butts," among ELM papers, HRC; ELM to Mencken, December 1, 1934 (meets Dorothy), NY Public; Diary 1935, March 14 (Buck ["Dodo" appears as "D" in the diary]).

16. Diary 1935, February 25, July 10, 18, and September 24 (*Invisible Landscapes*), April 25 and September 27 (*Lindsay*), June 24–July 25 (Ellen types autobiography); ELM to Brett, January 30, 1926 (threatens company with poor image in autobiography), HRC; Scribner's to ELM's agent G. Anne Brooks, June 19, 1934 ($500), HRC; John Hall Wheelock to Gerald Sanders, January 3, 1939 (3,000 copies), HRC.

17. Hilary Masters, *Last Stands,* 34–36.

18. Ibid., 32, 37–40, 42; Diary 1935, June 24–July 25 (autobiography).

19. ELM to Mary Bell Sloan, September 23, 1935 (leave in September), Dartmouth; ELM to Tom [Coyne], October 1, 1942 ("For days"), HRC; Diary 1935, June–August.

20. Harcourt Brace to ELM, September 17, 1935 (receives $25 for textbook poem), HRC;

Richard Walsh to ELM, January 14, 1935 (offers $50 for rights to magazine poem), HRC; National Poetry Center to ELM, July 6, 1936 (Gold Emblem), HRC; ELM to Anita Browne, National Poetry Center, May 21, 1936, misc. file C–Cz (refuses to go to award ceremony), HRC; ELM to Macmillan Company, February 1, 1936, and February 4, 1936 ($416, 896 copies of *Landscapes*), both HRC; [John Hall] Wheelock to ELM, December 3, 1935 (1,300 copies of *Lindsay*), HRC; Macmillan to Frank Dodd, August 20, 1935 (*Godbey* trade edition), HRC; Frank Dodd to James Putnam, August 22, 1935, Flaccus file 1935 (*Godbey* trade edition), HRC; "Masters Receives Twain Medal," *Publishers Weekly* 129 (Mar. 1936): 1177 ("preeminence"); ELM to Cyril Clemens, October 28, 1935 (will not go to Twain medal ceremony), NY Public; ELM to Arthur [Ficke], October 16, 1935 ("*Spoon River* has always"), Yale.

21. ELM to Mary [Bell Sloan], November 18, 1935 ("My own case"), Dartmouth; ELM to Jack [Powys], March 11, 1936, Flaccus file 1936 ("Far from falling"), HRC.

22. ELM to Dear Constance [Greene], September 12, 1935, Flaccus file 1935 ("Come here"), HRC; ELM, "Vernal Equinox," January 27, 1936, Flaccus file 1936 ("you unveiled," and "Your Hands"), HRC; ELM, "Age after Age," January 31, 1936, Flaccus file 1936 (lovers dead), HRC; ELM to Constance [Greene], August 13, 1936, Flaccus file 1936 ("friendship"), HRC.

23. Alice Davis, memoir (typist, first meeting, and date), Virginia; Gertrude Claytor, "Edgar Lee Masters in the Chelsea Years," *Princeton University Library Chronicle* 14 (Autumn 1952): 1 (second floor); ELM, biographical note on Alice Davis, n.d. (to Chelsea in June), HRC; picture P119C (physical appearance), photo archives, HRC; ELM, "Reflections," January 23, 1939 (Davis in room 1010), Harvard; ELM, "Hermaphroditus," June 17, 1937, Ficke Collection (born 1901, "Anita," physical appearance), Yale.

24. Diary 1935, November 11 and many other dates (male acquaintances); ELM, biographical note on Alice Davis, n.d. (affairs with at least three married men), HRC; Davis, memoir (from St. Louis), Virginia.

25. ELM, biographical note on Alice Davis, n.d. (born in Kansas, raised by grandmother), HRC; two poems written by Alice Davis are "How Do I Love Thee," July 1937, and "Cleopatra to Antony," July 10, 1937, both HRC; Alice Davis business card (specialist in research, advertising, copy writing), HRC; Alice to "Dearest" [ELM], September 23, 1936 (makes changes in manuscripts), HRC; ELM to "Dearest" [Alice Davis], November 18, 1938 (will make editorial changes she suggests), HRC; ELM to Alice Davis, September 20, 1936 (they will work jointly on poems about Alice), HRC; ELM to "Darling Girl" [Alice Davis], Christmas Day 1938 ("In all my life"), HRC; Elizabeth Henney, "Independence Day Marked by Latvian Envoy," *Washington Post*, November 19, 1938, p. 14 ("stunning figure"); Alice Davis to Mencken, February 1, 1945 (friend of Latvian official), NY Public.

26. Alice Davis, "Evenings with Edgar," 150A (death of Alice's mother), NY Public; ELM, "My Youth in the Spoon River Country," 244 (death of Pamela's mother), HRC; *ASR*, 298 (death of Tennessee's mother).

27. "Hen" to "Dearest Edgar Lee Bunny Buster Punkin and Cookie," n.d., HRC; Alice to ELM, September 1, [1936?] (arranges books on shelf), HRC; [ELM to Whom It May Concern], June 20, 1936 (note saying ELM has read Alice Davis's journal about him), HRC; ELM, biographical note on Dorothy Gardner, n.d. (sees "Dodo" in fall 1935, early 1936), HRC; Davis, "Evenings with Edgar," 71, 136 (ELM encourages journal), NY Public; Diary 1937, January 13 ("X and O to" and many similar examples); Diary 1935, December 25 (Lillian).

28. Diary 1935, April 6, July 5 (Oliver Herford), October 9, December 9 (Mrs. Herford), December 10 (holograph copy of *SRA* sold for $2,000), end paper (makes $2,700); Diaries 1935 and 1937 show much eating out; Diary 1937, June 8, 15 (loans Alice money); ELM to Mr. Decker, September 12, 1938, Flaccus file 1938 (received $2,000 for *SRA* ms.), HRC; ELM to Robert Hutchins, February 21, 1941 ($2,000 for *SRA*), HRC; ELM to Mr. Shiffrin, December 3, 1935 (only one holograph of *SRA*), HRC.

29. Davis, memoir (gourmet society, friends, sewing, travels, writings, readings, marriage, "Hen"), Virginia; ELM to Christian Gauss, September 29, 1936 ("secretary"), Princeton; Alice Davis to Mr. Straub, April 17, 1937 ("secretary to Mr. Masters"), HRC; ELM note, September 29, 1936 ("No law"), HRC; Hilary Masters to Herb Russell, June 11, 1997 (hen's head movements and fellatio); Davis, "Evenings with Edgar," 98 ($25 per week), 85 (both in love), NY Public.

30. ELM, "Sonnets in April (for Alice Davis)," April 1936, Flaccus file 1936, HRC; ELM, "Longum Illud Tempus," August 8, 1936 ("There is but one"), Yale; "Lute Puckett" [ELM], "My Hen," n.d. ("I think I never"), Dreiser Papers, University of Pennsylvania; [ELM], "Lyric" ("angel chicken"), Percy MacKaye Collection, Harvard; ELM, "The Hotel Chelsea," *The Chelsean,* April 1940, p. 1 ("All this will be"), Knox College.

31. Davis, memoir (Union College, Schenectady, Mohawk Drama Festival, August 18–22, ELM speaks on stage, pictures, press notices), Virginia; ELM to Charles Coburn, April 8, 1936 (no fee, 5 percent of movie or New York play), HRC.

32. Richard Gordon, "Anthology Wrath Fades as 25 Years Roll Past," unid. newspaper clipping, n.d., n.p., Flaccus file 1939 ("*Anthology* aristocracy"), HRC; ELM to Mencken, August 29, 1936 ("I'm off"), HRC; ELM to Frank [W. Allan], August 29, 1936 (Ellen and Hilary present), HRC; ELM to Charley [Coburn], August 4, 1936 ("I want my little boy"), HRC; "Homecoming, Pageant Feature Closing Day of City's Centennial," *Petersburg Observer,* September 11, 1936, p. 1 (Ellen speaks).

33. Hilary Masters to Herb Russell, conversation, 1993 (VIP treatment); ELM, "To the People of Petersburg and Lewistown," *The University Review* (Kansas City) 3 (Winter 1936): 107–8 ("To be here"); ELM to "Darling Anita" [Alice Davis], September 2, 1936 ("sweet village"), HRC; Hilary Masters, *Last Stands: Notes from Memory* (Boston: Godine, 1982), 34 (no family life between 1936 and 1944).

34. Hilary Masters to Herb Russell, December 31, 1992 (sexual habits of Ellen and Alice), June 11, 1997 (fellatio as "therapeutic").

35. Davis, "Evenings with Edgar," 160–214, 256, and 266 (the "Anita poems"), 128 (Library of Congress, "If he is remembered"), 201 ("Love's Philosophy"), NY Public.

36. ELM, *Invisible Landscapes* (New York: Macmillan, 1935), 77 ("And never"), 120 ("Those who"), 6 ("The invisible landscape").

37. D. Appleton-Century review notice, published August 1936, copy in author's possession; ELM to George Brett, January 14, 1922 (writing *Poems of People*), HRC; ELM to U.S. Register of Copyrights, January 5, 1923, HRC; ELM to President Roosevelt, September 19, 1936 (copy to president), HRC; unpub. chapter 27, p. 532 (began in 1922), HRC; Robinson, *ELM: An Exhibition,* 49 ("caught in the tangle"); ELM, *Poems of People* (New York: Appleton, 1936), 163 ("Peace in Loneliness"); ELM to [Clarence] Decker, November 28, 1936 (second printing), Dartmouth.

38. Robinson, *ELM: An Exhibition,* 50 (written in ten days in 1930); ELM, *The Golden Fleece of California* (Weston, Vt.: Countryman, 1936), 9 ("immersed"), [80] (signed edition of 550 copies); ELM to Carl Weinstein, August 11, 1936 (*Golden Fleece* published after *Poems of People*), Iowa; ELM, "My Youth," 21 (Henry Masters and McKendree), HRC; *ASR,* 43 (Missouri River), 208 (brother); Charles E. Burgess, "Edgar Lee Masters' Paternal Ancestry: A Pioneer Heritage and Influence," *Western Illinois Regional Studies* 7 (Spring 1984): 47–48 (Squire Davis helped build Illinois College).

39. ELM to Richard Minch, April 27, 1934 (offers to let high school print *Golden*), HRC; ELM to Vrest Orton, October 2, 1935 ("I keep producing"), HRC; John Lowell Pratt to ELM, August 13, 1937 ($364 from both editions), HRC; Robinson, *ELM: An Exhibition,* 50 (trade edition).

40. George Brett Jr. to ELM, September 12, 1935 (Ellen to make decision as to whether to publish autobiography), HRC; ELM to Wheelock, November 7, 1935 ("It is about"), HRC.

41. ELM to Wheelock, June 21, 1935 ("pleased"), Princeton; G. Anne Brooks to ELM, April 24, 1936 (libelous passages), HRC; ELM to John Farrar, May 23, 1936 (libelous passages), HRC; *ASR*, 165 ("exactly as Keats").

42. Graydon Regenos and Ada Regenos, eds., *Historic Fulton County* (Lewistown, Ill.: Mid-County, 1973), 16–17 (bridge picture and data).

43. Ellen Masters to Edith Masters, January 2, 1970, HRC; Joseph Tetlow, "The Intellectual and Spiritual Odyssey of Edgar Lee Masters" (Ph.D. diss., Brown University, 1970), 58, 65 (discusses *Who's Who* error).

44. "Information for *The National Cyclopedia of American Biography,*" form completed and signed by ELM, n.d., misc. file D–I, HRC.

45. ELM to Mr. Kennedy, February 3, 1927 ("he published his first book of verse"), HRC; Masters's handwriting on WJZ radio stationery, n.d., misc. file ("published" first book before thirty), HRC; ELM to [Robert Morss] Lovett, January 29, 1930 ("book was printed, bound, and ready," "never published"), HRC; ELM to [Gerald] Sanders, May 10, 1938 (first book reviewed in November 1898), HRC; *ASR*, 251 ("never published," book given to Masters); ELM, "My Youth," 187½ (*Maximilian* "first published"), HRC; "Book of Verses," *Chicago Evening Post*, November 26, 1898, p. 30 (review of ELM's first book); "ELM: MSR," ch. 7, p. 161 (first book reviewed in *Lewistown News* on November 21, 1898), Dartmouth; a review of *A Book of Verses* appears in the Knox College publication *Knox Student* dated January 10, 1898 (171, 173), but the date is a typographical error that should show "1899."

46. Hilary Masters to Herb Russell, December 31, 1992.

47. Lowell to ELM, January 2, 1917 (acknowledges receipt of biographical sketch), Harvard; ELM, [An Autobiographical Sketch], n.p., n.d., Harvard; ELM to Lowell, December 20, 1916 ("asked a man"), Harvard.

48. Diary 1930, April 18, August 17, 23.

49. ELM to Jack [Powys], April 25, 1939, Flaccus file 1939 ("daughters very indignant"), HRC; Davis, memoir (Hardin's sleeping), Virginia.

50. Bernard DeVoto, "Delphic Apollo in Illinois," *Saturday Review of Literature* 15 (Nov. 14, 1936): 5 ("it is, after all"); M. J. T., "Poet vs. Lawyer," *Christian Science Monitor*, November 11, 1936, p. 18 ("a life of appalling conflict"); John Holmes, "Edgar Lee Masters—Super Antagonist," *Boston Evening Transcript*, November 14, 1936, pt. 7, p. 2 ("Toward the end").

51. John T. Flanagan, *Edgar Lee Masters: The Spoon River Poet and His Critics* (Metuchen, N.J.: Scarecrow, 1974), 121–23 (summarizes commentary on *ASR*, Spiller); ELM to Mencken, April 10, 1943 ("wearisome"), NY Public.

52. Hilary Masters to Herb Russell, October 18, 1993 (hoped for money); ELM to [Barrett] Clark, May 15, 1936 (movie discussion), Yale; Farrar and Rinehart to ELM, January 18, 1937 (profits on *ASR*), HRC.

53. Holmes, "Edgar Lee Masters—Super Antagonist," pt. 7, p. 1 (unflattering picture and drawings, including ELM on pedestal); ELM to W. D. Howe, December 20, 1936 (sells four poems for $60), Princeton; ELM to John Farrar, June 5, 1936 (poetry judge), HRC.

54. Dow, "Introduction to Some Letters" ("When I look"), Newberry; Alice Davis to Mencken, February 16, 1944 (ELM looked to Mencken), NY Public; ELM to Anita Browne, May 21, 1936, misc. file C–Cz ("I always refuse"), HRC.

55. ELM to [Joseph Warren] Beach, February 14, 1939 ("communist mathematicians"), HRC; ELM to Jack [Powys], November 1, 1937, Flaccus file 1937 ("quack"), November 8, 1937, Flaccus file 1937 ("catered to the moron"), both HRC; ELM to G. Anne Brooks, October 1, 1936 ("the swine"), HRC; ELM to Arthur [Ficke], October 1, 1936 ("Nosey"), October 6, 1936 ("hogwash"), both Yale; ELM to Clarence Decker, November 29, 1936 ("iota-subscripts"), Dartmouth; Dow, "Introduction to Some Letters" ("all mixed up," "Yeats"), Newberry.

56. ELM to Jack [Powys], October 3, 1935, Flaccus file 1935 ("To call me"), HRC; Claytor, "Masters in the Chelsea Years," 10 (misquoted).

57. Claytor, "Masters in the Chelsea Years," 10 (timidity when speaking, Bryan); *ASR*, 211 ("It was as impossible," Petersburg speech); ELM to Brett, January 26, 1927 ("Dining, shaking hands"), HRC; ELM to Carter Davidson, December 6, 1936 (didn't "go in," refuses Knox), HRC.

58. Alice Davis to "Dearest Robby" [Roberta Grant], January 19, 1941 ("spoiled child," "purring," "friendliness"), Southern Illinois University; ELM to Bill Carlton[?], January 22, 1936, misc. file V–Z (buttermilk), HRC.

CHAPTER 18: A STRIP OF FADED CARPET AND AN OLD CLIPPING

1. Dreiser to ELM, February 3, 1940 ("outstanding"), HRC; Mencken to ELM, July 30, 1936 ("fecundity"), HRC; Witter Bynner to ELM, November 17, 1937 ("verbiaginous," "recapture"), HRC; ELM to Gerald Sanders, April 30, 1935 ("I turned"), HRC.

2. ELM to Jack [Powys], March 10, 1933, Flaccus file 1933 (ailanthus, sun, clouds), HRC; Clarence Decker to ELM, November 27, 1936 (book shelves, table), HRC; picture P243 (bay window, rockers), photo archives, HRC; Chelsea Hotel to ELM, September 14, 1937, misc. file A–B ($17.50, second floor), HRC; Kimball Flaccus, "Notes on Edgar Lee Masters," November 2, 1941, Flaccus file 24 (pictures of authors and Jefferson), HRC; ELM to Robert P. Tristram Coffin, November 18, 1937 ("quiet as a village"), HRC; Dorothy Dow, "An Introduction to Some Letters" (pictures crooked, lamps, drab, depressing), Newberry; Alice Davis, "Evenings with Edgar," 49 (phonograph, "Spoon River"), NY Public; Diary 1937, August 30 (room 214).

3. Selig Greenberg, "Edgar Lee Masters . . . ," *Providence Evening Bulletin*, May 4, 1936, p. 9 ("In appearance, dress, and manner"); "Bitter Poet on Sad Poet," *Time*, October 7, 1935, p. 67 ("Since he dresses"); Dow, "Introduction to Some Letters" ("pish," etc.), Newberry.

4. Dow, "Introduction to Some Letters" ("his hat," "He continued"), Newberry; Diary 1937, January 25 (swims); ELM to Mencken, January 6, 1937 (claims to swim daily), HRC; ELM to "Darling Girl" [Alice Davis], December 7, 1937 (pool across street), HRC.

5. Dow, "Introduction to Some Letters" (all quotations), Newberry.

6. Diary 1937, January 3 ("Took poem"), 11, 20, February 8 ("D. comes to write"), March 2 ("D. comes down"), May 31 ("Alone").

7. Picture of Alice Davis, ELM, and Dreiser dated May 8, 1938, in "Alice Davis" folder, among ELM papers, HRC; Alice Davis to ELM, June 4, 1943 (Mencken dinners), HRC; Diary 1937, April 12 (sandwich and drink), July 1 ("Love me"); lunches and dinners are indicated throughout Diary 1937; Davis, "Evenings with Edgar," 153 ("I love you"), NY Public.

8. Diary 1937, April 1 (Schopenhauer); ELM to Arthur [Ficke], October 12, 1937 ("Obscenia"), Yale; Tietjens Collection, Newberry, has examples of Masters's materials involving Chubb, Puckett, and other imaginary beings; Lillian Wilson to ELM, April 23, 1920 (Lillian knows of Chubb), HRC; ELM to Constance Greene, n.d., Flaccus file 1932 (ELM as Lucius Atherton), HRC; see broadside "Coming! Coming!" showing Chubb as LL.D., D.D., HRC; see broadside "Elmer Chubb LLD, Ph.D." for degrees, Chicago; ELM to Mencken, June 1, 1934 (ELM knew real Puckett in Lewistown), NY Public; William Marion Reedy, "Reflections," *Reedy's Mirror* 25 (Jan. 28, 1916): 1 (shows beginning of Percival Chubb's involvement in public morals); ELM to Percy [MacKaye], May 3, 1934 ("Pieces by Puckett"), Dartmouth.

9. Tietjens Collection (Prowler, Atherton, Chubb), Newberry; Monroe Collection (broadsides on Fem Vigoro, gland protectors, sinful sensations, "File with Masters"), Chicago; [ELM], *The Story of the Good Little Girl and the Bad Little Girl* (N.p., 1923).

10. Llewelyn Jones to [Kimball] Flaccus, August 8, 1953 (Brett wanted volume of Chubb), Georgetown; H. S. Latham (Macmillan) to ELM, July 27, 1922 (suggests volume of Chubb-related writings), HRC; Davis, "Evenings with Edgar," 126 (business card), 74 (poetry reading), 254 (good for Masters), NY Public.

11. Diary 1937, July 3–8 (men); Marshall Smith, "A Room with Ghost $4 and Up," unid. magazine clipping, 138 (Chase an artist), Western Illinois University; Davis, "Evenings with Edgar," 9–10 (Condon), NY Public.

12. Diary 1937 is replete with Masters's monitoring of Alice Davis; Diary 1937, June 9 ("not back").

13. Diary 1937, August 12–26.

14. Hilary Masters, *Last Stands: Notes from Memory* (Boston: Godine, 1982), 140 ("My God," "He was"); Ellen to Mencken, August 22, 1937 (passes master's exam), NY Public.

15. Ellen to Mencken, August 30, 1937 ("I don't know," "I should like"), NY Public; Mencken note, "Manuscripts by H. L. Mencken," folder 13, September 13, 1937 ("impossible"), NY Public; Diary 1937, September 2–7 (infantile paralysis).

16. Hilary [Masters] to ELM, n.d. [apparently August or September 1937] ("So sorry"), HRC; Hilary [Masters] to "My Dear Pa," n.d. [apparently fall 1937] ("This thing of just settin"), HRC.

17. "Spoon River Poet Called Great," *New York Times*, April 4, 1915, p. 7 ("natural child"); Wheelock to ELM, April 13, 1936 (suggests biography), HRC; ELM to Wheelock, April 21, 1936 ("No one would ever"), HRC; Scribner's to ELM, May 7, 1936 ($1,000 and 15 percent), HRC; ELM to Witter [Bynner], September 5, 1937 (read Whitman at eighteen), Harvard; unpub. chapter 26, p. 515 (visited Whitman house in 1923), HRC; Diary 1924, June 9 (sees house of Whitman).

18. ELM to Wister Institute, June 27, 1936 (seeks details on Whitman's brain), HRC; ELM to Wheelock, September 23, 1936 (previously unpublished picture of Whitman), HRC; Alice Davis, memoir (working on book by June 1936, typing, trip to Camden, nap), Virginia; Alice Davis photo credit is on dust jacket; ELM to Wheelock, June 17, 1937 ("She did research"), Princeton.

19. Scribner's to ELM, January 29, 1937 (March publication), September 3, 1937 (sells 1,500 copies), October 22, 1938 ($830), all HRC; Wheelock to Gerald Sanders, January 3, 1939 (3,000 copies), HRC; ELM, *Whitman* (New York: Scribner's, 1937), 309, 269, 271, 276, 299 (Frost and Robinson), 194 ("the literary gang"), 315, 171 ("prose poems"); ELM to Wheelock, November 12, 1941 ("didn't sell," "tricky"), Princeton.

20. ELM to "Dear Kid" [Ellen], October 11, 1931 (Dodd, Mead refuses), HRC; Harper and Brothers to Hewitt Howland, March 8, 1932 (refuses Masters's ms.), HRC; Simon and Schuster to G. Anne Brooks, March 23, 1934 (refuses Masters's ms.), HRC; Farrar and Rinehart to ELM, February 11, 1937 ($1,250), May 4, 1937 (editors see as muddle), June 29, 1937 (galley costs), August 2, 1937 (publication date), December 6, 1937 (poor sales), all HRC; ELM to John Farrar, December 24, 1936 (added 30,000 words in 1933), May 5 ("I can punctuate," "did not square"), both HRC.

21. ELM, *The Tide of Time* (New York: Farrar, 1937), 38–9 (academy), 323 (college), 528 (judgeship), 438 (Congress), 621 (mayor), 152 (Davis), 682 ("duty," "claims of the day"); John H. Wrenn and Margaret Wrenn, *Edgar Lee Masters* (Boston: Twayne, 1983), 96 ("son" of grandmother).

22. ELM, *The Tide of Time,* 350–420 (Sophronia), 217 (Adele attractive), 339 (Adele sensible), 281 (no passion), 233 (Byron), 218 (Keats and Shelley); *ASR,* 185–86, 214–16 (Honoria).

23. ELM, *The Tide of Time,* 341 (expected to marry), 546 ("imagined that men"), 339 ("Somehow it crept"), 420 (marries in haste).

24. Ibid., 304 ("Of one thing"), 611 (son dies).

25. Ibid., 639 ("The time never came"), 640 ("something was profoundly wrong").

26. ELM to Kimball [Flaccus], January 30, 1941, Flaccus file 1941 (used much of "Atlantis" in *The New World* [New York: Appleton, 1937], most extensive research), HRC; John L. B. Williams to ELM, September 23, 1937 (Pulitzer nomination), June 18, 1937 (galleys revised), both HRC; ELM to Carter Harrison, December 11, 1938 ("summation"), HRC; ELM to Mencken, August 3, 1937 (rewrote in 1933), NY Public; ELM to Roland and Elsie Farley, August 10, 1923 ("great work"), NY Public; "Old Man Spoon River," *Time,* November 22, 1937, pp. 80–81; "Poetry," *The Saturday Review of Literature* 17 (Jan. 1, 1938): 21; ELM to [John Gould] Fletcher, May 15, 1939 ("donkeys"), Arkansas.

27. ELM, *Hymn to the Unknown God* (Brown City, Mich.: New Age Ministry of Religious Research, n.d. [1937?]); ELM to Van Wyck Brooks, [September 1938], Flaccus file 1938 (initially thought well of poem, "it fails"), HRC; see also Herb Russell, "A 'New' Pamphlet by Edgar Lee Masters," *The Papers of the Bibliographical Society of America* 72 (Second Quarter 1978): 258.

28. Margaret Barker to ELM, October 11, 1937 (regarding plays), HRC; Ivan von Auw Jr. to ELM, October 1, 1937 (short story), HRC; ELM to John Farrar, April 23, 1937 (collection of poems), HRC; ELM to [John Hall] Wheelock, November 12, 1937, Flaccus file 1937 (book about Petersburg), HRC; Chadbourne, Wallace . . . to ELM, December 20, 1937 (lawsuit), HRC; ELM to Arthur [Ficke], October 14, 1937 (anti-anthologies), Yale; ELM, "America in 1937," with letter to Arthur Ficke, October 29, 1937, Yale.

29. ELM, "New Hope Meetinghouse," November 6–7, 1937, with Ficke papers, Yale; published in ELM, *More People,* 149–52.

30. Diary 1937, end papers ($5,500); ELM's federal tax return for 1937 (gross income of $3,744), property of Hilary Masters; Hardin Wallace Masters, *Edgar Lee Masters: A Biographical Sketchbook about a Famous American Author* (Rutherford, N.J.: Farleigh Dickinson University Press, 1978), 56 ("a son"); ELM to Senator [Robert] La Follette, December 16, 1937 (requests aid for artists), HRC; ELM to Editor, *Herald-Tribune,* December 19, 1937 ("legislation," "pensions"), HRC.

31. ELM to Hilary, October 27, 1931 (holiday gift), November 12, 1931 (toy), n.d. ("Mr. Ittie, I love de"), April 15, 1936 (*X*s and *O*s), December 21, 1930 ("Your ma"), September 11, 1930 ("bad people"), telegram, n.d. ("beah"), all Brown University. Some of Masters's letters were sent airmail and include references to money as a gift.

32. "Teacher at Ogontz," *Campuscope* (Pennsylvania State University's Ogontz Center), February 1956, pp. 7–8 (lectures); "Art Classes for 400," *Kansas City Times,* October 1, 1935, p. 7 (Ellen makes costumes); Ellen to Kimball Flaccus, April 21, 1951, misc. file, (ELM tried to prevent graduate education in January 1938), HRC; Diary 1938, January 31 ("Ellen blows in"), February 1 ("check[ed] out"); Elisabeth Earley, interview with Ellen Masters, December 2, 1970, p. 32 (master's degree in 1938), property of Hilary Masters.

33. Hilary Masters, *Last Stands: Notes from Memory* (Boston: Godine, 1982), 147 (divorce question, get-togethers to discuss Hilary, writing complaints).

34. Hilary Masters to Herb Russell, October 18, 1993 (living quarters, bookstore, Poconos), June 11, 1997 (Hilary at boy's camp); ELM to Jack [Powys], June 26, 1938, Flaccus file 1938 (to Poconos), HRC.

35. Diary 1938, January 15 (spat begins), end papers dated February 6 ("give D"), April 9 (dreams relation over), July 2 (last recorded sexual relations); Davis, "Evenings with Edgar," 130 ("probably taper off"), NY Public.

36. Diary 1937, January 10 and 22 (begins *Twain*), March 3 (finishes *Twain*); ELM to [John Hall] Wheelock, December 14, 1937, February 17, 1937 ($500 advance related to *Whitman* sales),

February 27, 1938 (Masters's book based on other biographies), all Princeton; John Hall Wheelock to Gerald Sanders, January 3, 1939 (3,000 copies), HRC.

37. Cyril Clemens, "A Chat with Edgar Lee Masters," *Hobbies* 55 (Aug. 1950): 123 ("read to tatters"); *ASR,* 78 (Hare Hummer); ELM, *Mark Twain: A Portrait* (New York: Scribner's, 1938) (parallels between ELM and Twain); Wrenn and Wrenn, *Edgar Lee Masters,* 18 (comments on some parallels between ELM and Twain).

38. ELM, *Mark Twain,* 92 ("de-Southernized"), 102 ("emasculated"), 113, 122, 137, 153; ELM to [John Hall] Wheelock, February 25, 1938 ("I attacked"), February 4, 1937 (King and Duke), both Princeton; ELM to Mencken, November 18, 1937 ("I have combed"), NY Public.

39. ELM to [John Hall] Wheelock, November 12, 1941 (*Twain* did not sell well), Princeton; Scribner's to ELM, n.d. [1938] (earnings sheet shows *Twain* published February 25, 1938), Princeton; [John Hall] Wheelock to Mr. Mers, June 12, 1950 (*Twain* made $432.50), Princeton; Scribner's to Leon Malraison, June 13, 1950, Flaccus file 1950 (*Twain* makes $432.50), HRC; Scribner's to ELM, September 14, 1938 (turns down new book), HRC.

40. ELM to Jack Powys, December 2, 1938 (neuritis, no magazine market), May 9, 1938 ("of all the human problems"), both HRC; *Esquire* to ELM, March 29, 1938 (ELM sells poem for $150), HRC; Ernest Briggs to ELM, December 19, 1938 (sends out offers to lecture), February 11, 1939 (junior college offer), March 1, 1939 (never heard of ELM), December 11, 1939 (refuse to consider lecture by ELM), all HRC; William Lyon Phelps to ELM, March 24, 1938 (lectures at Yale), HRC; ELM to W. W. Norton, May 17, 1938 (textbook), HRC; Henry Moe to ELM, January 20, 1939 (no grant), HRC; ELM to University of Chicago, November 19, 1938, misc. file A–B (tries to sell mss.), HRC; ELM to Brett, November 23, 1938 (*SRA* anniversary edition), HRC; carbon copy of chain letter, n.d., misc. file C–Cz, HRC; Daniel Henderson to ELM, November 18, 1938 ($250), HRC; Thomas P. Riggio, ed., *Dreiser-Mencken Letters: The Correspondence of Theodore Dreiser and H. L. Mencken, 1907–1945* (Philadelphia: University of Pennsylvania Press, 1986), 2:628 (arthritis); ELM to Margaret Bailey, April 21, 1938 (plays), Stanford.

41. ELM to Hardin Masters, November 17, 1938 ("My anxiety"), HRC; ELM to [Carter] Davidson, March 16, 1938 (turns down honorary status), HRC; ELM to Mencken, November 22, 1938 (Knox offers degree), HRC; ELM to Jack [Powys], March 5, 1939 (turned down honorary degree), HRC; Carter Davidson to ELM, March 13, 1939 (offers honorary faculty status), Knox College; Mencken to ELM, November 23, 1938 (Mencken dislikes honorary degrees), NY Public; Kimball Flaccus note, n.d., Additions to be Added to Main Collection (Carnegie Fund contributed over $5,000 to ELM's well-being between November 1938 and March 1950), Georgetown.

42. ELM to August Derleth, September 27, 1938, State Historical Society of Wisconsin; August Derleth, *Man Track Here* (Philadelphia: Ritten House, 1939), dedication; Diary 1939, October 27 and November 7 (Stuart); ELM to Gerald Sanders, September 23, 1938 (saw Wolfe at Chelsea bar), HRC; ELM to Mrs. Wheaton, November 26, 1938 (urged Wolfe to stay at Chelsea), HRC; ELM to Christian [Gauss], September 20, 1938 ("He used to"), HRC; "Wolfe Plaque at the Chelsea Hotel," *Thomas Wolfe Newsletter* 13 (Spring 1979): 24 (*You Can't Go Home Again*).

43. ELM to Jack [Powys], June 26, 1938, Flaccus file 1938 ("Man's journey," "When I think"), HRC; ELM to Hardin [Masters], November 17, 1938 ("I believe"), HRC.

44. Alice Davis, Christmas card, Christmas 1938 ("Edmund Pollard"), HRC; ELM to Constance Greene, March 6, 1939 ("There was a day"), HRC.

45. "Teacher at Ogontz," 15 (teaching job); Hilary Masters to Herb Russell, October 18, 1993 (Lincoln School of Columbia Teachers College); Elisabeth Earley, interview with Ellen Masters, December 2, 1970, p. 84 (Ellen did her practice teaching at Lincoln School in 1938; to get

a job, she had to take education courses in addition to those required for a master's), property of Hilary Masters.

CHAPTER 19: A LONELY OLD MAN IN NEW YORK

1. Diary 1939, January 24, April 20, 22, May 20, June 21 (sees Ellen or Hilary); Diary 1938, July 2 (final recorded sexual relations with Alice).

2. Arthur Davison Ficke, "Notes on Edgar Lee Masters, 1938–39," n.p., Yale.

3. Ibid.

4. Hardin Wallace Masters, *Edgar Lee Masters: A Biographical Sketchbook about a Famous American Author* (Rutherford, N.J.: Farleigh Dickinson University Press, 1978), 146 (afraid to cross street); Ficke, "Notes on Edgar Lee Masters," n.p. (Ficke's arm in traffic), Yale.

5. Diary 1938, end papers (shows income of $1,236 in 1938), August 4 (Alice Davis and money); Diary 1939, April 29 (gives food), May 6 (loans Alice Davis money); Alice Davis, "After *Spoon River*—What?" *Kansas Magazine*, 1939, pp. 109–13; Alice Davis, "Poet and Pleasant," *Knott Knotes*, February 1938, p. 11 (Alice's article in house newsletter).

6. Diary 1938, September 6 (Hilary to Kansas City), November 4–December 7 (Ellen with Hilary in Kansas City); Hilary Masters to Herb Russell, October 7, 1993 (erysipelas).

7. ELM to Cordell Hull, September 16, 1934 (seeks government post), HRC; Carter Harrison to ELM, December 28, 1938 (Harrison opens way to Ickes), HRC; Department of Interior to ELM, January 7, 1939 ("government secretary," transportation expenses of Ellen and Hilary to Virgin Islands), HRC; ELM to Carter Harrison, December 31, 1938 ($5,200–$6,000, "I have nerves"), February 21, 1939 (lists reasons for not going), both HRC; Carter Harrison, *Growing Up with Chicago* (Chicago: Ralph Fletcher Seymour, 1944), 350 (Harrison's federal job in Chicago); Robert Morss Lovett, *All Our Years* (New York: Viking, 1948), 268 ("greeter"); Hilary Masters to Herb Russell, October 18, 1993 (Ellen will not go to Virgin Islands), June 11, 1997 (concerned about Hilary's education); ELM to Mencken, January 27, 1939 ("I couldn't"), NY Public.

8. *Esquire* to ELM, January 23, 1939 (accepts article), April 20, 1939 (accepts article), both HRC; CBS to ELM, April 21, 1939 (gets $75 from broadcast of *SRA* poems), HRC; ELM to Caroline Shrodes, September 6, 1939 (*SRA* reprints), HRC; ELM to Jack Powys, April 7, 1939 ("scratching for money"), HRC; ELM to George Stokes, September 1, 1939 (ELM borrows $350), HRC; Arthur Ficke to ELM, September 4, 1939 (ELM borrows $100), HRC; ELM to Daniel Henderson, August 25, 1939 (asks for money from Authors Club), HRC; Library of Congress (Joseph Auslander) to ELM, August 17, 1939 (tries to sell mss.), HRC; ms. of the play "Spoon River," dated March 11, 1939, HRC; lecture contracts for Amherst, Massachusetts, October 9, 1939, and Ypsilanti, Michigan, September 11, 1939, both HRC; Rupert Hughes to ELM, January 23, 1939 ("mush"), HRC; Alice Davis to William Fadiman, Larney Goodkind, Margaret Holliwell, and William Bloom, all dated April 11, 1939 (urges *Spoon River* be accepted as a movie), all HRC; ELM, "Lincoln's New Salem: An Altar of Memory," *New York Times Magazine*, February 12, 1939, pp. 3, 14; ELM to August Derleth, January 15, 1939 (sifts through old mss.), State Historical Society of Wisconsin.

9. ELM to [John] Wheelock, January 10, 1939 ("New Salem" theft and Barrymore), Princeton; ELM to Sidney R. Fleisher, July 22, 1940 ("proceedings against Thornton"), HRC; Fleisher to ELM, July 27, 1940 (legal advice), HRC; ELM to Gerald [Sanders], October 31, 1941 ("I am robbed"), HRC.

10. Diary 1939, June 23 (proofs *More People*); ELM to Jack [Powys], August 28, 1936, Flaccus file 1936 (has enough unused poems from *Poems of People* to create a new volume), HRC; ELM to August Derleth, July 16, 1939 (*More People* to be published August 18), State Histor-

ical Society of Wisconsin; three poems—"Anson Harms," "Philosopher in Love," and "Transfusion"—show older man and young woman; ELM, *More People* (New York: Appleton, 1939), 190–91 ("Lands End," "Year after year imagination gathered"); ELM, "Lands End" (ms. dated August 23, 1938), Bobst Library; Alice Davis, "Evenings with Edgar," 505 (seventieth birthday), NY Public.

11. ELM to Theodore [Dreiser], April 19, 1939 ("worth $200,000"), University of Pennsylvania; picture P85 (shows ELM and Madeline on friendly terms at Hardin's home, 1936), photo archives, HRC; ELM to Jack [Powys], January 16, 1939 ("well-fixed," "I'd rather"), HRC; ELM to Agnes Lee Freer, April 23, 1928 (Madeline's marriage), Newberry; Marcia Lee Masters, "My Story," *LifeTimes* (Chicago), August 1989, p. 9 (relations with Marcia); Gary Panetta, "The Poet and His Daughter Connect through Verse," *Peoria Journal Star,* December 13, 1992, p. B-2 (Marcia's college).

12. Diary 1939, June 10–22 (Ellen and Hilary visit ELM prior to going to Poconos), September 18 ("Ellen comes"), end paper (Ellen's addresses); ELM to Jack [Powys], September 12, 1939, Flaccus file 1939 ("His face"), HRC; Hilary Masters to Herb Russell, October 18, 1993 (Ellen to Bentley), June 11, 1997 (hat-check work).

13. Diary 1939, December 9 (notified of medal); ELM to A. M. [Sullivan], December 19, 1939 ("While pleased"), HRC.

14. ELM to Theodore [Dreiser], January 27, 1940 ("On Thursday"), February 7, 1940 (Colum), both University of Pennsylvania.

15. Sanders to ELM, March 28, 1938 (at Ypsilanti), March 26, 1935 (begins bibliography), March 20, 1941 (plans trip to Library of Congress), July 17, 1941 (Sanders to central Illinois county seats seeking news articles by ELM), July 6, 1942 (last reference to active work on bibliography), March 24, 1940 ("crazy"), all HRC; Diary 1939, December 31 ("negligible year").

16. ELM, *The Triumph of Earth* (N.p., April 18, 1940); ELM to Dreiser, March 13, 1940 (has previously mailed a draft of *Triumph* to Dreiser), University of Pennsylvania; Ronald Primeau, "Shelley and Edgar Lee Masters' 'Amphimixis,'" *The Old Northwest* 1 (June 1975): 145 (private printing of *Triumph*); "ELM: MSR," ch. 4, p. 2 ("Triumph of Life" a favorite), Dartmouth.

17. ELM to Billy [William Lyon Phelps], April 8, 1940 (published March 13, 1940), Yale; ELM to Hewitt Howland, March 28, 1939 (Dreiser instrumental in getting Emerson book for Masters), HRC; Diary 1939, October 4 ($350 advance); ELM to Mencken, July 7, 1939 ("enjoyed immensely," "was a radical"), NY Public.

18. Ralph Waldo Emerson, *The Living Thoughts of Emerson,* selected and with an introduction by Edgar Lee Masters (New York: Longmans, Green, 1940), 2–3.

19. Ibid., 5 ("declarations").

20. Ibid., 61–62 ("Ever the instinct"), 58–59 ("The heart has"); ELM, *Whitman,* 104–5 ("sex . . . lifts"); *ASR,* 408 ("earth love").

21. Diary 1940, July 29 (contract), August 1 ($225), September 21, 22 (Hardin along); ELM, *The Sangamon,* intro. Burgess, 87 (misses roads, woods, farmstead, familiar tree, pond, disoriented), xx–xxi (Concord Church, nephew Thomas, Edith inherits); Charles Burgess, "Sandridge: A Masters Landscape Revisited," *Western Illinois Regional Studies* 14 (Fall 1991): 21 (house of grandparents); will of Squire Davis Masters, Menard County Courthouse (farm); Josephine Craven Chandler, "Mr. Masters' Spoon River," *University of Kansas City Review* 2 (Winter 1935): 96 (mill destroyed in middle 1930s); James T. Arnold to ELM, August 8, 1926 ("hard road"), HRC; "Widdle" [Wilbur Masters] to ELM, August 22, [1940] (blacktop road), HRC; ELM to Mrs. Lindsay, January 7, 1932 ("paradise lost"), HRC; ELM to Dreiser, October 2, 1940 (visits two gravesites), University of Pennsylvania.

22. Diary 1940, September 21 (Blane), 22 (Rutledge), 23 (Madeline and Marcia while with Hardin), 24 ("sad parting").

23. Diary 1940, June 20–22 (Alice Davis leaves her apartment, moves in with Masters), August 3 (Alice stays all night), September 5, 9, 10 (Alice searches for job), October 20 (Alice types), November 2 (Percy MacKaye), October 31 (Viereck), December 31 (Alice moves things out of ELM's room, no. 214); Alice Davis to ELM, September 16, 1940 (Ellen calls, gets Alice), HRC; Hardin Wallace Masters, *Edgar Lee Masters: A Biographical Sketchbook about a Famous American Author* (Rutherford, N.J.: Farleigh Dickinson University Press, 1978), 128 (room 214); John Dewey to Alice [Davis], January 4, 1937 (secretarial work for Dewey), Southern Illinois University; Diary 1937, end paper marked November 15 (mentions Wolfe and manuscripts and shows "D. will work for W").

24. Alice Davis, memoir (Alice and Sanders as coexecutors), Virginia; ELM to Gerald [Sanders], December 31, 1938 (Alice as executor would be offensive to Ellen), January 3, 1938, October 21, 1938, and November 15, 1941 (Sanders as literary executor), all HRC.

25. ELM to Frank [W. Allan], March 29, 1940 (Meyer dead), HRC; *Lewistown Evening Record* to ELM, November 28, 1940 (Reese dead), HRC; ELM to Mrs. Parke, July 30, 1941 (Stokes dies), HRC; Flaccus note, Flaccus file 1941 (McGaffey dies in 1941), HRC; Diary 1941, October 13 (Blane dies); ELM to Gertrude [Claytor], June 25, 1940 (Chiperfield dies), Princeton.

26. ELM to Lillian Wilson, June 27, 1923 (Reedy as biographer, "Before I went," "I have an"), HRC; ELM to John Cowper Powys, October 13, 1919 ("appraisal," "I have been," "article," "I have an"), March 19, 1919 ("I think you"), both University of Pennsylvania; John Cowper Powys, "The Real Edgar Lee Masters," typescript, Princeton; ELM to [Clarence] Decker, November 28, 1936 ("not satisfied"), Dartmouth.

27. Kimball Flaccus, "Edgar Lee Masters: A Biographical and Critical Study" (Ph.D. diss., New York University, 1952), i–ii (meets Masters, "a book about him"); Kimball Flaccus, "The Art of Edgar Lee Masters," *Voices,* no. 102 (Summer 1940): 43–45; Kimball Flaccus, "Masters: Poet of Affirmation, An Interview and an Estimate," *Common Sense* 9 (Oct. 1940): 13–15; Flaccus note, Flaccus file 1940 (to world's fair with ELM), HRC.

28. [John Hall Wheelock] to Henry Seidel Canby, April 15, 1941, Flaccus file 1941 (no chance for commercial success), HRC; ELM to Jack [Powys], April 28, 1941, Flaccus file 1941 ("hometown papers"), HRC; James A. Decker to Gerald Sanders, August 3, 1942 (500 copies at $2.00, fifty copies at $5.00, June publication), HRC (Masters's friend A. M. Sullivan had published with the press of James A. Decker before 1941, e.g., *Ballad of a Man Named Smith* and *New Jersey Hills,* both about 1940); Diary 1941, April 17, 25 (poems and contract).

29. Representative letters are Wilbur Masters to ELM, January 1, 1928 (neighbors, Sevigne Houghton and hogs), September 9, 1935 ("I see you yet"), both HRC; ELM to Jack [Powys], September 16, 1941 ("kept in the mood"), HRC.

30. ELM, *Illinois Poems* (Prairie City, Ill.: James A. Decker, 1941), 19–21 ("Petersburg"), 30 ("Gone is"), 66 (poem about Will).

31. "Poet Breaks Old Rule," *Kansas City Star,* January 27, 1942, p. 4; Poetry Society of America, *Official Bulletin,* February 1942, pp. 6–7 ("all of which were well," speech, and poems); ELM to A. M. Sullivan, February 20, 1942 (complains about press, program, names, angry with self), HRC; Poetry Society of America, "Annual Dinner," January 25, 1942 (program showing Bonner, Claytor, Flaccus), HRC.

32. FBI documents dated November 18 and November 19, 1954 (Stewart, "Are you for"), Federal Bureau of Investigation (copies in author's possession); FBI document dated May 6, 1946 ("the informant said," with several similar items), Federal Bureau of Investigation (copy in author's possession); Natalie Robins, *Alien Ink* (New York: Morrow, 1992), 288–89 (Masters for "Republican Spain," information still secret); ELM note to League of American Writers, February 1, 1938 ("I am for"), HRC; ELM, "The War in Spain," poem, n.d., HRC; ELM to Alice Davis, November 29, 1937 (reference to "a G man," although the context is not clear), HRC.

33. Davis, "Evenings with Edgar," 516 (Alice, ELM, Dreiser to League of American Writers meeting), 330 ("Trotsky"), 261 (Republican), NY Public; Davis, memoir (met Viereck in 1936), Virginia; Diary 1940, June 21 (Masters loses diary while at Viereck's); Diary 1941, April 4 ("FBI investigator"), October 17 ("about typing").

34. Rhoda Koenig, "Someone to Watch Over You," *New York,* March 9, 1992, p. 80 (Reed has first file); [Emma Goldman], "The Blood of the Prophets," *Mother Earth,* February 1907, pp. 41–43; ELM to Emma Goldman, April 24, 1935, HRC; Emma Goldman to ELM, April 20, 1935, HRC; Eugene Debs to ELM, December 9, 1922, March 12, 1926, both HRC; U.S. Department of Justice to ELM, April 14, 1942 (Takeshi Haga, "in the event"), HRC; Davis, "Evenings with Edgar," 155, 158 (Takeshi), NY Public; ELM, "Debs," a poem, February 1, 1926, E. P. Reese Collection, Illinois State Historical Library; Dorothy Dow, "Masters Letters and Notes," n.d. (Dexter a Marxist), Western Illinois University; Hilary Masters to Herb Russell, March 17, 1992 (Consumers Union, Dexter at Los Alamos); "Dexter Masters," *Contemporary Authors,* no. 127 (Detroit, Mich.: Gale, 1989), 293 (Dexter at MIT during World War II, atomic energy expert); Dexter Masters, *The Accident* (New York: Knopf, 1955), Author's Note and other pages.

35. ELM to [John Hall] Wheelock, December 4, 1942 (must fight Germany and Japan), May 10, 1938 ("It would be"), both Princeton; ELM to Jack [Powys], September 20, 1938, Flaccus file 1938 ("There is no respect"), HRC.

36. Nancy Johnson (American Academy of Arts and Letters) to Herb Russell, July 30, 1990 (ELM joined in 1918, resigned in 1931); ELM to Gerald [Sanders], May 4, 1942 (leaves when sees people he dislikes), HRC; Clayton Hamilton to Miss Geffen, March 12, 1943 (ELM refuses to pay annual dues of $5, resigns), American Academy of Arts and Letters.

37. Clayton Hamilton to Miss Geffen, March 12, 1943 ($500 loan, not repaid), American Academy of Arts and Letters; Assistant Treasurer to John Hall Wheelock, March 16, 1943 (ELM's loan will be the last), American Academy of Arts and Letters; certificate for Masters's $1,000 grant, "To Edgar Lee," signed by Stephen Vincent Benet, HRC; ELM to Dreiser, October 12, [1944] ("I refused"), University of Pennsylvania.

38. ELM, *The Sangamon,* intro. Charles E. Burgess (Urbana: University of Illinois Press, 1988), xv–xvi (Miller, Blane, Pond), xx (writing in October, November 1940); ELM to John Farrar, September 20, 1939 (offers history of Spoon and Sangamon Rivers), HRC; ELM to Nancy Parker, March 26, 1940 (wants to do history of Sangamon and Spoon), HRC; Erskine Caldwell to Nancy Parker, March 22, 1940 (wants broader geographic emphasis), HRC; ELM to Jack [Powys], January 26, 1941 (completes book in November 1940), HRC; Farrar and Rinehart to ELM, March 10, 1942 (last chapter omitted), HRC; ELM to Amy Bonner, September 10, 1942 (published in May 1942), Pennsylvania State University.

39. ELM, *The Sangamon,* 235 ("The Sangamon River!").

40. Ibid., 23 ("magical"), 116 ("The country").

41. Ibid., 44 ("the most beautiful"), 59 ("I know"), 26 ("My grandfather").

42. James A. Decker to ELM, November 2, 1948 (owed ELM royalties on both *Illinois Poems* and *Along the Illinois* [Prairie City, Ill.: James A. Decker, 1942]), October 9, 1941 (100 copies), November 11, 1941 ("Sandridge to Spring Lake"), all HRC; dust jacket, *Illinois Poems* ("largest publishing"); Catherine Davis to ELM, November 16, 1942 (details on Decker's press), HRC; ELM to Mrs. Harmon Marbold, January 14, 1942, Flaccus file 1942 (corresponds with Marbold and Fouche), HRC; ELM to Dell Fouche, February 19, 1942 (Fouche an early childhood sweetheart), HRC; picture caption, *Petersburg Observer,* August 20, 1970, p. 3 (Mrs. Harmon Marbold is sister of Mitch); unpub. chapter 24, p. 489 (Emily Marbold), HRC; Diary 1941, November 3 (getting ms. of "Sandridge to Spring Lake" together).

43. ELM, "River Towns," *Along the Illinois,* 19–21; James A. Decker to Gerald Sanders, Au-

gust 3, 1942 (published August 1942, 340 copies, $2), HRC; Alfred Kreymborg, "From Masters to Master Villa," *Saturday Review of Literature* 25 (Oct. 10, 1942): 17; ELM to August Derleth, August 24, 1942 (hopes to reprint two books of poems with New York publisher), State Historical Society of Wisconsin.

44. ELM to Gerald [Sanders], February 24, 1942 (bibliography unfinished, biography to be delayed), HRC; ELM to Brett, October 25, 1922, October 17, 1942 (wants standard edition of works), both HRC; ELM to Horace Liveright, May 6, 1924 (wants standard edition of works), HRC; Macmillan [Company] to ELM, October 16, 1942 (book plates to be melted, "bullets"), HRC; Francis S. Wilson to ELM, August 24, 1942 (history of court), HRC; ELM to Francis Wilson, October 19, 1942 (history of court not to be a book), HRC; ELM to [John Gould] Fletcher, March 24, 1942 (New York may be attacked), Arkansas.

45. ELM to Gertrude Claytor, October 18, 1942 ("to get up at 6"), September 24, 1942 ("adopted daughter," "I got a lawyer"), both Princeton; Ellen's notes on "petition for adoption" form (never attempted to adopt Alice), HRC; Hilary Masters to Herb Russell, conversation, January 5, 1993 (adoption a joke); Alice to ELM, February 22, 1943 ("adopted relative"), March 26, 1944 (Alice shown around by Wilbur), both HRC; Wilbur Masters to Ellen, August 27, 1944 (Alice shown around by Wilbur), HRC; Diary 1943, May 28 (St. Louis), June 12 (Alice in Petersburg).

46. ELM to Mencken, March 3, 1944 (merchant marines), NY Public; ELM to August [Derleth], April 9, 1943 (girlfriends, third floor), State Historical Society of Wisconsin; Diary 1943, January 25 (moves to third floor); ELM to Dreiser, June 4, 1943 (radios), University of Pennsylvania; Ellen to Gerald Sanders, August 3, 1949, misc. file (had lunches with ELM while separated), HRC; ELM to Gerald [Sanders], April 26, 1943 ("My morale"), HRC; Hilary Masters to Herb Russell, June 11, 1997 (Brewster); "Millikan Adds Time Capsule P.S.," *New York Times,* September 23, 1943, p. 24 ("meaningless").

47. ELM to August [Derleth], August 26, 1943 (engagement, Marcia in Chicago), September 2, 1943 ("Little Marcia"), September 7, 1943 (asks Derleth to write biography), all State Historical Society of Wisconsin; Davis, memoir (Marcia and daughter visit in 1942), Virginia; ELM to Dreiser, November 24, 1943 (Marcia to California), University of Pennsylvania; ELM to "Lamb" [Madeline], January 7, 1943, June 22, 1943, July 13, 1943, and July 21, 1943 (all show ELM on good terms with Madeline), letters property of Marcia Cavell; John Hall Wheelock to ELM, May 11, 1943, Flaccus file 1943 (Flaccus in navy), HRC; ELM to Mencken, May 8, 1943 (Hardin in army), NY Public.

48. Diary 1943, February 5 ("American Book of Portraits"), end papers (about $2,200); ELM to Wheelock, January 12, 1943 ("book of biographical gossip"), June 24, 1943 ("I suppose this ends"), both Princeton; Scribner's to ELM, January 14, 1943 (refuses autobiography merged with famous acquaintances), HRC.

49. ELM to Dreiser, November 1, 1943 ("eases my loneliness"), University of Pennsylvania; Farrar and Rinehart to ELM, August 3, 1943 (refuses Spoon River history), HRC; ELM to Gerald Sanders, June 30, 1943 (lectureship), HRC; ELM to [Josephine] Crane, August 1, 1943 (asks for $100), HRC; Josephine Crane to ELM, October 25, 1943 (sends $100), HRC; Poetry Society of America to ELM, October 27, 1943 ($75), HRC.

50. ELM to Doctor Large, October 1, 1926 (defers dental work), HRC; Alice Davis to Gerald Sanders, January 4, 1944 (ELM falls ill on December 9, Alice thinks he is not seriously ill, Ellen "took over"), HRC; Diary 1943 (shows poor diet); ELM to Mencken, February 8, 1937 (dislikes dental work), NY Public; Dorothy Dow, "An Introduction to Some Letters" (poor teeth, poor diet), Newberry; "Edgar Lee Masters, Famed Poet, Convalescing Near City Line," unid. news clipping (pneumonia and malnutrition), Virginia; ELM to Doc [Alexander Burke],

May 7, 1944 (falls ill on December 8), Pennsylvania State University; ELM to Art [Ficke], January 6, 1944 (falls ill on December 13), Yale; Hilary Masters, *Last Stands: Notes from Memory* (Boston: Godine, 1982), 166 (Nicolosi calls Ellen and calls ambulance).

CHAPTER 20: LAST CHAPTER

1. ELM to Jack Powys, February 4, 1928 ("cook famously"), University of Pennsylvania.

2. "Edgar Lee Masters, Famed Poet, Convalescing Near City Line," unid. newspaper clipping ("ill and penniless," "without funds"), Virginia; Hewitt Howland to ELM, February 8, 1944 ("ill and penniless"), HRC; Hilary Masters, *Last Stands: Notes from Memory* (Boston: Godine, 1982), 166–67 (Bellevue details).

3. Hewitt Howland to ELM, February 8, 1944 (*Life*), HRC; Genevieve Taggard to ELM, n.d. [1943] (Times Square, "POET"), HRC; "Poet Masters Not Destitute, says Daughter," unid. newspaper clipping, misc. file, HRC; ELM to Amy Bonner, February 29, 1944 (not broke), HRC; ELM to Harriet Monroe, March 29, 1944 (asks to refute stories of poverty), HRC; Hilary Masters to Herb Russell, June 11, 1997 (Brewster); Hilary Masters, *Last Stands,* 166–67 ("starving," "near death," exams); Harriet Monroe, "News Notes," *Poetry* 64 (May 1944): 116 ("poet plus").

4. "Edgar Lee Masters . . . Convalescing," (Bellevue, Park East), Virginia; "Poet Masters Not Destitute," (Park East, Hillcrest), HRC; Thomas Masters to ELM, December 23, 1943 (Bellevue, Park East), HRC; ELM to "Little" [Marcia Lee Masters], January 9, 1944 (at Hillcrest), HRC; [Ellen Masters to Hilary Masters?], October 14, 1971 (dental work), property of Hilary Masters; ELM to Art [Ficke], July 4, 1944 (accompanies Dreiser to academy), June 30, 1944 (Ellen director of camp, Hilary at Pocono Pines), both Yale; ELM to Amy [Bonner], April 24, 1944 (boardinghouse), August 16, 1944 (in Poconos), both Pennsylvania State University; ELM to Theodore [Dreiser], September 30, 1944 (to Charlotte), University of Pennsylvania; Hilary Masters, *Last Stands,* 172 (Hilary as counselor, Davidson); Hilary Masters, "Letters," *New York Review of Books* 38 (Nov. 21, 1991): 51 (Country Day School, health returns in spring).

5. ELM to Art [Ficke], July 7, 1944 ("literally nothing," "A doctor here"), Yale; ELM to Dudley [Nichols], December 4, 1944 ("I couldn't write a poem"), Yale; ELM to Amy [Bonner], April 6, 1944 ("tippy" table), Pennsylvania State University; ELM to Gertrude [Claytor], November 16, 1944 ("complete convalescence"), Princeton; ELM to [John Hall] Wheelock, September 30, 1944 (cannot stay awake after breakfast), Princeton; Thomas P. Riggio, ed., *Dreiser-Mencken Letters: The Correspondence of Theodore Dreiser and H. L. Mencken, 1907–1945* (Philadelphia: University of Pennsylvania Press, 1986), 2:714 ("275 years old").

6. Ellen Masters to Amy Bonner, September 7, 1949 ("His papers"), Pennsylvania State University; ELM to Theodore [Dreiser], October 20, 1944 (writing in 1944), University of Pennsylvania; John Hall Wheelock to ELM, November 8, 1944 (trunks not accessible), HRC; H. S. Latham to ELM, February 28, 1944, September 15, 1944 (Macmillan interested in ms.), both HRC; ELM to [John Hall] Wheelock, November 6, 1944 ("a hundred poems" misplaced), October 10, 1944 (would have produced new volume), both Princeton; Hilary Masters, *Last Stands,* 173 (writing in 1944).

7. [John Hall Wheelock] to Alfred Noyes, October 6, 1943, Flaccus file 1943 (nomination for Shelley Award), HRC; Old Colony Trust Company (Poetry Society of America) to ELM, January 10, 1944 ($554.09), HRC; Daniel Henderson (Authors Club) to ELM, May 15, 1944 ($375), HRC; Episcopal Actors Guild of America to ELM, May 19, 1944 ($200), HRC; Ellen Masters to Kimball Flaccus, January 26, 1953, misc. file (movie options), HRC; Sam Smith to ELM, February 12, 1944, misc. file ($10 from stranger), HRC; Dr. Alexander Burke to ELM, February 6, 1944 (sends check), HRC; Edna St. Vincent Millay to ELM, February 5, 1944 ($50

check [unendorsed]), HRC; Hilary Masters, *Last Stands*, 167 (Author's League); ELM to John [Hall] Wheelock, January 14, 1944 ("I can think"), Princeton.

8. Hilary Masters, *Last Stands*, 166 (call to Ellen), 167, 170 (week's income).

9. Alice Davis to ELM, March 26, 1944 (volume of poems), May 17, 1944 (to marry sailor), both HRC; Mencken to ELM, November 4, 1944 (Alice's marriage), HRC; Alice Davis to Gerald Sanders, January 14, 1944, misc. file (Alice and Mencken), HRC; Alice Davis to Mencken, December 19, 1943 (Alice handles ELM's correspondence), May 23, 1944 (married Clover), both NY Public; Mencken to Alice Davis, August 28, 1945 (Alice to divorce Clover), NY Public; Hilary Masters, *Last Stands*, 171 (Three Roses).

10. Correspondence letterheads show Selwyn Hotel, HRC; Hilary Masters to Herb Russell, conversation, 1994 (graduated at sixteen), July 11, 1997 (Davidson); Hilary Masters, *Last Stands*, 182, 192 ("We have," "There's good").

11. Hilary Masters, *Last Stands*, 182 ("Of course"), 188 ("What I am saying"), 189 ("Stand up").

12. Macmillan to ELM, August 10, 1944 ($100 for four poems for anthology), HRC; Lawrence Spivak to ELM, November 15, 1944 (reprint), HRC; ELM to John Valentine, May 31, 1944 (tries to sell book mss.), Lilly Library; ELM, "Fiddlers of the Ozarks," *Esquire*, November 1944; August Derleth, *Selected Poems* (Prairie City, Ill.: James A. Decker, 1944), ix–x, preface; ELM to Amy [Bonner], December 12, 1944 (memorial poem for Eunice Tietjens), Pennsylvania State University; ELM to Briggs, August 1, 1944 ("fifteen cents"), Princeton.

13. Kimball Flaccus, "Edgar Lee Masters: A Biographical and Critical Study" (Ph.D. diss., New York University, 1952), i–ii (meeting with Masters, navy); Kimball Flaccus to Ellen Masters, January 2, 1951 (ELM agreed to outline in 1942), HRC; ELM to John Hall Wheelock, March 2, 1944 ("I like Flaccus"), Princeton.

14. Mencken to ELM, March 5, 1945 (ELM drowsy), HRC; Daniel Henderson to ELM, June 8, 1945, May 15, 1944 (to receive check from Author's League), both HRC; ELM to Theodore [Dreiser], January 31, 1945 (does little writing), University of Pennsylvania; Hilary Masters, *Last Stands*, 192–93 (hotel room, Hilary); ELM to Gertrude [Claytor], n.d. [spring 1945] ("Ellen is well"), Princeton.

15. ELM to [John Hall] Wheelock, June 3, 1945, Princeton.

16. ELM to Gertrude [Claytor], November 26, 1945 (Ficke, Powys, and Dreiser ill), Princeton.

17. ELM to Harriet Monroe, May 27, 1927, Flaccus file 1927 (bust completed), HRC; Grace Ranney to John Hall Wheelock, March 17, 1943, Flaccus file 1943 ($1,000), HRC; Grace Ranney to Robert Hutchins, January 20, 1945 (metal shortages delayed bust), HRC; Nicolosi to ELM, February 28, 1945 (invites Masters to see bronze bust), HRC; Robert Hutchins to ELM, February 16, 1945 (plans presentation of bust), HRC; Ellen to Amy Bonner, April 3, 1947, Flaccus file 1947 (dedication), HRC; Judith Bond to [Kimball] Flaccus, May 27, 1953 (Ellen at dedication), Georgetown.

18. ELM to Art [Ficke], March 21, 1945 ("three articles"), Yale; Hal Trovillion to ELM, January 16, 1945, January 22, 1945 (books, Reedy, and Gillespie), both HRC; Kenneth Hopkins, "A Note on Hal Trovillion and the Powys Brothers," *ICarbS* 3 (Spring-Summer 1977): 97–101.

19. ELM to "Doc" [Burke], March 6, 1946 (almost eighteen years old), Pennsylvania State University; ELM to Amy [Bonner], February 19, 1946 (two years in navy), Pennsylvania State University; Hilary Masters to Herb Russell, June 19, 1997, conversation (navy).

20. ELM to Gertrude [Claytor], January 4, 1946 ("doing nothing," no desk), Princeton; ELM to Cyril Clemens, April 28, 1934 (agrees to do Shillaber introduction), HRC; Cyril Clemens, *Shillaber* (London: Laurie, 1946), xi–xvi (Masters's introduction).

21. Harcourt Brace and Company to ELM, [1946?] ($60 for two *Spoon River* poems), HRC; Kay Winn to ELM, October 5 [1946?] (seeks permission to air "Anne Rutledge" on radio broadcast, *Cavalcade of America*), HRC; Daniel Henderson to ELM, [1946] (receives financial support from Authors Club of New York), HRC; the Bryher Foundation to ELM, [1946?] ($250), HRC; Academy of American Poets (Marie Bullock) to ELM, April 15, 1946 (Bynner and Jeffers), HRC; "Gets Poet's Fellowship Carrying a $5,000 Grant," *New York Times*, April 12, 1946, p. 28; ELM to Tom [Mabbott], August 5, 1946 (in New York), Iowa; ELM to August Derleth, December 29, 1946 ("a book ready"), State Historical Society of Wisconsin.

22. Hilary Masters, *Last Stands*, 141 (Molly, soldier's home), 195–96 (apartment); Certificate of Death, Pennsylvania Department of Health, Bureau of Vital Statistics, March 6, 1950 (shows ELM had Parkinson's and hardening of the arteries from 1940 onward); ELM to "Doc" [Burke], December 27, 1946 ("Ellen with her college teaching"), Pennsylvania State University.

23. H. S. Latham to ELM, January 17, 1947 (ELM's new manuscript), HRC; August Derleth, *Three Literary Men: A Memoir of Sinclair Lewis, Sherwood Anderson, Edgar Lee Masters* (New York: Candlelight, 1963), 53 ("Far Horizons," "The trouble with," ms. will not be lost).

24. Hilary Masters, *Last Stands*, 197 (all quotations).

25. ELM to Gertrude [Claytor], August 2, 1947 (department head), Princeton; Ellen Masters to Gertrude [Claytor], n.d. [1947] (spine), Princeton; Mencken to Ellen, February 27, 1947, misc. file (Ellen's discomfort and chiropractor), HRC; ELM to Ellen, [December 25,] 1947 ("I am doing"), HRC; ELM to Witter [Bynner], May 7, 1948 (three operations), Harvard.

26. Ellen Masters to Amy [Bonner], March 22, 1948 (ELM collapsed, hospital, convalescent home), September 7, 1949 ("trained nurse," "pain," arthritis, feels crippled), both Pennsylvania State University; Ellen to Mencken, June 17, 1948 (college housing in 1948), NY Public; Ellen to Gerald Sanders, January 23, 1949, misc. file (first visit to Melrose Park), July 7, 1949 (second visit to Melrose Park in September 1948), both HRC.

27. ELM to Witter [Bynner], May 7, 1948 (shows ELM's hard-to-read signature), Harvard; Ellen to Kimball Flaccus, May 5, 1956, misc. file (no writing after 1948), HRC; James A. Decker to ELM, November 2, 1948 (seeks manuscript), HRC; Daniel Henderson to ELM, November 19, 1948, misc. file (Carnegie Fund), HRC; Hugo Winter to ELM, December 9, 1947 (proposes terms for *La Collina*), HRC; Flaccus file 1950 (*La Collina* plays in January 1950), HRC; Kimball Flaccus note, n.d., Additions to be Added to Main Collection (Carnegie Fund contributed over $5,000 between November 1938 and March 1950), Georgetown.

28. Ellen to Hardin Masters, September 7, 1949, misc. file ($3,000 per year), HRC; Gerald Sanders to Ellen, August 2, 1949, misc. file S–T (Sanders and Ellen work on poems), HRC; Ellen to Gerald Sanders, July 7, 1949, July 25, 1949 (Sanders to edit), both HRC (Sanders's incomplete bibliography of Masters's materials is at the HRC); ELM, "My Most Important Decision," *Cosmopolitan*, August 1949, p. 72; Ellen Masters to Amy Bonner, September 7, 1949 (poems to type and market), Pennsylvania State University; Kimball Flaccus to Daniel Henderson, March 28, 1953 (Ellen pays most bills, Hardin contributes little), Georgetown; Gerald Sanders to Kimball Flaccus, April 26, 1953 (to Georgia), Georgetown.

29. Ellen to Amy Bonner, September 7, 1949 (letters gone, "nearly all," "Someday"), Pennsylvania State University; Diary 1941, October 25 (Alice has access to Masters's papers).

30. D[orothy] D[ow] to ELM, February 28, 1950 (Byron letters), HRC; Ellen to Gladys Ficke, March 22, 1950 (Byron's letters and "quarrels"), Yale; ELM to Dreiser, May 5, 1943 ("As to God"), University of Pennsylvania; Certificate of Death, Pennsylvania Department of Health, Bureau of Vital Statistics, March 6, 1950 (bronchitis, pneumonia).

31. Although of course conjectural, this account of Masters's thoughts on his final night is based on his correspondence: "Widdle" [Wilbur Masters] to ELM, July 30, 1949 (fishing at

Sheep Ford), December 17, 1943 (riding Pepperdog or Molly, riding double, ELM opens gates), both HRC.

AFTERWORD

1. Hardin Wallace Masters, *Edgar Lee Masters: A Biographical Sketchbook about a Famous American Author* (Rutherford, N.J.: Farleigh Dickinson University Press, 1978), 58 (material goods).

2. ELM, *Illinois Poems,* 19 ("heart's home"); ELM to Mary [Bell Sloan], [May 16, 1925] ("It remains my spiritual home"), Dartmouth; ELM to Harriet Monroe, June 9, 1925 ("used to love me"), Chicago; ELM to Jack [Powys], November 11, 1938, Flaccus file 1938 ("I gave her"), HRC; Ellen to Amy Bonner, March 28, 1950, Flaccus file 1950 (Wilbur donates grave sites), HRC.

3. Hardin Masters, *ELM: A Biographical Sketchbook,* 28 (modest casket); Hilary Masters, *Last Stands: Notes from Memory* (Boston: Godine, 1982), 45 (Hilary flew); Hilary Masters to Herb Russell, conversation, March 1994 (Constance Greene is "Grace" of *Last Stands*), 26–30.

4. Hilary Masters, *Last Stands,* 49 ("old friends," *Life,* "family funeral").

5. Ibid., 45, 49; Hilary Masters to Herb Russell, conversation, June 19, 1997 (Helen at funeral home); W. S. Jewell, "Funeral and Burial of E.L. Masters," unpub. ms., n.d., n.p. (Helen at funeral home), Knox College.

6. ELM, "Lambert Hutchins," *SRA,* describes background; Julie Scott, "Oakland Cemetery in Petersburg," *Western Illinois Regional Studies* 14 (Fall 1991): 51 ("Lambert Hutchins" prototype owned house in which funeral was held); Edward Laning, "Spoon River Revisited," *American Heritage* 22 (June 1971); ELM to "Widdle" [Wilbur Masters], November 24, 1928 (considers rental of Laning house), HRC; Ellen to Mrs. Wheelock, March 23, 1950 (ELM and Ellen visited friends in Laning house), HRC.

7. Hilary Masters, *Last Stands,* 54–62 (funeral home details and service); Ellen to Cyril Clemens, April 11, 1950 (Beethoven, Chopin, Dvorak, Sibelius), NY Public; ELM, "Silence," *Selected Poems,* 351–53; John Dowling, "Edgar Masters Buried in Spoon River Grave," unid. news clipping (reader of "Silence" was State Representative G. William Horsley), Western Illinois University; "Illinois Town Mourns at Masters' Funeral," *Washington* [D.C.] *Evening Star,* March 11, 1950, p. 4 (the reader of the poem was Springfield attorney G. William Horsley, who portrayed Lincoln at New Salem pageants).

8. Hilary Masters, *Last Stands,* 54 (funeral home interior), 56 (flowers); Ellen Masters to Cyril Clemens, April 11, 1950 ("girls"), NY Public.

9. "Last Rites Held Here Friday . . . ," *Petersburg Observer,* March 17, 1950, p. 1 (funeral details); "Observations," *Petersburg Observer,* March 31, 1950, p. 6 (funeral details); ELM to L. P. Payne, July 21, 1925 (liked "Howard Lamson"), HRC.

10. "Last Rites Held Here," 1 (funeral details, pallbearers); "Observations," 6 (funeral details); Wilbur Masters to "Dear Gig" [ELM], September 30, 1943 (graveyard as "the hill"), HRC; note in Ellen Masters's hand on copy of letter of ELM to Cyril Clemens, May 4, 1947 (Clemens at ELM's funeral), HRC; Ellen to Ernestine and Dan [Henderson], June 16, 1948 (pallbearers will be from bar associations), HRC.

11. "To-Morrow Is My Birthday," *Reedy's Mirror* 26 (Sept. 14, 1917): 583–85; ELM, *Toward the Gulf,* 113–14; ELM to Arthur [Ficke], September 24, 1936 ("high water"), Yale; ELM to the Story Press, May 13, 1942 ("best"), Princeton; ELM to Gerald Sanders, March 27, 1935 ("best"), HRC; Edith Masters to Ellen, April 10, 1951, misc. file (Ellen handles epitaph), HRC; Reedy to ELM, September 12, 1917 ("wad," "Big Thing"), HRC; ELM to Kimball [Flaccus], October

9, 1941 ("Anne Rutledge" much anthologized), HRC; Charles E. Burgess, "Ancestral Lore in *Spoon River Anthology:* Fact and Fancy," *Papers on Language and Literature* 20 (Spring 1984): 204 ("Anne Rutledge" most anthologized).

12. Hardin Masters, *ELM: A Biographical Sketchbook,* 137 (Helen remained in love), 141 (Helen lived with Marcia); Dreiser to ELM, July 17, 1944 (Helen with Marcia), HRC; Helen Masters to Alice Gerstenberg, November 5, 1923 (reflects Helen's social status), Newberry; "Funeral Rites Saturday for Mrs. Masters," *Chicago Tribune,* November 28, 1958, pt. 3, p. 7.

13. Marcia Lee Masters, *Wind Around the Moon* (Georgetown, Calif.: Dragon's Teeth, 1986), front pages, [83] (biographical information); Marcia Lee Masters, *Looking Across* (Winnetka, Ill.: Thorntree, 1990), [91] (biographical information); Marcia Lee Masters, *Intent on Earth* (New York: Candlelight, 1965).

14. Marjorie Bordner, ed., *Fulton County Heritage* (Dallas: Curtis Media, 1988), 604–5 (Madeline and 1969 centenary; see the Edgar Lee Masters medal at the Western Illinois University Library).

15. Hardin Masters, *ELM: A Biographical Sketchbook,* 118 (banking), dust jacket (biographical information), 159 ("lovely lady").

16. Jerry Miller to Herb Russell, January 31, 1978 (shows Pamela's Grant County, Indiana, marriage license was issued on October 2, 1926); Betty Drook Shutt, *The Hostess House Story* ([Marion, Ind.]: Chronicle-Tribune, 1989), a pamphlet describing Lillian Wilson, her house, and her husbands; Dorothy Belle Hill to Herb Russell, telephone conversation, March 1994 (Lillian died in 1950s, moneyed, Park Avenue); Jean Rosen to Herb Russell, telephone conversation, February 1999 (unusual architecture).

17. Diana Haskell to Herb Russell, April 17, 1990 (Dow died 1989); Dorothy Dow, "An Introduction to Some Letters, 1950," Newberry.

18. ELM, *The Sangamon,* intro. Burgess, xix (Rev. Charles Tibbetts); Mencken to ELM, April 21, 1944 (advises ELM and Alice to give her journal to New York Public Library), November 1, 1944 (journal to New York Public Library), both NY Public; ELM to Gertrude [Claytor], January 7, 1944 (Mencken helps Alice deposit letters in New York Public Library), Princeton; Mrs. Norman Davis to Herb Russell, telephone conversation, January 5, 1996 (Alice Davis died in 1988).

19. "Teacher at Ogontz," *Campuscope* (Pennsylvania State University's Ogontz Center), February 1956 (interview).

20. Kimball Flaccus, "Edgar Lee Masters: A Biographical and Critical Study" (Ph.D. diss., New York University, 1952), i–ii (Flaccus offers to write book on ELM in 1940); Flaccus to Ellen, January 2, 1951 (ELM approved outline of biography in 1942), November 21, 1951 (Ellen refuses to name Flaccus as "authorized biographer"), October 1, 1958 (Ellen has not shared her Masters's papers with Flaccus), May 3, 1962, and September 22, 1969 (plans two volumes), February 20, 1971 (biography still underway, seems unaware that Ellen has transferred her ELM letters to University of Texas), all HRC; Scribner's to ELM, March 1, 1944 (ELM does not want Flaccus to write biography), HRC; Ellen to Flaccus, September 14, 1951 ("best equipped," refuses right to quote, "my position"), November 17, 1951 (refuses to name Flaccus as official biographer), May 18, 1970 (stamp ceremony, "I expect you"), all HRC; Alice Davis to Gerald Sanders, May 6, 1953 (Ellen tries twice to access Davis materials), HRC; ELM to August [Derleth], September 7, 1943 ("Flaccus was not"), State Historical Society of Wisconsin; Mencken to ELM, November 1, 1944 (Davis papers sealed), NY Public; Flaccus's unfinished ms., "Edgar Lee Masters: Man of Spoon River," is at Dartmouth.

21. ELM, *The Harmony of Deeper Music: Posthumous Poems of Edgar Lee Masters,* selected and edited and with an introduction by Frank K. Robinson (Austin: Humanities Research Center, University of Texas, 1976), 19–20.

22. Ibid., 42 ("They are wise"), [2] ("The leaves whisper").

23. Hilary Masters to Herb Russell, conversation, November 1996 (received power of attorney in 1988); conversation, June 2000 (biographical information); Hilary Masters, *Last Stands,* [213] (biographical material); Hilary Masters, *Success: New and Selected Stories* (New York: St. Martin's, 1992), 138–48 ("Ohm's Law"), dust jacket (biographical information).

24. ELM, "Percival Sharp," *SRA* ("true epitaph").

INDEX

Note: The abbreviation ELM is used for Edgar Lee Masters throughout the index.

HERBERT K. RUSSELL, the director for college relations at John A. Logan College, holds a B.S. in English literature from Eastern Illinois University and an M.A. and a Ph.D. in English literature from Southern Illinois University at Carbondale. He has edited three books on Illinois subjects and provided introductions for two more. His seventeen previous publications on Edgar Lee Masters include entries for the *Dictionary of Literary Biography* and the *Dictionary of Midwestern Literature.*

Typeset in 10.5/12.5 Adobe Minion
with Fenice Bold display
Composed by Jim Proefrock
at the University of Illinois Press
Manufactured by Thomson-Shore, Inc.

University of Illinois Press
1325 South Oak Street
Champaign, IL 61820-6903
www.press.uillinois.edu